The Progress of Management

HAROLD LAZARUS

Professor of Management
Graduate School of Business Administration
New York University

E. KIRBY WARREN

Professor of Management
Graduate School of Business
Columbia University

JEROME E. SCHNEE

Assistant Professor of Business
Graduate School of Business
Columbia University

Second Edition

The Progress of Management

PROCESS AND BEHAVIOR IN A CHANGING ENVIRONMENT

Prentice-Hall, Inc., Englewood Cliffs, New Jersey

Prentice-Hall International, Inc., London

Prentice-Hall of Australia, Pty. Ltd., Sydney

Prentice-Hall of Canada, Ltd., Toronto

Prentice-Hall of India Private Ltd., New Delhi

Prentice-Hall of Japan, Inc., Tokyo

10   9   8   7   6   5   4   3   2   1

Library of Congress Cataloging in Publication Data

Lazarus, Harold, comp.
       The progress of management.

       Includes bibliographies.
       1. Management—Addresses, essays, lectures.
I. Warren, E. Kirby, joint comp. II. Schnee, Jerome
E., 1941-   joint comp. III. Title.
HD31.L324 1972   658'.008   71-175519
ISBN 0-13-730606-7

The subtitle of this book, *Process and Behavior in a Changing Environment*, perhaps best explains the rationale for this the second edition of *The Progress of Management*. In the four years that have passed since the publication of the first edition, management has indeed progressed and adapted itself to its changing environment. Because of this, nearly three-quarters of the readings are new to this edition. These selections and some of the best ones from the previous edition offer the teacher, the student, the executive, and the management trainee a wide selection of important, original ideas advanced by distinguished authorities.

For professors and training directors, there are articles that investigate areas of controversy and analyze results of research in both large and small organizations. For executives, there are new approaches to the solution of complex management problems presented by experts who offer practical, easy-to-apply suggestions. For undergraduate and graduate students and for management trainees, there are case studies and introductory questions that stimulate thought and offer opportunity for self-testing and the exercise of decision-making skills. For all, there is the convenience of a one-volume anthology of contemporary management thought.

Although this book may be used alone or as a supplement to any management text, the editors feel that many readers will derive the greatest benefit from the selections if they are read in conjunction with the third edition of *The Process of Management: Concepts, Behavior, and Practice,* by

William H. Newman, Charles E. Summer, and E. Kirby Warren. In both books, the philosophy of administration is built around the following framework: *Social Role of Managers; Organizing: Structural Design; Human Factors in Organizing; Planning: Elements of Decision-Making; Planning: Decision-Making in an Enterprise; Leading; Measuring and Controlling;* and *Managing: An Adaptive Process.*

The editors wish to thank Raymond Mullaney, of Prentice-Hall, Ralph DiPietro, and Ron Rizzuto for their valuable assistance. We are also grateful to Elaine Hulunian and Lee Lustberg, our typists.

Harold Lazarus

E. Kirby Warren

Jerome E. Schnee

Contents

Social Role of Managers

In preparing this anthology, the editors selected articles, empirical studies, and portions of books with which they believe students of management and practicing managers should be familiar. Materials were chosen for significance, clarity of style, timeliness, and conciseness.

The selections are by scholars who know the road and by administrators who can drive the car. Their contributions represent several disciplines. The readings, seasoned with research findings, current trends, comparative analyses, useful techniques, and basic concepts, are almost entirely free of jargon. Because few selections can stand by themselves, the editors have supplied supporting links in the form of explanatory notes and bibliographies.

Managers are social beings who deal with other social beings, and so the process of management is a social process. A manager's actions are often guided by customs and shaped by the traditions of the society in which he operates and by his physical environment. For this reason, this introductory section explores the effect of the social and physical environment on executives. The first two selections offer the reader different views of the social role of managers and focus on some critical issues in the current debate concerning management's social responsibilities. If you gather together your own thoughts on this subject before reading selections 1 and 2, you will be able to observe the effects that the opposing opinions presented in these two readings will have upon your own attitudes.

Both selections are by contemporary economists—the first by Milton Friedman, a conservative, and the second by Paul Samuelson, a liberal. Friedman believes that the currently fashionable cloak of social responsibility worn by some executives could smother the market system. He also feels that managers should not injure stockholders in order to help society. For example, executives should spend money to reduce pollution only if this action is in the best interest of those whose assets are being used. Otherwise, management is generous with other people's money.

Executives who spend money to avoid pollution may be taking from stockholders without their consent, but what about executives who permit the pollution of our rivers? Are they not taking from the public without its consent? Friedman argues that managers do not have the right to involve corporations in activities that are *for* the general public. Do managers have the right to involve corporations in activities that are *against* the public?

After reading the first two selections, ask yourself why Friedman and Samuelson differ. What are their assumptions? Do they avoid any critical issues? Has either of them caused you to change your attitude toward corporate involvement in the major social problems of our time?

Perhaps before deciding what corporations *should* do, we ought to know what they *are* doing. Selection 3 summarizes the urban activities of 247 major corporations. After reading this selection, you will be better able to answer the question asked in its title, "Is business meeting the challenge of urban affairs?"

In a recent issue of *The New Yorker* magazine there was a Lorenz cartoon that depicted a beaming board chairman addressing a group of smiling stockholders at their annual meeting. Standing before a chart that shows an excellent trend in sales, the chairman tells his audience that, in spite of rising labor costs and increased government interference, management was again able to use deceptive marketing practices to earn an excessive profit. In recent years, consumer groups have tried to show that this type of attitude is too common in American industry.

Ralph Nader, a champion of consumer causes, is the author of selection 4. In his article, Nader urges professionals to take an active role in preventing what he calls "corporate or governmental negligence." Whether you agree with Nader or not, this article should invite insights about possible conflict between professional conscience and corporate loyalty.

The last reading in the section presents some thoughts on management's past, present, and future. In this article, Max Ways discusses some of the changes that management has undergone in the past fifty years and introduces some of the major schools of thought that are part of the literature of management theory. Could Andrew Carnegie, Henry Ford, or William Randolph Hearst manage a modern corporation? The ideas contained in selection 5 will help you to answer this question.

1

The Social Responsibility
of Business Is to Increase Its Profits

MILTON FRIEDMAN

Milton Friedman, a well-known economist, is the Paul Snowden Russell Distinguished Service Professor at the University of Chicago. In this article Friedman says that those who urge business to assume social responsibilities are "preaching pure and unadulterated socialism" and adds that those executives "who talk this way are unwitting puppets of the intellectual forces that have been undermining the basis of a free society." Is this criticism justified or is it merely name-calling? Is it really dishonest to call a certain action socially responsible if it can also be justified on grounds of self-interest?

Should executives be concerned only with maximizing the return to their companies, or should they also seek to benefit society in general? Friedman does not feel that they are trained to do the latter. Should they try, nevertheless?

Would respect for profits and for civil servants' power to tax encourage you to argue for effluent taxes that would make it unprofitable for corporations to pollute our water and our sky? Currently those who are downstream and downwind suffer from pollution and absorb some of the costs of cleaning the environment.

To what extent can we expect market forces to contribute to, or help stop, pollution of our environment? How should executives in business and government respond to problems of pollution?

Professor John Ullmann, head of the Department of Management, Marketing, and Business Statistics of Hofstra University, questioned Friedman's defense of self-regulation by corporations whose mission is (not to improve the quality of life on this planet but) to increase profits. Ullmann, in a letter to The New York Times, *argued that business pressure prevents laws on pollution from being enacted and enforced.*

The reader may be amused to learn in the following article that Friedman, a union-opposed, conservative economist, supports union leaders' inability or unwillingness to subordinate the interests of their members to more general social purposes. At the same time, a union-supported, liberal psychologist, Timothy Costello, takes the opposite point of view. Costello said recently: "I question whether all a union has got to do is protect employes, without delivering essential services, or raising the level of those services or making certain there is a contribution by the very people whom the union leaders are supposed to protect." What do you think are the social responsibilities of executives in labor organizations and business organizations?

Finally, if the business of business is to make a profit, who will eradicate the ills of our society and fight against air and water pollution? How will they do this? Why have they not succeeded in the past?

When I hear businessmen speak eloquently about the "social responsibilities of business in a free-enterprise system," I am reminded of the wonderful line about the Frenchman who discovered at the age of 70 that he had been speaking prose all his life. The businessmen believe that they are defending free enterprise when they declaim that business is not concerned "merely" with profit but also with promoting desirable "social" ends; that business has a "social conscience" and takes seriously its responsibilities for providing employment, eliminating discrimination, avoiding pollution and whatever else may be the catchwords of the contemporary crop of reformers. In fact they are—or would be if they or anyone else took them seriously—preaching pure and unadulterated socialism. Businessmen who talk this way are unwitting puppets of the intellectual forces that have been undermining the basis of a free society these past decades.

The discussions of the "social responsibilities of business" are notable for their analytical looseness and lack of rigor. What does it mean to say that "business" has responsibilities? Only people can have responsibilities. A corporation is an artificial person and in this sense may have artificial responsibilities, but "business" as a whole cannot be said to have responsibilities, even in this vague sense. The first step toward clarity in examining the doctrine of the social responsibility of business is to ask precisely what it implies for whom.

Presumably, the individuals who are to be responsible are businessmen, which means individual proprietors or corporate executives. Most of the discussion of social responsibility is directed at corporations, so in what follows I shall mostly neglect the individual proprietor and speak of corporate executives.

In a free-enterprise, private-property system, a corporate executive is an employe of the owners of the business. He has direct responsibility to his employers. That responsibility is to conduct the business in accordance with their desires, which generally will be to make as much money as possible while conforming to the basic rules of the society, both those embodied in law and those embodied in ethical custom. Of course, in some cases his employers may have a different objective. A group of persons might establish a corporation for an eleemosynary purpose—for example, a hospital or a school. The manager of such a corporation will not have money profit as his objective but the rendering of certain services.

In either case, the key point is that, in his capacity as a corporate executive, the manager is the agent of the individuals who own the corporation or establish the eleemosynary institution, and his primary responsibility is to them.

Needless to say, this does not mean that it is easy to judge how well he is performing his task. But at least the criterion of performance is straightforward, and the persons among whom a voluntary contractual arrangement exists are clearly defined.

Of course, the corporate executive is also a person in his own right. As a person, he may have many other responsibilities that he recognizes or assumes voluntarily—to his family, his conscience, his feelings of charity, his church, his clubs, his city, his country. He may feel impelled by these responsibilities to devote part of his income to causes he regards as worthy, to refuse to work for particular corporations, even to leave his job, for example, to join his country's armed forces. If we wish, we may refer to some of these responsibilities as "social responsibilities." But in these respects he is acting as a principal, not an agent; he is spending his own money or time or energy, not the money of his employers or the time or energy he has contracted to devote to their purposes. If these are "social responsibilities," they are the social responsibilities of individuals, not of business.

What does it mean to say that the corporate executive has a "social responsibility" in his capacity as businessman? If this statement is not pure rhetoric, it must mean that he is to act in some way that is not in the interest of his employers. For example, that he is to refrain from increasing the price of the product in order to contribute to the social objective of preventing inflation, even though a price increase would be in the best interests of the corporation. Or that he is to make expenditures on reducing pollution beyond the amount that is in the best interests of the corporation or that is required by law in order to contribute to the social objective of improving the environment. Or that, at the expense of corporate profits, he is to hire "hard-core" unemployed instead of better-qualified available workmen to contribute to the social objective of reducing poverty.

In each of these cases, the corporate executive would be spending someone else's money for a general social interest. Insofar as his actions in accord with his "social responsibility" reduce returns to stockholders, he is spending their money. Insofar as his actions raise the price to customers, he is spending the customers' money. Insofar as his actions lower the wages of some employes, he is spending their money.

The stockholders or the customers or the employes could separately spend their own money on the particular action if they wished to do so. The executive is exercising a distinct "social responsibility," rather than serving as an agent of the stockholders or the customers or the employes, only if he spends the money in a different way than they would have spent it.

But if he does this, he is in effect imposing taxes, on the one hand, and deciding how the tax proceeds shall be spent, on the other.

This process raises political questions on two levels: principle and consequences. On the level of political principle, the imposition of taxes and the expenditure of tax proceeds are governmental functions. We have established elaborate constitutional, parliamentary and judicial provisions to control these functions, to assure that taxes are imposed so far as possible in accordance with the preferences and desires of the public—after all, "taxation without representation" was one of the battle cries of the American Revolution. We have a system of checks and balances to separate the legislative function of imposing taxes and enacting expenditures from the executive function of collecting taxes and administering expenditure programs and from the judicial function of mediating disputes and interpreting the law.

Here the businessman—self-selected or appointed directly or indirectly by stockholders—is to be simultaneously legislator, executive and jurist. He is to decide whom to tax by how much and for what purpose, and he is to spend the proceeds—all this guided only by general exhortations from on high to restrain inflation, improve the environment, fight poverty and so on and on.

The whole justification for permitting the corporate executive to be selected by the stockholders is that the executive is an agent serving the interests of his principal. This justification disappears when the corporate executive imposes taxes and spends the proceeds for "social" purposes. He becomes in effect a public employe, a civil servant, even though he remains in name an employe of a private enterprise. On grounds of political principle, it is intolerable that such civil servants—insofar as their actions in the name of social responsibility are real and not just window-dressing—should be selected as they are now. If they are to be civil servants, then they must be selected through a political process. If they are to impose taxes and make expenditures to foster "social" objectives, then political machinery must be set up to guide the assessment of taxes and to determine through a political process the objectives to be served.

This is the basic reason why the doctrine of "social responsibility" involves the acceptance of the socialist view that political mechanisms, not market mechanisms, are the appropriate way to determine the allocation of scarce resources to alternative uses.

On the grounds of consequences, can the corporate executive in fact discharge his alleged "social responsibilities"? On the one hand, suppose he could get away with spending the stockholders' or customers' or employes' money. How is he to know how to spend it? He is told that he must contribute to fighting inflation. How is he to know what action of his will contribute to that end? He is presumably an expert in running his company—in producing a product or selling it or financing it. But nothing about his selection makes him an expert on inflation. Will his holding down the price of his product reduce inflationary pressure? Or, by leaving more spending power in the hands of his customers, simply divert it elsewhere? Or, by forcing him to produce less because of the lower price, will it simply contribute to shortages? Even if he could answer these questions, how much cost is he justified in imposing on his stockholders, customers and employes for this social purpose? What is his appropriate share and what is the appropriate share of others?

And, whether he wants to or not, can he get away with spending his stockholders', customers' or employes' money? Will not the stockholders fire him? (Either the present ones or those who take over when his actions in the name of social responsibility have reduced the corporation's profits and the price of its stock.) His customers and his employes can desert him for other producers and employers less scrupulous in exercising their social responsibilities.

This facet of "social responsibility" doctrine is brought into sharp relief when the doctrine is used to justify wage restraint by trade unions. The conflict of interest is naked and clear when union officials are asked to subordinate the interest of their members to some more general social purpose. If the union officials try to enforce wage restraint, the consequence is likely to be wildcat strikes, rank-and-file revolts and the emergence of strong competitors for their jobs. We thus have the ironic phenomenon that union leaders—at least in the U.S.—have objected to Government interference with the market far more consistently and courageously than have business leaders.

The difficulty of exercising "social responsibility" illustrates, of course, the great virtue of private competitive enterprise—it forces people to be responsible for their own actions and makes it difficult for them to "exploit" other people for either selfish or unselfish purposes. They can do good—but only at their own expense.

Many a reader who has followed the argument this far may be tempted to remonstrate that it is all well and good to speak of government's having the responsibility to impose taxes and determine expenditures for such "social" purposes as controlling pollution or training the hard-core unemployed, but that the problems are too urgent to wait on the slow course of political processes, that the exercise of social responsibility by businessmen is a quicker and surer way to solve pressing current problems.

Aside from the question of fact—I share Adam Smith's skepticism about the benefits that can be expected from "those who affected to trade for the public good"—this argument must be rejected on grounds of principle. What it amounts to is an assertion that those who favor the taxes and expenditures in question have failed to persuade a majority of their fellow citizens to be of like mind and that they are seeking to attain by undemocratic procedures what they cannot attain by democratic procedures.

In a free society, it is hard for "good" people to do "good," but that is a small price to pay for making it hard for "evil" people to do "evil," especially since one man's good is another's evil.

I have, for simplicity, concentrated on the special case of the corporate executive, except only for the brief digression on trade unions. But precisely the same argument applies to the newer phenomenon of calling upon stockholders to require corporations to exercise social responsibility (the recent G.M. crusade, for example). In most of these cases, what is in effect involved is some stockholders trying to get other stockholders (or customers or employes) to contribute against their will to "social" causes favored by the activists. Insofar as they succeed, they are again imposing taxes and spending the proceeds.

The situation of the individual proprietor is somewhat different. If he acts to reduce the returns of his enterprise in order to exercise his "social responsibility," he is spending his own money, not someone else's. If he wishes to spend his money on such purposes, that is his right, and I cannot see that there is any objection to his doing so. In the process, he, too, may impose costs on employes and customers. However, because he is far less likely than a large corporation or union to have monopolistic power, any such side effects will tend to be minor.

Of course, in practice the doctrine of social responsibility is frequently a cloak for actions that are justified on other grounds rather than a reason for those actions.

To illustrate, it may well be in the long-run interest of a corporation that is a major employer in a small community to devote resources to providing amenities to that community or to improving its government. That may make it easier to attract desirable employes, it may reduce the wage bill or lessen losses from pilferage and sabotage or have other worthwhile effects. Or it may be that, given the laws about the deductibility of corporate charitable contributions, the stockholders can contribute more to charities they favor by having the corporation make the gift than by doing it themselves, since they can in that way contribute an amount that would otherwise have been paid as corporate taxes.

In each of these—and many similar—cases, there is a strong temptation to rationalize these actions as an exercise of "social responsibility." In the present climate of opinion, with its widespread aversion to "capitalism," "profits," the "soulless corporation" and so on, this is one way for a corporation to generate goodwill as a by-product of expenditures that are entirely justified in its own self-interest.

It would be inconsistent of me to call on corporate executives to refrain from this hypocritical window-dressing because it harms the foundations of a free society. That would be to call on them to exercise a "social responsibility"! If our institutions, and the attitudes of the public, make it in their self-interest to cloak their actions in this way, I cannot summon much indignation to denounce them. At the same time, I can express admiration for those individual proprietors or owners of closely held corporations or stockholders of more broadly held corporations who disdain such tactics as approaching fraud.

Whether blameworthy or not, the use of the cloak of social responsibility, and the nonsense spoken in its name by influential and prestigious businessmen, does clearly harm the foundations of a free society. I have been impressed time and again by the schizophrenic character of many businessmen. They are capable of being extremely far-sighted and clear-headed in matters that are internal to their businesses. They are incredibly short-sighted and muddle-headed in matters that are outside their businesses but affect the possible survival of business in general. This short-sightedness is strikingly exemplified in the calls from many businessmen for wage and price guidelines or controls or incomes policies. There is nothing that could do more in a brief period to destroy a market system and replace it by a centrally controlled system than effective governmental control of prices and wages.

The short-sightedness is also exemplified in speeches by businessmen on social responsibility. This may gain them kudos in the short run. But it helps to strengthen the already too prevalent view that the pursuit of profits is wicked and immoral and must be curbed and controlled by external forces. Once this view is adopted, the external forces that curb the market will not be the social consciences, however highly developed, of the pontificating executives; it will be the iron fist of Government bureaucrats. Here, as with price and wage controls, businessmen seem to me to reveal a suicidal impulse.

The political principle that underlies the market mechanism is unanimity. In an ideal free market resting on private property, no individual can coerce any other, all cooperation is voluntary, all parties to such cooperation benefit or they need not participate. There are no "social" values, no "social" responsibilities in any sense other than the shared values and responsibilities of individuals. Society is a collection of individuals and of the various groups they voluntarily form.

The political principle that underlies the political mechanism is conformity. The individual must serve a more general social interest—whether that be determined by a church or a dictator or a majority. The individual may have a vote and a say in what is to be done, but if he is overruled, he must conform. It is appropriate for some to require others to contribute to a general social purpose whether they wish to or not.

Unfortunately, unanimity is not always feasible. There are some respects in which conformity appears unavoidable, so I do not see how one can avoid the use of the political mechanism altogether.

But the doctrine of "social responsibility" taken seriously would extend the scope of the political mechanism to every human activity. It does not differ in philosophy from the most explicitly collectivist doctrine. It differs only by professing to believe that collectivist ends can be attained without collectivist means. That is why, in my book "Capitalism and

Freedom," I have called it a "fundamentally subversive doctrine" in a free society, and have said that in such a society, "there is one and only one social responsibility of business—to use its resources and engage in activities designed to increase its profits so long as it stays within the rules of the game, which is to say, engages in open and free competition without deception or fraud."

2

Love That Corporation

PAUL A. SAMUELSON

Paul Samuelson, like Milton Friedman, is a distinguished economist. He is a Nobel prizewinner and a professor at the Massachusetts Institute of Technology. Although both Samuelson and Friedman are able economists, they disagree often. Here Samuelson disagrees with Friedman's attitudes toward the social responsibilities of business as presented in the preceding selection.

In Part Five of this book Blake, Mouton, and Bidwell tell us that the needs of organizations and of individuals are not necessarily in conflict. Can the same be said for the needs of society and the needs of individual companies?

Generally, Samuelson tends to favor prevention rather than cure. Prevention may be expensive and may require unpleasant inspection. However, it is often less costly and less unpleasant to avoid pollution than to clean it up. Similarly, it is often cheaper to prevent the onset of disease than to cure it through costly hospitalization.

Samuelson mentions Congressional reactions to the idea of a penalty tax on leaded gasolines. Do you favor such a penalty tax?

Finally, Samuelson suggests that the field of economics does not give us an ethical value system. Does the field of management?

Last Christmas I wrote a column on economics and love. Under the mistaken preconception that these, like oil and water, cannot mix, several people applauded either my innovation or my recantation.

Illustrative of this widespread misconception is the following typical query:

Reprinted from *The New York Times*, December 26, 1970, p. 17. Copyright 1970 by The New York Times Company. Reprinted by permission.

"Professor Samuelson, is it really a finding of economics that corporations should *solely* maximize their profits, disregarding any special obligation to the public interest or to the humanitarian needs of their workers and consumers?"

I was glad to be able to reply, ... "A large corporation these days not only may engage in social responsibility, it had damn well better try to do so."

Let me tell the ways.

First, let's forget the sterile problem of semantics as to whether the corporation is a person distinct from its employes and owners. As Descartes would say, the corporation holds committee meetings—therefore it exists. It pays taxes. It hires new people and after they are dead it continues to operate.

Second, we can dismiss the legal argument that the Board of Directors has no right to squander the shareowners' assets in Galahad causes. The stamp of legitimacy is on the other side.

The whole issue is what *are* the shareowners' assets? For decades the courts have upheld charitable giving by corporations. Today you'd be in more trouble with the authorities—the Stock Exchange, the S.E.C., the boys at the downtown eating club, to say nothing of the bailiff—if you tried to run a business along old-fashioned Sewall Avery lines of immediate profit than if you took account of the public interest.

Let me not overstate the case. It is true that Henry Ford 2d cannot operate today like Henry Ford, his grandfather. But neither can he operate like St. Francis of Assisi. The several hundred large corporations react to, and set, an evolving code of social conduct. So long as anyone does not depart too markedly from the ruling norm, it will not be penalized out of existence by market competition.

Thus, if International Harvester attempted by itself to solve the problem of general inflation, or even inflation in farm equipment prices—or if its board set out, by wage and price policy, to rectify the inequitable distribution of incomes in the United States—after a very few years International Harvester would be eliminated from the roster of Galbraithian giants. The elimination process would be a bit slower, but not less inexorable, if Allis Chalmers, Deere, Caterpillar, Dodge Trucks, and General Motors joined it in this unilateral crusade for social justice.

To advance the good cause, one must not expect too much of altruism. It is nonsense to look to General Motors, or even the Big Three, for voluntary solution of the problem of air pollution. It is only good sense to impose by the force of law—by regulation and taxation—an obligation for the auto makers to produce exhaust systems that lessen pollution of the environment.

Corporations, I am afraid, are persons, born like the rest of us imperfect and subject to sin. Thus, the small man is no better than the General Electric board. When I drove into a Los Angeles service station recently, I noted that the lead-free gas pump was neglected. I soon found out why: good people, men who love their wives and never fail to contribute to the collection plate, are not willing to pay more for gasoline which, if they alone use it, will only imperceptibly purify the atmosphere for the rest of the community. (Although not an admirer of Nixon economics, I must ask in this connection: why did Congress so cavalierly dismiss the President's suggestion of a penalty tax on leaded gasoline?)

I quote a final example from the recent book by William F. Buckley Jr. Lapsing for once into good sense, Buckley is arguing that coercive limitations can in such good causes as quarantine against plague add to total welfare and the algebraic total of human freedom:

"I asked Professor [Milton] Friedman, 'Is it your position that, assuming the community decided to license the whores, it would be wrong to insist that they check in at regular intervals for health certificates?' Yes, he thought that would be wrong—'After all, if the customer contracts a venereal disease, the prostitute having warranted that she was clean, he has available a tort action against her.' "

In response to a number of letters using this *reductio ad absurdum* as a reason for indicting economics, my reply is simply to demur. There is nothing in economics that leads to such a conclusion. Economics cannot tell us what to believe; it can help us to sort out the costs and benefits of various arrangements, as those costs and benefits are defined by the ethical value systems that we bring to economics.

Using civil suits to penalize undesired behavior *after* it takes place is indeed often a better social device than expensive and unpleasant inspection prior to behavior. But I cannot imagine a worse case to illustrate this purely tactical precept.

Thus, in principle, a venereal disease could be of irreversible type. Second, the courts would undoubtedly come to apply the doctrine of *caveat emptor*, let the buyer beware, to transactions such as these—what does it mean for a prostitute to warrant that she is "clean"? Finally, what are the assets against which the victorious plaintiff can levy? The mind boggles.

3

Is Business Meeting
the Challenge of Urban Affairs?

JULES COHN

In selection 3 we learn that corporations sometimes hire the hard-core unemployed because the supply of skilled workers has become almost exhausted in some of our cities. But when the government does not subsidize the training of the unemployed and when skilled workers are available are executives still justified in hiring the hard-core unemployed? Should companies seek government subsidies for their urban affairs programs?

In this reading Jules Cohn discusses several human-resource problems of our cities, but ignores crime, deficient housing, inadequate mass transportation, and poor educational facilities on the grounds that "relatively few corporations address themselves to these issues." Is this true, and should it be?

Cohn also mentions ways in which organizational climates change when firms enter the field of urban affairs. Do you approve of these changes? He also describes the shift in corporate donations away from colleges and churches and toward urban affairs groups and suggests that blacks may not always be willing to accept "payoffs" rather than programs.

In discussing the motives for starting urban affairs projects, Cohn mentions enlightened self-interest, corporate image, compliance with government requirements, prevention of violence, and new markets. Do you think that management should institute urban affairs programs? If so, for what reason? If such programs are introduced, what type of person should head these programs? To whom should the director of urban affairs report?

If you were placed in charge of urban affairs for a large corporation what would you try to accomplish? How would you go about setting limited, realistic goals? How would you try to reach these goals? What side effects would you attempt to avoid? Finally, how could you and top management evaluate the effectiveness of urban affairs programs?

In his article Cohn offers guidelines for those interested in developing, implementing, and evaluating a corporate urban affairs program.

Reprinted from the *Harvard Business Review*, March-April 1970, pp. 68-82. Copyright 1970 by the President and Fellows of Harvard College. All rights reserved.

13

American industry has long had a way of rising to challenges from unexpected quarters. In keeping with this tradition, the first responses of U.S. businessmen to public appeals for participation in the fight against urban problems were positive, optimistic, and self-confident. Today, nearly three years have passed since the first corporate urban affairs programs were launched in the wake of the 1967 riots and the shock waves generated by the Kerner Report.

What have these programs amounted to? How do their actual contributions add up against their original objectives? In what ways—if at all—have corporations and their managers been affected by exposure to urban affairs? And, in general, what have businessmen learned about their ability to cope with large-scale social problems?

Such questions are of increasing concern to chief executives who are looking for yardsticks with which to measure their own companies' experience, as well as to others who are seeking guidelines in this area. Yet to date little information on these questions has been available. The federal government provides some data about subsidized programs, but it is hard to obtain information about programs not receiving public funds, and industry spokesmen are sometimes better supplied with optimism than with solid information.

In an attempt to bridge the information gap, I recently undertook for McKinsey & Company a nationwide study of 247 major urban-based companies, all of which appear on *Fortune*'s list of the largest U.S. financial and industrial corporations. The sample included commercial banks, life insurance companies, retailing, transportation, utilities, and industrial companies (heavy manufacturing, light manufacturing, petroleum, aerospace, electronics, office equipment, and others).

Top executives in most of these companies were interviewed at length about their corporate efforts in urban problem solving; supplementary data were obtained by questionnaire. Information covered the history and current extent of corporate involvement, the kinds of programs under way, the organizational status of urban affairs activities, the problems encountered and successes achieved, and other aspects of urban affairs efforts. Representatives of community groups and local and federal government officials were also interviewed to get a broader range of opinions.

On balance, I found that the great majority of the survey respondents were candid and quite willing to cooperate with any inquiry that might help them fit their experiences into a useful frame of reference. This article reports the principal findings, offers tentative conclusions, and suggests key issues that should be of central concern to those interested in the development of effective corporate urban affairs programs.

Before taking a look at the picture today, however, let me briefly

Author's note: I would like to thank Maxine Nord of McKinsey's Research Department and J. Edward Massey of McKinsey's New York office for their valuable assistance.

mention a matter of semantics. To most companies, "the urban crisis" means the problems of the black ghettoes: the growth and expansion of enclaves of poverty, rising unemployment and underemployment among the black poor, mounting racial tensions, and the threat of violent conflict. Most urban affairs programs are explicitly directed at opening company doors, in one way or another, to more nonwhites than ever before.

Other problems, such as air and water pollution, deficient housing, transportation, and educational facilities, and problems of public safety, obviously contribute to the urban crisis, but there are relatively few corporate programs addressed to these issues, and thus treatment of them is beyond the scope of this article.

THE PICTURE TODAY

Broadly speaking, the extensive and sometimes intensive corporate activity in trying to meet the urban challenge is accompanied by much less rhetoric today than that heard three years ago. Top company officers are now trying to appraise both the value of their urban affairs activity and the direction that further effort ought to take. The current tendency toward reflection is explained by four factors:

1. After the two relatively "cool" summers of 1968 and 1969, public and governmental pressure on corporations to act to ameliorate the urban crisis has somewhat diminished.

2. Urban affairs programs have already proved a lot more costly than many corporate officials anticipated. A number of companies, including some that had initially declined offers of government aid, say they cannot expand their efforts—or, in some cases, even continue them—without government subsidy.

3. The complex tasks of planning and managing urban affairs programs require more thought and skill than many of their sponsors realized at the start. One chief executive officer said: "I don't think any of us really knew what we were getting into. We saw action was needed, and we moved fast, maybe too fast. The task turned out to be Herculean." Many others, likewise chastened by experience, are reluctant to set their hopes too high for future achievement, and some are despondent about how little they have been able to accomplish to date.

4. Some urban affairs programs have had unanticipated, frequently unwelcome, effects on the internal life of large companies. Some corporate managers are arguing that their companies need a transition period to adjust to these unexpected developments.

On the whole, I found few companies satisfied with the progress they have made. Nearly everyone would agree with the suggestion of HEW

Exhibit 1   The urban affairs program pattern.

Category	Number of Active Companies	Percentage
Donations of cash, staff, executive time, and/or facilities	175	70%
Minority-group hiring programs	110	44
Hard-core hiring programs	86	34
Hard-core training and upgrading programs	39	16
Other urban affairs activities	30	12

Secretary Robert H. Finch that many corporations reacted with more energy than discretion to government pleas for help in meeting the urban crisis. Even the most resourceful and powerful companies have encountered difficulties. No one says he wants to give up, but a large majority of the top executives interviewed feel it is time to reexamine commitments and, perhaps, recast programs.

Organized urban affairs programs are a relatively new development in the corporate world. Of the 247 companies in this sample, 201 currently have some sort of urban affairs programs under way, but only 4 of these were started before 1965.

For the purposes of the study, I classified urban affairs programs into five categories. This program pattern, the numbers of companies active in each category, and the percentage in each type of involvement are shown in *Exhibit 1*. Variation by industry with respect to type and degree of urban affairs involvement is, of course, to be expected. While certain industries tend to lead in certain types of programs, banks, utilities, insurance, and aerospace are in the vanguard in all or most of the categories. (See *Exhibit 2* which provides comparisons.)

MOTIVATION FACTORS

The principal motive offered by top executives in the 201 companies with urban affairs programs is:

Enlightened self-interest—virtually all companies feel that social responsibility in this area is essential for the company as well as for the community. "We believe that our urban affairs work is good for Chase Manhattan in a strictly business sense," said David Rockefeller; "our efforts are aimed at creating the healthy economic and social environment that is vital to the very existence of any corporation."

16

Additional motives for urban activities are also suggested by the data:

Appearance—for four fifths of the companies, strengthening corporate reputation and image is a key objective.

Compliance—two fifths adopted these programs at least partly to satisfy government requirements for equal opportunity in employment and in the awarding of contracts; for a few, this was the main reason. One executive said flatly, "Our policy against discrimination was adopted in response to the law—not conscience, civic spirit, or sentiment."

Insurance—a third of the companies feel that their programs will help discourage boycotts, violence, and other threats to company well-being—a much desired result. As one manager put it, "The last thing we need is a summer 'work-in' by SDS."

Profit—one eighth of the companies are explicitly interested in opening up new markets by attracting minority group customers, or in selling their services as trainers or consultants to government or other companies. Said an executive, "Urban affairs is a new market for us. The poverty program has brought us government contracts."

The reader should not conclude that the 46 companies without urban affairs programs either are uniformly insensitive to the foregoing considerations or oppose urban affairs activities in principle. In fact, most of them told me in effect, "We'd like to, but we simply can't afford it right now."

Only 5 took the position that the urban crisis is not their worry. The executive vice president of one company asserted that he and his managers have no time for activities not aimed directly at improving corporate earnings. "We serve our social function by increasing earnings per share," he said. Another of the company's officers declared, "In our type of business, we sell to affluent professionals—engineers, doctors, and chemists. Frankly, we don't have to worry about minority groups."

RANGE OF ACTIVITIES

As the preceding discussion and *Exhibit 1* indicate, the most popular types of corporate urban affairs activities are: (1) company donations, (2) intensified minority employment, (3) hard-core hiring, and (4) training and upgrading programs. I shall now discuss my findings for each of these program types in more detail.

Company Donations

Corporate civic conscience has traditionally been expressed in the form of contributions to colleges, churches, and conservative social welfare

Exhibit 2 Who's doing what?

A. Corporate donations programs

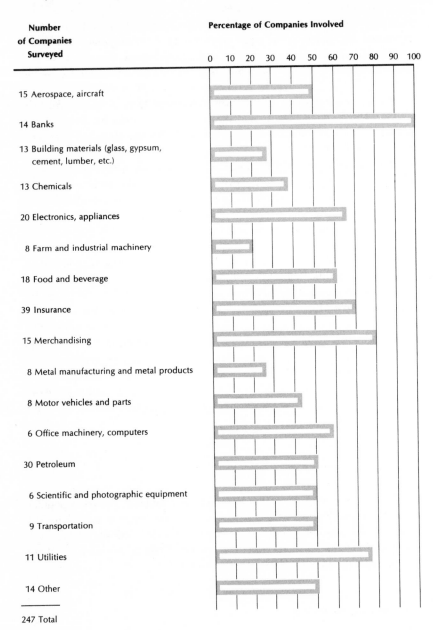

Number of Companies Surveyed	Percentage of Companies Involved

Source: McKinsey Survey of 247 Companies

Exhibit 2 Who's doing what? (cont.)

B. Corporate programs for minority-group employment

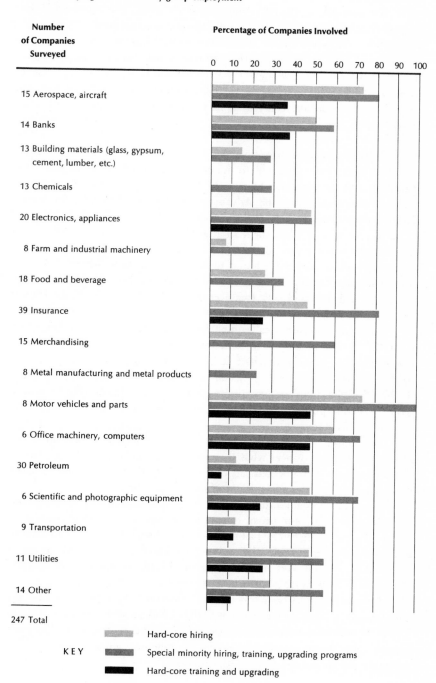

| Number of Companies Surveyed | Percentage of Companies Involved |

15 Aerospace, aircraft

14 Banks

13 Building materials (glass, gypsum, cement, lumber, etc.)

13 Chemicals

20 Electronics, appliances

8 Farm and industrial machinery

18 Food and beverage

39 Insurance

15 Merchandising

8 Metal manufacturing and metal products

8 Motor vehicles and parts

6 Office machinery, computers

30 Petroleum

6 Scientific and photographic equipment

9 Transportation

11 Utilities

14 Other

247 Total

KEY

▒ Hard-core hiring

▓ Special minority hiring, training, upgrading programs

█ Hard-core training and upgrading

19

agencies. Urban causes as such were seldom singled out. In the past three years, however, the urban crisis has brought about significant changes in the patterns and styles of corporate donations.

For example, of the 247 companies in the study, 175 have revised their annual donations lists since 1967 to include grants to national or local groups associated with urban affairs; at the same time, 45 of these companies have actually cut back on their donations to traditional charities. Amounts given to urban affairs activities since 1967 by individual companies have ranged from $10,000 to (in one case) $500,000 a year. The average figure was close to $175,000; according to my data, no company had given that much before 1967.

Shift of funds. Organizations benefiting most from corporate donations are those specifically oriented to minority-group problems. Both the Urban Coalition and the National Alliance of Businessmen are favored, as are the National Association for the Advancement of Colored People, the United Negro College Fund, and the Urban League.

Approximately one fourth of the 247 companies have added at least one of the latter three to their donations lists since 1967; another 23 companies, which had contributed to these organizations before 1967, are now giving significantly more. "We used to make a token contribution to the NAACP," said one company treasurer in a midwestern city. "Since 1968 it has received our largest grant."

Neighborhood and local community organizations, too, are benefiting from the change in corporate donations policies. Nearly one fifth of the companies have already donated funds for grass-roots self-help programs, neighborhood improvement projects, community education programs, and the like. Neighborhood or community group spokesmen, who might not have got past the receptionist five years ago, may find themselves ushered into the president's office today.

"We consider it most important to meet with neighborhood leaders and show them that we respect what they are doing," said one chief executive in San Francisco. "I think our attitude has helped us avoid the kind of demonstrations that have hurt a few of our competitors."

Some 27 companies did not wait to be approached; they went out and looked for worthy new urban causes and groups. A community leader in Watts, citing a phone call he had received from the public affairs officer of an aerospace company, said, "He wanted to know if we would accept a contribution. Would you believe some of the big companies are actually coming to us these days?"

Corporate liberality is less evident, however, where the more militant minority-group organizations such as CORE, SNCC, and the National Welfare Rights Organization are concerned. Out of 27 companies approached by such groups, only 3—an automobile maker, a computer manufacturer, and a national retail chain—responded with cash donations.

The accelerating shift of corporate donations to urban-oriented agencies, particularly those concerned with minority-group problems, has brought pressure on older charities to change their traditional approaches. "I didn't like to see our money being doled out to the same bland do-good groups," said the urban affairs officer of an aerospace company. "Our president saw my point and suggested to the local charities that they ought to involve themselves in neighborhood projects if they wanted our continued support."

(The United Fund is one well-known charity that recently reformulated its nationwide strategy in order to provide direct service on problems of poverty, health, and education in some communities rather than limiting itself to the role of coordinator among established agencies.)

Lack of evaluation. Despite the new patterns of donations, few companies have made a systematic effort to evaluate the large number of urban groups to determine what such groups do and whether to support their work. Board chairmen who formerly relied on personal acquaintanceships with the leaders of charities soliciting aid, or on lifelong familiarity with the work of establishment groups, are not likely to have rubbed elbows with black militants or to have a sense of who's who in the ghetto community.

But executives in charge of corporate donations programs know the high price of ignorance or naïveté when it comes to choosing among the many groups asking for company donations. Most of them have seen or experienced the political repercussions of an ill-informed decision about a grant. "We've been boycotted by groups on all sides of a major issue in this city because we gave money to all of them," said the president of a large paper products company.

Community groups are not the only source of protest worrying corporate donors. Companies that have updated their donations policies have also found themselves the target of criticism from shareholders and customers. "I don't think any of our stockholders has sold his stock yet because we gave to the Urban League, but I won't be surprised when it happens," said one top executive. But, as another put it, "You can't play it safe by not giving either." The consequences of turning down requests also have to be weighed very carefully. "A lot of the younger people on our staff have been telling me we ought to put our money where our mouth is," said the president of a Chicago-based company. "So we're about to announce substantial contributions for some ghetto projects right now."

Involvement of staff. In addition to funds, roughly one fourth of the companies donate staff and facilities as part of their urban affairs efforts. Typically, a company will have one or more executives serving on a community board, working with the Urban Coalition, advising on an antipoverty council or a Model Cities project, or on loan to the National Alliance of Businessmen.

Some of these officials work with black businessmen on management problems; others assist educators to improve school programs, lead youth groups in ghetto neighborhoods, or provide coaching in job-hunting techniques. Corporate staff specialists offer advice about financial management, administration, public relations, and manpower training to a wide variety of public or private urban affairs groups.

One well-known corporation set up a companywide service project under which employees volunteer for work in social agencies or with youth groups. In another company, employees serve after hours and on weekends in neighborhood renewal work and in a street academy program.

In all, nearly 40% of the 247 companies in the study encourage their staff members to help out in community projects, though less than half of these let them do so on company time.

John Gardner ... recently noted that many businessmen are uncomfortable at the thought of actually working with the poor. "We could get a lot more action if we told them they didn't have to sit down at a table with anyone but could just ... raise the money and then lob it over the walls of the ghetto," he said. Some of the top executives with whom I talked seemed to agree with this statement. They made clear that they prefer to make their community service contributions in cash rather than in time or the patience and tolerance demanded in community meetings.

Others prefer cash donations because they do not wish to be faced with the organization changes that are sometimes required by programs for unskilled new black hires. It is the possibility of organizational change rather than the dollar cost that worries them. When they choose the donations route, managers need not worry about the by-products of special hiring programs—new training requirements, new attitudes in hearing grievances, and new standards of employee behavior.

However, there are those who wonder whether companies can long afford not to set up special programs. "The question to me," said one executive, "is how long the blacks will be willing to accept payoffs rather than programs."

Minority Employment

In most companies, the expression "minority-group member" means a black or a Spanish-speaking American—though in some instances other minority-group members have also benefited from the new corporate equal opportunity programs.

Since 1967, 110 of the 247 companies have set up special programs to hire and upgrade minority-group members who, unlike the hard-core poor, are both skilled and qualified to fill jobs. And since the programs are significantly different for the two groups, I distinguish between them throughout this study. Companies in every industry group have set up new programs; 63 of the 110 companies with such programs concentrate on filling entry-level jobs and recruiting people between the ages of 18 and 30. Only a few companies are focusing their efforts on older recruits.

Recruitment programs for young blacks are often run in conjunction with community agencies, schools, and colleges. Banks and insurance and telephone companies, wrestling with increasingly serious manpower shortages, operate the largest number of such programs. "We aren't trying to find more blacks; we're trying to find more help," said a personnel director in a West Coast company.

His point was echoed by other company representatives, particularly those with plants located in urban areas whose ethnic composition has changed drastically in recent years. "We've always hired most of our people from right around here," said a factory manager in a large New Jersey city. "Twenty years ago there were not many Negroes in the neighborhood, so we had practically an all-white payroll. Now the area is nearly all black, and the labor force reflects the change."

Some executives conceded that their newly mounted minority-group hiring programs represented a sharp departure from previous unwritten policy. "I think we have reason to be a bit defensive about our past record," said a New York corporate official. "You can tell when a man was hired in this bank simply by the sound of his name. Thirty-five years ago we used to look for Germans and Swiss, even for the lowest level jobs. Then during World War II, we began to hire the Irish. By the time fighting broke out in Korea, we were taking Italians and Jews. And now, of course, we are actively recruiting blacks and Puerto Ricans."

Two thirds of the executives interviewed said they would like to see more minority-group executives in their organizations; but only 21 companies in the survey sample make special efforts to recruit minority-group members for managerial and executive positions.[1] However, 71 more have set up programs to train potential managers among minority-group' employees already on the payroll.

Problem of polarization. One consequence of sharply increased minority-group hires, though foreseen by most companies with these programs, has been the tensions created by employee resentment and hostility toward new black or Spanish-speaking workers.

In some cases, capable senior employees have quit in protest against real or imagined favoritism toward new black hires. Sometimes alleged backlash serves as convenient justification for lackadaisical hiring efforts. "I wish we could do more," said one manager, "but those men in the plant are such rednecks that we haven't dared to try."

[1] For a recent study of discrimination in executive selection, see Robert P. Quinn et al., *The Chosen Few* (Ann Arbor, Survey Research Center, University of Michigan, 1968).

More often, though, managers are genuinely concerned. "We've learned the hard way how important it is to be fair to our white employees and to give them the same breaks we try to give the blacks," said one executive. "We had a real backlash problem here until we made it clear that *everyone* was going to benefit from our program efforts."

Attempts to prevent polarization among employee groups get top priority in some companies, and many of the executives interviewed agreed that more needs to be done to motivate white employees to cooperate with minority hiring and training. I should point out that the National Alliance of Businessmen, like many of the private consulting firms that have sprung up around the urban problem, offers workshops, seminars, sensitivity sessions, and the like, for supervisors and managers whose companies are having problems of this kind.

Whether workshops alone or sensitivity training will solve the problems of overworked and overstrained supervisors remains an open question. There is evidence to support the view that companies will have to consider providing material incentives—that is, awards for reducing turnover and developing new workers, or even bonuses or pay increases for the extra work.

More pleasant atmosphere. Minority-group hiring programs have had other unanticipated consequences of a more welcome kind. Executives assigned to urban affairs functions, particularly those involved in training or supervising new minority-group employees, say that urban affairs involvement is changing their companies in an unexpected but pleasant way.

Mores governing job performance and advancement, as well as everyday behavior (dress, speech, decorum) after years of rigidity are becoming flexible. Where earlier newcomers to corporate life automatically submitted to company requirements, black employees in particular have successfully resisted the organizational ethic of conformity. There is evidence that a new chapter in corporate sociology is being written by blacks who, in an atmosphere that had always been strictly white-shirt and short-haircut, come to work wearing dashikis and Afro hairdos.

At least some of the executives and employees who work in companies undergoing ethnic and racial change consider themselves beneficiaries. "Urban affairs is fun," said one executive. "And we never had much of that around here. I was one of those obedient parochial-school types hired by this company a generation ago. I spent my first ten years keeping my mouth shut."

In some ways, of course, the new black employee has more bargaining power when it comes to advancement, as well as on personal matters like dress and behavior. For right or wrong, personnel directors and other supervisors in many companies think twice before summarily discharging or reprimanding minority-group workers. "I'll complain to the Equal Employment Opportunity people" is a threat to which more and more managers are sensitive.

The black man's presence in normally conservative banks, insurance companies, and other corporations often works as a force that relaxes, even in some degree humanizes, the atmosphere. Some companies see the change as a threat, but in others even the top men admit to enjoying the cool breeze of cultural variety.

Hard-core Hiring

Industry has been under the greatest pressure from government and private groups to participate in programs to hire and train the hard-core poor. Any serious effort in this direction introduces new costs, for training the hard-core is more expensive than training other new employees. For some companies training costs represent a budget item never before needed for filling entry-level jobs. Companies already maintaining training departments have found it necessary to add specialists and acquire new training materials. Other new expenses are incurred for counseling services, expanded medical services and basic education programs.

Intervention of government. Despite the increased cost connected with hard-core hiring, federal eligibility requirements have discouraged some executives from seeking training subsidies. They complain about having to hire from among candidates screened and certified as hard-core by the Concentrated Employment Program or the Employment Service. In addition, companies receiving government help must allow the examination of payroll records, personnel folders, and training and upgrading practices.

Some companies consider the intrusion of government inspectors more burdensome than bearing the cost of hiring and training the hard-core on their own. (Companies not participating in subsidized programs that claim to have hired hard-core workers have been accused of "skimming the cream" of the supply in order to avoid candidates with the worst problems.)

In my study, a little more than half of the companies that were operating hard-core training programs were doing so with the help of government funds.

Depending on the observer's perspective, the overall results of hard-core hiring programs can be ranked from highly encouraging to "just another numbers game." But there is consensus that the problem is a tough one, not only for the hard-core coming into jobs but also for the regular work force. Hiring people with long histories of economic and often emotional handicaps has presented employee and employer alike with an assortment of difficulties.

Training & Upgrading

Whatever the reasons—and there are many—only a third of the 247 companies are actively hiring the hard-core, and fewer than half of these provide special training and upgrading programs.

Aerospace companies, financial institutions, and computer manufacturers account for the largest number of hard-core hiring programs under way. This is a fact of which companies in other industries seem, in some cases, rather touchily aware.

"Don't compare us with those guys," said a vice president of a new conglomerate in explaining his company's modest urban efforts. "The insurance companies have more cash than we do, and aerospace has to bend over backwards to set up training programs as a way of holding on to government contracts."

Another observer insisted that "it wasn't until after the Detroit riots that the automobile makers got busy. If their factories were in East Cupcake, they wouldn't be so energetic about the hard-core."

While such explanations undoubtedly have some validity, it is also true that hard-core training and upgrading programs simply make more sense for certain industries than for others. A real need for unskilled workers is the best incentive to hire the hard-core. Some respondents made it clear that they would have invested in special training programs even if the riots had never occurred and the Kerner Report had never been written.

"We were willing to try anyone and anything," said the corporate personnel director of a Chicago-based utility. "Our traditional supplies of manpower were beginning to run dry. So we didn't have to be pushed to give the hard-core a try."

Training and upgrading programs fall into three basic categories: on the job, vestibule, and training in a specially set up subsidiary which in some instances is intended to be "spun off" to community groups.

On-the-job approach. This is by far the most prevalent kind of training and upgrading program found in the companies studied: 80% of all new hires in the 39 companies offering hard-core training are enrolled in programs of this type. The economics suggest the reason. The on-the-job approach does not require costly separate facilities or special training staffs. For the most part, the burden of providing for the needs of the new workers falls on the shoulders of line personnel. And, on the surface at least, companies can undertake such training without changing their production practices.

Even though special training is provided by fewer than half of the 86 companies that hire the hard-core, recognition of its importance is growing. Very high turnover of hard-core hires, particularly in the first weeks on the job, has brought home the message: adequate training may cost less than the high turnover associated with no training.

The automobile makers, who probably took on a larger share of the hard-core than any other industry in the year following publication of the Kerner Report, gradually came to realize the need for special training. At first, these companies assigned most of the new workers to jobs as operators and assemblers after only a few hours of orientation. The high attrition that immediately occurred convinced them to offer special training.

A major appliance manufacturer also modified its approach after initially placing employees on the job immediately. To cut down on turnover, it now provides a day of orientation, including a tour of the plant, introductions to supervisors and co-workers, and instructions for such run-of-the-mill requirements as punching time cards and taking coffee breaks. The company has also set up an on-the-job counseling program.

Vestibule technique. Conducted in a separate facility by a skilled training staff, this kind of program provides a sort of halfway house, designed to help the hard-core new hire adjust to the world of work and learn at least the rudiments of the job he has been hired to do. During the training period, new employees are insulated from the possible resentment of co-workers, and supervisors have the time and the responsibility to be sympathetic and offer advice on personal as well as work problems.

The vestibule technique helps build the morale of insecure, shy workers by offering the opportunity to rehearse with their peers before going into production jobs. Of the 247 companies I studied, 18 make use of this approach, which they view as less costly than on-the-job training in the long run.

Among the large automobile manufacturers, both Ford and Chrysler established vestibules. And Lockheed provides an example of an aerospace company that has converted hard-core training into a new business enterprise. It operates a successful training vestibule in Sunnyvale, California, where hard-core workers are trained for jobs in 41 companies that have formed a consortium in the area for the purpose of hard-core hiring.

Subsidiary method. Anyone who follows the business press is familiar with Aerojet-General's Watts Manufacturing Company in Los Angeles, North American Rockwell's NARTRANS (also in Los Angeles), Control Data's subsidiary in North Minneapolis, and Avco Manufacturing's printing plant in the Roxbury section of Boston. And there are more than two dozen other companies that have set up wholly owned subsidiaries or subsidiairies destined for eventual ownership and management by community groups.

Of the 247 companies in this study, 11 have set up such subsidiaries. Obviously, the number of employees trained and upgraded in such programs is small. However, the climate of acceptance and understanding which these plants provide for so-called unemployables constitutes what many consider the best milieu for training hard-core hires—as well as minority-group members who hold or will hold management positions.

Both the subsidiary approach and the vestibule, however, are vulnerable to community criticism on one point: in both cases, the company "quarantines" its hard-core workers and thus protects its regular operations from the organizational changes that might be needed if the new workers were brought into already existing operations. Thus vestibules and subsidiaries alike are segregated facilities by definition—and white-imposed segregation, however benevolent, has overtones which anger many in the black community.

Ghetto Programs

A relatively small number of the companies that participated in this study are involved in what can be classified as ghetto economic development programs. These activities include loans and other assistance for housing programs, schools, and transportation. Thus all 39 insurance companies in the study are participating in the mortgage fund put together by their national association to assist construction of low-cost housing. Most banks have set up new lending programs for small minority-group businessmen; some offer money-management courses for ghetto residents.

About 12% of the companies I studied are involved in special urban programs not directly concerned in any way with race or poverty. Most of these other programs are designed to increase income, as well as to assist the cities; they are based on the view that urban problems present a demand—or a market—for corporate services and products.

ORGANIZATIONAL STATUS

One indication of the importance of a function is the position of the box it occupies on the company organization chart. Accordingly, I examined the organizational position of urban affairs in each of the companies covered by the study (*Exhibit 3*). I also explored, wherever possible, the work background of the man who heads it.

Reporting Relationship

In all but 46 of the 247 companies, someone has been assigned full- or part-time responsibility for urban affairs; only 2 of these assignments date back earlier than 1967. Urban affairs is found most frequently in the personnel department (67 companies), followed by public relations (40), and public or government affairs (38). Personnel is an obvious choice for those companies which view urban affairs as primarily involving minority-group employment.

In such companies, the urban affairs director (sometimes called a minority-group adviser or an employee development officer) may be the company's inside troubleshooter for problems associated with recruiting, training, and developing minority-group members. He listens to their grievances and anticipates and prevents misunderstandings. Such a staff position was created in one company after black employees complained to

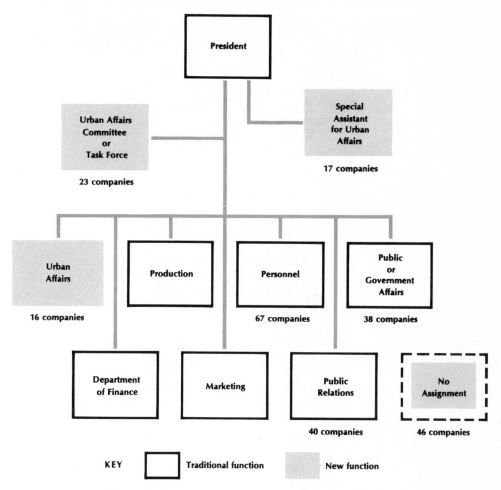

President

Urban Affairs Committee or Task Force

23 companies

Special Assistant for Urban Affairs

17 companies

Urban Affairs

16 companies

Production

Personnel

67 companies

Public or Government Affairs

38 companies

Department of Finance

Marketing

Public Relations

40 companies

No Assignment

46 companies

KEY Traditional function New function

Source: McKinsey Survey of 247 Companies

Exhibit 3 Urban affairs and the corporate organization chart.

their local human rights commission that their employer practiced discrimination in advancement policies.

Assigning urban affairs to public relations emphasizes, of course, an external focus. "My job is to smooth out troubles between the company and the community," said one urban affairs man in a public relations spot. Companies mainly concerned about contract compliance and other government relations see urban affairs as the province of the legislative liaison officer and the government relations staff, and also emphasize the external, reputational focus.

29

Urban affairs responsibilities in 23 of the companies have been handed to a task force of officers from several departments. "We didn't know where to put it, so we formed a committee," said a New York banker. Most of these companies called their committees a stopgap measure, to be replaced by assignment to an existing department or to a newly created one.

The spokesman for a nationwide supermarket chain described his company's committee situation. "We had accumulated a $200,000 urban affairs bill," he said. "We were conducting 14 training programs on the East Coast for cashiers and clerks, negotiating with three community groups who were boycotting us for selling California grapes, and shaping a new advertising campaign to convince our customers in low-income neighborhoods that we cared about them. Each of these activities was being monitored by different people in corporate headquarters, and we thought a coordinating structure was needed. So we set up a committee."

In 16 companies, some of which had previously tried the committee approach, the decision had been made to create a new department for urban affairs. "We didn't want our urban affairs man locked into personnel or PR work exclusively," said one senior executive; "urban affairs ought to have a niche of its own." Another reported, "Urban affairs officers can be buried as quickly as they're born. In this company, we could have accomplished that by assigning the man to Personnel. No one gets out of there alive."

Most of the new urban affairs departments were run by former personnel or PR officials.

A special assistant for urban affairs, reporting to the chief executive, has been designated in 17 companies. The duties of these assistants include speech writing, reviewing requests for donations, meeting with community groups, and interpreting the company's interest in urban affairs to line executives.

"I thought I'd like to have a right-hand man especially assigned to it," said one company president. "My urban affairs assistant keeps me up to date on all these problems and what we are doing about them. I'll probably bureaucratize him eventually and convert him and the assignment into a full-fledged department."

Most of the companies with an urban affairs activity on the organization chart staff it with one to three persons at the corporate level. When extensive training programs are offered, these are generally run by a training group in personnel.

The reporting relationship is often an indicator of the importance a company attaches to a function or unit. Urban affairs is no exception. When it reports at the presidential or vice presidential levels, its power is increased in most companies. In my study, besides the 17 companies with special urban affairs assistants to the president, 5 heads of urban affairs departments also report to presidents. A little less than half of the others report at the vice presidential level.

Executive Profile

To learn more about the men (there were no women) charged with urban affairs responsibilities, we talked with 61 of these executives and corresponded with many more. What are their backgrounds? Do they come from the business world or from the social sciences? Are they organization men with little personal interest in urban problems, or social reformers who have infiltrated the corporate world?

Typically, the urban affairs man is in his early 30's. He has served in other functions before moving into his current job, and he plans to move on to another, bigger job in the company eventually. The chances are 10 to 1 that he is white.

Several company presidents indicated that urban affairs is a job for young executives, not older, seasoned, or highly trained people. "Young people understand urban problems better than middle-aged line officers," said the chief executive of a San Francisco company known for its active work in urban affairs. "I think it's good training for junior executives."

While I found no fiery-eyed evangelists among corporate urban affairs officers, roughly half of the men interviewed expressed enthusiasm, even excitement, about their assignment. Some saw it as an opportunity to make the corporate structure more responsive to human needs.

"The message we're trying to get through to the top is that what's good for our hard-core trainees is good for all the employees," said one young urban affairs officer, "but I don't know if top management is hearing us." In this group, the enthusiasm was tempered mainly by some skepticism about top management's intentions to carry through on the program. "I'm afraid it may be a passing phase rather than a long-term commitment to social problem solving," said another young executive.

Most of the other younger people saw their jobs as a career opportunity—a place to get "exposure" and to make contacts, both within the company and on the outside. The older man seemed to see it as a good berth, after years of work in higher pressure jobs. Only seven urban affairs men planned to make their careers in this area. "If the action were in some other area, I'd be there," said a 30-year-old vice president of personnel; "and, when it moves, I'll hand urban problems over to someone else." The youngest officers in this group frequently expressed the opportunistic-cum-idealistic view that a stint in urban affairs is like a tour of duty in the Peace Corps: two years off to do some good.

Most urban affairs officers are amateurs in the field; only five of them had had experience or training that they themselves considered relevant—not that it is clear what "relevant" experience in such a new area might be. All are

31

college graduates, but their academic preparation had been mostly in business subjects; only a few majored in sociology, political science, or history.

A few companies, however, have sought specialists for their urban affairs departments, hoping to attract "new kinds" of people into the organization. One company's urban affairs executive is a Peace Corps alumnus; an airline recruited a former Congressional aide; a retail chain hired a city planner. Still other companies have hired a city manager, a college professor, and a lawyer for their urban affairs posts.

"The promise of urban affairs work helps us woo young people who otherwise would not be interested in us," said one company spokesman. But, in general, the business schools are providing recruits for urban affairs, along with other corporate jobs.

Appointment to an urban affairs position, according to some of these men, is not always an advancement or a career opportunity. "I'm not sure whether I was promoted or shoved aside," said the new urban affairs officer in a large petroleum company. He had been transferred from a marketing position in the field to head a new urban affairs headquarters staff.

Because of the ambiguity of the role, its tentative nature, and its newness in many companies, there is some anxiety about whether the job may be a dead end. "If I didn't really care about what I'm doing, it would be easy to see this as a road to nowhere," said one young urban affairs executive.

In some companies, of course, top management's strong interest in the new function makes the urban affairs role an important and desirable one. In 5 of the companies, the new urban affairs department was given a commitment of resources, funds, and talent thought of as impressive by company insiders, making it attractive to almost everyone on the way up.

LOOKING AHEAD

The optimism of businessmen about their ability to relieve the nation's urban crisis has been tempered as a result of their experiences in the past three years. My study found many corporate leaders distressed that urban affairs is still unfinished business in their companies. Though this reaction might seem natural for executives who expect to achieve superior track records on every project they undertake, it is probably not realistic.

After all, urban affairs is a new area of corporate involvement, abounding in hazards and imponderables. There are no formulas for success and no ready-made guidelines to follow. Business is only now beginning to learn which approaches have a chance of working and which might best be avoided.

If businessmen are depressed about what they have been unable to do, many of them are further disappointed by what they perceive as a waning of interest on the part of the federal government. Though measures to provide increased financial aid have often been discussed, few of these—such as new and easier to obtain subsidies, tax credits, and guarantees of government business—have actually been made available.

On the positive side, business is now beginning to realize some direct and tangible returns on its investment in urban affairs. A few companies (primarily those with training expertise) have been able to convert urban affairs into a market for their skills and products, and we can expect their number to increase as corporate understanding of urban problems grows and managerial experience deepens.

However, as business continues to involve itself in community problems, it is likely to learn that technology alone is not the answer; most of our urban dilemmas have moral, legal, and political dimensions. And solutions may require skills that are scarce in business and raise issues that not all businessmen are prepared to cope with. Thus, though a company might very well come up with a feasible way to construct low-cost public housing or an efficient and economical way to build new mass-transit systems, politicians and the electorate—not businessmen—must decide where the housing ought to be located and who should live in it, or whether economy and efficiency are the most important factors to weigh in solving our traffic problems.

Some would say that businessmen, most of whom are amateurs in politics, ought to continue playing a limited role in urban affairs by keeping their own houses in order through expanded employment and training programs, and by providing money for the cities through taxes and donations. Many businessmen, my findings indicate, would agree.

But whether a company opts for a more limited or a broader approach to urban affairs, greater sophistication about the issues involved in urban problem solving is likely to develop in the future.

Key Issues

Though it is too early to look for formulas or guidelines for success in urban affairs, this study does suggest some key issues that will need to be addressed by managers interested in running effective programs and avoiding major risks. As companies move into the next phase of the attack on urban problems, they are likely to find themselves pondering, in particular, six points.

1. *The need to arrive at realistic objectives.*

If urban affairs programs are going to be managed effectively, they have to be taken seriously as a corporate activity. And if they are to be taken seriously, viable objectives must be agreed on. What does the company want to accomplish through urban affairs activities? Is management mainly interested in reputation building? Does it seek to improve intergroup relations in the community? Does it principally want to tap a new source of labor? These questions need to be answered very early, on the basis of realistic, fact-founded analysis.

2. The need to explore alternative program possibilities.

There are many routes to take: expanded or new donations programs designed to make cash, staff time and expertise, and/or facilities available to carefully chosen outside groups; special minority employment (or employment and training) programs, ranging from expanded hiring to setting up subsidiaries; loans and other assistance to minority-group businessmen; "adoption" of schools; cooperation with local programs to upgrade housing, recreation, transportation facilities, and so on. Each has different implications in terms of cost, time, short- and long-range impact on company and community, and political risk. Companies need to understand the range of choice (and risk) before commitments are made.

3. The need to predict and allow for possible side effects.

A company that wants to undertake large-scale training activities ought to begin by analyzing the kinds of jobs for which it wants to train people, the kinds of people who will be trained and their aptitude levels, and the facilities that will be needed. If ongoing production activities will be affected, what steps will be necessary in order to prevent production slow-downs while training is under way? Will additional experienced employees have to be hired? What incentives will be necessary to motivate older employees?

4. The need to make a realistic inventory of available resources.

What will the budget allow? A hard look at the economic factors is especially important; some corporations that have undertaken large urban affairs commitments without fully facing up to cost considerations found themselves with unexpected bills to pay because of production time lost in new training programs. Sound business analysis presupposes the courage to look at the numbers and decide how much the company is really prepared to pay. "Unless social conscience includes a realistic appraisal of cost, we are likely to get only a window-dressing approach to urban problems by the private sector," states Frank Riessman of New York University, who has written extensively on techniques for training the hard-core.

5. The need to understand the political and sociological dimensions of urban problems.

Minority group training programs, as well as efforts to involve the company with community groups, will have implications for the internal life of the company. Sometimes management will be pressured to revise traditional personnel practices and scuttle long-established rules. Top executives may unexpectedly find their attitudes, values, and at times their very deportment challenged by the new breed of employees. Some businessmen will welcome such changes, but others will wish they had been warned.

6. The need to have workable organizational arrangements.

The kind of activity chosen, the objectives sought, the hazards to be avoided—all help to determine where urban affairs should fit into the corporate structure, and who should be put in charge. The urban affairs assignment can provide an attractive and challenging role that can enrich the internal life of the organization, as well as help solve community problems. But how the job is defined and how much support it receives will play a part in determining the kind of man (or woman) who will be willing to accept the responsibility.

Finally, it is well to remember that companies have many opportunities to participate in the fight against urban problems without creating an urban affairs department, donating to ghetto causes, or tackling the "other" urban crises. Significant participation in the battle against urban problems can be carried out through reappraising the company's ways of doing business.

For example, by setting aside some deposit funds for placement in minority-owned banks (or banks with active urban programs), by selecting suppliers (of paper clips or heavy machinery) on the basis of their equal employment records or other urban affairs activities, a company can have an influence on what happens in our cities. Influence can also be wielded in decisions on distribution policy and the selection of plant and facility locations.

In short, a company can create an impact simply by setting an example in its own industry and in the communities it serves. To the management more concerned with impact than image, such approaches will commend themselves—whether or not the company's human and financial resources permit it to take the more direct and dramatic routes reviewed in this article.

4

A Code for Professional Integrity

RALPH NADER

In the previous selection businessmen were treated as part of the solution to social problems. In this article, Ralph Nader considers them to be part of the problem. Here again we are reminded of a cartoon that appeared in a recent issue of The New Yorker. *The cartoon shows two prosperous executives sitting in overstuffed easy chairs in their club. One of the men tells the other that if being a major industrialist means being a major polluter, so be it.*

Nader feels that business and government organizations are sick and must change in fundamental ways. Minor modifications are not enough to get good service for the public. As a dissenter working outside the corporate and

Reprinted from *The New York Times*, January 15, 1971, p. 17. Copyright 1971 by The New York Times Company. Reprinted by permission.

governmental systems, Nader would like to encourage dissent within those systems. He assumes that dissent by knowledgeable, ethical professionals can have tremendous impact on the organizations for which they work.

Even though Nader does not discuss dissent by managers, there are signs that young executives are beginning to speak out against organizational misbehavior. Who would protect these dissenting executives? The Society for the Advancement of Management, the American Management Association, and the Academy of Management do not see this as their role. Should they?

Are professors more likely to express dissent than are other professional people? Is this related to their professional society's defense of academic freedom? To the system of tenure?

In the selection that follows, Nader recommends three basic changes designed to end the silence of professionals in the face of what he views as organizational illness. Would these changes make much of an impact on organizations? Would these changes actually offer protection to critics inside the system? Is prevention of punishment enough, or would potential critics also need some form of reward to motivate them.

Nader discusses the ideal mission of professionals such as physicians, lawyers, economists, engineers, and scientists who are employed in business and governmental organizations but does not discuss the mission of the professional manager. What is the mission of such a manager?

At what point should corporate or government scientists, engineers or other professionals dissent openly from their employer-organization's policy? If the professional does dissent, what is there to protect or defend his decision to place his professional conscience over what he believes is his organization's illegal, hazardous or unconscionable behavior?

These are important questions and they are rarely answered in the context of controversies such as the defoliation of Vietnam or the standards for constructing nuclear power plants. "Duty," said Alfred North Whitehead, "arises from our potential control over the course of events." Staying silent in the face of a professional duty, almost invariably articulated in the profession's canons of ethics, has direct impact on the level of consumer and environmental hazards. This awareness has done little to upset the slavish adherence to "following company orders."

Employed professionals are among the first to know about industrial dumping of mercury or fluoride sludge into waterways, defectively designed automobiles, undisclosed adverse effects of prescription drugs and pesticides. They are first to grasp the technical capabilities to prevent existing product or pollution hazards. But they are very often the last to speak out, much less refuse to be recruited for acts of corporate or governmental negligence or predation.

The twenty-year collusion by the domestic automobile companies against development and marketing of exhaust control systems is a tragedy, among other things, for engineers who, minion-like, programmed the technical artifices of the industry's defiance. Settling the antitrust case brought by the Justice Department against such collusion did nothing to confront the question of subverted engineering integrity.

A prime foundation for professionalism is sufficient independence to pursue a mission that could save lives, secure rights, or preserve property unjustly imperiled by the employer-organization. The overriding ethic of the professional is to foresee and forestall the risks to which he is privy by his superior access and knowledge, regardless of vested interests. Physicians should strive first to prevent disease; lawyers should apply the law to prevent auto casualties; economists should try to clarify product and service characteristics in the context of quality competition; engineers should make technology more humane as a condition of its use; scientists should anticipate the harmful uses of their genius.

All these ideal missions unfortunately possess neither the outside career roles for their advancement nor the barest of independence for the organizationally employed professional to exert his conscience in practice beyond that of the employer's dictates. The multiple pressures and sanctions of corporate and government employers are very effective to daunt the application of professional integrity. When on occasion such integrity breaks through these restraints, the impact is powerful, which might explain the organization's determined policy of prior restraint.

During the past half dozen years of disclosures about corporate and government injustices, the initiators have largely been laymen or experts who were outsiders to the system exposed. The list is legion—black lung, brown lung, DDT, mercury contamination, enzymes, phosphates and NTA in detergents, SST hazards ... MER-29, and nerve gas storage and disposal. Inside the systems, however, mum's the word.

Three basic changes are needed as a start.

First, Congress should enact legislation providing for safeguards against arbitrary treatment by corporations against employes who exercise their constitutional rights in a lawful manner. At a minimum, such an act would help Congress obtain expert witnesses for its hearings and authorize the courts to protect a professional's "skill rights" in a far more defined manner.

Second, employed professionals should organize to provide a solid constituency for the adoption by management of the requisite due process procedures, which the professional can appeal to or enforce in the courts.

Third, professional societies should clearly stake out their readiness to defend their colleagues when they are arbitrarily treated for invoking their professional ethics toward the corporate or government activity in which they were involved. Most of the established professional societies or associations never challenge corporate or governmental treatment of lawyers, engineers, scientists, or physicians as the American Association of University Professors has done on occasion for university teachers denied academic freedom. And where there is no willingness to challenge, there is less willingness for the employe to dissent.

To require an act of courage for stating perceived truth is to foster a system of self-censorship and the demise of individual conscience against the organization.

5

Tomorrow's Management: A More Adventurous Life in a Free-Form Corporation

MAX WAYS

As you read this selection, you might profitably think about your answers to several questions discussed therein. The first deals with the fact that proportionately there are many more managers in the United States than there are in the U.S.S.R. or Great Britain. How can you explain this difference? Do you agree with the author that the mission of executives is to manage change and that America's economy, because it is more dynamic and more innovative, therefore requires more managers? Will the number of American managers continue to expand faster than America's economy? The author believes that it will because the life cycle of products is becoming shorter, companies are accepting greater social responsibility, and there is increased international competition. Finally, what do you believe will be the impact of the new information technology on the number of persons in management and on the role of these managers? Mr. Ways argues that computers help to accelerate innovation and thereby increase the demand for managers. He further argues that the more managers know, the more they need to know in order to cope with the increasing complexity of their jobs.

What industrialization was to the nineteenth century, management is to the twentieth. Almost unrecognized in 1900, management has become the central activity of our civilization. It employs a high proportion of our educated men and determines the pace and quality of our economic progress, the effectiveness of our government services, and the strength of our national defense. The way we "manage," the way we shape our organizations, affects and reflects what our society is becoming.

The essential task of modern management is to deal with change. Management is the agency through which most changes enter our society, and it is the agency that then must cope with the environment it has set in turbulent motion. To carry out its active social role of adaptation, management itself, therefore, must be adaptable. Already the nature of management has undergone drastic alterations. As it stands today on the threshold of the final third of its first century, modern management seems pregnant with another metamorphosis. It is now possible to see in outline the shapes toward which the next generation of management will tend.

One of the more obvious questions of the last ten years has been whether the number of management men will continue to expand faster than the economy. Will many of the millions now pouring forth from the universities find that management is a contracting job market in which they will be surplus? The question is currently linked with predictions about the computer revolution. Without doubt, computers have taken over some work formerly done by middle management, and are capable of taking over much more. But this fact is only a part of the whole busy scene. Management is still expanding and probably will continue to expand as *new* tasks are created. Indeed, the new information technology represented by computers is one of the important factors creating the new tasks.

A less obvious question raised by the computers bears on the character, rather than the size, of future management. Will instant access by top management to operational information reverse the trend toward managerial decentralization, which has had the salutary effect of giving more independent scope to more people? It is easy to think of examples where authority now dispersed might be efficiently reconcentrated at the top with the aid of computers. But such reconcentration is not the main trend in organization today. Since the new information technology began coming into use in the Fifties, the trend toward decentralization has probably been accelerated, indicating that there were better reasons for decentralization than the lack of instant information at headquarters. Computers *can* be used to reinforce either a centralizing policy or its opposite; the probability increases that decentralization will in the coming decades be carried to lengths undreamed of ten years ago.

. . .

Assets, they say, make men conservative. Because language, incomparably the greatest of mankind's social assets, changes slowly, we are forced to describe the new and unfamiliar in terms drawn from the old and familiar. Since some change occurs in any period there is always a lag between actuality and the past-bound words we use to describe it. Where change is slow or is confined to a narrow segment of life, this language lag does no great harm. In the fast-changing twentieth century, however, the language lag causes untold confusion.

Corporations, government agencies, and scientific institutes are really quite different from tribes, families, armies, feudal estates, and monasteries, but our ideas of the newer organizations are distorted by an anachronistic vocabulary drawn from the older group. Business leaders of the late nineteenth century were called "captains of industry" or "robber barons." Government bureaus have "chiefs." Many present-day organizations still think they operate by "chains of command." From one point of view, management stands in the place of "the owner," a historically familiar figure; it is easy to slip into the habit of talking about a company as if it were merely a complicated kind of plantation with hundreds of "overseers" substituted for Mr. Legree.

As late as the 1920's some American law schools were handling what little they had to say about the internal life of corporations under the rubric of "the law of master and servant." The very word "manager" suggests—even more strongly than "management"—that the basis of the activity is power over other men. (In the 1950's, General Electric recognized that a large proportion of the people in management did not, in any literal sense, "manage." G.E. began to speak of management as made up of two groups: managers and "functional individual contributors." The number of "fics," who may be physical or social scientists, lawyers, or public-relations experts and who are often future managers or ex-managers, is increasing in nearly all large companies.) In short, the early image of the corporation was heavily loaded on the side of authoritarianism because the early vocabulary to management came from the patriarchal family, from military organization, from legal concepts of ownership, and from memories of the feudal hierarchy.

Upon this primal image of the corporation some less antique but equally misleading concepts were then superimposed. The science of economics developed in the nineteenth century when the public had become familiar with mechanical principles. Both classical and Marxist economics leaned heavily on mechanical analogies. The economists' model still in service today is a machine. Since humanity is that element in economics least susceptible to mechanical treatment and prediction, economics tends to suppress the human factors. "Economic man" is the most oversimplified of all views of our otherwise interesting species. Man's astounding capacities must be expressed in erglike units, man's even more astounding appetites must be reduced to chilly abstractions resembling Newton's gravitational pull, and man's most profound uncertainties must be ignored because they cannot be quantified. This dehumanized economists' model of the total economy, recast in compact form, merged with the older authoritarian myth of the corporation. The resulting popular image: a kind of life-with-father, automated.

BUREAUCRACY AS A MACHINE

Early in the twentieth century the great German sociologist Max Weber, noting common elements in business organizations, government bureaus, and the Prussian military structure, called the new organizational form "bureaucracy." In a bureaucratic system, public or private business was carried out "according to *calculable rules* and 'without regard for persons.' " Functionaries with specialized training learn their tasks better by practice. "Precision, speed, unambiguity ... unity, strict subordination, reduction of fraction—these are raised to the optimum point in the strictly bureaucratic administration, and especially in its monocratic form." Weber said the new form was succeeding because the "bureaucratic mechanism compares with other organizations exactly as does the machine with the nonmechanical modes of production." Around the same time, Frederick W. Taylor in the U.S. promulgated "scientific management" in which workers were regarded as parts of a corporate machine, the excellence of which was to be measured, of course, by its "efficiency."

It is against this persistent image of dehumanized modern organization that students today react with the sort of castration phobia expressed in the picket-sign slogan: "I am a human being; do not fold, bend, or mutilate." This fear and defiance of modern organization appears in scores of novels and plays, which restate Charlie Chaplin's *Modern Times*; the myth is the root of many antibusiness (and some antigovernment) attitudes; it even pervades management itself, souring fruitful careers with the sense that life is being sacrificed to a domineering and impersonal organization. The man who says, "I am a cog" does not thereby become a cog—but he may become an unhappy and "alienated" man.

BEYOND EFFICIENCY LIE THE HUMAN QUALITIES

Whatever of truth there once was in the myth of the modern organization as a tyrannical machine has been diminishing for fifty years. The myth never took account of the modern organization's essential involvement in change. As this involvement has deepened, reality and myth have drifted further apart. Around 1900 there was many a one-product manufacturer with a stable technology and a well-defined, reliable market. Such a company could increase its efficiency by routinizing more and more of its decisions into what Max Weber had called "calculable rules." Companies in this situation are exceedingly rare today: In the Sixties, a typical company makes scores, perhaps hundreds or thousands, of products, which it knows it will soon have to abandon or drastically modify; it must substitute others selected from millions of possibilities. Most of the actual and possible products are affected by rapidly changing techniques of production and distribution. Present and prospective markets are enticingly expansive, but fiercely competitive, loosely defined, and unstable.

In this situation, a company cannot be rigidly designed, like a machine, around a fixed goal. A smaller proportion of decisions can be routinized or precoded for future use. The highest activity of management becomes a continuous process of decision about the nature of the business. Management's degree of excellence is still judged in part by its efficiency of operation, but much more by its ability to make decisions changing its product mix, its markets, its techniques of financing and selling. Initiative, flexibility, creativity, adaptability are the qualities now required—and these are far more "human" than the old mechanical desideratum, efficiency.

The institutional system of the Soviet Union has been rigidly organized on the old bureaucratic model. Central authority fixes a definite goal, whether an increase in steel production or a vehicle to reach the moon. Material and human resources are mobilized around that goal. In terms of sheer efficiency certain aspects of the Soviet system work well. Yet we are right in regarding the U.S.S.R. as a "backward" country, and certain Russian leaders are justified in their recent efforts to move toward a more flexible and decentralized system. ... To cope with a very fluid technological and social environment such as that of the U.S., Soviet management would need much greater emphasis on the specifically human qualities.

Even U.S. governmental institutions, which are years behind our corporations in the evolution of management, are now using flexible approaches inconceivable in the U.S.S.R. The U.S. has consciously embarked on a huge effort to improve the quality of education without defining in any but the vaguest terms what that "improved" quality might be. We assume that through a highly decentralized educational system we may be able to grope our way "forward," step by step, forming new values and new targets as we proceed from choice to choice. In a similar spirit, we have begun an effort to improve the Appalachian region without knowing in advance what we want Appalachia to become. We have no centrally designed plan for Appalachia, but we believe that if the effort is "well managed," in the new (nonbureaucratic) sense of that phrase, a livelier Appalachia may result from the federal government's stimulation of changeful decisions by individuals, communities, and organizations in Appalachia. It is impossible to imagine the U.S.S.R.—or any other organization formed along the old authoritarian, machine-like lines—generating organized activity without first defining "the task."

MANAGEMENT AND CHANGE NEED EACH OTHER

U.S. corporations are pioneering the movement toward the new style of management because they are more heavily engaged than any other category of organization on the frontiers of actual social innovation. It is true, of course, that the main base of modern innovation lies in scientific discovery, most of which is—and all of which could be—carried on independently of business organizations. But the mission of science is to discover new truth; it is not organized to perform the additional and very different work of transforming discoveries into technological inventions; still less is it organized for the third stage of introducing these inventions into actual use. Usually, scientific discovery is the product of concentrated specialization in a field of study. Innovation, on the contrary, almost always requires various kinds of specialized knowledge drawn from many fields. One of the primary functions of modern management is to assemble various skills and coordinate them in production.

Science and technology, which make possible an ever increasing range of products and services, do not tell us which of these to produce. So another task of management is to mediate between the evolving wants of society and the evolving abilities for satisfying those wants. This mission, performed within a competitive market system, also requires many kinds of specialized knowledge—for example, market research, cost analysis—and very complex and delicate coordination. The whole process is suffused—as science is not—with questions of *value*, questions of whether the corporation and its customers want *A* rather that *B*. The judgments of management are relative and they are often intuitive—i.e., based upon incomplete and perhaps unreliable information. Management's hunger for knowledge on which to base decisions becomes ever stronger, but is fated to be forever unsatisfied. The advance of knowledge does not reduce the remaining body of ignorance because "possible knowledge" is not a finite quantity. In practical affairs, as in science, the more we learn the more questions confront us. Innovation does not wait until risk of failure has been eliminated by complete knowledge; in an era of radical change, management cannot be designed to work like a machine on the assumption that the goals and conditions that determined its design will remain constant.

Although statistical comparisons are impossible, it is almost certainly true that the numbers employed in "Management" have been growing more rapidly than the total economy during the past fifty years. If we apply the old bureaucratic machine standards of efficiency we are led to suppose that the vast increase in the numbers of management men represents the wasteful working of Parkinson's Law. But if the prime mission of management is to deal with change, then the size of management should be roughly proportionate to the rate of innovation rather than to the amount of physical output. This explains why the U.S. needs a proportionately larger managerial force than the less lively economy of the U.S.S.R. For years it has been obvious that in numbers and in quality British management was inferior to that of the U.S. and that Britain was not educating nearly enough men to fill its assumed management need. Yet no acute British "shortage" of management personnel exists in the sense that the market there places a very high price in money or prestige on management men; in fact, during the past twenty years a high proportion of men with the kind of training regarded as needed in management have emigrated from Britain, feeling their abilities to be in surplus in a relatively stagnant society. To take a more extreme example, the African nation of Gambia, which produces very few managerial types, would be the world's worst place to look for a job in management.

It appears that the need for management cannot be calculated on a simple supply-and-demand basis, because management creates change and change creates the need for management. As the "inventory" of management people in a society rises (in quantity and quality) the demand for still more management rises with it; or, to put it another way, the rate of innovation and the managerial function are interdependent. ...

Seen in this perspective, the computer revolution, by powerfully enhancing management's effectiveness in dealing with change, should have the long-range effect of increasing demand for management men. U.S. experience to date seems to support this theoretical expectation. Recruiting for management (of both managers, strictly so-called, and of such "functional individual contributors" as scientists, engineers, accountants) has never been more active, as any reader of newspaper advertisements is aware. More significantly, corporations are making increasing efforts to identify early the men with a high management potential, to train them rapidly, and to promote them to jobs of greater responsibility. This tendency seems especially marked in companies that have been quick to make use of computers. Probably the new information technology has had the effect of breaking bottlenecks that had restrained these companies from generating innovation and coping with the changing environment.

Not everyone expected this expansion of management. In 1958, when the computer revolution was young, two respected observers of management, Harold J. Leavitt and Thomas L. Whisler, wrote for the *Harvard Business Review* a much-discussed article entitled "Management in the 1980's." The article made a persuasive case for the proposition that the new information technology would reverse the trend toward decentralized and "participative" management. Leavitt and Whisler said: "In one respect, the picture we might paint for the 1980's bears a strong resemblance to the organizations of certain other societies—for example, to the family dominated organizations of Italy and other parts of Europe, and even to a small number of such firms in our own country. There will be many fewer middle managers, and most of those who remain are likely to be routine technicians rather than thinkers."

... Seven years later, with much more evidence to draw upon, H. Igor Ansoff, professor of industrial administration at Carnegie Institute of Technology, wrote for the *Harvard Business Review* a sort of answer to Leavitt and Whisler. In "The Firm of the Future," Ansoff said that the right question was not what the new information technology would do to management but "how will the manager use these extraordinarily powerful tools in furthering the objectives of the firm in its environment of the future." Since "the forces which will shape the future firm are already at work

... the shape of the firm in the 1980's ... need not be perceived dimly through a crystal ball [but] can be sketched by analyzing and projecting from the present." He listed three trends in the business environment: (1) *product dynamics*—"the life cycles of products will become shorter"; (2) *market dynamics*—"as superior technology displaces it from its traditional markets, the firm has to fight back by looking for new pastures" and the growing internationalization of markets will add to the competitive "turbulence"; (3) *firm and society*—governmental and social limits on the firm's behavior will increase so that "its search for profit will be strongly affected by an awareness of social consequences." The firm of the future would be able to program many of its activities, thus releasing management to deal with the increasing load of "nonprogrammable" decisions that would confront it in the new environment.

The manager to match these formidable new conditions would be "broader gauged than his present counterpart." He would need a grip on the firm's technology, but he would also have to deal with problems on "a combined economic-political-cultural level." The new environment would call for more managerial skill in human relations. "Increasing importance will be placed on the manager's ability to communicate rapidly and intelligibly, gain acceptance for change and innovation, and motivate and lead people in new and varying directions." Ansoff was not worried that management might be made obsolescent by new information technology. "The manager of the future will need all the computer help that he can get in coping with the greatly increased complexity of his job."

The fluid business environment of the future will demand not only a different kind of manager but a different organizational structure. Management's need to keep redefining "the nature of the business" applies not only to the product mix but also to the internal arrangements of the organization. One reason why men and their organizations may fail to adapt is that they cling to erroneous ideas about themselves and/or their situation. The late Douglas M. McGregor, of the Sloan School of Management of M.I.T., believed that the evolution of organizations was being retarded by a set of erroneous beliefs about man and his work which he called Theory X. The average man dislikes work, according to Theory X, and must therefore be coerced, directed, and controlled. He can be made to contribute to the achievement of organizational objectives only by a threat to the supply of his physiological needs. He seeks security and wishes to avoid responsibility for decisions. The old idea of authoritarian, paternalistic organizations fits Theory X; it is better for all concerned if power can be concentrated in the exceptional men at the top, who like responsibility.

Today men respond to certain stimuli that McGregor wrapped in a proposition called Theory Y. They take for granted the fulfillment of their basic material needs. "A satisfied need," McGregor said, "is not a motivator of behavior. Man is a wanting animal, [and his] needs are organized in a series of levels—a hierarchy of importance." A man whose stomach is satisfied by a secure supply becomes conscious of needs at a higher level. He seeks to feed his ego, which is more insatiable than any stomach, and to achieve a richer sense of his own identity. Many of these higher wants can best be satisfied by the kind of work that has a substantial content of intellectual activity and moral choice. Our society is by no means affluent in providing work of this sort, but more and more men in the professional and managerial category are finding their highest rewards in responsible work itself rather than merely in their pay.

Obviously, an organization based on the assumptions of Theory Y will array itself very differently from the old pyramid, where as much authority as possible was concentrated at the top. A Theory Y corporation would *prefer* to distribute responsibility widely among its managers, even if decision making could be centralized without loss of efficiency. A Theory X organization wants each individual to perform reliably the function assigned to him in the design of the total machine; a Theory Y organization wants an individual to be involved consciously in the relations between what he does and what others are doing; it wants him to seek ways of improving those relations in terms of his own expanding goals and the changing goals of the organization; it wants the individual to participate in setting goals for himself and for the organization.

What McGregor did was to put a [more solid] and more "human" base under older theories of "participative" management, which had slopped over into the dubious proposition (derisively referred to as "the contented-cow psychology") that the way to make workers efficient was to make them happy. McGregor's Theory Y allows plenty of room for discontent and tension; it provides, however, a realistic way to reconcile the needs of the individual with the objectives of the organization. The individual is no longer seen as entering a corrupt Faustian barter in which he abandons his "soul" in exchange for material satisfactions and power—a deal that will become increasingly repugnant to the more highly educated men that management will require. In short, the kind of management called for by Ansoff's projection of the future business environment could be provided under Theory Y much better than under Theory X.

Warren G. Bennis, McGregor's successor as chairman of the Organization Studies Group at M.I.T., asserts in a recent book, *Changing Organizations*, that during the past decade "the basic philosophy which underlies managerial behavior" has made a fundamental shift in the direction of Theory Y. Bennis discerns the philosophic shift in three areas:

1. A new concept on man, based on increased knowledge of his complex and shifting needs, which replaces the oversimplified, innocent push-button idea of man.
2. A new concept of power, based on collaboration and reason, which replaces a model of power based on coercion and fear.

3. A new concept of organizational values, based on humanistic-democratic ideals, which replaces the depersonalized mechanistic value system of bureaucracy.

Bennis is quick to say he does not mean that these transformations "are fully accepted or even understood, to say nothing of implemented in day-to-day affairs." But "they have gained wide intellectual acceptance in enlightened management quarters ... have caused a tremendous amount of rethinking on the part of many organizations, and ... have been used as a basis for policy formulation by many large-scale organizations." The shift in philosophy and the practical predicaments arising out of twentieth-century changes in the environment support one another in encouraging management to accelerate its own evolution. Business organizations, Bennis believes, are leading the way in replacing the old "bureaucratic mechanism," which was "capable of coordinating men and power in a stable society of routine tasks [but] cannot cope with contemporary realities."

... Management is the chief asset of the corporation rather than an overhead expense. "Investment for modernizing plant and equipment is often wasted unless there is a corresponding investment in the managerial and technical talent to run it," says M. J. Rathbone, former board chairman of Standard Oil (New Jersey). He notes that the valuation of a corporation's securities is based more upon appraisals of the quality of its management than upon the corporation's inanimate assets.

Many advanced companies engage in "total career development," a conscious policy of maximizing quality over the long run by balancing the old criterion of finding the best man for the job with some consideration of the best job for the development of the man. This policy is pursued even where it results in some short-run sacrifice of efficiency. Sears, Roebuck has for many years carried on an elaborate effort to identify as early as possible those individuals who have a high potential for development, and to measure as accurately as possible how they respond to various kinds of managerial challenges. Polaroid has taken a further step in the Theory Y direction; instead of having its top management planning the paths for executive careers, Polaroid uses a "posting system" in which its men are encouraged to compete for forthcoming job vacancies. General Electric's intense concern with the development of managers includes the belief that the man himself sets the objectives for his career and that the company must make an organized effort to keep open the means by which an individual can broaden his responsibilities, along lines he chooses himself.

The concern for broadening responsibilities goes all the way down to men recently recruited from college. Companies have noted with alarm that many young people, recruited after considerable effort, quit in the first year or two. The pay may be satisfactory, but they complain that their jobs are "too routine," or "not demanding enough." To meet this criticism, some companies are giving trainees jobs in which they can make costly mistakes. "There is no justification left for prolonged training procedures that prevent people from taking responsibility," says Frederick R. Kappel, chairman of A. T. & T. "There is no excuse for the timid doling out of oversupervised little jobs that allow a person no opportunity to show what he can do." Noting that many youngsters find business goals "too narrow" to fire their imaginations, Kappel counters with a broad one: In the "interaction of science and society," he says, "it is the goal of business management to translate discovery into use. Our job in industry is to assimilate the scientific revolution in such a way that practical values will flow to the public, to society at large, in the most orderly and economical way."

The structure of science is loose-jointed, nonpyramidal, nonauthoritarian. The same adjectives apply to the structure of modern "society at large." Working between science and society, two fluid and unpredictable worlds, corporations must not let their own structures petrify.

Companies alert to the danger, therefore, have set up continuous reviews of their organization charts. At least one company goes so far as to engage in periodic shake-ups, just to keep its structure from "freezing." A more intelligent way is represented by those companies (including U.S. Rubber and Kimberly-Clark) that have set up permanent analytical staffs to find out how parts of the company actually relate and figure out how they ought to relate. In the search for more flexible structures the old distinctions between staff and line and the old walls between specialists and between departments tend to blur. "The interesting part of the organization chart," says one management consultant, "is in the white space between the boxes. That's where the real activity goes on."

The organizations now evolving on the beliefs of Theory Y represent a shift from a mechanical to an organic model that confronts managers with more subtle and complex challenges. How, for instance, is the unity and coherence of the organization to be maintained in an evolving free-form structure of mobile individuals?

Transitionally, a lot of authority is still concentrated at "the top," but it exists as a reserve to deal with crisis, major internal conflict, and the fundamental decisions affecting the whole organization that cannot, under present conceptions, be made elsewhere. Some management analysts, searching for the shape of the future, are looking intently at large, diversified corporations whose divisions and subdivisions are now competing actively against one another within a loose corporate framework. Can this internal competition be stepped up by rewriting the rules of the game and improving the scoring system? If "the market" is a good way to organize the economy as a whole, why not deliberately make the corporation's internal structure more market-like? At present, the resources of the firm tend to flow toward those divisions where the return on investment has been highest; this "rule" may put too much emphasis on the past. Accountancy, concentrating on the record of what has happened, has not paid enough attention to projecting comparisons between the probable future prospects of several divisions of a company. The Defense Department's work in projecting the comparative cost effectiveness of different weapon systems not yet in being has given business a powerful impetus in the direction of a new kind of accountancy oriented toward the future. Computers, by simulating the results and costs of competing projects, can be of immense help in this kind of accountancy.

Thinking along the lines of an internal corporate market, Professor Jay Forrester of M.I.T. wants companies to get rid of the familiar budget centers, replacing them with profit centers. The budget-center system sets up a conflict between those groups (production, sales, research, etc.) whose interest is to spend and those groups whose function is to restrain spending, such as the controller's office. Because such conflicts can be resolved only at the top of the corporation, the budget-center system perpetuates the authoritarian form of organization. Internal profit centers, on the contrary, demand self-restraint because no group has an interest in spending, as such, or in saving, as such. Every group has an interest in the difference between them—i.e., profit.

Forrester would also break up such central services as purchasing and drafting rooms. Created in the name of efficiency, they can result in "internal monopolies" that tend to become somnolent and unresponsive to the need for change. Moreover, they confuse the accounting system within which internal competition is conducted. The economies of scale that they are supposed to produce are not worth what they cost in deadening the initiative and responsiveness of the corporation.

The substitution of structures in which more people exercise self-control fits with the broadest trends in modern society. Professor Bennis believes that "democracy is inevitable" because it "is the only system which can successfully cope with the changing demands of contemporary civilization." By democracy, Bennis means "a climate of beliefs" including "full and free communication, regardless of rank and power; a reliance on consensus, rather than ... coercion or compromise, to manage conflict; the idea that influence is based on technical competence and knowledge rather than on the vagaries of personal whims or prerogatives of power; [and] a basically human bias, one which accepts the inevitability of conflict between the organization and the individual but which is willing to cope with and mediate this conflict on rational grounds."

Not everybody would use the word *democracy* to describe this set of beliefs, but the contrast between this "climate" and that of the authoritarian machine-like organization is clear. It is also clear that the actual trends in U.S. management are moving in this direction and not back toward the shape forecast by Leavitt and Whisler, "the family dominated organizations of Italy and other parts of Europe."

"Professionalism" is here to stay a while. The scientist, engineer, and lawyer are indispensable to management and so are "professional" communicators and others whose skill lies in the coordination and leadership of specialists. The professional man in management has a powerful base of independence—perhaps a firmer base than the small businessman ever had in his property rights. The highly trained young man entering management today can look for corporate aid in enhancing his competence and hence his base of independence. He need not aspire to becoming *the* top officer of the firm, who holds the only "human" job in an organization conceived on the old line of a machine with all its decision-making initiative concentrated in the "operator" at the top. Today's management recruit can—and, in fact, does—have the more rational and less frustrating ambition of a life of ever-widening responsibility and choices. The prospect for a managerial career today is more adventurous than it ever was, because by the year 2000 there will be hundreds of thousands, perhaps millions, of Americans, whose influence on the quality of life in their more fluid society will be greater than that of any past "captain of industry."

FOR FURTHER READING

Allen, Louis A., *The Management Profession.* New York: McGraw-Hill Book Company, 1964.

Austin, Robert W., "Who Has the Responsibility for Social Change—Business or Government?" *Harvard Business Review*, Vol. 43, No. 4 (July-August 1965), 45-52.

Baumhart, Raymond, *Ethics in Business.* New York: Holt, Rinehart & Winston, Inc., 1968.

Bennett, K. W., "Pollution: Undigested Technology." *Iron Age*, Vol. 205, No. 13 (March 26, 1970), 57-58.

Berg, lvar, ed., *The Business of America.* New York: Harcourt, Brace, & World, Inc., 1968.

Berle, Adolph A., Jr., *Power Without Property.* New York: Harcourt, Brace & World, Inc., 1959.

_____ , and Gardner C. Means, *The Modern Corporation and Private Property.* New York: Commerce Clearing House, Inc., 1932.

Bowen, Howard R., *Social Responsibilities of the Businessman.* New York: Harper & Row, Publishers, 1953.

_____ , *Toward Social Economy.* New York: Rinehart & Company, 1948.

"Business: Bridge to Racial Progress." *Nation's Business*, Vol. 55, No. 10 (October 1967), 62-65.

"Business and the Urban Crisis." *Business Week*, No. 2005 (February 3, 1968), 57-72.

Davis, Keith, and Robert L. Blomstrom, *Business and Its Environment.* New York: McGraw-Hill Book Company, 1966.

De Bell, Garrett, ed., *The Environmental Handbook.* New York: Ballantine Books, 1970.

Drucker, Peter F., *Managing for Results*. New York: Harper & Row, Publishers, 1964.

Eells, Richard, *The Corporation and the Arts*. New York: The Macmillan Company, 1967.

――――, *The Meaning of Modern Business*. New York: Columbia University Press, 1960.

――――, and Clarence Walton., *Conceptual Foundations of Business*. Homewood, Ill.: Richard D. Irwin, Inc. 1969.

Elbing, A. O., and Carol J. Elbing. *The Value Issue of Business*. New York: McGraw-Hill Book Company, 1967.

Finley, Grace J., "Business Defines Its Social Responsibilities." *Conference Board Record*, Vol. 4, No. 11 (November 1967), 9-12.

Fortune, Vol. 77, No. 1 (January 1968). Special issue on business and the urban crisis.

Fortune, Vol. 81, No. 2 (February 1970). Special issue on the environment.

Friedman, Milton, *Capitalism and Freedom*. Chicago: University of Chicago Press, 1962.

Galliland, Charles E., Jr., ed., *Readings in Business Responsibility*. Braintree, Mass.: D. H. Mark Publishing Co., 1969.

Ginzberg, Eli, ed., *Business Leadership and the Negro Crisis*. New York: McGraw-Hill Book Company, 1968.

Goyder, George, *The Future of Private Enterprise*. Oxford: Basil Blackwell, 1951.

Greenwood, William T., ed., *Issues in Business and Society*. Boston: Houghton Mifflin Company, 1964.

Harbinson, Frederick, and Charles A. Myers, *Management in the Industrial World: An International Analysis*. New York: McGraw-Hill Book Company, 1959.

Harper, J. D., "Private Enterprise's Public Responsibility." *Public Relations Journal*, Vol. 23, No. 8 (August 1967), 8-18.

Heady, Ferrel, *Public Administration: A Comparative Perspective*. Englewood Cliffs, N.J.: Prentice-Hall, Inc., 1966.

Heider, David A., ed., *Business and the Urban Environment: A Guide to Cases and Other Teaching Materials*. Boston: Harvard University Graduate School of Business Administration, 1969.

Henderson, Hazel, "Should Business Tackle Society's Problems?" *Harvard Business Review*, Vol. 46, No. 4 (July-August 1968), 77-85.

Heyne, Paul T., *Private Keepers of the Public Interest*. New York: McGraw-Hill Book Company, 1968.

"Industry Cleans Up." *Nation's Business*, Vol. 56, No. 9 (September 1968), 57-78.

Johnson, H. L., "Socially Responsible Firms: An Empty Box or Universal Set?" *Journal of Business*, Vol. 39, No. 3 (July 1966), 394-399.

Koontz, Harold, "The Management Theory Jungle." *Academy of Management Journal*, Vol. 4 No. 3 (December 1961), 174-188.

Kuhn, W. J., and Ivar Berg, *Values in a Business Society*. New York: Harcourt, Brace & World, Inc., 1968.

Larson, John A., ed., *The Responsible Businessman*. New York: Holt, Rinehart & Winston, Inc., 1966.

Lazarus, Harold, ed., *Human Values in Management: The Business Philosophy of A. M. Sullivan*. New York: Dun & Bradstreet, Inc., 1968.

Levitt, Theodore, "The Dangers of Social Responsibility." *Harvard Business Review*, Vol. 36, No. 5 (September-October 1958), 41-50.

Linton, Ron M., *Terracide*. Boston: Little, Brown and Company, 1970.

McClanahan, Roger B., "More Money for Pollution Control." *Conference Board Record*, Vol. 5, No. 9 (September 1968), 26-29.

Mailick, Sidney, and Edwin Van Ness, eds., *Concepts and Issues in Administrative Behavior*, Englewood Cliffs, N.J.: Prentice-Hall, Inc., 1962.

Mason, Edward S., *The Corporation in Modern Society*. Cambridge, Mass.: Harvard University Press, 1960.

Merrill, Harwood, *Classics in Management*. New York: American Management Association, 1960.

Metcalf, Henry C., and L. Urwick, *Dynamic Administration: The Collected Papers of Mary Parker Follet*. New York: Harper & Row, Publishers, 1942.

Mitchell, William N., *The Business Executive in a Changing World*. New York: American Management Association, 1965.

Nader, Ralph, *Unsafe At Any Speed*. New York: Grossman Publishers, Inc., 1965.

"Needed: People Who See Administration Over-All." *Administrative Management*, Vol. 27, No. 1 (January 1966), 22-23.

Peters, Lynn, H., ed., *Management and Society*. Belmont, Calif.: Dickenson Publishing Co., Inc., 1968.

Petit, Thomas A., *The Moral Crisis in Management*. New York: McGraw-Hill Book Company, 1967.

Pollard, Sidney, *The Genesis of Modern Management*. Cambridge, Mass.: Harvard University Press, 1966.

Porter, Albert, "The Professional Executive of Tomorrow." *Personnel Administration*, Vol. 29, No. 1 (January-February 1966), 9-11.

Sheldon, Oliver, *Philosophy of Management*. New York: Pitman Publishing Corp., 1965.

Silberman, Charles E., *Crisis in Black and White*. New York: Random House, Inc., 1964.

Silver, I., "The Corporate Ombudsman." *Harvard Business Review*, Vol. 45, No. 3 (May-June 1967), 77-87.

Snively, W. D., Jr., *Profile of a Manager: A Descriptive Approach*. Philadelphia: J. B. Lippincott Co., 1965.

Spurrier, William A., *Ethics and Business*. New York: Charles Scribner's Sons, 1962.

Toffler, Alvin, *Future Shock*. New York: Random House, Inc., 1970.

Votaw, Dow, *Modern Corporations*. Englewood Cliffs, N.J.: Prentice-Hall, Inc., 1965.

Walton, Clarence C., *Corporate Social Responsibilities*. Belmont, Calif.: Wadsworth Publishing Co., 1967.

———, *Ethos and the Executive*. Englewood Cliffs, N.J.: Prentice-Hall, Inc., 1969.

"The War That Business Must Win." *Business Week*, No. 2096 (November 1, 1969), 63-74.

Wernette, J. P., *Executive Philosophy and Practice*. Ann Arbor, Mich.: The University of Michigan Press, 1966.

PART ONE

Organizing: Structural Design

The first management process we shall consider is formal organization—designing jobs and relations between jobs. This phase of management has been the chief focus of management writers and practitioners during the twentieth century. In fact some observers contend that organizing has frequently been overemphasized at the expense of planning, leading, and controlling. Nevertheless there can be little question that sound organization is vital if an enterprise is to achieve its mission.

In the past few years, two significant developments in formal organization have occurred. First, renewed research interest has produced valuable empirical findings on organization structure. Second, shifts in the environment, technology, and enterprise objectives have produced important new modifications in organization design. The reading selections in Part One reflect these two developments.

Three fundamental steps in building a total organization structure are: (1) identifying the key operating departments that fit the mission of the enterprise; (2) deciding the level at which operating decisions can be made most effectively; and (3) determining the nature and location of service and staff units.

To identify the key operating departments of an organization, we must focus on departmentation—the division of operating work. Departmentation involves the grouping of operating tasks into jobs, the combining of jobs into effective work groups, and the combining of groups into departments. The primary consideration at each of these levels is technology—the methods used to convert inputs into goods and services. Technology determines the nature of the work to be done; organization converts the work into jobs, groups, and major departments.

The pervasive effect of technology on organization has generated considerable interest in recent years. Some important research studies on this subject have provided new insights regarding the link between technology and organization. The first selection in this part, "Empirical Research on Organization Structure," summarizes the findings of these studies.

In order to decide the level at which operating decisions are to be made, we must resolve the issue of centralization versus decentralization. Decentralization is the division of administrative work so that decision-making is pushed to lower levels in the organization. The question of whether to centralize or decentralize is a recurring problem for management. Although this issue has been debated for years, it still remains very current and important for operating managers. In selection 7, "Centralization or Decentralization?" Antony Jay uses history and political science to identify the key factors in decentralization decisions.

The third step in shaping the overall organization structure is to decide on the nature and location of service and staff units. The use of staff has long been appealing to executives because staff personnel can perform work that the executive cannot do either because he is too busy or perhaps because he lacks the required technical expertise. However the use of staff also creates new responsibilities and problems for the manager. The sensitive nature of line-staff relationships has been treated at length in management and sociological literature. Selection 8, "Computers and Their Priests," by Robert Townsend, is a brief, readable warning concerning the special problems involved in the use of a computer and management-systems staff.

The organization design that emerges from a synthesis of departmentation, decentralization, and staff considerations is not a final static structure. Organization must be adapted to the changing needs of an enterprise. Five recent organization developments that result from changing company requirements are: (1) matrix organization, (2) external, independent staff, (3) office of the president, (4) interest representation, and (5) the impact of computers on organization.

Matrix organization is designed to provide both the coordinated action needed for unusual, complex projects and the specialized capabilities of functional departments. A project manager is appointed to direct each clear-cut mission, and specialists from each of the organization's functional departments are assigned to do the actual work. A functional specialist is "out on loan" to the project manager until the specialist's work on the project ends.

A second new organizational feature is the growth of external, independent staff. This type of staff group is used in large companies to check on major decisions involving huge commitments of resources. The external staff is not regarded as a substitute for the operating divisions' own internal staffs; instead, the external staff reviews annual and five-year plans of the operating divisions prior to central management's review.

A third innovation is the use of an office of the president as a means of relieving chief executives of some of their overburdening responsibilities. The need to lessen the number of time-consuming functions that presidents of large enterprises must perform is not new. Traditional alternatives for solving this problem include the use of administrative assistants, profit decentralization, and a full-time board of directors. An office of the president usually consists of a team of two to five senior executives who share the central management tasks.

A fourth frontier where social pressures are leading to new organization design is in the area of interest representation. Organized pressure-groups are seeking representation in the management of universities, school districts, urban renewal projects, and public utilities. These pressures force management to carefully reconsider the criteria for selection of personnel to serve on the board of directors or in key management positions. In addition, new mechanisms are required to establish and maintain effective two-way communication with each interest group.

The impact of computers on organizations has probably received the greatest attention. Up to now the principal effect of computers on organization has been the mechanization of clerical activities. Computers can also affect the degree of decentralization in an organization by virtue of their capability to rapidly transmit, analyze, and retransmit data. Because data can be fed from headquarters to the field or from the field to headquarters, computers can result in either more or less decentralization. The most controversial effect of computers, though, is on the management job itself. Several observers speculate that computers will eventually eliminate a large number of middle management positions. Others contend that the specific nature, rather than the number, of management jobs will change. The debate continues. Unfortunately the arguments regarding the impact of the computer usually proceed without the benefit of factual information. In selection 9, "The Impact of Information Technology on Organization Structure," Thomas Whisler remedies this situation somewhat by providing some important empirical evidence on this subject.

Selections 10 and 11 provide some insight into the practical application of concepts of organization design. "Organization Structure," by Paul E. Holden, Carlton A. Pederson, and Gayton Germane, integrates major organization design concepts and new developments by reporting top management practices in fifteen successful U.S. industrial companies. "G.E.'s Costly Ventures into the Future" describes how one company, which has pioneered in the area of organization, uses departmentation, decentralization, staff, and new organizational developments, such as an office of the president and external, independent staff.

We conclude Part One with a short selection from *Parkinson's Law*. Its author, C. Northcote Parkinson, is renowned for his satirical critiques of the imperfections of bureaucracy.

6

Empirical Research on Organization Structure

ALAN C. FILLEY AND ROBERT J. HOUSE

In this selection on formal organization, Professors Filley and House summarize the Woodward Studies, the Hall Study, the Sears, Roebuck Studies, and the Lawrence and Lorsch Study. Each of these studies provides valuable empirical evidence concerning the factors that affect organization design and the relationship between organization structure and organization success.

Joan Woodward's comparative study of British firms demonstrated the important link between technology and organization success. In contrast to Woodward's study of variations among organizations, R. H. Hall observed that differences in task technology produce structural variations within organizations. James Worthy's 1950 report of behavioral responses to organization structure at Sears, Roebuck is a classic statement of the dangers associated with narrow functional specialization and narrow spans of control. Lawrence and Lorsch examined how the stability of a firm's environment influences organization design. The most successful firms in their sample were those that maintained degrees of differentiation and integration consistent with environmental demands.

Consider the following questions in reviewing these four studies: (1) What key factors should be considered in choosing a basis for departmentation? (2) How much emphasis should be placed on specialization, as opposed to coordination, in organization design? (3) How much division of labor is desirable in an organization? (4) What are the advantages and disadvantages of a narrow span of control? (5) What major factors should be considered in determining the span of control? (6) Does organization structure affect organization performance?

· · ·

Comparative research on organizations is both relatively new and very difficult to conduct. The difficulty stems from the size of the unit to be analyzed and the formidable quantity of data to be collected and analyzed. In addition, the number of units available for comparison is usually very small; thus the comparisons may not be as meaningful as we would like them to be. Yet despite these difficulties, there are studies that throw light on the subject.

THE WOODWARD STUDIES

The studies reported by Joan Woodward are perhaps the most revealing comparative studies of organizational structures to date.[1] She and her associates employed a variety of research methods, including surveys, case studies, and longitudinal and historical analyses, to determine the ramifications of various types of organization in 100 British firms, all of which were manufacturing and selling products. The size of the firms ranged from 100 to 8,000 employes.

The foci of the studies were formal organizational structure and operating procedures. Researchers spent from half a day to a week in each firm, collecting information on:

1. The history, background, and objectives of the firm.
2. Manufacturing processes and methods.
3. Organizational structure and the operating routines.
4. Cost structure.
5. Labor structure.
6. The success of the firm as shown by economic facts and figures.

The firms were then divided into three groups, according to their degree of success: average, above average, and below average. In classifying a firm on the success scale, the researchers studied not only such factual material as annual reports, the fluctuation of shares on the stock exchange, and changes in share of market, but also the state of the industry of which it was a part. (Some industries were expanding; some operated in a stationary or contracting market; and some functioned in a more competitive environment than others. Hence, the comparative success of two firms in different industries could not be judged without considering the opportunities open to them.) Thus every attempt was made to base the assessment of success on factual material, although the researchers had to use their own judgment in weighing various factors.

After some preliminary attempts to correlate success with form and size of organization, Woodward's researchers hit upon the idea of classifying the firms into three groups according to complexity of technology: (1) unit and small-batch production; (2) large-batch and mass production; and (3) long-run process production of the same product, such as chemicals. Technological

---

[1] J. Woodward, *Industrial Organization: Theory and Practice* (London: Oxford University Press, 1965).

complexity thus ranged from the production of unit articles for individual customers' requirements (the oldest and simplest form of production) to continuous-process flow plants. Twelve firms had combined systems, and in these cases there was a tendency to organize each type of production independently.

When firms were classified according to technological complexity, a strong relation between organizational structure and success appeared within each group. The successful unit-production firms had organizational characteristics in common with each other, as did the above-average large-batch production firms and the above-average process production firms.

The successful firms at the top and bottom of the scale of technological complexity tended toward (1) less emphasis on clear-cut, written definition of duties, (2) greater delegation of authority, (3) more permissive management, (4) less tightly organized work forces, and (5) less organizational consciousness.

In the successful firms, line-staff organization was most highly developed in the middle ranges of technological complexity. Where the technology was relatively simple, the line supervisors were technically competent and there were few specialists. In highly technical process production, it was difficult to distinguish between executive and advisory responsibility.

The successful firms in the middle-technology group used more production administration and greater supervision of production operators. Control procedures were more elaborate, sanctions more rigorously applied, and written communications tended to be more frequent, than in the firms at either of the two technological extremes.

In the successful firms of each category, the spans of control of first-line supervisors tended to be close to the median for the technological category, whereas the spans for unsuccessful firms were either much smaller or much greater than the median group for each category. The median for the unit and small-batch firms was 23. In the below-average firms, on the other hand, spans ranged from 10 or fewer to 51 to 60. Similar results were shown for the firms in the other two technological groups. Moreover, similar trends appeared in figures on the spans of the chief executives, the number of levels in the chain of command, labor costs, and the various labor ratios.

Thus successful large-batch firms tended to be organized along classical lines, with duties and responsibilities clearly defined, unity of command, a clear distinction between staff and line, and a chief executive who confined his span of control to no more than five or six immediate subordinates. On the other hand, successful firms in the other two categories tended to have a less classical type of organization. As a result of these findings, Woodward suggests that the classical principles may have been drawn from observations of large-batch production industries, for many people tend to regard this type of industry as typical of modern times. Within this limited range of technology, she points out, the form of organization suggested by classical theory seems to be associated with success, but outside this range, the most suitable form or organization is not bound by the classical principles.

Following this analysis, the investigators selected twenty firms, each of which employed more than 250 people, for intensive study: six unit or small-batch production firms; six large-batch production firms; five process production firms; and three that combined mass production with the preparation of a product for sale. Nine of these firms had been classified as above average in success, eight as average, and only three as below average.

One or more members of the research team spent approximately a month in each firm selected for study, concentrating on various aspects of organization. The methods used were observation and interview; from 30 to 50 people were interviewed in each firm, the number depending on the size of the firm and the complexity of its formal organization. In this phase of the work, the investigators paid attention to organizational history and the evolution of the structure, and to the impact of individual prejudices and preferences on organizational decisions at various stages of the firm's development. They also studied in detail the nature and number of decisions made at different levels in the hierarchy.

In addition, a detailed study was made of three firms in which employment ranged from 2,000 to 4,000 persons and in which manufacturing methods were either changing or mixed. Woodward states that these three were selected because, if organization and technology are linked as the preliminary studies indicated, firms of this kind would be likely to face the most difficult organizational problems.

The researchers spent approximately six months in each of the three firms, observing until patterns of interaction became discernible. They interviewed all middle and top managers in all three firms. In Firm A, they also interviewed all first-line supervisors, and in Firms B and C half the first-line supervisors, randomly selected.

All these case studies not only confirmed the link between technology and the applicability of the organizational principles, but also demonstrated that this link is causal rather than coincidental. However, the studies also showed that the relationships were more complex than they had seemed from the preliminary study. Specifically, the investigators found that:

1. At the extremes of the technical scale, the physical work imposed very narrow restrictions on the type of organization possible.
2. In the middle range, the physical work set limits to what could be done organizationally, but left more range for management choice.

Thus Woodward says of the middle group:

> The separation of production administration from production operations, rationalization of the production processes, and attempts to push back the physical limitations of production resulted in the

emergence of a control system that depended in part on the physical work flow and in part on top management policy. In batch production, therefore, organization was not so much a function of technology as a function of the control system, the latter depending partly on technology and partly on social and economic factors ... (p. 66).

She also states that:

... situational demands impose themselves more rigidly and obviously at the extremes than in the middle of the scale. Those responsible for organization planning have less room for maneuver. There are few alternative ways or organizing production in a special-order production firm, and an unsatisfactory structure seems to show itself immediately in a decline in business success (p. 155).

THE HALL STUDY

A study by R. H. Hall contrasted organizational structures of two fundamentally different kinds in ten organizations, focusing on task technology at the departmental level rather than at the level of an entire organization.[2] His research was based on two hypotheses: (1) Departments dealing with uniform events and traditional skills (such as assembly-line work and standard clerical and routine administrative tasks) require different organizational arrangements than do departments engaged in tasks that require non-uniform and non-routine social and creative skills (such as research, sales, design, or advertising). (2) Hierarchical organizational levels whose tasks are not uniform require different organizational arrangements than those whose tasks are uniform.

Hall further hypothesized that departments and levels characterized by routine tasks are also characterized by Weber's bureaucratic model of organization. According to Weber, the most effective organization (the bureaucratic) has:[3]

1. A well-defined hierarchy of authority.
2. A division of labor based on functional specialization.
3. A system of rules covering the rights and duties of position incumbents.
4. A system of procedures for dealing with work situations.
5. Impersonality of interpersonal relationships.

[2] R. H. Hall, "Intraorganizational Structural Variation," *Administrative Science Quarterly*, Vol. 7, No. 3 (December 1962), 295-308.

[3] M. Weber, *The Theory of Social and Economic Organization,* trans. A. M. Henderson and T. Parsons (New York: The Free Press, 1947).

6. Selection for employment and promotion based on technical competence.

Note that, with the exception of No. 5, the classical model of organization includes every characteristic of Weber's bureaucratic model.

Hall examined the *degree* to which each of the above characteristics were present in different departments and at different organizational levels by conceiving of each characteristic as a *dimension*. He states that "The concept of a dimension assumes that the phenomena under study exists in the form of a continuum along the dimension." ...

Hall developed a scale for each dimension, designed to measure employe perceptions of the organization. These scales were administered to a random sample of personnel in the ten organizations: five were profit-making organizations, and five were government organizations.

By comparing responses from 16 departments, Hall found that, consistent with his first hypothesis, non-routine departments were perceived to be significantly different from routine departments in hierarchy of authority, division of labor, and specified procedure. No significant differences were found in the remaining three dimensions (specified rights and duties, impersonality, and criteria for hiring and promotion).

To test his second hypothesis, Hall administered his scale statements to 116 executives and 187 non-executives. Here he assumed that, because their work is less routine, executives work in a less bureaucratic setting. He found his assumption to be true for four of the six dimensions: emphasis on hierarchy, division of labor, specified procedure, and impersonality.

From the Woodward study we see variations *among* organizations: from the Hall study we see variations *within* organizations. Task technology within an organization appears to have an effect on organizational procedure similar to the effect of technology within an industry. ...

· · ·

THE SEARS, ROEBUCK STUDIES

James C. Worthy reported—from a study of employe morale conducted by Sears, Roebuck—some findings relative to organizational structure.[4] The findings were based on informal observations, interviews, and questionnaires of over 100,000 employes, working in several hundred different company units, both at Sears proper and at a number of other organizations as well. Worthy's report of the Sears findings does not present the data on any

[4] J. C. Worthy, "Organization Structure and Employee Morale," *American Sociological Review*, Vol. 15 (1950), 169-179.

specific issue, but rather consists of conclusions that summarize his own convictions and those of Sears management, based on the data and experience culled from the surveys. Following is a brief summary of these conclusions:

1. Overcomplexity in organizational structure is one of the most important and fundamental causes of poor management-employe relations in our modern economic system, and until this problem is faced and corrected, no substantial improvement in those relations is likely to be possible.

2. Where jobs are broken down too finely, there is a greater likelihood of low output and low morale. Conversely, the most sustained efforts are exerted by groups of employes who perform more complete sets of tasks (e.g., salesmen, supervisors, master mechanics) and they likewise exhibit the highest levels of morale and group loyalty. A major cause of overspecialization is the tendency of managers to separate organizations into functional divisions and to expand the size of the administrative component of the organization. "Much of industry's present vast scale of operation is required not so much by economic or technical factors as by an unhappy and unnecessary principle of organization (overspecialization)." This tendency toward overfunctionalization destroys the meaning of a job for the individual employe.

Overspecialization requires close and constant supervision at the work level. The supervisors themselves must be closely supervised and controlled to assure the necessary degree of coordination between the different units into which the organization has been subdivided. In a simpler type of organization, coordination can usually be achieved on a fairly informal basis because there are few artificial barriers in the form of departmental separation and lines of authority.

3. The growth of staff complicates the situation still further. An inevitable consequence is the elaboration of formal controls of various kinds to permit the staff to perform the functions and exercise the responsibilities that have been delegated to it or that it gradually assumes in an effort to strengthen its own position or extend its own authority.

4. "The significant point in all this, however, is that the over-complex, over-functionalized organizational structure is likely to require the driver type of leader; the overuse of pressure as a tool of supervision is thus related primarily to the character of the structure and only secondarily to the character of the individual at the head of it" (p. 177).

Worthy goes on to contrast "otherwise comparable units" of organizations which differ mainly in the complexity of their organizational structure and the degree to which authority and responsibility are effectively decentralized to those "further down the line." He reports that in more elaborate and complex organizations the individual supervisor is subject to constant control and direction and has little opportunity to develop the qualities of initiative and self-reliance.

According to Worthy, in organizations characterized by broad spans of control, the individual manager is thrown largely on his own to sink or swim on the basis of his own ability and capacity. He can rely only to a limited extent on those above him, and, by the same token, he cannot too severely restrict his own subordinates' growth and development by supervising and controlling them too closely.

On the other hand, in organizations characterized by many levels of supervision and elaborate systems of controls, not only does the individual have little opportunity to develop the capacities of self-reliance and initiative, but the system frequently weeds out those who do so. Furthermore, those who survive in this type or organization are likely, by virtue of the very qualities that enabled them to survive, to have personalities and ways of operating that do not make for great skill or for building employe teamwork and cooperation.

Worthy argues that two trends in particular make effective integration and voluntary coordination and cooperation difficult, and contribute to the progressive deterioration of management-employe relations. One is the trend toward increasing the size of the administrative unit; the other, that toward increasing the complexity of organizational structure. Both trends appear logical in terms of the widely held (classical) theory of business organization, but in both cases improvements in mechanical efficiency are at some point overbalanced by losses in the willingness and ability of employes to cooperate in the system. Moreover, the larger, more complex organizations are likely to become unadaptable and rigid, and to find it difficult to meet the requirements of economic and social change. Horizontal hierarchies in less complex structures, with a maximum of administrative decentralization, tend to create a potential for improved attitudes, more effective supervision, and greater individual responsibility and initiative among employes. Moreover, arrangements of this type encourage individual self-expression and creativity, which are necessary to the personal satisfaction of employes.

Since a department store's operation is at the lower extreme of technological complexity, it is interesting to note that Worthy's conclusions are consistent with Woodward's.

. . .

THE LAWRENCE AND LORSCH STUDY

As an attempt to answer the question "What kind of organization does it take to deal with various economic and market conditions?" a study by Lawrence and Lorsch provides a framework for integrating the studies just reviewed.[5]

[5] P. Lawrence and J. Lorsch, *Organization and Environment*, Division of Research, Graduate School of Business Administration, Harvard University, 1967.

Lawrence and Lorsch view the organization as an open system, whose internal characteristics must fit external demands from the environment. They describe the internal relationships of members of the organization as intertwined, and as influenced by "the nature of the task being performed, the form of relationships, rewards, and controls, and by the existing ideas within the organization about how a well-accepted member should behave." According to Lawrence and Lorsch, these internal factors must be integrated to function harmoniously if the organization is to perform effectively.

However, organizational differentiation, "the difference in cognitive and emotional orientation among members in different functional departments," also exists; that is, managers in various functional units can be expected to differ from one another in goal orientation, time orientation, and interpersonal orientation. Furthermore, formality of structure will differ between departments and between organizations. Thus, "because the members of each department develop different interests and differing points of view, they often find it difficult to reach agreement on integrated programs of action."

Lawrence and Lorsch argue that integration, which they define as "the quality of the state of collaboration," does not, as classical theorists assume, automatically follow from organizational design. For effective integration, the conflicts emerging from differing goal, time, and interpersonal differences must be resolved. The effectiveness of this resolution will depend on such factors as: (1) the formal position of liaison personnel who coordinate and integrate differentiated departments; (2) the influence of integrators and its source—knowledge, expertise, position, power, etc.; (3) the reward system for integrators; (4) the total level of influence in the organization; (5) influence centered at the required level in the hierarchy; (6) the modes of conflict resolution—confrontation, smoothing over, or forcing.

To Lawrence and Lorsch, the environment of the organization determines both the character and degree of differentiation and the mode of integration. In particular, they consider two aspects of the environment as dominant: the certainty of information or knowledge about events; and the dominant competitive issue in the industry. They therefore predicted that environmental uncertainty and competitive demand would affect the organization in terms of differentiation and integration: greater innovation and environmental uncertainty would be reflected in greater differentiation of goal, time, and interpersonal orientation and of organizational structure.

Research Strategy

Lawrence and Lorsch's research was carried out in two phases. First, a series of six detailed case studies were conducted among firms in the plastics industry. This phase provided a qualitative understanding of the relations among environment, differentiation, and integration. Second, a highly effective organization and less effective one in each of the plastics, food, and container industries were studied and compared. Lawrence and Lorsch chose the three industries because they displayed important differences among the environmental dimensions of certainty and competitive issue. The industries examined had a "different rate of technological change in both product and processes," and had dominant demands coming from different sectors of the environment.

Interviews and questionnaires were used to collect data. Interview data concerning internal matters were obtained from 30 to 50 upper and middle-level managers in each organization. Information concerning the outside environment was obtained from the top executives in each organization.

Environmental uncertainty was measured with a questionnaire, expressed in terms of clarity of information, uncertainty of cause-effect relationships, and the time span of definitive feedback: these scores were combined because they correlated to a significant degree.

Findings on Environmental Demands

Lawrence and Lorsch found that, in the plastics industry, continually emerging technological developments created an environment of high uncertainty in which the dominant competitive issue for firms was the capacity to innovate. The major competitive issue in the food industry was also innovation, but to a somewhat lesser extent. In the container industry, on the other hand, the main competitive issue was the ability to provide customer service. Lawrence and Lorsch also found that food and plastics firms worked under conditions of change and uncertainty; container companies worked under conditions of relative stability.

Findings on Differentiation

The goals of department managers in all three industries generally coincided with functional specialization. Thus manufacturing personnel were primarily concerned with cost reduction, process efficiency, and similar matters. Research and engineering personnel were oriented toward techno-economic goals and scientific matters. Marketing personnel were primarily concerned with customer problems, competitive activities, and other marketplace events. In the food industry, with its relatively greater sales orientation, all managers tended toward a somewhat more market-oriented view of goals.

With respect to time orientation, Lawrence and Lorsch found (as might be expected) that the managements of plastics firms, with their separate fundamental research divisions, had a slightly higher level of total time differentiation among functional departments than did the food firms.

The interpersonal orientations of managers were measured to determine whether a particular manager was personnel-relationship or task oriented. In the most uncertain industry, plastics, it was found that sales personnel were most highly relationship-oriented, production personnel were most task-oriented, and scientific personnel were about in the middle of the continuum. In the container industry, it was found that interpersonal orientation did not differ as greatly between managers: sales personnel were not as relationship-oriented, and production personnel were less task-oriented. The situation in the food industry was again affected by the importance of the sales function. Interpersonal differentiation here fell between the plastics and container extremes.

Differences in formal structure also reflected uncertainty and the diversity of environmental demands. The plastics industry required the greatest differentiation of interdepartmental structure: production, involving relatively routine procedures, was the most highly formalized department; sales, applied technology, and fundamental research had less formalized structures. Similarly, the environment which demanded the least diversity, that of the container industry, led to a lower level of differentiation along the structure dimension: all three departments were similar in structure. Again, the food industry fell between the plastics and container industries in this respect.

In summary, it was found that the actual amounts of goal, time, interpersonal, and structural differentiation were in line with the prediction that the environmental factors of uncertainty and motivation would be associated with increased differentiation.

Differentiation, Integration, and Performance

Lawrence and Lorsch found that "the most successful organizations tended to maintain states of differentiation and integration consistent with the diversity of the parts of the environment and the required interdependence of these parts." They judged performance by changes in profits and in sales volume over five years, and new products introduced as a percentage of sales over five years. In all three industries, high performing firms had fewer deviations from the theoretical amount of differentiation required by the environment. Lawrence and Lorsch conclude that "the more the parts of the environment differ in certainty and time span of feedback, and the less dominant any part was, the more differentiated were the pairs of the units in the high performing organizations."

In addition to effects on differentiation, environmental factors were found to require qualitative differences in modes of integration, as manifested by differences in the six integrative factors mentioned above. The highly differentiated plastics industry used formal integrating departments; the less differentiated food industry used individual integrators; and the least differentiated container industry used direct managerial contact (interestingly, the low-performing container firm used a formal integrating unit, and the high-performing container firm used direct managerial contact).

It was also found that all effective integrators or integrating units had positional influence, sufficient knowledge and information to make decisions, and influence based on competence; furthermore, they all used confrontation to resolve conflict, as opposed to smoothing over or forcing.

Environment was found to determine the relative influence of departments in the most effective organizations. For example, in the plastics industry, with its great need for integration, the integrating departments had the greatest influence. All members of the effective plastics and food firms reported having a high degree of influence over decisions. This finding is consistent with the prediction that the demands of an uncertain environment will require more decision making at lower levels. In the container industry, where the environment is relatively predictable, influence was found to be concentrated at the top of each organization, which was consequently less "democratic."

In organizations with effective integration, the reward system emphasized the achievement of *unified effort* rather than individual achievement.

Thus, relative to performance, the effective organization must exhibit the differentiation and integration demanded by the environment. As Lawrence and Lorsch say, "we have found that the state of differentiation in the effective organization was consistent with the diversity of the parts of the environment, while the state of integration achieved was consistent with the environmental demands for interdependence."

Relation to Other Studies

The findings of the Lawrence and Lorsch study provide an excellent framework for understanding and drawing together the other studies reported in this chapter.

In a relatively predictable environment, decisions are more effectively made at the top of the organization, and we might expect to find a classical type of formal structure. In a highly unpredictable type of situation, in which all levels of management need considerable influence to deal with environmental uncertainty, a more participative structure along the lines suggested by Likert would be advisable.[6] Recall that Woodward found in the advanced technological group (i.e., continuous process firms) hierarchies that were fully developed, with most decisions made at the top. Since continuous process technology is relatively predictable, her findings are consistent with those of Lawrence and Lorsch, and can be explained in terms of the relatively high degree of environmental certainty that accompanies process technology. Hall found that departments with predictable work had more hierarchical differentiation, greater division of labor, and more specified procedures than did the nonroutine departments, again in keeping with the Lawrence and Lorsch findings.

[6] R. Likert, *New Patterns in Management* (New York: McGraw-Hill Book Company, 1961).

7

Centralization or Decentralization?

ANTONY JAY

*"To centralize or not to centralize? The discussion is never resolved,
but the balance of emphasis is constantly shifting on the fulcrum of truth."
Antony Jay thus introduces his refreshing look at this age-old dilemma. This
selection is a chapter from Mr. Jay's best-selling book,* Management and
Machiavelli, *a witty and unique "inquiry into the politics of corporate life."*

*Early in this selection, the author stresses the recurring nature of
decisions on whether to centralize or decentralize. Certainly there is an
abundant, if not excessive, supply of management literature on this subject.
Enlightening discussions of corporate decentralization have been provided by
Ralph Cordiner, former chief executive of General Electric, in* New Frontiers
for Professional Managers, *and by Alfred P. Sloan, former chief executive of*
General Motors, in My Years With General Motors.

*Mr. Jay's approach is distinctive in that he avoids using the traditional
business examples of decentralization. Instead, he utilizes some interesting
examples of decentralization, or colonization, as carried out in the Roman
Empire and the Church. Many have argued that decentralization is especially
needed to overcome delays in communication. It is unlikely, however, that
any discussion is more vivid than Mr. Jay's description of how communication problems created a need for decentralization in the Roman Empire. Also
note the precautions taken by the Church and the Roman Empire to
internally "centralize" a man before allowing him to assume his decentralized
post. In our time, the prerequisites for effective decentralization, such as
comprehensive training and indoctrination in corporate policies, frequently
do not receive the attention they deserve.*

*Consider the following questions after reading this selection: (1) What
are the advantages and disadvantages of decentralization? (2) What factors
should be considered in resolving the centralization-versus-decentralization
dilemma? (3) What are some important prerequisites of effective decentralization?*

Reprinted from Antony Jay, *Management and Machiavelli*, pp. 60-69, by permission of
the publishers, Holt, Rinehart and Winston, Inc., New York, and Hodder and Stoughton
Ltd., London. Copyright 1967 by Antony Jay.

To centralize or not to centralize? The discussion is never resolved, but the balance of emphasis is constantly shifting on the fulcrum of truth. At present, decentralization is the fashionable idea; no doubt it will be superseded by centralization in a few years' time, when the evils of misguided or excessive decentralization begin to make themselves felt. But the illusion that one or the other is the right way to run a corporation is likely to persist.

In favor of the decentralizers, it can certainly be said that excessive centralization is a common error which can do extreme damage to an organization. Most people are familiar with the pattern: the ever-lengthening delays while head office makes up its mind, the futile attempts to lay down universal laws and procedures however inappropriate to the special circumstances of those affected, the top people growing more and more out of touch with the day-to-day realities, the men who work close to the products or customers having to refer decisions which they have the knowledge and experience to take correctly up to people who have neither, the stillbirth of enterprising ideas because of the frustration of waiting for the go ahead until it's too late, or getting it in time but hedged in with reservations and modifications which make success almost impossible. But, of course, the dangers of excessive decentralization are just as damaging: production schedules being drawn up without consulting a sales forecast, two representatives—one from the region and one from the product division—trying to sell the same product to the same customer while telling him conflicting facts about it, sales drives aimed at a volume of orders which the factories cannot in fact meet, good young managers bottled up in inadequate jobs because their bosses will not release them for promotion in other departments and have no vacancies in their own, and the general state of affairs where the planning department is an expensive joke and the firm has as many policies as managers.

Obviously, neither of these situations is desirable; equally obviously, a compromise which combines elements of both is not particularly desirable either. The trouble is that so often the argument between centralization and decentralization is the argument between two different kinds of bad management—the former nearly destroyed Ford, the latter nearly destroyed General Motors—and although they are both bad they are mutually exclusive—they cannot coexist in one firm. But that is not to say that good centralization and good decentralization cannot coexist, or that a corporation cannot have a great deal of both.

The nature of good decentralization can be seen most clearly in the way states used to establish colonies. Athens and Rome in antiquity, Venice and Genoa in the late Middle Ages, Spain and England after the Renaissance, as well as many other great empires, achieved greatness by colonization. There are other ways—conquest, for instance, when your nation defeats a weaker one, and its king submits to your rule and agrees to an annual tribute. That corresponds to a simple kind of takeover, where you do very little with the taken-over firm except appropriate its profit. Colonization is different; it is the opening up of virgin territory, or land that is sparsely populated and almost completely undeveloped. The founding country says to the colonists, in effect, "Off you go. Here's a map, and this is where you'll be founding your colony. From now on it's up to you. We don't really know what the potentialities of the place are, any more than you do, but from the reports of travelers they certainly look reasonable. Whether you stay as a little fishing community or build a great city as splendid as ours really depends on yourselves. You may even come running home in three months.

"Of course we'll help you if we can: If you need supplies or armed reinforcements, we'll send them if we have them to spare. But don't depend on us. The idea is that we shouldn't interfere at all, and that you should become rich enough to send money back to your families at home, and contribute a good chunk to the upkeep of our army and our fleet, for all our sakes. And at least there's more future for you in going than in staying here."

When a corporation alerts a small production and marketing group to a completely new product, or sends a small sales team out to a region or country where they have never tried to sell before—in any new situation where promotion prospects can be limitless, depending entirely on the success the team makes of the enterprise—this is colonization. It is by no means the same as running a department within a company or a division, and the difference is in the degree of freedom. The best example I have encountered of the opposite of a colony was my own position when I was head of a program production department in the BBC Television Service: If I wanted to take on a new production assistant or pay an incumbent one more money, I had to apply to the establishment department; if I wanted to promote him to producer I had to apply to the appointments department; if I wanted a film editor to work on Saturday I had to ask the film department; if I wanted to change a set designer I had to ask the design department; if I wanted new carpets or an extra office I had to ask the administration department; if I wanted to change studio rehearsal times I had to apply to engineering allocation; if I wanted to tell the press about a program, I had to do it through the publicity officer. There was no question of doing without an extra office so as to pay a producer more—all these budgets were unconnected, and none controlled by me. And none of the heads of these departments worked under the head of my own group, and many did not meet a common boss until three or four levels up in the hierarchy; three of them only met in the post of director-general. The opposite situation would be the owner of a small independent production company; he would have total control of the gross revenue, and total discretion as to how he applied it; he would take on and lay off free-lance designers, producers, and film crews entirely according to the needs of the program he was producing, and telephone the newspaper he chose whenever he had anything to talk about. Obviously the difference in degree of freedom between those two situations is very considerable, and the closer a man is to the second, the more truly can he be said to be building a colony; and unless he has quite a lot of these freedoms he cannot be said to be in a colony at all.

There are several reasons why it is advantageous for the corporation to put managers in charge of colonial groups. If a man knows that his salary, success, self-esteem, and status in the corporation are limited only by the limits to which he can raise his colony, he is likely to put more into it than if they are limited by his boss, company career policy, and the grading structure. Also, this sort of independence has a powerful liberating effect on latent or suppressed creative and leadership qualities. It may not always be possible to give this sort of independence, since many jobs are too closely integrated with others, but a reorganization can often create more jobs which are colonial in type at the expense of others which are more like departments of the civil service. One of the most important reasons for colonization is a by-product of the conventional management hierarchy; it was also one of the most important reasons for the founding of colonies by the states of the past; not the pull from without, but the push from within.

It is obvious that if a corporation needs to go into a new line or a new market it will need to form a colony. That is the pull from without. But it may be just as important for it to colonize for internal reasons, because of the push from within, and that is likely to be less obvious. But very often the cities and states started colonies because there was no scope, no land, for the young men within their own boundaries. Rome and Athens were surrounded with hills, and beyond there were other states or cities which made expansion impossible: the only way to make a fortune was to pack up, get on board ship, and sail off to a colony. The Norman invasion of England and the First Crusade thirty years later have both been ascribed to this push from within Europe because of increasing population and restless younger sons wanting wider opportunities than their homeland could supply. It was this urge to get away rather than the pull of a remote El Dorado which supplied the motive force for colonization, and acted as a safety valve to prevent mounting tension and internal strife.

The conventional management hierarchy is rather like an enclosed city-state: A young man can look around him and see the mountains which circumscribe his ambition. If you draw the diagram of the organization, you see at once that the higher you go, the fewer jobs there are; at every level, more and more people are squeezed out. Not necessarily forced to leave, but forced to reconcile themselves to not progressing beyond the level they have reached, or only one level beyond it. Each year the bright young men from the universities flock in in far greater numbers than there are top jobs that will need their abilities. A static hierarchic firm will watch some of them leave at the time when they are about to be of most value, and see others fail to grow to the stature of similar bright young men recruited by the firm in the days of its youth. Men grow to the stature to which they are stretched when they are young, and the ones who are not stretched will fail to grow; some will actually be diminished. Corporation executives may tell you that an organization cannot have too many good men, but they are wrong. What it cannot do is keep them good without constantly giving them tasks that match up to their abilities. This is why a firm may need to initiate projects for which there is no clear external reason, in order to make sure that staff of high quality stays with the firm—and stays of high quality.

So much for the nature of "good" decentralization, the foundation of colonies; it is close to the principle sometimes called federal decentralization, but its nature and advantages are better emphasized by thinking in terms of colonies than of the United States. There is, however, nothing inherent in colonizing which prevents the ill effects of bad decentralization, the fragmentation and conflicting objectives and practices referred to earlier. For this, good decentralization needs to be accompanied by good centralization; and so far from being in indirect proportion to each other, they are in direct proportion—the more you have of the latter, the more you can afford of the former.

It is arguable (though I have no intention of arguing it here) that one reason why the Roman Empire grew so large and survived so long—a prodigious feat of management—is that there was no railway, car, airplane, radio, paper, or telephone. Above all, no telephone. And therefore you could. not maintain any illusion of direct control over a general or a provincial governor, you could not feel at the back of your mind that you could ring him up, or he could ring you, if a situation cropped up which was too much for him, or that you could fly over and sort things out if they started to get into a mess. You appointed him, you watched his chariot and baggage train disappear over the hill in a cloud of dust, or his trireme recede over the horizon, and that was that. If there was a disaster you would know nothing about it until months later when a messenger came panting up from the port of Ostia or galloping in down the Via Appennina to tell you that an army had been lost or a province overrun. There was, therefore, no question of appointing a man who was not fully trained, or not quite up to the job; you knew that everything depended on his being the best man for the job before he set off. And so you took great care in selecting him; but more than that, you made sure that he knew all about Rome and Roman government and the Roman army before he went out. To become a general demanded a long apprenticeship in a highly trained and very well-organized army. To become a governor, a man had to be a proconsul, a former consul, in other words he had to have held the highest office of state, before he was entrusted with the government of a province. This ensured that he never needed policy guidance or rulings when he was on the spot, since in any case there was no means of his getting them. It had to be there, deeply ingrained in him, before he set out.

Of course you cannot run an empire without any communications—it will not be an empire, only a group of small, isolated states seeing occasional explorers. The Romans had an excellent communication system—command of the sea routes (a large part of the empire was maritime) and a superb network of roads. They could therefore move armies, send reinforcements, supply garrisons, and do all that was necessary to protect their frontiers, keep internal order, and hold the empire together. But they were never under the illusion that they could pick up the telephone and save the sum of things for the price of a trunk call.

In general, the long-distance telephone is a magnificent instrument for transmitting and receiving information and advice and suggestions, but an appalling one for exercising control. As a disgruntled British admiral growled after the Suez operation, "Nelson would never have won a single victory if there'd been a telex."

The good sort of centralization is where the man himself, the provincial governor or regional manager, is "centralized" within before he goes out to his decentralized post. St. Augustine once gave as the only rule for Christian conduct "Love God and do what you like." The implication is, of course, that if you truly love God, then you will only ever want to do things which are acceptable to Him. Equally, Jesuit priests are not constantly being rung up, or sent memos, by the head office of the Society. The long, intensive training over many years in Rome is a guarantee that wherever they go afterward, and however long it may be before they even see another Jesuit, they will be able to do their work in accordance with the standards of the Society. They may constantly face new situations and unfamiliar problems, but they will handle them exactly as the head of the Society would himself, because they are so efficiently centralized internally. Perhaps this concept was most neatly expressed by Reay Geddes, the head of Dunlop, when he was telling the head of their German organization how to lay out his new factory: "The trouble with you, Mr. Geddes," complained the German executive, "is that you will not let your subordinates have a mind of their own." "Mind, yes," replied Geddes, "will, no."

One of the great modern centralization/decentralization dilemmas was faced by Shell Oil, and they are said to have paid McKinsey's half a million dollars to sort it out for them. It is hard to see how the problem could have arisen at all, but for the telephone and the airplane. In essence, it was whether geographical regions (South America, Far East, etc.) should form the provinces of the Shell empire, or functional divisions (production, marketing, tankers, etc.). Obviously Rome would perforce have made the geographical unit the province, but while Shell were spending their half-million dollars with McKinsey's they might have invested a further dime in a phone call to the War Office. The British Army has exactly the same problem with its field commanders and its supporting arms—Artillery, Signals, Engineers, etc. Like the Romans and the Jesuits, the British Army takes great pains to make sure that field commanders are really deeply ingrained with the thinking of the army as a whole: tours of duty abroad, spells at home, staff college, all to ensure that when they take decisions on their own, they take the right ones, or at least the best the army knows. The Signals and Artillery people are more specialized, and so at every level they are a rank below the field commander, and "under command." The Signals officer at the War Office may replace his chief signals officer, but while he is "under command" he has to obey the man who is internally the most centralized, who is as it were trained, selected, and trusted by Rome to govern the province. Shell has in fact come to a similar conclusion, and it is the local manager who is in charge. A top executive has formulated the new setup in a way very similar to St. Augustine's: "Each local manager has a great deal of delegation, but he knows, by God, that he is a member of the group."

There is one further argument for delegation, that is, decentralization, of the right type, and in particular for starting colonies with considerable independence. It is that one day this small, experimental unit may turn out to be the great growth point of the corporation, and may even be its salvation. The decentralized, completely self-contained units of Christianity, the monasteries, were created by St. Benedict on this principle: that if everything in Christendom were destroyed except for one monastery, Christianity could still survive in that single cell, and it was in the monasteries of Ireland at the darkest hour of the Dark Ages that European learning and the Christian faith were preserved from the rising tide of Mohammedan and Viking conquest. The Roman Empire survived the fall of Rome because Constantine had already moved the center of the empire to the colony of Byzantium, like a punched card company which got into computers just in time to survive the crash of mechanical data processing equipment. But it had been Diocletian who started it, by taking the government of the empire around with him, wherever in the empire he happened to be visiting or fighting. He had seen, nearly 1,700 years ago, the answer to the problem of the huge, overgrown, overstaffed, extravagant, inefficient corporation steadily losing its share of the market: Move all the vital decision-making people and functions to another place, and let the old one cave in. If there is a promising, strong, self-contained subsidiary company to move to, the essentials can survive the disaster.

8

Computers and Their Priests

ROBERT TOWNSEND

Robert Townsend has called his immensely popular book a survival manual for successful corporate guerrillas and has given it a lengthy descriptive subtitle: "How to Stop the Corporation from Stifling People and Strangling Profits." The author firmly believes that big, successful institutions are not successful because of the way they operate, but in spite of it. The

Reprinted from Robert Townsend, *Up the Organization*, pp. 18-19, by permission of the publishers, Alfred A. Knopf, Inc., New York, and Michael Joseph Ltd., London. Copyright 1970 by Robert Townsend.

adjectives applied to the book range from "witty" and "iconoclastic" to "funny" and "outrageous."

This brief selection contains a set of warnings to executives concerning computer and systems staffs. Many experienced executives would contend that Mr. Townsend's views regarding the use of internal or external specialists and his guidelines for the indoctrination of computer specialists should apply to all staff groups, not merely to computer specialists. Do you agree?

First get it through your head that computers are big, expensive, fast, dumb adding-machine-typewriters. Then realize that most of the computer technicians that you're likely to meet or hire are complicators, not simplifiers. They're trying to make it look tough. Not easy. They're building a mystique, a priesthood, their own mumbo-jumbo ritual to keep you from knowing what they—and you—are doing.

Here are some rules of thumb:

1. At this state of the art, keep decisions on computers at the highest level. Make sure the climate is ruthlessly hard-nosed about the practicality of every system, every program, and every report. "What are you going to do with that report?" "What would you do if you didn't have it?" Otherwise your programmers will be writing their doctoral papers on your machines, and your managers will be drowning in ho-hum reports they've been conned into asking for and are ashamed to admit are of no value.

2. Make sure your present report system is reasonably clean and effective before you automate. Otherwise your new computer will just speed up the mess.

3. Rather than build your own EDP staff, hire a small, independent software company to come in, plan your computer system, and then get out. Make sure they plan every detail in advance and let them know you expect them to meet every dollar and time target. Systems are like roads. Very expensive. And no good building them until you know exactly where they're going to wind up.

4. Before you hire a computer specialist, make it a condition that he spend some time in the factory and then sell your shoes to the customers. A month the first year, two weeks a year thereafter. This indignity[1] will separate those who want to use their skills to help your company from those who just want to build their own know-how on your payroll.

5. No matter what the experts say, never, never automate a manual function without a long enough period of dual operation. When in doubt discontinue the automation. And don't stop the manual system until the

---

[1] Everybody including the chief executive had to go through the Avis rental-agent training school. I once saw the Ph.D. who was responsible for all Avis systems panic and run from an O'Hare rental counter at the approach of his first real customer.

non-experts in the organization think that automation is working. I've never known a company seriously injured by automating too slowly but there are some classic cases of companies bankrupted by computerizing prematurely.

9

The Impact of Information Technology on Organization Structure

THOMAS L. WHISLER

The effect that information technology has had on organization structure has attracted the attention of academics and managers alike. In 1958, Whisler and Harold Leavitt collaborated on a provocative and widely quoted article in which they made several predictions concerning the impact of information technology on organizations.* The major predictions were:

1. *Greater organizational centralization.*
2. *A reduction in the number of middle managers.*
3. *More programming of the jobs of middle managers.*
4. *The creation of a block to the movement of middle managers.*
5. *More emphasis in top management on innovation and the search for new goals.*

Several other writers, among them Herbert Simon, John Burlingame, John Dearden, and Melvin Anshen, have since issued further forecasts of the impact of information technology. All those who write on this subject speculate that information technology will cause changes in job content, organization structure, patterns of control, and skills necessary to work in computerized organizations. Yet considerable disagreement exists concerning the specific nature of organizational change that will take place.

Until recently there has been little empirical evidence concerning the probable directions of computer-induced organizational change. Conse-quently, Whisler's Information Technology and Organizational Change, *in which the author analyzes the findings of several recent empirical studies, is a valuable contribution. This particular excerpt deals specifically with the*

Reprinted from Thomas Whisler, *Information Technology and Organizational Change*, pp. 37-52, by permission of the publisher. Copyright 1970 by Wadsworth Publishing Company, Inc., Belmont, Calif.

**Harold J. Leavitt and Thomas L. Whisler, "Management in the 1980's," *Harvard Business Review*, XXXVI, No. 6 (November-December 1958), 41-48.*

impact of information technology on organization structure. The elements of organization design considered are organization size, the number of organizational levels, the span of control, and the basis for departmentation.

THE EFFECTS ON STRUCTURE

The General Impact: Consolidation and Shrinkage

The impact of computer systems on managerial productivity, mentioned earlier in this chapter, shows itself in a variety of ways. In some cases *shrinkage* is clearly visible; the number of people employed (not only managers but those working with them, such as clerks) declines quite clearly. This quantitative decline is usually accompanied by qualitative changes in the people and the jobs, which we will discuss later.

A decline in numbers is most obvious when outputs remain essentially fixed. In one division of a very large corporation, for instance, a decision was made to impose massive electronic data systems as quickly as possible in order to reduce costs; the division was losing money, and traditional efforts by consultants and others to rectify the situation had failed. Within three years comprehensive and integrated computer systems in production control, materials control, and accounting were programmed and installed. The shrinkage was dramatic; 34 percent of the managerial positions and about 20 percent of the nonmanagerial positions in these three areas disappeared.

In another large corporation a major division computerized its product-distribution function, initially for those products making up the bulk of its sales volume. Two hundred and ninety-three people were employed for this function before computerization; 102 were employed afterward despite a substantial increase in sales volume.

Quite often, computer-induced changes in employment are hidden by changes in output that occur during the period of computer installation. "Before-and-after" employment counts thus may be misleading. In an effort to deal with this difficulty, 15 life insurance companies were asked to estimate employment changes necessary at various levels were they to attempt *to accomplish their current output without their computer systems.* The results are shown in Table 1. A number of these same companies also were able to provide percentage estimates of the required employment changes. The average of these estimates is as follows:

Clerical	+60%
Supervisory	+ 9%
Managerial	+ 2%

This decline in the number of human inputs is often accompanied by the consolidation of activities. In the usual structure of an organization the

Table 1 Estimates from 15 companies of employment changes at different organization levels necessary if computers did not exist in presently computerized areas.

Organizational Level	Number of Companies Estimating That Employment Would:		
	Increase	Decrease	Not change
Clerical	14	0	1
Supervisory	8	1	6
Managerial	1	1	13

overall organizational operation is broken down into pieces sufficiently small to permit managers to cope with the flow of information and to solve the problems necessary to get the job done. When computers become partners with managers, the managers' capacity for handling information and solving problems is greatly increased. Consequently, it is not necessary to separate the organization into as many distinct groups as was necessary in precomputer days.

In the example mentioned above of the computerization of a product distribution organization, not only was the number of people reduced, but seven separate departments were consolidated into one called simply "distribution." This consolidation initially occurred in only one product area but soon spread across the three major corporate divisions, eventually resulting in the consolidation of all divisional distribution departments into one corporate distribution department. In another instance, a major U.S. shoe manufacturing corporation consolidated the vice presidencies of merchandising and production and their respective departments because of computerization.[1]

In a final example, a heavy equipment manufacturing firm, with three geographically separated manufacturing facilities, consolidated the control departments (material supply, production programming, and accounting) functioning separately at each of these facilities into equivalent departments located at divisional headquarters. This is a geographical consolidation, in contrast with the preceding two examples, which illustrated functional consolidations. Examples of both can often be found in a single company. Such horizontal consolidation almost invariably results in shifts in the control structure (to be discussed later) and changes in the basis of departmentation and the number of levels in the hierarchy.

[1] George P. Shultz and Thomas L. Whisler (eds.), *Management Organization and the Computer* (New York: Free Press of Glencoe, 1960), p. 160.

Reduction of Levels

The "geometry" of hierarchical organizations is imperfectly understood. Systematic efforts have been made only recently to study the formal structure of organizations.

Despite this lack of empirical study there are some "axioms" that arise from the modular structure of the hierarchy. In a hierarchy a group of individuals in a subordinate position report to another individual who is, in turn, a member of a group of subordinates reporting to still another individual, and so forth; if the number of individuals remains constant, the span of control (the average number of subordinates reporting to a superior) and the number of levels in the organization are inversely related. Should the size of the organization be reduced through displacement of individuals by a technology, either the number of levels or the span of control or both must decline. We shall point out in the next section that the span of control tends to be reduced. What happens to the number of levels as a consequence of computerization?

We have a modest amount of evidence that the number of levels tends to decline. Unfortunately, the data have been collected in such a way that we cannot determine if both the span of control and the number of levels decline in the same organization, or if one tends to substitute for the other. Only in the life insurance study, discussed at different points in this chapter, can we find evidence that in the same *set* of companies both span of control and number of levels tend to decline. While this relationship needs further study, we can point to some specific cases where large, integrated computer systems imposed on organizations in a short period of time reduced the number of levels.

One example is the application of the SAGE system to the North American Defense Command (NORAD). This command has the function of detecting and intercepting all unidentified aircraft on the North American continent and destroying hostile craft. Prior to the installation of the SAGE computer system, NORAD relied on World War II technology to carry out this function, using a complex of radar, radio, and plotting boards to work out the critical problem of the optimal deployment of interceptor weapons whenever an unknown aircraft appeared. The SAGE system is designed to solve this problem accurately, quickly, and automatically. As a consequence of SAGE installation, *the number of levels of command in NORAD was reduced from five to four.*

In private business we do not often find a broad computer system applied as rapidly as was SAGE. However, a similar effect appears when such an example is discovered. In the corporate division referred to in the previous section, where computer systems reduced the number of managerial positions by 34 percent, the number of organizational levels for production control was reduced from six to five. For accounting and cost control, no decline occurred.

In the life insurance study, firms were asked to report the effects of computers upon the number of levels in those parts of the organization using the computer systems. Some companies responded in terms of departments and others in terms of the entire affected area. The results are shown in Table 2. The missing cell in the table is the result of ambiguous reporting; a few companies indicated that no change in levels occurred in "the remainder of the departments," without specifying how many departments actually fall in this cell.

Based upon the small amount of evidence at hand, a reasonable conclusion is that if there is any change at all, the number of levels in the "chain of command" is more likely to decrease rather than increase as a consequence of computer use. This conclusion could surely be stated more strongly if in those studies, specific account had been taken of organizational growth. Virtually all the organizations were growing during the computerization period; this growth would naturally work to increase the number of levels.

The comment of one insurance executive illustrates this point:

> At the lower middle management level, division management and supervision, the chain of command has had a tendency to short-cut, with the compression directly related to the extent to which its functions were automated. It is at the upper middle management and senior officer levels that a marked increase in the chain of command has been noted. The planning and implementation for an accelerated and continuing program of automation has contributed to this expansion. It must also be recognized that our rapid rate of growth, coupled with increasing complexity of the business, has undoubtedly been the major factor for this increase in reporting levels above that of division manager.[2]

Table 2   Changes in the number of organizational levels in EDP-affected areas, reported by department and by company.

	By Departments	By Company
Decline in the number of levels	20	5
No change in the number of levels	—*	11
Increase in the number of levels	9	2

*See text for explanation.

[2] Thomas Whisler and Harald Meyer, *The Impact of EDP on Life Company Organization* (New York: Life Office Management Association, 1967).

The differential effects of computers at various stages of their development should also be noted in the above quotation. The organizational effects during the development phase, when systems analysis is under way and programs are being written, are likely to be different from the effects after the systems have been installed and all organizational adaptations made. In the insurance industry and in many other businesses, development has occurred from the bottom up, with lower-level people affected first and with often opposite effects on different levels at a particular point in time. This may explain some of the arguments about the consequences of information technology; the antagonists who buttress their arguments with apparently contradictory facts may simply be reporting effects at two different stages in the use of computers. ...

Reduction of Span of Control

The horizontal dimension of a hierarchy is usually measured in terms of the span of control—the number of individuals reporting to a supervisor. The average span of control has been used by a number of writers to indicate the degree of centralization of control in an organization. Since little empirical study has been done, however, to measure directly the relationship,[3] there is no universal agreement about what the association is; other critical factors affecting span of control, such as technology, make the search for evidence of this relationship very complex.

We do know logically that control must become less centralized as organizations get larger. We have a small amount of evidence to support this,[4] and furthermore we have some evidence showing that span of control increases with organizational size.[5] Thus, it is likely that control will be less centralized; because a supervisor's time is limited, the more people he must supervise, the less tightly—centrally—he will be able to control them. It is at least tenable, therefore, that centralization of control and span of control are related inversely, and control will become less centralized as the span of control increases. ...

Earlier in this chapter an example was given of a reduction in span of control at a high level of an organization, where two vice presidencies in a shoe manufacturing company were consolidated. The span of control immediately under the president was thus reduced. Most changes in span of control are concentrated in the lowest levels of management, however.

In the insurance company study, respondents were asked to report the

[3] One such study is T. L. Whisler, H. Meyer, B. H. Baum, and P. F. Sorensen, Jr., "Centralization of Organization Control: An Empirical Study of Its Meaning and Measurement," *Journal of Business*, Vol. 40, No. 1 (January 1967), pp. 10-26.

[4] Thomas L. Whisler, "Measuring Centralization of Control in Business Organizations," in W. W. Cooper, H. J. Leavitt, and M. W. Shelly, Jr. (eds.), *New Perspectives in Organization Research* (New York: John Wiley & Sons, Inc., 1964), pp. 326-330.

[5] See Harald Meyer, *A Theory of the Departmental Structure of the Formal Organization* (Unpublished dissertation, University of Chicago, 1967), p. 83.

effects of computers on span of control. Ten companies provided a department-by-department report on the effects, and ten gave reports on the EDP-affected segment as a whole. We also examined organization charts provided by individual companies, and compared the span of control before and after computers. The results are summarized in Table 3.

It can be seen that the results from examination of organization charts (first line) agree closely with the reports of the ten companies that provided a department-by-department report (third line). These figures differ somewhat from the estimates of companies reporting the affected segment as a whole. This discrepancy is probably a result of averaging and estimating (although it is possible there may be a real difference between the two groups).

The data do substantiate somewhat the expectation that span of control will decrease when information technology is utilized. It is also clear, however, that something else may at times increase the span of control or hold it constant in many departments.

Changes in the size of the organization may be one factor. We expect that span of control will increase as an organization grows. We might therefore expect that span of control would be reduced only slightly in those companies showing a high growth rate during the period of computer installation. However, if the computer does reduce the span of control, we would expect that the longer it has been in operation, the shorter span of control should be.

Table 4 shows these relationships in 19 insurance companies. The data are consistent with our expectations. Row A indicates the length of time the computer has been actively used in the corporation, and row B is a measure of growth. As anticipated, the largest declines in the span of control have

Table 3   Effects of EDP on average span of control as determined from three different sources of information.

Source of Information	Span of Control:		
	Decreased	Increased	Stayed the Same
Examination of organization charts of EDP-affected departments (n = 48)*	19 (40%)	15 (31%)	14 (29%)
Estimates from 10 companies† for EDP-affected segment of company (n = 10)	3 (30%)	0 (0%)	7 (70%)
Estimates from 10 companies† for EDP-affected departments, separately (n = 98)	44 (45%)	29 (30%)	25 (25%)

*These departments are in the same companies that provided estimates.
†Two mutually exclusive groups of 10 companies.

Table 4 Relationships between changes in span of control, the length of use of the computer, and the rate of growth of the firm in 19 companies.

	Firms with Largest Declines in Span of Control (n = 9)	Firms with Smallest (or No) Declines in Span of Control (n = 10)
A. Average number of years since first on-line run	5.4	4.2
B. Average percent growth in premium income (1960-1965)	30.7	33.3

occurred in those firms that have used the computer longest, and there is also evidence that the rate of growth of the company will offset the computer's effect on the span of control. Row B shows that the largest declines in the span of control have occurred in firms with lower growth rates. Had the computer not appeared, these companies' growth should have caused some growth in the span of control. We therefore interpret these data to mean that computers have reduced span of control even though corporate growth may offset this effect.

Insurance company data show that the changes occur at the lowest levels of the management hierarchy at the supervisory level. These findings are especially interesting when considered along with findings ... that the amount of interpersonal communication between superior and subordinate at these lowest levels has declined as a consequence of computer systems. One of our arguments for assuming that span of control will increase as centralization decreases was that because of limitations on a supervisor's available time, the more tightly (centrally) he controls, the fewer people he will be able to supervise. This argument assumes, however, that supervision is an interpersonal communication process and that with fewer people to oversee, the supervisor should be able to maintain a higher level of communication with his subordinates. The insurance data indicate instead that even with fewer subordinates, the supervisor spends less time communicating with them. He apparently spends his time in surveillance of the nonhuman system for which he is responsible. These findings raise doubts about the use of span of control as an indicator of centralization of control.

Changes in Departmentation

One of the great blanks in organization theory is a systematic and satisfactory explanation of the grouping of activities, jobs, and people in organizations, even though this is one of the fundamental problems to be solved by those responsible for an organization's effective functioning. Recent lines of investigation, however, suggest that the costs of communication are a fundamental determinant of the pattern of departmentation within any organization.[6] By trial and error, the organization seeks that structure which will minimize its costs, given the number and kinds of problems that it has to solve. These problems depend on the character and volume of its outputs.

The task of communication, of information handling, exists throughout the organization. No matter how departments are laid out, each one must gather and transmit information, analyze and transform it. With computer technology we would expect a pervasive change in the techniques and economics of information processing, and, as the technology grows, continuous changes in the arrangement of departments in the organization. Some idea of the magnitude of these changes is shown in Table 5. In 18 life insurance companies using computers for periods ranging from 18 months to ten years, 177 departmental changes were ascribed to the use of computer systems. These changes were concentrated in larger companies with longer experience, and with more extensive computer applications (see Table 6). It is not surprising that those that have used computers longest and have computerized more insurance functions show the greatest number of changes. The relationship to size is perhaps not so obvious, probably occurring because the equivalent of a shift of an entire section or department in a large firm is only the shift or partial redefinition of a single job in a small firm.

Are there systematic and predictable kinds of changes in these organizational rearrangements? We would expect that because the great speed and storage capacity of the computer make the consolidation of information handling activities economical,[7] previously separated information handling activities will move into the computer center. This concentration of information processing activities will reduce the size of some departments, and perhaps motivate a consolidation of these departments to economize on supervisory skills. Even if the size reduction is too small to encourage consolidation, consolidation might occur for another reason. The speed and capacity of the computer permits much wider analysis of information for decision and control purposes than was formerly possible. Under such circumstances, maintaining separate departments with a nominal degree of independence in decision making and control is awkward (recall the example of the merchandising and production vice presidents in the shoe manufacturing company). Where departments are performing sequential functions in the work of the organization, applying the high speed and capacity of information technology across this flow should have a tendency to make the definition of departmental boundaries broader.

Studies of organizational growth indicate that as firms get larger they

---

[6] Harald Meyer, *op. cit.*

[7] Martin B. Solomon, Jr., "Economics of Scale and the IBM System/360," *Communications of the ACM*, Vol. 9, No. 6 (June 1966) pp. 435-440.

Table 5 Number of kinds of changes in the organization structure as a result of EDP.

Type of Change	Number of Instances Reported	Percent of Total
(1) Creation of new departments	52	29
(2) Elimination of old departments	43	24
(3) Transfer of activities (departments) to EDP	33	19
(4) Other transfers of activities (departments)	21	12
(5) Consolidations (mergers) of departments	4	2
(6) Splits of departments	4	2
(7) Reorganization of parallel into functional departments	20	12
Total	177	100

Table 6 Relationship between number of changes in organizational structure induced by EDP applications, length of intensity of computer use, and company size, in 18 companies.

	Average Number of Years Since First On-Line Run	Average Number of Functions Computerized	Company Size (Number of Employees)
9 Firms with the greatest number of structural changes	5.9	16.4	6,593
9 Firms with the smallest number of structural changes	4.1	14.3	2,563

tend to disperse their activities geographically and to enlarge the range of services and goods that they produce. Because of this growth the problems of information transmission and transformation are greatly increased. Prior to the use of computers, one widely used solution was to restructure the organization so that it consisted of "parallel" departments, usually responsible either for a specific product line or for activities in a specific geographical area and controlling all or most of the functions related to that product line or area. This restructuring was characterized as a change from "functional" to "parallel" departmentation. The gains in effectiveness of decision making and information processing as a consequence of this rearrangement were offset in part by the loss of the earlier efficiency that resulted from specializing by function. As the computer greatly reduces the costs of information processing, however, specialization should again become more economic, and we would expect that parallel departmentation where it exists will shift to functional departmentation.

In the insurance study data shown in Table 5, we see that nearly one-fifth of the structural changes involve shifting activities to the department responsible for computer operation. The other transfers, shown in line 4, represent relocation of activities for more effective supervision, given the consolidation of information processing. We predicted both these changes. Unfortunately, only a few consolidations were reported. This may be due in part to semantic problems (as is often the case with questionnaires), since discussion of the collected data with the respondents indicated that some of the cases reported in line 2 as elimination of old departments were actually consolidations where the title of one department disappeared from the chart. Most companies also experienced considerable growth in total employment during the period covered by this study, probably inhibiting department mergers that might otherwise have occurred. Finally, the pressure to reduce the span of control brakes departmental consolidation.

The 20 reported examples of reorganization from parallel to functional departmentation is consistent with our expectations. For example, Company X (in life insurance) regrouped five parallel departments organized by geographical area and one service department into four functional departments as follows:

Before EDP	*After EDP*

Five parallel departments, organized by geographical area, each performing the functions of:
  Premium billing
  Agency report audit (on premium collection and commission payments)
  Premium loans
  Dividends
  Premium taxes, etc.
One service department
	Four functional departments:
	  Premium collection
	  Premium loan and accounting
	  Agency reports
	  Commission disbursement

Table 7 shows that the longer and more intensively companies use the computer, the greater is the tendency to move from parallel to functional departmentation. The table also compares the growth rate of those companies eliminating parallel departments with those showing no such change; the rate of growth of the first group is substantially lower than that of the second.

*Table 7   Elimination   of   parallel   departments   in   EDP-affected
areas as related to intensity of computer use and growth of firm
in 18 companies.*

	Average Number of Years Since First On-Line Run	Average Number of Functions Computerized	Average Percent Growth in Premium Income, 1960-1965
8 Firms showing elimination of parallel departments	6.1	16.5	26.3
10 Firms showing no elimination of parallel departments	4.7	13.5	35.6

Although there seems to be little question that computer systems precipitate rearrangements in the organizational structure, we need a more precise and comprehensive count and better identification of the kinds of changes that occur than is provided by the evidence shown in this chapter. The number of departments and firms that would need to be surveyed to provide this information would probably be five or six times the number of companies covered in the insurance study, however; such a large sample is necessary since controls have to be imposed for growth, geographical expansion, intensity of computerization, and length of exposure to the technology. With such a large sample and intense examination necessary, it is easy to see why we will not have a clear picture of the effects of information technology on departmentation until a major research project is completed.

Differences among Departments

In many organizations computers have been used extensively in certain departments with little visible change resulting in the structure of these departments. Since no systematic research has been done on this, however, we lack vital information about qualitative and quantitative differences in computer impacts on various departments.

It is always possible that lack of visible impact results either from the offsetting factors mentioned earlier, such as growth and diversification of product line, or from a lag in adaptation of organizational structure to the new systems. But the comments of a number of managers to the author, citing cases of extensive computerization coupled with little organizational change, make another analysis more attractive.

Certain kinds of departments dominate the list of those showing little structural change—engineering design, research and development, industrial relations, and advertising. If we compare these departments with those in which major changes are most often visible—production, accounting, premium billing, and product distribution—we can see some significant differences between the two groups. We summarize these differences as follows:

1. *Degree of job specializations.* Task specialization is more complete in some departments than in others, and in general has gone much further in the second group of departments cited above than in the first.

2. *The degree of job interdependence.* The degree of job interdependence—the degree to which the outcome of one member's effort depends upon the behavior of his fellow members—is largely a function of the degree of job specialization. Therefore, effort is substantially less interdependent in the first group of departments than in the second.

3. *The degree of management control and coordination required.* This is a function of both job specialization and job interdependence; in a highly specialized department, a high degree of management control is required to coordinate properly the efforts of those making up the department. Again, the first group of departments mentioned above would require less control and coordination than would the second.

4. *The character of departmental task—problem solving vs. problem definition.* Where organizational problems have been defined, and especially where they recur, it is feasible to develop a high degree of specialization, interdependence, and control and coordination. Where the task is primarily that of discovering which problems the organization must deal with, the ill-structured and one-time character of the task makes it difficult to extensively exploit specialization. The first group of departments above deals more with problem defining, the second with problem-solving (although there are obviously differences among departments in both groups).

5. *Time press.* In some departments deadlines are critical, accurately and precisely defined, and strongly enforced. In others, they are more vague and less stringent. These differences, again, correspond strongly with the degree of specialization; specialization itself is responsible for creating numerous deadlines as part of coordination. Furthermore, specialization permits telescoping time; having more people do many different parts of a large task simultaneously enormously reduces the total processing time. Under competitive pressure from other organizations one could expect that the time press on the second group of departments would be substantially greater than on the first.

We note that the tasks of communication and computation become complex and critical in those departments with a high degree of specialization, and it is in precisely these areas that information technology can play its greatest role. It becomes an integral part of control and coordination, often supplanting individuals who were earlier engaged in such activities and increasing the specialization of the remaining jobs. It is fast, and vast, and becomes a powerful tool in dealing with the myriad details of a department with high task specialization operating under stringent time press. Introducing a computer into a department of this kind makes a man-machine system out of a formerly human system, and its structural characteristics should be markedly changed.

In the other kind of department, there is little specialization, the basic task is problem definition, and organization tends to be "loose" with only modest control devices and arrangements. The time press is not as stringent as in the specialized department; jobs are large and consist of many bundles of skills. The impact of the computer is quite different. It will be an adjunct to an individual rather than part of the organization structure. The impact on some skills may be high, but the individual uses multiple skills; engineers may have to learn how to design products using elaborate computer programs, but they remain designers with similar responsibilities using many of the same skills. Larger individual outputs may be expected but the outputs are qualitatively similar. Interpersonal relations are not substantially affected because job interdependence is already relatively low. The control structure is little modified unless this department becomes closely tied to the operations of other departments through computer systems.

If this general analysis has some validity, we should not be too surprised to find that certain departments with enormous computer libraries in heavy use show little structural change. The lives of individuals in such departments may be considerably changed, nevertheless, and retraining and obsolescence problems appear. However, many of the problems of adaptation, "coordination," and relation of skills to one other are handled by the individual using his own professional judgment.

It is in the technical core[8] of the organizations with its carefully developed buffers against uncertainty that we expect to find information technology rearranging departmental structure, content of tasks, and individual skills. The second group of departments typifies the technical core of the modern industrial organization.

[8] The concept of "technical core" and "uncertainty buffers" is developed in James D. Thompson, *Organizations in Action* (New York: McGraw-Hill Book Company, Inc., 1967), pp. 3-83.

10

Organization Structure

PAUL E. HOLDEN, CARLTON A. PEDERSON,
AND GAYTON E. GERMANE

The book from which this selection is taken represents the continuation of a project originally begun in 1941 when Professor Paul E. Holden, together with Lounsberry S. Fish and Hubert L. Smith, published Top Management Organization and Control. *It presented the findings of an extensive field study of the then current top management practices of thirty-one large industrial companies in the United States.*

In 1968, Professor Holden collaborated with Carlton A. Pederson and Gayton E. Germane in publishing Top Management, *a book in which they reported the findings of a new study patterned after the one that was carried out in 1941. In this later study, the authors analyzed the top management practices of fifteen major American industrial companies in light of the many changes that had taken place in the external and internal environment of American industry since 1941. In the book, the authors seek to identify and evaluate the major changes that took place in top management policies and practices during the years between the two studies. They also attempt to interpret the implications of contemporary policies and practices and the probable trends in top management organization, direction, and control.*

The authors' survey of practice in the area of organization structure is particularly relevant to our examination of formal organization. They provide us with findings regarding the frequency of organization restructuring, approaches to organization design, and current practice as regards decentralization, the span of control, departmentation, and boards of directors. In addition, they comment on some new organization developments, such as management information systems, product managers, project managers, and program managers.

During the past quarter century, probably no area of top management involvement has evoked more discussion, written or oral, than that of corporate organization structure. Students of the subject, both practical and theoretical, have expounded at untold length by the printed page and from the platform at countless meetings. What have been the results? The findings of this study lead unquestionably to the conclusion that structuring a company's organization is still a very practical matter, and the theorists as yet have made no appreciable impact. Furthermore, the design of the basic structure continues to be a responsibility of the chief executive. Finally, organization planning is generally geared to corporate long-range planning, so that attainment of future objectives is not prevented by failure to have the appropriate organization structure in readiness.

The authors were privileged, in most of the companies included in this study, to examine organization charts over a long span of years. The subject of organization was discussed with appropriate top executives in each company. Out of these analyses and discussions certain developments, trends, and practices were observed, and these will be set forth in the following paragraphs.

ARRANGING THE STRUCTURE

The frequency with which basic or major structural changes are made follows no pattern whatsoever. A few of the companies are operating today under the same general organization plan that was adopted many years previously. Others have instituted fundamental modifications from time to time. Still others give the impression of maintaining their organization structure in virtually a constant state of flux. Finally, in an isolated instance, a complete reversal of organizational concept was recently carried out. Why this widely different situation in a group of large, successful, industrial enterprises? There are valid reasons for each grouping, and in no instance is there an unawareness of the vital importance of a company's organization structure nor an absence of perpetual surveillance.

In the first group are those companies that have adhered steadfastly to their early plans, doing so because there has been no justification for changing them. Through innate wisdom and incredible foresight, a prior generation of top executives devised patterns of organization that have stood the test of time. Not only have these organization structures accommodated growth, diversification, global expansion, and the inexorable advance of complexity of operation, but they have established philosophies adopted successfully by other top managements.

An attitude of complacency or "do not argue or tinker with success" is not evident in these cases. To the contrary, the several chief executives would, in the authors' judgment, be the first to restructure their companies' organizations if the existing plans gave indication of inadequacy or ineffectiveness. This latter statement presupposes, and rightly so, that a corporation's chief executive officer not only occupies the best vantage point from which to observe organizational weakness, but also is in the critical position and of the frame of mind to do something about it.

The second group—those who institute fundamental changes upon occasion—comprises the largest number of companies participating in this study. In fact, a substantial majority of all industrial enterprises would fall into this category. More often than not, the occasion for change has been the necessity to shift from a functional to a product or regional division basis.

As was pointed out in the earlier study, there comes a time in most manufacturing companies when the line of products, advance of technology, or spread of operations transcends the capacity of strictly functional executives to meet their full responsibilities. Another closely related occasion is brought about by acquisitions or mergers. An expanded product line may or may not be the impelling factor, but enlarged operations and additional management personnel necessitate a revamping of the organization structure. Whenever such occasions prompt a major reorganization, the second and usual practice is to devise a structure that will readily accommodate future developments and plans to the end that subsequent organizational changes are infrequent or minor of character.

Companies in the third group—those who make frequent changes—are exceptions and involve only a few. The underlying causes for frequent modification are several in number, usually occurring singly rather than jointly. Failure to gear organization planning to the long-range company plans is the most common cause. It can and does happen that while the "music" for future operations is well composed, the plans for organization are "played by ear." ...

A secondary cause for modification can occur when there are changes in top command. It is an accepted prerogative of the company's chief executive to have the pattern of organization that he wants and in which he believes. If the new head is brought in from the outside, he may have ostensibly good reasons to make modifications, one of which may well be an ineffective or inadequate plan of organization.

Still another cause, and one with some relevance to the preceding one, is the need to find an answer to an unsatisfactory or worsening situation. A possible cure is to change the organization structure, and if the new plan does not produce the desired results, try another one. Because of the disruptive effects of major organizational changes, it is fortunate that this third category is small in number and, where applicable, will undoubtedly attain a stabilized situation as the underlying causes disappear.

The single case that created a fourth category was a change from a basic decentralized structure to a highly centralized one with vertical functional direction. While this concept goes counter to general practice, the determination to make the 180-degree turn was a result of appropriate study and deliberation by top management, including final approval by the company's board of directors.

Aside from the attendant problems of adjustment, two disadvantages were recognized: (1) elimination of multiple profit centers and concentration on profit responsibility at one point—the chief operating officer; and (2) loss of the natural and built-in mechanism of developing executives with a general management orientation. The latter disadvantage can be overcome to some extent by providing multifunctional exposure at a fairly early period in the careers of promising young executives. On the plus side of the reorganization, several distinct benefits were contemplated and ultimately realized, as reported by the company: (1) improved coordination of long-range planning, (2) easier communication, (3) elimination of duplicated staff, (4) better facilities engineering, and (5) removal of two levels of management.

SPAN OF CONTROL

The number of people supervised by company officers has been a topic of interest for years to students and practitioners of organization. It has been surrounded by dogma in some circles. If corporate practice, currently and over a long period of time, may be accepted as a criterion, there most assuredly is no magic or immutable number of subordinates that should report to an immediate superior.

The appropriate span of control depends upon such variables as: similarity or dissimilarity of duties supervised, capacity of superior and capacity of subordinates, degree of decentralization and concomitant autonomy, age of the company and stability of the business, extent to which corporate objectives have been established and made known, and extent of policy coverage and promulgation.

If reference is confined to the position of chief executive officer, a highly varied situation is found among the companies in this study. The span of control for this topmost post ranges from one to fourteen, with ten being both the average and median.

A historical review of this organizational feature reveals a similar lack of uniformity for these same companies. In one instance, the span of control for the top officer has been as limited as three individuals and as extended as fifteen. In another case, the spread has been from a low of five to a high of twenty. There is, of course, nothing surprising or extraordinary concerning this variability. It simply points up the fact mentioned in the preceding paragraph, that the span of control can be and is far from a fixed figure and still represents desired practice by a given top management.

MULTIPLE EXECUTIVE VICE PRESIDENTS

In earlier years, the position of executive vice president, if such were present in an organization, had ordinarily just one import—the incumbent was the heir apparent to the presidency and held the second most important job in the company. Thus there was a single executive vice president as there was a single president.

The advent of the practice of having multiple executive vice presidents is of relatively recent occurrence, perhaps a decade or two ago. Despite its comparative newness, this organizational device has had wide acceptance among the companies studied. The application would be universal if the position of group vice president may be considered as virtually synonymous. The title of senior vice president, found occasionally, is not here regarded as comparable. The full connotation of "senior" often carries the implication of honorary.

Although the more common use of the title of "executive vice president" or "group vice president" pertains to a line position with jurisdiction over two or more product divisions, these same designations are occasionally applied to a position with supervisory responsibility over a number of central staff departments. In both instances, the organizational purpose is the same; viz. to decrease the administrative load of the chief executive officer and the chief operating officer or, as stated in the preceding section, to reduce the span of control for the two top executives. An obvious additional objective is to have several potential successors for the presidency rather than one.

One of the participating companies has for many years followed an unorthodox organization plan for the role of its two executive vice presidents. This has been done deliberately. The organization chart shows these two positions reporting to the president but with no specific assignment of functions or areas of responsibility. Traditionally these positions have been filled by incumbents with long company experience and with strong capability in functional areas complementing that of the president. The only authority attached to the two executive vice presidents is that of being authorities. They not only serve as advisors to the president but are an integral part of his office, and when traveling they represent and speak for the president. When the president is away, one of the executive vice presidents is always in residence.

VICE PRESIDENT FOR ADMINISTRATION

In the preceding section mention was made of an occasional instance of an executive vice president or a group vice president having a number of staff departments reporting to that position. This organizational scheme is quite prevalent among the cooperating companies, but the more common title designating the position is "vice president for administration." One company, several years ago, actually used the title "vice president and chief of staff."

There are several interesting questions arising from the actual use of this organizational device:

1. What would be considered a somewhat typical group of staff departments constituting the package of the vice president for administration?

2. For a given company, does the package remain reasonably stable insofar as contents are concerned?
3. What purposes are served by the device other than reducing the span of control for a chief executive?

It is not surprising to find that there is no typical package. The nearest approach to an answer is that the number of staff departments in the group is predominantly six, and the specific departments appearing most frequently are: employee relations, public relations, secretary, treasurer, and legal. Beyond these two measures of similarity the contents of the various packages are as unlike as if drawn from a grab bag. All in all, 28 different staff agencies were found in one or more groups. The makeup of a few groups would lead one to suggest that the executive in charge should be designated more appropriately as "vice president for miscellaneous!"

The answer to the second question in the preceding group is the typical one—yes and no. About one-half the participating companies have retained essentially the same group of staff agencies as a package under the vice president for administration. The opposite situation is true in the other half; the only difference within this second category is the frequency of change. In one company the package changed substantially five times during a ten-year period. An analysis of the organization charts reveals that where changes have occurred, the incumbents have also changed, which suggests the natural conclusion that to some extent at least an attempt has been made to tailor the position to an individual.

Beyond the obvious move to reduce the number of individuals reporting to a chief executive, the grouping of a number of staff departments under a single executive, by whatever title he is given, serves some additional purposes. Improved coordination between certain functions is a definite objective. Examples would be long-range planning and organization planning, purchasing and traffic, patent department and research and development. Another objective could be to provide a temporary home for a newly created department until a more permanent organizational arrangement is established; an example might be an operations research activity. Others might be giving administrative strength to a department until that requirement is met from within, a condition that might occur with a change of incumbents, or providing a home for an activity known in advance to have a short-lived mission. Finally, service as a group executive of the type under discussion can be, and is, used as a means of management development and evaluation.

OTHER DEPARTMENTAL GROUPINGS

Somewhat related to the preceding discussion are several interesting and rather new departmental groupings found among the cooperating companies. Under the title "director of marketing services," one company includes the following activities: product planning, advertising, pricing, sales financing, market research, parts depots, service, visitor services. The functions thus assembled are available to the worldwide operations of the company and provide the global marketing effort with a closely related support package.

In three other companies a deliberate attempt to focus on and accentuate the interface of the technical and commercial forces is achieved by assembling under a high-level executive the central corporate-wide functions of research, engineering, marketing, and market research. To this core group one company adds its patent department, another includes advertising and economic research, and two companies include manufacturing.

MANAGEMENT INFORMATION SYSTEMS

This term is used somewhat generically to embrace such corporate activities as electronic data processing, operations research, mathematical programming, quantitative analyses, and so forth. The broad subject area will be treated extensively in a subsequent chapter, but it is introduced here to take cognizance of its organizational implications and to underscore the fact that it is an exciting new field of top management involvement occurring since the prior study of more than twenty-five years ago.

Among the participating companies there was not a single instance where the advent of the computer resulted in any change or modification of the basic organization structure. Therefore, the only consideration at this point is the location in existing organizational arrangements of the hardware and software components of the management information systems.

Because most of the companies are divisionalized, either on a product or geographic basis, the predominant practice is to have a central computer center with lesser installations at the divisional or even the plant level. In one-third of the cases, the central computer center falls within the finance-accounting area. No other pattern prevails. There were several instances where jurisdiction over the computer center resided in an independent department reporting directly to either the chief executive officer or the chief operating officer.

Quite a different situation is found for statistical and mathematical applications. Only rarely are those individuals involved in such activities organizationally a part of the computer center. Operations research activities are often fragmented, but if centralized in a single group, they are often found in a central research or engineering department and located physically at a technical center. ...

PRODUCT MANAGERS

Significant organizational developments or innovations do not occur with notable frequency, but when they do there is manifest interest and, if applicable, a willingness by top management people to adopt or adapt. One such development is the position of product manager. Somewhat akin to but not identical with this position are others designated as project managers and program managers. There are certain similarities in the nature and scope of all three positions but some differences as well.

The *product manager*, as found in several of the participating companies, has essentially the role of planner, coordinator, and promoter of a single product or closely related family of products within an operating division producing and selling a range of products. His reporting relationship is to the divisional general manager. In most instances the product manager is held accountable for the profit of his line.

There is an inherent anomaly in the situation in that the product manager has no direct authority over the research and development, manufacturing, or sales personnel involved. His primary responsibility is relating his line of products to its market, and in that connection he usually has a strong voice in the nature and amount of advertising pertaining to his area of interest. He is expected to maintain a watchful eye on quality and service. One company characterizes the product manager as the customer's representative in the manufacturer's environment.

The *project manager*, on the other hand, although product- and market-oriented as is the product manager, is involved with an embryonic rather than an existing or ongoing venture. His assignment is ordinarily established when a product of research and development effort gives promise of worthwhile potential and may or may not be related to any division's current sphere of activity.

The project manager is placed in charge of a task force composed of research and development, manufacturing, and marketing people to carry the project forward to a point of proven viability or a justifiable decision to abandon. If the undertaking is successful, the project manager and his team may be taken over by a logical division, or a new division may be created. As one company expressed its experience with the project-manager concept, briefly described above, it has been the means of saving newly developed products from becoming "dropouts."

The *program manager* is an outgrowth of defense work and, in fact, is virtually a prerequisite to obtaining a contract of any appreciable magnitude. He is the principal contact with his counterpart in the procuring agency. Like the project manager, his involvement begins early, and if all goes well he continues his assignment until the contract is completed. Like the product manager, he reports to the head of his division and may be only one of several program managers in the division.

If, as is usually the case, the program is of substantial size and duration, he will carry a vice-presidential title and be supported by a small personal staff. He works through the functional organizations of his division, but has no authority over them. In essence the program manager is responsible for the successful completion of his program on schedule, within budget, and in accordance with required performance. The assignment is one with heavy responsibility but without direct concomitant authority.

To clarify this situation and establish a workable arrangement, one company has delineated the program manager's task as follows:

1. Approves plans covering program requirements, schedule, work tasks, and costs. This approved plan is, in essence, a contract between the program manager and the functional organization.
2. Approves program letters, as needed, defining major events or tasks, assigning responsibility and completion dates for accomplishing the events or tasks.
3. Establishes program priorities and policies. When these conflict with other programs, he seeks resolutions with other concerned program managers.
4. Participates in and approves all major technical, cost, schedule, and performance decisions.
5. Participates and concurs in the selection of major make or buy items and the selection of suppliers for those identified as buy.
6. Establishes report requirements and reviews reports and controls necessary for the evaluation of all phases of program performance.
7. Detects potential problems and determines or recommends corrective action.
8. Assists in establishment of program budgets and controls the allocation and reallocation of company resources assigned to him.
9. Periodically conducts program review meetings and issues action minutes.
10. Refers to a functional head for resolution of matters that should be decided by the functional head, even when such matters are specifically brought to him by functional personnel.
11. Is the prime contact with the customer's counterpart and other major representatives of the customer.
12. Establishes a relationship with the customer's representatives that will permit him to know the customer's plans, needs, ideas, and thinking on matters relating to the program. Keeps such representatives fully informed on the program.
13. Establishes and maintains an effective communications network of program information and progress with appropriate personnel.
14. Follows up branches, subcontractors, and others to assure that program events and tasks assigned to them are being satisfactorily accomplished within cost, schedule, and specification requirements, and, when necessary, that timely corrective action is effected.
15. Leads and motivates all personnel assigned to the program by the functional organizations to maximize program team effort.

16. Is alert to new contract requirements, government regulations and directives that might affect the work, cost, or management of the program, and initiates timely responsive action. Is alert also to competing products, programs, and companies that might affect the program.

Even with the foregoing "bill of rights" established and made known, to be successful the program-manager concept demands much coordination and understanding. Otherwise the lot of the director of manufacturing, for example, would be something less than utopian if he were involved constantly with several aggressive program managers.

ORGANIZATION PLANNING DEPARTMENTS

Over the past twenty-five years, the organization planning department as a top-level staff agency seems to have moved full cycle. When the prior top management study was made, there were only a few—four out of thirty-one, to be exact—participating companies that had established organization planning departments, and without exception the reporting relationship was to the chairman or to the president. Among the companies cooperating in this current study, only five have organization planning departments, and in no instance does the agency enjoy a top-level reporting status. In three cases, the agency is an adjunct of the personnel department; in one company it is under the direction of corporate planning; and in the fifth case it is attached to the office of corporate secretary.

During the period intervening between the two studies, most of the companies had at one time or another instituted organization planning departments. Why have these departments, to a large extent, disappeared? There are several reasons: (1) As corporate organization structures became relatively stabilized and were able to accommodate growth and diversification, the need for a full-time group of organization specialists no longer existed. (2) As companies decentralized operations, considerable autonomy was granted the product or geographic divisions, including the freedom to organize the division as the division manager saw fit. (3) If at some time there arose the necessity to change the basic corporate organization structure in any material way, the chief executive assumed the role of architect himself, perhaps calling upon outside consulting counsel. (4) Executives who attain high-level positions, including divisional general management, are well grounded in the principles of good organization practice and hence are not dependent upon staff service in this area.

The continued existence of a few headquarters organization planning departments prompts inquiry as to the justification. The most obvious reason is that the company's organization structure has not fully shaken down and is therefore still in a state of change. Then, too, some of the organization planning departments perform other functions such as manpower surveys, salary administration, and consulting services to divisions and subsidiaries, particularly foreign ones.

CENTRALIZATION VERSUS DECENTRALIZATION

Most large industrial enterprises in the United States operate on what might be termed "controlled" decentralization and have been functioning on this basis for many years. Decentralization takes the form of product divisionalization in those companies that produce and sell a diversified line of products. Regional divisionalization is the common practice for those companies with a single or quite limited range of end products but widespread geographic operations. There are frequent examples of a combination of these two basic types, such as oil companies with a substantial petrochemical involvement and doing business on a national or even global basis.

Participating companies whose organization structure is of the divisionalized pattern were asked what functions or activities were centralized. The response was unanimous as to the following items: setting corporate objectives, strategic planning, determination of basic policies, finance, accounting systems, basic research, consummation of mergers or acquisitions, approval of capital expenditures over prescribed limits, setting of executive salaries and bonuses above certain levels, and selection of individuals for positions down to specific echelons in the organization.

For the last three items there is complete acceptance of the need for centralized control but an absence of unanimity as to the dollar limits or position levels. The widest range occurs in the matter of capital-expenditure approval. A division general manager in one company has authority up to $10,000; in another company this same level of executive has authority up to $1,500,000. Usually there is a series of approvals and dollar amounts up to the chief executive officer. Equally wide is the range for capital expenditures when the executive committee or the board of directors exercises control—from $100,000 to $5,000,000.

The salary level at which the approval of the chief executive is required, while somewhat varied, is in general about the $20,000 figure. This would appear to be low and to deprive a divisional general manager of a natural prerogative, as in a large company there would be hundreds of individuals at or above this annual stipend. This rather widespread practice is simply a reflection of the interest and concern of the top executive in gaining and maintaining cognizance of the existing as well as the potential high-level management people in his company. In no instance did a chief executive feel that this involvement imposed any undue burden. Rather, it is universally regarded as a major obligation.

In most but not all cooperating companies a few additional activities are highly centralized. One of these is the setting of wage and fringe benefit guidelines for the decentralized bargaining that generally prevails. Were it not for this preventive or precautionary action, a whipsawing situation would develop in dealing, as some of the companies do, with up to as many as 80 unions. Similarly, in the matter of contributions and donations, limits or guidelines are established centrally both as a means of exercising appropriate control and of providing protection from local pressures on divisional managers. These limits or guidelines are in addition to the customary budgetary provisions.

Although in a number of the companies each division has its own public relations specialist, there is considerable influence, direction, and control residing in the central public relations department. An increasing awareness of and sensitivity to the external factors bearing upon corporate performance and actions has dictated this degree of centralization. In several instances it even includes tight surveillance over speeches given or articles written by an employee if the subject has any connection with the company's affairs.

With this rather broad recounting of the general practices of companies regarding the functions or activities carried out on a centralized basis, several questions appear germane. Is this a change from earlier practice? Has there been a substantial erosion of the divisional manager's autonomy? Does the fact that in several areas the pricing function, for example, no longer falls within the purview of the divisional manager make an anachronism of realistic profit and loss accountability? Does the present situation indicate a disenchantment with the concept of decentralization of operations? Has the computer been a factor in shifting the decision-making level upward in those specific instances of recent centralization of authority? What is the probable future trend?

Based on extensive interviews with top executives in the companies included in this survey, the following answers to the above questions represent a consensus. Current practice does reflect something of a change as environmental factors have had a definite impact on the need for more central responsibility. In addition, growth, complexity, and greater inter-dependence of divisions have accentuated the problem of coordination leading therefore to more action at headquarters.

Although there has been a gradual trend toward increasing control of certain activities on a centralized basis, there is no confirmation that the divisional manager's autonomy has been lessened to the extent that he has lost effectiveness. In prior times, when the division manager had more authority than is sometimes the case today, he never enjoyed a completely free hand, as most of the functions mentioned have always been centralized.

The top managements of those companies that have long operated under a divisionalized organization structure manifest no disillusionment as to the practicability of this concept. Whenever and whatever further centralization has developed, it has been a recognition of and accommodation to different conditions. In no instance was there acceptance of the idea that the computer has influenced this situation, nor is it expected to in the future. In other words, the levels of decision making will remain as at present.

Finally, what is the future outlook regarding centralization versus decentralization? Decentralization is unquestionably here to stay, at least as far ahead as any top executive cared to predict. Those companies operating under a divisionalized organization structure intend to continue with that pattern, and some of the companies not now operating in this fashion feel it is quite likely that they will move in the direction of decentralization.

. . .

COMMITTEES

Over the years no organizational feature has been as controversial as committees. Their faults and virtues have been discussed and debated with amazing persistency. This situation existed at the time of the earlier study of top management organization and control practices, and it is evident in the current study. The principal difference found between the two studies is that today there are fewer standing committees and a greater use of ad hoc task forces. Nevertheless, in virtually every one of the current participating companies high-level committees are in use. The number of such groups runs from one to six, and it was made quite clear that these agencies are fulfilling a genuine purpose.

The most common committee is the executive committee composed generally of inside directors of the company. The executive committee is invested with most of the authority of the entire directorate and is a powerful administrative body. In some instances it is a decision-making agency, although in other companies it is regarded as an advisory group to the chief executive officer on whom devolves the final responsibility for decisions. It could be reported that even under the latter condition decision making is by consensus, as only rarely would a chief executive officer go counter to the preponderant opposition of his top executive group.

In those companies having an executive committee composed, in part, of outside or nonofficer directors, there is usually a committee of top executives exercising extensive authority for direction and control of the enterprise. These committees frequently have the term "policy" in their designation, for example: policy committee, operations policy committee, operational policy committee. These committees, while lacking certain prerogatives of the board of directors, are frequently reported, like the aforementioned executive committees, as the agency that runs the business. This characterization is supported not only by the matters that come before such committees, but by the frequency of their meetings—usually weekly.

The value of committees as communication devices is well recognized by many of the cooperating companies. Variously termed administration committee, management council, executive council, operations review committee, these agencies have memberships considerably larger than the committees discussed in the preceding paragraphs.

In one company there are 36 top people who constitute its management council. As stated by one chief executive officer, "Our administration committee meets monthly, at which time actions taken at the last board of directors meeting are reviewed and reports are made by group vice presidents and staff vice presidents; the committee is essentially a communications device and a medium for passing policy information to the organization."

The executive council of another company meets twice a month "to discuss general corporate problems, to review what happened last month, to evaluate where we are now and to take a look at the immediate future; the council has no power, records no minutes, but does follow an agenda for each meeting; it is purely a communications device."

In a third company the management council meets monthly, at which time the chief executive officer reports on the last board of directors meeting and invites discussion of major changes, plans, and problems; the council is used as a means to encourage two-way communication.

A fourth company has 23 officers on its planning committee which meets weekly to review the current situation of its several product divisions. In the words of the company's chief executive officer, "We use this, as well as several other committees, for communications purposes, as there is a man present who will have to make the decisions."

The vital importance of the research effort and the magnitude of the budgetary support involved have been responsible for the creation of another top-level committee in a number of the companies in this study. These committees are composed of representation from top management (usually the chief executive officer), operating management, research management, and sometimes engineering and financial management.

These committees often have a fourfold mission: (1) establishment of policies and broad guidelines to provide direction to research and development programs, (2) coordination of the viewpoints of line management and technical management, (3) bringing to bear a wide range of judgment as to the wisdom of embarking upon a specific undertaking, (4) periodic review and monitoring of ongoing programs with a view toward recommending or even deciding to continue or abandon certain projects.

Although, as mentioned earlier in this section, the occurrence of committees is less widespread than a quarter-century ago, they still are considered to be a valuable, if not indispensable, organizational device. When they are set up to obtain collective judgment, to provide mature advice, to permit of an interchange of ideas and opinions, or to serve as a medium of communication, committees fulfill a purpose not so well met by any other means.

BOARDS OF DIRECTORS

A board of directors, although in every sense of the word a committee, is not subject to the polemical treatment that attaches to committees in general. The role of this organizational element in governing the conduct of an enterprise varies in substantial degree among companies, including those participating in this study. A critic of American business practice once opined that the average board of directors has about the same control over the direction of its company that a streetcar motorman has over the direction of his vehicle.

The implication of this allegation is quite clear, that is, this topmost agency often endorses the program laid out by the chief executive and his management team without serious debate or challenge. There can be little doubt that this "rubber stamp" characterization is true in some measure in most companies, but complete dominance by the operating officers (unless it is an inside board) is, to say the least, not common practice. If the streetcar analogy may be carried a bit further, the board as well as the motorman can always apply the brakes or can exercise control over acceleration and deceleration. In short, full abdication by the board of its trustee obligation is rarely, if ever, to be found in publicly owned corporations and those with nonofficer directors.

Interviews with the chief executive officers of the participating companies elicited such broad statements concerning the use of boards of directors as the following:

Our board is used primarily for soundings on policy.

We regard our board as an "advise and consent" group. It is recognized as a sounding board. The outside members provide a detached viewpoint that is not possible for inside members. The outsiders have greater objectivity, more completely represent stockholder interest, and do not lose sight of the need to declare appropriate dividends.

The board of directors must have perspective and the courage to speak up and suggest but should not be used as a crutch for management. If a company relies on its board to manage, then the company needs to obtain some new management people.

Our board is anything but a rubber stamp board. I, as chief executive officer, would be stupid to take highly controversial matters to the board of directors without prior discussion with individual board members. When you face people like we have on the board, you better have your homework done.

The most important function of the board is to ensure continuity of able management and to keep management productive and fully responsive. If the board of directors abdicates this to management, the company will come a cropper.

Any time a board of directors tries to run a company you have trouble. We believe the board should review, evaluate, and set policy. The officers should operate and run the business. It is the function of the board to see that the company is run right, and if it isn't the board should change management.

The main function of the board of directors is to monitor the performance of the chief executive.

The foregoing candid comments reflect some rather wide differences of opinion among top executives as to the role of the board of directors. It is obvious that the companies cited all had nonofficers on their boards and in most instances a preponderance of outsiders.

In somewhat similar vein, a few of these chief executives gave expressions to the qualifications looked for in outside directors.

In obtaining outside board members, we want people of outstanding character and stature from various parts of the country and the world. We like to have people of real competence in such fields as finance, science, marketing, and international trade. We do not care about their holding company stock—they should represent all stockholders. We want a board that is constructively critical and not given to *pro forma* action. That would be dangerous for me.

What we look for in outside directors is an independence of view and a willingness to protect the company from its management. This attitude and potential position is as important as the knowledge and experience they contribute.

In addition to demonstrated ability and broad business experience, we seek geographic representation in our outside directors. We also look for wide diversification of business connections. The principal difficulties we have in attracting the kind of outside directors we desire are availability of time, absence of a conflict of interest, and age—the latter because we have a retirement age of 72 for directors.

Regardless of the actual extent of board influence in company affairs, there are certain fundamental determinations that generally reside with the full board of directors: approval of basic policies; declaration of dividends; changes in the financial structure; approval of capital expenditures over predetermined limits; setting of salaries, bonuses, and other financial benefits to officers; approval of mergers, acquisitions, and joint ventures; and its own plan of organization, particularly board committees.

In the book that presents the findings of the previous study of top management practices, an extensive discussion of boards of directors was included. This discussion dealt at length with the composition, duties, compensation, committees, and other aspects of corporate boards. There would be no purpose in duplicating that information, as in many respects the situation today is little different.

Boards are about the same average size (fifteen) with much the same proportion of inside members (40 percent) having duties of similar nature, and with many of the identical committees that were then part of the board organization; viz. executive, finance, audit, investment, salary and bonus.

In the area of board compensation, however, considerable change has occurred. Fees are much higher, and the practice of having outside directors on an annual retainer is widespread. Another significant and growing change is the establishment of a compulsory retirement age for directors, whether former officers or nonofficers. Still another change is the practice of holding one or more board meetings each year at important divisional headquarters or technical centers of the company so that outside directors may obtain a better understanding of company operations and can meet at firsthand key executives in the field.

Regarding the future of boards of directors, there appears to be no desire or intent to alter the status quo. In a few cases it is likely that the proportion of outside members will be increased. This obviously would apply to those companies that now have a preponderance of board representation from the full-time executive ranks. Also, more companies may reduce the number of full board meetings to four per year instead of the more common twelve. Two reasons underlie this potential move: the better opportunity to attract the caliber of outside talent desired, and the volume of board business taken care of by board committees. Aside from these modest changes, no evidence was gathered that would indicate any probability of radical change in the posture of boards of directors.

11

G.E.'s Costly Ventures into the Future

ALAN T. DEMAREE

This selection by Alan Demaree is included to provide some insight into the practical application of organization design concepts. During the last two decades, General Electric, through its widely publicized use of decentralization and centralized corporate staff services, has been acknowledged as an innovator in organization design. Although this article is primarily devoted to an assessment of new G.E. ventures, it contains some interesting views on the company's current approaches to organization.

The firm's use of business departments, decentralization, an office of the president, external staff, and management selection and development are discussed. In particular, the description of G.E. as "the greatest unmobilized army in the world," whose executives lack "entrepreneurial flair" and "a sense of mission," poses some troubling questions. G.E.'s major changes of the 1950s were designed primarily to generate this elusive entrepreneurial spirit. Mr. Demaree indicates some of the reasons why these objectives have not been achieved and then describes how the present top management is responding to these problems.

As you read this selection, consider the following questions: (1) How should top management organize a firm as large and diverse as G.E. so as to generate the independent, entrepreneurial action required of managers at all levels? (2) What are some of the disadvantages of decentralization encountered by G.E.? (3) Does an office of the president, as utilized by G.E., appeal to you as a workable concept?

Behind the receptionist and the two trusted secretaries, in the gold-carpeted chief executive's office on the forty-fifth floor of the General Electric Building, Fred Borch keeps a secret plan locked tightly in his desk. Borch drew the plan privately, without consulting even his closest colleagues, when he took the reins from Ralph Cordiner seven years ago. It contains his goals for the largest and most diversified industrial conglomerate in the world, a company that is expected this year to sell some $9 billion of goods in nineteen of the nation's twenty-one basic manufacturing industries. These goals reach out to 1975, projecting sales and profits, key ratios like earnings

Reprinted from *Fortune*, October 1970, pp. 88ff., by permission of the publisher. Copyright 1970 by Time, Inc.

per share, and a less common figure that takes on tremendous importance at General Electric: the slice of profits Borch is willing to risk on new ventures.

Borch guards his plan like Cerberus at the gates of hell—he regards it as his own personal yardstick of achievement—but he concedes that G.E. has wandered erratically off course. When Ralph Cordiner was boss, he once said, "Quite a few of us ought to be fired" if G.E. didn't raise its profit margins above the then-current level of 11 percent. Margins have reached that figure only once in Borch's tenure, in 1965, and have dropped steadily since, to a low of 6.03 percent last year. And while Wall Street has traditionally viewed G.E. as a high-growth company, awarding it a price-earnings multiple of around 25, the actual rate of growth in G.E.'s earnings has ranked in the bottom third of *Fortune's* list of the 500 largest industrial corporations for several years. ...

More fundamentally, however, General Electric faces some paradoxical problems. The company has taken on grandiose ventures requiring new technical skills and business techniques that should imbue its people with spirit and élan. Yet many G.E. executives seem devoid of boldness and entrepreneurial flair, and lack a sense of mission. G.E. has taken on business risks that require tremendous long-term commitments. Yet in its day-to-day operations, and in its management-incentive program, the company is oriented toward short-term results. A visitor to the company's stodgy headquarters in New York detects a smugness that pervades much of top management and blocks any effective re-examination of accepted management principles that were developed in the Fifties. A Harvard Business School professor, familiar with G. E., ticks off the company's great strengths—the number of patents, the number of Ph.D.'s, the depth of research talent at the laboratory in Schenectady—and then adds regretfully: "I think G.E. is the greatest unmobilized army in the world, and it has something to do with the quality of top management."

THE LEADING LIGHT OF THE LAMP DYNASTY

Fred Borch, who leads the 400,000 G.E. troops, is a trim man of medium height, conservatively tailored, wearing cuff links and a fine golden chain restraining his tie. When he moves his hands to emphasize a point, the eye is attracted to his immaculately manicured fingernails. Brooklyn born but raised in Ohio, Borch joined General Electric fresh out of Western Reserve University in 1931 as a traveling auditor in the lamp division. Tremendously profitable, the lamp division virtually carried G.E. through the depression, and it became so independent that it was known throughout the company as the Irish Free State. For twenty years Borch worked his way steadily up through this fiefdom, where he was known as a decisive, no-nonsense executive. He reorganized the division as part of a company-wide decentralization plan in 1953, then went to New York as marketing vice president and headed the consumer-products group before succeeding Cordiner in 1963. He has since installed so many lamp-division executives in key jobs in New York that insiders talk of his regime as the Lamp Dynasty. And some wonder whether men reared in the prosaic lamp business can be comfortable making decisions about new, high-risk ventures.

Borch has a cocksure personality that at times borders on the arrogant. But he weighs his career in the sweep of corporate history, and has expressed concern to friends that he will be remembered as the man whose judgment on nuclear power cost stockholders millions. He sees himself as G.E.'s chief strategist and, in a way, its head of state. He spends about half his time on "external affairs—he is chairman of the Business Council, vice chairman of the Committee for Economic Development, etc.—and he stands aloof from the everyday detail of G.E.'s businesses. Five times a year he and his closest colleagues sit down separately with each of his eleven group vice presidents, who are in charge of large hunks of the business. One meeting is set aside to review the next year's budget, another the long-range budget, a third antitrust, and so on. As long as the many businesses perform "within the envelope" of their budgets, as Borch puts it, he sees little reason to interfere.

To reduce further the need for his own detailed involvement, Borch formed a corporate executive office in 1968, including besides himself three vice chairmen and "executive officers"—William H. Dennler, sixty, Jack S. Parker, fifty-two, and Herman L. Weiss, fifty-four. The total compensation, in cash and stock, of the members of the office was $1,285,000 last year, with Borch receiving $274,990 in cash and deferred stock payments worth $125,010. Each man has cognizance over several of G.E.'s groups, so the high-level strategic decisions are shared more than they were in Cordiner's day. Borch, of course, has ultimate responsibility, but his colleagues can remember no instance in which he has overruled their jointly held opinions.

"ELECTRIC CHARLIE'S" REVIVAL MEETING

In the early days of the company's history, every man from the president to the floor sweeper knew G.E. had a single mission—to electrify the world. This sense of mission held through World War II and into the reign of Charles E. "Electric Charlie" Wilson, whose sheer force of personality seemed to bind the company together. In those days, managers gathered each summer at a camp called Association Island, in the St. Lawrence River off Watertown, New York, to play softball, drink beer, and listen to the exhortations of their leaders beneath an ancient elm tree. On one such occasion, "Electric Charlie" announced to the assembled throng that he had heard rumors that Westinghouse was determined to catch up with G.E. "They should live so long," he declared. "Now let's all rise and sing *Onward Christian Soldiers.*" Recalls a G.E. old-timer: "You came out of there with tears in your eyes, ready to beat the world for General Electric."

Now this sense of community and unity of purpose has largely disappeared. G.E. has diversified into products as disparate as engineering plastics and industrial diamonds, a great change from the days when its business centered almost exclusively on the "benign circle" of products that produced, transmitted, and consumed electricity. The company has nearly quadrupled in size since Wilson's time, and it has *added* more dollars in sales in the past eight years alone than the *total* sales of Westinghouse in 1969. It would be naïve to expect that the simple corporate chauvinism of Wilson's day could or should remain a moving force in the company today. But now, without it, G.E. has somehow lost spark, excitement, and verve.

Ever since Cordiner, Wilson's successor, decentralized G.E. in the early Fifties, the company has made a fetish of structure and a catechism of management philosophy. Indeed Borch devoted much of his time for eighteen months to designing the structure adopted in 1968, under which G.E. is now broken down into some 180 departments, each run by a general manager who earns about $40,000 a year plus generous incentive compensation.

"AGGLOMERATION" UNDER THE "GROUPIES"

Ironically, when it comes to shaping departments, G.E. adopts the position that bigness is badness. The "theory of the case," to borrow from G.E.'s lexicon of management, is that a department should be the right size "for one man to get his arms around." The result often is a unit that would make about as much business sense if it had been stamped out with a cookie cutter. As Borch puts it, a department contains, on the average, three and one-half product lines, $50 million in sales. It may contain more than one business or, more frequently, a part of a business. Electric motors are divided into eight departments, for example, and home refrigerators into two, even though the only difference between the refrigerators they produce is the way the doors open. Department managers consequently tend to become oriented around a product line rather than thinking in terms of an entire market.

Departments are "agglomerated," as G.E. men say, into fifty-two divisions, often arbitrarily, and the divisions into eleven groups, each run by a group vice president, known as a "groupie," who reports to the corporate executive office. As much as any government agency, G.E. is a bureaucracy. If a department manager wants to get something done, he has to persuade a chain of people above him, which means he can hardly be fleet of foot. It took a G.E. committee four years to decide to raise the expense account allowance for automobile travel to 10 cents a mile.

In an attempt to get better control over G.E., Borch is now putting the company through another reorganization, this one with the help of McKinsey & Co., the management consultant. This summer he established a permanent corporate staff, whose task is to aid him in high-level strategic planning. And now he is installing staffs down through the levels below, hoping they can provide the kind of coherent business planning that the oddly constructed departments—containing only parts of businesses themselves—could not do on their own. Staffs had been anathema to Cordiner, who forbade their use at division or group level, save for a single financial analyst at each. This made strategic business planning next to impossible, and, as one executive puts it, G.E. went "wandering around like a loosely coordinated monstrosity." Even before this most recent reshuffling, Borch had begun to loosen up on the staff prohibition, installing a small planning staff of his own, and setting up numerous ad hoc task forces and high-powered "review boards" to watch over the high-risk businesses. But these measures had proved inadequate.

ACTION IN THE MANAGEMENT PIT

For all the attempts at reorganization, G.E. retains much of the personality it had in the Fifties. "We don't want geniuses," Borch says of his high-level managers; he wants men who can get other people to work. Most are engineers or people who came up through the financial side of the business. Few are recruited from outside the company, so those in important positions have generally followed the promotional ladder rung by rung.

Only recently has G.E. recruited outstanding business-school graduates from places like Harvard, Stanford, and Wharton, and so far it has been unable to attract the number it seeks. G.E. could "always hire the guys whose first question is 'What's your pension plan?'" says Charles Rieger, a former group vice president, who left to become president of Ebasco. "But the entrepreneurs go elsewhere." Rieger found it so hard to hire engineers for the power-generation business that he asked the head of the aerospace group to hire a hundred extra engineers a year; those who didn't work out in aerospace, Rieger took on.

G.E. clings steadfastly to a policy of rotating managers through diverse jobs every three or four years, and even more quickly in problem businesses. To make its managers "wonderfully mobile," as Cordiner once described them, the company indoctrinates them in this philosophy of management at Crotonville, G.E.'s private business academy on a beautiful Westchester estate, where they gather in a room called "the management pit." Borch defends fast rotation—"We'll switch 'em just as rapidly as we can switch 'em," he says—on grounds that it gives managers broad experience and prevents boredom. "You never really got to know the customers or the product too damned well," recalls a former G.E. man, now president of a midwestern manufacturing company.

One natural result of this game of musical chairs is that G.E. managers tend to emphasize short-term goals rather than the long-term future of their business. This tendency is reinforced by G.E.'s incentive compensation system, which most managers believe rewards them primarily on the basis of their short-term profitability. G.E.'s policies also produce what might be called "turnaround personalities,"· managers who have built reputations traipsing from one ailing business to another, putting them back in the black. This is no mean skill, of course, but sometimes the turnarounds prove to have been short-term repair work rather than solid, long-term reconstruction. And "turnaround personalities" are frequently promoted out of their jobs before they have lived through a product life cycle.

12

Parkinson's Law

C. NORTHCOTE PARKINSON

C. Northcote Parkinson achieved international acclaim with the publication of his eighteenth book, Parkinson's Law, *a satire on bureacracy. This selection consists of brief excerpts from that work. In this book and in later efforts he introduced such laws and axiomatic statements as:*

1. *Expansion means complexity, and complexity means decay.*
2. *Expenditures rise to meet income.*
3. *Work expands to fill the time available for its completion.*
4. *Executives multiply subordinates, not rivals.*
5. *Officials make work for each other.*

In an article Parkinson wrote for The Economist *before the publication of his famous book, he reports no correlation between the number of officials and the quantity of work to be done. The former tends to rise by more than 5 percent a year whether the volume of work increases, diminishes, or even disappears. For example, although the number of ships decreased by 67.7 percent over a given period, the number of Admiralty officials increased by 78.5 percent during the same period. Similarly, during Britain's period of imperial decline, there was a marked increase in the number of Colonial Office executives.*

Work expands so as to fill the time available for its completion. ... The importance of [this] Law lies in the fact that it is a law of growth based upon an analysis of the factors by which that growth is controlled. ... Omitting technicalities, we may distinguish at the onset two motive forces. They can be represented for the present purpose by two almost axiomatic statements, thus: (1) An official wants to multiply subordinates, not rivals, and (2) Officials make work for each other.

To comprehend Factor 1, we must picture a civil servant, called A, who finds himself overworked. Whether this overwork is real or imaginary is immaterial, but we should observe, in passing, that A's sensation (or illusion) might easily result from his own decreasing energy; a normal symptom of middle age. For this real or imagined overwork there are, broadly speaking, three possible remedies. He may resign; he may ask to halve the work with a colleague called B; he may demand the assistance of two subordinates, to be called C and D. There is probably no instance in history, however, of A choosing any but the third alternative. By resignation he would lose his pension rights. By having B appointed, on his level in the hierarchy, he would merely bring in a rival for promotion to W's vacancy when W (at long last) retires. So A would rather have C and D, junior men, below him. They will add to his consequence and, by dividing the work into two categories, as between C and D, he will have the merit of being the only man who comprehends them both. When C complains in turn of being overworked (as he certainly will) A will, with the concurrence of C, advise the appointment of two assistants to help C. But he can then avert internal friction only by advising the appointment of two more assistants to help D whose position is much the same. With this recruitment of E, F, G, and H the promotion of A is now practically certain.

Seven officials are now doing what one did before. This is where Factor 2 comes into operation. For these seven make so much work for each other that all are fully occupied and A is actually working harder than ever. ...

It is late in the evening before A finally quits his office. ... The last of the office lights are being turned off in the gathering dusk that marks the end of another day's administrative toil. Among the last to leave, A reflects with bowed shoulders and a wry smile that late hours, like gray hairs, are among the penalties of success. ...

FOR FURTHER READING

Anderson, J. W., "The Impact of Technology on Job Enrichment."*Personnel*, Vol. 47, No. 5 (September-October, 1970), 29.

Atchison, T. J., "The Fragmentation of Authority."*Personnel*, Vol. 48, No. 4 (July-August 1970), 8.

Baker, J. K., and R. H. Schaffer, "Making Staff Consulting More Effective." *Harvard Business Review*, Vol. 47, No. 1 (January-February 1969), 62-71.

Blau, P., and W. Scott, *Formal Organizations*. San Francisco: Chandler Publishing Co., 1962.

Brabb, George J., and Earl B. Hutchins, "Electronic Computers and Management Organization." *California Management Review*, Vol. 6, No. 1 (1963), 40.

Brink, V. Z., *Computers and Management*. Englewood Cliffs, N.J.: Prentice-Hall, Inc., 1971.

Carzo, R., "Some Effects of Organization Structure on Group Effectiveness." *Administrative Science Quarterly*, Vol. 7 (March 1963), 393-424.

Chapple, Elliot D., and Leonard R. Sayles, *The Measure of Management: Designing Organizations for Human Effectiveness*. New York: The Macmillan Company, 1961.

Clee, G. H., and W. M. Sachtjen, "Organizing a Worldwide Business." *Harvard Business Review*, Vol. 42, No. 6 (November-December 1964), 55-67.

Cleland, D. I., and W. R. King, *Systems Analysis and Project Management*. New York: McGraw-Hill Book Company, 1968.

Crozier, Michael, *The Bureaucratic Phenomenon*. Chicago: University of Chicago Press, 1964.

Dale, Ernest, *Planning and Developing the Company Organization Structure*. New York: American Management Association, 1957.

——, and Lyndall F. Urwick, *Staff in Organization*. New York: McGraw-Hill Book Company, 1960.

Dalton, M., "Conflicts Between Staff and Line Managerial Offices." *American Sociological Review*, Vol. 15, No. 3 (1950), 342-351.

Daniel, D. R., "The Team at the Top." *Harvard Business Review*, Vol. 43, No. 2 (March-April 1965), 74-82.

Davis, Keith, "Success of Chain-of-Command Oral Communication in a Manufacturing Management Group." *Academy of Management Journal*, Vol. 11, No. 4 (December 1968), 379-387.

Diebold, J., "Bad Decisions on Computer Use." *Harvard Business Review*, Vol. 47, No. 1 (January-February 1969), 14 ff.

Dubin, R., *Human Relations in Administration*, 3rd ed. Englewood Cliffs, N.J.: Prentice-Hall, Inc., 1968, Chaps. 9, 11-13.

Etzioni, Amitai, *A Comparative Analysis of Complex Organization*. New York: Free Press of Glencoe, 1962.

——, *Modern Organizations*. Englewood Cliffs, N.J.: Prentice-Hall, Inc., 1964, Chap. 9.

Fayol, Henri, *General and Industrial Administration*. London: Sir Isaac Pitman & Sons Ltd., 1949.

Filley, Alan C., and Robert J. House, *Managerial Process and Organizational Behavior*. Glenview, Ill.: Scott, Foresman & Company, 1969.

Goode, C. E., "Greater Productivity through the Organization of Work." *Personnel Administration*, Vol. 27, No. 1 (January-February 1964), 34-49.

Gouldner, Alvin, *Patterns of Industrial Bureaucracy*. New York: Free Press of Glencoe, 1955.

Gulick, L., "Notes on the Theory of Organization," in *Papers on the Science of Administration*, ed. L. Gulick and L. Urwick. New York: Institute of Public Administration, Columbia University, 1937.

House, Robert J., and J. B. Miner, "Merging Management and Behavioral Theory: The Interaction Between Span of Control and Group Size." *Administrative Science Quarterly*, Vol. 14 (1969), 451-464.

Juran, J. M., and J. K. Louden, *The Corporate Director*. New York: American Management Association, 1966.

Kast, F. E., and J. E. Rosenzweig, *Organization and Management*. New York: McGraw-Hill Book Company, 1970.

Koontz, Harold, "Making Theory Operational: The Span of Management." *The Journal of Management Studies*, Vol. 3, No. 3 (October 1966), 229-243.

———, and Cyril O'Donnell, *Principles of Management*, 4th ed. New York: McGraw-Hill Book Company, 1968.

Kover, A. J., "Reorganizing in an Advertising Agency: A Case Study of a Decrease in Integration." *Human Organization*, Vol. 22, No. 4 (Winter 1963), 252-259.

Krupp, Sherman, *Pattern in Organizational Analysis: A Critical Examination*. Philadelphia: Chilton Book Company, 1961.

Lawrence, Paul R., and Jay W. Lorsch, *Organization and Environment: Managing Differentiation and Integration*. Homewood, Ill.: Richard D. Irwin, Inc., 1967.

Learned, E. P., and A. T. Sproat, *Organization Theory and Policy*. Homewood, Ill.: Richard D. Irwin, Inc., 1966.

Leavitt, Harold J., and Thomas L. Whisler, "Management in the 1980's." *Harvard Business Review*, Vol. 36, No. 6 (November-December 1958) 41-48.

Litterer, J. A., *The Analysis of Organizations*. New York: John Wiley & Sons, Inc., 1965.

March, James G., and Herbert A. Simon, *Organizations*. New York: John Wiley & Sons, Inc., 1958.

Merton, Robert K., ed., *Social Theory and Social Structure*, rev. ed. New York: Free Press of Glencoe, 1957.

Mooney, J. O., *The Principles of Organization*. New York: Harper & Row, Publishers, 1947.

Myers, C. A., ed., *The Impact of Computers on Management*. Cambridge, Mass.: The M.I.T. Press, 1967.

Newman, William H., *Administrative Action*, 2nd ed. Englewood Cliffs, N.J.: Prentice-Hall, Inc., 1963.

Pelissier, R. F., "Successful Experiences in Job Design." *Personnel Administration*, Vol. 28, No. 2 (March-April 1965), 12-16.

Pfiffner, John M., and Frank Sherwood, *Administrative Organization*. Englewood Cliffs, N.J.: Prentice-Hall, Inc., 1960.

Presthus, Robert, *The Organizational Society*. New York: Alfred A. Knopf, Inc., 1962.

Rubenstein, A. H., and C. J. Haberstroh, *Some Theories of Organization*, rev. ed. Homewood, Ill.: Dorsey Press, 1966.

Schleh, E. H., *Management by Results*. New York: McGraw-Hill Book Company, 1961.

Simon, Herbert A., *Administrative Behavior*, rev. ed. New York: The Macmillan Company, 1958.

——, *The Shape of Automation for Men and Management*. New York: Harper & Row, Publishers, 1965.

——, Harold Guetzkow, George Kozmetsky, and Gordon Tyndall, *Centralization vs. Decentralization in Organizing the Controller's Department*. New York: Controllership Foundation, 1954.

Sloan, Alfred P., Jr., *My Years with General Motors*. Garden City, N.Y.: Doubleday & Company, Inc., 1965.

Soujanen, W. W., "The Span of Control—Fact or Fable?" *Advanced Management*, Vol. 20 (November 1955), 5-13.

Steiglitz, H., *Corporate Organization Structures*. New York: National Industrial Conference Board, Studies in Personnel Policy, No. 183, 1961.

——, "Optimizing Span of Control." *Management Record*, Vol. 24, No. 9 (September 1962), 25-29.

——, and A. R. Janger, *Top Management Organization in Divisionalized Companies*. New York: National Industrial Conference Board, Studies in Personnel Policy, No. 195, 1965.

Steiner, G. A., and W. G. Ryan, *Industrial Project Management*. New York: The Macmillan Company, 1968.

Thompson, Victor A., *Modern Organizations*. New York: Alfred A. Knopf, Inc., 1961.

Vance, S. C., *Boards of Directors: Structure and Performance*. Eugene, Oreg.: University of Oregon Press, 1964.

Vergin, Roger, "Computer Induced Organization Changes." *MSU Business Topics*, Vol. 15, No. 3 (Summer 1967), 61-67.

——, and Andrew J. Grimes, "Management Myths and EDP." *California Management Review*, Vol. 7, No. 1 (1964), 64-65.

Whisler, Thomas L., *The Impact of Computers on Organizations*. New York: Frederick A. Praeger, Inc., New York, 1970.

White, K. K., *Understanding the Company Organization Chart*. New York: American Management Association, 1963, pp. 60-61.

Wickesberg, A. K., *Management Organization*. New York: Appleton-Century-Crofts, 1966.

Woodward, Joan, *Industrial Organization: Theory and Practice*. London: Oxford University Press, 1965.

Worthy, J. C., "Organization Structure and Employee Morale." *American Sociological Review*, Vol. 15 (1950), 169-179.

PART TWO

Human Factors in Organizing

Although formal organization structure has an important influence on the behavior of people, a knowledge of this structure is not sufficient for understanding and predicting human behavior. Both individual motivation and the informal social relationships that develop within an organization modify the formal structure and influence organizational effectiveness.

The relationship between individual motivation and work has been examined by several behavioral scientists during the last two decades. Much of the emphasis has been on the role of work in relation to man's needs and man's capabilities. The new motivation theories that have been advanced usually relate, in one form or another, to Abraham Maslow's hierarchy-of-needs concept. Maslow postulated that human needs can be roughly categorized into physiological needs, security needs, social needs, ego needs, and self-actualization needs. These needs are arranged in a hierarchy with physiological needs at the bottom of the hierarchy and self-actualization needs at the top. As a person's most basic wants are satisfied, the next most important needs determine behavior. Physiological needs and other basic needs become dormant after they have been satisfied and provide little motivation until the need again becomes pressing.

Behavioral scientists, such as Chris Argyris and the late Douglas McGregor, have utilized the hierarchy-of-needs framework to criticize the organization design and management philosophy of modern industrial organization. They contend that such organizations create demands upon their members that are inconsistent with the needs of mature, healthy adults. The direct, or on-the-job, satisfactions in these organizations tend to satisfy only lower-level physiological and security needs. But workers seek to satisfy the higher-level needs in the Maslow needs hierarchy by striving for social belonging, independence, and personal growth. This mismatch between worker needs and direct job satisfaction causes workers to become alienated from their jobs. The motivationalists argue that the end result is a severe underutilization of human potential in modern industrial organization.

In selection 13, "Needs and Motivation," George Strauss presents a comprehensive review of motivation theory, evaluates important research studies, and suggests implications for management. The next selection, "Blue-Collar Blues on the Assembly Line," by Judson Gooding, reinforces the views of behavioral scientists by describing the dismaying extent of alienation among blue-collar workers.

A major outgrowth of research in behavioral science has been widespread interest in the subject of job design. Traditionally technology and production have been the primary considerations in designing individual jobs. Modern motivation theory has dramatically altered current thinking regarding job design. Today social scientists and managers are considering a variety of techniques for improving the motivational climate of the work situation.

Although there are multiple approaches to job design, they all have a common goal—to specify "the contents, methods and relationships of jobs in order to satisfy technological and organizational requirements of the jobholder."* The major job-design techniques are job enlargement, job rotation, job enrichment, the plan-do-control concept of work, and work simplification. These techniques are discussed in "Job Design: Methods and Models," an excerpt from a Conference Board Research Study conducted by Harold M. F. Rush. In selection 16, "Motivation Through the Work Itself," Robert N. Ford reports the results of the much publicized job-enrichment studies conducted at A.T. & T.

Studies of individual motivation on the job focus primarily on psychological factors in organizational behavior. Behavioral scientists have also examined social factors in the organization by studying the development of informal organization and its effect on behavior. Every organization develops its own distinctive subculture—the beliefs and patterns of conduct that are associated with working together in a given company. The informal social groups that develop whenever people work together strongly influence the subculture within an enterprise.

Men derive many of their day-to-day satisfactions on the job from the sociability provided by these informal groups. Informal social groups tend to create a pattern of common interests, beliefs, and attitudes. Group members usually feel pressure to conform to group standards and group routines. When a member deviates from group standards, group pressures to conform can be

---

*Louis E. Davis, "The Design of Jobs," *Industrial Relations,* October, 1966.

both substantial and unpleasant. This phenomenon has a significant impact on organizations, especially if group goals conflict with organizational goals. In such situations managers must focus on harmonizing the formal and informal organizations. Selection 17, "Independence and Conformity," by Harold Leavitt, graphically describes the various stages of group pressure exerted by an informal social group on a deviant member.

As noted in Part One, the impact of computers on formal organization has attracted widespread interest in recent years. There has been much speculation concerning the impact of information technology on organization size, job content, organization structure, and occupational skills. In contrast, the impact of computerized management information systems on individual motivation and informal social organization has received inadequate treatment. In the final selection in Part Two, "Management Information Systems: The Challenge to Rationality and Emotionality," Chris Argyris peers into the future and predicts the emotional impact of management-information systems.

13

Needs and Motivation

GEORGE STRAUSS

This selection introduces the reader to the mainstream of motivational theory. George Strauss has written several books on personnel, industrial relations, and human behavior. He begins this summary by outlining the major elements of the "personality vs. organization" hypothesis, as advanced by Chris Argyris and the late Douglas McGregor. Maslow's need hierarchy is identified as the theoretical basis of this hypothesis. Strauss notes that the Argyris view has gained implicit support from Frederick Herzberg's "motivation-hygiene" theory. Herzberg's imaginative and controversial research has stimulated some pioneering job-enrichment programs in industrial corporations such as A.T. & T. and Texas Instruments.

During the 1960s several doubts emerged concerning the universal validity of the "Theory Y" assumptions discussed in this selection. An earlier article written by Professor Strauss raised some major questions concerning the "personality vs. organization" hypothesis.* The major criticisms of the

Reprinted from George Strauss, "Organizational Behavior and Personnel Relations," *A Review of Industrial Relations Research*, I (1970), pp. 151-157, by permission of the author and publisher.
*George Strauss, "The Personality vs. Organization Theory," in *Individualism and Big Business*, ed. Leonard Sayles (New York: McGraw-Hill Book Company, 1963), pp.67-80.

Argyris-McGregor motivation theory have focused on the importance of personality, culture, and technology variables as determinants of job satisfaction. Professor Strauss reviews the major studies that have dealt with these variables. At the end of this selection, the author reviews some of the newer approaches to motivation.

NEEDS AND MOTIVATION

Researchers in this "psychological" area have been concerned with developing means by which human needs can be harnessed to achieve organizational objectives. The Hawthorne studies had shown that workers had social as well as purely economic needs. Later other needs were considered and by 1960 the contributions of individuals such as Argyris, Maier, Maslow, and McGregor had jelled into a fairly consistent view of motivation in industry and its consequences.

This view, which might be called the personality vs. organization hypothesis, in over-simplified form runs as follows: (1) Workers seek social belonging, independence, and personal growth (in other words, to climb the Maslow needs hierarchy ladder). (2) Organizations fail to recognize these needs and instead follow "Theory X" assumptions that workers dislike work and wish to avoid responsibility. In so doing they force workers to behave in an immature and dependent fashion. (3) As a consequence workers become alienated from the jobs. Either they fight back (through union activity, sabotage, or output restriction) or they withdraw and produce no more than a minimum amount of work. (4) The only consistent solution is for management to adopt "Theory Y" assumptions as to human nature, that people can enjoy work and can exercise self-control, and that they are imaginative and creative. Thus management should develop policies which promote intrinsic job satisfaction and individual development. Especially management should promote job enlargement, general supervision, strong cohesive work groups and decentralization.

Extensions and modifications

The above view, which was perhaps best expressed in Argyris' classic *Personality and Organization*, received considerable reinforcement, particularly during the early 1960's. McGregor's *Human Side of Enterprise* and his posthumous *The Professional Manager* both provided details as to the application of Theory Y. A considerable amount of empirical work has appeared generally consistent with the personality vs. organization theory. Kornhauser found an inverse relationship between job status and the mental health of Detroit workers: the lower one goes down on the status ladder, the poorer the adjustment of the workers. Similarly the work of Lyman Porter suggests that those lower down on hierarchy are less satisfied than those at higher levels, particularly in regards to egoistic and self-fulfillment needs.

In 1964 Argyris considerably softened his harshly pessimistic original view in his almost encyclopedic *Integrating the Organization and the Individual.* He recognized that many people seem to adjust satisfactorily to a challengeless work environment. Though such individuals may be psychologically "immature," their expectations of job satisfaction are low, and they suffer few overt pangs of aggression. They do routine jobs in an adequate manner, though their performance is not innovative and they are resistant to change. These workers may be not overtly dissatisfied but are still not motivated.

Implicit support for the Argyris view has come from the research of Frederick Herzberg and his colleagues.[1] On the basis of imaginative research (originally with accountants and engineers, but later extended to other occupations), Herzberg concluded that the job satisfaction and job dissatisfaction were not opposite points on a continuum but in fact two separate dimensions. "Extrinsic" factors, such as company policies, incompetent supervision, or unsatisfactory working conditions may lead to dissatisfaction. Such dissatisfaction may be reduced by hygienic measures such as fringe benefits, "human relations" training for foremen, or better company policies, but such measures won't make workers satisfied, only apathetic. For true satisfaction to be obtained, "intrinsic" factors must be provided, such as achievement, accomplishment, recognition, responsibility, and challenging work. Note that satisfaction is obtained primarily from the *content* of the work itself, dissatisfaction is derived from its *context* or environment. Only satisfaction relates to productivity. The presence of "dissatisfaction" may lead to low morale or absenteeism, but its elimination will not raise motivation or productivity.

Herzberg concludes that it is a mistake to emphasize traditional "hygienic," "extrinsic" measures which serve only to make the work environment more tolerable. Instead management should seek to enrich (not just enlarge) the job so as to make it seem interesting and important. (Note how Herzberg, along with Argyris, Likert, and Miles, has gone beyond human relations, with its emphasis on social satisfactions, and now stresses intrinsic, ego satisfactions.)

Herzberg's work has led to substantial controversy and considerable research. On the whole, those who have used his methodology have obtained his results; those who have used different methodologies have obtained different results. His work has been criticized as being "methodology bound ... , based on faulty research ... , inconsistent with past evidence ... , [and] an

[1] Frederick Herzberg, Bernard Mausner, and Barbara Snyderman, *The Motivation to Work* (New York: Wiley, 1960); Frederick Herzberg, *Work and the Nature of Man* (Cleveland: World, 1966). See also Robert F. Ford, *Motivation Through the Work Itself* (New York: American Management Association, 1969).

oversimplification of the relationship between motivation and satisfaction."[2]

Whatever the limitations of Herzberg's methodology, his research suggests that there can be a middle ground between harsh autocracy and fully participative management, a middle ground which Herzberg calls "hygienic management" and Miles calls "the human relations" model (in contrast to the Theory Y "human resources" model). Perhaps employee morale can be high and employees can do a steady "fair day's" work without Theory Y motivation. Indeed on many jobs it may be difficult or impossible to permit much ingenuity or self-direction without redesigning the technology and perhaps making it less efficient.

Personality, Culture, and Technology

The 1960's saw increasing questioning of some of the over-simplistic versions of the organization vs. personality hypothesis. Doubts were expressed about the universal validity of Theory Y assumptions.

One stream of research deals with personality and suggests that a substantial body of employees react negatively to opportunities for challenge and self-direction on the job. A study by Vroom, for example, suggests that it is chiefly people who have a high need for independence and weak authoritarian attitudes who are likely to respond positively to consultation by their superiors.[3] McClelland, Atkinson, and their disciples have stressed what they call "need achievement," the desire for achievement as measured by Thematic Apperception Tests. Persons high in need achievement react well to challenge; those who are low on this dimension are concerned primarily with playing it safe and avoiding failure. Presumably this latter group prefers direction to autonomy.

A second stream of research deals with cultural variables. McClelland argues that there are substantial differences in need achievement among cultures, that these differences are largely caused by variations in child-rearing practices, and further that there is a high correlation between economic growth in a given country and the strength of its managers' need achievement motive.

McClelland's work stems from clinical psychology. Another important series of intercultural studies—this time based on anthropology and linguistics—has developed from the work of William F. Whyte in Peru.[4] According to these studies Peruvian society is characterized by rigid status distinctions and low levels of interpersonal trust. The concept of leadership

[2] Robert J. House and Lawrence Wigdor, "Herzberg's Dual-Factor Theory of Job Satisfaction and Motivation: A Review of Evidence and a Criticism," *Personnel Psychology,* Vol. 20, No. 4 (Winter, 1967).

[3] Victor Vroom, *Some Personality Determinants of the Effects of Participation* (Englewood Cliffs, N.J.: Prentice-Hall, 1960).

[4] For a summary of the work so far, see his *Organizational Behavior* (Homewood, Ill.: Irwin, 1969), Chap. 32.

(as opposed to domination) is unknown in the language. Small wonder that, in sharp contrast to most American findings, close supervision is positively correlated with job satisfaction.

Recent research suggests that there are somewhat similar differences between rural and urban workers in the U.S. One of the great truths taught in the late fifties was that job responsibility was positively related to morale and that job enlargement was an almost surefire way to raise job satisfaction. The findings of Turner and Lawrence's *Industrial Jobs and the Worker* seriously challenged this verity. In a study conducted in 11 firms, these researchers sought to measure the relationship between job satisfaction and complexity of work. To their great surprise they discovered that small town workers reacted positively to more complex tasks (as expected) but that urban workers reacted negatively to them. This unanticipated finding was further supported by a series of articles by Hulin and Blood reporting on research with 1,900 workers in 21 plants in a wide variety of communities.[5] Where urban and slum characteristics were high, the correlations between blue-collar satisfaction and job skills were low or negative, the reverse was true in more rural areas, while nature and location of community seemed to make no difference for white-collar workers.

These findings are hard to explain (and the research is subject to some criticism). There may be some basic cultural differences between urban and city life, differences which may even affect personality variables such as need achievement. Turner and Lawrence, for example, offer as one explanation for their findings the fact that their city workers were mostly Catholic and their rural workers were mostly Protestant, suggesting that these two religions had different values toward work. Hulin and Blood suggest that rural workers adhere to the Protestant ethic of achievement through work, while urban workers look upon the job merely as a means of obtaining satisfactions off the job.

This research generally suggests that workers' attitudes toward their job are influenced by a much larger number of variables than a simple view of Theory Y would imply. While McGregor is undoubtedly right that some workers seek self-actualization through work, for other workers the job is merely a means for earning money or the locus of a rich social life. If we are to understand how to motivate desired behaviors on the job, more complex theories are required.

A final stream of research dealt with technology. It suggested that technology may be as important a determinant of job satisfaction as managerial style. Vroom's study of a parcel delivery service indicated that drivers, who see their boss only a few minutes each day, are more likely to

[5] The work is summarized in Charles Hulin and Milton R. Blood, "Job Enlargement, Individual Differences, and Worker Responses," *Psychological Bulletin*, Vol. 69 (1968), pp. 41-55. Some serious questions as to the methodology here have been raised by Kornhauser. See also Jon M. Shepard, "Functional Specialization, Alienation, and Job Satisfaction," *Industrial and Labor Relations Review*, Vol. 23 (January, 1970), pp. 207-219.

prefer bosses with strong authoritarian attitudes, whereas dock workers, who are in close contact with their boss all day long, prefer those who are not authoritarian.[6] Robert Blauner's important *Alienation and Freedom* starts with Marx's definition of alienation and presents evidence showing that the kinds of alienation which capitalism (and Theory X) is supposed to induce seems to be most prevalent in assembly-line work.[7] Alienation is considerably less in both craft (printing) and automated (chemicals) work. His findings about automation are encouraging because they seem to contradict the hypothesis that blue-collar work must inevitably become psychologically less meaningful over time.

Blauner's typology is concerned solely with various forms of manufacturing industry. Etzioni has adopted a much broader typology which is based primarily on the means used by the organization to motivate its participants.[8] His main thesis is that in the *typical* case (he discusses exceptions as well) there is a close relationship between organizational goals, the nature of the power and sanctions used to induce motivation, and the forms of involvement of its members. Thus normative power, which relies on "manipulation of esteem, prestige, and ritualistic symbols," is appropriate chiefly where organization goals are value-oriented (as in a university, church, or political movement), and its participants identify with the organization and internalize its goals. Similarly, in organizations producing economic goods, the rewards are "material" and involvement is "calculative." All of this may be merely a fancy way of making an obvious point: the kind of involvement with work required to make Theory Y valid may be easier to obtain when organizational goals are idealistic rather than materialistic.

Newer Approaches to Motivation

As the foregoing discussion suggests, it has become increasingly clear that no one form of motivation is universally appropriate for all personalities, cultures, and technologies. This realization has led to attempts to develop "field" theories which would take these and other factors into account—theories which would explain, for example, the conditions under which Theory Y would be appropriate. Among the leaders here have been Vroom and Lawler and Porter.[9]

Early human relations theory was not well worked out, but it seemed to suggest that high morale would lead to harder work. Yet, as Brayfield and Crockett pointed out in 1955, the empirical evidence suggests that the

[6] Victor Vroom and Floyd C. Mann, "Leader Authoritarianism and Employee Attitudes," *Personnel Psychology*, Vol. 13, No. 3 (Summer, 1960), pp. 125-140.

[7] Robert Blauner, *Alienation and Freedom* (Chicago: University of Chicago Press, 1964).

[8] Amitai Etzioni, *Complex Organization* (Glencoe: Free Press, 1961).

[9] Victor Vroom, *Work and Motivation* (New York: Wiley, 1964) and Lyman Porter and Edward Lawler, *Managerial Attitudes and Performance* (Homewood, Ill.: Irwin, 1968).

correlation between job satisfaction and productivity is very low (though the impact of satisfaction on absenteeism and turnover is quite apparent).

The new theories, in effect, reverse the direction of causation. Using "paths-goal" analysis the new theories suggest that people will work harder when they perceive that harder work is a path toward a goal they desire, or more explicitly that higher production will in turn lead to a reward which will satisfy a need important to them. Note that this chain of causation may break down at any point: there may be no perceived relationship between effort and production (as on the assembly line); higher production may not be rewarded (promotion may be based on seniority rather than productivity; productivity may be difficult to measure); the reward may not be of particular value to the employee (it might be praise when he wants pay); finally, any of these relations may exist but not be perceived as existing (there must be accurate feedback).

Stated in this form the theory is consistent with both Taylor's Scientific Management and McGregor's Theory Y. One emphasizes piece-work, the other self-direction, yet in both cases if the previously mentioned conditions are met, high productivity will result. However, the theory also permits us to specify the conditions under which various forms of motivation might be successful. Long before 1960 we knew that monetary or other "Theory X" incentives worked well only under relatively restricted conditions. Obviously there are other, but essentially similar, constraints on Theory Y variables. For example, if sense of achievement is to operate as a successful motivator, then the following conditions, among others, may have to be attained: (1) the employee in question must have an active or latent high need achievement motive; (2) the task in question must be viewed as a meaningful challenge (it must not be too easy, too hard, or irrelevant to his interests); (3) the employee must have some feedback as to whether in fact he completed the task. And so forth.

14

Blue-Collar Blues on the Assembly Line

JUDSON GOODING

The "personality vs. organization" hypothesis contends that the inconsistency between organization demands and worker needs leads to alienation on the part of workers. This alienation, in turn, results in absenteeism, turnover, output restriction, and sabotage. This selection

Reprinted from *Fortune*, July 1970, pp. 69ff., by permission of the publisher. Copyright 1970 by Time, Inc.

supports the view that there is substantial alienation among U.S. blue-collar workers. Judson Gooding reports on the extent of alienation among the 740,000 hourly paid workers in the automobile industry. Based on interviews with workers and management, Gooding concludes that auto workers, particularly those under thirty, find job discipline harsh and uninspiring. They vent their feelings through absenteeism, high turnover, shoddy work, and often sabotage.

Gooding notes that job-performance statistics in the auto industry are very discouraging. Absenteeism has doubled at General Motors and Ford during the past ten years. An average of 5 percent of G.M.'s hourly workers are missing from work without explanation every day; the figure goes as high as 10 percent on some days, notably Mondays and Fridays. The complaints about the monotony of work, tight job discipline, lack of possibilities for advancement, and absence of personal time off add to the grim picture. In the article one worker complains: "You're tied down. You do the same thing every day, day in, day out, hour after hour. You're like in a jail cell—except they have more time off in prison. ... "

The managers interviewed by Mr. Gooding recognize the need to build more worker satisfaction into jobs; the true challenge is to improve worker motivation within the constraints imposed by technology. This dilemma has heightened interest in the subject of job design, which will occupy our interest in the following two reading selections.

This article was the first of a two-part series that Mr. Gooding prepared for Fortune *magazine. In the September 1970 issue of* Fortune, *Mr. Gooding reported on job design efforts in U.S. industry in "It Pays to Wake Up the Blue-Collar Worker."*

I Spend 40 Hours a Week Here —Am I Supposed to Work Too?

Sign in tavern near Ford Dearborn plant

Detroit knows a lot about building new cars, but there's a lot it doesn't know about the new young men building them. This failure to understand the men who do the work has meant, increasingly, failure to get the work done with maximum efficiency. The problem is particularly serious because the understanding gap, curiously reminiscent of the gaps between parents and children and between universities and students, faces off the nation's biggest industry against a very substantial percentage of its workers. There is labor unrest on many fronts this year, but nowhere else do venerable production techniques and a fractious new work force collide quite so dramatically. Among the unpleasant possibilities for Detroit is a major strike when union contracts expire this fall.

Of the 740,000 hourly paid workers building cars today, 40 percent are under thirty-five. The automobile industry, justly proud of its extraordinary record of past accomplishments, is totally committed to the assembly line which comes down from that past, and its heroes are veteran production men who know how to "move the iron." At the plant level, managers are trying to build cars by the old methods with new workers they don't understand and often don't much like. While at headquarters top executives are beginning to worry about "who's down there" on those assembly lines, what "they" are like, what "they" want from their jobs, there is still a comprehension gap. This gap would be dangerous at any time, but it is particularly so in a grim sales year, a period of intensifying foreign competition, and a time of swift social change.

Somewhat belatedly perhaps, management is attempting to ease its labor problems in a variety of ways, from sensitivity training for supervisors to the greatly increased degree of automation being built in at G.M.'s new Lordstown, Ohio, plant. Such changes will show results only over the long range, though, and contracts with the United Automobile Workers expire September 14. Negotiating a new agreement without precipitating a strike will be even more difficult than usual because of that angry mood down on the production line.

The central fact about the new workers is that they are young and bring into the plants with them the new perspectives of American youth in 1970. At the beginning of this year, roughly one-third of the hourly employees at Chrysler, General Motors, and Ford were under thirty. More than half of Chrysler's hourly workers had been there less than five years. The new workers have had more years in school, if not more of what a purist would call education: blue-collar workers between twenty-five and forty-four years old have completed twelve years of school, compared to ten years for those forty-five to sixty-four. It doesn't sound like much of a difference, but it means an increase of 20 percent. The new attitudes cut across racial lines. Both young blacks and young whites have higher expectations of the jobs they fill and the wages they receive, and for the lives they will lead. They are restless, changeable, mobile, demanding, all traits that make for impermanence—and for difficult adjustment to an assembly line. The deep dislike of the job and the desire to escape become terribly clear twice each day when shifts end and the men stampede out the plant gates to the parking lots, where they sometimes actually endanger lives in their desperate haste to be gone.

For management, the truly dismaying evidence about new worker attitudes is found in job performance. Absenteeism has risen sharply; in fact it has doubled over the past ten years at General Motors and at Ford, with the sharpest climb in the past year. It has reached the point where an average of 5 percent of G.M.'s hourly workers are missing from work without explanation every day. Moreover, the companies have seen only a slight dip in absenteeism since car production started declining last spring and layoffs at the plants began. On some days, notably Fridays and Mondays, the figure goes as high as 10 percent. Tardiness has increased, making it even more difficult to start up the production lines promptly when a shift begins—after the foreman has scrambled around to replace missing workers. Complaints about quality are up sharply. There are more arguments with foremen, more complaints about discipline and overtime, more grievances. There is more turnover. The quit rate at Ford last year was 25.2 percent (this does not mean one worker in four quit, but simply that there was very heavy turnover among a small but volatile fraction, primarily of the younger ones). Some assembly-line workers are so turned off, managers report with astonishment, that they just walk away in mid-shift and don't even come back to get their pay for time they have worked.

TOOL HANDLES IN THE FENDERS

The result of all this churning labor turmoil is, inevitably, wasted manpower, less efficiency, higher costs, a need for more inspections and repairs, more warranty claims—and grievous damage to company reputations as angry consumers rage over flaws in their glistening but all too frequently defective new cars. In some plants worker discontent has reached such a degree that there has been overt sabotage. Screws have been left in brake drums, tool handles welded into fender compartments (to cause mysterious, unfindable, and eternal rattles), paint scratched, and upholstery cut.

General Motors has taken the initiative in bringing the problem out into the open. Some suspect this may be because G.M. is expected to be the target of the United Automobile Workers if negotiations this fall break down and a strike is called against one of the companies. In his Christmas message to G.M.'s 794,000 employees, Chairman James Roche laid into those workers who "reject responsibility" and who "fail to respect essential disciplines and authority." He hit harder, and attracted wide attention, in a February speech celebrating G.M.'s fiftieth anniversary in St. Louis. "Management and the public have lately been shortchanged," he said bluntly. "We have a right to more than we have been receiving." G.M. had increased its investment per hourly employee from $5,000 in 1950 to $24,000 in 1969, he said, "but tools and technology mean nothing if the worker is absent from his job." He stressed the domino effect of absenteeism on co-workers, on efficiency, on quality, and on other G.M. plants with related production. "We must receive the fair day's work for which we pay the fair day's wage."

The problem was thus clearly enunciated. The trouble is no one is really certain why the absentees are absent, why the tardies are tardy, why the discontented are discontent. It *is* known that the great majority of the hourly workers are reasonably faithful in attendance and that chronic absenteeism is concentrated among only 10 to 15 percent of the employees at each plant. It is these regularly irregular performers who have made the absentee rate jump to double the former figure; some of them miss one or more days each week.

The reasons they give cover the predictable stumbling blocks of life: car wouldn't start, wife sick, alarm clock didn't go off. Some candidly cite pressing amorous engagements that preclude their appearance at the plant. Doctors' certificates are popular because when absence is for a proved medical cause, pay is not docked. As a result, there is a thriving market for stolen prescription pads from doctors' offices—and medical excuses are viewed with skepticism. One personnel man called a doctor to check on an excuse the physician had written, and the doctor, misunderstanding the purpose of the call, assured the official, "Sure, send me anyone you got. I'll fix them up for five bucks apiece."

DISCIPLINE VERSUS PERMISSIVENESS

Absenteeism is notably higher on the less desirable late shifts, where there are more of the newer and younger employees. Lacking any precise knowledge of why the absentees stay away, beyond their often feeble excuses, the conclusion has to be that by staying out they are saying they don't like the job. The reasons for this are not yet known precisely either, but there are some useful clues.

First, it is significant that the absentee problem is especially severe in the automobile industry, where unskilled and thus less motivated workers constitute 70 percent of the labor force, compared to an average of only 10 percent unskilled in all industry. Automobile manufacturing is an old, entrenched industry with old, ultrasimplified methods originally designed not only to avoid waste motion but to accommodate unschooled immigrant labor and farm youths. It has a lot of old-line executives who have worked their way up for thirty and forty years. These men are used to dealing with engineers and machines in absolutes, not with fragile contemporary psyches. They tend to see the problem in basic terms, distrusting theorists and social scientists who claim the work is "monotonous" and "lacking in motivation factors." Earl Bramblett, the G.M. vice president for personnel, says absenteeism occurs not because the jobs are dull, but because of the nation's economic abundance, and the high degree of security and the many social benefits the industry provides. He cites the impressive gains labor has made and deplores the younger workers' insistence on even more benefits and improvements, thinks instead they should show more appreciation for what they have. At the same time, too, top management is well aware that the young recruits, coming from today's more permissive homes and schools, often get their first real experience with discipline on the factory floor.

Further, the automobile industry lacks the relative glamour, the involvement and satisfaction of newer industrial jobs such as those at Polaroid or Texas Instruments or I.B.M. It seems fairly certain that, given a choice, most young auto workers would prefer jobs in those future-oriented firms. Automobile making is paced, in most of its production operations, by the inexorable demands of the assembly line, usually turning out about fifty-five cars per hour, leaving the men no flexibility of rhythm. At some plants there are sternly detailed work rules that would make a training sergeant at a Marine boot camp smile with pleasure. The rules prohibit such offenses as catcalls, horseplay, making preparations to leave work before the signal sounds, littering, wasting time, or loitering in toilets.

Another special handicap for the carmakers is that they are tied to big-city areas by their capital investments and their reliance on the inner city for a large pool of unskilled labor. Working conditions in the plants, some of which are gloomy and old, do not match those in many other industries; the setting is often noisy, dirty, even smelly, and some jobs carry health hazards. The pace of the line and the separation of work stations limit the amount of morale-sustaining camaraderie that can develop. The fact that 100,000 of the 740,000 auto workers were laid off for varying periods this year has, of course, added to discontent.

ABOVE THE BEADS, CURIOUS EYES

In this rather somber setting it is hardly surprising that the injection of tens of thousands of hopeful young workers during recent years has caused some conflict. They both know more and expect more. Many have never experienced economic want or fear—or even insecurity. In the back of their minds is the knowledge that public policy will not allow them to starve, whatever may happen.

Walter Reuther pondered the industry's problem with youth in an educational-television interview a few weeks before his death. Young workers, he said, get three or four days' pay and figure, "Well, I can live on that. I'm not really interested in these material things anyhow. I'm interested in a sense of fulfillment as a human being." The prospect of tightening up bolts every two minutes for eight hours for thirty years, he said, "doesn't lift the human spirit." The young worker, said Reuther, feels "he's not master of his own destiny. He's going to run away from it every time he gets a chance. That is why there's an absentee problem."

The visual evidence of a new youthful individuality is abundant in the assembly plants. Along the main production line and in the subassembly areas there are beards, and shades, long hair here, a peace medallion there, occasionally some beads—above all, young faces, curious eyes. These eyes have watched carefully as dissent has spread in the nation. These men are well aware that bishops, soldiers, diplomats, even Cabinet officers, question orders these days and dispute commands. They have observed that demonstrations and dissent have usually been rewarded. They do not look afraid, and they don't look as though they would take much guff. They are creatures of their times.

Management has tended to assume that good pay with a good fringe is enough to command worker loyalty and performance. For some, it is.

General Motors has issued to all its workers an elaborate brochure informing them that even its lowest-paid hourly employees are in the top third of the U.S. income spectrum. (The average weekly wage at G.M. is $184.60.) But absenteeism continues, and learned theoreticians take issue with the automobile executives about money as a reward, arguing that men work for more than pay and that their other psychological needs must be satisfied. Since pay alone demonstrably does not work, management must study the lessons offered by absenteeism, just as others have had to study the lessons of campus and political dissent among youth. One of the first things management must learn to do, as college presidents and politicians have had to learn, is to listen.

"I DON'T LIKE NOTHIN' BEST"

What the managers will hear is a rumbling of deep discontent and, particularly from younger production workers, hostility to and suspicion of management. A black worker, twenty-two years old, at Ford in Dearborn, says he dislikes "the confusion between the workers and the supervisor." By "confusion" he means arguments. He would like to set his own pace: "It's too fast at times." The job is "boring, monotonous," there is "no glory"; he feels he is "just a number." He would not want to go any faster, he says, "not even for incentive pay." A white repair man in the G.M. assembly plant in Baltimore, twenty-nine years old, says, "Management tries to get more than a man is capable of. It cares only about production."

A black assembly worker at Chrysler who shows up for work regularly and at twenty-four, after Army service, gets $7,400-a-year base pay, says, "I don't like nothin' best about that job. It really ain't much of a job. The bossman is always on our backs to keep busy."

Talks with dozens of workers produced few words of praise for management. There is cynicism about possibilities for advancement. "Promotion depends on politics in the plant," a twenty-seven-year-old trim worker for Ford said, and others expressed similar views. "They tell you to do the job the way it's wrote, even if you find a better way," says an assembly worker, thirty-two, at Cadillac.

Complaints about the lack of time for personal business recurred in different plants. "You're tied down. You do the same thing every day, day in, day out, hour after hour," says a union committeeman, thirty-one, who worked on the line twelve years. "You're like in a jail cell—except they have more time off in prison. You can't do personal things, get a haircut, get your license plates, make a phone call." With the increased complexity of life, including more administrative and reporting obligations, more license and permit requirements, more insurance and medical and school forms, workers tied to the production line have difficulty keeping up. Unable even to phone in many cases, as their white-collar brethren can, they feel frustrated, and one result is they sometimes take a whole absentee day off to accomplish a simple half-hour chore. The problem affects everyone similarly, but here as in other areas of discontent, the young workers are quicker to complain, and more vociferous.

A prominent and somewhat surprising complaint is that companies have required too much overtime. Workers, particularly the younger ones with fewer responsibilities, want more free time and want to be able to *count* on that time. Overtime diminished or disappeared after the slowdown this year, but it will again become a problem when demand for cars increases. U.A.W. Vice President Douglas A. Fraser says, "In some cases high absenteeism has been caused almost exclusively by high overtime. The young workers won't accept the same old kind of discipline their fathers did." They dispute the corporations' right to make them work overtime without their consent, he says, feeling this infringes on their individuality and freedom. Fraser recommends overtime be optional, not mandatory.

NOBODY LIKES THE FOREMAN

The foremen, as the most direct link between management and the workers, draw heavy criticism, most of it from the younger men. They are accused, variously and not always fairly, of too close supervision, of inattention or indifference, of riding and harassing men, of failing to show them their jobs adequately.

A young apprentice diemaker at Fisher Body says, "They could let you do the job your way. You work at it day after day. They don't." A General Motors worker in Baltimore, twenty-nine and black, says, "The foreman could show more respect for the workers—talk to them like men, not dogs. When something goes wrong, the foreman takes it out on the workers, who don't have nobody to take it out on."

There is also an increasing number of complaints by whites alleging favoritism or indulgence by foremen toward blacks—and similar complaints by blacks about whites. However, open clashes along racial lines are rare, even though blacks now constitute around 20 percent of the hourly force (varying by geographical location). The liberal leadership of the U.A.W. has a powerful influence on attitudes and as a result bigotry is generally concealed, if not eliminated. But black workers in some plants do tend to stick to themselves, and it is not uncommon for a black to converse by shouts with a brother twenty feet down the line rather than with the white across from him and only a yard away.

The more serious split that has developed in the plants is between the young and old. The tendency of the younger men to speak out rather than bottle up their grievances is contagious, and the older men, too, complain more than in the past. In this contentious atmosphere, young turn on old, and old on young. A young apprentice diemaker at Fisher Body says, "The older guys sit back and take it easy, because they got their time in. They razz the kids a little." A Baltimore worker denounces older men for catering to the company: "They do all they can to follow instructions when the company tries one more speedup."

Some of the older workers are just as bitter. A forty-three-year-old diemaker is angry at the diminished sense of craftsmanship among the young. "They make me sick," he says, adding angrily that a third-year apprentice he knows, "who is a dummy," is making only $300 a year less than he is. Another says, "The older men feel the young are cocky, that they better watch themselves." A thirty-eight-year-old worker on the Cadillac transmission line says flatly, "I resent the younger ones. They feel they should come in and not take turn in seniority—they want the big jobs right away."

The antagonism between young and old, although by no means universal, is reflected in union affairs as well. The union leadership is of another generation, and some of the younger workers feel they are a constituency without a voice. They are suspicious of what they see as close ties between union delegates and management. A Baltimore Chevrolet worker, twenty-nine and black, says, "Sometimes it looks like the company and the union had gotten together on a matter when maybe they shouldn't."

In this kind of climate, the difficulties of the tightrope act the union must perform in the forthcoming negotiations become apparent. (The death of Walter Reuther adds another burden, putting his successor Leonard Woodcock on the spot to prove himself to the membership.) A fundamental problem is that while younger members want union negotiators to concentrate on immediate pay and benefit increases, older members want more emphasis placed on retirement goals.

The contract demands already set forth by the U.A.W. reflect the union's anxious desire to come up with something for everybody, young and old. The list includes more holidays, longer vacations, elimination of compulsory overtime, retirement after thirty years' service with a minimum of $500 per month, full cost-of-living protection, year-end cash bonuses, payment of dental bills, reduction of pollution—and of course, higher pay. Such a package would be fantastically expensive, and the companies are prepared to resist, point by point. For their part, the younger workers, in their present temper, would probably like nothing better than to down tools for a rousing great strike.

"THEY HATE TO GO IN THERE"

The morale of the young workers is summed up grimly by Frank E. Runnels, the thirty-five-year-old president of U.A.W. Local 22 at Cadillac: "Every single unskilled young man in that plant wants out of there. They just don't like it." Runnels, who put in thirteen years on the assembly line, says there has been a sharp increase in the use of drugs and that heavy drinking is a continuing problem. "This whole generation has been taught by their fathers to avoid the production line, to go to college to escape, and now some of them are trapped. They can't face it; they hate to go in there."

Much of the blame for present problems goes to industry managers who have done little to make the jobs more rewarding. "They haven't tried to build motivators into the jobs," says the Reverend E. Douglas White, associate director of the Detroit Industrial Mission, a labor counseling group. Gene Brook, director of labor education at Wayne State University, blames the young auto workers' anger on "the guy's feeling that he is not a part of anything," that he is an interchangeable cog in the production process. "Workers who want a sense of self-development, and want to contribute," says management consultant Stanley Peterfreund, "instead are made to feel unimportant." Campus and factory ferment have similar origins, in the opinion of Fred K. Foulkes, an assistant professor at the Harvard Graduate School of Business Administration. "People want more control, more autonomy. They want to be the acting agent rather than acted upon." Foulkes, author of *Creating More Meaningful Work*, stresses that the discipline of the assembly line adds a special problem. "People *have* to be there," he says. "There's no relief until relief time comes around. The whole situation, therefore, is inconsistent with what seems to be going on in society—and it's too costly to change the technology. So the question remains: How do you permit men to be individuals?"

John Gardner, in his new book *The Recovery of Confidence*, says, in an observation that might have been crafted to order for the automobile business, "An important thing to understand about any institution or social system is that it doesn't move until it's pushed." The push applied to the carmakers has been the sharp surge of absenteeism, dissension, and shoddy workmanship in their plants. Admittedly, the industry managers are hampered in their efforts to meet the demands, spoken and unspoken, of their youthful new employees because they are boxed in by the givens within which they operate. The old plants, the urban setting, the tyranny of the assembly line, all make solutions more difficult. But the industry has become increasingly aware of the problems facing it, has considered a wide variety of approaches, and is moving ahead on several of them.

WORKING IT OUT ON THE FLOOR

One attack is being made at the level where management and hourly workers meet, on the plant floor, through the foremen. On the average there is one foreman to thirty production workers, and the majority of foremen have come up from the hourly ranks themselves. All of the big three auto companies operate training programs for foremen designed to increase their effectiveness as leaders. Pontiac takes foremen off on weekends to various resorts for specially tailored sensitivity training and discussion of the problems new workers face. At Chrysler a special consultant instructs foremen on the difficulties black workers encounter when starting work in an auto plant.

Since late in 1968, General Motors has operated a "New Work Force" program for foremen in plants across the country. The title was chosen to indicate General Motors' awareness that there is indeed a new and different work force, not so homogeneous as in the past, including blacks and whites old and young, persons with little education and of various cultures, some with criminal records, many who would once have been considered unemployable. The program gives managers a look at the lives of such workers, takes them into ghetto areas, puts them in role-playing situations in which they act out the workers' parts in orientation and disciplinary interviews. Supervisors are shown how to reduce new employees' tensions, feelings that if unresolved can cause a new man to quit, stay away from work, or rebel in some other fashion. Ford, too, conducts human-relations programs at various plants to guide supervisors in dealing with motivation, work control, costs, and quality.

Some of the foremen have been hard to convince, particularly those who have been threatened with violence or even death (such threats are not uncommon in connection with firings, according to the foremen). But the message about the need for a new approach is getting through. Reflecting the change, one chassis-assembly foreman at Cadillac said, "I try to work *with* them, not threaten them. The old-type tactics of being a supervisor don't work with these guys." A foreman in Pontiac's foundry division said, "I try not to use the discipline route. I tell the man the pocketbook effect on him. Some of this absenteeism is for simple reasons, like the foreman didn't smile right or turned his back when you were talking. Or family reasons, the wife is sick." He gets questioned on assignments, he says, "but I try to anticipate the questions and explain why. That way, if he wants to argue, he has to meet me head on."

General Motors runs a vigorous, well-financed suggestion program as a way of creating and sustaining employee initiative. Last year 324,647 ideas came in and the company paid out more than $17 million for the 279,461 suggestions adopted. Ford has just put into distribution to its plants a new film in *cinéma verité* style aimed at new employees. It is designed to show them what production work is really like, so that when they step out on the clangorous floor on that first day of work they won't be dismayed. It has an unusual title, *Don't Paint It Like Disneyland*, and, as a Ford official said, 'It's an unusual industrial film. We don't have the chairman of the board giving a speech about working for Ford, either at the beginning or at the end." It is unusual, too, in its candor. In it one production worker says, "It's a drag at first, but you realize you got to do it; so you do it." Another looks up from his job on the line and says in a puzzled way, "I got a good job—but it's pretty bad."

Ford is also looking hard for ways to give workers more feeling of responsibility and authority in their work. One tactic being applied at all Ford assembly plants is an established technique with a new name. It is called the "positive-buy" inspection. The inspector puts his initials on the inspection sheet for each car he passes. This indicates personal approval and ensures active examination rather than passive acceptance. Various plant managers are experimenting with other motivational approaches such as job rotation, group or team work, and self-set quotas, but they are hampered by the inflexible nature of the automobile-assembly process, and by the reluctance of many workers to change familiar routines.

THE DISCIPLINE ROUTE

At the Chevrolet assembly plant in Baltimore, where absenteeism has gone up steadily from just over 3 percent in 1966 to 7.5 percent today. management is trying a whole array of tactics. The basic approach there, too, is through the foremen, who are told to make every effort to know their workers as individuals and to try to make them *want* to do their jobs. Workers needing time off for personal business are urged to ask in advance, so that management can plan ahead to replace them. The problem here is that not all such requests can be granted—not everyone can leave during Maryland's deer season, for example—and refusal can create more resentment.

The next stage beyond motivation is what Baltimore plant management terms "the discipline route." Workers and union officials say that there has been a definite "tightening of the reins," including more reprimands, more "time off" (meaning disciplinary suspension without pay), and more dismissals. One Friday on the second shift (three-thirty to midnight) last April, more than 200 employees were absent, out of the shift force of 2,700 hourly workers. Management decided to shut down the plant after four hours, a decision that meant those who had come to work lost half a day's pay, through no fault of their own. The union cried foul, claiming management took the absenteeism as a money-saving excuse to cut production because of lower sales. To get back at management, dozens of workers canceled their savings-bonds and community-chest deductions, both ardently advocated by the company.

Plant manager H. H. Prentice had letters mailed to every worker, addressed "Dear Fellow-employee and Family," explaining why the closing was necessary, urging "your best effort in being at work every day on time," and expressing certainty that "most of our employees want to be at work every day to provide for themselves and their families." Thus to the "discipline route" was added "the family route." With cooperation from employees, Prentice ended, "we will avoid the necessity of harsh disciplinary measures." The threat seemed sufficiently clear.

Two quite sweeping methods have been suggested by various managers and theoreticians for dealing once and for all with worker discontent. One is to keep the jobs as dull as they are, and hire dull men to fill them. This seems a backward-looking course at best, even if such a large, docile labor force still existed anywhere in this country. At the other extreme are the proposals for automating the plants completely, throwing out the old assembly line in the process, and eliminating the dull jobs altogether. Unfortunately, this solution is not feasible either with present technology.

LOOKING AHEAD AT LORDSTOWN

The more central course, which many advocate, would have managers find ways to make the jobs varied and interesting through both motivation and technology. The industry is certainly looking. On the motivational side, some G.M. plants have even tried rewarding regular attendance with Green Stamps, or initialed drinking glasses. G.M. is taking some long steps toward more complete automation in planning for production of its low-cost Vega 2300, which will go on sale this year. The production line being built at Lordstown, Ohio, is designed to permit assembling a hundred cars per hour, compared with the usual fifty-five, and surpassing even the ninety-one Oldsmobiles built each hour at Lansing. Since labor input must be reduced if G.M. is to make a profit building these smaller, cheaper cars, every phase of the assembly operation is being restudied and much of it is being redesigned. For example, the Vega chassis will be raised and lowered automatically as it moves along the line, to speed assembly and make the workers' jobs easier.

Whatever is done, says G.M.'s director of employee research, Delmar L. Landen Jr., it must be remembered that absenteeism and allied production problems are only symptoms of the trouble. For too long the automobile industry has "assumed economic man was served if the pay was okay," says Landen, who has a doctorate in industrial psychology and fourteen years experience with G.M. "It didn't matter if the job was fulfilling. Once the pay is good, though, higher values come into play." Other satisfactions are required. "One thing is sure: if they won't come in for $32.40 a day, they won't come in for a monogrammed glass." In Landen's view, a greater sense of participation must be built into the job; he does not know just how. He is currently completing a major survey of foremen to learn the exact dimensions of, and the basic reasons for, low worker morale. The study has been in preparation for more than a year. From the findings, he will develop specific recommendations. At this point he is surprisingly optimistic. "We are having very vital, critical changes in our society," he says. "And the question is how we can capitalize on this, how we can exploit the forces of change and profit from them."

Nobody disputes that these new workers are the brightest, best-educated labor force that ever came into the plants. If their potential were somehow fully released, they would be an asset instead of a problem. But it is clear, too, that solutions will not be quick and easy. A new challenge to the industry has quite clearly been thrown down. Old familiar plants that once taught industrial efficiency to the world have, almost unnoticed, undergone a change of season. In the new climate young workers have created, top management must increasingly think of its workers and the satisfactions they can and should derive from their work. Failure to do so would mean failure, ultimately, in management's basic responsibilities to its stockholders as well.

15

Job Design: Methods and Models

HAROLD M. F. RUSH

This selection is taken from a research study published by The Conference Board, an independent nonprofit business research organization that has conducted studies in the fields of business research and business management for more than fifty years. This report is an outgrowth of an earlier Conference Board research study, also conducted by Harold Rush, of the application of behavioral science concepts in industry. As a result of widespread interest in the application of job design concepts, this study was undertaken to examine how companies are implementing job design. The report discusses the historical and theoretical influences on the job-design movement, the principal methods of job design, and an analysis of company and union experience with job-design applications.

In his introduction, Rush notes that initially he planned to investigate the implementation of job enrichment. Early in the study, it became obvious that job enrichment is only part of the broader concept of job design, which is concerned with the whole relation of the work performed to employee motivation. Job design may include a variety of approaches, depending upon the technology, the nature of the work force, the product or service requirements, and the managerial philosophy of the firm. The author notes that he uses the term "job design" in his report to connote a behaviorally oriented approach to designing work.

In the excerpt that follows Mr. Rush examines several approaches to job design: job rotation, job enlargement, job enrichment, plan-do-control, and work simplification. The relationship between these techniques and other management approaches, such as management-by-objectives and the Scanlon Plan, are explored.

Reprinted from *Job Design for Motivation*, pp. 11-17, by permission of the publisher. Copyright 1970 by The Conference Board, N.Y.

In a subsequent section of his report, not included here, Mr. Rush reviews the reasons why few organizations have made any sustained effort at job design. He states that "Job design for motivation is a manifestation of a philosophy of management. In some organizations, it is a built-in part of the management style. It is viewed as the most effective way—sometimes, indeed the only way—to operate."

The design or redesign of jobs may be said to have a single purpose, though it is a purpose with a double edge: to increase both employee motivation and productivity. That purpose, however, is but a nebulous catch phrase unless it is translated into more specific goals in relation to the job itself and the person performing it. Both theorists and managers who have had experience with job design usually cite concrete objectives that provide the stimulus for undertaking it. The objectives vary with the approach a company takes, the form the job design takes, the production and attitudinal situation, and, ultimately, with what the company hopes to accomplish.

PURPOSES AND INTENT OF JOB DESIGN

Obviously, a company may employ many means, both subjective and objective, to evaluate its job design projects. There are several objectives or variables that appear singly or in concert with others when a company seeks to measure the success of failure of its experiments. Some of the most common are given below.

Increase Employee Motivation

The stimulus for a job design project may be management's perception or experience of employee apathy or boredom. There may be subjective or intuitive recognition that morale is poor and that employees are disinterested in their jobs; or there may be observable, concrete evidence in the form of grievances, complaints, slowdowns, or interpersonal conflict between peers or between superiors and subordinates. While all of these may be apparent without quantitative measurement, to pinpoint specific problem areas, a firm may try to assess morale and motivation by surveying employee attitudes or job reaction.

If job dissatisfaction is apparent and the firm undertakes a project to improve motivation, the expectation is that the dissatisfying or restraining forces will be reduced or removed by improving the job. To substantiate a cause-and-effect relationship, the company also takes a reading of job reaction and motivation during and following the job modification.

Raise Productivity

Productivity, as a measure of the efficient use of human and material resources, is more than production output. The qualifying difference is the word "efficient," which implies maximum, or at least optimum, utilization of the resources available. Job design is undertaken to increase either machine output or human output, or both.

Improve Quality or Quantity of Goods and Services

Higher production of goods or services may be the principal goal of job design. In other instances, higher quantity is not the primary aim at all. For example, improved quality may be the objective—to eliminate or reduce the number of rejects or customer complaints—even if this means lower production of goods or services.

Reduce Operating Costs

Reduction of operating costs may be viewed as a function of increased productivity or improved quality of goods and services. Analysis of the technology and of how human effort is being used can result in elimination of unnecessary equipment, processes, or jobs.

Reduce Turnover and Training Costs

Job satisfaction is believed to have a direct bearing on motivation and productivity. It is also believed to be reflected in reduced turnover—voluntary and involuntary—and studies have shown a link between the employee's job satisfaction and his speed and ability in acquiring skills on the job. Reduced turnover and accelerated learning rates would naturally reduce training costs.

Accommodate to New Technology

Most job design is redesign, but technological changes or the introduction of new processes may sometimes require teaching new skills or making use of existing skills in a different way. Job design offers a means to meet the demands of new technology. Some firms begin their job design efforts at this point because there is no resistance to change, since there was no "traditional" way of doing the job.

METHODS OF JOB DESIGN

Although the ultimate goals or purposes of job design are, by and large, similar, there are multiple approaches to it and just as many opinions about the relative merits of each approach. Each seems to have its partisans who champion the validity and efficacy of their particular school of thought. The manager who is trying to improve the efficiency of his operation and build motivational factors into jobs may even be uncertain about the denotations and connotations of the terminology of the several job design techniques. The field of job design, as it exists in the socio-technical sense or as managers know it today, is relatively new. Yet there are various techniques and approaches that together characterize the state of the art. Among them are *job enlargement, job rotation, job enrichment*, the *"plan-do-control"* concept of work, and *work simplification*.

Job Enlargement

Job enlargement is the expansion of the job from a central task to include other related tasks.

In other words, tasks that normally would be done by several employees are combined into a sequence of tasks performed by a single employee. Job enlargement implies a lengthening of the time cycle required to complete a unit of the operation and a reduction of the degree of specialization.

Research on job enlargement indicates that an employee's job satisfaction can be increased by increasing the number and variety of his tasks. Job enlargement alters the job content by varying the operations, and seeks to reduce repetitiveness and monotony. Supporting research indicates that efficiency is improved and interest in the work is increased when fatigue associated when repetitiveness is lessened.

Job enlargement in this sense does not attempt to *deepen* an employee's responsibility for his work; instead, it *widens* the number of tasks for which he is responsible. For this reason, job enlargement is often referred to as "horizontal loading." (See Exhibit 1.)

Job Rotation

Job rotation often implies rotating an employee through a series of departments or jobs for short time periods for the purpose of orientation, especially in management-development programs or in career-path planning. Job rotation, in the job design sense, has some similarity. However, in job

Exhibit 1   Horizontal job loading—job enlargement.

design the rotation usually centers on a core job and is undertaken not only to give the employee broader perspective but to increase his skills and knowledge about that job and related jobs. The aim is flexibility within a prescribed series of tasks; the jobs themselves are not redesigned or modified, and the worker's responsibility is for the specialized or fractionalized part of the operation that he performs at any given time.

    While job rotation is usually within a single department or work unit, it is also used as a training or development tool in moving an employee through a series of operations to broaden his knowledge and perspective of the total operation. Proponents of job rotation cite advantages similar to those of job enlargement: variety that relieves boredom, and the broadening of skills.

Job Enrichment

    Job enrichment usually means delegating to the worker some functions generally thought to be managerial. The traditional role of the manager is to plan, organize, lead, and control the work of others, while the worker does the "doing" of the job. Job enrichment implies that the worker assumes some

Exhibit 2   Vertical job loading—job enrichment.

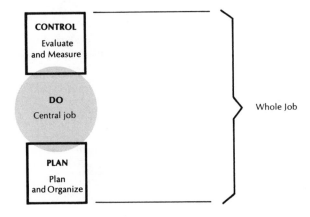

of the planning and control aspects of his job, as well as the doing. This is referred to as "vertical job loading," as contrasted with the "horizontal job loading" of job enlargement. (See Exhibit 2.) The job content or basic task may remain unchanged, but the worker plans and controls his performance. Job enrichment usually implies also that the level of difficulty or complexity of the job is raised, and quite often the number and variety of tasks are increased as well. The result is a combination of horizontal and vertical job loading.

Herzberg's "motivation-hygiene" theory of motivation is the foundation for most job enrichment projects. Jobs are designed to provide "satisfiers" or motivating factors of achievement, recognition, interesting work, responsibility, advancement, and growth. Herzberg insists that real motivation will result only when the job has the potential to satisfy these upper-level needs, which translate into job enrichment. Horizontal job loading, in his view, has little if any motivational impact—"two or three meaningless activities do not add up to a meaningful one."

Chris Argyris's research on job design and motivation generally supports Herzberg's contention that horizontal job loading has little real motivational influence. Argyris says: "In order for the individual to express more of his knowing and feeling abilities, he requires a work environment over which he has greater control, where he can make decisions concerning goals, policies, and practices. This type of job enlargement cannot be restricted to the tasks found along the flow of work. The employee must be provided more 'power' over his *own work environment* and therefore he must be given responsibility, authority, and increased control over the decision making that affects his immediate work environment. He must become self-responsible."[1]

Argyris, however, uses the term *job enlargement* to mean vertical job loading and, unlike Herzberg whose motivation-hygiene theory portrays supervision, interpersonal relations, and environmental factors as merely maintenance factors, he stresses the importance of supervisory style, peer relationships, and environmental factors in motivation toward work.

Plan-Do-Control

The plan-do-control concept is a model of job design developed by M. Scott Myers, whose validation of the motivation-hygiene theory at Texas Instruments resulted in large-scale job redesign within the firm.[2] Basically, the plan-do-control concept is a model of job enrichment, and it stresses the motivational factors as postulated by Herzberg.

Myers's research, however, indicates that the "satisfiers" and "dissatisfiers" are not always as discrete as Herzberg claims. For example, Myers found that meaningful work is a motivator, but he also found that the lack of meaningful work demotivates. Another point of difference between Myers and Herzberg is the relative importance of some of the "hygiene" or

[1] Chris Argyris, *Personality and Organization.* (New York: Harper & Brothers, 1957)
[2] See M. Scott Myers, *Every Employee a Manager.* (New York: McGraw-Hill, 1970)

maintenance factors in motivation. While Myers agrees that job content and self-reliance are integral to real motivation, he also stresses the influence of interpersonal competence, helpful systems, meaningful goals, and the opportunity for self-actualizing work.[3] Myers, unlike Herzberg, stresses the importance of employee participation and the interpersonal aspects of superior subordinate relationships. In this respect, the Myers view of job enrichment, though roughly paralleling Herzberg's, is more closely allied with Argyris's concepts.

The plan-do-control theory posits that the worker *must* have a considerable degree of control over all three aspects of his work if the job itself motivates. The planning phase includes planning and organizing and consists of problem-solving and goal-setting for the use of manpower, material, and systems. The doing phase is the implementation of the plan through coordinated expenditure of physical and mental effort and the utilization of aptitudes and special skills. The controlling phase includes measurement, evaluations, and correction of the work. In other words, it is the feedback process for evaluating success or failure of achievements as measured against goals.

Work Simplification

Work simplification is a matter of examining a job—literally, taking it apart, studying the various steps, and working to redesign it more efficiently. This procedure makes use of "methods improvement," a process for the analysis of the utilization of material and physical facilities; but it goes a step further by analyzing the human effort that goes into the use of material. Work simplification has its roots in Taylorism, in that it uses industrial-engineering techniques to study jobs and break them down into their smallest possible segments. To many managers, work simplification still connotes fractionalization of jobs into the simplest and most repetitive operations. However, the basic aim is not fractionalization but the attainment of more efficient processes by eliminating unnecessary steps and combining steps wherever possible—a kind a job enlargement.

Work simplification is a term whose coinage is attributed to Erwin Schell of M.I.T., but its chief proponent today is Allen Mogensen, an industrial engineer who teaches the technique at the Work Simplification Conferences (chiefly at Lake Placid, New York). Attendees are encouraged to design jobs by asking: What steps can be eliminated completely? What steps can be combined? Should the job sequence be changed? What can be simplified? A cursory look at work simplification indicates that this technique belongs more in the industrial-engineering disciplines than in the behavioral sciences. It is, indeed, used in industrial engineering, but it is also

[3] See Harold M. F. Rush. "Behavioral Science—Concepts and Management Application," *Studies in Personnel Policy*, No. 216. National Industrial Conference Board, 1969. (Case study on Texas Instruments pp. 139-156)

widely used in job design projects that have their roots in behavioral science concepts, and especially in "job enrichment" projects. When work simplification is used in this context, it is usually an adjunct to a larger motivational effort. Employee participation in the improvement of their own jobs is viewed as an aspect of participative managing.

MODELS OF JOB DESIGN IN APPLICATION

Values, theories, and techniques all underlie job design. They remain hypothetical or academic until they are translated into design of jobs in a workaday situation. For a variety of reasons that stem from technological, financial, and attitudinal considerations, the translation process is often difficult.

. . .

Clearly, job design has many faces and a company's venture into it may take many forms. How each of the methods of job design might be employed in combination with the others may be shown by analyzing the functioning of an "autonomous work group" or a "semiautonomous work group"—an idealized organizational construct that some job design proponents dream about, but that rarely exists in its "pure" form in practice.

Autonomous Work Group

The terms "autonomous" or "semiautonomous" can be misleading in an organizational context; the degree of autonomy is relative. Both groups may be viewed as self-sufficient or autonomous relative to former controls or in comparison with work units in most other firms; however, they are also subject to major corporate or divisional restraints, and their objectives are within the larger framework of the company's objectives.

The rationale is that employees can more easily identify with a smaller organizational component, and the results of their efforts—individual and collective—are more easily observed and measured as a group with interdependent roles and relationships.

The work group is organized as a "work family," or the grouping of people into a work unit with a common product or service requirement. There is in the semiautonomous work group a boss or manager who belongs to it and also serves as its communication link with the rest of the organization. Typically, several steps or operations, and a variety of jobs and skills, are required for completion of the product or service. Individual members are accountable to the group; the group, as a whole, is accountable to management.

Since the group operates with a relative degree of autonomy as a work family, it may decide how its objectives will be established and met, and who does what, and when. As a rule, each member acquires the skills to perform all the tasks within the group. This enables any member to do a variety of related operations, and the group may decide within a given time span to divide labor to provide *job enlargement* for its members. *Job rotation* is facilitated by the same broadening of skills; to break up the monotony of repetitive "assembly line"-type tasks, a group member may do one specialized job for awhile, then exchange jobs with another member. Both job enlargement and job rotation may be used to help the group meet its objectives more effectively. For example, if a member of the group leaves the company or is absent for awhile, another member can step in and do the job, or the job may be assumed in addition to a regularly assigned job.

The group sets its objectives within the larger requirements of the company's objectives and in line with its own functional assignments and capabilities. Goal-setting, division of labor, assignment of tasks, and measurement of the quantity and quality of effort are all done by the group themselves. They *plan-do-control* their activities, and usually some time is set aside for problem-solving, goal-setting, and interpersonal feedback. In other words, in order to function as a group or team, they expend special effort on team-building.

While group members work in proximity and the product or service is their common objective, the labor can be divided to allow some members to perform various "doing" functions, while others inspect for quality and measure productivity. However, all phases of the operation may occasionally be performed by one person, if the product or service requirements permit. He may plan his work sequence, do the various jobs required, and inspect his own work, a process that results in individual *job enrichment*.

Within the group, each member's contribution, performance, and effectiveness is measured on an individual basis for personal evaluation, as well as on the basis of how his effort relates to the total group effort. Since the group usually has over-all responsibility and accountability for its output and internal operation, it seeks ways to improve the job and to get rid of bottlenecks and unnecessary or combinable tasks. The principles and techniques of *work simplification* or work improvement are commonly utilized in the group's problem-solving, goal-setting sessions.

JOB DESIGN ASPECTS OF ADJUNCT SYSTEMS

Job design principles are adapted to many situations, some of them recognizable in manipulation of specific job content, as in job enlargement and job enrichment. However, the principles of broadened jobs and deepened levels of responsibility appear in other forms that might not commonly be considered job enlargement or job enrichment. If one takes the "plan-do-control" concept as a base for building greater employee commitment and involvement, job design principles are in operation in several management or work systems.

For example, when the so-called managing-by-objectives concepts are used as a system of managing that goes beyond the "appraisal by results" practice, real job enrichment may exist.[4] In fact, job enrichment itself is objectives-oriented, and there may be only a fine line of distinction between what one firm calls managing by objectives and what another calls job enrichment. Job enrichment can be viewed as pushing the concepts of managing by objectives down to the lowest possible level of the organization to embrace low-skilled jobs as well as professional and managerial ones. Managing by objectives, while most often applied to managerial and professional jobs, is actually part of the operation of the "autonomous work group," which may include employees in entry-level jobs. Autonomous work groups participate in setting goals and objectives against which they are measured, by themselves as well as by management. Managing by objectives, when it is indeed a full system of managing, shares with job enrichment the principles of *planning* (objectives or goal-setting), *doing* (carrying out the objectives), and *controlling* (measuring effectiveness in meeting objectives). Both concepts stress individual initiative and self-control as means of increasing job motivation, productivity, and personal growth.

While the current interest in job design takes into consideration material or monetary awards, most of the focus is on the intrinsic or self-actualizing rewards associated with meaningful work. Most behavioral scientists and managers who are concerned about building motivational factors into work have stressed financial incentives but little, if at all, in the belief that the economic needs of man are important but unidimensional. However, one type of incentive program that has intrigued behavioral scientists since it was first developed is the Scanlon plan, named for its "inventor," the late Joseph N. Scanlon, former professor (Massachusetts Institute of Technology) and onetime union official (United Steelworkers of America).[5]

Generically, the Scanlon plan is a group incentive plan. What sets the Scanlon plan apart from other incentive or profit-sharing plans is its provision for plant-wide standards and participation of employees at all levels. It can be very complex, but its two basic parts are a means of sharing the results of increased productivity on a plant-wide basis, and a provision that no one benefits individually from a suggestion, thereby eliminating possible conflict among originators of the suggestion. Furthermore, the Scanlon plan goes beyond most suggestion-system incentive plans in that participation—on a group basis—is its hallmark. Groups may be established to solve problems of

[4] For a comprehensive treatment of management by objectives in concept and practice, see Walter S. Wikstrom. "Managing by—and with—Objectives," *Studies in Personnel Policy*, No. 212, National Industrial Conference Board, 1969.

[5] See F. G. Lesieur (ed.), *The Scanlon Plan.* (Cambridge: M.I.T. Press, 1958)

cost reduction, production flow, waste, quality control—*key factors within their control.* If their efforts result in higher production or lowered costs, all employees share the gains. In this sense, employees plan, do, and control their jobs, and are rewarded tangibly for the application of their abilities toward work improvement and job design.

Scanlon was not a behavioral scientist, nor was his aim to increase employee motivation through participation, per se, but many behavioral scientists have lauded his work as truly consistent with, and conducive to, real job enlargement or enrichment. McGregor devoted a chapter of *The Human Side of Enterprise* to an evaluation of the Scanlon plan as a means of participative management.[6] Argyris, among other behavioral scientists, has cited the Scanlon plan for providing a means for employees to use many of their more important abilities, to be less dependent, passive, and subordinate toward management, and to have increased control over their own immediate work environment.[7]

Participation of another kind, which also involves employee control over work environment, may be found in the use of task forces or *ad hoc* groups. These task forces are usually composed of persons from several levels of the organization who become a group for any number of reasons and who function participatively on a temporary basis. They typically have a specific organizational problem or set of problems to attack, and they are charged with analyzing the situation, recommending or taking action, and measuring results in terms of organizational improvement. There are plan-do-control implications in their jobs, and an additional motivational factor, namely, skills and personal growth, is one hoped-for consequence of their participation.

[6] Douglas McGregor, *The Human Side of Enterprise.* (New York: McGraw-Hill, 1960)
[7] Argyris, *op.cit.*, p. 182.

16

Motivation Through the Work Itself

ROBERT N. FORD

In the introduction that preceded the previous selection, we noted that company experience with the application of job-design concepts has been limited. There are, however, some large-scale job-design projects that are notable exceptions to this general observation. One such "classic" in job design is the set of job-enrichment studies conducted by Robert N. Ford and his associates at the American Telephone and Telegraph Company.

Reprinted from Robert N. Ford, *Motivation Through the Work Itself*, pp. 185-199, by permission of the publisher. Copyright 1969 by the American Management Association, Inc.

The specific problem that precipitated the studies at A.T. & T. was high employee turnover. Since 1960, annual turnover rates had been on the rise throughout the Bell System. In 1964, Ford and his associates initiated job enrichment trials in A.T. & T.'s Treasury Department. Frederick Herzberg's motivation-hygiene concept of work motivation provided the theoretical basis for the A.T. & T. studies. The results of the initial studies were highly successful and encouraged the company to conduct eighteen replications of the original study in various departments throughout the Bell System.

This selection is the concluding chapter of Mr. Ford's book. In the first part of the selection, the author states the original problem and reviews the job-enrichment strategy and the study results. He then concludes by interpreting the data and speculating on the future of job-enrichment studies.

This closing chapter consists solely of the author's ideas and opinions, not those of the Bell System, although the corporation does not necessarily disagree with the basic position set forth here. The statement of the problem, the strategy employed to meet it, and the results are scarcely open to question. But the final sections of the chapter are interpretations of data and one man's point of view about the nature of work.

THE PROBLEM OF JOBS

The problem that precipitated these studies is employee dissatisfaction with work, which is evidenced in steadily mounting turnover rates. That this problem is widespread was shown by the many inquiries about these studies from other businesses.

Careful exit interviewing brought out the usual wide range of reasons for quitting—inadequate pay, undesirable hours, bad transportation, home problems, poor supervision, and undesirable work. The Bell System has worked reasonably hard to correct these problems or, when they cannot be corrected, to alleviate them. Take night work, for example. Night tours of duty for some employees are facts we have to live with in any business that operates around the clock every day, without time off even for Christmas. This is a limiting factor in any effort to decrease dissatisfaction. Does this limiting condition apply to the *jobs* we do, also? Must they, like the tours of duty, be what they are? Are they causing trouble unnecessarily?

STRATEGY FOR IMPROVING JOBS

The work of Professor Herzberg and others suggested strongly that the work itself was a powerful motivator of employees under certain conditions. The Herzberg survey study of 200 management men probed the causes of job satisfaction and dissatisfaction. A.T. & T.'s experimental studies started where the Herzberg study left off; they involved several thousand employees in achieving groups spread across nine different nonsupervisory jobs in ten associated companies of the Bell System.

In all cases the work itself—the task—was the variable in the experimental groups and was held as constant as possible in the control groups. In both experimental and control groups the factors that surround the work itself—variously labeled maintenance or hygiene items—were also held constant.

In each of the experimental trials, a family of immediate supervisors tried to solve this problem: How can we shape a particular job so that the job incumbent has, not more work, but more responsibility for the work? How can we make him feel that a part of the business is his alone, that he can make decisions regarding it and personally identify with it? If we can do this, the employee will have a heightened chance for individual achievement and for recognition of his achievement. In addition, he will have a chance to learn and to grow on his job, perhaps to be promoted. Furthermore, if we can do this, we can make the employee's working life a more meaningful human experience. If we succeed, he will not feel impelled to look elsewhere for good work or to become so unproductive as to be useless to the company.

Here are two illustrations of how employees are given *more* responsibility. In the first, a service representative usually decided when a customer's service should be cut off for failure to pay a bill. She reported her decision to her supervisor, who checked the facts and the reasoning and usually obtained the signature of someone still higher in management. Then service was discontinued until the customer paid his bill. In the work-itself program, after the representative has repeatedly demonstrated her good judgment, she orders the cutoff directly. If the customer pays the overdue bill, the representative involved can really feel that *she* was successful. And if she has made an error in judgment, it is her error, not the supervisor's. Thus responsibility, a major motivator, is increased for the employee.

The second illustration comes from a large foreign chemical company where six studies similar to those reported in this book are in progress. Although the sales volume in dollars is high for a certain line of chemicals, the profit margin is dropping. The salesmen have been doing an excellent job of selling chemicals that have low margins and competitively favorable prices but they have not done well at selling lines with better profit margins. However, the salesmen were not aware of this.

In this project, the experimental group was given pricing information, including the lower and upper bounds that have to be observed in setting the price of any chemical. Next, they were acquainted with the profitability problem and were asked, in effect, to "act for the company. Set the price at the level that you think will result in a sale and help to overcome the profitability slide." After six months of applying this technique the experimental group is reported to be running almost three-quarters of a million dollars ahead of the control group in profitability of sales. The control group, in contrast, is still merely following the book in setting prices. In the service representative illustration and in this one, the challenge is to find ways, big or little, whereby an employee can earn the right to act for the company.

As these sessions with families of supervisors proceeded (never cross-sectional or interdepartmental groups), the technique of greenlighting was developed whereby highly specific items or ideas were produced to make a job more meaningful and more interesting. For competent people with demonstrated ability, jobs can be improved by steps such as these:

1. Give the employee a good module of work.
   - Pull responsibilities back down to this job level if they have been assigned higher up only for safety's sake.
   - Gather together the responsibilities that are now handled by people whose work precedes or follows, including verifying and checking.
   - Push certain routine matters down to lower-rated jobs.
   - Automate the routine matter completely if possible.
   - Rearrange the parts and divide the total volume of work, so that an employee has a feeling of "my customers," my responsibility."
2. Once an employee has earned the right, let him really run his job.
3. Develop ways for giving employees *direct* individual feedback on their own performance (not group indexes).
4. Invent ways of letting the job expand so that an employee can grow psychologically. ("There's always something new coming up on this job!")

Such steps as these four principles of job improvement should result in better jobs for employees. Since employees want meaningful work, they should like the improved job better, and turnover should drop in locations where it once was high. In other jobs that are handled by older people who don't quit but who do give other evidences of job dissatisfaction (low productivity, grievances, and so on) improvement should be attainable simply by concentrating on the question: How can we make this as good a task or assignment as possible and practical?

SOME SURPRISINGLY GOOD RESULTS

Of the nineteen studies nine were rated "outstandingly successful," one was a complete "flop," and the remaining nine were "moderately successful." The most striking single piece of evidence was a 13 percent drop in the turnover rate among a large sample of service representatives at a time when the control group rate increased by 9 percent. Other technical results (productivity, quality of performance, customer reaction, and so on) either improved slightly or at least held their own. If the turnover rate across the Bell System could be dropped by only 10 percentage points (to use a conservative figure) the savings in training costs on this one job alone would be in millions of dollars.

The biggest error one could make in interpreting the data would be to contend that these good results came from increased skill at "keeping people busy." In the first place, a typical service representative is never "unbusy." She is always very busy indeed. But supervisors in the test locations found ways of letting trained service representatives be *more* responsible for their customers in a meaningful way than they had ever been before. As a result, the desire to quit apparently dropped and other indicators improved slowly.

While permanence of the gains is still to be established for 18 of the 19 studies, the original Treasury Department results show *excellent* long-range promise. After three years, the Treasury correspondents' service index for all units (achieving and control alike) is now in the upper 90's.

No claim is made that these 19 trials cover a representative sample of jobs and people within the Bell System. For example, there were no trials among the manufacturing or laboratory employees, nor were all operating companies involved. There are more than a thousand different jobs in the Bell System, not just the nine in these studies. What to make of the results, then?

Even this limited sample of the universe of jobs shows that significant changes can be made in some jobs and that striking improvements will result. In other cases, not much will happen, although no losses will occur in the effort to improve jobs. These are the most likely probabilities if we take more samples of the same jobs, but there is no way of predicting whether good results will occur with a new job.

THE FUTURE OF THE EFFORT

What will be done with the findings in the companies that conducted the studies? The reaction throughout the Bell System has generally been, "We don't see how we can afford not to go ahead." There is to be no crash program; we made it clear that these results usually required eight months to a year of patient, persistent work. In general, any department in any location, systemwide, may go ahead *with the active support and concurrence of headquarters.* Men in all departments at headquarters have been made available to help start either projects or programs in the field.

For the most part, however, the project stage is past. Most departments, both at headquarters and in the field, now ask to start *programs.* This implies that no data will be collected from a control group; that is, no group will be asked to "hold still" for a year. Therefore, evaluation will generally be in terms of a group's own past performance.

A small manpower utilization group with these explicit responsibilities has been set up at A.T. & T. headquarters.

1. Spread current knowledge and techniques.
2. Act as consultants on current job structures.
3. Continue to probe for new understanding of the reasons jobs go wrong; get the principles refined.
4. Serve as consultants to field people who are setting up new jobs, a never-ending process in such an expanding industry as communications.

Quite clearly A.T. & T. is settling down for the long haul. Seventy-seven new programs have been started. No one expects all jobs to be equally improvable, nor is every job in need of assistance. And, since there are so many requests, the accepted view is, "Don't push any manager who is uncertain or lukewarm in his interest. Reach him later."

At this writing, more than 50 companies outside the Bell System have requested further information about the studies. Some were already conducting their own studies; others have now started here in the United States and abroad. A reasonably safe prediction is that much more information will be available within the next ten years as to how one bridges the gap from theory to fact. Experimental studies, not surveys, will probably make the difference as knowledge in this field accumulates.

SOME TRUTHS ABOUT WORK

One reason not all managers rush into this program is that it means extensive change and not trivial change at that. Placing his photograph above each employee's work position won't suffice, but it is a project that could be set up in one "crash" week. Making basic changes in a well-established job is hard work, mentally and emotionally. After working on improving the jobs of the people they supervise, managers have often been heard to say, "What am I doing to my own job!"

Many a supervisor rose to his present job by performing well on each job in turn on the way up. To have kept these jobs rather than to have become a turnover statistic himself might be viewed as a reflection on his own ability. But, in spite of the likelihood of emotional involvement when changing a familiar job, personal feelings do not get in the way very frequently either in workshop sessions or among the highly placed managers when proposals for change are brought to them. Even the man who may be responsible for the fix a job is in is usually glad to find a solution. Occasionally, a particular executive has struggled too hard to save an old job rather than accept the changes proposed by lower-level supervisors in the greenlight sessions, but this is the exception.

There are no villains, no evil people who deliberately deprive employees of job satisfaction. When past steps have resulted in inadvertent job denuding, these steps were usually taken to achieve other desirable ends.

Still another basic truth is uncovered when we ask, "Why have these projects gone well?" We let it be known that six new projects were needed in order to check out the original Treasury study. We got three times that number in a matter of weeks, even though the executive level had only the results of one study to judge by. And, since the new programs are doing very well indeed, many other managers want to start.

The basic truth here is that managers *want* employees to do well and to have good jobs. "After all," one said, "I work here too." John W. Gardner suggests that *there can be no institutional change without aspiration.*[1] The fact that managers reach toward the work-itself goal indicates that they do aspire to present their employees with rich job opportunities.

The aspiration of good jobs for all employees is matched by similar aspirations for the other two legs of the corporate stool. There is no doubt at all that a sensible corporation aspires to give better service to *customers* also. More than 15,000 employees in the Bell Telephone Laboratories, for example, are working essentially toward new and better services. And on the *shareholder's* side, in an era when his equity can erode because of rapid inflation, the corporation has given repeated evidence that it aspires to keep its shareholder financially above the tide of inflation.

There is a direct connection between job improvement projects and one of Gardner's statements:

> The release of human potential, the enhancement of individual dignity, the liberation of the human spirit—those are the deepest and truest goals to be conceived by the hearts and minds of the American people. And those are ideas that sustain and strengthen a great civilization—if we believe in them, if we are honest about them, if we have the courage and the stamina to live for them.[2]

What is the connection? The studies were founded on the premise that jobs could be improved—and then set out to do it by releasing human potential more completely. In Gardner's words:

> Of all the ways in which society serves the individual, few are more meaningful than to provide him with a decent job. ... It isn't going to be a decent society for any of us until it is for all of us. If our sense of responsibility fails us, our sheer self-interest should come to the rescue.[3]

[1] John W. Gardner, *No Easy Victories,* Harper & Row, New York, p. 44.
[2] *Ibid.,* p. 16.
[3] *Ibid.,* p. 25.

Some people may assume that Gardner was talking about the hard-core unemployed. Actually, he was talking about a just society for all; but in any case his words amply support the aphorism, "A difference which makes no difference is not different."

A statement of deep truth that appeared at the time of these studies was made by the Negro psychologist Kenneth B. Clark, who said:

> The roots of the multiple pathology in the dark ghetto are not easy to isolate. They do not lie primarily in unemployment. In fact, if all of its residents were employed it would not materially alter the pathology of the community. More relevant is the status of the jobs held ... more important than merely having a job, is the kind of job it is.[4]

Ultimately there is no truth for the black employee that is not equally a truth for the white. To help a hard-core person get started management may want to take a job apart for a while. It may at first give him not the whole module or task—the installation and repair of telephones, for example—but the recovery of telephone handsets that were left in apartments, homes, or offices when tenants moved. Then he can learn how to install a telephone and eventually perform the more difficult task of figuring out why an instrument refuses to work.

Nothing more will be said here about minority problems, differences between male and female employees, or college graduates versus high school or grade school graduates simply because we have not found (*in these studies*) that the differences make a difference. Even the question of how to improve jobs for older employees as distinct from younger ones has not proved to be a critically important problem. *The major problem* is how to improve the job for any human being. That's why work itself, not the manipulation of people, has been repeatedly presented as the crucial variable.

And Gardner is quite right when he says, "our sheer self-interest should come to the rescue." This is one employee program that can be cost-free in as little as one year. In contrast, most employee programs end up as added costs of doing business.

There are still some people who would debate these issues. One spokesman explicitly said that these work-itself studies are misdirected. In his opinion, what employees need is "more close-order drill, more discipline." He said that the lack of discipline in American industry today is causing excessive turnover, grievances, and strikes. Although he made no suggestion as to how to achieve this discipline, one might observe that all it takes is military conscription (a kind of compulsory employment office), prisons for poor performers and objectors to the proposed employment, and, in some countries, a wall against which to stage executions.

Still another view of work that needs to be dealt with holds that the

---

[4] Kenneth B. Clark, "Explosion in the Ghetto," *Psychology Today*, September 1967.

"work ethic" or "Protestant ethic" idea is outdated. By 1985, Americans will be able to live at the level of their present standard of living by working only six months a year. Or, alternatively, if a man chooses to work year-round, he will be able to retire from work at age 38.[5] Enough rise in the gross national product is expected to make this feasible. People must get ready for handling leisure, and the unmistakable implication of the report is that the work ethic has prepared us poorly for such a life.

And so it has. The disputable point is not the accuracy of the prediction; it is the implication that work is not or cannot be as enjoyable as is a hobby or a sport such as golf or fishing. Gardner states the case for the potential satisfactions of work:

> What could be more satisfying than to be engaged in work in which every capacity or talent one may have is needed, every lesson one may have learned is used, every value one cares about is furthered?
>
> No wonder men and women who find themselves in that situation commonly overwork, pass up vacations, and neglect the less exciting games such as golf.
>
> It is one of the amusing errors of human judgment that the world habitually feels sorry for overworked men and women—and doesn't feel a bit sorry for the men and women who live moving from one pleasure resort to the next. As a result, the hard workers get not only all the real fun but all the sympathy too, while the resort habitués scratch the dry soil of calculated diversion and get roundly criticized for it. It isn't fair.[6]

What seems likely is that people of the future will learn to struggle against jobs that are unnecessarily bad. The willingness of management in many companies to improve the work itself should give courage to those who believe men should not write off the work portion of their lives while getting ready for the new leisure. Obviously one portion yields money, the other does not. But the point is this: Both the work *and* the leisure portions should be and can be challenging and interesting. The right mix will vary from person to person.

HOW LONG WILL IT LAST?

The concept of work just outlined grew out of the studies, as have the views as to how long a person will find his job improved, a question that arises repeatedly. In the first place, not all jobs have equal potential for yielding satisfaction. Some will be fairly routine even when we have reshaped

---

[5] *The New York Times,* April 7, 1968, report of a new study conducted by Southern California Research Council.

[6] Gardner, *op. cit.,* p. 32.

them as best we can. In this case, the goal is still to give the employee all the responsibility possible in running the job.

A woman in one of our studies volunteered to take on a routine clerical assignment that recurred four times a year, a job that involved replacing lost, mislaid, or mutilated checks—the sort of job that automation can never eliminate. When asked why she volunteered for a second time to perform this "dum-dum" job, she replied, "Well, it may be a dum-dum job, but at least it's *my* dum-dum job the way we now run it." An important implication of these studies is that routine work, especially if everyone recognizes that it must be done, can be made more acceptable if we maximize the personal responsibility component. Although this may not be the world's greatest job, employees will find it worthwhile if they are allowed to run it in a self-responsible way.

The substantial reduction in turnover indicates that we can slow down the onset of dissatisfaction. Part of the long-range job of a supervisory family is to plan a *series* of steps so that an employee can feel he is still learning, still growing. He should be able to advance within his current job, as well as upward to the next job level. Unless a job has very elastic boundaries and psychological growth and learning can occur, it will eventually bore its incumbents. People, like plants, may need to be repotted occasionally, at least until the pot is big enough for the specimen to grow without stunting. Once we have done our best to make a good and challenging job, the onset of boredom will vary with the ability of the incumbents. For some, the job may be good for a lifetime; for others, only a few years. If we have been reasonably good at selection, placement, and training, as well as job shaping, no one will be bored in only a few weeks or months.

The whimsical "Peter Principle" holds that men rise in a business hierarchy until they reach their own level of incompetence. There they stay, since they are incompetent to go ahead. If a battle of principles were to break out, we would present in opposition the Ford Principle, which is that "a man tends to repot himself until he finds a pot that is big enough." Not all people succeed in finding such a pot, of course. This puts men (or employees) into three classes.

Class 1—Men in pots that are too big for them (as suggested by the Peter Principle).
Class 2—Men in pots that are just right.
Class 3—Men in pots too small for them.

Class 1 is no cause for worry; surely not too many men are in it. Those men in Class 2 are to be envied. It's Class 3 that is bothersome.

Applying the Ford Principle, we should not cut men down to fit the pots we need to fill; we should instead get bigger pots—enlarge the jobs—and let our men grow to fill them. To put it another way, if our round pegs (people) do not fit our square holes (jobs) ream the holes to the pegs; don't ram the pegs into the holes any which way or cut them down to fit. In other words, change the shape of the jobs and you improve the level of employee satisfaction; cut the employees down to fit the job and you perpetuate existing troubles and perhaps breed new ones.

WILL FUTURE STUDIES TURN OUT AS WELL?

Progress over the past two or three years has led us to conclude that the measured results, are an understatement of what can be achieved eventually. Some handicaps were built into the study designs for scientific reasons, such as the need to minimize the Hawthorne effect. Experience shows that if employees know that they are part of a special study or campaign, results drop off again when the campaign is over. Therefore, we never told the employees that studies were under way or that we were going to try to improve their jobs. We simply did it, at first not very expertly. In 16 of the 19 studies, we did not tell even the first-level supervisors that systematic approach to job improvement was under way simply to block their being either for or against the idea of improving motivation through the work itself.

In the future, either projects or programs *should* provide richer yields for these reasons:

1. First-level supervisors can be informed, along with upper levels. The complete family will have better greenlight ideas than the smaller supervisory family we used (second, third, and fourth levels). Acts inconsistent with the principles will occur less frequently once the immediate supervisor is both informed and included.
2. The topmost levels should be informed also so that inconsistent ideas, orders, and plans do not come down from above.
3. Sometimes good ideas for improving one job are blocked unless other jobs, even other departments, are involved. In the project stage, we had to forgo involving other jobs and departments; but they should be involved in future programs.
4. When supervisory people in *many* locations are working simultaneously to reshape a given job, cross-fertilization of ideas actually occurs. In only one study were we able to take advantage of this.
5. The training workshops have improved because of the early trials.
6. Only after the studies were well along did we discover the crucial importance of devising feedback schemes for individual employees (as opposed to group indexes).

Considering all these factors, future efforts should be more productive than the original trials, especially if they are programs available to any supervisory family, rather than limited to a trial or project group. This does not imply that a program will be *any easier* than the trials; good greenlight items will always be hard to come by. But results should be at least as striking, if not more so.

THE PRINCIPLES OF JOB ENRICHMENT

At the start of this series of studies, many tape recordings were made wherein employees talked about their jobs, especially upon quitting. Many remarks were heard repeatedly: "I'm tired of being treated like a child." "I didn't think this would be like school, but it is." "I don't want to be simply a 'hey-boy' for someone else." There is no indication that times will change, that people will once again come to employment offices begging for work, or that they will stay when they don't want to, as they have at times in the past. The roots of the disenchantment must be dealt with. Much of the disenchantment can be traced to the early 1900's, when industry went through a period of job engineering and stopwatch analyses of work flow. Then job designs, job specifications, job rules, job regulations, and highly detailed work practices were developed. In many interviews, employees specifically complain about being caged in by these rules.

In such a work situation, the supervisor's job may seem to be that of keeper of the caged-in people. And his major motivational task might be viewed as that of rattling the cages so that the drowsy animals "look alive." In this analogy motivation is from *outside*: the keeper does it. Many managers now believe that this approach to work motivation has had its day.

How to go forward, then? How to view employees? The data from these studies show that it is possible to get an order-of-magnitude change, not just a small increment. Modern employees are bright, healthy, well fed, and well educated compared to those in the time-and-motion study days. They will not accept dull jobs unless the jobs are their very own. We must set the conditions of work so as to gradually maximize the responsibility thrust upon the worker. To do this we must ask ourselves these questions:

- What do I do for him that he could now do for himself?
- What thinking can he now do for himself?
- What goals could we now set *jointly*?
- What advanced training or skill could he now have?
- What job could he work toward now? How could I help him?
- Is there a way of combining this job with another one that he would like? Is the module right?
- Is there anything he does that could be given to a lower-rated job?
- Can anything be automated out of the job?

The trouble, then, with a straight engineering approach to work flow, job layout, and job specifications is that employees won't stay on these jobs—as evidenced by turnover rates for highly rationalized, tightly structured jobs. We must learn to trade off engineering economies for human values and not to assume that this will be costly. Actually, every day beyond the old median length of tenure that a service representative, for example, stays on a newly reshaped job is of cash value to the business. We are quite sure that she *will* stay if she can get more satisfaction from her work.

Job satisfaction is hard to describe, hard to visualize. It will not make an employee go around with a big, happy grin on his face. More typical of his expression would be that of the golfer, the athlete, the chess player, trying to make a good shot or to perform well. The face and attitude of any well-motivated worker confronted by a difficult, challenging situation are more like those of the athlete than those of the relaxed watchers in the stands.

Job satisfaction may or may not be tied to happiness. But we will know that we are doing something right if we can change the conditions of the job so that employees will stay on and work productively. For the older workers, the test will be whether they are with us in spirit as well as in body. The way to achieve this end, for new or old employees, is not to confront them with demands, but to confront them with demanding, meaningful work. And the employee will always have the last word as to whether the work is meaningful.

17

Independence and Conformity

HAROLD LEAVITT

This selection is a chapter taken from the revised edition of Managerial Psychology, *by Harold Leavitt. In the preface, Professor Leavitt notes that there was real doubt in 1957, when he completed the first edition of his book, whether a book labeled as "an introduction to individuals, groups, and industrial organizations in terms of modern psychology" would be of use to anyone in management. Surprisingly, the notion that the social sciences might find a home in management education was both radical and doubtful as recently as the late 1950s. By the time the revised edition of* Managerial Psychology *was published in 1964, the question was not whether social science belonged in the curriculum of a management education program but how it could best be taught.*

Professor Leavitt begins this selection with an illustration of how painful and difficult it often is for an individual to resist pressures to conform

Reprinted from Harold Leavitt, *Managerial Psychology*, rev. ed., pp. 268-282, by permission of the publisher. Copyright 1964 by the University of Chicago Press.

to group standards. He uses the setting of a committee of executives for his example. Yet the pressures applied to the deviant executive are not all that different from the pressures we have all experienced in the family, in school groups, and extracurricular committees. The four stages of group pressure are: (1) reasonable, rational discussion, (2) emotional seduction, (3) attack, and (4) ostracism. The importance of the group objective and the cohesiveness of the group determine whether, and how rapidly, a group passes through these four stages.

Many observers strongly criticize a group's tendency to demand conformity from group members, but Professor Leavitt presents a more balanced discussion of the pros and cons of this subject. He notes that, because our society values individuality and nonconformity, the deviant is usually considered to be a hero. However, many of society's complex tasks are carried out by groups, and achievement of objectives often depends on obtaining agreement and cooperation from all members. Thus, the group's aim is to complete a task, not to apply pressure arbitrarily to deviants.

Here is a problem:

You are a member of a committee. It doesn't matter what sort of a committee; you may be trying to select new products, or working out a strategy for up-coming negotiations with the union, or allocating space in the new laboratory, or deciding which of several men to promote to a new job. It is a committee made up mostly of people at about your level, chaired by a man who is intelligent and reasonable and rather well liked by all of you. He has circulated an agenda in advance of your next meeting, and you have thought a good deal about it and arrived at a position on the very first item,—a position you feel rather strongly about.

When you arrive at the meeting room, a few of the eight members have not yet shown up, so you and four or five others chat about this and that until things get under way. After the late arrivals show up and you exchange a few pleasantries, the chairman gets things started and gradually one member after another begins to express his views about the first item on the agenda. By the time you get into the act, it has become pretty clear that most members seem to share one opinion—*an opinion very different from yours.* Most people seem to be nodding their heads and saying, "Yes, method X suggested by Joe Blow looks like a pretty good solution."

Then you come in rather strongly for method Y. Nobody seems very upset. Everybody listens politely. Some of the fellows ask you questions and make comments that are partially supportive and partially in disagreement. And the discussion goes on.

After a while the chairman says, "Well, we've been at this for awhile; let's see where we stand." And he tries to summarize the two positions that have been taken, essentially Joe Blow's position X and your position Y. It's all done informally, but one after another, each in his own style, the members go along with X rather than Y. As one after another of the members goes this way, you begin to feel some discomfort. People seem to be turning toward you, psychologically if not physically; and the chairman casts an inquiring look your way. This is a committee that likes to operate informally, and you approve of this informality. You know that the chairman doesn't want to have to put this issue up to a formal vote and say, "We have decided seven to one in favor of X over Y." On the other hand, in your opinion, Y is right and X is wrong.

So the pressure begins to build and the spotlight begins to focus on you. The chairman says, "Well look, gentlemen, we've got a little time. Why don't we talk a little longer." And turning to you, he says, "Why don't you give us a rundown on the reasons for your position?" So you do. You lay it out in a way that sounds (to you) forceful and reasonable and correct.

The rest of the committee, which is now focusing rather intently on you, asks questions. It's as though you are the center of a star communication net. Everybody is turning towards you and talking to you. They are not shouting at you; they are not angry at you; they are simply asking you "rationally" to prove your position.

This goes on for a while and then people begin to get a little fidgety. Finally, one of the members turns to you and says, "Perhaps our differences aren't as big as they look. Perhaps it's all really just a matter of words. Sometimes differences that are really small begin to blow up to look like something bigger than they are." And the chairman adds, "Well gentlemen, it is getting rather late and in the interests of getting this job done, I think we have to arrive at some kind of conclusion." Then somebody laughs, turns to you, and says, "Why don't you just come along for the ride, and then we can all go out and have a cup of coffee?"

You are no dope. You can really feel the pressure now. You know that what these people are really saying is, "You are one of us. We want to get going. Don't hold us up any longer."

But you're a tough and rugged individualist. You're a man of principle. Position Y is right, by golly, and you say so again rather forcefully. There is a long silence. Then one of the members says something forceful in reply: "Oh for Chrissakes! You've been riding that horse for about three-quarters of an hour now, and you haven't come up with a single new reason. Why the hell are you being so stubborn?" As though this first opening is a signal, others join in on the attack. People go at you from all sides. They point out that you've been wrong before when you've held out in situations like this. They attack your loyalty to the group. After all you know this group likes to operate by consensus, and that it is important to all the rest of them that you all agree. They hit you with everything they've got. Even the chairman seems to be joining in.

But still you hold out. You just can't bring yourself to accept position X when it is so patently clear to you that Y is the only reasonable answer. So there you sit thinking that this is a little like how it must feel to be interrogated by the Gestapo. Your mouth is dry and you seem to be all alone inside your own thin skin. But you've been raised right! You also think of individuality and honor. And so you grit your teeth and fight back. And the clock ticks along.

What comes next?

Pretty far down inside you, you know damn well what will come next. The floodlights will be turned off; but not to give you relief. Finally (and rather suddenly), one of the members turns to the chairman and says, "We've been at this for almost an hour and a half. We have other business at hand. I think we should adopt position X, and then go on about our business." And other people turn their chairs, facing one another and the chairman; and no longer facing you. They summarize the arguments for position X and someone says, "Okay, we've decided to do X; now let's go on with the next item."

You've been quiet for the last few minutes because people haven't been talking to you. You have listened to the summary of the reasons for accepting position X, and since one of them is clearly absurd, you open your mouth to say something about it. A couple of people in the group turn and look at you as you talk, but they don't say anything in return. The others don't even look, and the chairman finally says, "Let's get on to the next problem on the agenda." And the group goes ahead.

You know what's happened. You have been psychologically amputated. As far as the group is concerned, you are no longer there. When you say things, you are no longer heard. Your influence is now zero. This is the last stage in the process by which groups deal with deviating, nonconforming members. You have been sealed off.

The story we have just told is probably reasonably familiar to almost every adult. It is not limited to committees of executives in industry. We encountered the same pressures when we were kids in the family, in street corner gangs, and in school groups. We met it again as teenagers, when we were pressed to conform to group standards of dress and deportment—standards we often tried to resist. And we keep hitting it.

THE STAGES OF GROUP PRESSURE

But the fact that we have encountered it often doesn't make the pain and the pressure any less. In fact, our experience has taught this so well that we can foretell early in the process what we will be in for if we buck the group. We know they are likely to start out being reasonable and rational, discussing the pros and cons of the issue. But even at that stage, it is implicitly quite clear that the deviant, not the group, is expected to change.

We can sense what comes next, too. We know the seductive pat-on-the-back routine. We know that some members of the group will be friendly and smile and joke with us. They will, in effect, tell us how much they love us and remind us of how valuable the group is to us. They will behave like a woman who wants a mink coat from a man, chucking us under the chin and making up to us.

And we also know what is likely to happen if we don't come across.

Groups, like (some) women, are likely to get tired of playing games rather quickly. At some point, they will decide that they have wasted enough time on that tactic. Then the silken glove will come off to expose the iron fist. If reason won't work, and seduction won't work, then the group moves to stage 3, attack. Now they try to beat us into submission. They pull out all stops; the mask is off.

But even that isn't the last stage in the process of exerting pressure on the deviating individual. The last stage is amputation. It's as though the members of the group were saying, "Let's reason with him; if that doesn't work, let's try to tease him by emotional seduction; and if even that doesn't work, let's beat him over the head until he has to give up. Failing that, then we'll excommunicate him; we'll amputate him from the group; we'll disown him."

This last and final stage is for most of us a very serious and frightening possibility; the more frightening, the more we value the group. The threat of isolation, physical or psychological is a very grave threat indeed. We don't want to be abandoned by our families, nor by our friends, nor by our business associates.

Perhaps it is because we can foresee this ultimate stage that even mild and early pressures can often cause us to change positions or beliefs or attitudes. Most of us don't get all the way through meetings like the one we described at the beginning of this chapter. We are apt to give in a good deal earlier in the game. We "work things out" when we are still at the reasoning level or at the emotional seduction level. For the paradox in this process is that the greater the pressure the group exerts on the deviant through these steps, the more difficult it is for the deviant to give in. The stage at which we can give in most easily (and still save face) is the first stage; the reasonable, rational stage. If we say "yes" in response to the chucking under the chin and the love-making, we are apt to feel a little sheepish, but that isn't terribly embarrassing. To give in under a beating is a lot more painful, and a lot weaker and more shameful. And to give in after we have been amputated is darn near impossible because nobody is there to accept our surrender.

IS THE GROUP BEING CRUEL AND CAPRICIOUS?

So far we have been viewing the group's pressures on the deviant from the deviant's perspective. For most of us the individual who holds out is the hero, whether he wins or loses. For we value individuality and nonconformity in our society, or at least we say we do. We identify with the underdog, with the deer attacked by wolves. But it is useful to view this same problem from the other perspective, that of the group. We may ask: Why are these people doing this? Why are they reasoning, seducing, attacking, amputating? Is it just a malicious, devilish kind of behavior to satisfy some sadistic needs of the group members? Not usually. If we think of the times we ourselves have been members of the majority, we can begin to see the other side of the picture.

Here is a group that is trying to get a job done. To get the job done well depends in large part on getting wholehearted agreement and co-operation from all members of the group. But there is a clock, and there are other constraints imposed by the world.

We go about the problem in good spirit, trying to cooperate, trying to understand, trying to work out a solution that we can all accept and to do it in a reasonable time. And we get very close to an answer. Everybody seems to be in perfect agreement except for that one character there.

Then what shall we do? As reasonable men, we do not steam-roller a person because he thinks differently from us. We listen to him, and we ask him to listen to us. So we go through that ritual. We reason with him. But that doesn't work; he just doesn't seem to be able to see it our way. The clock is ticking away.

What next? Why then we try to appeal to him on emotional grounds, on grounds of loyalty or decency. We almost beg him to agree. This is a difficult thing for us to do, but we want to get the job done and we don't want to hurt him. We appeal to him to join up, to go along, to maintain a solid front. But he stubbornly refuses even to go with that one.

Now what? So now we hit him. Now we *really* are mad at him, so we let him have it. Maybe if we all jump up and down on him, he will have sense enough to come around. And the clock ticks on. But the stupid, stubborn s.o.b. still holds out.

What then? Well, then we must take a step that is as painful for us as it is for him. We must dismember our group. We must amputate one of our own members, leaving us less than whole, less than intact, but at least capable of coming to a conclusion. With this recalcitrant, stubborn, impossible member, this group cannot remain a group. To preserve it, we have no choice but to cut him out.

Viewed this way, the deviant individual is not such a hero. Much of the world's complex work is done by groups. When a group exerts pressure on an individual, it may thus not constitute an arbitrary imposition of power, but rather a set of increasingly desperate efforts to try to hold the group together in order to get the work done.

DOES THE DEVIANT DO ANYBODY ANY GOOD?

Besides the argument that it is good and wholesome and healthy for individuals to be independent thinkers—an argument that is not *always* as sensible as it sounds—is there any other good argument for encouraging individuals to take deviant positions if they believe in them, and for encouraging groups not to clobber people who deviate?

The answer, of course, is that there is at least one very good practical reason, in addition to all the moral reasons. It is the fact that deviants stimulate groups to think about what they are working on. Deviants, whether they are themselves creative or not, generate creativity in groups.

The process is simple enough and understandable enough. When like-minded people get together to talk over an issue, they are likely to come to agreement pretty quickly and then to pat one another on the back and go out and drink beer. When the same people get together in the presence of a person with quite different ideas, they are forced to re-examine their own beliefs, to go over them in detail, to consider sides and aspects of the problem which they never had to consider before. They must do this in order to argue effectively with the deviant, in order to attack him, in order to reason with him. As a consequence, they end up knowing more about their own problem than they would have if the deviant hadn't been there. It costs the group time and sweat. But what they earn is greater understanding, broader search, more knowledge of their own subject matter.

CAN THE DEVIANT EVER WIN?

We now come to the next question in this logical sequence: Suppose the deviant is right? Does he have a chance? Or will his presence simply cause the group that is already wrong to believe more strongly but more sophisticatedly in its wrong position?

The answer to this one is rather complicated. There is rather good research evidence that people can and will distinguish better answers from worse ones. And a deviant who comes up with a clearly better answer, even in the face of a large group that has agreed upon another answer, has a very good chance of getting his answer accepted. Such is the case at least for problems with a clear logical structure. If I can demonstrate to you a clearly easier way to add a column of figures than the way all of you are now adding them, it will not be hard for me to swing you over to my method. So the deviant who comes up with a new solution—one that other people had not even thought of, but clearly a good solution—is likely to have little trouble getting it through.

Unfortunately, many problems, probably *most* problems, tackled by groups aren't quite of that nature. They are fuzzily outlined judgmental problems, in which ordering the quality of solutions is not so easy. The "normal" problems are problems like selecting or promoting personnel, or allocating funds among several departments, or deciding on a promotion. On those kinds of issues the deviant doesn't have much of a chance in most groups.

And here we encounter another paradox. The guy with the different ideas, the deviant, is apt to have a better chance of getting his ideas accepted by a group that isn't very solid, isn't very cohesive, hasn't worked together very much; than by a group that is solid, whose members do know and like one another. So the executive may find himself faced with what looks like a strange dilemma. On the one hand he wants solidity, loyalty, high morale in his group. On the other hand, he may want the creativity he can get from the deviant. And yet it is precisely the high-morale, cohesive group that will go after the deviant hard and fast; that will clobber him even more quickly than the new group or the unsure group.

But the paradox may be more apparent than real. In a way all we are saying is that the guy with different ideas may be able to pull a snow job on a bunch of people who feel shy and uncertain with one another. He has a chance of influencing them, of getting his ideas through, more readily than he could in a solid group. But he is likely to get his ideas through, not because a pick-up group will examine and consider those ideas more rationally or more seriously than a solid group; but rather because they are constrained, uncertain, unwilling to open up themselves for fear of attack by others. So the aggressive deviant, the one who talks loud and fast, may be able to get to them.

On the other hand, when faced with a solid, self-assured group, the snow job is almost impossible. The deviant will have to prove his case and prove it rather thoroughly. But, of course, the probability of his being able to prove it to a group that is solid and self-assured is not very great. For they are not likely to break ranks unless the logic of the case is so clear, so rational, so obviously better than their own solution, that only a fool could reject it.

WHAT KIND OF DEVIANT CAN SURVIVE?

Interestingly enough, even powerful deviants don't seem to have much chance against a strong and solid group. As all of us know, a member of the group who is already peripheral and uninfluential—the new, young member of a street corner gang, for example—is in a poor position to try to push a new idea through. But we are apt to think that if a man is strong and central in the group—the leader of the street corner gang—then he should be omnipotent, and capable of getting the group to accept even extremely different ideas. The fact of the matter seems to be, however, that even strong men in groups, men with authority or with personal influence and power, have a very tough time pushing a group very far from its own standards. Even the kingpin has to move slowly, by bits and pieces, to get the gang to stop stealing apples and start playing basketball. If he doesn't move slowly, he will get the same treatment as any other deviant and eventually find himself amputated.

The same thing seems to be true in industry. Even the powerful boss will meet a good deal of trouble in pushing a very different idea through a solid group of subordinates. If he is a real Machiavellian manipulator, he will work first on individuals when he is trying to bring about a radical change, rather than on the face-to-face group.

THE LONELY EXECUTIVE

It may seem a shockingly soft thing to say, but one can interpret most of the research and common-sense analysis of conformity as essentially a problem of loneliness. Group pressures can be exerted on individuals—lone individuals—much more effectively than they can be exerted on pairs or subgroups. It is when the deviant finds himself alone, without a twig of support, without even another deviant (even one who deviates in quite different directions), that the pressures of the group are apt to become overpowering. It may be this fear of isolation, of singleness, that permits a group to press the individual to conform, even if that individual has authority or other kinds of power. Even the president seems to want and need some sources of support, some assurance of psychological backing from his people. He may need very little but he needs not to be alone. In fact, much of the effect of group pressure can be washed out in the sort of case we talked about at the start of this chapter, by the simple expedient of having just *one* other member of the group back up the deviant.

Thus again we encounter a paradox. For now we are saying that it is loneliness that will force a man to conform to the group. Which implies that he will feel less pressure to conform (and therefore feel more independent) if he is *in* the group—a member of it—and thus not at all lonely. So how now are we to answer the earlier question: Does the group force the individual to fit into its mold, thereby reducing his individuality, thereby brainwashing him? Or is it only when he is a psychologically secure member of the group that he can express his individuality without feeling pressure and restraint?

The answer begins to become a little clearer. It seems to be true that people need psychological support, an environment free from the fear of loneliness. But if that support is bought at the price of constricting conformity, the individual loses his individuality no matter which way he goes. So the critical issue becomes the nature of the group. To what extent does it demand conformity, and on what dimensions of behavior? Does it demand, as the price of support, that he dress as they dress? that he believe as they believe? Or does it set more open standards, requiring conformity in fewer dimensions and perhaps less critical ones? requiring, perhaps, that everyone conform to certain time demands and certain demands of procedure, but consciously avoiding requirements of conformity in opinion or belief?

Since the individual needs the group, the group can exploit the individual, forcing him to bend to its demands. But individuals make groups, and it is possible to make groups that can work while exerting tolerable pressures on procedure without constraining beliefs and ideas.

IN SUMMARY

Groups put pressure on members who deviate. Usually the pressure moves through several stages, from rational argument through emotional seduction to attack and finally to amputation of the deviant member. But the process is not usually capricious or sadistic. From the group's side, they exert pressure in an effort to survive intact and to get the job done.

Group pressures work mostly when the deviant feels all alone. Given any kind of minimal support, he can hold out much more effectively. And though a powerful deviant has a better chance than a weak one, no deviant can try to push a solid group very far very fast and expect to get away with it.

Clearly, deviants make groups think, even when they don't change the groups' mind. But we need to temper two prevalent notions about deviation: The first is the notion that nonconformity is somehow always better than conformity. We must remember that much of the world's work can only be done by conforming to agreed-upon standards. The second is the notion that groups kill individuality by exerting pressures to conform. We need to remember that most of us feel freer to be ourselves in groups where our position and membership are secure, than in settings in which we feel alone and unsupported.

18

Management Information Systems:
The Challenge to Rationality and Emotionality

CHRIS ARGYRIS

Considerable attention has been focused on the impact of computerized management information systems (MIS) on organization. The debate regarding the potential effects of these systems centers on technical questions dealing with the capability of these systems to take over managerial decision-making tasks from humans.

In this selection,* Chris Argyris, a noted behavioral scientist, explores the emotional impact of management information systems on people. Professor Argyris considers the following question: What would happen if management information systems were developed that could achieve their designers' highest expectations by performing many critical management functions? Because these systems would make all important managerial decisions, they would limit the autonomy and discretion of managers. As a result, managers would begin to experience the frustrations that manu- facturing employees have experienced in the past because of narrowly designed jobs. Managers would also feel that they are less essential to the enterprise.

These experiences of executives would as a result create resistance to management information systems. Professor Argyris' study of a management information group in a multibillion-dollar corporation convinced him that "MIS specialists ... are not presently equipped to cope with the emotional problems caused by their systems. They react over rationally ... and have difficulty in coping with their own and the executives' feelings and behavior."

Consider the following questions in connection with this selection: (1) Do you agree with Professor Argyris' pessimistic view of the prospects for implementing sophisticated management information systems? (2) What approaches would be helpful for coping with the problems identified by

Reprinted from *Management Science*, February 1971, pp. 275 ff., by permission of the publisher.

*In explanatory notes at the beginning of the original version of this article, *Management Science* indicated that the original manuscript was received in December 1969 and was revised in July and September 1970. In addition, Mr. Argyris made the following statement: "The author would like to express his deepest appreciation to the members of the management services division who participated in this study. Their excellent support helped him immensely. He is also indebted to Professor Robert Fetter for his advice during the research and his helpful comments on the manu- script."

Professor Argyris? (3) What will be the eventual impact of computerized management information systems on organization?

Management science theorists and practitioners would tend to agree that some day management information systems (MIS) will probably be designed that perform many critical managerial functions. Many also would agree that the realization of this potential is a long way off.

What would happen if an MIS system were developed that could achieve this potential? How would individuals react to increased rationality in their lives? Will they think as many humanists believe, namely that information science rationality can lead to a mechanistic and rigid world which, because of its narrow concept of efficiency, will dominate man and eclipse his humanness?[1] Will individuals believe, as many futurists argue, that the scope of our society has become so great and the interdependence so pervasive, that without the rationality possible from sophisticated information systems we run the risk of losing control over our everyday life and our destiny?

These critical questions require much research from many different perspectives. We have chosen to focus on these issues by conducting empirical research in actual settings where they are being played-out (or, more accurately, fought out). The setting is the study of a management services division in a multibillion dollar corporation. One objective of the division is to introduce new management information systems into certain management processes, that are now possible with the advent of more sophisticated management information systems, within the firm. The professionals in the management services division see themselves as consultants to the entire corporation with the mission of unfreezing "This colossus and pushing it into the twenty first century." They genuinely believe, like the futurists noted above, that organizations have become so complex and cumbersome that the only (best?) answer for effectiveness is management through the expanded and deepened rationality possible from sophisticated information systems.

What has caused organizations to develop internal processes that lead to increased ineffectiveness? In order to shed light on this question, we need to focus on the pyramidal structure which is the most dominant organizational design in use. It assumes that within respectable tolerances man will behave rationally, that is, as the design requires him to behave.[2]

THE FORMAL ORGANIZATION
AND ITS IMPACT ON THE PARTICIPANTS

There are three aspects of the formal organizational design that are important in generating work requirements for the participants at all levels.

[1] Argyris, C., "How Tomorrow's Executives Will Make Decisions," *Think*, Vol. 33, No. 6 (1967), pp. 18-26.

[2] Argyris, C., *Personality and Organization*, Harper & Row, Publishers, 1957.

They are (1) work specialization, (2) chain of command, and (3) unity of direction. These properties of formal organization have been shown to place (especially the lower level employees) in situations where they tend to be dependent upon and submissive to their superiors; where they experience a very short time perspective and low feelings of responsibility about their work.

Those employees who prefer to experience some degree of challenge, to have some control, to make some decisions will tend to feel frustration and a sense of psychological failure. They may adapt to the frustration and failure by such activities as apathy, indifference, work slow downs, goldbricking, the creation of unions, absenteeism and turnover. Those employees who do not prefer challenging work or control over their work activities will not tend to feel frustrated. They will tend to report satisfaction and involvement, but the latter will not be deep or enduring.

The impact of task specialization, chain of command, and unity of direction is different at the upper levels. At the upper levels the formal design tends to require executives who need to manage an intended rational world, to direct, control, reward and penalize others, and to suppress their own and others' emotionality. Executives with these needs and skills tend to be ineffective in creating and maintaining effective interpersonal relationships; they fear emotionality and are almost completely unaware of ways to obtain employee commitment that is internal and genuine. This results in upper level systems that have more conformity, mistrust, antagonism, defensiveness, and closedness than individuality, trust, concern and openness.

As these dysfunctional activities become embedded in the system and as the defenses that hide their original causes are rigidified and locked into place, there is a tendency in the system to reduce the probability that accurate information will flow through the system. Top management reacts by establishing further controls which feed back to reinforce the original condition that began this causal sequence.

These reactions again tend to reinforce the initial conditions, and so there is a closed loop creating a system with increasing ineffectiveness in problem solving, decision making, and implementation. *In the social universe, where presumably there is no mandatory state of entropy, man can claim the dubious distinction of creating organizations that generate entropy, that is, slow but certain processes toward system deterioration.*

To some readers this analysis may seem overly pessimistic; to others overly optimistic. John Gardner,[3] for example, has gone so far as to suggest that the "dry rot" in organizations will become so bad that they eventually will collapse (a view shared by the writer). Admittedly empirical research is needed if the analysis is to become convincing.

The relevant point for the operations researcher-management scientist however is that his field has been born at the very time our institutions are

[3] Gardner, J., "America in the Twenty-third Century," *The New York Times,* July 27, 1968.

becoming increasingly ineffective. This will place his professional wares in high demand. It will also have the (temporary) advantage of increasing the probabilities that even his early and primitive modelling attempts will be useful. To put it somewhat coarsely, things are so bad that the only way is up. The success however may come as much as a result of the hard thinking and the facing of reality that is required if one attempts to model the world as it does from the use of the models developed. This advantage is not to be disparaged. All of us working in these new fields need all the honeymoon period that we can get.

The difficulty in being born at this time stems from the very advantage just described. As organizations become increasingly ineffective, they tend to produce *valid* information for the *unimportant* and programmed problems and *invalid* information for the important and nonprogrammed problems.[4] The development and successful introduction of a sophisticated MIS is an example of an important and nonprogrammed problem. Thus the climate of rationality needed for the effective construction of an MIS may be very difficult to create.

The Properties of Management Information Systems (MIS) and Their Impact on Management

We are concerned with MIS whose usage can alter significantly the way top managers make important decisions (not those that deal with trivial data that are easily programmable). These are the MIS that help the executive to order and understand the complexity of the present. They are the systems that provide the executive with an opportunity to experiment with different possible future states of his environment and to learn what might be the possible consequences for each state. These are the systems therefore that a top executive may use to simulate the future so that he can increase the probability that his decision processes will produce outcomes which are in some sense fulfilling prophecies.

It is agreed that such systems may be a long way off. However, it seems useful to study these systems as if they existed in order to identify some of the problems that may accompany their introduction and use. Thus the MIS studied in this project, as is the case for many such models, is far from constituting complete systems of this kind. The state of the art is too primitive for such claims. However, in studying the human problems associated with the introduction and acceptance of MIS to management, it is acceptable to focus on the potential of the MIS and the extent of its realization in an application such as this because executives react to the potential as much as (if not more than) to our present delivery capabilities.

---

[4] Argyris, C., "On the Effectiveness of Research and Development Organizations," *American Scientist*, Vol. 56, No. 4 (1968), pp. 344-355.

MIS, like formal pyramidal organizations, are based upon the assumption that organizations are, and should continue to be, intendedly rational. Whereas the traditional scientific management designer of organization attempts to construct organizational structures as they ought to be (forgetting provisionally, at least, the personality interpersonal and group factors) the designer of MIS is more interested in modelling the system in accordance with how individuals actually behave. He focuses on aspects of the functional *and* dysfunctional activities described above. In doing this he acknowledges the relevant formal *and* informal activities. The important criterion for inclusion is that the factors are relevant to solving the problem at hand.

(1) *Reduction of space of free movement.* Whereas the traditional management expert limits his plans to the formal system, the MIS expert enlarges his domain of interest to all relevant factors. Consequently, the MIS expert may ask that behavior, policies, practices and norms that have been operating covertly be surfaced so that their contributions to the problem be made explicit. This requirement can be threatening because what has been hidden may be incriminating to some participants.

Equally important however is that, as the informal is made explicit, it comes under the control of the management. The result may be that the participants will feel increasingly hemmed-in. In psychological language the participants will experience a great restriction of their space of free movement. Research suggests that a restriction of the (psychological) space of free movement tends to create feelings of lack of choice, pressure and psychological failure. These feelings, in turn, can lead to increasing feelings of helplessness and decreasing feelings of self-responsibility resulting in the increasing tendency to withdraw or to become dependent upon those who created or approved the restriction of space of free movement.

(2) *Psychological failure and double bind.* The second impact of MIS upon management is related to the eventual thrust of the MIS on what Carroll has called "global real time" or "on-line, real-time." The salient characteristics of this structure are formal and continuous flows of global information throughout the system and machine involvement in all decision making. The system makes all the important decisions. If the local decision maker sees an opportunity to alter the plan, he asks the console to evaluate his idea and give him a yes or no response. The real-time decisions are made centrally. Ultimately, the real-time decisions will be automated completely.[5] Moreover future planning will be a continual activity primarily carried out by MIS as it is fed information about possible changes.

The impact of such a system can be eventually to create a world for the local decision maker where his daily goals are defined for him, the actions to achieve these goals will be specified, and the level of aspiration will be

[5] Carroll, D. C., "On the Structure of Operational Control Systems," *Operations Research and the Design of Management Information Systems,* John F. Pierce, Jr. (Ed.). Special Tech. Association Publication Stap. No. 4, Chapter 23 (1965), pp. 398-402.

determined, and the performance evaluated, by a system that is external to him. These conditions may lead individual managers to perform as expected. However, they will also lead to a sense of psychological failure (Lewin, Dembo, Festinger, and Sears).[6] Psychological failure occurs whenever someone else defines the individual's goals, path to his goals, his level of aspiration, and criteria for success. Psychological failure, in turn, leads those managers who aspire toward challenging work that requires self-responsibility to be frustrated while those who prefer less challenge and less responsibility are satisfied. The former may leave, fight, or psychologically withdraw; the latter usually stay and withdraw. The manager, in short, because of the MIS, will now tend to experience the frustrations that the employees have experienced in the past as a result of the industrial and quality control engineers who have designed their work and monitored their performance.

The sense of psychological failure is distasteful to human beings such as successful managers who have been accustomed to psychological success. The manager is now in a double bind. If he follows the new rationality he will succeed as a manager and fail as a human being. He is damned if he refuses to obey, and he damns himself if he does obey.

(3) *Leadership based more on competence than on power.* A third impact that the MIS can have upon management is its emphasis upon the use of valid information and technical competence, rather than formal power, to manage organizations. It is not accidental that in models of the actual flow of work events, there is rarely a hierarchy of power positions independent of the work flow. If a decision maker exists, he is in the diagram along the work flow and not above it, as is the case in the traditional models. McDonough and Garrett have described this characteristic of MIS as emphasizing what and how things are done, whereas in traditional models there was an equal, if not greater, emphasis upon who did it.[7]

The MIS is not, however, completely devoid of emphasis on power. In defining a "good criterion" Hitch has been quoted as saying, "The criterion for good criteria is consistency with a good criterion at a higher level."[8] With this definition the MIS expert places himself under the control of the upper levels of management; an action that probably helps to account for his "acceptance" by the upper levels given the problems that we have discussed above and will discuss below.

The difficulties with making valid information and technical competence the new currency for power are several. First, one greatly reduces the probability that managers can order others simply because they have power. This may be threatening to executives who have, up till now, been free to

---

[6] Lewin, K., Dembo, T., Festinger, L., and Sears, P. S., "Level of Aspiration," in J. M. V. Hunt (Ed.), *Personality and the Behavior Disorders*, Ronald Press, New York, 1944, pp. 333-378.

[7] McDonough, A. M., and Garrett, L. J., *Management Systems*, R. D. Irwin and Co., 1965, pp. 18-19.

[8] *Ibid.*

make the organization "move" even if they had incomplete or invalid information.

Second, as we have seen above, is the tendency for organizations to produce invalid information about important issues. An effective MIS will ask the executives to produce precisely that information that they may have learned to withhold (until the appropriate moment) in order to survive.

Thirdly, organizations with properties described above require those executives who enjoy ambiguity, the manipulation of others, and the making of self-fulfilling prophecies. The latter skill is a particularly important one. One of the marks of a successful executive has been that he was able to marshal human and financial resources to make his decisions come true even if others felt that the decision could not be accomplished. These executives enjoyed, indeed needed, to feel that they were fighting and confronting and overcoming a system.[9]

(4) *Decreasing feelings of essentiality.* As MIS becomes more sophisticated there will be less need for ambiguity and self-fulfilling prophecies; there will be less need for "taking hold of the goddam place and turning it around and tightening it up." These activities will now be carried out in a planned and rational way by the MIS.

In other words success, in the past, may have come from selecting an admittedly ambiguous course of action but, with resources and power, making it come to reality. The manager, therefore, had good reason to feel essential and powerful. If a decision was successful, he could point to where his influence was important. With optimal ambiguity and fluidity he could also reduce the probability of being convicted of incompetence if the decision was not successful. The ambiguity and fluidity could have helped him to protect himself from his competitors *and*, when successful, made it possible to assign the feelings of success to himself. The use of sophisticated quantitative models therefore could tend to reduce this protection and the feelings of essentiality on the part of the line manager. One might argue that a line manager could take more risks with an MIS because he could blame the model or those who develop it. Our research suggests such an action is not a psychological risk to the individual. Moreover a line executive would not enhance his position with those above him if his strategy is to blame others.

(5) *Reduction of intra and inter group politics.* Fourthly, a mature MIS reduces the need for organizational politics within but especially among departments. The basic assumption of traditional organizational theory is that the subordinate should focus on fulfilling his departmental responsibilities. It is the superior's task to integrate the several departments into a meaningful whole. Because of such factors as competition, lack of trust, and win-lose dynamics, the subordinate tends to build walls around his department to protect it from competing peers or arbitrary superiors. Given the

[9] Argyris, C., *Integrating the Individual and the Organization,* John Wiley and Sons, 1964; Bennis, W. G., *Changing Organizations,* McGraw-Hill, 1966; and Dalton, M., *Men Who Manage,* John Wiley and Sons, 1958.

interdepartmental rivalries and barriers, interdependence becomes only partially effective, and success may come primarily from constant monitoring by the superior.

Researchers have documented the existence of interdepartmental rivalries where one side must lose and the other win.[10] Competition for scarce resources is high. Indeed many managers believe that interdepartmental competition is healthy. They see it as the best way to assure that departments will make the best possible demands upon the management. This "rabble hypothesis" of management can be shown to have many dysfunctional effects upon interdepartmental cooperation. It is probably the major cause of subordinates developing and maintaining a departmental view whereas their superiors wish that they had a concern for the whole.

The reduction of organizational politics for managing the whole system requires that the relevant departments provide valid information and abide by decisions made by the MIS. The sophisticated MIS no longer views the organization as an aggregate of "hungry, competitive, and angry" units but as a set of interrelated activities that have to be meshed into a whole. In order to do this, the MIS follows a principle that most managers agree with in theory but seldom follow in practice. "The idea is that the activity of any part of an organization has some effect on the activity of every other part. ... Therefore, in order to evaluate any decision of action ... it is necessary to identify all the significant interactions and to evaluate their *combined* impact on the performance of the organization as a whole, not merely on the part originally involved."[11] In order to capture the wholeness of the problem, the technology must deal not only with the behavior of each department, but also with the interrelationships among the departments. This leads the information scientist to seek information from the parts about their relationship with each other and the whole. He hopes to build a model that will show how the departments can be integrated into a fully functioning whole. To succeed means that the departments which have been locked into win-lose conflicts will have to learn to cooperate with each other. Departments with a long history of survival through combat will understandably be skeptical and cautious about being "required" to cooperate.

(6) *New requirements for conceptual thinking.* Finally the sophisticated MIS will require of managers a different level of intellectual and conceptual competence. However, the historical emphasis upon power over competence and fuzziness over explicitness has naturally attracted executives with qualities and competence that are different than those needed if one is to manage with a sophisticated management information technology.

One major difference is the level of conceptualization they are able to employ. In the past, when data was very incomplete much of the intuition

[10] Blake, R. R., Shepard, H. A., and Mouton, J. S., *Managing Intergroup Conflict in Industry,* Gulf Publishing Co., Houston, 1964.

[11] Ackoff, R. L. (Ed.), *Progress in Operations Research,* Vol. 1, John Wiley and Sons, 1961, p. 26.

used by a manager was to fill in the many blanks with possible valid data. This meant that managers focussed on immersing themselves "in the facts" especially as revealed by past practice.

A sophisticated management information system is able to develop a much richer set of data or facts. Past and present experience can be efficiently summarized and presented. The new skill that may be required is for the manager to deal with the interdependence among the facts. But since he has many facts and these produce complex interdependences and since the human mind is a finite information processing system, the demand will be for more effective conceptualization of the data in higher order concepts.[12] This skill typically has been lacking with many managers.[13]

Management science specialists might wish to point out, at this time, that the ultimate goal of a valid information science system is to free the manager from the routine data and permit him to focus on being creative and innovative. Indeed, as Ackoff states, the objective of a valid management information system is to reduce the overabundance of irrelevant information because many managers suffer from information overload. The writer agrees.

Unfortunately, our studies so far indicate that the majority of managers still do not know how to use models as the basis for creative experiments. This is partly due to the fact that experimentation, risk taking and trust, as we say above, have been largely drummed out of managerial systems. This, in turn, tends to assure that men who do not enjoy experimenting will become managers. And for those few brave souls who prefer to experiment, they will probably be faced with an array of control systems to keep their innovations "within bounds."

To summarize: Line management and MIS experts probably agree upon the necessity for organizations being essentially rational phenomena. However, the MIS experts' view of rationally designing systems could lead to some basic changes in the present world of management. The managers may find themselves (1) experiencing increasing amounts of psychological failure yet system success and therefore more double binds; (2) being required to reduce interdepartmental warfare and intradepartmental politics; and (3) finding that the concept of managerial success changes its base from one of power, ambiguity, and self-fulfilling prophecy to valid information, explicitness, and technical competence.

Therefore, sophisticated MIS that introduce in organizations a quantum jump in rationality represent a stressful and emotional problem to the participants.

[12] Miller, G. A., "The Magical Number Seven Plus or Minus Two," *Psychological Review*, Vol. 63 (1956), pp. 81-97.
[13] Anshen, M., "The Management of Ideas," *Harvard Business Review* (July-August 1969), pp. 99-107.

The "New" Degree of Rationality
Creates a "Deeper" Degree of Emotionality.

How would MIS professionals tend to react to stress and emotions?

Before an attempt is made to answer this question a caveat seems in order. The analysis, to date, has attempted to predict the world if and when MIS were fully mature. No claim is made that we have reached such a state or indeed ever will. The position is that as MIS become more sophisticated they will tend to create the conditions described above. However, as we shall point out below, man need not be reactive and submissive to a system. Indeed, it will be our argument that if the MIS were used effectively, they could actually free the manager rather than restrict him. Our pessimistic prediction is that man will not tend to use MIS effectively because of the norms of the existing world and the way he has programmed himself to be more incompetent than competent in dealing with people.

. . .

Some Thoughts on Coping
with the Problems Identified

The reader may ask what can the MSOR Team members and the line executives do to reduce the problems identified above and to increase the probabilities of effective introduction of MIS? The first step is that both groups become aware that the MIS per se is *not* the basic problem. The basic problem is that modern organizations, as we indicated at the outset, are designed with power centralized at the top, with specialization of tasks which results in many concealed dysfunctional components that are revealed by a MIS and that MIS implies a different design for organizations, one where competence is more important than power and collaboration and interdependence are more important than competition. This tends to create many fears and resistances on the part of individuals, groups, and intergroups.

In order for valid advice to become available, much empirical research is needed on the differential impact of the different degrees of these consequences. Rubenstein *et al.* have identified ten variables that could be used in such studies.[14] They are:

---

[14] Rubenstein, A. H., Radnor, M., Baker, N. R., Heiman, D. R., and McColly, J. B., "Some Organizational Factors Related to the Effectiveness of Management Science Groups in Industry," *Management Science*, Vol. 13, No. 8 (April 1967), pp. B508-B518.

1. Level of management support
2. Client receptivity
3. Organizational and technical capability of the OR/MS person or group
4. Organizational location
5. Influence upon organization
6. Reputation
7. Adequacy of the resources
8. Relevance of projects
9. Level of opposition
10. General perception of the level of success

Many researchers have suggested that one way to reduce these problems is to teach managers the basic knowledge about management information science technology. Others suggest that both managers and MIS professionals need to be taught to hold a "mutual understanding." Under such conditions both react to each other in order to enhance their personal gains.[15] The difficulty with these suggestions is that no one, to the writer's knowledge, has ever shown that if such learning is achieved it transfers to real situations when the individuals are fighting a win-lose game and are under high stress. Indeed, our data show that the MIS people, who are well educated in information sciences, have similar emotional problems with each other. They frequently challenge each other's work which leads to the same kinds of strains that exist between themselves and the line managers.

Suggestions to bridge the two cultures by placing line managers in MIS groups and vice versa may help. However, in the writer's experience, when these "fully" educated men enter the arena of conflict and win-lose they may use their knowledge about the other side to decrease the probability that they will win.

In the organization studied, the strategy used was to place a member of the line management on the MIS team to act as a liaison. He was in constant touch with both groups. He made significant inputs into the development of the model. However, these men reported great role strain. They described themselves as men-in-the-middle trying to please and help both sides only to wind up as a hero or a traitor (depending upon which way the decision went).

Others have suggested that MIS may be helped if the team is housed in a management services division, if it has easy access to influential top management, and if it has adequate funds to support some of its activities on a research basis. This group was housed in a management services division and was encouraged by top management to take on a few jobs, primarily on a research basis. The access to the top management however was not easy. But it is not clear what such an access could have achieved. Perhaps both sides

[15] Churchman, C. W., and Schainblatt, A. H., "The Researcher and the Manager: A Dialectic of Implementation," *Management Science*, Vol. 11 (February 1965), pp. B69-B87.

would hesitate to go to the top because the nature of their win-lose intergroup dynamics and lack of communication would become evident to the highest officers.

The primary difficulty with all these strategies is that they assume the problem can be solved rationally. Education and structural rearrangements assume that people will respond rationally to the new stimuli these learnings and changes create. This assumption is valid up to the point where people begin to threaten each other and are in conflict. Then both sides regress and respond ineffectively. Rational solutions may delay the moment of conflict, but they do not get at the underlying problem, namely, no one has been able to program human activity significantly to eliminate or reduce conflict and threat. Moreover, in the cases where it has been attempted the "success" has been due to the fact that the protagonists got the message and suppressed the expression of conflict in front of top management.

This does *not* mean that rational solutions such as education and structural changes will never work. The strategy being suggested is that the competence of *both* managers and MIS professionals in dealing with emotionality and strain in interpersonal and intergroup problems must be raised. As their interpersonal competence in these areas increases they will naturally turn to education and structural changes. We would predict, on the basis of other research, that their commitment to education and the changes will then be internal, not merely external (imposed).[16] Under these conditions the participants would also tend to develop a responsibility of continually monitoring their solutions to correct the failures. In short, the team members may need to be helped to modify their behavior.

Behavioral science research suggests that in order to increase one's interpersonal competence the individual needs to be aware of his self and his defenses. Next, it is helpful if the individual strives to attain a minimum of psychological conflict and an acceptance of his self so that he can create conditions that lead to trust, openness, risk taking, and effective confrontation of conflict.[17]

The focus on interpersonal relations and the expression of feelings should *not* be interpreted to mean that rationality should be substituted for emotionality and interpersonal competence for technical competence. As Rubenstein *et al.* pointed out, a reputation for professional excellence is central to the success of an MIS unit. Openness requires a particular combination of rational *and* emotional communication. Openness does *not* mean that each individual should express whatever is on his mind regardless of any concern for the feelings of others. The aim is to create a situation in which the MSOR Team members can express how they feel in such a manner as to help the line executives express themselves in a similar open manner.

[16] Argyris, C., *Organization and Innovation*, R. D. Irwin and Co., 1965, and Argyris, C., "Interpersonal Barriers to Decision-Making," *Harvard Business Review*, Vol. 44, No. 2 (1966), pp. 84-97.

[17] Argyris, C., *Intervention Theory and Method: A Behavioral View* (in press).

The theory is that emotional problems within organizations do not simply disappear when they are not faced; rather they tend to obstruct the carrying out of rational plans.

Also, the utilization of behavioral science technology requires an awareness of, and competence in, the use of a different set of concepts and conceptual schemes. These schemes, primitive as they may be, are presently either unknown or incompletely known to the MSOR Team members. Moreover, to learn these concepts in such a way that the individual can use them he would be required to undergo learning experiences that may be somewhat painful to him. Concepts about human behavior are most effectively learned by first experiencing them and later relating the concepts to the experience.[18] This means that the learning situations can be designed to help individuals experience and openly talk about their feelings regarding many different complex emotions. But, as we have seen, the expression and exploration of feelings was not one of the strengths of the MSOR Team members.

Developing and increasing interpersonal competence includes becoming aware that high competence is maintained by constant feedback of valid information from others about one's own impact on the others. In order to get relatively valid feedback from others, one must help to create conditions for minimal defensiveness for one's self and the others. These conditions include (1) reducing the formal power of the superior, (2) focussing more on interpersonal competence as a basis for influence, and (3) creating conditions where others can feel free to confront one's self and others on the difficult interpersonal and substantive issues. Such a relationship is significantly different from the way the various team members dealt with authority and influence. They were consistent with their line executives who tend to be controlling and directive.

Finally, there is a necessity to recognize and deal openly with interpersonal interdependence. Individuals are incomplete without others. Again this tends to be at variance with the feeling and beliefs of most of the MSOR Team members. They felt "completed" by relating themselves to a world of symbols, models, and concepts. They tended to resist getting into interpersonal interdependence.

The point being made is that the introduction of a sophisticated information technology is as much an emotional human problem that requires interpersonal competence (as well as technical competence) and that requires knowledge about the human aspects of organizations such as personality, small groups, intergroups, and living systems of organizations norms. Those of us working in these fields are painfully aware of the inadequacy and primitive state of our knowledge. We need help from the management scientist-operations research professional if the relationships between thought and action, as played out in this world, are to be understood and made more effective.

[18] Schein, E. H., and Bennis, W. G., *Personal and Organizational Change Through Group Methods: The Laboratory Approach,* John Wiley and Sons, 1965.

FOR FURTHER READING

Alderfer, Clayton, "An Empirical Test of a New Theory of Human Needs." *Organizational Behavior and Human Performance*, Vol. 4 (1969), 142-175.

Applewhite, Philip B., *Organizational Behavior.* Englewood Cliffs, N.J.: Prentice-Hall, Inc., 1965.

Argyris, Chris, *Interpersonal Competence and Organizational Effectiveness.* Homewood, Ill.: Richard D. Irwin, Inc., 1962.

———, *Personality and Organization.* New York: Harper & Row, Publishers, 1970.

Armstrong, John A., "Sources of Administration Behavior: Some Soviet and Western European Comparisons." *American Political Science Review*, Vol. 59, No. 3 (September 1965), 643-655.

Athos, Anthony, and Robert Coffey, *Behavior in Organizations: A Multidimensional View.* Englewood Cliffs, N.J.: Prentice-Hall, Inc., 1968.

Barnard, Chester I., *The Functions of the Executive.* Cambridge, Mass.: Harvard University Press, 1968.

Bass, Bernard M., and K. M. Thiagarajan, *Transnational Study of Management: Final Report to the Ford Foundation, 1966-69.* Rochester, N.Y.: Management Research Center, Rochester University, 1969.

Bassett, Glen A., *Practical Interviewing: A Handbook for Managers.* New York: American Management Association, 1965.

Bell, Gerald, *Organizations and Human Behavior.* Englewood Cliffs, N.J.: Prentice-Hall, Inc., 1967.

Bennis, Warren G., *Changing Organizations.* New York: McGraw-Hill Book Company, 1966.

———, *et al.,* eds., *Planning of Change,* 2nd ed. New York: Holt, Rinehart & Winston, Inc., 1969.

Berelson, Bernard, and Gary A. Steiner, *Human Behavior: An Inventory of Scientific Findings.* New York: Harcourt, Brace & World, Inc., 1964.

Blake, Robert R., and Jane S. Mouton, "Initiating Organization Development." *Training Directors Journal*, Vol. 19, No. 10 (October 1965), 25-28, 30-32, 34-36, 38-41.

Bruner, J. S., *On Knowing: Essays for the Left Hand.* New York: Atheneum Publishers, 1965.

Buchanan, Paul, "Laboratory Training and Organization Development." *Administrative Science Quarterly*, Vol. 14, No. 3 (September 1969), 467-479.

Burke, Ronald J., "Methods of Resolving Superior-Subordinate Conflict: The Constructive Use of Subordinate Differences and Disagreements." *Organizational Behavior and Human Performance*, Vol. 5, No. 4 (July 1970), 393-411.

Converse, Elizabeth, "The War of All Against All: A Review of the 'Journal of Conflict Resolution,' 1957-1968." *Journal of Conflict Resolution,* Vol. 12, No. 4 (December 1968), 471-532.

Davis, Keith, and George R. Allen, "Length of Time That Feelings Persist for Herzberg's Motivational and Maintenance Factors." *Personnel Psychology,* Vol. 23, No. 1 (Spring 1970), 67-75.

Davis, Keith, *Human Relations at Work,* 2nd ed. New York: McGraw-Hill Book Company, 1962.

De Greene, Kenyon B., ed., *Systems Psychology.* New York: McGraw-Hill Book Company, 1970.

Dickson, G. W., and J. K. Simmons, "The Behavioral Side of MIS." *Business Horizons,* Vol. 13, No. 4 (August 1970), 59-71.

Drucker, Peter, *The Age of Discontinuity.* New York: Harper & Row, Publishers, 1969.

Etzioni, Amitai, *Modern Organizations.* Englewood Cliffs, N.J.: Prentice-Hall, Inc., 1964.

Evans, M. G., "Herzberg's Two-Factor Theory of Motivation: Some Problems and a Suggested Test." *Personnel Journal,* Vol. 49. No. 1 (January 1970), 32-35.

Festinger, Leon, and Daniel Katz, eds., *Research Methods in the Behavioral Sciences.* New York: The Dryden Press, 1953.

Finkle, Robert, and William Jones, *Assessing Corporate Talent: A Key to Managerial Manpower Planning.* New York: John Wiley & Sons, Inc., 1970.

Ford, Robert N., and Edgar F. Borgatta, "Satisfaction with the Work Itself." *Journal of Applied Psychology,* Vol. 54, No. 2 (April 1970), 128-134.

Foss, Laurence, "The Psychedelic Seventies: New Life Styles for Those In Business." *Management of Personnel Quarterly,* Vol. 9, No. 2 (Summer 1970), 2-10.

Foulkes, Fred K., *Creating More Meaningful Work.* New York: American Management Association, 1969.

Gellerman, Saul W., *Motivation and Productivity.* New York: The Macmillan Company, 1968.

Ginsburg, Woodrow L., E. Robert Livernash, Herbert S. Parnes, and George Strauss, *A Review of Industrial Relations Research,* Vol. 1, Madison, Wis.: Industrial Relations Research Association, 1970.

Golembiewski, Robert, and Arthur Blumberg, eds., *Sensitivity Training and The Laboratory Approach: Readings About Concepts and Applications.* Itasca, Ill.: F. E. Peacock Publishers, Inc., 1970.

Goode, William J., and Paul K. Hatt, *Methods in Social Research.* New York: McGraw-Hill Book Company, 1952.

Greenwood, William T., *Management and Organizational Behavior Theories: An Interdisciplinary Approach.* Cincinnati: South-Western Publishing Co., 1965.

Guest, Robert H., *Organizational Change.* Homewood, Ill.: Richard D. Irwin, Inc., 1962.

Hage, Jerald, "An Axiomatic Theory of Organizations." *Administrative Science Quarterly*, Vol. 10, No. 3 (December 1965), 289-320.

_____, and Michael Aiken, *Social Change in Complex Organizations.* New York: Random House, Inc., 1970.

Hardin, W. G., Jr., and L. L. Byars, "Human Relations and Automation." *Advanced Management Journal*, Vol. 35, No. 3 (July 1970), 43-49.

Heany, Donald, "Introducing New Management Techniques Into Your Organization." *Stanford Graduate School of Business Bulletin*, Vol. 34, No. 2 (Autumn 1965), 18-23.

Hershey, Robert, "The Grapevine ... Here To Stay But Not Beyond Control." *Personnel*, Vol. 43, No. 1 (January-February 1966), 62-66.

Hill, Walter A., and Douglas Egan, *Readings in Organization Theory: A Behavioral Approach.* Boston: Allyn and Bacon, Inc., 1967.

Hoglund, Bengt, and Vilian U. Jorgen, *Conflict Control and Conflict Resolution.* New York: Humanities Press, Inc., 1970.

Homans, George C., *Social Behavior: Its Elementary Forms.* New York: Harcourt, Brace & World, Inc., 1961.

House, Robert J., "T-Group Training: Good Or Bad?" *Business Horizons*, Vol. 12, No. 6 (December 1969), 69-77.

House, William C., "Effects of Group Cohesiveness on Organization Performance." *Personnel Journal*, Vol. 45, No. 1 (January 1966), 28-33.

Hunt, J. G., and J. W. Hill, "The New Look in Motivation Theory for Organizational Research." *Human Organization.* Vol. 28 (1969). 100-109.

Hyman, R., *The Nature of Psychological Inquiry.* Englewood Cliffs, N.J.: Prentice-Hall, Inc., 1964.

Kelly, Joe, *Organizational Behavior.* Homewood, Ill.: Richard D. Irwin, Inc., 1969.

Korman, Abraham K., *Industrial and Organizational Psychology.* Englewood Cliffs, N.J.: Prentice-Hall, Inc., 1971.

Knudson, Harry R., Jr., *Human Elements of Administration.* New York: Holt, Rinehart & Winston, Inc., 1963.

Kuriloff, Arthur H., and Stuart Atkins, "T Group for a Work Team." *Journal of Applied Science*, Vol. 2, No. 1 (January, February, March 1966), 63-93.

Lambert, William W., and W. E. Lambert, *Social Psychology.* Englewood Cliffs, N.J.: Prentice-Hall, Inc., 1963.

Lawrence, Paul R., and Jay W. Lorsch, *Organization and Environment: Managing Differentiation and Integration.* Homewood, Ill.: Richard D. Irwin, Inc., 1967.

Lawrence, Paul R., and Jay W. Lorsch, *Developing Organizations: Analysis and Action.* Reading, Mass.: Addison-Wesley Publishing Co., Inc., 1969.

Lawrence, Paul R., and John A. Seiler, *Organizational Behavior and Administration: Cases, Concepts, and Research Findings.* Homewood, Ill.: Richard D. Irwin, Inc., 1965.

Leavitt, Harold J., *Managerial Psychology*. Chicago: University of Chicago Press, 1964.

Levinson, H., *et al.*, *Men, Management, and Mental Health*. Cambridge, Mass.: Harvard University Press, 1962.

Likert, Rensis, *New Patterns of Management*. New York: McGraw-Hill Book Company, 1961.

Lippitt, Gordon L., "Emerging Criteria For Organization Development." *Personnel Administration*, Vol. 29, No. 3 (May-June 1966), 6-11.

————, *Organizational Renewal: Achieving Viability in a Changing World*. New York: Appleton-Century-Crofts, 1969.

Locke, Edwin A., "What Is Job Satisfaction?" *Organizational Behavior and Human Performance*, Vol. 4, No. 4 (July 1969), 309-336.

McClelland, David C., and David G. Winter, *Motivating Economic Achievement*. New York: The Free Press, 1969.

McGregor, Douglas. *The Human Side of Enterprise*. New York: McGraw-Hill Book Company, 1960.

McLuhan, H. M., "The End of Jobs, the Return to Roles." *Administrative Management*, Vol. 31, No. 1 (January 1970), 40.

Maier, Norman R. F., *Psychology in Industry*, 3rd ed. Boston: Houghton Mifflin Company, 1965.

Mann, John, *Changing Human Behavior*. New York: Charles Scribner's Sons, 1965.

Marks, Samuel B., *Breaking the Barriers of Occupational Isolation*. New York: Skill Advancement, Inc., 1966.

————, *Some Factors Influencing the Rating of Professional and Technical Personnel*. Ann Arbor, Mich.: University Microfilms, 1965.

Mead, Margaret, *Anthropology, A Human Science: Selected Papers, 1939-1960*. Princeton, N.J.: D. Van Nostrand, Co., Inc., 1964.

Mockler, R. J., "Theory and Practice of Planning." *Harvard Business Review*, Vol. 48, No. 2 (March-April 1970), 148-150.

Murray, E. J., *Motivation and Emotion*. Englewood Cliffs, N.J.: Prentice-Hall, Inc., 1964.

Murrell, K. F. H., *Ergonomics: Man and His Working Environment*. New York: Barnes & Noble, Inc., 1969.

Myers, Scott M., *Every Employee A Manager: More Meaningful Work Through Job Enrichment*. New York: McGraw-Hill Book Company, 1970.

Odiorne, George S., "A Systems Approach to Training." *Training Directors Journal*, Vol. 19, No. 10 (October 1965), 11-19.

Olson, Mancur, Jr., *The Logic of Collective Action: Public Goods and the Theory of Groups*. Cambridge, Mass.: Harvard University Press, 1965.

Orth, C. O., J. C. Bailey, and F. W. Wolek, *Administering Research and Development, The Behavior of Scientists and Engineers in Organizations*. Homewood, Ill.: Richard D. Irwin, Inc., 1964.

Paterson, T. T., "Organization Theory and the Personnel Manager." *Personnel Management*, Vol. 47, No. 374 (December 1965), 207-211.

Peter, Lawrence J., and Raymond Hull, *The Peter Principle: Why Things Always Go Wrong.* New York: William Morrow & Co., Inc. 1969.

Porter, Lyman, and Edward Lawler, *Managerial Attitudes and Performance.* Homewood, Ill.: Richard D. Irwin, Inc., 1968.

Rigby, Paul H., *Conceptual Foundations of Business Research.* New York: John Wiley & Sons, Inc., 1965.

Rush, Harold M. F., "The Language of Motivation." *Conference Board Record,* Vol. 3, No. 1 (January 1966), 41-46.

Sampson, Robert G., *Managing and Managers: A Realistic Approach to Applying the Behavioral Sciences.* New York: McGraw-Hill Book Company, 1965.

Sayles, Leonard R., *Individualism and Big Business.* New York: McGraw-Hill Book Company, 1963.

Schein, Edgar H. *Organizational Psychology.* Englewood Cliffs, N.J.: Prentice-Hall, Inc., 1965.

————, *Process Consultation: Its Role in Organization Development.* Reading, Mass.: Addison-Wesley Publishing Co., Inc., 1969.

Selltiz, Claire, Marie Jahoda, Morton Deutsch, and Stuart W. Cook, *Research Methods in Social Relations.* New York: Holt, Rinehart & Winston, Inc., 1960.

Simon, Herbert A., *The Shape of Automation for Men and Management.* New York: Harper & Row, Publishers, 1965.

Smelser, Neil J., *The Sociology of Economic Life.* Englewood Cliffs, N.J.: Prentice-Hall, Inc., 1963.

————, and William T. Smelser, eds., *Personality and Social Systems,* 2nd ed. New York: John Wiley & Sons, Inc., 1970.

Stolz, Robert K., "Executive Development—New Perspective." *Harvard Business Review,* Vol. 44, No. 3 (May-June 1966), 133-143.

Sturmthal, A. F., *Workers Councils: A Study of Workplace Organization on Both Sides of the Iron Curtain.* Cambridge, Mass.: Harvard University Press, 1964.

Summer, Charles E., Jr., and Jeremiah J. O'Connell, eds., *Managerial Mind: Science and Theory in Policy Decisions,* rev. ed. Homewood, Ill.: Richard D. Irwin, Inc., 1968.

Tanenbaum, Robert, Irving R. Wechsler, and Frederick Massarik, *Leadership and Organization.* New York: McGraw-Hill Book Company, 1961.

Turner, Arthur N., and Paul R. Lawrence, *Industrial Jobs and the Worker: An Investigation of Response to Task Attributes.* Boston: Harvard Business School, 1965.

Walker, C. R., *Steeltown: An Industrial Case History of the Conflict Between Progress and Security.* New York: Russell & Russell Publishers, 1970.

————, and R. H. Guest, *Man on the Assembly Line.* Cambridge, Mass.: Harvard University Press, 1952.

Walker, James, "Manpower Planning, An Integrative Approach." *Management of Personnel Quarterly,* Vol. 9, No. 1 (Spring 1970), 38-42.

Walton, Richard E., *Interpersonal Peacemaking: Confrontations & Third Party Consultation.* Reading, Mass.: Addison-Wesley Publishing Co., Inc., 1969.

Warren, D. I., "The Effects of Power Bases and Peer Groups on Conformity in Formal Organizations." *Administrative Science Quarterly,* Vol. 14, No. 4 (December 1969), 544-556.

Whisler, Thomas L., *The Impact of Computers on Organizations.* New York: Frederick A. Praeger, Inc., 1970.

Whyte, William F., *Organizational Behavior: Theory and Application.* Homewood, Ill.: Richard D. Irwin, Inc., 1969.

————, and E. L. Hamilton, *Action Research for Management.* Homewood, Ill.: Richard D. Irwin, Inc., 1965.

Winstanley, N. B., "Management 'Incentive' Bonus Plan Realities," *Conference Board Record,* Vol. 7, No. 1 (January 1970), 35-39.

Zand, Dale E., Fred I. Steele, and Sheldon S. Zalkind, "The Impact of an Organizational Development Program on Perceptions of Interpersonal, Group, and Organization Functioning." *Journal of Applied Behavioral Science,* Vol. 5, No. 3 (1969), 393-410.

PART THREE

Planning: Elements of Decision-Making

Clearly, one of the most important talents any manager must possess is the ability to make sound business decisions. To be sure, many key managerial activities must precede and follow the making of decisions. The decision itself, however, its timeliness, as well as its validity with respect to the numerous forces which prompt it, remains *a*, if not *the*, central, or focal, point of managerial effectiveness.

Although this probably always has been true, until recently relatively little attention was focused in the management literature on operational principles for making decisions. What was written tended for the most part to restate long-accepted concepts generally subsumed under the heading "the scientific method." In recent years, however, there has been a rash of books, articles, and courses that carry titles such as "Managerial Decision-Making."

One of the primary reasons for this increased attention stems from two relatively recent and closely related phenomena. First is the increased success and ensuing acceptance of quantitative techniques developed by those working in the fields of operations, or systems, research. Second is the increased availability of high-speed computers and program support, which permit quantification of many elements of the decision-making process. Although these forces have tended to focus more attention on the process of making decisions, they have done so largely because they forced re-examination, if not changes, in the ways managers approached the making of decisions. To utilize, or in some cases defend themselves against, these "new" techniques, many managers were forced to spend more time considering how they had been approaching this key task.

Much of the recently published material on the subject of decision-making has been written by operations researchers, industrial engineers, and econometricians. Their offerings included such standard "concert pieces" as queuing theory or linear programming applied to particular types of decision problems. This was soon followed by more comprehensive concepts like Neo-Baysian probability theory, game theory, and econometric types of model-building techniques.

What troubled many practitioners, who sought first to understand and then to apply these concepts to business decisions, was the gap between those able to develop and apply mathematical techniques, and those who possessed both the bulk of the information needed for making decisions and the responsibility for their implementation. Although much has been done on both sides to narrow this gap, a great deal remains to be done.

Even with this recent progress and optimistic forecasts about further narrowing of the gap, many hold that the quantitative techniques presently available are useful only for certain parts of the decision-making process. Most decisions begin with the identification of a problem or unrealized opportunity. Quantitative techniques may be of value in this first step to the extent that they are used in measurement and control of past performance and in forecasting anticipated conditions. Quantitative approaches may also prove useful in projecting and analyzing the cost-benefit implications of alternative decisions and, therefore, may be of value in assisting the decision-maker in his final choice.

Such quantitative devices, however, are of far less value in moving from first-level identification of problems and unrealized opportunities to a fuller diagnosis of the situation. Much work, which resists the precision of quantification, forces the decision-maker to refine the diagnosis by determining the causes of problems and by flushing out the relationships between the particular decision under consideration and other aspects of the business. Similarly, the value of quantitative techniques for projecting the implications of alternatives in a form that assists in the making of a decision must be preceded by the creative development of alternatives and tempered by nonquantifiable elements of choice.

Partly as a result of the increased focus on managerial decision-making arising from the growth of quantitative techniques, and partly as a result of its increasing stature in the business community, another "voice"—that of the behavioral scientist—is falling on more receptive ears. It is true that much of the material on business decision-making coming from the fields of psychology, sociology, and recently, anthropology, has been directed primarily toward *organizational* aspects of decision-making. In Part Four of this book, which deals with decision-making in the enterprise, this material will be considered. In Part Three, which focuses on the individual manager, we will look, instead, at what the behavioral scientists have to say about so-called "rational" models of *individual* decision-making.

Although there may be as many viewpoints as there are writers on the subject, there appears to be one criticism of the "rational" models common to all who represent the behavioral viewpoint; namely, the definition of rationality. Such writers hold that rationality typically is defined, in these models, solely in terms of economic and company values. Because of such assumptions about the "economic man" and/or the "organization man," behavioralists maintain that so-called "rational" models are too narrowly conceived to have much validity. The failure of quantitative approaches to reflect individual and group differences in values may create serious problems. This is so, behavioralists feel, because the errors in early "intuitive" approaches, which stemmed from oversimplification about values and rationality, may now be hardened in the concrete of quantification with which the mathematician builds his models.

To the behavioralist, models of individual decision-making must reflect more of the psychological aspects of how individuals behave in decision-making situations. The models must reflect findings from studies on perception, concept formation, and resolution of conflict.

It is not our purpose to reconcile the differences among those presenting the several schools of thought dealing with decision-making. We have tried, through the selection of representative readings, to reflect the major viewpoints and to highlight areas of agreement and disparity. In the pieces that follow, you will find such representation. We leave the task of integration, if not to the reader, to more venturesome theorists and practitioners.

19

Why the Rational View?

DONALD SCHON

We begin this section with a selection from Donald Schon's much acclaimed book, Technology and Change. *In this work, which is a very thoughtful and critical analysis of technological change in industry and its impact on various aspects of American society, Schon pauses to ask why, in the face of much evidence to the contrary, so many of us cling to what he considers the "myth" of rationality as a progenitor of innovation.*

Because he believes that "nonrationality and uncertainty" are so much a part of innovative planning, Schon feels that any superimposition of a rational approach to invention would be self-defeating.

Reprinted from Donald A. Schon, *Technology and Change*, pp. 37-41, by permission of the publisher. A Seymour Lawrence Book/Delacorte Press. Copyright 1967 by Donald A. Schon.

As you read this section try to separate Schon's views into two groups: those that apply to decision-making in general and those that pertain to elements of decision-making that concern the generation of truly innovative alternatives. Is Schon guilty of considering decision-making or planning in terms of only one of its key elements, namely, generating innovative alternatives? Or, in your opinion, do his points apply equally to all aspects of decision-making and planning?

In view of [all the evidence to the contrary] ... we must ask why so many in industry have believed the rational myths of invention and innovation.

There is more than one answer. One key to the question lies in the very nonrationality and uncertainty of invention and innovation. A man may state the rational view when he is describing a process in which he has no part, or when he is trying to tell others how to do it, or to exhort others to do it, or, again, when he is reassuring himself about it. It may function, in short, as a device. It is then an idealized, after-the-fact view of invention and innovation—invention and innovation as we would like them to be so that they can be controlled, managed, justified—rather than invention and innovation as they are. It is a view designed to calm fears, gain support or give an illusion of wisdom.

This attraction of the rational view is easy to understand. Uncertainty is frightening. If the development of new products and processes is unavoidable—as it is coming to seem in a growing number of corporations—it is cold comfort that most new products fail, that invention is full of unanticipated events, that innovation is inherently uncertain and subject to a treacherous cost curve. It is far more cheering, even apparently necessary, to believe that invention and innovation are essentially rational, deliberate processes in which success is assured by intelligent effort. As a result, uncertainty becomes taboo, unmentionable, especially in the context of important corporate decisions. It may seem necessary then to have a clear and rational view of where we have been and where we are going and to believe that the future is essentially predictable and controllable, if only we gather the right facts and draw the right inferences from them. We suppress the surprising, uncertain, fuzzy, treacherous aspects of invention and innovation in the interest of this therapeutic view of them as clear, rational and orderly. Armed with this myth, managers make decisions and mobilize resources. They and their subordinates must then live out the actual uncertainty of the process.

But there is another answer to the question, Why the rational view?, which focuses on its partial truth and on its utility.

For one thing, the rational view of invention and innovation is more nearly correct for more nearly marginal inventions. The less significant the invention, the more the process tends to be orderly and predictable. The more radical the invention, the less rationality and predictability.

We can represent the universe of new products and processes by a target-like diagram (Figure 1). In the outer rings are those inventions whose acceptance requires least change. They are hardly inventions at all, in the usual sense of the term: a new cake-mix flavor, a new package design, a slightly different fabric weave. These inventions require little or no change in the technology. They do not significantly advance the state of the art. They require no modification of scientific theory. Production equipment can be made to handle them with only minor change. Little or no rethinking of the corporate organization or approach is required.

As we move toward the center of the diagram, however, we encounter inventions like synthetic fibers, transistors, freeze-drying, television. These carry with them major changes in technology; their introduction goes hand in hand with change in scientific theory. They command new concepts in marketing and new marketing organization, as well as radically different production equipment and major new investments. They force corporate organization itself to undergo major change.

Between these extremes are inventions like powder metallurgy, stretch fabrics, polyethylene-coated paper and fiberglass boats.

Figure 1   Comparison of equal cost alternatives.

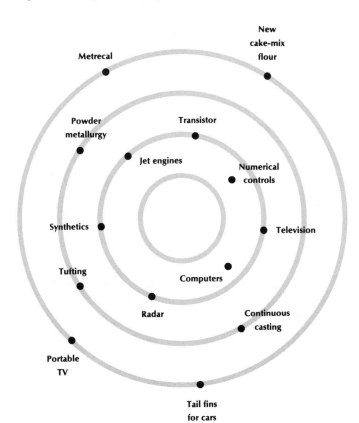

Needless to say, these assignments within the diagram are only approximate. The question of degree of novelty is complex. A technically insignificant invention, like individually packaged food products, may require major changes in marketing. A major technological invention, nylon, required surprisingly little change in textile machinery. A corporation's decision to market a product, new for it but old for the industry, may require major corporate reorganization. Radical novelty in *any* of these senses may be fraught with uncertainties and surprise. There is also an unusual optical effect: what looks like trivial change from afar may appear monumental close-up and from within. The decision to go national with a regional product or to market a "king-size package" may require considerable change in several corporate domains.

Degree of novelty should not be confused with magnitude of effort. A relatively small development—for example, a new electronic component—may require for its acceptance major change in technology and in corporate structure. A large-scale effort, such as a new missile system, may require little more than a scaling up of proved engineering devices and principles, entailing little disruption of the technology and little organizational change.

In any case, the more peripheral the development, the less change required for acceptance, the more the development tends to conform to the rational view of invention.

It is also true that relatively unlimited dollars available for development tend to blur the nonrational character of invention and innovation. When, for all practical purposes, money doesn't matter—as in the case of the development of a crucial weapon in time of war—an objective can be stated at the outset and many parallel paths to its attainment undertaken. Unexpected failures, unexpected twists in the development process, can be put aside or exploited. After success has been achieved, the history of the development may be rewritten to display the straight line connecting means and end, familiar in the historical revisionism common to the field of innovation. Surprises and uncertainties may be drowned in a sea of dollars.

It is, of course, disappointing when such developments are taken as models for more normal, limited industrial efforts. The Manhattan Project, which exercised such an influence on industrial research after World War II, makes a poor model for technical innovation in industry.

But there is another sense in which belief in the rational view may be justified. There may be utility in acting *as if* it were true.

The process of planning, which assumes the rational view, may be useful even though plans are bound to be inadequate. The formulation of objectives for technical effort provides direction for the effort and a stimulus for action, even though the objectives will have to be modified in light of discoveries made in the process. There is utility in the formulation of such objectives, provided this flexibility is allowed and expected; otherwise, they strangle invention. There is utility in mapping out stages in the development process and identifying checkpoints along the way, even though the development plan will require radical revision. Provided that such revision is not required as a confession of failure, plans of this sort may give discipline for evaluation and direction of effort; otherwise, such plans stand in the way of invention.

Planning the process of invention and innovation, which assumes the goal-directed, orderly structure of the rational view, has utility as a programing device. It is useful when treated as something from which to deviate. It is false and harmful when treated as a hard-and-fast methodology or an accurate description of the process of innovation. We must add that so strong is the attraction of the rational view, plans that begin as flexible programing devices frequently congeal as master plans or myths about the process.

Planning in the flexible sense, and with it, assumption of the rational view for planning purposes, does not change the nonrational character of invention or the character of innovation as a confrontation with uncertainty requiring leaps of decision. It is, rather, a way of living with those very characteristics.

20

How to Make an Intelligent Decision

ROBERT L. HEILBRONER

In contrast to some of the views expressed by Schon in the previous selection, consider this short and most readable piece. One of the most concise statements on the basic steps to take in producing rational decisions, this selection offers a decidedly different perspective on how to approach a decision in an orderly way without having rationality become an obstacle to imagination.

Pay particular attention to the author's observations on potential psychological obstacles to decision-making and relate them to selection 23, in which Charles Lindblom offers several concrete suggestions on how to channel certain types of decisions through a looser framework of rationality in the hopes of accomplishing Heilbroner's objectives in the light of real-world obstacles to ordered analysis.

There is nothing in the world so common and ordinary and yet so agonizingly difficult as a tough decision. Most of us have marched up to some crossroad in our lives—whether or not to get married, to change jobs, to

Reprinted from *Think* magazine, December 1960, pp. 2-4, by permission of the publisher and the author. Copyright 1960 by the Reader's Digest Assn., Inc., Pleasantville, N.Y.

choose this or that career—and experienced the awful feeling of not knowing which route to choose. Worse yet, many of us have known what it is like, after a paralyzing wait, to start down one road with the sinking sensation that we've picked the wrong one.

Ever since Adam and Eve made the wrong one, decisions have been bedeviling people. Damn-fool decisions and half-cocked decisions lie behind much of the unhappiness of life. More pathetic yet is the misery caused by no decision. "Everything comes to him who waits," writes Bill Gibson, in *The Seesaw Log*, "—too late."

What makes us decide things badly, when we "know better"? What is it that sometimes stalls our decision-making machinery entirely? There is no single or simple reason why decisions are the pitfall of our lives. A high school senior who sits with his pencil wavering between the True and False answers on an examination may be baffled by the difficulty of the questions, or may simply be reduced to a blue funk by the pressure of taking an exam. A young woman in the throes of indecision over a marriage proposal may be trying to weigh the pros and cons of a tangled life situation, or may be panicked by the thought of marriage itself. Foolish decisions and indecision are the consequence not only of the complexity of the world about us, but of the complicated crosscurrents of the world within us.

Whatever their causes, the agonies of decision making are often magnified because we go about making up our minds so ineffectively. Faced with a hard choice, we allow our thoughts to fly around, our emotional generators to get overheated, rather than try to bring our energies to bear as systematically as we can.

There is no ABC for decision making. But there are a few guidelines that have helped others, and we can use them to help ourselves.

MARSHAL THE FACTS

A lot of the mental anguish of decision making comes because we often worry in a factual vacuum. An endless amount of stewing can be avoided if we do what all good executives do with a problem that can't be settled: send it back for more data. Dale Carnegie once quoted a distinguished university dean as saying, "If I have a problem that has to be faced at three o'clock next Tuesday, I refuse to try to make a decision about it until Tuesday arrives. In the meantime I concentrate on getting all the facts that bear on the problem. And by Tuesday, if I've got all the facts, the problem usually solves itself."

But just gathering facts won't solve hard problems. "The problem in coming to a firm and clear-sighted decision," says Lt. General Thomas L. Harrold, veteran infantry commander and now commandant of the National War College, "is not only to corral the facts, but to marshal them in good order. In the Army," General Harrold explains, "we train our leaders to draw up what we call an Estimate of the Situation. First, they must know their objective. Unless you know what you want, you can't possibly decide how to get it. Second, we teach them to consider *alternative* means of attaining that objective. It's very rarely that a goal, military or any other, can be realized in only one way. Next we line up the pros and cons of each alternative, as far as we can see them. Then we choose the course that appears most likely to achieve the results we want. That doesn't guarantee success. But at least it allows us to decide as intelligently as the situation permits. It prevents us from going off on a half-baked hunch that may turn out to be disastrous."

Some people, however, *misuse* the idea of fact-collecting. They go on and on getting advice, gathering data, and never seem to be able to clinch the case. When we find ourselves assembling more and more facts without coming to any clear conclusions, without acting, it's time to be suspicious. Frequently we are merely waiting for the "right" fact which will rationalize a decision we have already made.

An executive of a New York placement agency tells of a young man who couldn't make up his mind whether or not to take a job that involved a move out of town. He kept coming back for more and more information until one day he learned that the company had had tough sledding during the '30's and nearly closed down. That clinched it. With obvious relief the young man "reluctantly" turned the job down.

"Actually," the placement official comments, "it was clear that he didn't want to move. But he had to find a 'fact' to make his decision respectable in his own eyes."

When we reach this point, it is time to stop fact-collecting.

CONSULT YOUR FEELINGS

The psychiatrist Theodore Reik, when still a young man, once asked Sigmund Freud about an important decision he had to make. "I can only tell you of my personal experience," Freud replied. "When making a decision of minor importance I have always found it advantageous to consider all the pros and cons. In vital matters, however, such as the choice of a mate or a profession, the decision should come from the unconscious, from somewhere within ourselves. In the important decisions of our personal life, we should be governed, I think, by the deep inner needs of our nature."

We can usually tell when a decision accords with our inner nature by the enormous sense of relief that it brings. Good decisions are the best tranquilizers ever invented; bad ones often increase our mental tension. When we have decided something against the grain, there is a nagging sense of incompletion, a feeling that the last knot has not been pulled out of the string.

TIMING

We must learn to distinguish between our deep-running characters and our transient moods. There is an old rule that we should sleep on big decisions, and contemporary psychological research has established that the rule is sound.

Data from questionnaires answered by some 500 persons at Columbia University's Bureau of Applied Social Research show that our behavior is affected by our passing moods. When we are blue, low, our actions tend to be aggressive and destructive; when we are in good spirits, all fired up, our behavior swings toward tolerance and balance. Everyone knows that the boss is more apt to make lenient decisions when he's in a good mood, and that it's no time to ask him for a raise when he comes into the office glowering. We do well to take account of our emotional temperatures before we put important decisions on our *own* desks. On paydays, for example, we are all apt to be a little happy-go-lucky, especially about money decisions; on days when we've had a run-in with our wife or the day's work has gone all wrong, we are apt to decide things harshly, pessimistically, sourly.

A sense of timing also requires that we know when *not* to make a decision. "In surgery," says Dr. Abram Abeloff, surgeon at New York's Lenox Hill Hospital, "a doctor often studies a situation for days or even weeks until he feels reasonably confident to go ahead. Time itself is an essential component of many decisions. It brings uncertain situations to a head. Premature decisions are the most dangerous a person can make."

Consciously postponing a decision—deciding not to decide—is not the same as indecision. As Chester I. Barnard, first president of the New Jersey Bell Telephone Company, has put it in a famous book on business leadership, *The Functions of the Executive*: "The fine art of executive decision consists in not deciding questions that are not now pertinent, in not deciding prematurely, is not making decisions that others should make."

In ordinary life, as well as in business and medicine, many of the most involved and difficult decisions are best not "made," but allowed to ripen. Facts accumulate, feelings gradually jell and, as Barnard says, other people take a hand in the situation. By holding ourselves back—refusing to plunge in the moment our adolescents ask us, "Should I go to college?" "Should I enlist in the Army now, or should I wait?"—we give complicated situations a chance to work themselves out, and sometimes save ourselves a great deal of exhausting and useless brain-cudgeling.

FOLLOW-THROUGH

We all know that decisions do not mean much unless we back them with the will to carry them out. The alcoholic decides a thousand times to give up drink; the smoker vows again and again that this is his last cigarette. Many times an inability to make up our minds reflects just such an unwillingness to *go through* with a decision. "Thinking," wrote the great Swiss psychiatrist Otto Fenichel, "is preparation for action. People who are afraid of actions increase the preparation."

Thus, indecision can sometimes help us *clarify* our minds. It can be the signal flag that forces us to look beyond the immediate point at issue into the follow-through that a decision demands of us. Frequently, when we make fools of ourselves at a retail counter, trying to decide which gift to buy, we are wrestling with a quite different problem such as our unconscious feelings about the person for whom we're selecting the gift. At a more serious level, an unhappily married woman, endlessly debating with herself whether or not to ask for a divorce, may in fact be avoiding the more difficult question of what she would do with her life if she *were* divorced.

FLEXIBILITY

Part of the worrisomeness of decision making comes from a natural tendency to overstress the *finality*, the once-for-allness of our choices. There is much more "give" in most decisions than we are aware. Franklin D. Roosevelt, for example, was a great believer in making flexible decisions. "He rarely got himself sewed tight to a program from which there was no turning back," his Secretary of Labor, Frances Perkins, once observed.

"We have to do the best we know how at the moment," he told one of his aides. "If it doesn't turn out all right, we can modify it as we go along."

Too many of us find decisions painful because we regard them as final and irrevocable. "Half the difficulties of man," Somerset Maugham has written, "lie in his desire to answer every question with yes or no. Yes or no may neither of them be the answer; each side may have in it some yes and some no."

Sometimes, naturally, we have to answer a question with a firm yes or no. But even then it is often possible to modify our answer later. That's why some advisers counsel: "When in doubt, say no. It's a lot easier to change a no to a yes, than vice versa."

THE FINAL INGREDIENT

Finally, there is one last consideration to bear in mind. In making genuinely big decisions we have to be prepared to stand a sense of loss, as well as gain. A student who hesitates between a lifetime as a teacher or as a businessman, a talented young girl trying to make up her mind between marriage and a career, face choices in which sacrifice is involved, *no matter what they do*. That's one reason why big decisions, in contrast to little ones, do not leave us exhilarated and charged with confidence, but humble and prayerful.

It helps to talk big decisions over with others—not only because another's opinion may illumine aspects of the dilemma that we may have missed, but because in the process of talking we sort out and clarify our own thoughts and feelings. Talk, as a clergyman and the psychiatrist both know, has a cathartic effect; it gives vent to feelings which may otherwise be expressed, not always wisely, in actions.

After this, meditation, reflection—letting the problem stew in its own juice—can also help. But in the end, after talk and thought, one ingredient is still essential. It is courage.

"One man with courage makes a majority," said Andrew Jackson; and this was never more true than in the election of our minds where the one vote we cast is the deciding one.

21

Do Managers Find Decision Theory Useful?

REX V. BROWN

Several years ago a number of concepts emerging from the growing field of operations research were linked together in a sequential approach to decision-making that came to be known as "decision theory" or "decision-theory analysis." This approach has now been tried in countless organizations on a wide variety of decisions and with rather mixed success.

Brown offers an excellent description of this approach and a critical review of its application. Consider, as you read this selection, the degree to which the approach may lend itself to certain types of individuals as well as to certain types of decisions. Do you feel Brown's conclusions support or contradict Schon's concerns? Do they persuade you that decision theory analysis is a logical extension of Heilbroner's approach, or do you feel that the necessary precision and need to quantify conflict with the philosophy that underlies Heilbroner's recommendations? You may find it helpful in answering these questions to read on and consider the suggestions contained in the Miller and Starr selection.

For thousands of years, businessmen have been making decisions in the face of uncertainty about the future. Such decisions have often served to separate "the men from the boys" in business—and perhaps always will. In

Reprinted from the *Harvard Business Review*, May-June 1970, pp. 78-89. Copyright 1970 by the President and Fellows of Harvard College. All rights reserved.

Author's note: I wish to acknowledge the assistance of Paul Vatter, Howard Raiffa, Stanley Buchin, and Robert Buzzell in arranging contacts for the survey discussed in this article.

recent years, however, the problem executives face has been altered by the introduction of a set of techniques of quantitative analysis which I shall refer to here as Decision Theory Analysis (DTA). ...

As might be expected when a radically new approach is used, business executives have often found DTA methods frustrating and unrewarding. Nevertheless, there is a steadily growing conviction in the management community that DTA should and will occupy a very important place in an executive's arsenal of problem-solving techniques. Only time can tell if, as some enthusiasts claim, decision theory will be to the executive of tomorrow what the slide rule is to the engineer of today. But clearly, in my opinion, the *potential* impact of DTA is great.

The primary purpose of this article, which is based on a survey of 20 companies made in 1969, is to present some of the experiences of practitioners who have been exploring various applications of DTA techniques to management decision making. ...

...The companies included three organizations with several years of active experience with DTA (Du Pont, Pillsbury, and General Electric); a sampling of corporations that have taken up DTA in the past two or three years and are now quite active in employing it (e.g., General Mills and Inmont Corporation); one or two organizations whose experience with DTA has been disappointing; a few companies (such as Ford Motor and Time, Inc.) where there is a definite interest in DTA but—at least, as of 1969—little application; and a couple of consulting firms with well-known expertise in the area (notably Arthur D. Little, Inc. and McKinsey & Company).

During the course of the survey, particular attention was focused on such questions as the following, which will be discussed in this article:

○ What tangible impact does DTA have on how businesses are run and on how individual decisions are made?

○ What areas of decision making is DTA best suited for?

○ What practical benefits result?

○ What trends in usage are apparent?

○ What obstacles and pitfalls lie in the way of more effective usage?

○ What organization steps should management take to use DTA more effectively?

○ What remains to be done in developing and expanding the usefulness of DTA?

DTA IN REVIEW

Before turning to the findings of the survey, let us review some of the elements of DTA. (The theory does not, by the way, always go under this name. Sometimes it is called "Personalist Decision Theory" or "Bayesian Decision Theory.")

First, what information does DTA demand of the executive? It requires such inputs as executive judgment, experience, and attitudes, along with any "hard data," such as historical records. In particular, the executive is asked to:

1. Stipulate what decision alternatives are to be considered in the analysis of a problem.
2. Make a probabilistic statement of his assessment of critical uncertainties.
3. Quantify some possible consequences of various actions and his attitudes toward these consequences.

The logically preferred decision can then be derived routinely according to the highly developed statistical theory that underlies DTA, using decision trees, computer programs, and/or other computational devices.

The use of DTA is not restricted to investment, marketing, or other types of business decisions. Potential and actual applications are also to be found in the area of medical, military, engineering, and governmental decisions. The most ambitious application of decision theory yet reported apparently was employed in the hypothetical problem of whether to push the nuclear button if the President receives different kinds of ambiguous evidence of an impending Russian attack on the United States.

The analyst does not need to keep in his head all the considerations that are taken into account, and, indeed, all the considerations do not need to be evaluated by the same person (although whoever makes the decision must *accept* the evaluations). For instance:

○ The company president might determine the company's attitude toward risk in new product planning.
○ The vice president of marketing might choose the business decisions to be compared.
○ The director of research might provide information on development times, likely success in solving technical problems, and so on.
○ The probable costs might come from the controller's office.
○ The probable sales might come from a sales manager or forecasting specialist.

Contentious elements in the analysis can be lifted out, and revised assessments substituted for them, without the analyst's having to reconsider every issue.

. . .

While, in principle, any decision problem *can* be analyzed by DTA methods, this is a very far cry from arguing that it always *should* be. In various instances, traditional decision making may be more economical, practical, and sound than modern methods of quantitative analysis. ...

Growing Use

Only a few U.S. companies appear to have used DTA in operations for any length of time. Two of these companies are Du Pont, which got started with the approach in the late 1950's, and Pillsbury, which got started in the early 1960's. However, there has been a dramatic increase in DTA activity since about 1964.

. . .

□ General Electric set up an intensive study of DTA by a high-level committee that led to major changes in plant appropriation methods.

□ Ford Motor and other companies put literally hundreds of their middle and senior managers through training programs varying in length from a few days to several weeks.

□ Other companies, including General Mills, began to introduce DTA on a project-by-project basis.

IMPACT ON DECISION MAKING

Since the companies in the survey were selected on the basis of their actual or imputed use of DTA, no special significance can be attached to the fact that most of them do indeed use the tools. What is significant, in my opinion, is that even these companies, leaders though they are, do not show drastic changes in their general decision-making procedures as a result of DTA. However, *individual* decisions are often profoundly affected. Examples from the experience of the most active companies interviewed—Du Pont, Pillsbury, GE, and Inmont—give some measure of how DTA is being used by managers.

Application at Du Pont

Substantial DTA activity is going on throughout the Du Pont organization, stimulated by staff groups in the Development Department and elsewhere. Managers in the various departments have shown increasing interest in the staff groups' services (which are supplied for a fee) during the past ten years. Yet, even after all this time, Dr. Sig Andersen, manager of one of the consulting groups and perhaps the most prominent figure in the application of DTA, says he feels that DTA has not yet reached the point where it really has a major impact at the general manager level in Du Pont. J. T. Axon, Manager of the Management Sciences Division, says:

"I think [Andersen and his colleagues] have indeed been pioneers and missionaries on behalf of DTA within Du Pont, and I share with them the conviction that their work has improved the quality of numerous decisions around the company. Their impact has been seriously limited, however, by the absence of appropriate educational efforts aimed at the decision makers. Even at this date, we have in Du Pont, in my judgment, very few key decision makers who are "alive" to the possibilities of DTA and comfortable in its use. It is this lack that has dragged down the Du Pont effort."

At Du Pont middle and even senior managers increasingly will take action or submit recommendations that include DTA along with more conventional analyses, but the presentation to top management is likely to be supported by more informal reasoning, not DTA. Thus:

☐ In the case of a new product which had just reached the prototype stage at Du Pont, the question before management was: On what scale should initial pilot production be carried out? Critical uncertainties involved the reliability of the military demand for which the prototype had been originally designed, and the amount of supplementary commercial business that would be generated.

DTA was performed on a computer to produce "risk profiles" of return on investment for various plant sizes and pricing strategies. The inputs included probability assessments of demand for each possible end-use of the product (based on market research), as well as assessments of cost and timing. The analysis indicated that, on the basis of the assessments used, a certain price was optimal, and a $3-million pilot plant would have the highest expected rate of return.

When this conclusion was transmitted to top management, it was couched in the language of informal reasoning, not of DTA. Management opted for a smaller, $1-million plant, but adopted—unchanged—the pricing recommendation of the study. It appears that top management, without explicitly disagreeing with the assumptions underlying the analysis, possessed an aversion to risk which was not assumed in the analysis.

Pillsbury's Approach

James R. Petersen, Vice President of The Pillsbury Company and General Manager of the Grocery Products Company, uses decision trees regularly in evaluating major recommendations submitted to him. More than a dozen marketing decisions a year are approved by him on the basis of the findings of detailed DTA. (Many more decisions in his divisions are rendered after first using a skeletal decision tree to clarify the key problem issues.)

Typically, a middle manager in the Grocery Products Company will spend a week or so developing a DTA approach, often with the help of a staff specialist. When the middle manager's recommendation comes to be considered by Petersen, this analysis is the vehicle for discussion. For instance:

◻ In one case, the issue before management was whether to switch from a box to a bag as a package for a certain grocery product. Petersen and his sales manager had been disposed to retain the box on the grounds of greater customer appeal. The brand manager, however, favored the bag on cost considerations. He supported his recommendation with a DTA based on his own best assessments of probable economic, marketing, and other consequences. Even when the sales manager's more pessimistic assessments of the market impact of a bag were substituted for the brand manager's, the bag still looked more profitable. Petersen adopted the recommendation, the bag was introduced, and the profits on the product climbed substantially.

During the course of discussions, some Pillsbury executives urged that the bag be test-marketed before management made a firm decision. The original DTA showed, however, only a one-in-ten chance that the bag would prove unprofitable—and if that occurred, it would probably be not too unprofitable. A simple, supplementary DTA showed that the value of making a market test could not remotely approach its cost. Accordingly, no test marketing was undertaken. Management's confidence in the analysis was later confirmed by the bag's success.

Uses at GE

At General Electric there has recently been a formal head office requirement that all investment requests of more than $500,000 be supported by a probabilistic assessment of rate of return and other key measures. In the wake of this requirement, and largely in the area of plant appropriations, more than 500 instances of computerized DTA have been recorded over the past four years.

Heavy use is made of a library of special DTA programs developed largely by Robert Newman, Manager of Planning Services, who works with managers in other GE operations on a consulting basis. The consulting relationship, no doubt enhanced by Newman's own experience in line management, often has an impact on issues beyond the scope of the originating inquiry, as this example shows:

◻ One GE division was faced with a shortage of manufacturing capacity for a mature industrial product. Using the information and assessments supplied by the division manager (including a suspicion that the product was obsolescent), Newman spent a few hours on a DTA which suggested that the division should not increase capacity, but raise prices. Both the consultant and the manager felt uneasy about this conclusion.

Further discussion yielded new but confidential information that the division was developing a product which promised to supplant the old one. This intelligence, plus various estimates of the probability of success and related matters, led to a new DTA (which employed GE's pre-packaged computer programs). This study pointed to the conclusion that research and development expenditures on the new product should be increased by a factor of 20. The recommendation was adopted, the new product went into production two years later, and it achieved highly profitable sales of some $20 million a year.

Inmont's Programs

Although Inmont Corporation's usage of DTA is less extensive than that of the three companies just discussed, James T. Hill, President, comments that he often uses computer simulations in evaluating potential acquisition candidates. Preliminary information available on such candidates is programmed into a model by his assistant. This model is part of a prepackaged DTA simulation program which merges Inmont and the acquisition candidate according to the specific purchase strategy that Inmont is contemplating. The computer prints out detailed information as to the cost to Inmont and the return to the individual shareholders of the acquired company, including a pro forma balance sheet and income statement both before and after conversion of convertible securities.

Once the results are reviewed by Hill and his top executives, any alternative financing schemes that have been suggested can be explored in a matter of minutes in order to determine the best financial plan. Computer terminals are available at strategic decision-making locations in the head office, and the program is designed so as to enable any executive's secretary to put in data for different possible modes of acquisition. It is an easy matter, therefore, for alternative strategies to be evaluated quickly at any stage in the decision-making process.

When the most desirable financial approach has been determined, a second program can be utilized to run projected pro forma balance sheets and income statements for any period into the future. This program uses probability theory to arrive at the "best guess" as to the outcome of various operating strategies. It also enables executives to determine the factors most crucial to the future return on investment of a proposed merger. This "sensitivity analysis" thus focuses on the critical questions with which Inmont's management would have to deal if it were to undertake the acquisition.

This is what Hill says about Inmont's use of the procedure:

"The two programs, together, help ensure that the decision as to a potential acquisition is made after a comprehensive analysis of alternatives. It is not necessary to choose only one method of financing or one method of operation, for example. Rather, it is possible to explore, in a very short period of time, numerous strategies to discover that which will maximize the benefits to the merged companies. It is understood that the decision is no better than the reliability of the inputs, including the assigned probabilities."

Various other companies responding to my survey report that they are using DTA on a more-or-less systematic basis for marketing and allied decisions, most frequently in the area of new product selection and development, but also in promotion, pricing, test marketing, and other activities. In fact, about 50 specific applications of DTA to marketing problems are noted—and some of these will be mentioned subsequently in this article.

OBSTACLES AND PITFALLS

Enthusiasm for DTA is very great in many quarters. For example, Robert Newman of General Electric predicts:

"Within 10 years, decision theory, conversational computers, and library programs should occupy the same role for the manager as calculus, slide rules, and mathematical tables do for the engineer today. The engineer of Roman times had none of these, but he could make perfectly good bridges. However, he could not compete today, even in bridge building, let alone astro-engineering. Management is today at the stage of Roman engineering. Needless to say, managers will still use specialists, just as engineers use heat transfer experts."

While Newman's time schedule may be optimistic, my survey findings in no way contradict the substance of his view. However, a number of more or less serious obstacles—many no doubt attributable to inexperience in using DTA—lie in the path of a major revolution such as Newman envisages.

Personal Competence

It is clear that companies will experience only limited success with a new analytical approach like DTA unless they have executives who are alive to its possibilities and use it effectively. While there is a substantial and rapidly expanding number of DTA-oriented executives in positions to influence management decisions, they represent a tiny fraction of the total managerial pool. The momentum of educational processes will remedy this problem in time—but it will take time. ...

. . .

However, even if there were no manpower shortage, serious obstacles to successful and expanding use of DTA would still exist. Removing them may require more deliberate initiative and research on management's part than will correcting the lack of line and staff training.

Uncertainty over Return

For one thing, no substantial personal or corporate benefits of using the technique may be apparent to the potential user. Many effective managers have a "show me" attitude toward new decision-making techniques, and as yet there is little to show. Indeed, no firm evidence is available to prove that DTA *does* have widespread practical value. The evidence from my survey is encouraging, but far from conclusive; enough disappointments have been reported to sustain the doubts harbored by many businessmen. For example:

□ A central staff team for an international manufacturer of industrial components carried out a sophisticated and competent DTA designed to help a regional subsidiary choose which of several alternative markets to compete in. When the DTA part of the study was presented to the subsidiary's president, however, he perceived it as having little relevance to him in his decision making. He told me that the market forecast and other input data gathered for the analysis were certainly of substantial value to him, but he could not see that the DTA itself added much that was useful. Indeed, while the market data provided a basis for much of the subsidiary's subsequent strategy, no specific action appeared to be traceable to the DTA part of the study (though some people in the company felt that the analysis had some diffuse influence on several decisions).

The managers of the subsidiary are seeking to adapt the DTA to meet their needs, and the prospects look encouraging. Moreover, the staff team from the head office has since introduced DTA to *other* subsidiaries with, it seems, substantial success.

Note that this experience was the first the company had had with DTA. Almost all of the most successful users of DTA have started out with one or more disappointing experiences. What accounts for such disappointments? Let us take the international manufacturer again as a case example. Its experience is typical of that of several other companies I know about:

1. The logic and language of DTA was unfamiliar to the president and his senior executives, and they could not readily and comfortably incorporate it into their normal mode of thinking. A more gradual introduction of the complex technology would surely have been more digestible.

2. The decision options addressed by the DTA turned out *not* to be the ones the president was concerned about. (For example, he was more interested in deciding *how* to develop a particular market sector than in *whether* to be in it at all.) Fuller and earlier communication between executive and staff analysts helps to counter this very common problem experienced in applying DTA.

3. The DTA was initiated and performed by "head office" people over whom the subsidiary had no direct control, and the subsidiary president may have felt some threat to his autonomy. Having such an analysis performed or commissioned by his own people would have removed the threat.

4. The subsidiary president told me that the way to make money in his business was to get good data and implement decisions effectively. He had little interest in improved ways of *processing* data to make decisions, which is, of course, the special province of DTA.

Diffused Decision Making

At Ford Motor Company, some 200 senior executives have passed through a brief DTA-oriented program during the past five years; the program has been followed up in some divisions by intensive workshops for junior executives. And yet, according to George H. Brown, former Director of Marketing Research at Ford headquarters, usage of DTA at Ford has been negligible in the marketing area, and the prospects unpromising, at least as of the time of this survey. In his opinion, large organizations with diffuse decision-making processes (like Ford) are not as well suited to the effective use of DTA as, say, the small or one-man organization is.

John J. Nevin, now Vice President of Marketing for Ford, adds the following observations:

"I am not sure that there is any reason to be discouraged by the fact that, in many companies, DTA may be far more accepted and far more utilized by middle management. Maybe all analytical tools sneak into general usage through the back door. It does not seem to me to be improbable that the middle management people, who are more comfortable with these techniques and are using them on very specific technical problems today, will, as they grow to top management positions, feel as uncomfortable switching to some new decision-making process as many of today's managers feel in switching to a more disciplined analysis."

He also notes that the average executive has difficulty picking up all of the variables in a complex decision-making problem. He attributes this in large part to the executive's inability to discipline himself to use a new technique.

Nevertheless, several Ford divisions are now exploring DTA applications at their most senior executive levels. Since my survey began, early in 1969, there have been some cases of successful implementation. For instance:

□ At Ford Tractor, a product policy decision was recently required. In a regional market suffering from competitive inroads, the main options were to reduce prices or to introduce one of several possible new models; a modest DTA was carried out on these choices. Several runs incorporating assessments and modifications advanced by the marketing manager, the assistant general manager, and the general manager were made. The somewhat controversial conclusion to introduce a certain model was presented in DTA form to the general manager, who adopted it and initiated the necessary engineering studies.

Organizational Obstacles

If there is one dominant feature that distinguishes the successful from the less successful applications of DTA, judging from the findings of this survey, it is the organizational arrangements for offering DTA. The most successful appears to be the "vest pocket" approach, where the analyst works intimately with the executive and typically reports directly to him (Pillsbury's Grocery Products Company and Inmont Corporation provide excellent examples of this approach).

At the other end of the spectrum is the arms'-length approach, which is characteristic of much operations research. In this approach the analysis is performed by a staff group which is organizationally distant from the executive being served. In such instances, the executive may feel threatened rather than supported by DTA, and critical weaknesses may thus develop in the communication of the problem and its analyses.

. . .

Technical Questions

A further obstacle to the widespread use of DTA has to do with the logical underpinnings of DTA. Some potential users, especially in staff positions, take the position that where information about an uncertain quantity is weak, there is no point in *attempting* to measure that uncertainty. This amounts to a rejection of a basic tenet of DTA, viz., that subjective judgment, however tenuous, must be taken into account *somehow* by the decision maker, and that a DTA approach may do the job more effectively than unaided intuition.

In addition, increase in the effectiveness of DTA is to some extent dependent on the state of the art. The development and propagation of economical and quick routines utilizing inputs and outputs that can be readily communicated will no doubt be a major factor. Such routines affect the practicality and appeal of DTA in a management setting. However, it seems clear that purely theoretical developments are not holding up further application of DTA; the frontiers of the technology are way ahead of the applications, in most cases.

REALIZING THE POTENTIALS

How beneficial is a DTA to a company? Does it lead to "better" decisions than other approaches to decision making? Logic alone cannot give us the answer. However, it seems clear that DTA may *not* be the best approach if:

1. The subjective inputs required for the analysis are inaccurately measured and recorded. (Executives, as Meal suggests in the comment quoted earlier in this article, may not explicitly admit to uncertainty about some critical variable, whereas they may take it into account in their informal reasoning.)

2. The DTA does not incorporate all the considerations which the executive would informally take into account—for example, some nonmonetary side effect like goodwill. (Where there is good communication between executive and analyst, the executive often can and does make "eyeball" adjustments for anything that has been left out of the analysis. Sometimes, though, such adjustments are so substantial that they swamp and thereby invalidate the entire DTA.)

Considering all the angles and factors that bear on a good DTA (or any other analysis) is time-consuming and sometimes quite frustrating. Clearly, though, it is one of the prerequisites of making this approach. The following experience should suffice to make the point:

□ A corporate staff team at General Mills evaluated an acquisition opportunity by means of a DTA computer program that took four months to develop and another two months to run with successively modified inputs corresponding to new assessments and assumptions made by the researchers and executives. In all 140 computer runs were made before arriving at a recommendation to make the acquisition and to adopt a specific marketing and production strategy. The recommendation was rejected by top management, however, when the company's legal counsel advised against the acquisition on certain legal grounds. The lawyers discovered that a critical consideration had been omitted from the analysis which rendered it unusable for the purpose at hand.

It should be noted that this was the company's first major attempt at applying DTA, and the experience performed a valuable function in exposing line and staff to the scope and pitfalls of DTA. The company's record with DTA since then has been quite successful.

Costs vs. Benefits

The costs of applying DTA are by no means inconsequential. It is true that the out-of-pocket costs for technicians and computers, even for a large-scale analysis, may be relatively trivial. Moreover, these costs can be expected to decline as DTA technology becomes more streamlined. Other, less obvious costs, however, are not trivial and are unlikely to become so. For example:

□ Critical decisions may be unacceptably delayed while an analysis is being completed. (When General Mills does not use DTA for market planning decisions, this is cited as the most common reason.) A busy executive needs to devote some of his valuable time to making sure that all of the relevant judgments he can make have been fed into the analysis.

□ Even more serious a "cost" is the discomfort an executive feels as he forces his traditional way of thinking into an unfamiliar mold and lays bare to the discretion of a DTA specialist the most delicate considerations that enter into his decision making. These considerations sometimes include confidential information (as in the GE new product example previously noted), admissions of uncertainty (which often run counter to the prevailing managerial culture), and embarrassing motivations. In one instance of an elaborate analysis of possible locations for a European subsidiary, the actual decision was dominated by the fact that key personnel wanted to be near the International School in Geneva. Somehow, that consideration seemed too noneconomic and nonrational to be fed into the analysis.

However, such costs are by no means prohibitive if management's approach to DTA is sound and thorough. When that is the case, the advantages claimed by users of DTA are material and persuasive:

○ It focuses informal thinking on the critical elements of a decision.

○ It forces into the open hidden assumptions behind a decision and makes clear their logical implication.

○ It provides an effective vehicle for communicating the reasoning which underlies a recommendation.

Many of the executives most satisfied with DTA value it as a vehicle for communicating decision-making reasoning as well as for improving it. My own feeling is that DTA's contribution to the quality of decision making often seems to come more from forcing meaningful structure on informal reasoning than from supplementing it by formal analysis. For instance, in the Pillsbury Grocery Products Company, for every DTA pushed to its numerical conclusion, there are half a dozen cases where only a conceptual decision tree has been drawn. Such a tree is used to focus attention on the critical options and uncertainties, and is then dropped in favor of informal reasoning.

Suggestions for Starting

After reflecting on the experiences of successful and unsuccessful users of DTA, I want to offer some suggestions for the executive intent on trying out DTA in his organization:

□ Ensure the sympathetic involvement of the chief executive of the company (or operating unit).

□ Make sure that* at least a few key executives have a minimal appreciation of what DTA can do for them and what it requires of them. (This might be done by means of one of the short DTA orientation courses currently available.)

□ Make at least one trial run on a decision problem—preferably a live one—with the help of a DTA specialist. Use the exercise as a training vehicle for your executives and staffers, without expecting immediate pay-offs.

□ Plan on recruiting or developing in-house staff specialists to do the detail on subsequent analyses. The specialists should report directly to you, not to part of an organizationally distant operations research group.

□ Wean yourself and your staff from outside specialists as soon as possible, using them only as residual technical resources.

□ On any particular DTA, follow the analysis closely enough to make sure that the problem which gets solved is the problem you have, and that you accept *all* of the underlying assumptions. This will probably mean a less sophisticated analysis than would gladden the heart of the typical technician. It will also probably mean you spend more time with the analysis than you think you can afford.

CONCLUSION

What efforts are needed to make DTA a more effective tool for the executive? It may be helpful to think of DTA as in some way analogous to an industrial product and to ask ourselves, What aspects of its "manufacture" or "marketing" stand most in need of attention?

The "fundamental research" and "product design" aspects (corresponding to statistical decision theory and the development of special analytical devices) appear to be in rather good shape. Rare are the instances in which successful use of DTA is held up through shortcomings in the purely technical state of the art. Of course, there are areas where improved DTA techniques need to be developed, such as the extraction of probability assessments, handling risk aversion and nonmonetary criteria for action, and accommodating group decision making. But, even so, it is clear that greater use of DTA does not depend on such refinements. The tools that exist are well in advance of the capacity of most companies to use them.

Improvements in "production technique"—i.e., in the ability to deliver competent DTA at an acceptable cost—appear to be somewhat harder to achieve. In one major analysis of a pricing problem, the only reason that subjective probabilities were not introduced explicitly was that the computer cost would have been too high. However, we can be confident that within a few years progress in computer technology will largely eliminate this deterrent.

The manpower costs and delays involved in performing a reasonably complete analysis are usually more intractable. With the emergence and propagation of generalized computer programs of the type developed independently by each of the leaders (notably General Electric) in the DTA field, such costs can also be expected to decline—but the improvement will be gradual during the next five to ten years.

The inadequacy of "production facilities"—that is, the ability of DTA analysts to use available methods and concepts—is another temporary obstacle. Solving this problem will take more formal education and increased awareness of the issues and techniques that others have learned. Certainly help to this end will come from university programs and professional publications. Need for access to physical facilities, such as computer services, does not seem to be a serious limiting factor.

"Promotion" and "packaging" are areas requiring serious attention because they have been more neglected. It is true that the "product awareness" needed to stimulate management demand has been created by publications and executive development programs. But willingness to *try* the product (DTA) requires communicating to a potential user the benefits he can expect. These benefits need to be ascertained and documented in a far more effective way than by incomplete testimonials from satisfied—and not so satisfied—users (as in a survey like the present one).

"Repeat buying" on the part of experimental users requires an attractive and convenient "package" so that an executive can contribute judgments and estimates with less pain and confusion, and also so that the conclusions of a DTA can be presented in a more effective, appealing manner. Confusing computer print-outs and technical reports account for many indifferent receptions to what are otherwise very adequate DTA's.

Somewhat allied to the packaging problem, and still more critical, is the question of how DTA should be *used* in the context of a company's operation. This raises the whole issue of how to organize the DTA function, how to implement recommendations, and how to identify suitable applications. Kent Quisel, a senior analyst at Du Pont, comments that he spends a third of his time on what he calls "user engineering," and that this amount is still not enough. At companies less experienced in DTA than Du Pont is, the proportion of time spent in this way is generally much less than a third, to the almost invariable detriment of DTA's effectiveness.

Possibly the most important area of all for study is "product evaluation." Just how good a product *is* DTA? How deserving is it of intensive development and promotion? The survey findings leave no doubt in my mind that many users are pleased with DTA, and with good cause. What is much less clear is just how important its impact can be on business as a whole. After all, only a very minute fraction of companies have so much as experimented with DTA. Can it really revolutionize management as mathematics has revolutionized engineering? Or will it forever be an occasionally helpful side calculation in a decision-making process that remains essentially unchanged?

The answers are clearly of major importance to businessmen and, indeed, depend in large measure on the businessmen themselves. How eager are they to improve the quality of their decision making? What scope for improvement is there? The answers to these questions are the key to many of the issues raised in this article.

22

When Is a Problem Worth Solving?

DAVID W. MILLER AND MARTIN K. STARR

Among the plethora of books and articles written in recent years on operations research and quantitative approaches to decision-making, one would have to search long and hard to find a selection that doesn't suggest that such material offers the long-awaited answers to all managerial decision problems. Perhaps the missionary fervor of the Mathematical "Peters" who have sought to bring the "word" to those who still worship nonquantitative idols accounts for this unusual lack of humility in most recent management science works. Whatever the reason, Miller and Starr, clearly two men extremely well versed in the new mathematical catechism, are among the few to offer a humble and helpful guide to deciding where and how such techniques best may be used or not used.

This excerpt from Miller and Starr's The Structure of Human Decisions *is almost unique in that it offers a clear and, delightfully, almost jargon-free set of guides to where and how logic and, where appropriate, quantitative techniques may be applied among the many problems that face a decision-maker.*

Granted the general usefulness of operations research, management science and other logical, systematic and quantitative methods of approaching decision problems, it still does not follow that the manager should focus them upon every aspect of his organization. When, then, should he?

WHAT IS A PROBLEM?

. . .

There is considerable agreement among people on some of the *general characteristics* of problems. Very often the existence and nature of a problem can be diagnosed by means of some obvious questions. Why should this activity be done? Why should it be done in that way? How else can this be done? How should this be done? When should this be done? Who should do this? These questions, and others like them, are *problem-pointers*. The act of questioning indicates the *possible existence* of a problem. By no means does it demonstrate the *real existence* of a problem. We usually use the word *problem* when someone is endeavoring to come to grips with one or more of these questions. To find suitable answers is to *solve* the problem. ...

... One cannot come to grips with a problem until he is aware of its existence. The awareness of a problem is the first prerequisite to dealing with it.

How does one become aware of a problem? There are obviously a multitude of ways, and we do not propose to catalogue them all. But it will be worth mentioning a few of the more common ways.

HEAD-ON CONFRONTATION

First, sometimes we become aware of a problem because reality is so obstreperous that it literally hits us head-on with the problem and there is no conceivable way that we could avoid being aware of it. Examples of this kind of awareness are, unfortunately, particularly numerous. Consider national problems. Only the erosion of millions of acres of farmland leads to an awareness of the problem of soil conservation. Or, the devastation of a hurricane is required before we become aware of the problem of an adequate storm-warning system. Horrifying mid-air collisions produce an awareness of the need for total systems control of aircraft.

There are also many business examples. The manager who becomes aware of the problem posed by a new competitive product because his sales slump to the vanishing point is one case. ...

PRECAUTIONARY MONITORING

Second, some kinds of problems are highlighted by our way of looking at reality. With forethought we are always watching for certain signs. We have called our way of looking at reality "models" of reality. We are now saying that our models of reality generally put some kinds of problems into bold relief. An outstanding example is the administrator's accounting model of his organization. The accounting model is designed to quickly call the administrator's attention to problems signaled by unbalanced cash flow, decreased demand, unit cost increases, higher inventory investments, and a host of similar problems.

. . .

Our models can function as blinders instead of aids to better vision. By giving the illusion of a "total" early-warning system, when in fact it is only "partial," a great disservice may be done. Susceptibility to such illusions is one of the greatest ills that human minds are heir to. Classical economic theory is a good example. The classical economists had a model of the economic activities of society which included only marketplace phenomena. They were so delighted with this model that they resolutely refused to admit the relevance to economics of social problems that were a direct consequence of economic policies. The indefatigable persistence with which some of the classical economists adhered to this position can only be marveled at. Fortunately, the labor of subsequent economists has resulted in economic models that more adequately reflect reality.

In the business world the same kind of thing can happen. Let us consider the accounting model in this regard. Inventory carrying charges are reasonably accessible. There is, however, no entry for profit lost because of unfilled orders, nor is there an entry for the loss of customer goodwill because of out-of-stocks. All kinds of direct costs are emphasized, but there is no place for opportunity costs. Such examples can be multiplied easily. We are not criticizing the accounting model for omitting something it was never intended to do. Rather, we want to point out that an executive who leaned too exclusively on this one model would miss problems that he should be aware of. ... The executive must always remember that all models should serve as problem-pointers not as problem-blinders.

EXTERNAL PERTURBATION

Third, awareness of a problem can result from the fact that someone whose role is external to the immediate system discovers its existence. ... The "outsider" becomes aware of the problem and presents his discovery with such irresistible logic that others become aware through his efforts. Such contributions to our perception of problems frequently reflect creative genius of a high order. As an example, we can cite Frederick W. Taylor's discovery of the "real" problems of production. The success with which he promulgated his concepts is recorded history. ...

RANDOM SEARCHING

Fourth, and last, one can become so problem-oriented that when no problems can be discovered by any other means one goes looking for them. Such a search is usually predicated on the proposition that "things can't be perfect." Few organizations are without some *problem-finding* group (it may be called a methods department or a value analysis group). ... History provides ample evidence that functions such as these have a significant role to play.

Nevertheless, the basis for "looking-for-trouble" is not without its own liabilities. The belief that organized searching will uncover real problems is, in the case of many organizations, only too often justified by the fact that *the searching process creates its own problems.* Such self-justifying processes provide continual reasons for their own existence without necessarily contributing to the organizational well-being. A number of subsequent remarks will be relevant to the question of when one can reasonably initiate a search for problems.

These are some of the major ways in which one can become aware of problems. But is is obvious that not all persons view the same things as problems even when they are faced with the same kinds of situations. Some persons will come to grips with the issues and attempt to resolve them. Others will ignore or defer the issues, i.e., they will not make any effort to solve the problem. For them there is only a problem-pointing question, not a real problem in our sense of the word. Let us consider the reasons for this difference.

· · ·

PROBLEMS AND THE SIZE OF ORGANIZATIONS

The question we have raised above can be typified by an example. Company *A* produces electronic equipment for a *local market*. It is small and profitable. The company has a problem situation in the form of too high a turnover in the plant labor force. Having become aware of the problem, *A*'s plant manager calls a meeting of his foremen and discusses the problem with them for an hour. Finding no answers, he closes the meeting by ordering the installation of a suggestion box. Then he returns hastily to other, more pressing problems. Company *B* produces electronic equipment for the *national market*. It is large and profitable. It, too, has a problem in the form of too high a turnover in the plant labor force. Having become aware of the problem, *B*'s vice-president in charge of production calls in a team of consultants, which includes industrial psychologists, sociologists, and an applied anthropologist. After a reasonably lengthy investigation they will probably make some good recommendations as to how the problem can be resolved. The responses of the two companies to the same problem are totally different.

The kind of situation typified by this example is so common that similar examples are probably familiar to anyone acquainted with organizational realities. Our question is: Why does this difference occur in response to identical problems?

The answer, speaking generally, is that the *returns* that result from solving a problem *tend to be proportional to the size, income, sales, or profit* of the organization, while the *cost* of solving the problem *tends to be a fixed amount.* We want first to justify this answer and then to discuss how it affects organizational attitudes toward problems.

The first part of the answer is that the returns that result from solving a problem tend to be proportional to some measure of the organization's involvement in the area of the problem. Such measures are income, sales, budgets, operating costs, profit, and the like. This requires but little demonstration. An organization with extra labor costs of $100,000 per year owing to high turnover may save $25,000 or $50,000 from cutting the amount of turnover. But they certainly can't save more than $100,000. Another organization with an extra labor cost of $1,000,000 owing to high turnover could easily save more than $100,000 by cutting the amount of turnover. Furthermore, comparable amounts of improvement in the two organizations would probably save comparable percentages of the respective total extra costs. This is what is meant by the statement that returns tend to be proportional to the measure of the organizational involvement in the problem area. The measure of involvement here is the extra cost owing to the high turnover. And lest it be objected that this measure wouldn't be known, let us hasten to add that the same conclusion would follow if total labor costs were used as the measure.

The same kind of argument applies to most kinds of organizational problems. The solution of a marketing problem might increase sales by any reasonable range of amounts, but the increase would generally be proportional to the sales. A company with ten times the annual sales of another company that solved the same problem would probably get around ten times the amount of return in sales units, or about the *same percentage* return. It is exceptions to this statement that demand explanation rather than the statement itself.

The second part of the answer is that the cost of solving a problem tends to be a fixed amount. This requires justification because it is certainly an overgeneralization and is false in some cases. Nonetheless, it is generally a reasonable approximation to the facts. The important word is "tends"—we are not stating an equation. The major reason why the cost of solving a problem tends to be a fixed amount is that the amounts of information and analysis required are more nearly a *function of the problem than they are of the size of the organization* that has the problem.

Consider an analysis of an inventory problem as an example. A small firm may have two or three thousand items in inventory, whereas a large firm may have 200,000. But what will be typically required, in either case, will be a careful analysis of a relatively small selection of items. Once an inventory system has been worked out it will generally be up to the organization's personnel, with a little coaching, to get the system installed on all the items. Much of the time spent in analysis will be used in careful studies of generic problem characteristics as they apply to the special circumstances and needs of the organization. This represents a general cost of the study which will be applicable regardless of the number of items studied. Add to this the fact that a fair amount of the time will be spent in establishing the necessary working relationships and channels of communication. The result is that a large percentage of the cost of solving the inventory problem is fixed, and only a small percentage depends on the number of items. This is the hallmark of an essentially fixed cost, which is exactly our thesis. Similarly, consider the case of a problem involving the allocation of salesmen's time. The fact that one company has ten times the number of salesmen another company has does not necessarily make the study of the first company's problem more expensive. The study of customer characteristics will be required in either case and the same mathematical models will be tried in both cases. The fixed costs, in short, are high. A great number of organizational problems are of this sort.

There are, of course, problems for which the cost of a solution is directly proportional to the size of the organization. An outstanding example of this kind of problem is one in the area of information flow. These are the problems that prompt systems analysis in the hope of improvement by redesign of the organization's communication network. The communication network consists of links between various processors of information. If all possible links existed (between every pair of information-processors) the number of links would increase in proportion to the square of the number of information-processors. Generally this isn't the case, but the number of links certainly increases as fast as the number of information-processors. The work, and hence cost, of an analysis of such a system depends on the number of such links. Therefore, a large organization, having more information-processors and more links, can expect a systems study to cost more money than it would for a small organization. Despite exceptions, it appears that the majority of problems are such that their *solutions involve high fixed costs.*

What does this imply in terms of company attitudes to problems? The main consideration involves company size. Let's take a problem in marketing for which a solution would involve a 2 per cent increase in sales for one year. In accord with our argument we will suppose that a solution will cost $50,000. If we assume a 10 per cent gross profit on sales, it follows that a company's sales would have to be at least $25,000,000 per year—since ($25,000,000) (0.02) (0.1) = $50,000—before it would be profitable to undertake the study. Smaller companies would be equally delighted to gain 2 per cent of their sales by solving the given problem, but it is simply not economical for them to have it solved. Similarly, in the case of the two manufacturers of electronic equipment (*A* and *B*), with which we commenced this section, equivalent percentage improvements might result if the problem were solved in the two cases. But the difference in the amount of involvement in the problem area makes it economical for the larger company to undertake an expensive analysis of the problem, which would be completely uneconomical for the smaller company.

. . .

Some further ramifications of the same argument are worth discussing. First, we have assumed in the above discussions that the solution to the problem is assured if only the search is undertaken. This, of course, is a very bad assumption. A manager's life would be delightfully easy if he knew that each of his problems could be solved by retaining some suitable consultants or by employing his own specialists. Unfortunately, this is far from true. The manager may invest considerable sums in an attempt to solve a problem and may find no solution at all. In this event he still has his problem plus the realization that he has wasted resources in a vain effort to solve it.

This situation can be described by saying that a search for a problem solution has some probability of being successful. The possibility of making an immediate and realistic estimate of this probability must be questioned. For the present, it will be sufficient to observe that there is some probability of finding a solution, whether we know what it is or not. Now, since there is usually a continual succession of problems in any organization, it follows that a succession of choices must be made. For any problem, one can attempt to find the solution, or else ignore the problem. The situation also might be immediately resolved by utilizing managerial intuition.

At present, let us note that there are two available possibilities: (1) undertake a search for the solution to the problem, which will cost some particular sum and which will have some specified probability of success, or (2) do something else that will not involve expenditures to find the solution (including decision by default) to the problem. These choices are available for each problem and there is a constant succession of problems. So formulated, the situation of an organization regarding its problems bears a striking resemblance to that of a gambler making wagers on some chance device. The problems are the successive wagers and, like the gambler, the managers are not forced to make a bet. The sum required to search for the problem solution is the amount of the wager, and the return that results if the solution is found represents the amount won if the wager is successful. Finally, the probability that a solution will be found is the probability of winning. The analogy is complete and we might expect that probability theory, which has much to say about gambler's chances, might have something to say about the organization's policy regarding its problems, which in fact it does.

In probability theory this problem is treated under the descriptive title, "The Problem of the Gambler's Ruin." The organization that is establishing a policy for dealing with its problems is not a gambler, and it is not often in a position where it is really risking ruin by attempts to solve its problems. However, because of the analogies we have pointed out, it is possible to consider the organization's situation in the light of the results available from an analysis of this intriguing comparison. Rational managers should recognize, and take account of, the fact that the allocation of funds to a search for problem solutions bears a strong *family* resemblance to the problem facing a gambler with a limited capital. This does not mean that managers and administrators need be experts in probability theory. The point is simply that their allocation of problem-solving funds should be weighted in the direction indicated by the theory.[1]

Two points remain to be mentioned in this brief discussion of the effect of an organization's size on the approach to problems. First, most returns from solutions to problems are not lump sums received upon implementation of whatever is indicated by the problem solution. Instead they are in the form of some increment to income over a period of years. Ordinarily the number of years cannot be assumed to be too great because future changes in conditions will either require a new solution or will render the whole problem irrelevant. But, even so, the future income stream must be discounted back to present worth before any conclusions can be drawn concerning the advisability of searching for a solution. From the standpoint of the smaller organization, the effect is to require a greater margin of safety (as compared to the larger one) against the possibility of a bad-luck streak. The spreading of the possible return over a number of years means that there is less chance of one good solution's sustaining the available funds against several failures. This requires a greater relative increase in the safety margin for the smaller organization than it does for the larger one.

Second, as soon as probabilities of gains and losses enter the picture the question of the utility of money arises. ... When due account [is] taken of differing utilities for money, the organization with larger resources [can] assume risks that a smaller one could not. Precisely the same effect results in this case. The introduction of utilities for money will result in the smaller organization's having to forego still more searches for solutions to problems, which the larger enterprise can easily undertake.

. . .

WHAT IS A PROBLEM SOLUTION WORTH?

This question is obviously a complex one. But it is equally obvious that it is the key to a rational analysis of the decision problem of whether or not to undertake a search for a solution. The main difficulty results from the large variety of ways in which the manager might profit from a search for a solution. Let us list some of them.

1. He may profit from the mere fact of a search for a solution even if no solution is found. For example, a study of productive efficiency sometimes results in greater efficiency purely because of the response of the personnel to the fact that their efficiency is being studied.

[1] See David W. Miller and Martin K. Starr, *Executive Decisions and Operations Research* (Englewood Cliffs, N.J.: Prentice-Hall, Inc., 1960), pp. 370-74.

2. He may profit from a search that doesn't find a solution by discovering that some factor that he had been considering important is not so important. As a result, he will no longer have to worry about that factor. For example, a company that undertakes a study to minimize direct-mail duplication may not discover the solution, but as a result of the investigation it may learn that duplication is not large enough to warrant further attention.

3. He may profit because the range of the possible states of nature is narrowed. Any successful search for improved predicting methods is an example.

4. He may profit because the number of strategies that he needs to consider is decreased. Often this results because the complex system involved in the problem is found to depend on some key component. Only those strategies which affect this key part need be considered.

5. He may profit by discovering a more suitable measure of effectiveness.

6. He may profit by obtaining good estimates of the probabilities of the states of nature. An example would be that of a company considering a sizable expansion in a foreign country. Such a company might undertake a study to ascertain the probabilities of war, revolution, socialization, and other relevant states of nature.

7. He may profit by discovering the correct evaluation of the payoff measure. As an example we can cite studies made of the optimal allocation of salesmen's time in which it has been found that the payoff measure (sales, for example) is related to the allocation of time in ways that are far from obvious.

Still other kinds of returns from solutions could be given. But it is not worthwhile to try listing all of them, even assuming that this could be done. We cannot discuss every possible gain that might be derived from a search for a solution. The important thing to note is that the process of searching for a solution can produce peripheral benefits that help to justify the decision to solve the problem. In other cases, the side effects may not be beneficial. This occurs, in particular, when an efficient process must be disturbed to collect information necessary for the solution of the problem. The decision-maker must consider the pros and cons of the side effects that might result from the decision to solve a problem.

Basically, the value of a solution can be treated in much the same way as any other value problem. We can distinguish at least three different types of value situations. In the first place, we have the situation in which the solution to a problem has a value determined by the supply and demand for solutions. For example, the demand for oil and the frequency with which varying quantities of oil are found permit us to specify the value of this solution. Similarly, the value of the solution to the problem of finding an adequate number of engineers depends upon the supply of engineers and the company's demand for them. The second type of value situation is the one in which there is an imputed value for the solution that is independent of the supply and demand for such solutions. For example, when an air-sea rescue operation is undertaken to locate a pilot downed at sea, the combined cost of all of the equipment and personnel employed in the search provides at least a lower bound for the imputed value of the pilot's life. In business, imputed values must be used when a numerical equivalent cannot be found. This is the case for employee morale, company goodwill, community relations, and so forth. The third type of value situation we will mention is one in which the value of the solution is basically a measure of improved efficiency. As we have previously stated, it is sometimes possible to estimate an upper limit for efficiency, in which case, if the organization knows its present efficiency it is able to estimate the probable value of a solution. The estimate depends upon the anticipated effectiveness of the strategies (techniques) that will be employed. Consequently, the appraisal of techniques is of great importance in the estimation of the value of a solution. With standard techniques and methods, and an evaluation of the data that are used, it is possible to estimate the degree to which the best possible result will be approximated. With nonstandard techniques, it is necessary to approach this problem in stages. At each stage, the previous results and additional information gained can be used to reestimate the probable value of the solution that will result if the problem-solving procedure is continued.

It is not unusual for the solution of one problem to bring to light the value to be gained from solving another problem. However, many problems are not involved in such mutual relationships, and it is necessary to find still other means for estimating the worth of a solution.

The general procedure we would like to be able to follow is clear. We must attempt to estimate the payoffs that result from solutions. Since we will often have an estimate of the maximum possible improvement that could result, it may be most convenient to express the different payoffs as percentages of this maximum. Then, by determining the effect of a percentage-point improvement on some convenient dollar measurement (sales, costs, profit, and the like), it will be possible to convert the payoff measures to dollars, which can be included directly with the dollar cost of the search in evaluating the expected returns of the strategies. This, of course, is far easier said than done, but it is quite straightforward for many problems. In estimating the payoffs it is often possible to utilize published studies showing the improvements that resulted from similar searches for solutions. In this context it may be noted that the smaller organization has an advantage here. In accordance with our previous argument it is likely that the smaller organization will be dealing with problems that have a direct and large effect on its primary objectives. These are the problems which have most often been handled by other organizations and, hence, for which the greatest amount of information on resulting improvements is available. The larger organization may be dealing with a specialized problem that has never, or rarely, been dealt with before. This makes it more unlikely that any significant amount of information concerning improvements will be available.

One rule of thumb is worth noting in connection with the fact that some problems have always been recognized as being decision problems (although no formal search has been made to find a solution); others have not been considered to be decision problems. The first kind of problem will have had the attention of a decision-maker. If he has had the benefit of an accurate measure of the payoff from his decisions he will have had the opportunity to develop his own methods for approaching an optimal selection of strategy. Under usual conditions he will have done so—and with a fair degree of success if the problem is not exceedingly complex. Thus, a solution for a problem of this kind is not likely to produce nearly so much improvement as will a solution to the other kind of problem.

To illustrate the difference we will contrast three problems. First, consider a transportation problem involving factories and warehouses. Here the costs are given and the total cost of any shipping strategy is immediately available. Any conscientious manager would approach the minimum-cost strategy for this problem, over a period of time, even for a large number of factories and warehouses. Second, consider an inventory problem. Here the manager will rarely receive the information necessary to completely evaluate his own decisions. He will not, therefore, be so likely to improve his decisions beyond a certain point—even with practice. Third, consider a problem in plant location that has never arisen before. Clearly, there is no basis for improving performance on a unique problem. Generally speaking the relative improvements resulting from solutions will be smaller in the first case, larger in the second, and largest in the third. We must emphasize the word "relative." It means the improvement as a percentage of the cost of the decision-maker's unaided decision. We cannot say anything about the absolute improvements because this measure depends on the specific circumstances of the problems. The moral is simple: Never underestimate the ability of the manager to approach the optimal strategy *if* he is given an adequate feedback of information.

In the attempt to evaluate the return from a solution, one of the greatest difficulties results from the fact that a solution may be found but the determining factors may be outside the manager's control. This would essentially eliminate the possibility of a return from the solution. For example, the labor-turnover problem might be analyzed at considerable expense only to find that the main contributing factors were sociological conditions over which the organization had no control. There is no certain way of handling this difficulty, but it is possible in many cases to estimate the hazard. Usually the manager has reasonable knowledge of the factors that he controls. This being so, he may be able to discover, either from his own organization's experience or from that of similar ones:

1. That the quantitative measure of his objective in the past has varied, while the factors under his control remained essentially constant, or

2. That the quantitative measure of his objective in the past has remained fairly constant, while the factors under his control varied.

In either case, one can assume that the factors under his control are not sufficient to determine the objective measure (payoff). Hence, there is a good chance a solution will disclose that the important factors in determining his payoff are outside his control. However, it is known that feedback systems can produce variation although a constant strategy is being maintained. In this case, the lack of sufficient information about the system could mislead the decision-maker into believing that he has no control over the situation, when in fact he does have control but he doesn't know how it works.

Similarly, there is a problem with respect to the second point. The quantitative measure of the objective may remain constant while the control factors are varied, but the time lag may be so great that the effect of varying the controls cannot be observed. For example, changing advertising effort may not affect short-term sales but profoundly affect long-term sales. Consequently, the manager must evaluate the kind of situation that prevails when he attempts to determine how much control he exercises in obtaining a solution.

Whenever a situation arises in which the decision-maker appears to have no strategy available that will permit him to utilize the results of a solution, the value of that solution would be nil. For example, the fact that a company knows who its potential customers are will be of limited value unless specific means are available for reaching these customers. If no medium exists that includes a larger proportion of potential customers in its audience than exists in the general population, the characterization of potential customers is valueless—at least for selecting optimal media. Sometimes persistence and imagination can succeed in devising a strategy that will give value to a solution. This depends on the caliber of the men who attempt to resolve the problem. It is not our intention to discuss such questions as the kind of men needed to provide creative and resourceful ideas with respect to the utilization of solutions. Still, the value of a solution will frequently increase because an ingenious way has been found for putting the result to work.

One additional factor should be mentioned that affects the value of a solution. Competitive incentives exist that are difficult to evaluate. Many times a value must be imputed for being the first to achieve something. Frequently, a company that is second benefits at the expense of the first. In many other cases, the advantage of being first gives the company that pioneers the solution a lead that cannot be overcome. The position of a company with respect to its competitors and the characteristics of the market must, therefore, be considered when attempts are made to place a value on a solution.

We can see that the value of a solution is a function of many factors. If it can be represented on a single scale, such as dollars, then a direct decision can be made between possible alternative problems to be studied. If it is not possible to estimate the value of a solution on a single scale, then it is necessary to use the methods that we have discussed for comparing outcomes in terms of the multiple objectives of the organization.

23

The Science of Muddling Through

CHARLES E. LINDBLOM

Although Shakespearean scholars may shudder at the application of the appellation "classic" to an article on business decision-making, we feel it is deserved in this case.

The Lindblom article offers a clear set of alternatives to the kind of rational models presented in the previous three selections in this section and seems to add support for the Schon position presented in selection 19. What does an administrator do, the author asks, when the situation in which he works makes the application of the scientific method impractical? Lindblom outlines the commonly accepted steps in the scientific method and tries to show where and why they are often untenable in many administrative decision-making situations. For these situations, he offers his "muddling through," or "branch," approach. The reader will profit by testing Lindblom's criticisms of scientific-method models against the suggestions contained in the Schon, Heilbroner, Brown, and Miller and Starr selections. Where does his approach really differ? What is the nature of the differences? Do you, as a reader, see ways of integrating his views with those of the authors of the first four selections?

Suppose an administrator is given responsibility for formulating policy with respect to inflation. He might start by trying to list all related values in order of importance, e.g., full employment, reasonable business profit, protection of small savings, prevention of a stock market crash. Then all possible policy outcomes could be rated as more or less efficient in attaining a maximum of these values. This would of course require a prodigious inquiry into values held by members of society and an equally prodigious set of calculations on how much of each value is equal to how much of each other value. He could then proceed to outline all possible policy alternatives. In a

Reprinted from the *Public Administration Review*, the journal of the American Society for Public Administration, Vol. 19, No. 2 (Spring 1959), by permission of the publisher.

third step, he would undertake systematic comparison of his multitude of alternatives to determine which attains the greatest amount of values.

In comparing policies, he would take advantage of any theory available that generalized about classes of policies. In considering inflation, for example, he would compare all policies in the light of the theory of prices. Since no alternatives are beyond his investigation, he would consider strict central control and the abolition of all prices and markets on the one hand and elimination of all public controls with reliance completely on the free market on the other, both in the light of whatever theoretical generalizations he could find on such hypothetical economies.

Finally, he would try to make the choice that would in fact maximize his values.

An alternative line of attack would be to set as his principal objective, either explicitly or without conscious thought, the relatively simple goal of keeping prices level. This objective might be compromised or complicated by only a few other goals, such as full employment. He would in fact disregard most other social values as beyond his present interest, and he would for the moment not even attempt to rank the few values that he regarded as immediately relevant. Were he pressed, he would quickly admit that he was ignoring many related values and many possible important consequences of his policies.

As a second step, he would outline those relatively few policy alternatives that occurred to him. He would then compare them. In comparing his limited number of alternatives, most of them familiar from past controversies, he would not ordinarily find a body of theory precise enough to carry him through a comparison of their respective consequences. Instead he would rely heavily on the record of past experience with small policy steps to predict the consequences of similar steps extended into the future.

Moreover, he would find that the policy alternatives combined objectives or values in different ways. For example, one policy might offer price level stability at the cost of some risk of unemployment; another might offer less price stability but also less risk of unemployment. Hence, the next step in his approach—the final selection—would combine into one the choice among values and the choice among instruments for reaching values. It would not, as in the first method of policy-making, approximate a more mechanical process of choosing the means that best satisfied goals that were previously clarified and ranked. Because practitioners of the second approach expect to achieve their goals only partially, they would expect to repeat endlessly the sequence just described, as conditions and aspirations changed and as accuracy of prediction improved.

BY ROOT OR BY BRANCH

For complex problems, the first of these two approaches is of course impossible. Although such an approach can be described, it cannot be practiced except for relatively simple problems and even then only in a somewhat modified form. It assumes intellectual capacities and sources of information that men simply do not possess, and it is even more absurd as an approach to policy when the time and money that can be allocated to a policy problem is limited, as is always the case. Of particular importance to public administrators is the fact that public agencies are in effect usually instructed not to practice the first method. That is to say, their prescribed functions and constraints—the politically or legally possible—restrict their attention to relatively few values and relatively few alternative policies among the countless alternatives that might be imagined. It is the second method that is practiced.

Curiously, however, the literatures of decision-making, policy formulation, planning, and public administration formalize the first approach rather than the second, leaving public administrators who handle complex decisions in the position of practicing what few preach. For emphasis I run some risk of over-statement. True enough, the literature is well aware of limits on man's capacities and of the inevitability that policies will be approached in some such style as the second. But attempts to formalize rational policy formulation—to lay out explicitly the necessary steps in the process—usually describe the first approach and not the second.[1]

The common tendency to describe policy formulation even for complex problems as though it followed the first approach has been strengthened by the attention given to, and successes enjoyed by, operations research, statistical decision theory, and systems analysis. The hallmarks of these procedures, typical of the first approach, are clarity of objective, explicitness of evaluation, a high degree of comprehensiveness of overview, and, wherever possible, quantification of values for mathematical analysis. But these advanced procedures remain largely the appropriate techniques of relatively small-scale problem-solving where the total number of variables to be considered is small and value problems restricted. ...

Accordingly, I propose in this paper to clarify and formalize [a] second method, much neglected in the literature. This might be described as the method of *successive limited comparisons*. I will contrast it with the first approach, which might be called the rational-comprehensive method.[2] More impressionistically and briefly—and therefore generally used in this article— they could be characterized as the branch method and root method, the former continually building out from the current situation, step-by-step and by small degrees; the latter starting from fundamentals anew each time, building on the past only as experience is embodied in a theory, and always prepared to start completely from the ground up.

[1] James G. March and Herbert A. Simon similarly characterize the literature. They also take some important steps, as have Simon's recent articles, to describe a less heroic model of policy-making. See *Organizations* (John Wiley and Sons, 1958), p. 137.

[2] I am assuming that administrators often make policy and advise in the making of policy and am treating decision-making and policy-making as synonymous for purposes of this paper.

Let us put the characteristics of the two methods side by side in simplest terms.

Rational-Comprehensive (Root)	Successive Limited Comparisons (Branch)
1a. Clarification of values or objectives distinct from, and usually prerequisite to, empirical analysis of alternative policies.	1b. Selection of value goals and empirical analysis of the needed action are not distinct from one another but are closely intertwined.
2a. Policy-formulation is therefore approached through means-end analysis: First the ends are isolated, then the means to achieve them are sought.	2b. Since means and ends are not distinct, means-end analysis is often inappropriate or limited.
3a. The test of a "good" policy is that it can be shown to be the most appropriate means to desired ends.	3b. The test of a "good" policy is typically that various analysts find themselves directly agreeing on a policy (without their agreeing that it is the most appropriate means to an agreed objective).
4a. Analysis is comprehensive; every important relevant factor is taken into account.	4b. Analysis is drastically limited: i) Important possible outcomes are neglected. ii) Important alternative potential policies are neglected. iii) Important affected values are neglected.
5a. Theory is often heavily relied upon.	5b. A succession of comparisons greatly reduces or eliminates reliance on theory.

Assuming that the root method is familiar and understandable, we proceed directly to clarification of its alternative by contrast. In explaining the second, we shall be describing how most administrators do in fact approach complex questions, for the root method, the "best" way as a blueprint or model, is in fact not workable for complex policy questions, and administrators are forced to use the method of successive limited comparisons.

INTERTWINING EVALUATION
AND EMPIRICAL ANALYSIS (1b)

The quickest way to understand how values are handled in the method of successive limited comparisons is to see how the root method often breaks down in *its* handling of values or objectives. The idea that values should be clarified, and in advance of the examination of alternative policies, is appealing. But what happens when we attempt it for complex social problems? The first difficulty is that on many critical values or objectives, citizens disagree, congressmen disagree, and public administrators disagree. Even where a fairly specific objective is prescribed for the administrator, there remains considerable room for disagreement on sub-objectives. Consider, for example, the conflict with respect to locating public housing ... disagreement [may occur] despite the clear objective of providing a certain number of public housing units in the city. ...

Administrators cannot escape these conflicts by ascertaining the majority's preference, for preferences have not been registered on most issues; indeed, there often *are* no preferences in the absence of public discussion sufficient to bring an issue to the attention of the electorate. Furthermore, there is a question of whether intensity of feeling should be considered as well as the number of persons preferring each alternative. By the impossibility of doing otherwise, administrators often are reduced to deciding policy without clarifying objectives first.

Even when an administrator resolves to follow his own values as a criterion for decisions, he often will not know how to rank them when they conflict with one another, as they usually do. Suppose, for example, that an administrator must relocate tenants, living in tenements scheduled for destruction. One objective is to empty the buildings fairly promptly, another is to find suitable accommodation for persons displaced, another is to avoid friction with residents in other areas in which a large influx would be unwelcome, another is to deal with all concerned through persuasion if possible, and so on.

How does one state even to himself the relative importance of these partially conflicting values? A simple ranking of them is not enough; one needs ideally to know how much of one value is worth sacrificing for some of another value. The answer is that typically the administrator chooses—and must choose—directly among policies in which these values are combined in different ways. He cannot first clarify his values and then choose among policies.

A more subtle third point underlies both the first two. Social objectives do not always have the same relative values. One objective may be highly prized in one circumstance, another in another circumstance. If, for example, an administrator values highly both the dispatch with which his agency can carry through its projects *and* good public relations, it matters little which of the two possibly conflicting values he favors in some abstract or general sense. Policy questions arise in forms which put to administrators such a question as: Given the degree to which we are or are not already achieving the values of dispatch and the values of good public relations, is it worth sacrificing a little speed for a happier clientele, or is it better to risk offending the clientele so that we can get on with our work? The answer to such a question varies with circumstances.

The value problem is, as the example shows, always a problem of adjustments at a margin. But there is no practicable way to state marginal objectives or values except in terms of particular policies. That one value is preferred to another in one decision situation does not mean that it will be preferred in another decision situation in which it can be had only at great sacrifice of another value. Attempts to rank or order values in general and abstract terms so that they do not shift from decision to decision end up by ignoring the relevant marginal preferences. The significance of this third point thus goes very far. Even if all administrators had at hand an agreed set of values, objectives, and constraints, and an agreed ranking of these values, objectives, and constraints, their marginal values in actual choice situations would be impossible to formulate.

Unable consequently to formulate the relevant values first and then choose among policies to achieve them, administrators must choose directly among alternative policies that offer different marginal combinations of values. Somewhat paradoxically, the only practicable way to disclose one's relevant marginal values even to oneself is to describe the policy one chooses to achieve them. Except roughly and vaguely, I know of no way to describe—or even to understand—what my relative evaluations are for, say, freedom and security, speed and accuracy in governmental decisions, or low taxes and better schools than to describe my preferences among specific policy choices that might be made between the alternatives in each of the pairs.

In summary, two aspects of the process by which values are actually handled can be distinguished. The first is clear: evaluation and empirical analysis are intertwined; that is, one chooses among values and among policies at one and the same time. Put a little more elaborately, one simultaneously chooses a policy to attain certain objectives and chooses the objectives themselves. The second aspect is related but distinct: the administrator focuses his attention on marginal or incremental values. Whether he is aware of it or not, he does not find general formulations of objectives very helpful and in fact makes specific marginal or incremental comparisons. Two policies, X and Y, confront him. Both promise the same degree of attainment of objectives a, b, c, d, and e. But X promises him somewhat more of f than does Y, while Y promises him somewhat more of g than does X. In choosing between them, he is in fact offered the alternative of a marginal or incremental amount of f at the expense of a marginal or incremental amount of g. The only values that are relevant to his choice are these increments by which the two policies differ; and, when he finally chooses between the two marginal values, he does so by making a choice between policies.[3]

As to whether the attempt to clarify objectives in advance of policy selection is more or less rational than the close intertwining of marginal evaluation and empirical analysis, the principal difference established is that for complex problems the first is impossible and irrelevant, and the second is both possible and relevant. The second is possible because the administrator need not try to analyze any values except the values by which alternative policies differ and need not be concerned with them except as they differ marginally. His need for information on values or objectives is drastically reduced as compared with the root method; and his capacity for grasping, comprehending, and relating values to one another is not strained beyond the breaking point.

RELATIONS BETWEEN MEANS AND ENDS (2b)

Decision-making is ordinarily formalized as a means-ends relationship: means are conceived to be evaluated and chosen in the light of ends finally selected independently of, and prior to, the choice of means. This is the means-ends relationship of the root method. But it follows from all that has just been said that such a means-ends relationship is possible only to the extent that values are agreed upon, are reconcilable, and are stable at the margin. Typically, therefore, such a means-ends relationship is absent from the branch method, where means and ends are simultaneously chosen.

Yet any departure from the means-ends relationship of the root method will strike some readers as inconceivable. For it will appear to them that only in such a relationship is it possible to determine whether one policy choice is better or worse than another. How can an administrator know whether he has made a wise or foolish decision if he is without prior values or objectives by which to judge his decisions? The answer to this question calls up the third distinctive difference between root and branch methods: how to decide the best policy.

THE TEST OF "GOOD" POLICY (3b)

In the root method, a decision is "correct," "good," or "rational" if it can be shown to attain some specified objective, where the objective can be specified without simply describing the decision itself. Where objectives are defined only through the marginal or incremental approach to values described above, it is still sometimes possible to test whether a policy does in fact attain the desired objectives; but a precise statement of the objectives

[3] The line of argument is, of course, an extension of the theory of market choice, especially the theory of consumer choice, to public policy choices.

takes the form of a description of the policy chosen or some alternative to it. To show that a policy is mistaken one cannot offer an abstract argument that important objectives are not achieved; one must instead argue that another policy is more to be preferred.

So far, the departure from customary ways of looking at problem-solving is not troublesome, for many administrators will be quick to agree that the most effective discussion of the correctness of policy does take the form of comparison with other policies that might have been chosen. But what of the situation in which administrators cannot agree on values or objectives, either abstractly or in marginal terms? What then is the test of "good" policy? For the root method, there is no test. Agreement on objectives failing, there is no standard of "correctness." For the method of successive limited comparisons, the test is agreement on policy itself, which remains possible even when agreement on values is not.

It has been suggested that continuing agreement in Congress on the desirability of extending old-age insurance stems from liberal desires to strengthen the welfare programs of the federal government and from conservative desires to reduce union demands for private pension plans. If so, this is an excellent demonstration of the ease with which individuals of different ideologies often can agree on concrete policy. Labor mediators report a similar phenonemon: the contestants cannot agree on criteria for settling their disputes but can agree on specific proposals. Similarly, when one administrator's objective turns out to be another's means, they often can agree on policy.

Agreement on policy thus becomes the only practicable test of the policy's correctness. And for one administrator to seek to win the other over to agreement on ends as well would accomplish nothing and create quite unnecessary controversy.

If agreement directly on policy as a test for "best" policy seems a poor substitute for testing the policy against its objectives, it ought to be remembered that objectives themselves have no ultimate validity other than that they are agreed upon. Hence agreement is the test of "best" policy in both methods. But where the root method requires agreement on what elements in the decision constitute objectives and on which of these objectives should be sought, the branch method falls back on agreement wherever it can be found.

In an important sense, therefore, it is not irrational for an administrator to defend a policy as good without being able to specify what it is good for.

NON-COMPREHENSIVE ANALYSIS (4b)

Ideally, rational-comprehensive analysis leaves out nothing important. But it is impossible to take everything important into consideration unless "important" is so narrowly defined that analysis is in fact quite limited.

Limits on human intellectual capacities and on available information set definite limits to man's capacity to be comprehensive. In actual fact, therefore, no one can practice the rational-comprehensive method for really complex problems, and every administrator faced with a sufficiently complex problem must find ways drastically to simplify.

. . .

In the method of successive limited comparisons, simplification is systematically achieved in two principal ways. First, it is achieved through limitation of policy comparisons to those policies that differ in relatively small degree from policies presently in effect. Such a limitation immediately reduces the number of alternatives to be investigated and also drastically simplifies the character of the investigation of each. For it is not necessary to undertake fundamental inquiry into an alternative and its consequences; it is necessary only to study those respects in which the proposed alternative and its consequences differ from the *status quo*. The empirical comparison of marginal differences among alternative policies that differ only marginally is, of course, a counterpart to the incremental or marginal comparison of values discussed above.[4]

Relevance as Well as Realism

It is a matter of common observation that in Western democracies public administrators and policy analysts in general do largely limit their analyses to incremental or marginal differences in policies that are chosen to differ only incrementally. They do not do so, however, solely because they desperately need some way to simplify their problems; they also do so in order to be relevant. Democracies change their policies almost entirely through incremental adjustments. Policy does not move in leaps and bounds.

. . .

Since the policies ignored by the administrator are politically impossible and so irrelevant, the simplification of analysis achieved by concentrating on policies that differ only incrementally is not a capricious kind of simplification. In addition, it can be argued that, given the limits on knowledge within which policy-makers are confined, simplifying by limiting the focus to small variations from present policy makes the most of available knowledge. Because policies being considered are like present and past policies, the administrator can obtain information and claim some insight.

[4] A more precise definition of incremental policies and a discussion of whether a change that appears "small" to one observer might be seen differently by another is to be found in my "Policy Analysis," 48 *American Economic Review* 298 (June, 1958).

Non-incremental policy proposals are therefore typically not only politically irrelevant but also unpredictable in their consequences.

The second method of simplification of analysis is the practice of ignoring important possible consequences of possible policies, as well as the values attached to the neglected consequences. If this appears to disclose a shocking shortcoming of successive limited comparisons, it can be replied that, even if the exclusions are random, policies may nevertheless be more intelligently formulated than through futile attempts to achieve a comprehensiveness beyond human capacity. Actually, however, the exclusions, seeming arbitrary or random from one point of view, need be neither.

Achieving a Degree of Comprehensiveness

Suppose that each value neglected by one policy-making agency were a major concern of at least one other agency. In that case, a helpful division of labor would be achieved, and no agency need find its task beyond its capacities. The shortcomings of such a system would be that one agency might destroy a value either before another agency could be activated to safeguard it or in spite of another agency's efforts. But the possibility that important values may be lost is present in any form of organization, even where agencies attempt to comprehend in planning more than is humanly possible.

The virtue of such a hypothetical division of labor is that every important interest or value has its watchdog. And these watchdogs can protect the interests in their jurisdiction in two quite different ways: first, by redressing damages done by other agencies; and, second, by anticipating and heading off injury before it occurs.

In a society like that of the United States in which individuals are free to combine to pursue almost any possible common interest they might have and in which government agencies are sensitive to the pressures of these groups, the system described is approximated. Almost every interest has its watchdog. Without claiming that every interest has a sufficiently powerful watchdog, it can be argued that our system often can assure a more comprehensive regard for the values of the whole society than any attempt at intellectual comprehensiveness.

· · ·

Mutual adjustment is more pervasive than the explicit forms it takes in negotiations between groups; it persists through the mutual impacts of groups upon each other even where they are not in communication. For all the imperfections and latent dangers in this ubiquitous process of mutual adjustment, it will often accomplish an adaptation of policies to a wider range of interests than could be done by one group centrally.

Note, too, how the incremental pattern of policy-making fits with the multiple pressure pattern. For when decisions are only incremental—closely related to known policies—it is easier for one group to anticipate the kind of moves another might make and easier too for it to make correction for injury already accomplished.[5]

Even partisanship and narrowness, to use pejorative terms, will sometimes be assets to rational deicision-making, for they can doubly insure that what one agency neglects, another will not; they specialize personnel to distinct points of view. The claim is valid that effective rational coordination of the federal administration, if possible to achieve at all, would require an agreed set of values[6]—if "rational" is defined as the practice of the root method of decision-making. But a high degree of administrative coordination occurs as each agency adjusts its policies to the concerns of the other agencies in the process of fragmented decision-making I have just described.

For all the apparent shortcomings of the incremental approach to policy alternatives with its arbitrary exclusion coupled with fragmentation, when compared to the root method, the branch method often looks far superior. In the root method, the inevitable exclusion of factors is accidental, unsystematic, and not defensible by any argument so far developed, while in the branch method the exclusions are deliberate, systematic, and defensible. Ideally, of course, the root method does not exclude; in practice it must.

Nor does the branch method necessarily neglect long-run considerations and objectives. It is clear that important values must be omitted in considering policy, and sometimes the only way long-run objectives can be given adequate attention is through the neglect of short-run considerations. But the values omitted can be either long-run or short-run.

SUCCESSION OF COMPARISONS (5b)

The final distinctive element in the branch method is that the comparisons, together with the policy choice, proceed in a chronological series. Policy is not made once and for all; it is made and re-made endlessly. Policy-making is a process of successive approximation to some desired objectives in which what is desired itself continues to change under reconsideration.

Making policy is at best a very rough process. Neither social scientists, nor politicians, nor public administrators yet know enough about the social world to avoid repeated errors in predicting the consequences of policy moves. A wise policy-maker consequently expects that his policies will achieve only part of what he hopes and at the same time will produce

[5] The link between the practice of the method of successive limited comparisons and mutual adjustment of interests in a highly fragmented decision-making process adds a new facet to pluralist theories of government and administration.

[6] Herbert Simon, Donald W. Smithburg, and Victor A. Thompson, *Public Administration* (Alfred A. Knopf, 1950), p. 434.

unanticipated consequences he would have preferred to avoid. If he proceeds through a *succession* of incremental changes, he avoids serious lasting mistakes in several ways.

In the first place, past sequences of policy steps have given him knowledge about the probable consequences of further similar steps. Second, he need not attempt big jumps toward his goals that would require predictions beyond his or anyone else's knowledge, because he never expects his policy to be a final resolution of a problem. His decision is only one step, one that if successful can quickly be followed by another. Third, he is in effect able to test his previous predictions as he moves on to each further step. Lastly, he often can remedy a past error fairly quickly—more quickly than if policy proceeded through more distinct steps widely spaced in time.

Compare this comparative analysis of incremental changes with the aspiration to employ theory in the root method. Man cannot think without classifying, without subsuming one experience under a more general category of experiences. The attempt to push categorization as far as possible and to find general propositions which can be applied to specific situations is what I refer to with the word "theory." Where root analysis often leans heavily on theory in this sense, the branch method does not.

The assumption of root analysts is that theory is the most systematic and economical way to bring relevant knowledge to bear on a specific problem. Granting the assumption, an unhappy fact is that we do not have adequate theory to apply to problems in any policy area, although theory is more adequate in some areas—monetary policy, for example—than in others. Comparative analysis, as in the branch method, is sometimes a systematic alternative to theory.

Suppose an administrator must choose among a small group of policies that differ only incrementally from each other and from present policy. He might aspire to "understand" each of the alternatives—for example, to know all the consequences of each aspect of each policy. If so, he would indeed require theory. In fact, however, he would usually decide that, *for policy-making purposes*, he need know, as explained above, only the consequences of each of those aspects of the policies in which they differed from one another. For this much more modest aspiration, he requires no theory (although it might be helpful, if available), for he can proceed to isolate probable differences by examining the differences in consequences associated with past differences in policies, a feasible program because he can take his observations from a long sequence of incremental changes.

· · ·

THEORISTS AND PRACTITIONERS

This difference explains—in some cases at least—why the administrator often feels that the outside expert or academic problem-solver is sometimes not helpful and why they in turn often urge more theory on him. And it explains why an administrator often feels more confident when "flying by the seat of his pants" than when following the advice of theorists. Theorists often ask the administrator to go the long way round to the solution of his problems, in effect ask him to follow the best canons of the scientific method, when the administrator knows that the best available theory will work less well than more modest incremental comparisons. Theorists do not realize that the administrator is often in fact practicing a systematic method. It would be foolish to push this explanation too far, for sometimes practical decision-makers are pursuing neither a theoretical approach nor successive comparisons, nor any other systematic method.

It may be worth emphasizing that theory is sometimes of extremely limited helpfulness in policy-making for at least two rather different reasons. It is greedy for facts; it can be constructed only through a great collection of observations. And it is typically insufficiently precise for application to a policy process that moves through small changes. In contrast, the comparative method both economizes on the need for facts and directs the analyst's attention to just those facts that are relevant to the fine choices faced by the decision-maker.

With respect to precision of theory, economic theory serves as an example. It predicts that an economy without money or prices would in certain specified ways misallocate resources, but this finding pertains to an alternative far removed from the kind of policies on which administrators need help. On the other hand, it is not precise enough to predict the consequences of policies restricting business mergers, and this is the kind of issue on which the administrators need help. Only in relatively restricted areas does economic theory achieve sufficient precision to go far in resolving policy questions; its helpfulness in policy-making is always so limited that it requires supplementation through comparative analysis.

SUCCESSIVE COMPARISON AS A SYSTEM

Successive limited comparisons is, then, indeed a method or system; it is not a failure of method for which administrators ought to apologize. Nonetheless, its imperfections, which have not been explored in this paper, are many. For example, the method is without a built-in safeguard for all relevant values, and it also may lead the decision-maker to overlook excellent policies for no other reason than that they are not suggested by the chain of successive policy steps leading up to the present. Hence, it ought to be said that under this method, as well as under some of the most sophisticated variants of the root method—operations research, for example—policies will continue to be as foolish as they are wise.

Why then bother to describe the method in all the above detail? Because it is in fact a common method of policy formulation, and is, for complex problems, the principal reliance of administrators as well as of other policy analysts.[7] And because it will be superior to any other decision-making method available for complex problems in many circumstances, certainly superior to a futile attempt at superhuman comprehensiveness. The reaction of the public administrator to the exposition of method doubtless will be less a discovery of a new method than a better acquaintance with an old. But by becoming more conscious of their practice of this method, administrators might practice it with more skill and know when to extend or constrict its use. (That they sometimes practice it effectively and sometimes not may explain the extremes of opinion on "muddling through," which is both praised as a highly sophisticated form of problem-solving and denounced as no method at all. For I suspect that in so far as there is a system in what is known as "muddling through," this method is it.)

One of the noteworthy incidental consequences of clarification of the method is the light it throws on the suspicion an administrator sometimes entertains that a consultant or adviser is not speaking relevantly and responsibly when in fact by all ordinary objective evidence he is. The trouble lies in the fact that most of us approach policy problems within a framework given by our view of a chain of successive policy choices made up to the present. One's thinking about appropriate policies with respect, say, to urban traffic control is greatly influenced by one's knowledge of the incremental steps taken up to the present. An administrator enjoys an intimate knowledge of his past sequences that "outsiders" do not share, and his thinking and that of the "outsider" will consequently be different in ways that may puzzle both. Both may appear to be talking intelligently, yet each may find the other unsatisfactory. ...

If this phenomenon is a barrier to communication, an understanding of it promises an enrichment of intellectual interaction in policy formulation. Once the source of difference is understood, it will sometimes be stimulating for an administrator to seek out a policy analyst whose recent experience is with a policy chain different from his own.

This raises again a question only briefly discussed above on the merits of like-mindedness among government administrators. While much of organization theory argues the virtues of common values and agreed

[7] Elsewhere I have explored this same method of policy formulation as practiced by academic analysts of policy ("Policy Analysis," 48 *American Economic Review* 298 (June, 1958)). Although it has been here presented as a method for public administrators, it is no less necessary to analysts more removed from immediate policy questions, despite their tendencies to describe their own analytical efforts as though they were the rational-comprehensive method with an especially heavy use of theory. Similarly, this same method is inevitably resorted to in personal problem-solving, where means and ends are sometimes impossible to separate, where aspirations or objectives undergo constant development, and where drastic simplification of the complexity of the real world is urgent if problems are to be solved in the time that can be given to them. To an economist accustomed to dealing with the marginal or incremental concept in market processes, the central idea in the method is that both evaluation and empirical analysis are incremental. Accordingly I have referred to the method elsewhere as "the incremental method."

organizational objectives, for complex problems in which the root method is inapplicable, agencies will want among their own personnel two types of diversification: administrators whose thinking is organized by reference to policy chains other than those familiar to most members of the organization and, even more commonly, administrators whose professional or personal values or interests create diversity of view (perhaps coming from different specialties, social classes, geographical areas) so that, even within a single agency, decision-making can be fragmented and parts of the agency can serve as watchdogs for other parts.

24

The Purloined Letter

EDGAR ALLAN POE

This short excerpt from one of Poe's classic mysteries offers a refreshingly different look at one of the psychological aspects of decision-making; namely, in competitive situations, sizing up your adversary. In addition, Poe, speaking through Dupin, touches on the field of perception theory and offers several interesting views on training in mathematics or in the arts as a basis for creative problem-solving.

. . .

"The Parisian police," Dupin said, "are exceedingly able in their way. They are persevering, ingenious, cunning, and thoroughly versed in the knowledge which their duties seem chiefly to demand. Thus when G_____ detailed to us his mode of searching the premises at the Hotel D_____ , I felt entire confidence in his having made a satisfactory investigation—so far as his labours extended."

"So far as his labours extended?" said I.

"Yes," said Dupin. "The measures adopted were not only the best of their kind, but carried out to absolute perfection. Had the letter been deposited within the range of their search, these fellows would, beyond a question, have found it."

I merely laughed—but he seemed quite serious in all that he said.

"The measures, then," he continued, "were good in their kind, and well executed; their defect lay in their being inapplicable to the case, and to the man. A certain set of highly ingenious resources are, with the Prefect, a sort of Procrustean bed, to which he forcibly adapts his designs. But he perpetually errs by being too deep or too shallow, for the matter in hand; and many a schoolboy is a better reasoner than he. I knew one about eight years of age, whose success at guessing in the game of 'even and odd' attracted universal admiration. This game is simple, and is played with marbles. One player holds in his hand a number of these toys, and demands of another whether that number is even or odd. If the guess is right, the guesser wins one; if wrong, he loses one. The boy to whom I allude won all the marbles of the school. Of course he had some principle of guessing; and this lay in mere observation and admeasurement of the astuteness of his opponents. For example, an arrant simpleton is his opponent, and, holding up his closed hands, asks, 'are they even or odd?' Our schoolboy replies, 'odd,' and loses; but upon the second trial he wins, for he then says to himself, 'the simpleton had them even upon the first trial, and his amount of cunning is just sufficient to make him have them odd upon the second; I will therefore guess odd';—he guesses odd, and wins. Now, with a simpleton a degree above the first, he would have reasoned thus: 'This fellow finds that in the first instance I guessed odd, and, in the second, he will propose to himself, upon the first impulse, a simple variation from even to odd, as did the first simpleton; but then a second thought will suggest that this is too simple a variation, and finally he will decide upon putting it even as before. I will therefore guess even';—he guesses even, and wins. Now this mode of reasoning in the schoolboy, whom his fellows termed 'lucky,'—what, in its last analysis, is it?"

"It is merely," I said, "an identification of the reasoner's intellect with that of his opponent."

.   .   .

"And the identification," I said, "of the reasoner's intellect with that of his opponent, depends, if I understand you aright, upon the accuracy with which the opponent's intellect is admeasured."

"For its practical value it depends upon this," replied Dupin; "and the Prefect and his cohorts fail so frequently, first, by default of this identification, and, secondly, by ill-admeasurement, or rather through nonadmeasurement of the intellect with which they are engaged. They consider only their *own* ideas of ingenuity; and, in searching for anything hidden, advert only to the modes in which *they* would have hidden it. They are right in this much—that their own ingenuity is a faithful representative of that of *the mass*; but when the cunning of the individual felon is diverse in character from their own, the felon foils them, of course. This always happens when it is above their own, and usually when it is below. They have no variation of principle in their investigations; at best, when urged by some unusual emergency—by some extraordinary reward—they extend or aggravate their old modes of *practice*, without touching their principles. What, for example, in this case of D——— , has been done to vary the principle of action? What is all this boring, and probing, and sounding, and scrutinizing with the microscope, and dividing the surface of the building into registered square inches—what is it all but an exaggeration *of the application* of the one principle or set of principles of search, which are based upon the one set of notions regarding human ingenuity, to which the Prefect, in the long routine of his duty, has been accustomed? Do you not see he has taken it for granted that *all* men proceed to conceal a letter,—not exactly in a gimlet-hole bored in a chair-leg—but, at least, in *some* out-of-the-way hole or corner suggested by the same tenor of thought which would urge a man to secrete a letter in a gimlet-hole bored in a chair-leg? And do you not see also, that such *recherchés* nooks for concealment are adapted only for ordinary occasions, and would be adopted only by ordinary intellects; for, in all cases of concealment, a disposal of the article concealed—a disposal of it in this *recherché* manner,—is, in the very first instance, presumable and presumed; and thus its discovery depends, not at all upon the acumen, but altogether upon the mere care, patience, and determination of the seekers; and where the case is of importance—or, what amounts to the same thing in the policial eyes, when the reward is of magnitude,—the qualities in question have *never* been known to fail. You will now understand what I meant in suggesting that, had the purloined letter been hidden anywhere within the limits of the Prefect's examination—in other words, had the principle of its concealment been comprehended within the principles of the Prefect—its discovery would have been a matter altogether beyond question. This functionary, however, has been thoroughly mystified; and the remote source of his defeat lies in the supposition that the Minister is a fool, because he has acquired renown as a poet. All fools are poets; this the Prefect *feels*; and he is merely guilty of a *non distributio medii* in thence inferring that all poets are fools."

"But is this really the poet?" I asked. "There are two brothers, I know; and both have attained reputation in letters. The Minister I believe has written learnedly on the Differential Calculus. He is a mathematician, and no poet."

"You are mistaken; I know him well; he is both. As poet and mathematician, he would reason well; as mere mathematician, he could not have reasoned at all, and thus would have been at the mercy of the Prefect."

"You surprise me," I said, "by these opinions, which have been contradicted by the voice of the world. You do not mean to set at naught the well-digested idea of centuries. The mathematical reason has long been regarded as *the* reason *par excellence*."

.   .   .

"I dispute the availability, and thus the value, of that reason which is cultivated in any especial form other than the abstractly logical. I dispute, in particular, the reason educed by mathematical study. The mathematics are the science of form and quantity; mathematical reasoning is merely logic applied to observation upon form and quantity. The great error lies in supposing that even the truths of what is called *pure* algebra, are abstract or general truths. And this error is so egregious that I am confounded at the universality with which it has been received. Mathematical axioms are *not* axioms of general truth. What is true of *relation*—of form and quantity—is often grossly false in regard to morals, for example. In this latter science it is very usually *un*true that the aggregated parts are equal to the whole. In chemistry also the axiom fails. In the consideration of motive it fails; for two motives, each of a given value, have not, necessarily, a value when united, equal to the sum of their values apart. There are numerous other mathematical truths which are only truths within the limits of *relation*. But the mathematician argues, from his *finite truths*, through habit, as if they were of an absolutely general applicability—as the world indeed imagines them to be. Bryant, in his very learned 'Mythology,' mentions an analogous source of error, when he says that 'although the Pagan fables are not believed, yet we forget ourselves continually, and make inferences from them as existing realities.' With the algebraists, however, who are Pagans themselves, the 'Pagan fables' *are* believed, and the inferences are made, not so much through lapse of memory, as through an unaccountable addling of the brains. In short, I never yet encountered the mere mathematician who could be trusted out of equal roots. ...

"I mean to say," continued Dupin, while I merely laughed at his last observations, "that if the Minister had been no more than a mathematician, the Prefect would have been under no necessity of giving me this check. I knew him, however, as both mathematician and poet, and my measures were adapted to his capacity, with reference to the circumstances by which he was surrounded. I knew him as a courtier, too, and as a bold *intriguant*. Such a man, I considered, could not fail to be aware of the ordinary political modes of action. He could not have failed to anticipate—and events have proved that he did not fail to anticipate—the waylayings to which he was subjected. He must have foreseen, I reflected, the secret investigations of his premises. His frequent absences from home at night, which were hailed by the Prefect as certain aids to his success, I regarded only as *ruses*, to afford opportunity for thorough search to the police, and thus the sooner to impress them with the conviction to which G———, in fact, did finally arrive—the conviction that the letter was not upon the premises. I felt, also, that the whole train of thought, which I was at some pains in detailing to you just now, concerning the invariable principle of policial action in searches for articles concealed—I felt that this whole train of thought would necessarily pass through the mind of the Minister. It would imperatively lead him to despise all the ordinary *nooks* of concealment. *He* could not, I reflected, be so weak as not to see that the most intricate and remote recess of his hotel would be as open as his commonest closets to the eyes, to the probes, to the gimlets, and to the microscopes of the Prefect. I saw, in fine, that he would be driven, as a matter of course, to *simplicity*, if not deliberately induced to it as a matter of choice. You will remember, perhaps, how desperately the Prefect laughed when I suggested, upon our first interview, that it was just possible this mystery troubled him so much on account of its being so *very* self-evident."

"Yes," said I, "I remember his merriment well. I really thought he would have fallen into convulsions."

". . . Again: have you ever noticed which of the street signs, over the shop-doors, are the most attractive of attention?"

"I have never given the matter a thought," I said.

"There is a game of puzzles," he resumed, "which is played upon a map. One party playing requires another to find a given word—the name of a town, river, state or empire—any word, in short, upon the motley and perplexed surface of the chart. A novice in the game generally seeks to embarrass his opponents by giving them the most minutely lettered names; but the adept selects such words as stretch, in large characters, from one end of the chart to the other. These, like the overlargely lettered signs and placards of the street, escape observation by dint of being excessively obvious; and here the physical oversight is precisely analogous with the moral inapprehension by which the intellect suffers to pass unnoticed those considerations which are too obtrusively and too palpably self-evident. But this is a point, it appears, somewhat above or beneath the understanding of the Prefect. He never once thought it probable, or possible, that the Minister had deposited the letter immediately beneath the nose of the whole world, by way of best preventing any portion of that world from perceiving it.

"But the more I reflected upon the daring, dashing, and discriminating ingenuity of D_____ ; upon the fact that the document must always have been *at hand*, if he intended to use it to good purpose; and upon the decisive evidence, obtained by the Prefect, that it was not hidden within the limits of that dignitary's ordinary search—the more satisfied I became that, to conceal this letter, the Minister had resorted to the comprehensive and sagacious expedient of not attempting to conceal it at all. ...

FOR FURTHER READING

Ackoff, Russell L., *A Concept of Corporate Planning*. New York: John Wiley & Sons, Inc., 1970, Chap. 1.

_____ , and Patrick Rivett, *A Manager's Guide to Operations Research*. New York: John Wiley & Sons, Inc., 1963.

Alexis, M., and C. Z. Wilson, *Organizational Decision Making*. Englewood Cliffs, N.J.: Prentice-Hall, Inc., 1967.

Anshen, Melvin, "The Manager and the Black Box." *Harvard Business Review*, Vol. 38, No. 6 (November-December 1960), 85.

Beer, S., *Decision and Control*. New York: John Wiley & Sons, Inc., 1967.

Bierman, Harold J., and Seymour Smidt, *The Capital Budgeting Decision*. New York: The Macmillan Company, 1960.

Boulden, James B., and Edward S. Buffa, "Corporate Models: On-Line, Real-Time Systems." *Harvard Business Review*, Vol. 48, No. 4 (July-August 1970), 65.

Boulding, Kenneth, "Ethics on Rational Decision." *Management Science*, Vol. 12, No. 6 (January 1966), 161.

Bower, Joseph, "Group Decision Making: A Report of an Experimental Study." *Behavioral Science*, Vol. 10, No. 4 (July 1965), 277.

Braybrooke D., and C. E. Lindblom, *A Strategy of Decision*. New York: The Free Press, 1963.

Churchman, C. W., and A. H. Schainblatt, "The Researcher and the Manager: A Dialectic of Implementation." *Management Science*, Vol. 11, No. 4 (February 1965), 69-70.

Dean, J., *Capital Budgeting*. New York: Columbia University Press, 1951.

Emory, C. W., and P. Niland, *Making Management Decisions*. Boston: Houghton Mifflin Company, 1968, Chap. 5.

Etzioni, A., "Mixed-Scanning: A 'Third' Approach to Decision-Making." *Public Administration Review*, Vol. 27, No. 6 (November-December 1967).

Greiner, Larry E., D. Paul Leitch, and Louis B. Barnes, "Putting Judgment Back into Decisions." *Harvard Business Review*, Vol. 48, No. 2 (March-April 1970), 59.

Goldman, T. A., ed., *Cost Effectiveness Analysis: New Approaches in Decision-Making*. New York: Frederick A. Praeger, Inc., 1967.

Gore, William J., *Administrative Decision Making: An Heuristic Model*. New York: John Wiley & Sons, Inc., 1964.

———, and J. W. Dyson, *The Making of Decisions: A Reader in Administrative Behavior*. New York: The Macmillan Company, 1964. A Free Press Book.

Gregory, C. E., *The Management of Intelligence: Scientific Problem Solving and Creativity*. New York: McGraw-Hill Book Company, 1967.

Gruber, H. E., ed., *Contemporary Approaches to Creative Thinking*. New York: Atherton Press, Inc., 1962.

Hammond, John S., III, "Better Decisions with Preference Theory." *Harvard Business Review*, Vol. 45, No. 6 (November-December 1967), 123.

Haynes, W. W., *Managerial Economics*, rev. ed. Austin, Tex.: Business Publications, Inc., 1969, Chaps. 2 and 10.

Hertz, David B., "Risk Analysis in Capital Investment." *Harvard Business Review*, Vol. 42, No. 1 (January-February 1964), 95.

Hinkle, Charles L., and Alfred A. Kuehn, "Heuristic Models: Mapping the Maze for Management." *California Management Review*, Vol. 10, No. 1 (Fall 1967), pp. 59-68.

Jones, Curtis H., "At Last: Real Computer Power for Decision Makers." *Harvard Business Review*, Vol. 48, No. 5 (September-October 1970), 75.

Jones, M. H., *Executive Decision Making*, rev. ed. Homewood, Ill.: Richard D. Irwin, Inc., 1962, Chaps. 1 and 3.

Kepner, C. H., and B. B. Tregoe, *The Rational Manager*. New York: McGraw-Hill Book Company, 1965.

Magee, John, "Decision Trees for Decision Making." *Harvard Business Review*, Vol. 42, No. 4 (July-August 1964), 126.

Malcolm, Donald G., "On the Need for Improvement in Implementation of O.R." *Management Science*, Vol. 11, No. 4 (February 1965), 48-58.

Miller, David W., and Martin K. Starr, *Executive Decisions and Operations Research*, 2nd ed. Englewood Cliffs, N.J.: Prentice-Hall, Inc., 1969.

Milton, G. A., "Group vs. Individual Problem Solving and Decision Making." *Canadian Public Administration*, Vol. 68, No. 3 (September 1965), 301-306.

Parnes, S. J., and H. F. Harding, eds., *A Source Book for Creative Thinking*. New York: Charles Scribner's Sons, 1962.

Pounds, William F., "The Process of Problem Finding." *Industrial Management Review* Vol. 11, No. 1 (Fall 1969), 1-19.

Raiffa, Howard, *Decision Analysis*. Reading, Mass.: Addison-Wesley Publishing Co., Inc., 1968.

Rugg, H., *Imagination: An Inquiry into the Sources and Conditions That Stimulate Creativity*. New York: Harper & Row, Publishers, 1963.

Schlaifer, Robert O., *Analysis of Decisions Under Uncertainty*. New York: McGraw-Hill Book Company, 1969.

Schon, D. A., *Invention and the Evolution of Ideas*. London: Associated Book Publishers Ltd., 1967.

Shillinglaw, G., *Cost Accounting*, rev. ed. Homewood, Ill.: Richard D. Irwin, Inc., 1967.

Shuchman, A., ed., *Scientific Decision Making in Business*. New York: Holt, Rinehart & Winston, Inc., 1963.

Starr, Martin K., *Management: A Modern Approach*. New York: Harcourt Brace Jovanovich, Inc., Parts 1 and 2.

Stein, M. I., and S. J. Heinze, *Creativity and the Individual*. Glencoe, Ill.: Free Press of Glencoe, 1960.

Steiner, Gary, *The Creative Organization*. Chicago: University of Chicago Press, 1965.

Vandell, Richard, "Management Evolution in the Quantitative World." *Harvard Business Review*, Vol. 48, No. 1 (January-February 1970), 83.

Vatter, William J., "The Use of Operations Research in American Companies." *The Accounting Review*, Vol. 42, No. 4 (October 1967), 721-730.

Wagner, Harvey M., *Principles of Management Science*. Englewood Cliffs, N.J.: Prentice-Hall, Inc., 1970.

Walton, C. C., *The Ethos and the Executive*. Englewood Cliffs, N.J.: Prentice-Hall, Inc., 1969.

Woods, Donald H., "Improving Estimates That Involve Uncertainty." *Harvard Business Review*, Vol. 44, No. 4 (July-August 1966), 91-98.

Zani, William, "Blueprint for MIS." *Harvard Business Review*, Vol. 48, No. 6 (November-December 1970), 95.

PART FOUR

Planning: Decision-Making in an Enterprise

During the early stages of industrial development in the United States, the study of planning would have generated little interest in business circles. In fact, planning far ahead was contrary both to the temperament of the entrepreneurs who built American industry and to the needs of the time.

In a nation of vast resources and unparalleled opportunity, isolated from the economic and political turmoil of Europe, formal planning was relatively unimportant. Many resources could be, and were, squandered, and opportunities ignored. The truly scarce "resources" were tough, hard-driving men of action who had the capacity to organize the untapped wealth of America to meet its growing needs.

During this period, business planning was equated with rapid and economical *adaptation* to change. The relatively slower rate and magnitude of change permitted managers to wait until change had taken place. Quick, imaginative *reactions* were often successful substitutes for planning.

With the continuing growth of both domestic and international competition, U.S. managers have found that the increased speed, magnitude, and complexity of economic, social, and technological change make adaptation a costly substitute for real planning. These changes combine to lengthen the decision-making process, while concurrently shortening the economic or profitable life of any single business decision. Today, most business leaders recognize that the best way to meet this challenge, to shorten the decision-making process and find faster, less disruptive answers to changing conditions, is through more and better planning.

In Part Three attention was directed to models of individual decision-making. We focused on the individual manager and sought to examine the steps *he* must take and the factors *he* must consider in making business decisions. As indicated in the introduction to Part Three, concepts and techniques generated in the fields of operations research and the behavioral sciences, to pick just two, have increased the amount of attention given to *formalized* approaches to planning. Even if only one man in an organization did all the planning, he still could profit from these "formalizing" concepts.

A second type of pressure has increased the attention given to more formalized planning approaches. It stems from the fact that, typically, no one person is responsible for all the preparation for any one decision, nor does one person make all the decisions. The increased size of organizations, coupled with the complexity of the problems requiring solutions, has created a need for planning in a way that first draws on the several parts of the organization that must contribute to the planning process, and, second, communicates the plans to those who must implement them.

The second, organizational, type of pressure makes the use of informal, *ad hoc*, approaches to planning difficult, even when the talents of individual decision-makers permit it. As a result, in this section, we focus on the elements of planning that must be considered when the task moves from the level of the individual manager to that of planning in the framework of the enterprise. Hopefully, an understanding of these concepts will lead us back to models of individual decision-making in order to modify them so that they reflect organizational pressures and constraints.

The most difficult problem we faced in seeking to implement these objectives was selecting from the vast amount of material published on planning in recent years. Because the traditional texts on management contain a great deal of material on terminology, we decided to omit such material in order to focus on aspects of planning in the enterprise that only recently have received the attention due them. These are:

1. The importance and the implications of identifying overall corporate strategy and philosophy as a first key step in planning within the enterprise.
2. The problems arising as a result of conflicts among overall organizational goals, conflicts among the more specific goals of the subunits of the organization, and conflicts that face the individuals who man these subunits in trying to balance both personal and subgroup goals with higher-order corporate goals.

Toward these ends, we have chosen the selections appearing in Part Four.

25

The Management of Ideas

MELVIN ANSHEN

Selected by a jury of management experts as one of the two best articles published in the Harvard Business Review *in 1969, this insightful article by Melvin Anshen has been chosen to keynote our section on decision-making in organizations. The author combines in this piece the insight of a visionary philosopher with the critical awareness of one who has spent years advising executives on matters of top-level policy formulation. Anshen pushes away with one arm the busy concerns of the "mechanics" of management who clamor for executive attention as they vie to sell the latest "how-to tools" while with the other arm he sweeps away the purveyors of platitudes who offer vague conceptual schemes for ordering the process of strategy formulation. In place of these, he offers guides to what top managers must think about and suggestions on how they should think about them in order to develop a basis for knowing which tools or conceptual schemes to use.*

As you read this article, consider what types of courses a man or woman preparing for a career in management should take. What types of books, articles, and/or seminars should the practitioner seek out to provide the growing breadth and intellectual stamina required for those who aspire to shape and implement the kinds of strategic decisions that may alter the direction and success of large organizations?

A profound change in the main task of top management is emerging as a result of the accelerating dynamics of technologies, markets, information systems, and social expectations of business performance. If this projection is correct, the threat of obsolescence of managers will pass swiftly from today's conversational shocker to tomorrow's operating reality. Executives best prepared to survive this challenge may turn out to be those equipped to think like philosophers—a type of intellectual skill not ordinarily developed in business schools or by the common work experiences of middle management.

The roots of this radical transformation of the general management job can be identified in recent business history:

☐ *Resources*—Up to about the last two decades the main task of top management could fairly be described as the efficient administration of physical resources. The focus was essentially short-range and unifunctional, and the dominant decision criteria were economic. The highest demonstration of management skill was the successful manipulation of revenues and costs in the production and distribution of materials, machines, and products.

☐ *People*—Beginning in the 1930's this concern with managing physical things was enlarged by a growing interest in managing people. This was enlargement, rather than change, because the ultimate goal of effective people management was still effective thing management, with top executives extending their grasp over resources by means of their ability to organize and motivate people. The focus of management attention remained within short-term horizons and unifunctional activity.

☐ *Money*—After World War II, in a business environment marked by rapid growth in corporate size, product and market diversification, accelerated technological development, and shortened product life cycles, the principal task of top management evolved from concentration on physical and human resources to a major concern with money. This shift was accompanied by an extension of planning horizons and a transition from a unifunctional to a multifunctional view of a company's activities.

· · ·

☐ *Ideas*—We are now beginning to sense that a focus on managing money, although broader than the earlier focus on physical and human resources, still fosters a dangerous sort of tunnel vision. The world of management is in a revolutionary phase. Within the company, racing technologies destroy both their own foundations and inter-technological boundaries. Outside the company, the environment is moving faster (in market evolution and consumer behavior), exploding in geographic scope (from nation to world), and reflecting the demands and constraints of a new society in which the traditional role of private business and traditional criteria of management performance are challenged by new concepts and standards.

At the same time, new analytical techniques, largely quantitative and computer-based, are presenting a management opportunity that is unique in at least two important ways. First, they provide an administrative capability without parallel in breadth, depth, and speed. Second, for their full and efficient utilization they press management to establish a unified command over the totality of a business, including the dynamic interface of external environment and internal activities. These changes are defining a novel view of management itself as a universally applicable resource, readily transferred from one business to another, from one industry to another, from one technology to another, from one country to another.

In this emerging management world, what will be the main task of management, common to top-level administrators in all types and sizes of companies? I suggest a combination of spatial and temporal intellectual vision, with the ability to transform vision into operating results through the flexible administration of physical, human, and financial resources in any environment. This might be described as applied conceptualization—or, more simply, as the management of ideas.

. . .

CENTRAL FOCUS FOR IDEAS

Skill in generating and manipulating ideas is precisely the skill of the great philosophers—the ability to universalize from here and now to everywhere and always. If it is true that top executives in the years ahead are going to be tested above all by their ability to manage ideas, then they are going to have to understand what it means to think like philosophers and develop skill in doing it. This has implications for management education, training, and selection, especially at the higher levels of administration. It also carries a substantial threat of obsolescence for managers now holding broad responsibilities whose talent, education, and experience have not equipped them to use their intellects in this manner.

The implications are not limited to the purely intellectual demands placed on general managers. They also extend to corporate purpose, organization, and function. A business devoted to the identification of central ideas and the formulation of strategies for moving swiftly from ideas to operations will differ in structure and activity from a business primarily concerned with management of money, or of physical and human resources.

Management of ideas is a broader concept than either management by objectives or long-range planning. The use of objectives and planning are techniques equally relevant for any major management task, whether it be a focus on physical resources or money, or a principal concern with ideas.

Management of ideas also goes beyond the concept of strategy. Just as there are alternative strategies for attaining an objective, so there are alternative strategies for executing an idea that defines the central purpose of a business. Focusing on the management of ideas contributes to more realistic planning, more appropriate objectives, more relevant strategies.

Ideas for Technology

One example of how an idea may be viewed as the central focus for management attention can be found in industries characterized by advanced, dynamic technologies.

Soft answers: In this arena, it is attractively easy to frame a soft answer to the hard question of how to organize resources for maximum effectiveness. A typical soft answer:

"In our fast-moving technological environment, the big winners will be those companies with large investments in research and development, because out of R&D come the new products that capture markets and generate high return on investment. Therefore we should invest every available dollar in R&D."

The inadequacy of this operating design is suggested by the common management complaint in these industries that it is difficult to establish rational control over investment in, and performance of, R&D, difficult to measure payback on R&D investment, and difficult to concentrate research efforts on projects with high potential payoffs.

Hard answers: However, there are few companies in high-technology industries in which such complaints rarely arise. These are the companies whose top managers have done the thinking that develops hard, rather than soft, answers. They have observed that a commitment to R&D without a specific central concept for total organization effort is a clumsy, even a meaningless, commitment. But by resolute probing, they have found an opportunity for defining a core idea around which total company effort can be designed. This opportunity can be described in terms of three specific idea options:

1. To mobilize all of a company's resources around the concept of becoming a creative technological leader—the first in the industry to discover, develop, and market new products at the leading edge of moving technology.

2. To organize resources around the central idea of becoming an early imitator and adapter of the successful innovations of the industry's creative leader.

3. To become a low-price mass producer of established products, sacrificing the high margins (and high risks) of innovation for the high volume (and limited risks) of low-price imitation.

Each of these options carries specific implications for the kind of investment in product and market research, as well as for organization structure, information network, scale of activity and risk, and many other aspects of a company's physical, personal, and financial resources. In short, out of each of these idea options can be derived a total scheme for operating a business. This total scheme will be uniquely determined by the central idea and will represent the top management choice among alternative strategies for executing the idea throughout the business.

. . .

Other Examples

Still other examples of central ideas may be cited briefly:
○ A shift in the definition of a business from one concerned with the

sale of a product to one concerned with the delivery of a complete system of customer values—as in airlines' marketing of packaged vacations, computer manufacturers' marketing of systems to solve customers' information problems, and consumer hard-good companies' marketing of assured lifetime performance of products.

o The discovery, almost the invention, of new industries—such as environmental hygiene and control, education as a lifespan need, and the profit-oriented performance of traditional public services such as urban redevelopment or even urban creation.

o The abandonment of accepted notions of industry boundaries—as in the transformation of a steel company into a materials company or of a petroleum company into an energy company.

o The evolution of "scrambled merchandising" in retail stores which focus on a pattern of consumer needs and buying habits rather than on historic product categories such as groceries or drug products.

Each of these ideas is the energized core of a unique design for a business. The exploitation of each idea requires a comprehensive intellectual grasp of the totality of a business viewed as an interacting system that includes both internal resources and functions and external distribution systems and markets. From such a comprehensive vision will issue a flow of strategic options for products, services, costs, prices, technology, organization structures, responsibilities, information networks, and motivations for all levels of management.

NEW WAYS OF THINKING

Thinking in terms of such ideas, from initial concept through full implementation, is a difficult intellectual task. It is no assignment for second-rate minds, or even for first-rate but narrowly oriented minds. Moreover, it demands the special intellectual ability to visualize the translation of ideas and strategies into controlled operating systems responsive to dynamic change.

The need for these unusual talents is the inevitable outcome of radically new conditions within and outside the corporation. The critical new condition is an acceleration in the rate of change of such magnitude that change itself becomes the central object of management attention. Up to now, with rare exceptions, the administration of change has been handled as a supplement to the administration of established ongoing activities. In this context, the future evolves from the present at a controllable pace, and it is reasonable for managers to concentrate mainly on targets of efficiency and to treat adapting to market challenges as a subsidiary element within a larger administrative responsibility.

. . .

Preparing for Change

At this point, it becomes more important to make correct decisions about the direction, timing, and implementation of change than to attain a high level of efficiency in administering steady-state operations. However, few business organizations have been designed to give primary support to this unfamiliar ordering of goals. In most companies the values, organization, responsibility, control systems, information networks, and performance standards are not well adapted to this requirement.

Most companies, including many with reputations for being well managed, are organized primarily to administer yesterday's ideas. Investments and operations are measured by efficient performance, with relatively short-term targets for achievement, and a primary focus on taut administration of existing resources and markets. This was an appropriate corporate design concept when the rate of changes within and outside the company was slow.

The weakness of such organizations is revealed, however, whenever a new opportunity or a forced adaptation is sensed by a single department. Rapid exploitation of new markets usually increases production costs, and is therefore resisted by managers whose performance will be adversely affected in any shift in ongoing efficient activities. Less common, but equally possible, is resistance from the marketing people to innovation in production technology with its risk of cost, quality, and delivery uncertainties.

But even this view is simplistic. For in spite of the current touted commitment to a marketing orientation in management, the performance record in many companies suggests that leadership by the marketing function frequently generates little more than better adaptation of existing products to better defined existing markets. This may be a move in the right direction in the short run. But it is not good enough in a period when new technology may erode established market positions or capture untouched markets "overnight."

Inherent in the concept of core ideas for top management is a total business orientation, rather than a market-oriented administration (or a technology-oriented or any "other-oriented" administration). A total business orientation views the company as a system of physical, financial, and human resources in dynamic interaction with a changing environment. It views swift response to opportunities and problems as more important for long-run success than efficient control of current operations. It values the future above the present. Such an orientation has revolutionary implications for many management designs and tasks.

• • •

Information Revolution

[An] example of revolutionary change in administrative design can be found in the area of information generation and use.

A few words about computers are in order at the outset. The history of computer applications in the 17 years since their introduction to the business market reveals two distinct stages in management concepts of their potential.

1. Initially, most managers viewed computers as electronic clerks. The primary use of computers was therefore in familiar tasks.

2. Recently, a second stage of management thinking can be discerned. This has been marked by a superficial popularization of the concept of the integrated information system which calls on the storage, retrieval, and manipulative capability of large computers to bring the total information requirements of a business within an integrated decision network. (This does not imply a computerized decision system, but simply an organized information system, computer-based, to assist comprehensive human decision making.)

While the notion of the integrated information system has been widely described and explored in technical and management journals, several probes of management practice suggest that few companies have made a sustained attempt to operate in this way, and few managers have any real grasp of what the concept means in either theoretical or operating terms. There is, to be sure, a growing number of fractional, single-function information systems, such as those linking production, inventory, and procurement activities. And there is a growing disposition to talk about comprehensive management information systems. But the operational application is a long way from the discussion, with many unresolved conceptual and technical problems in between.

It would be a gross misconception to view this gap as the familiar one between software and hardware. The primary task ahead is not to develop programs that will utilize the capabilities of the machines. Rather it is to develop management concepts that define integrated systems. It will then be possible to describe the principal data requirements to make such systems operational, including clear delineation of relationships among the components of a dynamic system responsive to external and internal feedback. The next step will be the design of computer programs to store and manipulate data for management needs.

At present, most top managers have yet to approach even the initial stage of developing basic concepts. The skeptic may be inclined to say: "But this can't be true! Managers are running companies, and this means that they are running systems, with whatever crude tools, including the human brain, they may have at hand." To which the appropriate reply is:

"True enough, managers are running companies. But examination of the typical management decision process reveals that what is happening is in no sense total system analysis. Problems are usually fractionated within the total company system—partly to reduce them to a size and order of simplicity that are manageable with available analytical tools, and partly to follow familiar routines and utilize familiar rules of thumb."

What is defined here is not a technical requirement, but an intellectual requirement. This is essentially a command of logical design. The basic design building blocks are:

1. Identification of critical areas of initiating change that generate effects in one or several operating areas.

2. Rough measures of the magnitudes of the primary cause-effect relationships.

3. Identification of the principal feedbacks.

4. Rough measures of these feedbacks.

For purposes of concept formulation and testing the degree of precision ordinarily required is modest because this is not primarily a quantitative exercise. One does not need numbers to design a business system. In fact, the truth is quite the reverse. One first needs a concept of a system in order to identify the kinds of numbers needed to work the system.

Furthermore, it is unlikely that any comprehensive business system can be completely quantified in the sense of converting all decision inputs into a set of manipulatable numbers. The objective is limited and practical. It is simply to use both quantitative and qualitative analysis to extend management's decision horizon to the total business viewed as a dynamic system, and thereby to improve the quality of decisions. The improvement will be reflected in the ability to make decisions that are broadly consistent with the basic concept of the business, sensitive to impacts and feedbacks throughout the business, and rapidly and flexibly adaptive to changing conditions within and outside the company.

FOCUS ON THE FUTURE

A [second] example of the impact of revolutionary change is the need for upgrading management's ability to forecast the shape of things to come. During the last 20 years economic forecasting has made the transition from favorite parlor game of professional economists to favorite reading matter of professional managers. The prognostications of accredited economic forecasters are a mandatory item on every trade association agenda, while discussions of the economic outlook clog the pages of management magazines.

But economic change is only one of several environmental areas important to managers. Three other areas are equally significant: technological change, social change, and political change. Few companies and few individual managers have addressed themselves in a serious and organized way to the problems of forecasting trends in these areas. Yet changes in the years ahead, coming more rapidly than ever before, will be loaded with opportunities for the forewarned, and with threats for those who have not cast their minds forward and formulated offensive and defensive strategies.

The requirement is for more than a freshened interest in the future. The evolution of economic forecasting to its present significant role in management planning resulted from the invention of sophisticated tools of analysis. One cannot predict economic trends with a useful level of confidence until the significant economic variables have been identified and their interacting dynamics at least roughly measured. Forecasting of technological, social, and political changes (including both trends and rates of movement) will require a comparable intellectual achievement. Large rewards will be realized by organizations that can anticipate developments in these areas with enough confidence to incorporate their forecasts in strategic planning.

Technological Forecasting

In the area of technology an essential conceptual adaptation must be to extend management thinking beyond the base to which it is commonly tied, that is, the view that improvements will be regularly generated from developments in the technologies that have been their historical foundation. This is an understandable but limiting and risky framework for forecasting.

Analysis of recent technological advances clearly identifies two related phenomena of great importance to management. One is the application of "foreign" technologies in process and product areas where they have played no significant prior role. The other is the erosion, often the disappearance, of traditional industry and product boundaries. Together, they lay down a requirement that technological forecasting be treated broadly.

It will not be safe for a manager to project the shape of technological changes by extrapolating trends in existing applications. Some of the most significant developments affecting both production and marketing are likely to be spawned within technologies that are not currently applicable in his industry and company.

Technological forecasting of this breadth and sophistication will not progress far without the development of a new kind of professional expertise, comparable to that of professional economists. It will be a prime responsibility of enlightened managers to encourage qualified scientists and engineers to address themselves to the assignment, and to build their own ability to communicate with and guide this new corps of professionals.

In addition, just as the sophisticated manager needs the skill to translate economic forecasts into signals of opportunity and threat for his company's future operations, so will he need a parallel skill to translate technological forecasts into meaningful guides for business strategies. This task cannot safely be left to the technicians. There should be little need to emphasize this warning to managers who have grasped, often after painful experience, the need to guide the work of computer specialists to assure that they mobilize information specifically relevant for management control and decision.

A prime ingredient in translating technological projections into business applications will be a thorough understanding of the difference between technical feasibility and economic feasibility. Technology determines what can be done. Economics determines what will be done. Managers must be familiar with this distinction. Many of today's naive forecasters of the technological outlook who are writing in the popular press certainly are not.

Social Forecasting

Forecasting of social trends covers such topics as changing social structure (including racial and ethnic components), evolution of living patterns and related spending patterns, and shifting values and priorities (for example, between work and leisure, between risk assumption and security).

The full implications of the opportunities presented by recent social trends have been grasped by few companies. For instance, managers of a number of financial institutions reveal a persistent preoccupation with superficial economic phenomena of consumers' saving and investment patterns, rather than a probing analysis of the financial service needs of a society marked by widespread affluence, multiple options in discretionary spending, confidence in long-range income security, and rising concern about permanent inflation.

A well-known example of the powerful application of social (appropriately combined with economic) forecasting is the course pursued by Sears, Roebuck and Co. since World War II. The dramatic divergence of this company's performance from that of its direct competitor, Montgomery Ward & Company, Inc., needs no description for a management audience. But the important contribution made by a projection of fundamental social changes and the translation of that forecast into market opportunities deserves to be noted.

Sears made an aggressive exploitation of social perspective through a core institutional idea. The results have been as spectacular as was the comparable grasp of a new business opportunity evoked by socioeconomic change evidenced in the implementation of a core management idea by General Motors under Alfred P. Sloan's direction in the 1920's.

The extension of management's conceptual competence in the area of social dynamics calls for knowledge and perceptiveness that have not been required hitherto. As in the field of technology, managers will be dealing with professional specialists whose work must be directed and interpreted. Competence in doing this will build the confidence to use social projections in designing business strategies that open the way to radical innovations in organization and operations.

Political Forecasting

The principal business element in political forecasting is the shifting boundary between the private and public sectors of the economy. Until recently, the prevailing management view of this area was a superficial conclusion that a transfer of activities was occurring from the private to the public sector, directly by intervention or indirectly by control.

Current developments are beginning to suggest that this is a naive judgment. Movement in the opposite direction can also be discerned, for example, in education, research, and construction. New, mixed public-private enterprise forms, such as Comsat, are being invented. More developments of this sort may be anticipated. Moreover, changes in the domain of private enterprise, in pure or mixed form, are not totally a result of decisions taken within government. Business initiative can open the door to private expansion, particularly where the public performance has been lethargic, unimaginative, or grossly inefficient.

The pejorative descriptive phrase "socialization of American society," indiscriminately applied to developments in such diverse fields as health, insurance, transportation, housing, or even protection of consumer interests, has a dangerous potential for stultifying thinking about the central issues. A more open view might recognize that an industrialized, urbanized, high-technology society, in which a dramatically visible gap appears between the actual and the potential quality of life, is a society ripe for changes in traditional public-private relationships.

The changes may move in either direction: toward public invasion of the private sector or toward private invasion of the public sector. The direction and rate of these changes will be powerfully influenced by managers who can deal confidently with new ideas in areas where businessmen have seldom allowed their minds to be engaged. The political environment, there can be little doubt, will be redesigned. But those who believe that environment is created by forces outside their control will not be in an intellectual position to participate in the redesign. An environment will be imposed on them which, however reluctantly, they will be compelled to accept.

On the positive side, a rising interest and skill in forecasting political relationships will identify opportunities for private enterprise to invent new environmental concepts. Formulating these concepts, and relating them to profitable resource investment, will require an intellectual adventure in the world of ideas such as few managers have so far experienced. Part of the process will surely be fresh definitions of the words "private" and "public," which, as applied to business and government activities, have been largely emptied of meaning by emotional abuse.

As in forecasting social change, it is not easy to perceive shifts in the private-public balance, or potential for inducing shifts by initiatives from the private sector. We lack even the professional discipline to generate the knowledge and develop a reliable analytical base for management thinking. Traditional political science is oriented toward the problems of governing men and the performance of institutions for public legislation and administration. The new issues are closer to those implied by the classic term "political economy" and involve concepts of social design on the grand scale.

PHILOSOPHER-EXECUTIVE

The emerging dominance of ideas as a central concern for top management raises critical questions about the education, selection, and development of candidates for high-level assignments in the years ahead. Neither business school education nor in-company experience is presently structured to emphasize the manager-as-philosopher concept. Rather, the principal thrust in school and company environments is toward new analytic techniques, both quantitative and qualitative, and their application in rational decision making and control.

There is good reason to doubt that students in professional schools are at a stage of their intellectual development where they would benefit from a major emphasis on the role of central ideas in top management responsibilities. Moreover, the relevant technical input to their education is so important and growing so rapidly that any sharp curtailment would constrain their ability to handle management tasks in junior executive positions.

The education of middle-level managers is another matter, however. There are opportunities at this stage to expose selected high-potential executives to the significance of core ideas in the design of long-range corporate strategies and in the adaptation of organization and resources to their implementation. The opportunities arise in planned job experiences and management education programs, both in-house and university. Imaginative action at this level will produce two important benefits. One is the preparation of a cadre of potential top executives for the broad new responsibilities that the future business environment will thrust on them. The other is a new selection criterion for top-level positions, based on specific performance in mid-career assignments where the ability to think conceptually and to relate ideas to applied management can be tested.

Today's development programs give principal emphasis to new techniques for analysis and control in functional areas, and to strategic planning of resource utilization at the general management level. It would be desirable to curtail the technical content to some degree and introduce material on dynamic environmental change (markets, technologies, social, political), on the role and manipulation of ideas, and on the impact of change on corporate strategy.

A related effort to enrich idea-management experience on the job and test executives' abilities would require more opportunities below the top management level for assignments that require imaginative projection, assessment of the total environmental outlook, and relevant strategic decision. Corporations which move in this direction will fortify their management ability to cope powerfully and speedily with a radically new business world.

26

The World of Program Budgeting

G. H. FISHER

One of the most recent frameworks offered for increasing rationality in the formulation and implementation of decisions is the Program Budgeting approach conceived by the U.S. Department of Defense. Although many managers were introduced to this approach as a requirement for doing business with the Department of Defense, as they grew to understand it, they turned to it for its value in coordinating the many elements of key nondefense-related planning. This selection by Fisher offers a clear and concise description and illustration of the key elements of this technique.

In going over these concepts consider some of the questions raised by Schon and Lindblom in Part Three.

To what degree do you feel the techniques for linking "rational" inputs taken from numerous parts of an organization offer answers to the objections Schon and Lindblom raise?

Suppose that you are vice-president in charge of corporate planning for a large automobile manufacturing firm. Suppose further that your planning staff comes into your office to present its plan for the future involving the introduction of several new car lines several years hence. Since the lead time in the automobile industry from conception of a new design until display on the showroom floor is about 4 or 5 years, the planners are talking about a time horizon of at least five years into the future.

Reprinted from *Long Range Planning,* the journal of the Society for Long Range Planning, Vol. 2, No. 1 (September 1969), 50-60, by permission of the publisher and the author. Copyright 1969 by Pergamon Press Ltd., London.

The staff starts with a "Madison Avenue" type presentation regarding the beauties of the styling of these proposed new vehicles. They also present information about performance characteristics. Numerous color slides are flashed on a screen to emphasize the possible appeal of these new models. Finally, some quantitative exhibits are presented, of which the following are representative:

(1) A table showing the dollar investments required in the *forthcoming year* (1969) to initiate the new program:
Research and development
New plant investment
New equipment investment
etc.

(2) The total shown in (1) for 1969 broken down into the major *organizations* of the company: the engine and transmission division, the stamping division, the final assembly division, etc.

(3) The same total broken down in terms of contractual services, in-company labour, materials, overhead, etc.

End of presentation. You, as vice-president in charge of planning, are now supposed to agree to the proposed plan before it is taken to higher levels. At this point, if you are an experienced executive you will be exasperated and you might decide to give your staff a little lecture containing remarks like the following:

1. As strategic planners we are supposed to consider the basic objectives of this company, and to develop and evaluate numerous alternative possible ways of attaining these objectives in the future. Our hard core quantitative objective is to develop, produce, and sell good car lines across the total spectrum of the automotive market: economy class, intermediate price range, and luxury class. The basic problem is to devise ways of penetrating these markets more deeply than we are right now. Ultimately, we want to do this in a way that will tend to maximize the company's net income in the long run, but subject to certain constraints. Some of these constraints are qualitative—e.g., preserving our public image in various directions. Now, your [the planning staff's] presentation did not tell me very much about any of these things.

2. To be more specific: Your presentation contained a *single* plan, and even that was not defined in terms very meaningful from a strategic planning point of view. You gave me no indication whatever of the *alternatives* that were considered and what their respective impacts on attainment of basic company objectives might be. Also, you might even have used a little more imagination and asked yourselves whether the currently held and projected *objectives* ought to be revised; and if so, the alternatives that might be considered to attain *those* objectives.

In sum, you have given me no substantive basis for making a decision. I don't know whether your proposed plan is better than some other alternative or not. In fact, you haven't told me anything about the relevant alternatives.

3. While your vehicle styling presentations were rather impressive from a sales point of view, your other exhibits were not very informative. For example, you show me what the investment costs are for the *on-coming* year—the "down payment" so to speak. But by definition our problem has at least a 5-year time horizon into the future. Ideally, I would like to see projections of estimated total costs (both investment and operating) *and revenues,* time phased by fiscal year over the total time horizon. And I would like to see this for *each of the alternatives* you considered. Only then would I have some of the key quantitative inputs that would help me weigh the merits of the alternatives in terms of estimated costs and benefits (and hence net company income) over the relevant span of years.

4. The particular identifications you use in your cost exhibits, while relevant, are not the most important from a planning point of view. In addition to the time horizon being too short, you stress only organizational and functional (labour, material, overhead, etc.) break-outs. These, of course, are very important when it comes to implementing the plan administratively and operationally. However, from a planning decision point of view, I would want to see much more emphasis placed on objectives-oriented identifications. For example, we could visualize a summary table having down the side the major market areas we must try to penetrate in the future, and the various car lines that are being proposed within each area. The column headings would contain the fiscal years over the total planning horizon, and for each year we could show the estimated costs and revenues for each market area and the car lines within each area [Figure 1]. Of course, there would be backup exhibits to the summary; and again, I would like to see such a presentation for *each* alternative plan considered.

The above "lecture" contains the basic elements of the *World of Program Budgeting.* The preceding example is purely hypothetical. The U.S. automobile industry does not conduct its planning activities in the manner portrayed by the planning staff in the example. The planning is done much more along the lines suggested in the vice-president's "lecture."

A DEPARTMENT OF DEFENSE EXAMPLE

. . .

If we had examined the U.S. Department of Defense's planning, programming and budgeting activity prior to 1961, in terms of budget format, we would have found something like that shown in Figure 1a.

Notice that the time horizon is only one fiscal year into the future. Thus, essentially no information is conveyed about the future implications of decisions made to date. With respect to budget categories, it is clear that the particular set of identifications used sheds little or not light on issues pertaining to national security objectives, or on the instrumentalities to be used in pursuing those objectives. In short, the format is not very meaningful from a planning and programming point of view.

An illustrative program budget format for the Department of Defense is portrayed in Figure 2. Figure 2 is far more meaningful than Figure 1—particularly from the standpoint of planning and programming. Of course the planned projected forces are an integral part of Figure 2. This, of course, makes sense; and one might ask how it could be any other way. The fact is, however, that prior to 1961 there was not a clear relationship among plans, programs, and budgets. While at the present time some problems still exist on this score in the Department of Defense, a great amount of progress has been made since 1961. The Department is well on the way toward attaining an integration of budgeting considerations on the one hand, and planning and programming considerations on the other.

Figure 1   Summary of estimated revenues and cost for Plan No. 1.

Market Area and Car Line	1966 Revenue	1966 Cost	1967 Revenue	1967 Cost	1968 Revenue	1968 Cost
Economy class Car line X_1 Car line X_2 : :						
Total						
Intermediate price market range Car line Y_1 Car line Y_2 : :						
Total						
Luxury price class Car line Z_1 Car line Z_2 : :						
Total						
Grand Total						

THE MAJOR CHARACTERISTICS
OF A PROGRAM BUDGETING SYSTEM

Let us turn now to the problem of trying to define rather explicitly the major considerations involved in a total program budgeting activity. While the basic ideas are very simple and straightforward, we do find semantic problems in attempting to discuss what is meant by the term "program budgeting." Even at the present time the term often means very different things to different people.

... The conception of the subject is also essentially the one adopted by the Bureau of the Budget at the present time. The primary considerations involved in program budgeting may be summarized under three main heads:

(1) Structural or format
(2) Analytical process
(3) Data or information systems

	1971		Total 1966-1971		
...	Revenue	Cost	Revenue	Cost	Net Revenue
...	———	———	———	———	———
...	———	———	———	———	———
...	———	———	———	———	———
...	———	———	———	———	———
...	———	———	———	———	———
...	———	———	———	———	———

Figure 1a

Budget Category	Obligational Authority (in dollars)		
	Past Fiscal Year	Current Fiscal Year	Oncoming Fiscal Year
R&D			
Procurement			
Construction			
Operations and maintenance			
Military personnel			
.			
.			
.			
etc.	———	———	———
Total			

Let us elaborate briefly on each of these topics.

The *structural* aspects of program budgeting are concerned with establishing a set of categories (a program and program element structure) oriented primarily toward "end-product" or "end-objective" activities that are meaningful from a long-range planning point of view.[1] In such a context emphasis is placed on provision for an extended time horizon—some five, ten or more years into the future, depending upon the nature of the activities of the organization under consideration. These characteristics are in marked contrast with conventional governmental budgeting which until recently has tended to stress functional and/or "object class"[2] categories and a very short time horizon (one or two years).

Analytical process considerations pertain to various study activities conducted as an integral part of the program-budgeting process and within the framework of the structure mentioned above. The primary objective of this type of analytical effort is to systematically examine alternative courses of action in terms of utility and cost, with a view to helping to clarify the relevant choices (and their implications) open to the planning decisionmakers in certain problem areas.

Information system considerations are aimed at support of the first two items. There are several senses in which this is important, the primary ones being: (1) progress reporting and control, to give an indication of how well (or poorly) major program decisions are being carried out in the process of implementation; and (2) providing data and information to serve as a basis for

[1] In many instances, end products may in fact be *intermediate* products, especially from the point of view of the next higher level in the decision hierarchy.

[2] In the case of the Federal Government, object classes consist of categories like the following: personnel compensation; travel and transportation of persons; transportation of things; rent, communications, and utilities; printing and reproduction; supplies and materials; etc.

the analytical process—especially to facilitate the development of estimating relationships and analytical models which will permit making estimates of benefits and costs of *future* alternative courses of action.

It takes all three of the items discussed above to make a complete program-budgeting system, and it would be difficult to say which is the most important. However, in many cases people have tended to focus on the structural (format) and progress reporting aspects, to the relative neglect of the analytical part of the system. This is a great mistake. Many of the most important advantages of a program budgeting system cannot be realized without setting up a substantive analytical activity to generate and specify alternative future courses of action, to systematically explore the implications of the alternatives in terms of possible benefits and costs, and to present the results to the planning decisionmakers in such a way as to sharpen their intuition and judgment.

· · ·

THE ROLE OF ANALYSIS IN PROGRAM BUDGETING

Now we must turn to the subject of *analysis* in the program budgeting process. First of all we must be very clear about what the *purpose* of analysis really is—particularly in a long-range planning decision context. Contrary to what some of the more enthusiastic advocates of quantitative analysis may think, we tend to visualize analysis as playing a somewhat modest, though very significant, role in the overall decisionmaking process. In reality most major long-range planning decision problems must ultimately be resolved primarily on the basis of intuition and judgment. However, the main role of analysis should be to try to provide a better basis for exercising this intuition and judgment. In practically no case should it be assumed that the results of the analysis will "make" the decision. The really interesting problems are just too difficult, and there are too many intangible (e.g. political, psychological, and sociological) considerations that cannot be taken into account in the analytical process, especially in a quantitative sense. In sum, the analytical process should be directed toward assisting the decisionmaker in such a way that his intuition and judgment are better than they would be without the results of the analysis.[3]

---

[3] Apparently this view is held by Dr. Alain Enthoven, Assistant Secretary for Systems Analysis, Department of Defense. He writes: "Where does this leave us? What is operations research or systems analysis at the Defense policy level all about? I think that it can best be described as a continuing dialogue between the policy-maker and the systems analyst, in which the policy-maker asks for alternative solutions to his problems, makes decisions to exclude some, and makes value judgments and policy decisions, while the analyst attempts to clarify the conceptual framework in which decisions must be made, to define alternative possible objectives and criteria, and to explore in as clear terms as possible (and quantitatively) the cost and effectiveness of alternative courses of action.

"The analyst at this level is not computing optimum solutions or making decisions. In

Figure 2 Illustrative program budget format for the U.S. Department of Defense.

Program Element Structure	Projected Force Structure (No. of Force Units)					Projected Program Cost (Total Obligation Authority and/or Expenditures) Research & Development				
	1966	1967	1968	...	1972	1966	1967	1968	...	1972
General war forces										
B-52 bomber system										
Minuteman system										
Polaris system										
.										
.										
etc.	___	___	___	...	___	___	___	___	...	___
Total general war	___	___	___	...	___	___	___	___	...	___
Limited war forces										
Armored divisions										
Infantry divisions										
Carrier task forces										
F-111 tact. A/C system										
.										
.										
etc.	___	___	___	...	___	___	___	___	...	___
Total limited war	___	___	___	...	___	___	___	___	...	___
Mobility forces										
C-141 transport system										
C-5A transport system										
Navy rapid development										
Logistics ships										
.										
.										
etc.	___	___	___	...	___	___	___	___	...	___
Total mobility	___	___	___	...	___	___	___	___	...	___
.										
.										
etc.	___	___	___	...	___	___	___	___	...	___
Grand total	___	___	___	...	___	___	___	___	...	___

fact, computation is not his most important contribution. And he is helping someone else to make decisions. His job is to ask and find answers to the questions: 'What are we trying to do?' 'What are the alternative ways of achieving it?' 'What would they cost, and how effective would they be?' 'What does the decisionmaker need to know in order to make a choice?' And to collect and organize this information for those who are responsible for deciding what the Defense program ought to be."
(Source: *The Armed Forces Comptroller*, Vol. IX, No. 1, March 1964, p.39)

Projected Program Cost (Total Obligational Authority and/or Expenditures)														
Investment					Operating Cost					Total				
1966	1967	1968	...	1972	1966	1967	1968	...	1972	1966	1967	1968	...	1972
—	—	—	...	—	—	—	—	—	...	—	—	—	—	...	—
—	—	—	...	—	—	—	—	—	...	—	—	—	—	...	—
—	—	—	...	—	—	—	—	—	...	—	—	—	—	...	—
—	—	—	...	—	—	—	—	—	...	—	—	—	—	...	—
—	—	—	...	—	—	—	—	—	...	—	—	—	—	...	—
—	—	—	...	—	—	—	—	—	...	—	—	—	—	...	—
—	—	—	...	—	—	—	—	—	...	—	—	—	—	...	—
—	—	—	...	—	—	—	—	—	...	—	—	—	—	...	—

Given this view, then, what do we mean by analysis? Numerous analytical approaches may be used to support the program budgeting decision process. Here we will focus on the one that is likely to be most important in helping the decisionmakers grapple with major program decision problems. The approach is currently identified by numerous labels: cost-benefit analysis, cost-effectiveness analysis, systems analysis and the like. In order to

273

avoid a discussion of semantics pertaining to these labels, we will invent our own term—*cost-utility analysis*—and define it.

Cost-utility analysis may be viewed as an approach having the following major characteristics:

(1) A most fundamental characteristic is the systematic examination and comparison of alternative courses of action which might be taken to achieve specified objectives for some future time period. Not only is it important to systematically examine all of the relevant alternatives that can be identified initially, but also to *design additional ones* if those examined are found wanting. Finally, the analysis, particularly if thoroughly and imaginatively done, may at times result in modifications of the initially specified objectives.

(2) Critical examination of alternatives typically involves numerous considerations; but the two main ones are assessment of the cost (often in the sense of economic resource cost) and the utility (the benefits or gains) pertaining to each of the alternatives being compared to attain the stipulated objectives.

(3) The time context is the future—frequently the distant future (five, ten or more years).

(4) Because of the extended time horizon, the environment is one of uncertainty—very often great uncertainty. Since uncertainty is an important facet of the problem, it should be faced up to and treated explicitly in the analysis. This means, among other things, that wherever possible the analyst should avoid the use of simple expected value models.

(5) Usually the context in which the analysis takes place is fairly broad (often very broad) and the environment very complex with numerous interactions among the key variables in the problem. This means that simple, straightforward solutions are the exception rather than the rule.

(6) While quantitative methods of analysis should be utilized as much as possible, because of items 4 and 5,[4] purely quantitative work must often be heavily supplemented by *qualitative* analysis. In fact, we stress the importance of good qualitative work and of using an appropriate combination of quantitative and qualitative methods.

Now how does one go about doing an analysis of this type? The fact is that at the current stage of development of analytical concepts and methods, cost-utility analysis is most definitely an art rather than a science. The really significant problems to be tackled are each in a sense unique, with the result that it is not possible to give a specific set of rules on how to do an appropriate analysis. All that can be done is to give some guidelines, principles, and some illustrative examples. But books, or major parts of

[4] And also because of inadequate data and information sources.

books, have been written on this subject. Here the treatment must of necessity be much more limited.

Some important guidelines to be followed in carrying out a cost-utility analysis (not necessarily in order of relative importance) are as follows.[5]

(1) Proper Structuring of the Problem and Design of the Analysis

This by far is the most important of the guidelines. From an incredibly complex environment, that which is relevant to the problem at hand must be included, and that which is irrelevant excluded. Here, there are no formal rules to guide us. The experience, skill, imagination, and intuition of the analyst are paramount. It is at this point—the *design* of the analysis—that most cost-utility studies either flounder hopelessly or move ahead toward success. In sum, if we can structure the problem so that the *right questions* are being asked, we shall be well on the way toward a good analysis. This sounds trite; but it really is not. There are all too many instances of large amounts of effort being expended on an analytical exercise addressed to the wrong questions.[6]

Another point is that typically the problem and the design of the analysis may well have to be re-structured several times. Considerations that were initially thought to be important may, after some preliminary work, turn out to be relatively unimportant—and vice versa. Finally, in the process of doing some of the analytical work new questions and new alternatives may come to mind.

(2) The Conceptual Framework

In general there are two principal conceptual approaches:

Fixed-utility approach. For a specified level of utility to be attained in the accomplishment of some given objective, the analysis attempts to determine that alternative (or feasible combination of alternatives) which is likely to achieve the specified level of utility at the lowest cost.

Fixed-budget approach. For a specified budget level to be used in the attainment of some given objective, the analysis attempts to determine that alternative (or feasible combination of alternatives) which is likely to produce the highest utility for the given budget level.[7]

[5] Observance of these guidelines will not in itself produce a good analysis, but it will most surely help. ...

[6] Incredible as it may seem, there have been studies that started out by asking questions about which alternative would maximize gain and at the same time minimize cost—clearly an irrelvant and impossible situtation.

[7] The fixed level of utility or budget is usually specified by someone "outside the analysis"; i.e. it is usually a given datum to the analyst. Very often several levels (e.g. high, medium and low) may be used to investigate the sensitivity of the ranking of the alternatives to utility or budget level.

Either (or both) of these approaches may be used, depending upon the context of the problem at hand. In any event, the objective is to permit *comparisons* to be made among alternatives, and for this purpose something has to be made fixed.

(3) Building the Analytical Model

Here the term "model" is used in a broad sense. Depending upon the nature of the problem at hand, the model used in the analysis may be formal or informal, very mathematical or not so mathematical, heavily computerized or only moderately so, and so on. However, the main point is that the model need not be highly formal and mathematical to be useful. In any event, the following are some important points to keep in mind:

(a) Model building is an art, not a science. It is often an experimental process.
(b) The main thing is to try to include and highlight those factors which are relevant to the problem at hand, and to suppress (judiciously!) those which are relatively unimportant. Unless the latter is done, the model is likely to be unmanageable.
(c) The main purpose in designing the model is to develop a meaningful *set of relationships* among objectives, the relevant alternatives available for attaining the objectives, the estimated cost of the alternatives and the estimated utility for each of the alternatives.
(d) Provision must be made for explicit treatment of uncertainty. (More on this later.)
(e) Since by definition a model is an abstraction from reality, the model must be built on a set of assumptions. These assumptions must be made *explicit*. If they are not, this is to be regarded as a defect of the design.

(4) Treatment of Uncertainty

Since most really interesting and important decision problems involve major elements of uncertainty, a cost-utility analysis of such problems must provide for explicit treatment of uncertainty. This may be done in numerous ways.

For purposes of discussion, two main types of uncertainty may be distinguished:

(A) Uncertainty about the state of the world in the future. Major factors here are technological uncertainty, strategic uncertainty, uncertainty about a firm's competitors and their reactions to the firm's own policies, and the like.

(B) Statistical uncertainty. This type of uncertainty stems from purely chance elements in the real world. It would exist even if uncertainties of the first type were zero.

Type (B) uncertainties are usually the least troublesome to handle in cost-utility studies. When necessary, Monte Carlo and/or other techniques may be used to deal with statistical fluctuations; but these perturbations are usually swamped by Type (A) uncertainties which are dominant in most long-range planning problems. The use of elaborate techniques to treat statistical uncertainties in such problems is likely to be expensive window dressing.

Type (A) uncertainties are typically present in most long-range decision problems, and they are most difficult to take into account in a cost-utility analysis. Techniques which are often used are sensitivity analysis, contingency analysis and *a fortiori* analysis. Let us comment briefly on each of these in turn:

Sensitivity Analysis. Suppose in a given analysis there are a few key parameters about which the analyst is very uncertain. Instead of using "expected values" for these parameters, the analyst may use several values (say, high, medium and low) in an attempt to see how sensitive the results (ranking of the alternatives being considered) are to variations in the uncertain parameters.

Contingency Analysis. This type of analysis investigates how the ranking of the alternatives under consideration holds up when a relevant change in criteria for evaluating the alternatives is postulated, or a major change in the general environment is assumed. (For example, in a military context, the enemy is assumed to be countries A and B. We might then want to investigate what would happen if C joins the A and B coalition.)

A Fortiori Analysis. Suppose that in a particular planning decision problem the generally accepted intuitive judgment strongly favors alternative A. However, the analyst feels that A might be a poor choice and that alternative B might be preferred. In performing an analysis of A vs. B, the analyst may choose deliberately to resolve the major uncertainties in favor of A and see how B compares under these adverse conditions. If B still looks good, the analyst has a very strong case in favor of B.

Creation of a New Alternative. While the three techniques listed above may be useful in a direct analytical sense, they may also contribute indirectly. For example, through sensitivity and contingency analyses the analyst may gain a good understanding of the really critical uncertainties in a given problem area. On the basis of this knowledge he might then be able to come up with a newly designed alternative that will provide a reasonably good hedge against a *range* of the more significant uncertainties. This is often difficult to do; but when it can be accomplished, it may offer one of the best ways to compensate for uncertainty.

(5) Treatment of Problems Associated with Time

More likely than not, the particular problem at hand will be posed in a dynamic context; or at least the problem will have some dynamic aspects to it. While a "static" type analysis can go a long way toward providing the decisionmaker with useful information, very often this has to be supplemented by analytical work which takes time into account explicitly.

A case in point is with respect to the treatment of the estimated *costs* of the alternatives for a fixed level of utility.[8] The nature of the problem may be such that the costs have to be time-phased, resulting in cost streams through time for each of the alternatives. The question then arises about whether the decisionmaker is or is not indifferent with respect to the time impact of the costs. If he is not indifferent concerning time preference, then the cost streams have to be "discounted" through time, using an appropriate rate of discount.[9] Determining specifically what rate to use can be a problem; but it is usually manageable. If it is not, an upper bound rate and a lower bound rate may be used to see whether it really makes any difference in the final conclusions of the problem.

It should be pointed out that the analyst pays a price for introducing time explicitly into an analysis.

(A) It complicates the analysis by increasing the number of variables and hence the number of calculations. If we put time in, we may have to take something else out.

(B) As implied above, it complicates the selection of a criterion for evaluating alternatives: solution X may be better for 1966 and worse for 1970; solution Y may be just reverse.

(6) Validity Checking

In the preceding paragraphs we have discussed building the analytical model, "exercising" the model (sensitivity and contingency analysis), and the like. Another important consideration—often relatively neglected—is validity

---

[8] Maintaining a fixed level of utility *through time* is often a difficult problem in itself. We cannot go into this matter in the present limited discussion.

[9] One may raise the question regarding under what conditions the decisionmaker *would* be indifferent. Economic theorists might argue that there probably should not be any such condition. However, in practice decisionmakers often find themselves in an institutional setting (like the Department of Defense, for example) where it is customary to be indifferent regarding time preference, and hence discounting of cost streams through time is not done. This is not to say that the decisionmakers are correct in principle.

It should be emphasized that the type of discounting under discussion here is purely to equalize cost streams through time with respect to time preference—not to compensate for risk and for uncertainty.

checking of the model. Since the model is only a *representation* of reality, it is desirable to do some sort of checking to see if the analytical procedure used is a reasonably good representation, within the context of the problem at hand. This is difficult to do, especially in dealing with problems having a time horizon five, ten, or more years into the future.

In general we cannot test models of this type by methods of "controlled experiment." However, the analyst might try to answer the following questions:

(A) Can the model describe known facts and situations reasonably well?
(B) When the principal parameters involved are varied, do the results remain consistent and plausible?
(C) Can it handle special cases where we already have some indication as to what the outcome should be?
(D) Can it assign causes to known effects?

(7) Qualitative Supplementation

We have already stressed the importance of qualitative considerations in cost-utility analysis—particularly qualitative *supplementation* of the quantitative work. Introduction of qualitative considerations may take several forms:

(A) Qualitative analysis *per se,* as an integral part of the total analytical effort.
(B) Interpretation of the quantitative work.
(C) Discussion of relevant non-quantitative considerations that could not be taken into account in the "formal" analysis.

The latter item can be particularly important in presenting the results of a study to the decisionmaker. The idea is to present the results of the formal quantitative work, interpret these results, and then to say that this is as far as the formal quantitative analysis per se will permit us to go. However, there are important *qualitative* considerations that you (the decisionmaker) should try to take into account; and here they are (listed by the analyst). Finally, relevant questions about each of the qualitative items can be raised, and important interrelations among them discussed.

So much for guidelines for carrying out a cost-utility analysis. Let us now turn to examples of problem areas where cost-utility types of analyses may be applied.

SOME EXAMPLES

At this point, the reader may be wondering about the types of problem areas where cost-utility analysis may be applied. The following is a list—illustrative only, and certainly not complete—of problem areas where a cost-utility type of analysis has been done in the past, is being done currently, or is planned to be done in the future:

(1) Analysis of proposed water resources projects (reservoirs) in terms of their costs and benefits (effects on underground water supply, farm incomes, and limiting flood damage).

(2) Examination of the problem of measuring the benefits of government expenditures on outdoor recreation.

(3) High school dropouts: analysis of the costs and benefits of prevention programs.

(4) Analysis of the transportation problems of the Northeast corridor (from Boston to Washington, D.C.): the costs and benefits of possible alternative "mixes" of private cars, public buses, railroads, airplanes, etc., in order to try to get some notion about what the preferred mix might be in the future.[10]

(5) Studies of the commercial aviation problem in the 1970 decade: e.g., should the U.S. develop a supersonic transport (SST) or not? What are the estimated costs and benefits of SST systems vs. second generation subsonic jet aircraft systems?[11]

(6) A comparison of alternative ways to deal with urban transportation problems in large cities—e.g., the estimated costs and benefits of freeways (surface, below surface, above surface), rail rapid transit systems (surface, below surface, above surface), buses, etc.; and various mixes of these instruments of transportation.

(7) The "large city" problem in general, including schools, urban transportation, poverty, urban renewal, etc.[12]

(8) Analysis of public health problems; e.g., costs and benefits of syphilis control programs.[13]

(9) Studies to explore the costs and benefits of proposed future Office of Economic Opportunity programs.[14]

(10) Application of cost-utility analyses to crime and delinquency problems, waste disposal, pollution, water conservation, etc., for the State of California.[15]

Let us now turn to a different kind of example. We wish here to illustrate a point made earlier: that the main role of analysis is to provide a

[10] Studies in this area are being conducted currently, sponsored by the U.S. Department of Transportation and other agencies.

[11] The Federal Aviation Agency has sponsored numerous studies of this type in the past. Recent FAA studies tend more in the direction of trying to determine the optimum configuration of an SST system—given that the U.S. wants to develop an SST.

[12] The City of New York has established a program budgeting activity for the city. This activity includes analytical studies of alternative ways to deal with the city's problems in the future. As an example of an analysis of the urban renewal problem.

[13] The U.S. Department of Health, Education and Welfare has conducted studies of alternative health programs in several areas. ...

[14] An analytical staff of the OEO is currently conducting such studies.

[15] Most of this work has been done for the State by various aerospace corporations.

Figure 3 A decision between alternative water resources projects.

Figure 3 A decision between alternative water resources projects.

Analytical Factor	Proposed Projects 1 2 3 4 ... n

(1) Present worth* ($):
  (a) Discounted @ 2½% (50 yr)
  (b) Discounted @ 5% (50 yr)
  (c) Discounted @ 8% (50 yr)
(2) Possible variability of outcome:
  (a) "Most likely" range of present worth (low-high $)
  (b) Range of present worth outside of which outcome is "very unlikely" to fall
(3) Effect on personal wealth distribution:
  (a) Number of farms affected
  (b) Average value of land and buildings per farm in the watershed ($)
  (c) Average net benefit per farm owner ($)
(4) Effect on regional wealth distribution:
  (a) Average increase in per family income in the Basin ($)
  (b) Percentage increase in average income in the Basin due to project.
(5) Internal rate of return of project (%)†

*Present value of estimated benefits minus present value of estimated costs.
†The rate of discount which reduces present worth to zero.

better basis for exercising the intuition and judgment of the decisionmakers; and that often a considerable amount of help can be provided, even where anything approaching "hard core" optimization is not possible (the general case in most really significant major decision problems).

Suppose that we are concerned with deciding among alternative proposed water resources projects, and that we have a given budget to spend on such projects in the future. The budget is such that all of the proposed projects cannot be undertaken. We therefore want to choose the "preferred mix." Suppose further that we have an analytical staff and that it comes up with a summary of results of cost-utility analyses of the problem in Figure 3.

Assume that in addition to the quantitative data presented in the table, the analytical staff has supplemented the numerical calculations with *qualitative* discussion of some of the more relevant nonquantifiable issues involved in the decision: e.g., political factors, non-quantifiable "spillover" effects, and the like.

Now decision problems regarding alternative water resources projects are usually very complex. The analyst can rarely come up with a preferred solution—particularly in the sense that one mix of alternatives completely dominates all others. Even in such a context, analytical results of the type portrayed above can go a long way toward sharpening the intuition and judgment of the decisionmakers. In the above illustrative case, the

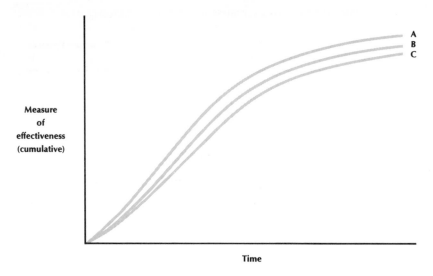

Measure of effectiveness (cumulative)

Time

Figure 4 Comparison of equal cost alternatives.

decisionmakers would be better off if they had the results of the analytical effort than if they did not have such information. Their decision is likely to be a more informed one. That is the goal of analysis.

Let us now turn briefly to another example to illustrate a somewhat different point. We have in mind here the results and conclusions of a study that was actually performed by one of the military departments in the Department of Defense and submitted to the Secretary of Defense and his staff. We need not get into the substantive national security issues involved in the study to illustrate the methodological points that we wish to emphasize.

The structure of the analysis was an actual cost comparison of several alternative future courses of action; that is, for a specified budget level to be devoted to a particular military mission area, the alternatives were compared on the basis of their estimated effectiveness in accomplishing the stipulated task. The final quantitative results took the form shown in Figure 4.

The stated conclusion of the study, based almost exclusively on these quantitative results, was that alternative C is preferred over A and B for a wide range of circumstances and contingencies. (The context of the study involved a time period some 10-15 years into the future.) Yet the difference in estimated effectiveness of the alternatives (for a constant budget level) was *at most 15 per cent!* Now my point is simply that the context of the problem was clouded by so many uncertainties and the model used in the analysis was so aggregative, that calculated differences among the alternatives averaging less than 15 per cent *just cannot be regarded as significant.* Thus, the stated conclusions of the study, if taken literally, could in a real sense be misleading to the decisionmakers.[16] In decision problems of this type where uncertainties are very great, the analyst is generally looking for much larger differences among the alternatives being examined. How great? There is no general rule. However, in the past when experienced analysts have been dealing with problems of this type, differences in the neighborhood of a *factor* of 2 or 3 have been sought. In most long-range planning problems where major uncertainties are present, quantitative differences among alternatives must be *at least a factor of two* before we can even begin to have any confidence that the differences are significant. In any event, when they are smaller than that, the analyst must exercise extra caution in interpreting the results, and he must not make statements that are likely to mislead the decisionmakers.

There is another side to the coin, however. When quantitative differences among alternatives fall within a relatively narrow range, does this mean that the study is of no use to the decisionmaker? Not necessarily. If the quantitative work has been carried out in a reasonably competent manner and the differences among alternatives do tend to be relatively small, this fact in itself can be of considerable interest to the decisionmaker. This is especially true if sensitivity analyses have been made showing that as key parameters in the problem are varied over their relevant ranges, the final results are still within relatively narrow ranges. Given results of this kind, the decisionmaker may then feel somewhat more comfortable about focusing more of his attention on the *qualitative* aspects of the problem—political, psychological, sociological considerations. In fact, if the analyst has done a reasonably thorough job, he might include a discussion of these factors in a qualitative supplementation to the purely quantitative part of the study.

The main point here is that while one of the main goals of analysis is to search for "preferred alternatives" characterized by quantitative results *significantly* different (better) from other alternatives, the fact that a strong case cannot be made for a preferred alternative does not mean that the study is worthless. The results, and the sensitivity analysis supporting the results, can still be very enlightening to the decisionmaker. This is the main purpose of analysis.

So much for the role of analysis in the total program budgeting process. Let me turn now to a different subject.

CONSIDERATIONS AND PROBLEMS
IN IMPLEMENTING A PROGRAM BUDGETING SYSTEM

If an executive is convinced that program budgeting might be a good thing, he may well ask about some of the considerations and problems

---

[16] Needless to say, the Secretary of Defense and his analytical staff were *not* misled in this case. They are too experienced in interpreting the results of analytical studies to be overly impressed by small differences.

involved in implementing such a system. Here are a few comments which, hopefully, might have general applicability:

1. Do not expect the task to be easy. Particularly in a large organization, the substantive issues themselves are likely to be difficult; and these difficulties no doubt will be intensified by internal political problems—e.g., in the form of resistance to change by certain groups.

2. Do not rush in rapidly to try to implement a poorly planned scheme; but on the other hand, do not wait too long to take positive, well thought out *initial* implementation action for at least *part* of the system. To wait too long keeps elements of the bureaucracy in a suspended state of waiting and also gives opposition forces too much time to consolidate positions.

3. In the context of point (2) with respect to program and program element structure, about two months or so of intensive work should be spent in developing the initial structure. Then it should be put into operation, with the clear understanding that modifications will be made in areas where actual use dictates changes in the original structure. One could spend many months and even years trying to develop the "perfect" program structure before implementation; but since a perfect structure does not exist anyway, it is best to try to come up with something reasonable (though far from perfect) soon, get it into operation, and then let it evolve over time. Also, we should remember that even under ideal conditions, the program and program element structure should not stay the same. The structure should change as the nature of planning problems and the decisionmaking context of the organization change over time.

4. The analytical part of the total program budgeting system should be set up early—preferably simultaneously with the process of establishing the program structure. Actually, one can make a very strong case for starting the analytical work *first*, and then letting the analytical people play the leading role in setting up the program and program element structure. Clearly, there are strong interactions (or should be) between structure and analysis; and this is something that should be preserved as the total system develops over time. In some instances there is a tendency toward separation of the two elements as time passes. The program structure becomes "fixed in concrete" and dominated by the accountants and the progress control people; and the analytical people proceed with their planning study work, more or less independently of the formal structure.

5. With regard to the progress reporting and control function, this part of the system should be implemented last, and not until considerable experience has been accumulated in using the program/program element structure. This makes sense for two reasons: (a) the original structure is likely to be modified considerably as implementation progresses; and (b) the top management should have some time to determine those elements which are most important and hence should be subjected to progress reporting and

control. On this latter point, an attempt should *not* be made to "progress report and control" on *everything*. Here, the classical accounting concept of a complete enumeration of everything is not appropriate. The accountants should not be permitted to dictate the main characteristics of the system. This leads to another important point.

6. Everyone—not only the accountants and particularly the top management—should have a clear understanding about what a program budgeting system really is, and what it is not. Program budgeting is focused primarily toward the planning and programming realm, to assist decision-makers in making *major program and planning decisions*. It is not designed *primarily* as a tool to assist operating managers in day-to-day management of operations—though it can help in this area to some degree. Top management especially should understand that the main thrust is in the direction of the major program decision process, and that a program budgeting system should not be used as a vehicle for trying to control the *implementation* of programs *in detail*—a task that is best delegated to the lower levels of management in the operating structure of the organization. To try to utilize the system in this way is a misuse of program budgeting, and it can lead to over-centralization with its tendency to dampen incentives at lower levels in the organization.

27

A Summary of Basic Concepts in the Behavioral Theory of the Firm

RICHARD M. CYERT AND JAMES G. MARCH

We have chosen to reproduce this chapter from Cyert and March's landmark book, A Behavioral Theory of the Firm, *because of the skill with which the authors have captured the essence of those concepts that lead to their nontraditional theory of what constitutes the framework of decisions called "the firm."*

Because they elaborate on these concepts in the chapters that follow this one, the material presented here is rather cryptic and cries for examples and illustrations. We selected this piece, despite its somewhat formal and difficult style, because it pinpoints so many of the key behavioral concepts necessary to understanding and dealing with decision-making in today's large, multiproduct firms operating under uncertainty in oligopolistic markets.

Reprinted from Richard M. Cyert and James G. March, *A Behavioral Theory of the Firm*, pp. 114-127, by permission of the publisher. Copyright 1963 by Prentice-Hall, Inc., Englewood Cliffs, N.J.

In its classic form, economic theory is simply a language designed to provide a systematic framework within which to analyze economic problems. Such a role was assigned to theory by Marshall and is clearly implicit in contemporary theory. In this view theory performs two major functions. On the one hand, it is an exhaustive set of general concepts. Any variable observed in the system can be assigned to an appropriate niche. The theory is a set of filing cabinets with each drawer bearing the title of an economic concept. Within each file drawer there is a set of folders for each economic variable relevant to the concept. Within each folder there is a further breakdown in terms of the factors affecting the variable. At the same time, the theory is a statement of critical relations among system variables. These relations may be assumptions about interdependence among variables, about the functional form of the interdependences, or about broad structural attributes of the system.

As an example in classic theory, consider the concept of market demand. The usual treatment of demand involves (1) a description of demand in terms of a "demand curve," (2) the decomposition of the market demand curve into individual demand curves, and (3) the specification of individual demand in terms of individual preference orderings and the concept of utility. Within such a filing system we establish relations between external events and demand phenomena (for example, a relation between demand for a particular commodity and money income) by introducing relational concepts (for example, income elasticity).

One of the most important requirements for the usefulness of theory conceived in this general way is the requirement that all important variables in the system be conveniently represented within the concepts of the theory. The theory of the firm seems to meet this requirement reasonably well for the kinds of problems with which it has usually been faced (for example, the perfectly competitive market). However, the theory has not been adequate to cope with oligopolistic markets. The theory outlined [here] specifies an alternative framework and an alternative set of key relations for dealing with the modern "representative firm"—the large, multiproduct firm operating under uncertainty in an imperfect market.

GOALS, EXPECTATIONS, AND CHOICE

The basic framework for analysis we have proposed, like the classic one, has two major organizing devices: (1) It has a set of exhaustive variable categories; (2) it has a set of relational concepts. ... We can analyze the process of decision making in the modern firm in terms of the variables that affect organizational goals, the variables that affect organizational expectations, and the variables that affect organizational choice.

Organizational goals. Quite simply, we have identified two sets of variables affecting the goals of an organization. The first set influences the *dimensions* of the goals (what things are viewed as important). Within this set of variables, we can cite the composition of the organizational coalition, the organizational division of labor in decision making, and the defintion of problems facing the organization. Thus ... organizational goals change as new participants enter or old participants leave the coalition. ... The operative goals for a particular decision are the goals of the subunit making that decision. Finally ... goals are evoked by problems. The second set of variables influences the *aspiration level* on any particular goal dimension. Here we have identified essentially three variables: the organization's past goal, the organization's past performance, and the past performance of other "comparable" organizations. The aspiration level is viewed as some weighted function of these three variables.

Organizational expectations. Expectations are seen as the result of drawing inferences from available information. Thus, we consider variables that affect either the process of drawing inferences or the process by which information is made available to the organization. With respect to inference drawing, we have not attempted to reflect all of the recent efforts in the psychology of individual choice. However, we have identified some simple pattern-recognition variables (for example, linear extrapolation) and the effect of hopes on expectations. With respect to the process by which information is made available, we have cited particularly variables affecting search activity within the firm. Affecting the intensity and success of search are the extent to which the goals are achieved and the amount of organizational slack in the firm. Affecting the direction of search are the nature of the problem stimulating search and the location in the organization at which search is focused.

Organizational choice. Choice takes place in response to a problem, uses standard operating rules, and involves identifying an alternative that is acceptable from the point of view of evoked goals. Thus, the variables that affect choice are those that influence the definition of a problem within the organization, those that influence the standard decision rules, and those that affect the order of consideration of alternatives. The standard decision rules are affected primarily by the past experience of the organization and the past record of organizational slack. The order in which alternatives are considered depends on the part of the organization in which the decision is being made and past experience in considering alternatives.

... We have tried to elaborate on this simple structure in order to develop meaningful and useful theories of organizational goals, expectations, and choice. We think it is possible to subsume any variable within the theory of business decision making under one or more of these categories.

FOUR MAJOR RELATIONAL CONCEPTS

In the course of developing the three subtheories, we have developed a relatively small number of relational concepts. In many respects, they represent the heart of our theory of business decision making. The four major concepts used in the theory are (1) quasi-resolution of conflict, (2) uncertainty avoidance, (3) problemistic search, and (4) organizational learning. In this section we review briefly the meaning of each of these concepts. ...

Quasi-resolution of Conflict

In keeping with virtually all theories of organizations, we assume that the coalition represented in an organization is a coalition of members having different goals. We require some procedure for resolving such conflict. The classic solution is to posit an exchange of money from some members of the coalition to other members as a way of inducing conformity to a single, consistent set of goals—the organizational objective.

We propose an alternate concept of organizational goals and an alternate set of assumptions about how conflict is resolved. Basically, we have argued that most organizations most of the time exist and thrive with considerable latent conflict of goals. Except at the level of nonoperational objectives, there is no internal consensus. The procedures for "resolving" such conflict do not reduce all goals to a common dimension or even make them obviously internally consistent.

Goals as independent constraints. In our framework, organizational goals are a series of independent aspiration-level constraints imposed on the organization by the members of the organizational coalition. These constraints may include nonessential demands (that is, demands that are already satisfied when other constraints are met), sporadic demands (that is, demands that are made only occasionally), nonoperational demands (that is, demands for which there are no operational measures), as well as essential, continuous, operative goals. In general, although we recognize the importance of goals that are nonessential (because they might become essential), of goals that are ordinarily sporadic (because they occasionally are enforced), and of goals that are nonoperational (because they sometimes can be made operational), we will focus on those constraints that are essential, continuous, and operative.

Specifically, in the case of price and output models of the business firm, we assume a profit goal, a sales goal, a market share goal, an inventory goal, and a production goal. In any particular firm we expect some subset of these objectives to be essential, continuous, and operative. Moreover, we expect that subset to pose problems for the organization in the form of potential conflict. Thus, we require assumptions about procedures for resolving conflict. We assume that conflict is resolved by using local rationality, acceptable-level decision rules, and sequential attention to goals.

Local rationality. We assume that an organization factors its decision problems into subproblems and assigns the subproblems to subunits in the organization. From the point of view of organizational conflict, the importance of such local rationality is in the tendency for the individual subunits to deal with a limited set of problems and a limited set of goals. At the limit, this reduces to solving one problem in terms of only one goal. The sales department is primarily responsible for sales goals and sales strategy; the production department is primarily responsible for production goals and production procedures; the pricing department is primarily responsible for profit goals and price decisions; and so on.

Through delegation and specialization in decisions and goals, the organization reduces a situation involving a complex set of interrelated problems and conflicting goals to a number of simple problems. Whether such a system will in fact "resolve" the conflict depends, of course, on whether the decisions generated by the system are consistent with each other and with the demands of the external environment. In our theory, consistency is facilitated by two characteristics of the decision process: (1) acceptable-level decision rules; (2) sequential attention to goals.

Acceptable-level decision rules. In the classic arguments for decentralization of decision making, we require strong assumptions about the effectiveness of the "invisible hand" in enforcing proper decisions on a system of local rationality. Consistency requires that local optimization by a series of independent decision centers result in over-all optimization. On the other hand, we are persuaded that organizations can and do operate with much weaker rules of consistency (that is, we require that local decisions satisfying local demands made by a series of independent decision centers result in a joint solution that satisfies all demands). Such rules are weaker in two senses: (1) There will ordinarily be a large number of local decisions that are consistent with other local decisions under such a rule. The demand constraints do not uniquely define a solution. (2) Any such system will tend to underexploit the environment and thus leave excess resources to absorb potential inconsistencies in the local decisions.

Sequential attention to goals. Ordinarily when we talk of "consistency" of goals or decisions we refer to some way of assessing their internal logic at a point in time. As a result, in classic theories of organizations we are inclined to insist on some consistency within a cross section of goals. Such an insistence seems to us inaccurate as a characterization of organizational behavior. Organizations resolve conflict among goals, in part, by attending to different goals at different times. Just as the political organization is likely to resolve conflicting pressures to "go left" and "go right" by first doing one and then the other, the business firm is likely to resolve conflicting pressures to "smooth production" and "satisfy customers" by first doing one and then the other. The resulting time buffer between goals permits the organization to solve one problem at a time, attending to one goal at a time.

Uncertainty Avoidance

To all appearances, at least, uncertainty is a feature of organizational decision making with which organizations must live. In the case of the business firm, there are uncertainties with respect to the behavior of the market, the deliveries of suppliers, the attitudes of shareholders, the behavior of competitors, the future actions of governmental agencies, and so on. As a result, much of modern decision theory has been concerned with the problems of decision making under risk and uncertainty. The solutions involved have been largely procedures for finding certainty equivalents (for example, expected value) or introducing rules for living with the uncertainties (for example, game theory).

Our studies indicate quite a different strategy on the part of organizations. Organizations avoid uncertainty: (1) They avoid the requirement that they correctly anticipate events in the distant future by using decision rules emphasizing short-run reaction to short-run feedback rather than anticipation of long-run uncertain events. They solve pressing problems rather than develop long-run strategies. (2) They avoid the requirement that they anticipate future reactions of other parts of their environment by arranging a negotiated environment. They impose plans, standard operating procedures, industry tradition, and uncertainty-absorbing contracts on that environment. In short, they achieve a reasonably manageable decision situation by avoiding planning where plans depend on predictions of uncertain future events and by emphasizing planning where the plans can be made self-confirming through some control device.

Feedback-react decision procedures. We assume that organizations make decisions by solving a series of problems; each problem is solved as it arises; the organization then waits for another problem to appear. Where decisions within the firm do not naturally fall into such a sequence, they are modified so that they will.

Consider, for example, the production-level decision. In most models of output determination, we introduce expectations with respect to future sales and relate output to such predictions. Our studies indicate, to the contrary, that organizations use only gross expectations about future sales in the output decision. They may, and frequently do, forecast sales and develop some long-run production plans on paper, but the actual production decisions are more frequently dominated by day-to-day and week-to-week feedback data from inventory, recent sales, and salesmen.

This assumption of a "fire department" organization is one of the most conspicuous features of our models. Under a rather broad class of situations, such behavior is rational for an organization having the goal structure we have postulated. Under an even broader set of situations, it is likely to be the pattern of behavior that is learned by an organization dealing with an uncertain world and quasi-resolved goals. It will be learned because by and large it will permit the organization to meet the demands of the members of the coalition.

Negotiated environment. Classical models of oligopoly ordinarily assume that firms make some predictions about the behavior of their environment, especially those parts of the environment represented by competitors, suppliers, customers, and other parts of the organization. Certainly such considerations are important to any decisions made by the firm. Our studies, however, lead us to the proposition that firms will devise and negotiate an environment so as to eliminate the uncertainty. Rather than treat the environment as exogenous and to be predicted, they seek ways to make it controllable.

In the case of competitors, one of the conspicuous means of control is through the establishment of industry-wide conventional practices. If "good business practice" is standardized (through trade associations, journals, word of mouth, external consultants, etc.), we can be reasonably confident that all competitors will follow it. We do not mean to imply that firms necessarily enter into collusive agreements in the legal sense; our impression is that ordinarily they do not, but they need not do so to achieve the same objective of stability in competitive practices.

For example, prices are frequently set on the basis of conventional practice. With time, such variables as the rate of mark-up, price lines, and standard costing procedures become customary within an industry. ... The net result of such activity with respect to prices (and comparable activity with regard to suppliers and customers) is that an uncertain environment is made quite highly predictable.

Such negotiation among firms is not obviously collusion for profit maximization. Rather, it is an attempt to avoid uncertainty while obtaining a return that satisfies the profit and other demands of the coalition. The lack of a profit-maximizing rationale is suggested by (1) the stability of the practices over time and (2) the occasional instances of success by firms willing to violate the conventional procedures (for example, discount houses in retailing).

In a similar fashion, the internal planning process (for example, the budget) provides a negotiated internal environment. A plan within the firm is a series of contracts among the subunits in the firm. As in the case of industry conventions, internal conventions are hyperstable during the contract period and tend to be relatively stable from one period to the next (for example, in resource allocation). As a result, they permit each unit to avoid uncertainty about other units in making decisions.

Problemistic Search

In the framework proposed ... the theory of choice and the theory of search are closely intertwined. Necessarily, if we argue that organizations use acceptable-level goals and select the first alternative they see that meets those goals, we must provide a theory of organizational search to supplement the concepts of decision making. In our models we assume that search, like decision making, is problem-directed. By *problemistic search* we mean search that is stimulated by a problem (usually a rather specific one) and is directed toward finding a solution to that problem. In a general way, problemistic search can be distinguished from both random curiosity and the search for understanding. It is distinguished from the former because it has a goal, from the latter because it is interested in understanding only insofar as such understanding contributes to control. Problemistic search is engineering rather than pure science.

With respect to organizational search, we assume three things:

1. *Search is motivated.* Whether the motivation exists on the buyer or seller side of the alternative market, problemistic search is stimulated by a problem, depressed by a problem solution.
2. *Search is simple-minded.* It proceeds on the basis of a simple model of causality until driven to a more complex one.
3. *Search is biased.* The way in which the environment is viewed and the communications about the environment that are processed through the organization reflect variations in training, experience, and goals of the participants in the organization.

Motivated search. Search within the firm is problem-oriented. A problem is recognized when the organization either fails to satisfy one or more of its goals or when such a failure can be anticipated in the immediate future. So long as the problem is not solved, search will continue. The problem is solved either by discovering an alternative that satisfies the goals or by revising the goals to levels that make an available alternative acceptable. Solutions are also motivated to search for problems. Pet projects (for example, cost savings in someone else's department, expansion in our own department) look for crises (for example, failure to achieve the profit goal, innovation by a competitor). In the theory we assume that variations in search activity (and search productivity) reflect primarily the extent to which motivation for search exists. Thus, we assume that regular, planned search is relatively unimportant in inducing changes in existing solutions that are viewed as adequate.

Simple-minded search. We assume that rules for search are simple-minded in the sense that they reflect simple concepts of causality. Subject to learning (see below), search is based initially on two simple rules: (1) search in the neighborhood of the problem symptom and (2) search in the neighborhood of the current alternative. These two rules reflect different dimensions of the basic causal notions that a cause will be found "near" its effect and that a new solution will be found "near" an old one.

The neighborhood of symptom rule can be related to the subunits of the organization and their association with particular goals and with each other. A problem symptom will normally be failure on some goal indicator. Initial reaction, we assume, will be in the department identified with the goal. Thus, if the problem is the failure to attain the sales goal, the search begins in the sales department and with the sales program. Failing there, it might reasonably proceed to the problem of price and product quality and then to production costs.

The neighborhood of existing policy rule inhibits the movement of the organization to radically new alternatives (except under circumstances of considerable search pressure). Such an inhibition may be explained either in terms of some underlying organizational assumptions of continuity in performance functions or in terms of the problems of conceiving the adjustments required by radical shifts.

When search, using the simple causal rules, is not immediately successful, we assume two developments. First, the organization uses increasingly complex ("distant") search; second, the organization introduces a third search rule: (3) search in organizationally vulnerable areas.

The motivation to search in vulnerable areas stems from two things. On the one hand, the existence of organizational slack will tend to lead search activity in the direction of slack parts of the organization. On the other hand, certain activities in the organization are more easily attacked than others, simply because of their power position in the system. One general phenomenon is the vulnerability of those activities in the organization for which the connection with major goals is difficult to calculate concretely (for example, research in many firms). In either case, a solution consists in either absorbing slack or renegotiating the basic coalition agreement to the disadvantage of the weaker members of the coalition.

Bias in search. We assume three different kinds of search bias: (1) bias reflecting special training or experience of various parts of the organization, (2) bias reflecting the interaction of hopes and expectations, and (3) communication biases reflecting unresolved conflict within the organization. Bias from prior experience or training is implicit in our assumptions of search learning (below), local specialization in problem solving (above), and subunit goal differentiation (above). Those parts of the organization responsible for the search activities will not necessarily see in the environment what those parts of the organization using the information would see if they executed the search themselves. The bias in adjusting expectations to hopes has the consequence of decreasing the amount of problem-solving time required to solve a problem and of stimulating the growth of organizational slack during good times and eliminating it during bad. We assume that communication bias can be substantially ignored in our models except under conditions where the internal biases in the firm are all (or substantially all) in the same direction or where biases in one direction are located in parts of the organization with an extremely favorable balance of power.

Organizational Learning

Do organizations learn? To assume that organizations go through the same processes of learning as do individual human beings seems unnecessarily naïve, but organizations do exhibit (as do other social institutions) adaptive behavior over time. Just as adaptations at the individual level depend upon phenomena of the human physiology, organizational adaptation uses individual members of the organization as instruments. However, we believe it is possible to deal with adaptation at the aggregate level of the organization, in the same sense and for the same reasons that it is possible to deal with the concept of organizational decision making.

We focus on adaptation with respect to three different phases of the decision process: adaptation of goals, adaptation in attention rules, and adaptation in search rules. We assume that organizations change their goals, shift their attention, and revise their procedures for search as a function of their experience.

Adaptation of goals. The goals with which we deal are in the form of aspiration levels, or—in the more general case—search equivalence classes. In simple terms, this means that on each dimension of organizational goals there are a number of critical values—critical, that is, from the point of view of shifts in search strategy. These values change over time in reaction to experience, either actual or vicarious.

We assume, therefore, that organizational goals in a particular time period are a function of (1) organizational goals of the previous time period, (2) organizational experience with respect to that goal in the previous period, and (3) experience of comparable organizations with respect to the goal dimension in the previous time period. Initially at least, we would assume a simple linear function,

$$G_t = a_1 G_{t-1} + a_2 E_{t-1} + a_3 C_{t-1}$$

where G is the organizational goal, E the experience of the organization, C a summary of the experience of comparable organizations, and where $a_1 + a_2 + a_3 = 1$. The parameters in this goal adaptation function are important attributes of the organization. a_3 reflects the organization's sensitivity to the performance of competitors or other comparable organizations. a_1 and a_2 reflect the speed at which the organization revises goals in the face of experience. In some cases, we will want to define two values for a_3—one for when comparative experience exceeds the organization's goal and a different one for when it is below the goal. Similarly, we may want to allow the effect of the organization's experience to depend on whether it exceeds or is below the goal.

Adaptation in attention rules. Just as organizations learn what to strive for in their environment, they also learn to attend to some parts of that environment and not to others. One part of such adaptation is in learning search behavior, which we will consider in a moment. Here we wish to note two related, but different, adaptations:

1. In evaluating performance by explicit measurable criteria, organizations learn to attend to some criteria and ignore others. For example, suppose an organization subunit has responsibility for a specific organizational goal. Since this goal is ordinarily stated in relatively nonoperational terms, the subunit must develop some observable indices of performance on the goal. Among the indices objectively available to the subunit, which will be used? Observation suggests this is a typical case of learning. Subunits in the short run do not change indices significantly. However, there are long-run shifts toward indices that produce generally satisfactory results (that is, in this case, usually show the subunit to be performing well).

2. Organizations learn to pay attention to some parts of their comparative environment and to ignore other parts. We have assumed that one of the parameters in the goal adaptation function is a parameter reflecting the sensitivity of the organization to external comparisons. This parameter is not fixed. We would expect it to change over time as such comparisons do or do not produce results (in the form of goals) that are satisfactory to the important groups in the coalition. At the same time, we have represented by C in the goal adaption function a summary description of comparable organizations. Concealed in such an abstract form is organizational learning with respect to what is properly comparable. With which attributes of which organizations should we compare ourselves? Although in a relatively short-run model we might reasonably consider this fixed, we would expect that in the long run we would require a model in which such attention factors changed.

Adaptation in search rules. If we assume that search is problem-oriented, we must also assume that search rules change. Most simply, what we require in the models are considerations of the following type: when an organization discovers a solution to a problem by searching in a particular way, it will be more likely to search in that way in future problems of the same type; when an organization fails to find a solution by searching in a particular way, it will be less likely to search in that way in future problems of the same type. Thus, the order in which various alternative solutions to a problem are considered will change as the organization experiences success or failure with alternatives.

In a similar fashion, the code (or language) for communicating information about alternatives and their consequences adapts to experience. Any decision-making system develops codes for communicating information about the environment. Such a code partitions all possible states of the world into a relatively small number of classes of states. Learning consists in changes in the partitioning. In general, we assume the gradual development of an efficient code in terms of the decision rules currently in use. Thus, if a decision rule is designed to choose between two alternatives, the information code will tend to reduce all possible states of the world to two classes. If the decision rules change, we assume a change in the information code, but only after a time lag reflecting the rate of learning. The short-run consequences of incompatibilities between the coding rules and the decision rules form some of the more interesting long-run dynamic features of an organizational decision-making model.

THE BASIC STRUCTURE OF THE ORGANIZATIONAL
DECISION-MAKING PROCESS

We have described four basic concepts that seem to us fundamental to an understanding of the decision-making process in a modern, large-scale business organization. The quasi-resolution of conflict, uncertainty avoidance, problemistic search, and organizational learning are central phenomena with which our models must deal. In our judgment, the natural theoretical language for describing a process involving these phenomena is the language of a computer program. It is clear that some parts of the theory are susceptible to representation and solution in other forms, but the general structure of the process can be conveniently represented as a flow chart. Such a flow chart is outlined in its most general form in Figure 1....

Figure 1 is intended to illustrate two things. On the one hand, it shows abstractly the step-by-step decision process. For convenience, we have started the process at the point of receiving feedback from past decisions. Since the decision process is continuous, this start is arbitrary. Starting from the feedback, the figure shows the sequence of steps taken by a particular subunit in the firm with respect to a specific decision and a specific goal. Other decisions by other subunits using other goals would occur in parallel with this one. Loose connections among the subunits and decisions are secured by the environmental feedback and (when indicated) by expanded search.

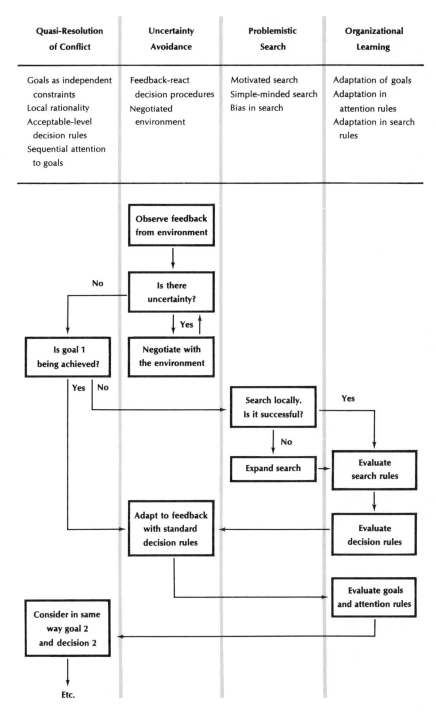

Quasi-Resolution of Conflict	Uncertainty Avoidance	Problemistic Search	Organizational Learning
Goals as independent constraints Local rationality Acceptable-level decision rules Sequential attention to goals	Feedback-react decision procedures Negotiated environment	Motivated search Simple-minded search Bias in search	Adaptation of goals Adaptation in attention rules Adaptation in search rules

Observe feedback from environment

No

Is there uncertainty?

Yes

Is goal 1 being achieved?

Negotiate with the environment

Yes | **No**

Search locally. Is it successful? **Yes**

No

Expand search

Evaluate search rules

Adapt to feedback with standard decision rules

Evaluate decision rules

Evaluate goals and attention rules

Consider in same way goal 2 and decision 2

Etc.

Figure 1 Organizational decision process in abstract form.

At the same time, the figure shows (by the vertical columns) the relation between the basic concepts of the theory and the decision process flow chart. At a general level, each of the concepts is represented in a decision process having this structure. Obviously, when a specific decision in a specific content is considered, this abstract description of the process must be substantially elaborated with specific content.

Clearly, models based on these concepts will deviate significantly from models based on the approach of classical economics. Such differences are not surprising. We have emphasized the fact that the behavioral theory of the firm is designed to answer a set of questions different from those to which traditional theory of the firm is directed. We think that these concepts will prove useful in dealing with organizational decision making as it is reflected in business firms.

28

The Decision

JOHN F. PFIFFNER AND FRANK P. SHERWOOD

Our major reason for choosing this selection is because it is a marvelously concise presentation and critical analysis of the pioneering work of Herbert Simon and others at Carnegie-Mellon University on the relationship between organization structure and decision-making. By beginning with Simon's basic hypothesis, which holds that organization structure and function are determined in large part by human problem-solving processes, the authors allow us to examine another view of a relationship noted in earlier selections. That is, much of the material written on the relationship between organization structure and decision-making focuses on how organizational design shapes decision-making in the firm. The material in this selection reverses that focus.

The significance of the decision as a primary orienting point in organization theory has long been central to the approach and philosophy of Herbert Simon. Like Bakke at Yale, Simon for more than two decades has been pondering these questions and evolving his own formulations. His first important work in this field was undertaken in association with Clarence

Ridley, then executive director of the International City Managers' Association. These two refined and expanded an earlier effort by Ridley to provide a basis for decision making in the municipality. Published in 1937, the monograph was entitled *Measuring Municipal Activities.*[1] It was in 1945, however, that Simon's pioneering and perhaps most significant work, *Administrative Behavior,* was published. With the decision as his basic frame of reference, he took to task most of the earlier propositions on organization, labeling them ambiguous and useless. Since *Administrative Behavior,* Simon has concentrated with his colleagues on the sharpening of his basic theory. This has involved considerable research at Carnegie Institute of Technology and has resulted in such publications as *Centralization versus Decentralization* (1954), *Models of Man* (1957), and *Organizations* (1958).

SIMON'S BASIC IDEAS

While it is perhaps possible to construe the decision concept in rather narrow, mechanistic terms, this has not at all been the Simon approach. Like the group at Yale, Simon has seen the organization problem in its total social and psychological context. His basic assumption has been that the features of organization structure and function derive from the characteristics of human problem-solving processes and rational human choice.[2] Thus the members of an organization are not to be viewed as mere mechanical instrumentalities. They must be regarded as individuals who have wants, motives, and drives, and are limited in their knowledge and in their capacities to learn and to solve problems. The organization is, in these terms, an extension of individuals making choices and behaving on the basis of their understanding of their environment and their needs.

The Organization

Human organizations are regarded by Simon as systems of interdependent activity, encompassing at least several primary groups. There are three *levels* of multiperson units: (1) the *smallest* is the primary group; (2) the *largest* is the institution, such as the state, economic system, etc.; and (3) systems *in between* are organizations. In such a definition there is a great deal of ambiguity, as Simon has pointed out. Organizations may exist *within*

[1] Clarence Ridley and Herbert Simon, *Measuring Municipal Activities* (Chicago: International City Managers' Association, 1937). Many writers have since joined Simon in placing emphasis on the decision. Harold J. Leavitt has suggested that this will be the predominant orientation of organization theory in the future: *Managerial Psychology* (Chicago: University of Chicago Press, 1958), p. 301.

[2] James G. March and Herbert A. Simon, *Organizations* (New York: John Wiley & Sons, 1959), p. 169.

organizations—"a whole agency, a bureau, or even a section of a large department may be regarded as *an* organization."[3]

In later writings Simon has placed increased emphasis on the human organism. Adaptive behavior, largely in terms of "one thing at a time," is basic to the existence of organization structure. Such structure exists only as patterns of behavior which are relatively stable and change slowly. People do not want to tackle too many problems at once. By necessity they must settle on some habits of conduct. These, then, constitute organization *structure;* and it is in the development of these patterns, which obviously involve decision making, that attention can be concentrated profitably.

The Decision

In the very first paragraph of *Administrative Behavior,* Simon has indicated how significant the decision is to his system of thinking. He has written that traditional discussions of administration emphasize the action process, getting things done; and so-called principles are laid down to aid in achieving such action. In all such discussion scant attention has been paid to the choice which prefaces all action, to decide what is to be done rather than how to do it.[4]

The first step in building an adequate theory of organization (and hence a model) is the development of an appropriate unit of analysis. That is why Simon has placed so much emphasis on the decision. He has concluded that the analysis of the *role* played by individuals in an organization is not precise enough; similarly a study of acts or actions remains too general. He regards the decision *premise* as a much smaller unit of analysis and therefore more appropriate. Many premises are involved in any specific decision or action and are incorporated in the definition of a single role. "The central notion," he has written, "is that a decision can be regarded as a conclusion drawn (though not in any strict logical sense) from premises; and that influence is exercised by transmitting decisions, which are then taken as premises for subsequent decision."[5]

In this view there is not an expectation that decision making is necessarily rational. As a matter of fact Simon has appeared to become less sure over the years that even the rationality he assumed in *Administrative Behavior* was appropriate.[6]

The really critical factors in the decision process, then, are (1) the availability of information and (2) the computational capacities available to

[3] Herbert A. Simon, "Comments on the Theory of Organization," *American Political Science Review,* Vol. 46, No. 1130 (December 1952).

[4] Herbert A. Simon, *Administrative Behavior,* 2nd ed. (New York: The Macmillan Company, 1957), p.1.

[5] Simon, "Comments on the Theory of Organization," p. 1132.

[6] "I now feel that ... I yielded too much ground to the omniscient rationality of economic man." Simon, *Administrative Behavior,* p. xxxv.

deal with the information. Man should not be regarded as even "intendedly" rational, as the models of economic man and administrative man suggest. We should substitute the concept of a "choosing" organism of "limited knowledge and ability."[7]

The point of reference that Simon uses to analyze organization behavior is, then, a human organism capable of choosing, problem solving, and decision making. But it does not possess infinite powers, it is limited to doing a few things at a time and can deal with only a small part of the information stored in its memory or existing in its environment.[8]

General Comments

How can such an emphasis on decision be applied to a more general model of organization? Note that decision premises arise largely out of information and the ability of the individual to handle that information. Thus the key to this approach to organization is identification (1) of the decision centers, and (2) of the channels by which communications are carried. Put in the words of March and Simon:

1. Communication traverses definite channels, either by formal plan or by the gradual development of informal programs.
2. Information and stimuli move from sources to points of decision; instructions move from points of decision to points of action; information of results moves from points of decision and control.
3. Rational organization design would call for the arrangement of these channels so as to minimize the communication burden.[9]

The manner in which this type of analysis can provide a foundation for the structuring of organization may be seen in the following hypotheses suggested by March and Simon:

- As one moves toward the top of a hierarchy, the possibilities of rationality decline. He must deal with phenomena in grosser and more aggregative form.

- The division of work according to purpose (or subgoals) tends to foster insularity by building in a subgoal bias. Other subgoals and other aspects of the goals of the larger organization tend to be ignored in the decisions of the subunit, even though conflicts may exist.

---

[7] Herbert A. Simon, "A Behavioral Model of Rational Choice," *Models of Man* (New York: John Wiley & Sons, Inc., 1957), p. 241.

[8] March and Simon, *Organizations,* p. 11.

[9] Quoted from March and Simon, *Organizations,* pp. 166-67; *numbering added.*

- Division of work on the basis of process (subprograms rather than subgoals) will be carried furthest in stable environments. It is likely, too, that organizations, in order to permit a greater degree of process specialization, will devise means for increasing stability and predictability of the environment.
- Specialization is most apt to be found when the organization has stability and is not continually adapting to a rapidly changing environment.
- The degree of local autonomy may reflect the precision of coordination. When communication is poorly developed and control from the center made difficult, there is very apt to be a considerable degree of local discretion for the reason that little else is possible.
- The influence structure in an organization is set in large part by its communication system. More precisely, it is suggested that the "locus of uncertainty absorption" is extremely significant. Thus, persons closest to the reality communicate their "facts," which cannot be checked, as a conscious or unconscious means of acquiring and exercising power.
- The greater the communication efficiency of a channel, the greater its usage. Further, channel usage tends to be self-reinforcing. Once the channels have been well established, their pattern will have an important influence on decision-making processes and, particularly, upon nonprogrammed activity.

. . .

29

Organized Improvisation

ALBERT SPEER

More and more today it has become evident that in the formulation of plans within an organization, consideration must be given to the values and motives of those who act as interpreters of the corporate will. The many persons who participate in setting objectives, formulating strategies, and designing the network of policies, procedures, and methods that are supposed to reach those objectives bring to their task values and personal ambitions that may be more significant than the technical skills they have to offer.

In looking inside the Third Reich through the aging eyes of one of its prime architects, Albert Speer, we are offered a rare opportunity to glimpse

Reprinted from Albert Speer, *Inside the Third Reich,* by permission of The Macmillan Company and George Weidenfeld & Nicolson Ltd. Copyright 1969 by Verlag Ullstein G.m.b.h. Copyright 1970 by The Macmillan Company.

both the moral perversion and organizational form that gave that perversion its awesome thrust.

As you read this section of Speer's autobiography, question the degree to which the organizational means of arriving at and implementing decisions were responsible for so distorting "normal" values to permit the atrocious efficiency of Nazi Germany. Or were the ways in which objectives were set and plans carried out a function of the values of the men and women who emerged from the conditioning process that preceded Hitler's rise to power?

In trying to answer these questions read the next selection by Kuhn and Berg. It may help in trying to sort out the "truth" from among Speer's recollections and rationalizations.

As I rode through the suburbs of the capital with their factories and railroad yards, I was overcome by anxiety. How would I be able to contend with this vast and alien field, I wondered. I had considerable doubts about my qualifications for this new task, for coping with either the practical difficulties or the personal demands that were made upon a minister.

. . .

My work began immediately. Field Marshal Erhard Milch, state secretary of the Air Ministry, invited me to a conference in the great hall of the Ministry, to be held on Friday, February 13, at which armament questions were to be discussed with the three branches of the services and with representatives of industry. When I asked whether this conference could not be postponed, since I first had to get the feel of my job, Milch replied with a counterquestion typical of his free and easy manner and the good relations between us: The top industrialists from all over the Reich were already on their way to the conference, and was I going to beg off? I agreed to come.

. . .

I sensed that something unusual was awaiting me at Milch's conference. Since I still felt by no means secure and since Hitler was still in Berlin, I informed him of my anxieties. I knew, from the little episode with Goering at the time of my appointment, that I could count on his backing. "Very well," he said. "If any steps are taken against you, or if you have difficulties, interrupt the conference and invite the participants to the Cabinet Room. Then I'll tell those gentlemen whatever is necessary."

The Cabinet Room was regarded as a "sacred place"; to be received there would inevitably make a deep impression. And the fact that Hitler would be willing to address this group, with whom I would be dealing in the future, offered me the best possible prospects for my start.

The large conference hall of the Air Ministry was filled. There were thirty persons present: the most important men in industry, among them General Manager Albert Vogler; Wilhelm Zangen, head of the German Industry Association; General Ernst Fromm, chief of the Reserve Army, with his subordinate, Lieutenant General Leeb, chief of the army Ordnance Office; Admiral Witzell, armaments chief of the navy; General Thomas, chief of the War Economy and Armaments Office of the OKW; Walther Funk, Reich Minister of Economics; various officials of the Four-Year Plan; and a few more of Goering's important associates. Milch took the chair as representative of the conference host. He asked Funk to sit at his right and me at his left. In a terse introductory address he explained the difficulties that had arisen in armaments production due to the conflicting demands of the three services. Vogler of the United Steel Works followed with some highly intelligent explanations of how orders and counterorders, disputes over priority levels, and constant shifting of priorities interfered with industrial production. There were still unused reserves available, he said, but because of the tugging and hauling these did not come to light. Thus it was high time to establish clear relationships. There must be one man able to make all decisions. Industry did not care who it was.

Thereafter, General Fromm spoke for the army and Admiral Witzell for the navy. In spite of some reservations they expressed general agreement with Vogler's remarks. The other participants likewise were convinced of the necessity for having one person to assume authority in economic matters. During my own work for the air force I too had recognized the urgency of this matter.

Finally Economics Minister Funk stood up and turned directly to Milch. We were all in essential agreement, he said; the course of the meeting had revealed that. The only remaining question, therefore, was who the man should be. "Who would be better suited for the purpose than you, my dear Milch, since you have the confidence of Goering, our revered Reich Marshal? I therefore believe I am speaking in the name of all when I ask you to take over this office!" he exclaimed, striking a rather overemotional note for the occasion.

This had clearly been prearranged. Even while Funk was speaking, I whispered into Milch's ear: "The conference is to be continued in the Cabinet Room. The Fuehrer wants to speak about my tasks." Milch, quick-wittedly grasping the meaning of this, replied to Funk's proposal that he was greatly honored by such an expression of confidence, but that he could not accept.

I spoke up for the first time, transmitting to the assembled group the Fuehrer's invitation and announcing that the discussion would be continued on Thursday, February 18, in my ministry, since it would probably deal with my assignment. Milch then adjourned the session.

Later Funk admitted to me that on the eve of the conference Billy Korner, Goering's state secretary and associate in the work of the Four-Year Plan, had urged him to propose Milch as the authority for final decisions.

Funk took it for granted that Korner could not have made this request without Goering's knowledge.

Hitler's invitation alone must have made it clear to those familiar with the balance of power that I was starting from a stronger position than my predecessor had ever possessed.

Now Hitler had to make good on his promise. In his office he let me brief him on what had taken place and jotted down some notes. He then went into the Cabinet Room with me and immediately took the floor.

Hitler spoke for about an hour. Rather tediously, he expatiated on the tasks of war industry, emphasized the need for accelerated production, spoke of the valuable forces that must be mobilized in industry, and was astonishingly candid on the subject of Goering: "This man cannot look after armaments within the framework of the Four-Year Plan."

It was essential, Hitler continued, to separate this task from the Four-Year Plan and turn it over to me. A function was given to a man and then taken from him again; such things happened. The capacity for increased production was available, but things had been mismanaged.

(In prison Funk told me that Goering had asked for this statement of Hitler's—which amounted to stripping him of some of his powers—in writing so that he could use it as evidence against his use of forced labor.)

Hitler avoided touching on the problem of a single head for all armaments production. Similarly, he spoke only of supplies for the army and navy, deliberately excluding the air force. I too had glossed over this contested point in my words with him, since the matter involved a political decision and would have brought in all sorts of ambiguities. Hitler concluded his address with an appeal to the participants. He first described my great feats in construction—which could scarcely have made much of an impression on these people. He went on to say that this new job represented a great sacrifice on my part—a statement which did not have much meaning in view of the critical situation. He expected not only cooperation on their part but also fair treatment. "Behave toward him like gentlemen!" he said, employing the English word, which he rarely used. What exactly my assignment was, he did not clearly state, and I preferred it that way.

Heretofore Hitler had never introduced a minister in this way. Even in a less authoritarian system such a debut would have been of assistance. In our state the consequences were astonishing, even to me. For a considerable time I found myself moving in a kind of vacuum that offered no resistance whatsoever. Within the widest limits I could practically do as I pleased.

．　．　．

Equipped with Hitler's grant of full authority, with a peaceable Goering in the background, I could go forward with my comprehensive plan of "industrial self-responsibility," as I had sketched it in my outline. Today it is generally agreed that the astonishingly rapid rise in armaments production was due to this plan. Its principles, however, were not new. Both Field Marshal Milch and my predecessor Todt had already adopted the procedure of entrusting eminent technicians from leading industrial firms with the management of separate areas of armaments production. But Dr. Todt himself had borrowed this idea. The real creator of the concept of industrial self-responsibility was Walter Rathenau, the great Jewish organizer of the German economy during the First World War. He realized that considerable increases in production could be achieved by exchange of technical experiences, by division of labor from plant to plant, and by standardization. As early as 1917 he declared that such methods could guarantee "a doubling of production with no increase in equipment and no increase in labor costs." ...

We formed "directive committees" for the various types of weapons and "directive pools" for the allocation of supplies. Thirteen such committees were finally established, one for each category of my armaments program. Linking these were an equal number of pools.

Alongside these committees and pools I set up development commissions in which army officers met with the best designers in industry. These commissions were to supervise new products, suggest improvements in manufacturing techniques even during the design stage, and call a halt to any unnecessary projects.

The heads of the committees and the pools were to make sure—this was vital to our whole approach—that a given plant concentrated on producing only one item, but did so in maximum quantity. Because of Hitler's and Goering's continual restiveness, expressed in sudden shifts of program, the factories had hitherto tried to assure themselves of four or five different contracts simultaneously, and if possible, from different branches of the services, so that they could shift to alternative contracts in case of sudden cancellations. Moreover, the Wehrmacht frequently assigned contracts only for a limited time. Thus, for example, before 1942 the manufacture of ammunition was checked or increased depending on consumption, which came in sudden bursts because of the blitz campaigns. This state of affairs kept the factories from throwing all their productive energy into making ammunition. We provided contractual guarantees of continued procurement and assigned the types we needed among the various factories.

By dint of these changes, the armaments production of the early years of the war, which had been on a more or less piecework basis, was converted to industrial mass production. Amazing results were soon to show up. ... I regarded my task principally as one of tracking down and defining problems so far screened by long years of routine; but I left their solution to the specialists. Obsessed with my task, I did not try to keep down the extent of my responsibilities, but rather to take in more and more areas of the economy. ... After all, at thirty-six I was the youngest minister in the Reich. My Industry Organization soon comprised more than ten thousand assistants and aides, but in our Ministry itself there were only two hundred and eighteen officials at work. This proportion was in keeping with my view of the Ministry as merely a steering organization, with the chief thrust of our operation lying in "industrial self-responsibility."

The traditional arrangement provided that most matters would be submitted to the minister by his state secretary. The latter functioned as a kind of sieve, deciding the importance of things at his own discretion. I eliminated this procedure and made directly subordinate to myself more than thirty leaders of the Industry Organization and no less than ten department chiefs[1] in the Ministry. In principle they were all supposed to settle their interrelationships among themselves, but I took the liberty of intervening in important questions or whenever differences of opinion arose.

Our method of work was just as unusual as this form of organization. The old-line officials of the government bureaucracy spoke disdainfully of a "dynamic Ministry" or a "Ministry without an organization plan" and a "ministry without officials." It was said that I applied rough-and-ready or "American" methods. My comment, "If jurisdictions are sharply separated, we are actually encouraging a limited point of view," was prompted by rebellion against the caste mentality of the system, but also bore some resemblance to Hitler's notions of improvised government by an impulsive genius.

Another principle of mine also gave offense. This had to do with personnel policy. As soon as I assumed my post I gave instructions, as the Fuehrer's Minutes of February 19, 1942, record, that the leading men in important departments who were "over fifty-five years old must be assigned a deputy who is no older than forty."

Whenever I explained my organizational plans to Hitler, he showed a striking lack of interest. I had the impression that he did not like to deal with these questions; indeed, in certain realms he was altogether incapable of distinguishing the important from the unimportant. He also did not like establishing clear lines of jurisdiction. Sometimes he deliberately assigned bureaus or individuals the same or similar tasks. "That way," he used to say, "the stronger one does the job."

. . .

[1] All department heads under my direction were empowered to sign orders as "deputized by" the minister rather than "in behalf of" the minister. This was a technical breach in the rules of the state bureaucracy, for it implied that they were authorized to act independently, a power usually reserved to state secretaries. I ignored the protests submitted by the Minister of the Interior, who was responsible for preserving the regular procedures of government administration.

I brought the head of the Planning Department, Willy Liebel, from Nuremberg, where he had been mayor. The director of the Technical Department, Karl Saur, had risen from the intermediate ranks of party functionaries, after previously occupying a subordinate position in industry. The head of the Supply Department, Dr. Walter Schieber, was a chemist by profession; he was typical of the older party member in the SS and party who had had previous experience as specialists. Xaver Dorsch, my deputy in the Todt Organization, was our oldest party member. The head of the department responsible for consumer goods production, Seebauer, had also joined the party long before 1933.

Aside from all organizational innovations, things went so well because I applied the methods of democratic economic leadership. The democracies were on principle committed to placing trust in the responsible businessmen as long as that trust was justified. Thus they rewarded initiative, aroused an awareness of mission, and spurred decision making. Among us, on the other hand, all such elements had long ago been buried. Pressure and coercion kept production going, to be sure, but destroyed all spontaneity. I felt it necessary to issue a declaration to the effect that industry was not "knowingly lying to us, stealing from us, or otherwise trying to damage our war economy."

The party felt acutely challenged by that attitude, as I was to find out after July 20, 1944. Exposed to sharp attacks, I had to defend my system of delegated responsibility in a letter to Hitler.

Paradoxically, from 1942 on, the developments in the warring countries moved in an opposite direction. The Americans, for example, found themselves compelled to introduce an authoritarian stiffening into their industrial structure, whereas we tried to loosen the regimented economic system. The elimination of all criticism of superiors had in the course of years led to a situation in which mistakes and failures, misplanning, or duplication of effort were no longer even noted. I saw to the formation of committees in which discussion was possible, shortages and mistakes could be uncovered, and their elimination considered. We often joked that we were on the point of reintroducing the parliamentary system. Our new system had created one of the prerequisites for balancing out the weaknesses of every authoritarian order. Important matters were not to be regulated solely by the military principle, that is by channels of command from top to bottom. But for such "parliamentarism" to work, of course, the committees mentioned above had to be headed by persons who allowed arguments and counterarguments to be stated before they made a decision.

Grotesquely enough, this system met with considerable reserve on the part of the factory heads. Early in my job I had sent out a circular letter asking them to inform me of their "fundamental needs and observations on a larger scale than previously." I expected a flood of letters, but there was no response. At first I suspected my office staff of withholding the mail from me. But actually none had come in. The factory heads, as I learned later, feared reprimands from the Gauleiters [district leaders of the German National Socialist party].

There was more than enough criticism from above to below, but the necessary complement of criticism from below to above was hard to come by. I often had the feeling that I was hovering in the air, since my decisions produced no critical response.

We owed the success of our programs to thousands of technicians with special achievements to their credit to whom we now entrusted the responsibility for whole segments of the armaments industry. This aroused their buried enthusiasm. They also took gladly to my unorthodox style of leadership. Basically, I exploited the phenomenon of the technician's often blind devotion to his task. Because of what seems to be the moral neutrality of technology, these people were without any scruples about their activities. The more technical the world imposed on us by the war, the more dangerous was this indifference of the technician to the direct consequences of his anonymous activities.

In my work I preferred "uncomfortable associates to compliant tools." The party, on the other hand, had a deep distrust for non-party leaders. ...

. . .

The longer I fought the typically German bureaucracy, whose tendencies were aggravated by the authoritarian system, the more my criticism assumed a political cast. This matter became something of an obsession with me, for on the morning of July 20, 1944, a few hours before the attempted assassination, I wrote to Hitler that Americans and Russians knew how to act with organizationally simple methods and therefore achieved greater results, whereas we were hampered by superannuated forms of organization and therefore could not match the others' feats. The war, I said, was also a contest between two systems of organization, the "struggle of our system of overbred organization against the art of improvisation on the opposing side." If we did not arrive at a different system of organization, I continued, it would be evident to posterity that our outmoded, tradition-bound, and arthritic organizational system had lost the struggle.

30

Businessmen: Entrepreneurs or Bureaucrats?

JAMES W. KUHN AND IVAR E. BERG

This selection was chosen because it ties closely to the preceding selection, which raises some of the most "spine tingling" questions contained in management literature—that is, "spine tingling" to anyone who can conceive of the efficiency that was mobilized behind the monster that was Nazi Germany. For American business to maintain a position of esteem within our society, it cannot rest on assurances that the sterile efficiency of the objectiveless bureaucrat is being nurtured. Instead we must seek those organizational forms that give rise to plans that have woven into their very fabric the means of making objectives sufficiently visible so that they may be carefully considered and then supported or rejected by all those concerned.

Reprinted from James W. Kuhn and Ivar E. Berg, *Values in a Business Society: Issues and Analysis,* pp. 183-190, by permission of the publisher. Copyright 1968 by Harcourt Brace Jovanovich, Inc., New York.

Kuhn and Berg attempt to identify the factors that move the leadership of an organization from the pioneering individualism of an entrepreneur to the sheeplike tramp of the bureaucrat and leave it ripe for the manipulative hand of an industrial demagogue or the slow suffocation of prolonged bureaucracy.

Businessmen and union leaders not infrequently argue that the power they are believed to possess is merely putative. The chief executive officer of a large national manufacturing firm once complained that he and his managers were in an almost hopeless situation; they were buffeted so severely by circumstances, opponents, and competitors that he foresaw only a dark future for his firm and the industry. First, they had suffered a long and costly strike and had then had to settle without gaining their demands to be able to operate their plants more efficiently. Second, the government was threatening to impose price guidelines upon them, and the antitrust division of the Justice Department was continually lurking about, looking for an excuse to prosecute. Third, foreign competition had made large inroads into the firm's markets abroad, and at home substitute products were eating away at sales. In sum, he saw no relief, no room for maneuver, and no chance for initiative. He and his associates were hemmed in and restricted—powerless pawns of a society that no longer encouraged efficient, profit-seeking business.

The particular complaints of this businessman may have been born of temporary setbacks to the company and his own ineptitude, but their general tone is not untypical. Most business and union leaders probably also feel that they act as conditions and situations dictate rather than as men who impress their will upon events and give them direction. So convinced are businessmen and union leaders—like almost all managers within large bureaucracies—of their limited power that they seldom identify those who act or make decisions within the organization. Things happen, decisions are made, and transactions are accomplished, but these proceed apparently without the help of personalities. The people involved become puppets of circumstances or of tendencies and forces within the industry. Although muckraking journalists and biographers once pictured swashbuckling captains of industry who shaped their industrial as well as their political and social environment, businessmen today are inclined to portray themselves as competent professionals who adapt themselves to forces set in motion by others.

There are, of course, constraints on the businessman's freedom of action and on his power; many considerations must enter into his judgments and decisions, among them the power and demands of politicians, organized consumer groups, and employees. Such realities, and not simply the self-pity of businessmen, were reflected in the popularity of an article published in the *Harvard Business Review* that described how even routine business decisions could only be made in consultation, almost hourly, with government representatives.[1] And James R. Hoffa of the Teamsters Union could undoubtedly tear a similar page from his own calendar to reveal the magnitude of limitations on union leaders in conducting what he not unrealistically terms "the union business." Indeed, the prolonged legal battle he carried on with the Department of Justice might well have intimidated and frustrated a person of less initiative and imagination.

In addition to the objective constraints they actually face, however, managers also operate in an environment of values and beliefs that reinforces their self-image of essentially passive response. The thought that businessmen, along with angry Presidents, aggressive trustbusters, and hard-bargaining unionists, might be accountable for even some of the major developments in our society is not readily entertained by most citizens. The idea that the business community responds to the initiative of others is perpetuated by the news media as they regularly report "Wall Street reactions" to Presidential press conferences, the statements of labor leaders, and other significant events. The pictures occasionally drawn of businessmen as "robber barons," "malefactors of great wealth," or "economic royalists" have never replaced the less colorful one of the businessman as a manager who minds his own business, adjusting its detailed operations to meet contingencies triggered by others. Indeed, if we omit the Progressive era and the Great Depression, we can generalize that businessmen have usually been regarded as rational economic agents who simply make decisions "at the margins" guided by the best information available to them, straightforward criteria of profitability, and their individual consciences.

The crucial factor influencing business judgment is now commonly thought to be the degree of "confidence" in the state of the economy. Americans are influenced in this belief more by the reasoning of academic economists than by the judgment of social critics. Arthur F. Burns, chairman of the Council of Economic Advisors during the Eisenhower Administration, president of the National Bureau of Economic Research, and a Columbia University economist, has emphasized the importance of business confidence and lent his support to the view that the individual businessman is an "intervening variable" who is almost totally dependent on and vulnerable to the acts, demands, and even attitudes of others. In a sweeping appraisal of the performance of the American economy in the postwar era, Burns related changes in the economy to variations in the level of business confidence, which in turn he linked in detail to specific public policies, union demands, and Presidential attitudes toward the business community.[2] We need not

---

[1] Gilbert H. Clee, "The Appointment Book of J. Edward Ellis," *Harvard Business Review*, 40 (November-December, 1962), 79-92. Some readers were given pause by the editorial blurb at the beginning of this article that identified the author as the director of a leading consulting firm who had not permitted the annoyance of having to keep appointments with bureaucrats to prevent him from the successful "reorganization of foreign and domestic states."

[2] Arthur F. Burns, *The Management of Prosperity*, "The 1965 Fairless Lectures" (New York: Columbia University Press and Carnegie Press, 1966).

examine here the kinds of congressional policies, Presidential attitudes, or union postures that Professor Burns believes heighten business confidence and that are conducive to socially beneficial investment and managerial decisions. The important point is that the views of Burns and other economists reinforce the image of the businessman as a technician who has little freedom in shaping the character of American life.[3]

Professor Burns' view of the businessman is completely consistent with—indeed, it is a corollary of—the priority assigned the market mechanism in economic theory. According to the theory, competitive pressures operate *in the long run,* so as substantially to limit the discretionary range and effect of business decisions. However, as John Maynard Keynes pointed out, in the long run we are all dead. In the short run, businessmen sometimes enjoy considerable discretion and find ample room for initiative. We do an injustice to the boldness, the genius, and the imagination of businessmen to describe their work as merely the outcome of grinding market forces. Consider the following description by a Supreme Court Justice of the massive merger of 37 steel companies into the United States Steel Corporation in 1901; it was, he said,

> an evolution, a natural consummation of the tendencies of the industry on account of changing conditions, practically a compulsion from "the metallurgical method of making steel and the physical method of handling it," this method, and the conditions consequent upon it, tending to combinations of capital and energies rather than diffusion in independent action. And the concentration of powers ... was only such as was deemed necessary, and immediately manifested itself in improved methods and products and in an increase of domestic and foreign trade. Indeed an important purpose of the organization of the corporation was the building up of the export trade in steel and iron. ...[4]

To describe the creation of U.S. Steel as the result of "natural tendencies" and "technological compulsions" is to overlook the carefully plotted strategies and inspired maneuvers of such men as Charles M. Schwab who worked hard to bring about the merger. We need not be surprised, however, that the men involved accepted its description as an impersonal, natural event. To introduce people into the drama would raise awkward questions about the power amassed by the men who controlled the $1.4 billion corporation that produced half the pig iron, 60 per cent of the structural steel, and 90 per cent of the bridge steel in the nation. From certain points of view, such questions might be better left unexplored or even unasked.

[3] This image is perpetuated in literature, film, and in TV "Easterns," in which the businessman is typically portrayed as an "organization man," a "Babbitt," a "tired businessman," or a "man in a grey-flannel suit" rather than as a swashbucking entrepreneur.

[4] "Opinion of the Court," Justice McKenna, United States v. U.S. Steel Corporation, 251 U.S. 419, 437-38.

There are several important qualifications to acceptance of the theories of general business helplessness in the face of events and government action. The interaction between government and business has often been clearly very profitable for business. Much of the entrepreneurial skill displayed by business in the prosperous period dating from the end of World War II has been dedicated to making imaginative and inventive use of the opportunities afforded by government subsidies, tax reductions, contracts, and investments in such things as airports, roads, schools, and research.[5] Indeed, one can hardly begin to account for the enormous gains in the American economy since 1945 without recognizing the business initiative that imaginatively combined these and other welfare benefits with private funds and managerial expertise. The business leaders that *Fortune* admiringly calls the "New Breed" have learned to capitalize upon the opportunities offered them in the form of governmental programs. Gilbert Clee concludes his tale in the *Harvard Business Review* about the depressing web of government bureaucracy and red tape with the somewhat ironic observation that managers must learn to negotiate more effectively the labyrinthian corridors of political power. And the investment firm of Merrill Lynch, Pierce, Fenner & Smith, in a pamphlet on the investment prospects arising from America's growing efforts to solve pressing domestic problems, extolls "the economic virtues of a free society" and reminds its clients of "the lucrative markets created by forthcoming social problems."[6]

Another reason for discounting the modesty of top industrial leaders about their impact on the economy is the estimate of their importance implicit in the salaries they pay themselves. In one year, the 66 highest executives of the General Motors Corporation received more income from salaries, bonuses, and other financial benefits than the combined total salaries of the President and the Vice President of the United States, the members of the Cabinet, the Supreme Court, the Senate, the House of Representatives, and 48 state governors.

Antitrust cases, pricing conspiracies, and the other scandals that are reported with oppressive monotony in the daily pages of the *Wall Street Journal* constitute a further argument against believing that consumers, political figures, and labor leaders determine economic processes, while business leaders are merely passive instruments. The degree to which it is possible, for example, to build stout, though perhaps illegal, shelters against the chill winds of the marketplace suggests that businessmen have a good deal more power than is acknowledged in their rhetoric.

Consider the situation that came to light when the price conspiracy in the electrical equipment industry was revealed. In 1959 the Tennessee Valley Authority asked for bids to deliver a 500,000 kilowatt turbo-generator and

---

[5] Business has also profited from government pollution control and stockpiling programs. With respect to antipoverty projects, see Ivar Berg and Marcia Freedman, "Job Corps: Business Bonanza," *Christianity and Crisis*, 25 (May 31, 1965), 115-19.

[6] "The New American Horizon," Securities Research Division, Merrill Lynch, Pierce, Fenner & Smith, Inc., New York, May, 1966.

awarded the contract to C. A. Parsons & Co., Ltd., of England. General Electric, whose bids had been eliminated as too high, complained that the English firm's bid was unfair because its labor costs were 40 per cent lower than comparable American wages. This wage differential, GE maintained, accounted for the more than $6 million difference between the American bids and the lower bid by Parsons. In answering these charges of unfairness, TVA's chairman, General Herbert Vogel, calculated that the British firm's bid would have been $4 million to $5 million lower even if General Electric had paid its labor—including engineers, draftsmen, and other salaried personnel, as well as hourly rated factory workers—nothing!

It is by no means clear that the two American companies that bid in the TVA competition were subject to the discipline of the marketplace as they set their prices for turbo-generators. At the very least, the market had failed to promote efficient production. The companies could not come within striking distance of Parsons' bid even though the British firm had to overcome the handicaps of a tariff of $1.5 million (about the size of its wage bill) and a "Buy American" requirement that foreign bids had to be at least 20 per cent lower than any domestic bid for a government agency to accept them.

The normal pricing policies in several American industries suggest as strongly as the sporadic instances of outright price conspiracies elsewhere that businessmen have considerable power to shape their destinies. Deftly analyzing the incomplete data on automobile pricing disclosed in congressional hearings and other sources, Daniel Bell concluded that the management of General Motors sets automobile prices so that they will return a profit even when production may be no more than 35 per cent or 40 per cent of capacity. When sales are high, economies of scale beome operative and unit costs dip below those used in the low sales years as a basis for determining prices, thus insuring the automaker substantial profits.[7] Similarly, in the steel industry, the break-even figure in the 1960's has been reliably reported at 48 per cent of capacity. Presumably prices could be lowered to reflect the economies that set in when high levels of production are achieved; instead, profits soar as prices remain stable or even rise.

Stories of old-fashioned initiative, business acumen, and entrepreneurial derring-do on the American economic scene still appear often enough to constitute a final reason for rejecting the theory that businessmen are helpless. By no means are all managers tired bureaucrats, as the case of one company that had been losing money will illustrate. Anxious to avoid a financial failure, the managers of this company wondered what to do with a large and useless inventory of wallpaper cleaner that would not sell. With intelligence—and no little sense of humor—they relabeled it "Play-dough" and in the first two years alone sold several million dollars' worth of it across toy counters.

If the role of business leaders in making vital economic decisions needs to be reexamined in an atmosphere cleared of foggy ideologies, at least as

[7] *New York Review of Books*, 3 (September 10, 1964), 12.

much attention should be focused on the role of union leaders. Union officials claim that they are hamstrung by the combined workings of union democracy, government surveillance of their financial operations, rapid technological change that stalks after the jobs they seek to control, and unemployment rates that exert downward pressure on wages. Like some business managers, however, some labor leaders have capably turned events and challenges into opportunities and advantages, so no general theory of the natural weakness of union leadership can be taken at face value.

Thus, when employers and congressmen sympathetic with them insisted, in the Taft-Hartley Law of 1947, that labor-management agreements be construed as legal contracts, the union cause seemed at first to have suffered a setback. Employers anxious to avoid pressures from the organized segments of the labor market and wishing to obtain government aid in achieving greater stability in their complex business operations had wanted "no strike" clauses in labor agreements, coupled with provisions for the arbitration of disputes, to be made enforceable in the courts; with the Taft-Hartley Act they were successful. Union leaders were not slow to see the advantages of property ownership that the construal of agreements as contracts implied, however; they have since managed successfully to husband their members' investments in their jobs by contesting unilateral managerial decisions to modify work procedures and to relocate production facilities. What at first seemed government persecution of unions was recognized as an opportunity and was turned to good use by alert labor leaders.

Union leaders are also a good deal less the victims of changing technology than they portray themselves to be in disputes with their counterparts in corporations over such issues as work loads, crew sizes, and working rules. For example, Harry Bridges, president of the West Coast longshoremen's union,[8] negotiated with an employer group a ground-breaking "modernization and mechanization" agreement that opened the way for far-reaching technological changes in the manner of loading and unloading seagoing cargo. The stevedoring companies were enabled by the agreement to cut crew sizes, use larger sling loads, and employ forklift trucks and other mechanical devices. As a result of these reforms, turn-around time for West Coast-based ships has been substantially reduced, and longshoremen share—in accordance with the terms of the original agreement—a portion of the benefits that accrue to the companies. Only the slowness of some of the employers to take advantage of the permissive clauses in the contract has kept the union from enjoying even greater returns on its forward-looking policies.

Another leader who has refused to be daunted by changing technology is Edward Swayduck, president of the Amalgamated Lithographers Union of New York. Swayduck is an even more individualistic entrepreneur than Bridges and has led his union on an independent course in pursuit of the opportunities for growth in the areas of his members' interests. His union regularly finances research on new methods and applications of lithography.

[8] The International Longshoremen's & Warehousemen's Union.

The union's contributions to the art of packaging alone have been notable; it has also added a great deal to the advertising industry's array of techniques for catching the eye and the interest of the consumer.

Not all union leaders grasp opportunities to exploit their business environment, of course, any more than business executives typically exploit all the opportunities afforded them by the presence of unions. Some formerly aggressive union leaders have now virtually given up in the face of the difficulties and pressures that confront the labor movement in America. Unions have not achieved much influence as representatives of the swollen ranks of white-collar workers, and they have been less than completely successful in preventing rank-and-file members brought into the fold in earlier periods from embarrassing defections, secessions, and even occasional subversions of their bargaining efforts. Whether unions have even succeeded in raising wage levels in America is a matter of considerable dispute among economists. As for their social impact, the vulnerability of many unions to criticism from congressional investigating committees and militant civil rights leaders is by now a matter of public record.

In sum, we may well be skeptical of the bland innocence and agonized helplessness that have become central themes in the rhetoric of businessmen and union leaders. The captains of industry are not merely "dependent variables" in reality, whatever place economists may assign them in the world of their elegant but oversimplified equations. Business managers are neither as powerless nor as rational as they and others often claim. Nor are union leaders as subversive of capitalist institutions and values nor as omnipotent as their critics would have us believe. Their own complaints against the effects of laws are less than compelling; their exploitation of the market and its price systems are sometimes impressive; their capacity for consolidating or expanding their organizational gains are perhaps less than their abilities to manage their organizations with bureaucratic expertise.

At the same time that we make room for a better differentiated view of business and union leaders than that offered by conventional stereotypes, it is well to note that a new breed of politically astute entrepreneurs, outside both unions and corporations, has appeared, almost unnoticed on the American scene. Little attention has yet been given to the heads of private foundations, the university scholars, and the government leaders who have quietly moved to become initiators in recent years. The Ford Foundation has played a major role in the economic development of the new countries of Africa; the Carnegie Foundation has regularly broken new ground in education, which, in turn, figures very significantly in the growth of the U.S. economy; the Atomic Energy Commission, the National Aeronautics and Space Administration, and the Department of Agriculture have contributed enormously to the peaceful application of nuclear energy, the development of computer technology and "miniaturization," and an unbelievable output of foodstuffs, respectively. Clark Kerr, formerly president of the University of California at Berkeley, and George Taylor of the University of Pennsylvania have broken numerous impasses between corporations and unions while teaching the nation much about effective leadership of large organizations.

A host of quasi-public agencies gives testimony to the fact that old-fashioned entrepreneurship is appearing in some new guises. A noted economist reminds us that the Tennessee Valley Authority, the many turnpike authorities, port authorities, and regional "conferences," and a number of housing and urban renewal agencies represent new forms of "enterprise structures." "These structures have become so large and extensive," he writes, "that when Robert Moses, a New York civil servant, was at the height of his activity in the middle 1950's, he had the best claim to the title of the nation's outstanding entrepreneur."[9] A review of Mr. Moses' activities and relationships is indeed suggestive of the variety of entrepreneurial opportunities still present in America. One of the newest enterprise structures is the Communications Satellite Corporation; it was invented by public servants and politicians, working in collaboration with private citizens, to capitalize on space-age opportunities.

Initiative and creativity are of significance to our economic system wherever they are found, and economic doctrines that overlook the importance of entrepreneurial "bureaucrats" in governmental and quasi-public agencies ought to be modified to fit current reality.

[9] Eli Ginzberg, "The Passing of an Economy That Never Was," *Columbia Journal of World Business.* 1 (Summer, 1966), 133-38.

FOR FURTHER READING

Ackoff, Russell L., *A Concept of Corporate Planning.* New York: John Wiley & Sons, Inc., 1970, Chap. 2.

———, "The Meaning of Strategic Planning." *Management Review*, Vol. 55, No. 10 (October 1966), 20-24.

Aharoni, Y., *The Foreign Investment Decision Process.* Boston: Harvard Business School, 1966.

Ammer, Dean S., "The Side Effects of Planning." *Harvard Business Review*, Vol. 48, No. 3 (May-June 1970), 32.

Anderson, T. A., "Coordinating Strategic and Operational Planning." *Business Horizons*, Vol. 8, No. 2 (Summer 1965), 44-58.

Ansoff, H. Igor, *Corporate Strategy.* New York: McGraw-Hill Book Company, 1965.

———, "Planning as a Practical Management Tool." *Financial Executive*, Vol. 32, No. 6 (June 1964), 34-37.

Berg, T. L., and A. Shuchman, eds., *Product Strategy and Management.* New York: Holt, Rinehart & Winston, Inc., 1963, pp. 569-86.

Branch, Melville C., *The Corporate Planning Process.* New York: American Management Association, 1962.

Capon, F. S., "Essentials of Corporate Planning." *The Controller,* Vol. 28, No. 5 (May 1960), 218.

Chandler, A. D., Jr., *Strategy and Structure.* Cambridge, Mass.: The M.I.T. Press, 1962.

Cotton, D. B., *Company-Wide Planning.* New York: The Macmillan Company, 1970.

Cyert, Richard M., and James G. March, *A Behavioral Theory of the Firm.* Englewood Cliffs, N.J.: Prentice-Hall, Inc., 1963.

Emery, J. C., *Organizational Planning and Controls Systems.* New York: The Macmillan Company, 1969, Chap. 5.

England, G. W., "Organizational Goals and Expected Behavior of American Managers." *Academy of Management Journal,* Vol. 10, No. 2 (June 1967), 107-117.

Ewing, David, ed., *Long-Range Planning for Management.* New York: Harper & Row, Publishers, 1968.

Gilmore, F. F., and R. Brandenburg, "Anatomy of Corporate Planning." *Harvard Business Review,* Vol. 40, No. 6 (November-December 1962), 61-69.

Glans, T. B., *et al., Management Systems.* New York: Holt, Rinehart & Winston, Inc., 1968.

Granger, C. H., "The Hierarchy of Objectives." *Harvard Business Review,* Vol. 42, No. 3 (May-June 1964), 65-74.

————, "How to Set Company Objectives." *Management Review,* Vol. 59, No. 7 (July 1970).

Gross, B. M., "What Are Your Organization's Objectives?" *Human Relations,* August 1965.

Haas, Raymond M., *Long-Range Planning for Small Business.* Bloomington, Ind.: Indiana University Press, 1969.

Hardwick, C. T., and B. F. Landuyt, *Administrative Strategy and Decision Making,* 2nd ed. Cincinnati: South-Western Publishing Co., 1966.

Higginson, M. V., *Management Policies I and II.* New York: American Management Association, 1966.

Hughes, Charles L., *Goal Setting: Key to Individual and Organizational Effectiveness.* New York: American Management Association, 1965.

Le Breton, Preston P., and Dale A. Henning, *Planning Theory.* Englewood Cliffs, N.J.: Prentice-Hall, Inc., 1961.

Leontief, Wassily W., "Proposal for Better Business Forecasting." *Harvard Business Review,* Vol. 42, No. 6 (November-December 1964), 166-182.

Litschert, R. J., "The Structure of Long-Range Planning Groups." *Academy of Management Journal,* Vol. 14, No. 1 (March 1971), 33-43.

Mace, Myles L., "The President and Corporate Planning." *Harvard Business Review,* Vol. 43, No. 1 (January-February 1965).

Miller, David W., and Martin K. Starr, *Executive Decisions and Operations Research,* 2nd ed. Englewood Cliffs, N.J.: Prentice-Hall, Inc., 1969.

Miller, E. C., *Advanced Techniques for Strategic Planning.* New York: American Management Association, 1971.

————, *Objectives and Standards*. New York: American Management Association, 1966.

Mockler, R. J., "Theory and Practice of Planning." *Harvard Business Review*, Vol. 48, No. 2 (March-April 1970), 148-150.

Neuschel, R. F., *Management by System*. New York: McGraw-Hill Book Company, 1960.

Newman, W. H., and J. P. Logan, *Strategy, Policy, and Central Management*. Cincinnati: South-Western Publishing Co., 1971.

O'Donnell, Cyril, "Planning Objectives." *California Management Review*, Vol. 6, No. 2 (Winter 1963), 3-10.

Payne, Bruce, *Planning for Company Growth*. New York: McGraw-Hill Book Company, 1963.

Ross, Ronald J., "For LRP—Rotating Planners and Doers." *Harvard Business Review*, Vol. 40, No. 1 (January-February 1962), 105-115.

Simon, Herbert A., "On the Concept of Organizational Goal." *Administrative Science Quarterly*, Vol. 9, No. 1 (June 1964), 1-22.

Steiner, George A., ed., *Managerial Long-Range Planning*. New York: McGraw-Hill Book Company, 1963, p. 17.

————, "Rise of the Corporate Planner." *Harvard Business Review*, Vol. 48, No. 5 (September-October 1970), 133.

————, *Top Management Planning*. New York: The Macmillan Company, 1969.

Summer, Charles E., Jr., "The Future Role of the Corporate Planner." *California Management Review*, Vol. 3, No. 2 (Winter 1961), 17-31.

————, and Jeremiah J. O'Connell, eds., *Managerial Mind: Science and Theory in Policy Decisions*. Homewood, Ill.: Richard D. Irwin, Inc., 1968.

Thompson, Stewart, *How Companies Plan*. New York: American Management Association, 1962.

Valentine, Raymond F., "Laying the Groundwork for Goal Setting." *Personnel*, Vol. 43, No. 1 (January-February 1966), 34-41.

Vancil, Richard, "The Accuracy of Long-Range Planning." *Harvard Business Review*, Vol. 48, No. 5 (September-October 1970), 98.

Warren, E. K., *Long-Range Planning: The Executive Viewpoint*. Englewood Cliffs, N.J.: Prentice-Hall, Inc., 1966.

PART FIVE

Leading

Leadership is the management process that concerns the personal, man-to-man relationship between a supervisor and his subordinates. Men have always been fascinated by the various aspects of leadership. The increased complexity of modern industrial organization has placed a premium on competent leadership during the last fifty years. Although research into leadership has grown significantly during the last two decades, we still know little about the factors that make a leader effective or ineffective.

There have been two major theoretical approaches to the study of leadership: trait theory and situational theory. Proponents of trait theory feel that successful and effective leaders have identifiable traits that differentiate them from less effective leaders. Early leadership research attempted to identify these distinguishing traits by studying the leader's intellectual, social, emotional, physical, and personal makeup. Trait theory has had no appreciable success in developing a generalized and valid explanation of leadership. The limitations of trait theory are perhaps best expressed in "The True Executive," a poem by Dr. Richard Armour that first appeared in *The Management Review*:

> From what I've read in magazines
> And seen in sundry movie scenes,
> The true executive is he
> Who delegates authority,
> Who resolutely, firmly acts,

But only when he has the facts,
Who speaks well, writes a splendid letter,
But also listens even better,
Who cares about his men, their wives,
But doesn't meddle in their lives,
Who knows details, yet keeps his eye
On goals beyond minutiae,
Who works as long as anyone,
And leaves his desk clear, tasks all done,
Who even on the darkest days
Can summon up a word of praise
And bravely smile amidst disaster,
Who goes to church, and knows the pastor,
Who chairmans P.T.A. and Chest,
Who, hale and hearty, needs no rest,
But is, of course, a sportsman too,
Topnotch with golf club, gun, canoe.
The true executive, in short,
Is good at work and good at sport,
Resourceful, charming, man of talents,
Possessed of perfect poise and balance,
His words and deeds and aims all mesh. ...
I'd like to see one in the flesh.

In the 1950s the study of leadership was heavily influenced by the human relations movement. Discouraged by the limitations of trait theory, students of leadership sought to explain leadership on the basis of what the leader does. Numerous studies were conducted in the belief that behavior patterns, observable by others, make up a leadership pattern. The general presumption was that the effective leader was people-centered rather than production-centered. He was supportive, gave few orders, and allowed his subordinates to participate in important decisions.

Gradually, over the last fifteen years, this general view of the value of the supportive leader has given way to situational theory. Situationists claim that leadership can best be explained in terms of the interaction between the leader, those being led, and the type of work situation and have conducted leadership research in order to identify those situational variables that either allow or cause certain kinds of leader characteristics and behavior to be effective. The conclusions of these studies suggest that it is inappropriate to talk about effective leaders; it is far more correct to talk about leaders who are effective in certain situations and ineffective in other situations.

The first three selections in Part Five provide the reader with a broader and more detailed perspective on the major leadership theories and factors underlying the choice of a leadership style. Selection 31, "Leader Behavior," by Paul Hersey and Kenneth H. Blanchard, contrasts trait theory with situational theory by reviewing the most significant leadership research of the last two decades. The next selection, "Managerial Grid," explains a very popular and valuable framework for describing leadership styles and relating them to theoretical concepts of leadership. In "A Theory of Leadership Effectiveness," Fred Fiedler shifts the reader's focus from the broad range of leadership theories to a highly promising situational theory of leadership and discusses the implications of his leadership contingency model for leadership selection, leadership training, and organizational improvement efforts.

The primary purpose of a leader is to guide and motivate the behavior of subordinates so that their actions fit established jobs and plans. Because the use of power is likely to have some detrimental side effects on worker motivation and two-way communication, a leader generally should rely on voluntary cooperation rather than on the use of power. A leader's success in developing voluntary cooperation depends on the manner in which he deals with his subordinates on a day-to-day basis. However a subordinate's willingness to cooperate also depends on his feelings toward the job and the company. A sound management structure is therefore prerequisite to a high degree of voluntary cooperation.

A first structural prerequisite to voluntary cooperation is the incorporation of direct personal satisfactions into jobs. Task-teams, committees, job enrichment, and decentralization tend to increase the willingness of subordinates to cooperate. Similarly, clear understanding of duties and authority and proper manpower planning to match men to jobs help engender a spirit of cooperation. Other structural prerequisites include effective communication networks, sound objectives, workable standing plans, and balanced control systems.

In selection 34, "Every Employee A Manager," M. Scott Myers discusses the strong cooperative feelings that are generated by self-managed jobs. He explains how a sound job enrichment program produces some important changes in the role of the supervisor.

Organizational growth, changes in technology, and dynamic competitive conditions continually impose new demands on managers. In addition, new managers are needed because of retirements, promotions, and other normal attrition. These two needs—the new demands on existing managers and the necessity to fill managerial positions with new personnel—have caused a great deal of attention to be focused on methods for developing managerial talent. The emphasis placed on management development is attested to by the substantial resources devoted to management development programs by corporations, government agencies, and nonprofit organizations. As the size of the investment in management development has increased, several questions have been raised concerning the best way to develop managers.

Two key questions that influence the choice of a strategy for the development of managers are: (1) What is an effective manager? and (2) What is the best way for people to learn to be an effective manager? The first question is intimately related to leadership theory. When trait theory dominated the study of leadership, many people believed that the characteristics of effective leaders could be taught to aspiring managers. At present, situational theory suggests that there is no such thing as a universally effective manager. The effectiveness of a manager is situation-bound. Consequently there is not an idealized managerial prototype to guide management development.

Most organizations have selected formal classroom training as the answer to the second question. Formal executive programs account for the major portion of the investment in management development. Executives have, however, become increasingly aware of the value of the job environment itself as a development influence. A more permanent and effective type of management development seems to occur in organizational climates that provide managerial aspirants with growth-inducing jobs. In selection 35, "The Enlargement of Competence," Saul Gellerman compares the *education, agricultural,* and *jungle* theories of management development by examining how each of these approaches solves questions regarding the definition of managerial effectiveness and the choice of teaching method.

One management development technique that has continued to generate controversy is sensitivity training. The advocates of sensitivity training contend that it is a useful and well-tested method for effecting lasting behavioral change. Critics contend that sensitivity training has no permanent impact on participants, lacks clearly identified terminal behavior, and holds substantial risks for certain types of participants. In selections 36, 37, and 38, Chris Argyris, an advocate, and George Odiorne, a critic, debate the educational merits of sensitivity training.

31

Leader Behavior

PAUL HERSEY AND KENNETH H. BLANCHARD

This selection is taken from Hersey and Blanchard's Management of Organizational Behavior, *a book that is designed to help practitioners and students become more effective in their everyday interaction with other people. The authors stress the importance of effective leadership by noting that the achievement of objectives through leadership applies to all organizations—businesses, educational institutions, political groups, military units, hospitals, or families. They seek to synthesize behavioral findings and*

Reprinted from Paul Hersey and Kenneth H. Blanchard, *Management of Organizational Behavior,* pp. 59-73, by permission of the publisher. Copyright 1969 by Prentice-Hall, Inc., Englewood Cliffs, N.J.

to combine them into operational frameworks that can be applied in both a diagnostic and predictive manner.

In describing the leadership process, the authors provide historical perspective by tracing the concern with tasks and with human relationships back to the scientific management and human relations movements, respectively. The authors emphasize the situational approach to leadership because they believe that this approach has proved more productive than the trait approach. They cite Eugene E. Jennings' conclusion that "Fifty years of study have failed to produce one personality trait or set of qualities that can be used to discriminate leaders and nonleaders."

Professors Hersey and Blanchard include summaries of the Ohio State Leadership Studies, the Michigan Leadership Studies. The Tannenbaum-Schmidt framework, the Group Dynamics Studies, the Managerial Grid, the Likert Studies, and the Leadership Contingency Model in their extensive review of leadership theory. Two of the studies that they discuss will be treated at greater length in subsequent reading selections—the Managerial Grid, in selection 32, and the Leadership Contingency Model, in selection 33.

The successful organization has one major attribute that sets it apart from unsuccessful organizations: dynamic and effective leadership. Peter F. Drucker points out that managers (business leaders) are the basic and scarcest resource of any business enterprise.[1] Statistics from recent years make this point more evident: "Of every 100 new business establishments started, approximately 50, or one half, go out of business within two years. By the end of five years, only one third of the original 100 will still be in business."[2] Most of the failures can be attributed to ineffective leadership.

On all sides there is an almost frenzied search for persons who have the necessary ability to enable them to lead effectively. This shortage of effective leadership is not confined to business but is evident in the lack of able administrators in government, education, foundations, churches, and every other form of organization. Thus, when we decry the scarcity of leadership talent in our society, we are not talking about a lack of people to fill administrative or executive positions; we have plenty of administrative "bodies." What we are agonizing over is a scarcity of people who are willing to assume significant leadership roles in our society and can get the job done effectively.

[1] Peter F. Drucker, *The Practice of Management* (New York: Harper & Row, Publishers, 1954).
[2] George R. Terry, *Principles of Management*, third edition (Homewood, Illinois: Richard D. Irwin, Inc., 1960), p. 5.

LEADERSHIP DEFINED

According to George R. Terry, "Leadership is the activity of influencing people to strive willingly for group objectives."[3] Robert Tannenbaum, Irving R. Weschler and Fred Massarik define leadership as, "interpersonal influence exercised in a situation and directed, through the communication process, toward the attainment of a specialized goal or goals."[4] Harold Koontz and Cyril O'Donnell state that "leadership is *influencing* people to follow in the achievement of a common goal."[5]

A review of other writers reveals that most management writers agree that leadership is *the process of influencing the activities of an individual or a group in efforts toward goal achievement in a given situation*. From this definition of leadership, it follows that the leadership process is a function of the *leader*, the *follower*, and the *situation*, $L = f(l,f,s)$.

TRAIT VS. SITUATIONAL APPROACH
TO THE STUDY OF LEADERSHIP

For many years the most common approach to the study of leadership concentrated on leadership traits per se, suggesting that there were certain qualities, such as physical energy or friendliness, that were essential for effective leadership. These inherent personal qualities, like intelligence, were felt to be transferable from one situation to another. Since all individuals did not have these qualities, only those who had them would be considered to be potential leaders. Consequently this approach seemed to question the value of training individuals to assume leadership positions. It implied that if we could discover how to identify and measure these leadership qualities (which are inborn in the individual), we should be able to screen leaders from nonleaders. Leadership training would then be helpful only to those with inherent leadership traits.

A review of the research literature using this trait approach to leadership has revealed few significant or consistent findings. As Eugene E. Jennings concluded, "Fifty years of study have failed to produce one personality trait or set of qualities that can be used to discriminate leaders and non-leaders."[6] Empirical studies suggest that leadership is a dynamic

---

[3] Terry, *Principles of Management*, p. 493.

[4] Robert Tannenbaum, Irving R. Weschsler, and Fred Massarik, *Leadership and Organization: A Behavioral Science Approach* (New York: McGraw-Hill Book Company, 1959).

[5] Harold Koontz and Cyril O'Donnell, *Principles of Management*, fourth edition (New York: McGraw-Hill Book Company, 1968).

[6] Eugene E. Jennings, "The Anatomy of Leadership," *Management of Personnel Quarterly*, I, No. 1 (Autumn 1961).

process, varying from situation to situation with changes in leaders, followers, and situations. Current literature seems to support this situational or leader behavior approach to the study of leadership.[7]

The focus in the situational approach to leadership is on observed behavior, not on any hypothetical inborn or acquired ability or potential for leadership. The emphasis is on the behavior of leaders and their group members (followers) and various situations. With this emphasis upon behavior and environment, more encouragement is given to the possibility of training individuals in adapting styles of leader behavior to varying situations. Therefore it is believed that most people can increase their effectiveness in leadership roles through education, training, and development. From observations of the frequency (or infrequency) of certain leader behavior in numerous types of situations, theoretical models can be developed to help a leader make some predictions about the most appropriate leader behavior for his present situation. For these reasons, in this chapter we will talk in terms of leader behavior rather than leadership traits, thus emphasizing the situational approach to leadership.

LEADERSHIP PROCESS

We have defined leadership as the process of influencing the activities of an individual or a group in efforts toward goal achievement in a given situation. In essence, leadership involves accomplishing goals with and through people. Therefore a leader must be concerned about tasks and human relationships. Although using different terminology, Chester I. Barnard identified these same leadership concerns in his classic work, *The Functions of the Executive,* in the late 1930's.[8] These leadership concerns seem to be a reflection of two of the earliest schools of thought in organizational theory—scientific management and human relations.

Scientific Management Movement

In the early 1900's one of the most widely read theorists on administration was Frederick Winslow Taylor. The basis for his *scientific management* was technological in nature. It was felt that the best way to increase output was to improve the techniques or methods used by workers. Consequently, he has been interpreted as considering people as instruments or machines to be manipulated by their leaders. Accepting this assumption,

[7] John K. Hemphill, *Situational Factors in Leadership*, Monograph No. 32 (Columbus, Ohio: Bureau of Educational Research, The Ohio State University, 1949).

[8] Chester I. Barnard, *The Functions of the Executive* (Cambridge, Mass.: Harvard University Press, 1938).

other theorists of the scientific management movement proposed that an organization as rationally planned and executed as possible be developed to create more efficiency in administration and consequently increase production. Management was to be divorced from human affairs and emotions. The result was that the people or workers had to adjust to the management and not the management to the people.

To accomplish this plan, Taylor initiated time and motion studies to analyze work tasks in order to improve performance in every aspect of the organization. Once jobs had been reorganized with efficiency in mind, the economic self-interest of the workers could be satisfied through various incentive work plans (piece rates, etc.).

The function of the leader under scientific management or classical theory was quite obviously to set up and enforce performance criteria to meet organizational goals. His main focus was on the needs of the organization and not on the needs of the individual.[9]

Human Relations Movement

In the 1920's and early 1930's, the trend initiated by Taylor was to be replaced at center stage by the *human relations* movement. This was initiated by Elton Mayo and his associates. These theorists argued that in addition to finding the best technological methods to improve output, it was beneficial to management to look into human affairs. It was claimed that the real power centers within an organization were the interpersonal relations which developed within the working unit. The study of these human relations was the most important consideration for management and the analysis of organization. The organization was to be developed around the workers and had to take into consideration human feelings and attitudes.[10]

The function of the leader under human relations theory was to facilitate cooperative goal attainment among his followers while providing opportunities for their personal growth and development. His main focus, contrary to scientific management theory, was on individual needs and not the needs of the organization.

In essence, then, the scientific management movement emphasized a concern for task, while the human relations movement stressed a concern for relationships (people). The recognition of these two concerns has characterized the writings on leadership ever since the conflict between the scientific management and human relations schools of thought became apparent.

[9] Frederick W. Taylor, *The Principles of Scientific Management* (New York: Harper and Brothers, 1911).

[10] Elton Mayo, *The Social Problems of an Industrial Civilization* (Boston: Harvard Business School, 1945).

Authoritarian-Democratic-Laissez Faire
Leader Behavior

Past writers have felt that concern for task tends to be represented by authoritarian leader behavior while a concern for relationships is represented by democratic leader behavior. This feeling was popular because it was generally agreed that a leader influences his followers by either of two ways: (1) he can tell his followers what to do and how to do it, or (2) he can share his leadership responsibilities with his followers by involving them in the planning and execution of the task. The former is the traditional authoritarian style which emphasizes task concerns. The latter is the more nondirective democratic style which stresses the concern for human relationships.

The differences in the two styles of leader behavior are based on the assumptions the leader makes about the source of his power or authority and human nature. The authoritarian style of leader behavior is often based on the assumption that the leader's power is derived from the position he occupies and that man is innately lazy and unreliable (Theory X), whereas the democratic style assumes the leader's power is granted by the group he is to lead and that men can be basically self-directed and creative at work if properly motivated (Theory Y). As a result, in the authoritarian style, all policies are determined by the leader, while in the democratic style, policies are open for group discussion and decision.

There are, of course, a wide variety of styles of leader behavior between these two extremes. Robert Tannenbaum and Warren H. Schmidt depicted a broad range of styles on a continuum moving from very authoritarian leader behavior at one end to very democratic leader behavior at the other end[11] as illustrated in Figure 1.

Leaders whose behavior is observed to be at the authoritarian end of the continuum tend to be task-oriented and use their power to influence their followers while leaders whose behavior appears to be at the democratic end tend to be group-oriented and thus give their followers considerable freedom in their work. Often this continuum is extended beyond democratic leader behavior to include a laissez-faire style. This style of behavior permits the members of the group to do whatever they want to do. No policies or procedures are established. Everyone is let alone. No one attempts to influence anyone else. As is evident, this style is not included in the continuum of leader behavior illustrated in Figure 1. This was done because it was felt that in reality, a laissez-faire atmosphere represents an absence of leadership. The leadership role has been abdicated and therefore no leader behavior is being exhibited.

[11] Robert Tannenbaum and Warren H. Schmidt, "How to Choose a Leadership Pattern," *Harvard Business Review* (March-April 1957), pp. 95-101.

In recent years, research findings indicate that leadership styles vary considerably from leader to leader. Some leaders emphasize the task and can be described as authoritarian leaders while others stress interpersonal relationships and may be viewed as democratic leaders. Still others seem to be both task and relationships oriented. There are even some individuals in leadership positions who are not concerned about either. No dominant style appears. Instead various combinations are evident. Thus task-orientation and relationships-orientation are not either/or leadership concerns as the preceding continuum suggests. These concerns are separate and distinct dimensions which can be plotted on two separate axes, rather than a single continuum.

Ohio State Leadership Studies

The leadership studies initiated in 1945 by the Bureau of Business Research at Ohio State University attempted to identify dimensions of leader behavior through the development of the Leader Behavior Description Questionnaire.[12] This instrument was designed to describe *how* a leader carries out his activities.

[12] Roger M. Stogdill and Alvin E. Coons (eds.), *Leader Behavior: Its Description and Measurement*, Research Monograph No. 88 (Columbus, Ohio: Bureau of Business Research, The Ohio State University, 1957).

Figure 1   Continuum of leader behavior.

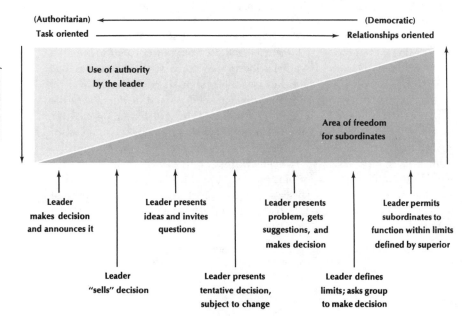

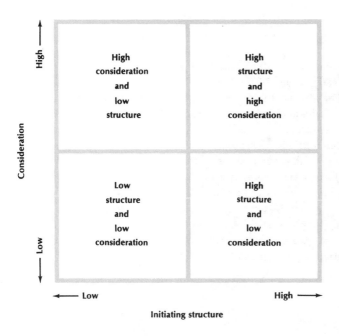

Figure 2   The Ohio State leadership quadrants.

The staff, defining leadership as the behavior of an individual when he is directing the activities of a group toward a goal attainment, eventually narrowed the description of leader behavior to two dimensions: *initiating structure* and *consideration*. Initiating structure refers to "the leader's behavior in delineating the relationship between himself and members of the work-group and in endeavoring to establish well-defined patterns of organization, channels of communication, and methods of procedure." On the other hand, consideration refers to "behavior indicative of friendship, mutual trust, respect, and warmth in the relationship between the leader and the members of his staff."[13]

Initiating structure seems to be task-oriented. This dimension emphasizes the needs of the organization. At the same time consideration is relationships-oriented and tends to emphasize the needs of the individual.

In studying leader behavior the Ohio State staff found that initiating structure and consideration were separate and distinct dimensions. Thus it was during these studies that leader behavior was first plotted on two separate axes, rather than a single continuum. Four quadrants were developed to show various combinations of initiating structure (task) and consideration (relationships)—see Figure 2.

[13]Andrew W. Halpin, *The Leadership Behavior of School Superintendents* (Chicago: Midwest Administration Center, The University of Chicago, 1959), p. 4.

Michigan Leadership Studies

Occurring almost simultaneously with the Ohio State Leadership Studies were the early studies of the Survey Research Center at the University of Michigan.[14] The attempt there was to approach the study of leadership by locating clusters of characteristics which seemed to be related to each other and tests of effectiveness. The studies identified two concepts which they called *employee orientation* and *production orientation*.

A leader who is described as employee-oriented stresses the relationships aspect of his job. He feels that every employee is important. He takes interest in everyone, accepting their individuality and personal needs. Production orientation emphasizes production and the technical aspects of the job, viewing employees as tools to accomplish the goals of the organization. These two orientations parallel the Ohio State Leadership dimensions of initiating structure and consideration.

Group Dynamics Studies

Dorwin Cartwright and Alvin Zander, based on the findings of numerous studies at the Research Center for Group Dynamics, claim that all group objectives fall into one of two categories: (1) the achievement of some specific group goal, or (2) the maintenance or strengthening of the group itself.[15]

According to Cartwright and Zander, the type of behavior involved in goal achievement is illustrated by these examples: The manager "initiates action ... keeps members' attention on the goal ... clarifies the issue and develops a procedural plan."[16]

On the other hand, characteristic behaviors for group maintenance are: The manager "keeps interpersonal relations pleasant ... arbitrates disputes ... provides encouragement ... gives the minority a chance to be heard ... stimulates self-direction ... and increases the interdependence among members."[17]

Goal achievement seems to coincide with the task concepts discussed earlier (initiating structure and production orientation), while group maintenance parallels the relationships concepts (consideration and employee orientation).

[14] D. Katz, N. Maccoby, and Nancy C. Morse, *Productivity, Supervision, and Morale in an Office Situation* (Detroit, Michigan: The Darel Press, Inc., 1950); D. Katz, N. Maccoby, G. Gurin, and Lucretia G. Floor, *Productivity, Supervision and Morale Among Railroad Workers* (Ann Arbor, Michigan: Survey Research Center, 1951).

[15] Dorwin Cartwright and Alvin Zander, *Group Dynamics: Research and Theory* (Evanston, Illinois: Row Peterson and Co., 1960).

[16] *Ibid.*, p. 496.

[17] *Ibid.*

Managerial Grid

In discussing the Ohio State, Michigan, and Group Dynamics Leadership studies, we have been concentrating on two theoretical concepts. Robert R. Blake and Jane S. Mouton have popularized these concepts in their Managerial Grid and have used them extensively in organization and management development programs.[18]

In the Managerial Grid, five different types of leadership based on concern for production (task) and concern for people (relationships) are located in the four quadrants identified by the Ohio State studies [Figure 3].

Concern for production is illustrated on the horizontal axis. Production becomes more important to the leader as his rating advances on the horizontal scale. A leader with a rating of 9 on the horizontal axis has a maximum concern for production.

Concern for people is illustrated on the vertical axis. People become more important to the leader as his rating progresses up the vertical axis. A leader with a rating of 9 on the vertical axis has maximum concern for people.

The five leadership styles are described as follows:

[18]Robert R. Blake and Jane S. Mouton, *The Managerial Grid* (Houston, Texas: Gulf Publishing, 1961).

Figure 3   The Managerial Grid leadership styles.

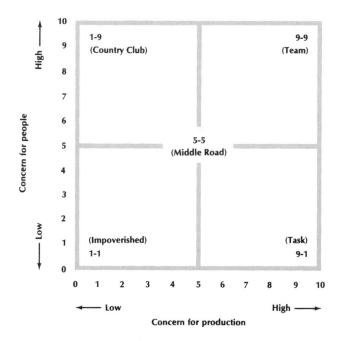

Impoverished—Exertion of minimum effort to get required work done is appropriate to sustain organization membership.

Country Club—Thoughtful attention to needs of people for satisfying relationships leads to a comfortable friendly organization atmosphere and work tempo.

Task—Efficiency in operations results from arranging conditions of work in such a way that human elements interfere to a minimum degree.

Middle-of-the-Road—Adequate organization performance is possible through balancing the necessity to get out work while maintaining morale of people at a satisfactory level.

Team—Work accomplishment is from committed people; interdependence through a "common stake" in organization purpose leads to relationships of trust and respect.[19]

In essence, the Managerial Grid has given popular terminology to five points within the four quadrants of the Ohio State studies. A diagram combining the two theories could be illustrated as shown in Figure 4.

[19]Robert R. Blake *et al.*, "Breakthrough in Organization Development," *Harvard Business Review* (November-December 1964), p. 136.

Figure 4 Merging of the Ohio State and the Managerial Grid theories of leadership.

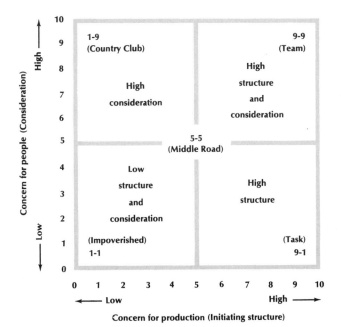

IS THERE A BEST STYLE OF LEADERSHIP?

After identifying the two central concerns of any leadership situation, task and relationships, the researchers discussed earlier have recognized the potential conflict in satisfying both concerns. Consequently, an attempt has been made to find a middle ground which will encompass both concerns. Chester Barnard recognized this fact when he purposely included both concerns as necessary factors for the survival of any organization.[20]

According to Warren G. Bennis, theorists like Barnard who express concern for both task and relationships are called "revisionists."

> The revisionists are now concerned with external, economic factors, with productivity, with formal status, and so on, but not to the exclusion of the human elements that the traditional theorists so neglected. So what we are observing now is the pendulum swinging just a little farther to the middle from its once extreme position to balance and modulate with more refinement in the human organization requirements.[21]

Andrew W. Halpin, using the Leader Behavior Description Questionnaire in a study of school superintendents, found that the administrators he interviewed had a tendency to view consideration and initiating structure as either/or forms of leader behavior. "Some administrators act as if they were forced to emphasize one form of behavior at the expense of the other."[22] Halpin stressed that this conflict between initiating structure and consideration should not necessarily exist. He points out that according to his findings, "effective or desirable leadership behavior is characterized by high scores on both Initiating Structure and Consideration. Conversely, ineffective or undesirable leadership behavior is marked by low scores on both dimensions."[23]

From these observations, Halpin concludes that a successful leader, "must contribute to both major group objectives: goal achievement and group maintenance (in Cartwright and Zander's terms); or in Barnard's terms, he must facilitate cooperative group action that is both effective and efficient."[24] Thus the Ohio State Leadership studies seem to conclude that the high consideration and initiating structure style is theoretically the ideal or "best" leader behavior, while the style low on both dimensions is theoretically the "worst."

[20] Barnard, *The Functions of the Executive.*
[21] Warren G. Bennis, "Leadership Theory and Administrative Behavior: The Problems of Authority," *Administrative Science Quarterly*, IV, No. 3 (December 1959), p. 274.
[22] Halpin, *The Leadership Behavior of School Superintendents*, p. 79.
[23] *Ibid.*
[24] *Ibid.*, p. 6.

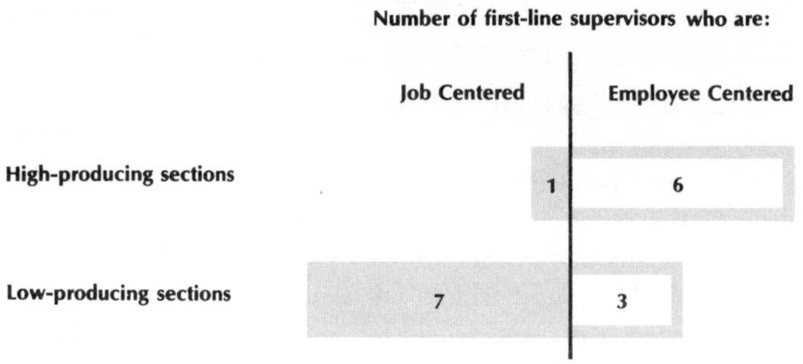

	Job Centered	Employee Centered
High-producing sections	1	6
Low-producing sections	7	3

Figure 5 Employee-centered supervisors are higher producers than job-centered supervisors.

The Managerial Grid also implies that the most desirable leader behavior is "team management" (maximum concern for production and people). In fact, Blake and Mouton have developed training programs to change managers toward a 9-9 management style.[25]

Using the earlier Michigan Studies as a starting place, Rensis Likert did some extensive research to discover the general pattern of management used by high-producing managers in contrast to that used by the other managers. He found that: "Supervisors with the best records of performance focus their primary attention on the human aspects of their subordinates' problems and on endeavoring to build effective work groups with high performance goals."[26] These supervisors were called "employee-centered." Other supervisors who kept constant pressure on production were called job-centered and were found more often to have low-producing sections.[27] Figure 5 represents the findings from one study.

Likert also discovered that high-producing supervisors "make clear to their subordinates what the objectives are and what needs to be accomplished and then give them freedom to do the job."[28] Thus he found that general, rather than close, supervision tended to be associated with high productivity. This relationship, found in a study of clerical workers,[29] is illustrated in Figure 6.

The implication throughout Likert's writings is that the ideal and most productive leader behavior for industry is employee-centered or democratic. Yet his own findings raise questions as to whether there can be an ideal or single normatively good style of leader behavior which can apply in all leadership situations. As the preceding figures revealed, one of the eight job-centered supervisors and one of the nine supervisors using close

[25] Blake *et al.*, "Breakthrough ... ," p. 135.
[26] Rensis Likert, *New Patterns of Management* (New York: McGraw-Hill Book Company, 1961), p. 7.
[27] *Ibid.*
[28] *Ibid.*, p. 9.
[29] *Ibid.*

336

supervision had high-producing sections; also three of the nine employee-centered supervisors and four of the thirteen supervisors who used general supervision had low-producing sections. In other words, in almost 35 per cent of the low-producing sections, the suggested ideal type of leader behavior produced undesirable results and almost 15 per cent of the high-producing sections were supervised by the suggested "undesirable" style.

Further evidence suggesting that a single ideal or normative style of leader behavior is unrealistic was provided when a similar study was done in an industrial setting in Nigeria.[30] The results were almost the exact opposite to Likert's findings. In that country the tendency is for job-centered supervisors who provide close supervision to have high-producing sections, while the low-producing sections tend to have employee-centered supervisors who provide general supervision. Thus a single normative leadership style does not take into consideration cultural differences, particularly customs and traditions as well as the level of education and the standard of living. These are examples of cultural differences in the followers and the situation which are important in determining the appropriate leadership style to be used. Therefore, based on the definition of leadership process as a function of the leader, the followers, and other situational variables, the desire to have *a single ideal type of leader behavior seems unrealistic*.

ADAPTIVE LEADER BEHAVIOR

This desire to have an ideal type of leader behavior is common. Many managers appear to want to be told how to act. It is also clear from the preceding discussion that many writers in the field of leadership suggest some normative style. Most of these writers have supported either an integrated leadership style (high concern for both task and relationships) or a permissive,

[30] Paul Hersey, an unpublished research project, 1965.

Figure 6   Low-production section heads are more closely supervised than high-production heads.

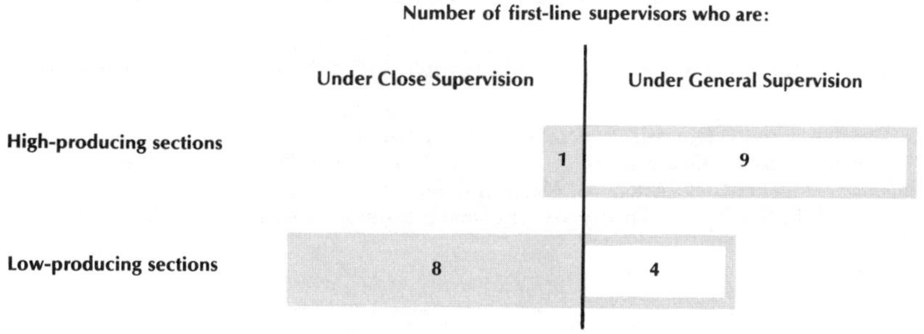

Number of first-line supervisors who are:

	Under Close Supervision	Under General Supervision
High-producing sections	1	9
Low-producing sections	8	4

democratic, human relations approach. These styles might be appropriate in some industrial or educational settings in the United States, but they also may be limited to them. Effective leader behavior in other institutions such as the military, hospitals, prisons, churches, might very well be entirely different. Perhaps our formula should be modified to read: $E = f(l,f,s)$. The "E" stands for effectiveness. An effective leader is able to adapt his style of leader behavior to the needs of situation and the followers. Since these are not constants, the use of an appropriate style of leader behavior is a challenge to the effective leader. "The manager must be much like the musician who changes his techniques and approaches to obtain the shadings of total performance desired."[31] The concept of *adaptive leader behavior* might be stated as follows:

> The more a manager adapts his style of leader behavior to meet the particular situation and the needs of his followers, the more effective he will tend to be in reaching personal and organizational goals.[32]

Leadership Contingency Model

The concept of adaptive leader behavior questions the existence of a "best" style of leadership: It is not a matter of the best style, but of the most effective style for a particular situation. The suggestion is that a number of leader behavior styles may be effective or ineffective depending on the important elements of the situation.

According to a Leadership Contingency Model developed by Fred E. Fiedler, there are three major situational variables which seem to determine whether a given situation is favorable or unfavorable to a leader: (1) His personal relations with the members of his group (leader-member relations); (2) The degree of structure in the task which the group has been assigned to perform (task structure); and (3) The power and authority which his position provides (position power).[33] Leader-member relations seems to parallel the relationships concepts discussed earlier, while task structure and position power, which measure very closely related aspects of a situation, seem to be related to task concepts. Fiedler defines the *favorableness of a situation* as "the degree to which the situation enables the leader to exert his influence over his group."[34]

In this model, there are eight possible combinations of these three

---

[31] Koontz and O'Donnell, *Principles of Management.*

[32] Paul Hersey, *Management Concepts and Behavior: Programmed Instruction for Managers* (Little Rock, Arkansas: Marvern Publishing Co., 1967), p. 15.

[33] Fred E. Fiedler, *A Theory of Leadership Effectiveness* (New York: McGraw-Hill Book Company, 1967).

[34] *Ibid.*, p. 13.

situational variables that can occur. As a leadership situation varies from high to low on these variables, it will fall into one of the eight combinations (situations). The most favorable situation for a leader to influence his group is one in which he is well liked by the members (good leader-member relations), has a powerful position (high position power), and is directing a well-defined job (high task structure): for example, a well-liked general making inspection in an army camp. On the other hand, the most unfavorable situation is one in which the leader is disliked, has little position power, and faces an unstructured task: an unpopular chairman of a voluntary hospital fund-raising committee.

Having developed this model for classifying group situations, Fiedler has attempted to determine what the most effective leadership style—task-oriented or relationships-oriented—seems to be for each of the eight situations. In a re-examination of old leadership studies and analysis of new studies, in terms of his model, Fiedler has concluded that:

1. *Task-oriented* leaders tend to perform best in group situations which are either very favorable or very unfavorable to the leader.
2. *Relationships-oriented* leaders tend to perform best in situations which are intermediate in favorableness.[35]

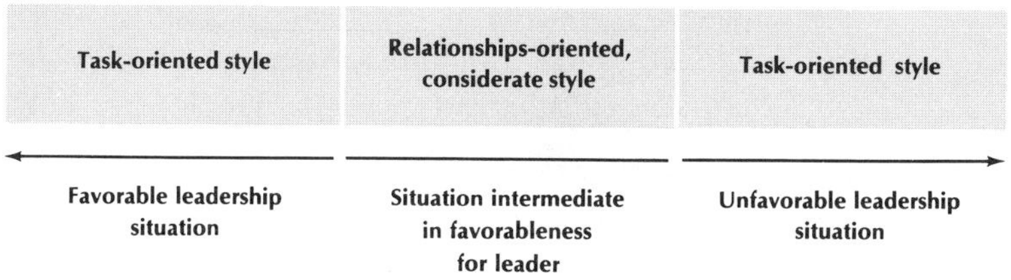

Task-oriented style	Relationships-oriented, considerate style	Task-oriented style
Favorable leadership situation	Situation intermediate in favorableness for leader	Unfavorable leadership situation

Figure 7   Leadership styles appropriate for various group situations.

While Fiedler's model is useful to a leader, he seems to be reverting to a single continuum of leader behavior, suggesting that there are only two basic leader behavior styles, task-oriented and relationships-oriented. It is felt that most evidence indicates that leader behavior must be plotted on two separate axes, rather than a single continuum. Thus a leader who has a high concern for tasks does not necessarily have a high or low concern for relationships. Any combination of the two dimensions may occur.

[35] Adapted from Fiedler, *A Theory of Leadership Effectiveness*, p. 14.

32

Managerial Grid

ROBERT R. BLAKE, JANE SRYGLEY MOUTON,
AND ALVIN C. BIDWELL

This reading describes in greater detail one of the leadership concepts summarized by Professors Hersey and Blanchard in the previous selection. Dr. Robert R. Blake, Dr. Jane Srygley Mouton, and Mr. Alvin C. Bidwell describe the Managerial Grid, which is a graphic framework for classifying and analyzing leadership styles. The grid also proves useful for summarizing theoretical leadership ideas, such as the Ohio State, Michigan, and Group Dynamics Leadership Studies. In selection 31, Professors Hersey and Blanchard discussed the link between the Managerial Grid and the Ohio State Leadership Studies.

The Grid has also been used for describing organizational climates and for communicating ideas about management methods and organizational environment. As a result, the Managerial Grid has been used extensively in organization and management development programs. A more detailed discussion of the application of the Grid in management development programs can be found in Blake and Mouton's Corporate Excellence through Grid Organizational Development *(Houston, Texas: Gulf Publishing Co., 1968).*

The selection that follows describes the relationship between the Managerial Grid and seven managerial theories. In addition, the authors explain how managers with different leadership styles handle conflict. Readers may wish to study the Grid as a diagnostic device for identifying, evaluating, and changing their own styles of supervision.

The purpose of this article is to compare seven managerial theories in terms of how each deals with (1) organizational needs for production and profit and (2) human needs for mature and healthy relationships.

Five of these seven are shown in the chart, "The Managerial Grid."[1]

Reprinted from *Advanced Management-Office Executive*, September 1962, pp. 12-16, by permission of the publisher.

[1] The line of thinking that leads to the generalized version of the Managerial Grid is consistent with work by Rensis Likert, "Developing Patterns of Management," AMA General Management Series (New York: American Management Association No. 178, 1955), pp. 32-51; Edwin A. Fleishman, Edwin F. Harris, and Harold E. Burtt, *Leadership*

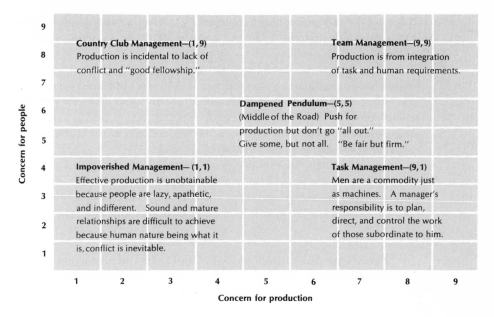

Figure 1   The Managerial Grid.

[See Figure 1.] They are referred to as *country club management, impoverished management, dampened pendulum, team management, and task management.* The remaining two are combined forms.

The term *concern for,* as used in the Grid, is a theoretical variable which reflects basic attitudes or styles of control. ... The horizontal axis of the Grid represents concern for production and profit. The vertical axis represents concern for mature and healthy relations among those engaged in production. Each axis is on a 1 to 9 point scale, with the 1 representing minimum interest or concern and the 9, maximum concern.

In the discussion that follows, the emphasis is on analysis of the corners and mid-point of the Grid, although these extreme positions are rarely found in pure form in the working situation.

In several of the theories, the concerns for production and those for people will be seen in conflict. In three of the theories, the assumption is that attention to needs of individuals does not contribute automatically to production requirements.

Turning again to the chart, note that the lower right-hand corner

---

and Supervision in Industry (Columbus, Ohio: Bureau of Educational Research, Ohio State University, 1955); Chris Argyris, *Personality and Organization* (New York: Harper & Row, Publishers, 1957); and Douglas McGregor, *Human Side of Enterprise* (New York: McGraw-Hill Book Co., Inc., 1960).

represents the task management approach (9,1). Here, primary concern is for output of the enterprise.[2] People are viewed solely in terms of their contribution to production.

This theory is based on the notion that a manager's central responsibilities are to achieve production objectives.[3] Those who are engaged in planning and controlling, in other words, are not those who carry out the actions directly. Under the task management theory, a job is a job and someone has to do it. Like machines, people are seen as production tools, obligated to comply when told what they are to do.

At lower levels, concern for production may be thought of as actual output. Concern for production at the managerial levels is just as critical as units of output are among operators. The following kind of advice, which was given to managers in the middle levels, is characteristic of a task management orientation.[4]

> For an executive to challenge orders, directions and instructions, policy and procedures, rules and regulations, etc., smacks of insubordination or lack of cooperation. It shows his failure to understand the need for decisions at higher levels and for direction and control.

Thoughts, attitudes, and feelings are given little or no attention. When interpersonal conflict arises, the way to handle it (as well as all types of feelings) is to suppress it through disciplinary types of actions. Under the task management theory, if people don't comply after a certain amount of control has been applied, they should be replaced. Thus, this theory has been referred to as an impersonal approach to managing.

The task management theory tends to produce unsound relationships among those who should be operating in an interdependent way within the organizational structure.[5] Since Chris Argyris has hammered home the negative consequences of this theory, little more needs to be said here.[6]

PRODUCTION INCIDENTAL TO SATISFACTION

The country club management theory (see 1,9, upper left-hand corner of the chart) is the reverse of the task management theory in a number of respects. In the former, production is incidental to satisfaction through social relations, good fellowship, and fraternity. Goal of this theory of management

---

[2] W. R. Spriegel, *Principles of Business and Operation*, 3rd ed. (Englewood Cliffs, N.J.: Prentice-Hall, Inc., 1960), pp. 540-541.

[3] Frederick Winslow Taylor, *The Principles of Scientific Management* (New York: Harper & Row, Publishers, 1947), pp. 36-38.

[4] Milton Brown, *Effective Work Management* (New York: The Macmillan Company, 1960), pp. 14-15.

[5] Likert, *op. cit.*, p. 32.

[6] Argyris, *op. cit.*, pp. 123-163.

is to achieve harmony even though needs for output may suffer as a result. Assumption is that contented people will produce as well as contented cows, if given the chance.[7]

This theory is not well suited to organizations which strive for increased effectiveness. When, because of outside forces, the organization has to increase efficiency, it is frequently unable to respond to the demands. The country club theory does tend to flourish in organizations that approach monopolies and in bureaucratic structures.

Under the country club theory, too, executives are aware of the need to be nice. Moreover, the people in the system sense the phony quality in *good* human relations which are *not* related to conditions of work and production.

The be-nice approach leads to few overt production or personnel problems, because conflict is smothered and denied. The manager is seen as a likable fellow, a good Joe, or a big brother. He is prepared to make his subordinates happy, carefree, and satisfied at almost any economic price.

Also, the country club approach is unlikely to achieve any meaningful human-relations gains, since conflict and frustration are smoothed over, not dealt with. This is the style which is sometimes called *soft* management, in contrast with *hard* management. Frequently the only alternative seen by hard managers is the country club theory.

The impoverished management theory (1,1) is shown in the lower left corner of the chart. The manager at this position de-emphasizes concerns for production, with just enough being done to get by. He also disregards or diminishes the importance of human relationships. He takes the ostrich approach to feelings—instead of suppressing or denying them, he ignores them.

Within the executive level an impoverished management orientation can be found in circumstances in which a person has been passed by repeatedly. Rather than looking elsewhere, he adjusts to the work setting by giving minimal performance, seeking satisfaction elsewhere.

This managerial style is not so prevalent throughout an entire company. In a competitive economy, a company operated under this style is unlikely to stay in business long. On the other hand, many individuals who manage in the impoverished management style are able to survive in bureaucratic organizations[8] and in country club managerial structures where the rule is that "no one gets fired."

Three approaches to management consider the task (9,1), the country club (1,9) or the impoverished (1,1) types simultaneously. All stem from the notion that needs of mature individuals and organizational requirements of production oppose each other.

---

[7] N. R. F. Maier, *Psychology in Industry*, 2nd ed. (Boston: Houghton Mifflin Co., 1955), pp. 138-139.

[8] Maurice Stein, Arthur J. Vidich, and David M. White, "The Meaning of Work in a Bureaucratic Society," in *Identity and Anxiety*, by B. Rosenberg and J. Bensman (Glencoe, Ill.: The Free Press of Glencoe, 1960), pp. 182-185.

The wide-arc pendulum theory, for example, describes a relationship between the task (9,1) and the country club (1,9) positions as: When management tightens up to get increased output, as often happens under recession pressures, it does so consistently with the task (9,1) attitude. Later, relationships become so disturbed that production suffers. Then management feels forced to ease off and to start being concerned with the thoughts, feelings, and attitudes of people.

Because of the negative results of the task approach, a swing in the direction of the country club position takes place. Output pressures are lessened to make people feel that management's intentions are good. Thus, the pendulum tends to swing from the one position to the other.

When a degree of confidence in management has been restored among the people, the tightening up occurs again to regain the losses in production suffered during the previous pendulum swing. Cracking down to get efficiency and easing up to restore confidence is the pendulum swing from hard to soft.

Another kind of pendulum swing within an organization is one associated with task management (9,1) pressures for production. In this cycle, as described by Robert L. Katz,[9] top management's plans and commands lead to lower management's reacting in an impoverished manner (1,1), with indifference, apathy, and minimal output.

The failure of middle and lower levels of management to respond with concrete contributions to production is followed by top management's redoubling of its efforts to tighten up. Once successful influence from top to middle has been achieved, the middle tries to tighten up on lower levels. Thus the cycle goes from the task, to the impoverished, and back to the task management theory.

In the center of the Managerial Grid is shown the dampened pendulum (5,5) or the middle-of-the-road theory. This theory says, push enough to get acceptable production, but yield to the degree necessary to develop morale. When the happy medium is achieved, don't expect too much production. Recognize that one must be flexible and must give. Under the dampened pendulum theory, it is believed that by clever string-pulling, management can prevent either of the two concerns from blocking the complete attainment of the other.[10]

In a number of respects it would appear that managements which have abandoned the task theory tended over time to slide toward the dampened pendulum position. However, the shift is not a healthy one because the dampened pendulum position retains the theory of work direction contained in the task management position. The shift adds the theory of human relations of country club management. The dampened pendulum approach

[9] Robert L. Katz, "Towards a More Effective Enterprise," *Harvard Business Review* (September-October 1960), pp. 80-102.

[10] W. H. Knowles, *Personnel Management* (New York: American Book Co., 1955), pp. 188-189.

does not solve the problem. Rather, a live-and-let-live situation is created under which the real problem is muted.[11]

Paternalistic management pushes for output in a task management way, but in time it recognizes feelings of alienation that separate the workers from the management. Therefore, an additional step is taken to satisfy lower management levels and workers. Concern for people is expressed through *taking care of them* in a country club management fashion. Organizational members are *given* ... things—good pay, excellent benefit programs, recreational facilities, retirement programs, and even low-cost housing.

However, these are not given to acknowledge contribution to output. They are given to *buy* subservience.[12] A paternalistic executive retains tight control in work matters, but is benevolent in a personal way. In other words, he treats his junior executives as part of his managerial family. Paternalism is a more or less stable mix of two anchor positions. Although it has failed repeatedly to solve the basic problems of getting production through people, it is still current in managerial thinking.[13, 14]

ACCEPT CONFLICT AS INEVITABLE

All the managerial styles just described accept conflict between concerns for production and concerns for people as inevitable. Each attempts to deal with the assumed basic incompatibility in a different way. ...

The middle-of-the-road, or dampened pendulum, and the paternalistic modes try to achieve some sort of balance. Under the impoverished management approach, the manager does the minimum. Only under the team approach, a description of which follows, is an integration achieved where the goal is production through people.

In the team management position (9,9), the building block in the organization is the team. It is not the individuals on a one-to-one basis, as though isolated from one another.[15] To a country club style manager, the style of a task manager and that of a team manager seem similar, since both express a high concern for production. However, the way in which production is achieved is vastly different.

A team manager describes his philosophy on work planning as:

[11] R. C. Davis, *The Fundamentals of Top Management* (New York: Harper & Row, Publishers, 1951).

[12] A. J. Marrow, *Making Management Human* (New York: McGraw-Hill Book Co., Inc., 1957), pp. 75-76.

[13] Robert N. MacMurray, "The Case for Benevolent Autocracy," *Harvard Business Review* (January-February 1958), pp. 82-90.

[14] John Perry, *Human Relations in Small Industry* (New York: McGraw-Hill Book Co., Inc., 1954), pp. 131-139.

[15] McGregor, *op. cit.*; Katz, *op. cit.*; and Rensis Likert, "Measuring Organizational Performance," *Harvard Business Review* (March-April 1958).

> When a change is required, I meet with my work group, present the picture, discuss and get reactions and ideas, *build* in their ideas, commitment, and ownership. Together we set up procedures and ground rules and assign individual responsibilities. The work group sets goals and flexible schedules.

Planning, as but one example, is a product of team effort rather than of individual skill. In a well-integrated team operation, all voices carry weight in final positions.

Gaining effective integration among members of multilevel teams is seen as another important task of leadership. Here, joint effort is centered on production, and members share responsibilities for planning, directing, and controlling.

A third key objective of team management is that of linking teams into effective communication and problem-solving systems which have a peer relationship with one another. Union and management or correlated divisions in different departments would be examples.

Knowledge of human relations needed under the team management theory is far greater than most managers possess today. When problems of feelings and emotions arise in the working relationships, the manager who uses the team approach recognizes the problems and confronts them directly. He deals with and works through conflict as it appears.

MORALE ACHIEVED IS TASK RELATED

The manager who uses the task management approach finds it difficult to distinguish team management from country club management because both reflect high concern for people. Yet the concern expressed by the country club manager is more in terms of satisfaction based on nonwork aspects of the situation, such as good social relations. The team manager seeks to integrate people around production. The morale achieved under team management conditions is task-related.

Also, the manager who uses the team approach must have greater appreciation of and skill in unleashing individual motivation than managers using any other approach. Behavioral-science theory and research findings have identified many of the conditions of team management.[16] In addition, the theory and ways of teaching are available for the manager who wants to shift from any of the other approaches to the team situation.

Many organizational efforts of the past 15 years have intuitively aimed toward improving the achievement of production through people in a team

[16] Thomas G. Spates, *Human Values Where People Work* (New York: Harper & Row, Publishers, 1960), pp. 176-187, and A. Zaleznik, C. R. Christensen, F. J. Roethlisberger, *The Motivation, Productivity and Satisfaction of Workers* (Boston: Harvard University Press, 1958), pp. 387-432.

management approach. Without explicit managerial theory available to guide them, many efforts have been built on trying to shore up bad human relations brought about by the task management approach.

One result has been what is called phony human relations. All too frequently, managers have adopted a managerial strategy in the country club area of the Managerial Grid as a soft approach.[17] They have been led down this path by the assumption that there must be a conflict between the organizational requirements and needs of individuals. Other managers have confused the emphasis on using the team as the building block with that of destroying individual self-expression and freedom.[18]

By now, in a number of instances, managerial effort has successfully employed behavioral-science concepts and methods as the basis for moving toward a team managerial orientation. Some have used team training with specific development of the Managerial Grid for setting meaningful organization objectives to which all team members are committed.[19, 20]

[17] Robert Tannenbaum, Irving R. Weschler, and Fred Massarik, *Leadership and Organization* (New York: McGraw-Hill Book Co., Inc., 1961), pp. 6-22.
[18] Malcolm P. McNair, "Thinking Ahead: What Price Human Relations," *Harvard Business Review* (March-April 1957), pp. 15-22.
[19] *An Action Research Program for Organization Improvement* (Ann Arbor, Mich.: The Foundation for Research on Human Behavior, 1960), p. 71.
[20] A. C. Bidwell, J. J. Farrell, and Robert R. Blake, "Team Job Training—A New Strategy for Industry," *ASTD Journal* (1961), 15, pp. 3-23.

33

A Theory of Leadership Effectiveness

FRED FIEDLER

Fred Fiedler and his associates at the University of Illinois have devoted over fifteen years of research to a study of leadership effectiveness. Professor Fiedler has developed a situationist approach to leadership that he calls the leadership contingency model. In this excerpt from his book A Theory of Leadership Effectiveness, *Professor Fiedler discusses the implications of the leadership contingency model for leadership selection, leadership training, and organizational improvement efforts.*

The leadership contingency model is built around two measures of leadership style: "assumed similarity between opposites" (ASO) and "the least preferred coworker" (LPC). ASO measures the degree to which a leader perceives as very similar his most and least preferred coworkers. A perception of close similarity between the two suggests that the leader is not discriminating in his preferences about coworkers. LPC measures the degree to which the leader sees even a poor coworker in a relatively favorable manner. Both factors, which are highly correlated, are therefore measures of a supervisor's leniency. A supervisor with a high LPC rating or high ASO is presumed to be "permissive, human-relations oriented, and considerate of the feelings of his men."

According to the leadership contingency model, the appropriate style of leadership in any given situation depends on whether (1) the leader is accepted by the group, (2) the group's task is structured, and (3) the leader has strong formal position power. Directive leadership is most appropriate in situations that are relatively high or low on all three of these components; a more permissive leadership style works best when the situation is somewhere in the middle on all three components. Professor Fiedler concludes that it is not meaningful to speak of an effective leader or an ineffective leader; it is more correct to speak of a leader who tends to be effective in one situation and ineffective in another.

The Contingency Model postulates that leadership effectiveness depends upon the appropriate matching of the individual's leadership style of interacting and the influence which the group situation provides. What are the implications of this theory and our findings for the selection and recruitment of leaders for training and for the management of organizations?

The major point of this theory is that leadership effectiveness—that is, effective group performance—depends just as much on the group situation as it does on the leader. If the theory is right this means that a personnel program that deals only with the personality aspects of the leader or only with the situational aspects of the organization is bound to fail. One style of leadership is not in itself better than the other, nor is one type of leadership behavior appropriate for all conditions. Hence, almost everyone should be able to succeed as a leader in some situations and almost everyone is likely to fail in others. If we want to improve organizational performance we must deal not only with the leader's style but also with the factors in the situation which provide him with influence. While one can never say that something is impossible, and while someone may well discover the all-purpose leadership style or behavior at some future time, our own data and those which have come out of sound research by other investigators do not promise such miraculous cures. And if leadership performance is in fact a product of both the individual's leadership style and the leadership situation then it is logically impossible that one leadership style could serve in every context. On the other hand, it also follows from this theory that we can improve group or organizational performance either by changing the leader to fit the situation or by changing the situation to fit the leader.

Industrial psychologists and personnel men typically view the executive's position as fixed and immutable and the individual as highly plastic and trainable. When we think of improving leadership performance we generally think first of training the leader. Yet, we know all too well from our experience with psychotherapy, our attempts to rehabilitate prison inmates, drug addicts, or juvenile delinquents—not to mention our difficulties with rearing our own progeny—that our ability to change personality has its limitations.

A person's leadership style, as we have used the term, reflects the individual's basic motivational and need structure. At best it takes one, two or three years of intensive psychotherapy to effect lasting changes in personality structure. It is difficult to see how we can change in more than a few cases an equally important set of core values in a few hours of lectures and role playing or even in the course of a more intensive training program of one or two weeks.

On the other hand, executive jobs and supervisory responsibilities almost always can be modified to a greater or lesser extent both by the incumbent of the position and, even more readily, by his organization. In fact, organizations frequently change the specifications of a management job to make it more appealing to the executive whom the organization wishes to attract or whom it wishes to retain. If anything, many organizations change executive jobs and responsibilities more often than might be necessary.

Executives at higher echelons are well aware of the fact that they must take account of the strengths and weaknesses of their subordinate managers. One man may operate most effectively when his authority is strictly defined and circumscribed while another must be given considerable leeway and discretion. Some executives excel in staff work while others perform best in line positions; some are known as specialists in trouble-shooting who thrive on turmoil and crisis while others perform best as administrators of well-running subunits of the organization. Our theory provides a conceptual framework and a preliminary set of guidelines for determining how to match the leadership situation and the man. While cookbook prescriptions are still a task for the future we can indicate here some of the major directions which our theory indicates. The basic methods in managing executive and managerial talent have been by leadership recruitment and selection and by leadership training. We shall add to these an organizational engineering approach and discuss these three approaches in light of the theory and the data which this book has presented.

LEADERSHIP RECRUITMENT AND SELECTION

The classical and "time-tested" method for maintaining a cadre of executives calls for the recruitment of men who not only have the technical experience and background which the job requires but also the personality attributes and abilities which will make them effective leaders. Given a candidate who has the technical and intellectual qualifications, the recruiter then tries to predict the individual's leadership potential from his background and possibly from psychological tests.

However, previous leadership experience is likely to predict future performance only if the past leadership situation was nearly identical to the leadership situation for which the individual is to be selected. And all too frequently the recruiter knows very little about the leadership situation the individual is likely to face. He knows next to nothing about what he will do two or five years later. And no system of leadership selection is likely to work without this knowledge as long as leadership performance varies from situation to situation or from task to task.

. . .

We must emphasize that management and administrative functions, or being a "good executive," are not identical with leadership. Management is more than leadership. It includes routine administration and the maintenance of communications with other departments or other agencies; it requires knowledge of organizational procedures and regulations. It usually involves negotiating and bargaining functions between the manager and his own superior or with others at his level to maintain the status of his department within the total organization (see for example Barnard, 1938; Katz and Kahn, 1965). It also requires the motivation to seek and accept executive responsibilities. Some of these factors of administrative skill may well be predictable by personality and achievement tests. Leadership ability—the knack of getting any group to perform in a highly efficient manner—is not currently predictable. Considering the fact that years of effort have failed to produce any generally valid leadership tests, and that these tests would fly in the face of all currently available evidence, it seems safe to say that they are not likely to appear in the future.

If our theory is correct then the recruitment and selection of leaders can be effective only when we can also specify the relevant components of the situation for which the leader is being recruited. There is no reason to believe that this cannot be done, or that this should not be done in specific cases. Difficulties arise because leadership situations change over time. The organization must then be aware of the type of leadership situations into which the individual should be successively guided, but this is basically no different than seeing that an electrical engineer does not get assigned to bookkeeping duties.

LEADERSHIP TRAINING

Because the leader is seen as the key to organizational success, be this in government, in educational institutions, in sports, in the military, or in business and industry, it is not surprising that these organizations have unstintingly devoted substantial time and money to leadership training. These training programs, supervisory and leadership workshops, and residential courses have enjoyed widespread popularity for many years both in the United States and abroad.

These programs frequently provide instruction in administrative procedures, in organizational policy, and such various other fields as accounting, cost control, and legal responsibilities of the organization. As before, our discussion deals only with leadership training per se, that is, with the skills that can be measured in terms of group and organizational effectiveness. We recognize that these training programs often provide a number of other benefits. These may range from giving the executive a welcome break from his routine or widening his intellectual horizon to raising his own morale and that of his subordinates. Whether or not an executive development program or a leadership training workshop can be justified in these terms is a matter of administrative judgment.

Of relevance is the fact that many of these programs are primarily designed to increase the individual's leadership skills. It might also be pointed out that the yearly amount expended for training programs of this sort in the United States is likely to stagger the imagination. It is all the more unfortunate, therefore, that the development of these programs, as well as the utilization of other leadership selection devices, has not been matched by an appropriate number of adequate evaluation studies. Organizations have been more than happy to spend money on training programs but they have been considerably less eager to find out whether the training really does any good. Moreover, personnel research has been severely handicapped by the fact that the criteria of group and departmental effectiveness are only vaguely spelled out and defined in many organizations, and even less frequently are they measured with any degree of reliability.

. . .

Most leadership training programs are designed either to change the trainee's attitudes and behaviors in the direction which will make him more task-oriented, managing, and directive, or in the direction which will make him more human-relations oriented, permissive, and nondirective. If we assume that these training programs are effective in changing the behavior in the desired direction, and if the Contingency Model is an accurate mapping of reality, then about half the trainees would have come out with an inappropriate leadership style no matter which type of program they attended. Those trained to be directive, managing, and task-oriented would be well suited for leadership situations which are very favorable or else very unfavorable, but they would be unsuited for the situations intermediate in favorableness. Those trained to be relationship-oriented, permissive, and nondirective would be well suited for the situations intermediate in favorableness but poorly suited for the very favorable or the very unfavorable situations. This assumes, of course, that a training program actually can effect more than temporary modifications in the individual's leadership style and concomitant behavior, which still remains to be established.

If leadership training is to be successful, the present theory would argue that it should focus on providing the individual with methods for diagnosing the favorableness of the leadership situation and for adapting the leadership situations to the individual's style of leadership so that he can perform effectively. It should be relatively easy to develop methods which would indicate to the leader whether or not the situation fits his particular style. ... It should also be possible to construct a measure which would indicate to the leader how good his relations are with his group members. We can then instruct the leader in making the necessary modifications in the leadership situation so that the situation will match his style. While this sounds simple in principle a number of difficulties will need to be resolved before a procedure of this type can be put into general practice.

The alternative method would call for training the leader to develop a flexible leadership style and to adapt his leadership style to the particular situation. The author is highly pessimistic that this training approach would be successful. There may well be some favored few who can be effective in any leadership situation, and some unfortunate few who would even find it difficult to lead a troop of hungry girl scouts to a hot-dog stand. However, our experience has not enabled us to identify these individuals. Nor have we found it possible to identify those who can switch their leadership style as the occasion demands. It would seem more promising at this time, therefore, to teach the individual to recognize the conditions under which he can perform best and to modify the situation to suit his leadership style.

ORGANIZATIONAL ENGINEERING

The Contingency Model suggests one important alternative method for improving leadership performance. This is predicated on the belief that it is almost always easier to change a man's work environment than it is to change his personality or his style of relating to others. Experienced managers have long been aware of the fact that an executive who performs poorly in one situation might be excellent in another. However, there has been no rationale for changing an executive from one job to another, nor for changing the dimensions of a given job in order to make him more effective. The comment is often heard that one manager has too much responsibility, that another needs more rank in order to function effectively, or that a third is an excellent staff officer but a poor line executive. The Contingency Model permits us to place these evaluations into a theoretical frame of reference and to determine a priori what kinds of changes might be required to obtain maximum performance from various men in positions of leadership.

It might appear at first blush that it would be a very formidable task to change the situation so that it will fit the man's leadership style; that we surely cannot reorganize a company every time a new manager is hired; and that such organizations as military units simply cannot be changed at all. It may indeed be impractical or impossible to modify some situations to fit them to the leader's style. Yet, in the overwhelming number of cases, including military organizations, it should be possible to make some relevant changes. Here again our conjectures far outstrip our data but it seems profitable to indicate the ways in which various leadership situations could be modified.

1. In some organizations we can change the individual's task assignment. We may assign to one leader very structured tasks which have implicit or explicit instructions telling him what to do and how to do it, and we may assign to another the tasks which are nebulous and vague. The former are the typical production tasks, the latter are exemplified by committee work, by the development of policy, and by tasks which require creativity.

2. We can change the leader's position power. We not only can give him a higher rank and corresponding recognition, we can also modify his position power by giving him subordinates who are equal to him in rank and prestige or subordinates who are two or three ranks below him. We can give him subordinates who are expert in their specialties or subordinates who depend upon the leader for guidance and instruction. We can give the leader the final say in all decisions affecting his group, or we can require that he make decisions in consultation with his subordinates, or even that he obtain their concurrence. We can channel all directives, communications, and information about organizational plans through the leader alone, giving him expert power, or we can provide these communications concurrently to all his subordinates.

3. We can change the leader-member relations in the group. We can have the leader work with groups whose members are very similar to him in attitude, opinion, technical background, race, and cultural background. Or we can assign him subordinates with whom he differs in any one or several of these important aspects. Finally, we can assign the leader to a group in which the members have a tradition of getting along well with their supervisors or to a group which has a history and tradition of conflict.

The concept of organizational engineering requires that the average performance of groups be independent of the favorableness of the group situation. When we correlate leader LPC and group performance for various levels of group favorableness, we are dealing with group performance scores in relative terms. However, we must also consider group performance in absolute terms if we hope to improve group performance by increasing or by decreasing the favorableness of the group situation.

It would seem reasonable to expect, on a commonsense basis, that the average level of group performance will be lower as the favorableness of the group situation decreases. That is, we would expect poorer performance of groups in which leaders have very little influence than in groups in which they have much influence. If this is the case there would be little advantage in changing the leadership situation to make it fit the leader. We would only need to make the situation as favorable as possible, whatever the leadership style of the executive.

As already indicated in previous chapters, this typically is not the case: the average level of group performance is very little affected by the favorableness of the situation.

... The data suggest, therefore, that it should be possible in most cases to improve the effectiveness of a leader even though this may require making the leadership situation less favorable.

In fact, the leader, himself, may sometimes change the leadership situation in a less favorable direction. A leader may decide to work on a vague and unstructured assignment before tackling a highly structured task; he may voluntarily relinquish or not fully utilize the power of his position by seeking the group's advice or by announcing that he will not make decisions without his group's concurrence. If the leader is made aware of his strengths and weaknesses as well as possible remedies, he may not only be able to modify group situations to match them with his leadership style, he may also learn how to avoid group situations which are incompatible with his style and seek out those in which he is most likely to succeed. A man who is able to avoid situations in which he is likely to fail is likely to be a success.

A major potential advantage of the organizational engineering approach is that it enables the manager at the second or third level of the organization to provide a situation for his subordinate managers which will utilize their leadership potential to the fullest. It should be possible to train the higher level manager to diagnose the leadership situation of his subordinates and, knowing his subordinates' leadership style, to modify the task, the position power, or the group relations in a way which will make it compatible with the leadership style of the executive. While we are admittedly speculating on the basis of very incomplete evidence, these modifications could be accomplished by the organization without fanfare and on a basis sufficiently gradual to provide close control over the effects.

When a valued executive performs poorly in his position, or when the outstanding specialist, the expert in his field, or the particularly knowledgeable member of the organization is unable to deal with his leadership responsibilities, the organization is faced with the dilemma of getting rid of the man or shifting him to another job in the hope that he may improve in time. It is essential that we realize that poor performance in a leadership position is likely to be as much the function of the leadership situation which the organization provides as it is the function of the individual's personality structure. An alternative to discarding the poorly functioning leader is then to engineer the organizational dimensions of the leadership job so that the specialist can function effectively not only as a technical expert but also as a manager and leader. In view of the increasing scarcity of highly trained executive manpower, an organizational engineering approach may well become the method of necessity as well as of choice.

34

Every Employee a Manager

M. SCOTT MYERS

M. Scott Myers has conducted pioneering research and experimentation in job enrichment during his ten years in personnel research at Texas Instruments.

In his book Every Employee A Manager, *Dr. Myers provides practical guidance on how to redefine the jobs and the roles of both employees and supervisors in order to make every employee a manager. The following excerpt from Dr. Myers' book provides a valuable link between leadership theory and the selections on the subject of job design in Part Two. Dr. Myers describes how the role of the supervisor shifts when the "plan-do-control" job enrichment concept is implemented. As workers' jobs are enriched, the supervisor must shift from authority-orientation to goal-orientation. Similarly, management prerogatives, which are exclusive rights based on authority, give way to responsibility. The influence of official supervisory authority is replaced by the unofficial influences of all members of the group based on their competence and commitment to goals.*

Although the manager has a vital role in increasing human effectiveness, he must rely on the voluntary compliance of the group rather than on formal authority. As Dr. Myers puts it: "The manager who insists on using the influence of official authority in today's enlightened society will increasingly be frustrated by negative reaction to his attempted use of arbitrary direction and control."

To make every employee a manager through the creation of meaningful work requires supervisory sophistication not common in most enterprises. The author acknowledges that many managers experience difficulty in assuming this new supervisory role. He feels that organizational climate factors such as delegation, innovation, authority orientation, goal orientation, and communication are key determinants of the willingness of supervisors and subordinates to make every employee a manager.

Reprinted from M. Scott Myers, *Every Employee a Manager*, pp. 96-117, by permission of McGraw-Hill Book Company. Copyright 1970 by McGraw-Hill, Inc.

Management of change is the key function of the manager, in regard to both human effort and technology. The responsibility is not new, of course, but it is becoming increasingly complicated by the accelerating rate of change in all media. Because change requires adaptation at all levels of the organization, the manager is confronted with the circular problem of encouraging innovation, while introducing changes in a manner that will not threaten the innovators. Being human, the manager, too, is vulnerable to change, and he must be able to monitor and evaluate his own effectiveness and take measures to prevent his own obsolescence. Through the media of supervisory style, management systems, and other factors affecting the organization's climate, he must gradually shift the source of influence from authority to competence so that initiative and freedom at all levels of the organization will find responsible expression.

He is challenged further by the requirement for applying principles of human effectiveness in operations in other cultures. The role of the American abroad is defined, with particular reference to his relationships with indigenous personnel. In part, the role of the American abroad is a response to Servan-Schreiber,[1] who sees America's industrial invasion as a threat to other countries' economic and cultural sovereignty, and articulates a plea for Europeans and other international associates to unite against the omnipresent expatriate American entrepreneur.

THE ROLE OF THE SUPERVISOR

The preceding chapter presents a framework to erase the management-labor dichotomy and give substance to the slogan "Every employee a manager"—a manager being defined as one who manages a job. A self-managed job is one which provides a realistic opportunity for the incumbent to be responsible for the total plan-do-control phases of his job. Though many jobs in their present forms cannot be fully enriched, most can be improved and some can be eliminated. Whether the supervisor's mission is to enrich, to improve, or to eliminate the job, he achieves it best by utilizing the talents of the incumbents themselves.

The supervisor must be able to understand the conditions which promote and inhibit expression of talent in terms of interpersonal competence, meaningful goals, and helpful systems, as defined [earlier]. In satisfying these conditions, he must be able to hold the mirror up to himself and see himself objectively—to find out what new responsibilities and activities he should be involved with, and which of his traditional roles should be modified or discontinued. As he is human, changes in his role are unsettling or threatening, particularly if they are imposed by authority. His dilemma is ameliorated if he himself is the initiator and agent of his changing role.

[1] J.-J. Servan-Schreiber, *The American Challenge*, Atheneum Publishers, New York, 1969.

When production supervisors in Texas Instruments introduced the problem-solving-goal-setting process, they did so in an attempt to invoke the talent of their groups in achieving difficult production goals. Their efforts were rewarded when the job-enrichment process led to the successful attainment of goals. Moreover, they noted that, in addition to the increase in production, the quality of workmanship improved; complaints about maintenance factors decreased; and absenteeism, tardiness, and trips to the health center, restrooms, and personnel department diminished. In some cases, they found commitment so high it became essential to remind employees to take the legally required rest periods in midmorning and midafternoon.

With their increased freedom and involvement in managing their own work, operators began working directly with the engineers in methods improvement, value analysis, and rearranging their work place. Supervisors permitted these new work roles of the operators primarily because they resulted in improved performance. But the operators' activities did not always of necessity involve the supervisors, who became understandably uncomfortable with the resultant ambiguity of their own roles. One supervisor's anxiety reached a new high when a problem-solving group told him that he was free to attend to other matters and that they would keep him posted on their progress. Consequently, a group of these disfranchised supervisors, with the assistance of the division training director, undertook the task of defining their new role.

Role Redefinition

The results of this group's efforts are reflected in Figure 1. Initial efforts of the group produced the traditional authority-oriented role detailed in the left column—not because they were committed to this role, but, rather, because their anxiety and haste regressed them temporarily to the typical textbook definition of the role of supervision. After evaluating and then rejecting this traditional role as an inaccurate description of their emerging role, they restated their supervisory responsibilities, thereby defining the goal-oriented role column.

Though most of the items in the left column are acceptable in the light of tradition, their collective effect tends to reinforce the authority-oriented relationship, depicted in the diagram at the foot of the column, in which people conform to the plan-lead-control directions received from their supervisors. Items in the goal-oriented column do not differ completely from those in the authority-oriented column, but their net effect provides opportunity for people to manage the full plan-do-control phases of their work, involving supervisors as resources.

During the discussion of the emerging role of the supervisor, the group concluded that an effective supervisor is one who provides a climate in which people have a sense of working for themselves. In terms of their day-to-day relationships, they defined the supervisor's role as:

- □ Giving visibility to company goals.
- □ Providing budgets and facilities.
- □ Mediating conflict.
- □ Staying out of the way to let people manage their work.

Figure 1 The role of supervision.

Authority-Oriented	Goal-Oriented
Set goals for subordinates; define standards and results expected.	Participate with people in problem solving and goal setting.
Give them information necessary to do their job.	Give them access to information which they want.
Train them in how to do the job.	Create situations for optimum learning.
Explain rules and apply discipline to ensure conformity; suppress conflict.	Explain rules and consequences of violations; mediate conflict.
Stimulate subordinates through persuasive leadership.	Allow people to set challenging goals.
Develop and install new methods.	Teach methods-improvement techniques to job incumbents.
Develop and free them for promotion.	Enable them to pursue and move into growth opportunities.
Reward achievements and punish failures.	Recognize achievements and help them learn from failures.

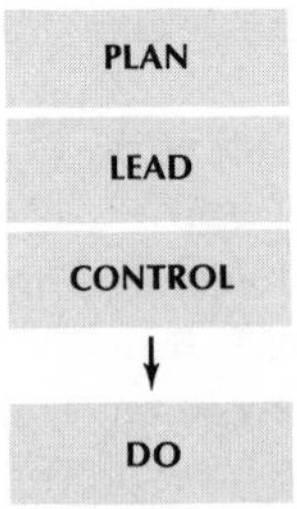

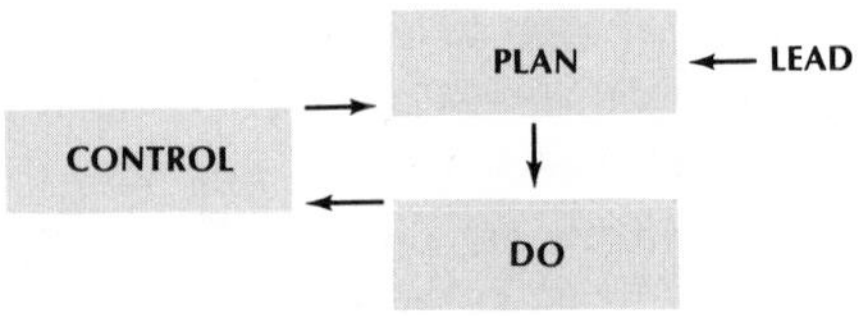

Giving visibility to company goals means sharing information with the members of the group who are to be involved in achieving a specific customer goal. In a production line, for example, it means defining the group's mission to provide a product for a customer, including cost, quality, and schedule requirements. It means detailing the overhead, materiel, and labor costs associated with providing the product or service, showing the percentage each contributes to the total cost, and distinguishing between the fixed and variable costs. All members of the group should be able to see the problem essentially as the supervisor sees it and should have access to any information needed to achieve their goal. The key to this function is emphasizing the facts that everyone has a customer, whether this customer is the ultimate customer or another department or assembly line within the company, and that the group goal is to satisfy the customer's need.

Providing budgets and facilities does not mean financing every improvement or capital investment suggested by the members of the group. It does mean sharing with them the rationale for managing a budget and, if a capital investment is suggested, explaining the amortization process and exploring with them its application to a suggested expenditure. When the group is involved in assessing a proposed investment in terms of increased efficiency, the duration of the project, change in quality, etc., they can see whether or not it is a sound economic investment, and a decision to buy or not to buy is a matter of logic rather than an arbitrary decision based on authority.

The mediation of conflict is an ongoing and often misunderstood role of supervision. Conflict always exists; however, the nature of conflict varies. In the environment of meaningless or oppressive work, conflict naturally arises as a form of displaced aggression or as a means of breaking the monotony. In an environment of challenging and interesting work, conflict may arise as a result of competition and efforts to overcome barriers to individual and group goals. This type of conflict is not harmful, as long as it is surfaced and group members are able to cope with it. Supervisors too often believe that conflict is undesirable and must be suppressed—not realizing that such a strategy deals only with symptoms.

Staying out of the way to let people manage their work does not mean abandoning the group, but it does mean being sensitive to the needs of individuals in regard to their desire and ability to be responsible for many planning and control functions of their job. When delegation is done successfully, people are not subjected to imposed direction and control, but have the freedom to pursue goals which they have helped define. They will seek help from any source to achieve this goal, including the supervisor if he has earned their acceptance and has something to contribute in the nature of needed business information or technical competence. The intervention of authority in a team effort is usually felt more as an inhibiting than as a facilitating influence.

Goals Replace Conformity

This redefinition of the supervisor's role to provide opportunity for people to manage their own work is portrayed in Figure 2. In contrast to the authority-conformity-oriented roles of the supervisor and operator shown [earlier], each now has a goal-oriented role in which the revised *do* phase of the supervisor and *plan* phase of the operator compose the realm of interface between them. Figures 1 and 2 both show the goal-oriented supervisor to be a resource person whose involvement is invoked primarily at the initiative of the operator.

This role of the leader, evolved initially to illustrate the relationship between the foreman and operator, is a model representing ideal supervisory relationships at any level. Furthermore, enriching the operator's job has changed higher-level jobs, in some cases making it possible to reduce the number of levels in the management hierarchy. The foreman, now freed of many detailed maintenance and control functions, has more time to be involved with his supervisor in higher-level planning functions and is also more available to meet his responsibility as a mediator and resource person when needed by the natural work group under his supervision.

The application of meaningful work offers substantial short-range incentive for managers to support it. Judged as they are, periodically, in terms of profit, cost reduction, cash flow, share of the market, and return-on-investment criteria, job enrichment is valued as a process for achieving success. But it offers even greater rewards on a long-term basis, particularly if criteria of success are broadened to include aspects of human effectiveness such as better utilization of employee talent, responsible civic and home relationships, and the profitable and self-renewing growth of the organization.

Responsibility Replaces Prerogatives

Gone are management prerogatives. Management prerogatives, by definition, are exclusive rights based on authority. The specifying of "management" prerogatives evokes a requirement for "labor" prerogatives. Evaluation of labor prerogatives shows them to be unaligned with, or contradictory to, company goals. ... Hence, it is self-defeating to articulate and act through the authority of management prerogatives. The divine rights of "King Supervisor" are being relinquished under the self-imposed pressures of enlightenment. The price of management prerogatives in terms of quashed initiative, alienation, and unachieved goals is much too high for all but those seeking satisfaction of pathological needs for power and manipulation.

Prerogatives have given way to responsibility—to customers, share-

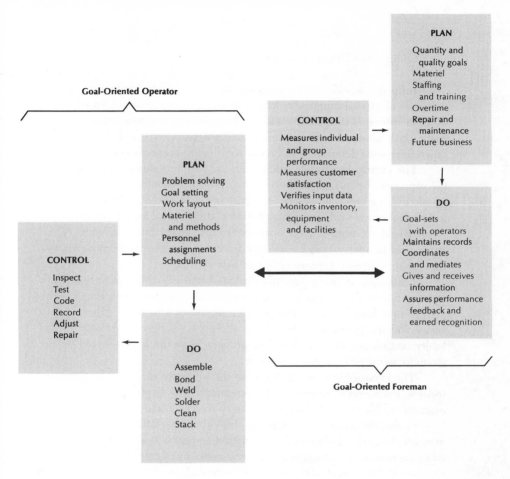

Figure 2   Goal-oriented relationship between foreman and operator.

holders, employees, and the community. To the *customer* the manager is responsible for delivering a superior product or service at minimum cost. To the *shareholder* or owner he is responsible for maximizing return on investment. To the *employee* he is responsible for providing a meaningful life at work. And the manager's impact is made on the *community* by the emulation in homes of his leadership patterns on the job. Democratic and autocratic managers began the development of their management styles in democratic and autocratic homes under parents whose styles of supervision were often copied from the job situation. Hence, industry represents a potent medium for influencing the philosophy of a culture.

361

Competence Replaces Authority

Influence is still needed to satisfy this new role; however, it is not the influence of official supervisory authority but, rather, the unofficial influence of all members of the group based on their competence and commitment to goals. Both kinds of influence exist in all organizations, and the manager's supervisory style determines and indicates which is predominant.

For practical purposes, what really matters in industry is not whether the supervisor has official authority or not, but whether he is accepted by the people in his group. The supervisor whose behavior has earned the acceptance and respect of his work group has, in effect, transformed his official authority to unofficial acceptance. He is both the formal and the informal leader of the group, and he succeeds as a leader not by virtue of authority from above, but through the willing acceptance of those below.

Leadership is not a psychological trait but a function of the situation and the nature of the group. In a given situation, the effective leader is the person most fitted to take charge. The supervisor who is the official group leader will try to see to it that he is accepted willingly as the appropriate leader in that situation, rather than grudgingly as the leader forced on the group by virtue of his formal authority.

The manager who insists on using the influence of official authority in today's enlightened society will increasingly be frustrated by negative reactions to his attempted use of arbitrary direction and control. No matter how technically correct and logically insightful the direction given by the manager, his style of dispensing information and influencing the group will be a key determinant of his success. The successful manager has learned to avoid the use of official authority and succeeds through the constructive harnessing of his group's competence. He knows how to organize his materiel and manpower in ways that allow free expression of talent in defining problems, in setting goals, and in managing resources for achieving these goals.

The new role of the supervisor is not always accepted easily. Testimonials from others who solve production problems with the help of operators are often received with mixed reactions. For some managers, the involvement of subordinates in solving management problems is seen as an expression of weakness that is bound to cause loss of respect from subordinates. Such managers oppose worker involvement, as capitulation or as relinquishment of management prerogatives. Reactions of this type are not uncommon, as authority-oriented relationships fostered in many homes, schools, military organizations, and other institutions find natural expression in most job situations. A supervisor does not switch styles by edict or as an immediate consequence of reading a book or hearing an inspiring speech. An intellectual message may sensitize him to his problem, but he must work through the process of self-evaluation, self-acceptance, adjustment of values, and change of behavior at his own pace, in his own way, and only in a climate conducive to change. The pressure of an edict to "be democratic" will only regress him to familiar old authority-oriented patterns, from which stance he will obediently recite the official intellectual message.

Supervisory effectiveness results from job enrichment as a circular phenomenon. In the first instance, job enrichment requires action (or discontinuation of previous action) on the part of the supervisor to supply conditions of human effectiveness. The results of this action in turn reinforce it and encourage its application by others. Its application brings about subtle changes in the perceptions, the values, and finally, the habits of the supervisors, so that in a gradual branching and multiplying process a new way of life at work is put into motion which simultaneously changes and effects changes through the supervisor. Hence, the supervisor is the originator of and the medium for change—providing conditions for the development of others and thereby bringing about his own self-development or obsolescence.

. . .

ORGANIZATIONAL CLIMATE

Every organization can be said to have a climate which colors the perceptions and feelings of people within their work environment. A company's climate is influenced by innumerable factors such as its size, the nature of its business, its age, its location, the composition of its work force, its management policies, rules and regulations, and the values and leadership styles of its supervisors. Many of the factors influencing an organization's climate are dynamic and interactive, resulting in ever-changing "weather" within the organization. However, some factors remain relatively constant, tending to stabilize other factors around a modal or characteristic climate for the organization. Some of these pivotal factors are defined below.

Growth Rate

Rate of growth is a climate factor. In a rapidly expanding organization, the sense of urgency and speed of change create rich opportunities for individual growth, achievement, responsibility, and recognition. Domineering supervisors who would seem oppressive in a stable organization are tolerated in the growth climate, perhaps because their roles are seen as transitory. Also, the sheer pressure of expanding responsibility reduces the authoritarian manager's ability to maintain tight controls, and delegation occurs, if only by default.

In the stabilized or retrenching organization, a condition which often coincides with economic pressures, managers frequently resort to reductive supervisory practices. Delegation is curtailed and growth opportunities are interrupted or deferred, and the more talented members of the work force become impatient and discouraged. Eager to forge ahead, they seek greener pastures, and gradually abandon the organization to those who have less ability either to relocate themselves or to revive the organization. The loss of top talent to competitor organizations, of course, further handicaps the plateaued organization. Hence, growth itself is needed if for no other reason than to retain the talented personnel upon whom the continuing success of the organization depends.

Delegation

Delegation, as a climate factor, is expressed both through style of supervision and through organization structure. Managers operating on the basis of goal-oriented assumptions ... delegate naturally and willingly—particularly managers who are themselves the recipients of delegated authority. Authority-oriented managers, in contrast, fail to delegate and do little to encourage delegation below them.

The business organized around decentralized semi-autonomous product-customer centers tends to foster delegation better than the functionally layered organization. In a functionally layered organization, for example, the manager of manufacturing with five plants under his jurisdiction has limited freedom to exercise his judgment in setting goals and managing plant resources if another manager is responsible for the sale of his products and another is responsible for research in the five plants. In contrast, a plant manager who has the threefold responsibility of creating, making, and marketing products or income-producing services has more flexibility in managing his resources and in making decisions necessary for organizational success. He is less hampered by the bureaucratic constrictions of poorly coordinated jurisdictions, and can more naturally delegate to others the freedom necessary for building an empire on a foundation of entrepreneurial principles.

Innovation

The spontaneous and constructive expression of creativity is a desirable characteristic of an organization's climate—in the management process as well as in the laboratory. Though managers readily enough accept the principle that they are managers of innovation, few plan for it or demonstrate constructive creativity in their normal day-to-day behavior. Worse yet, official commitment to the support of innovation may foster formidable official systems for "managing innovation" which tend to quash it. Rewards in the form of raises, bonuses, and promotions more often go to those who support the "system," while those who might be involved in the constructive departure from the *status quo* tend to be punished or expelled from the system.

Innovation exists in great abundance in every organization, but not always to the benefit of the organization. In the democratic organization in which people at all levels have opportunity to receive information, solve problems, and set goals, innovation finds positive expression. In organizations characterized by tight supervision, inflexible rules, engineered labor standards, and other authority-oriented controls, creativity finds reactive expression, usually to the detriment of the organization. The tighter the controls, the more innovativeness is directed toward circumventing them. Hence, the problem is not one of evoking innovativeness as much as it is one of providing outlets which give positive expression to innovativeness.

Constructive innovation is encouraged not only by style of management, but also by appropriate systems for managing innovation. The hierarchy of objectives, strategies, and tactical action programs described [earlier] provides a framework in which the efforts of task forces can find creative expression in achieving organizational goals. The work-simplification process ... teaches problem-solving-goal-setting techniques and philosophy to give expression to creativity at all levels of the organization. The task-force analysis of attitude survey results ... in a system for better utilization of talent at all levels. A climate of innovation is also enhanced by the avoidance of authority-based systems such as engineered labor standards, chain-of-command communication, defensive expense reporting, and elaborate status symbols.

Authority Orientation

An organization's climate may be described in terms of goal orientation or authority orientation. An employee may be described as goal-oriented if he understands his job in terms of what it does for the customer, but he is authority-oriented if he performs his job in blind obedience to an order from his boss.

The reductive use of authority ... is not an indictment of authority per se. Authority is freedom to act, and it is needed by every member of the organization. However, it is damaging when people at higher levels, deliberately or in ignorance, create systems or behave in ways that deprive people lower in the organization of the information and freedom necessary for goal orientation.

Without deliberate efforts to prevent it, growing organizations drift inexorably toward an authority-dominated climate. The worker parks on the company parking lot according to rules established by a nebulous "management," and the lower his rank, the farther out his parking space. He records his entry and departure from the plant by official timekeeping procedures, he is told by his supervisor what his job is and perhaps by his union steward what his job is not. Industrial engineering defines "correct" procedures and specifies his quantity and quality goals. A signal bell authorizes the beginning and ending of his coffee break and lunch period, and posted notices tell him he cannot eat or smoke in the hallways. Information is dispensed by management through the public-address system, official bulletins, the company newspaper, and bulletin boards. His pay is determined through the value judgment of supervision, and his paycheck is prepared by computer, minus deductions authorized by Federal and state laws, the union, and management. His supervisor may review his performance with him, detailing his strong and weak points, and prescribe remedial actions. The United Fund and Savings Bond Drives for "voluntary" participation are administered through a process which would make his nonparticipation threatening to those above him, and hence to him. His recourse in case of injustice is a grievance procedure which he hesitates to use because of the possibility of alienating his superior and incurring subtle reprisals. His request for time off must be justified to his supervisor by what is sometimes a humiliating detailing of personal information. When he seeks transfers and promotions, or decides to terminate, his dependency on his supervisor's goodwill is inescapable. Though deliberate strategies can prevent or counter the oppressiveness of authority in an organization's climate, few large organizations have succeeded in doing so.

Goal Orientation

Goal orientation is the motivational force which gives direction to the systems and relationships defined throughout this book. It is the climate factor created by processes which give visibility to broad organizational goals, and it allows access to information and freedom to act so that individual initiative finds expression in setting goals and measuring achievements. A goal-oriented person manages his job, in contrast to the authority-oriented person who feels he is managed by his job. Goal orientation depends on an integrated balance of meaningful goals, helpful systems, and interpersonal competence. ... Deliberate and systematic attempts are made in goal-oriented organizations to minimize the status symbols which tend to sensitize people to authority. Dining facilities are shared by all employees; employee identification badges do not reflect rank; parking privileges, office space, and furnishings are assigned on the basis of factors other than organizational level. Mode of attire is not standardized and is often informal. People address each other on a first-name basis and tend to communicate through the informal and fluid grapevine which exists in every organization. The unwritten, but apparent, ground rule followed by members of the organization is that individuals treat each other with the mutual respect and informality of social peers. The supervisor's influence is not a manifestation of arbitrary direction and control but, rather, results from his role as an adviser, consultant, and coordinator. The net effect of such a system is to enable people to relate to each other on a competence basis in the pursuit of common goals, rather than to sensitize them to, and sandwich them into, an authority hierarchy.

Status

Climates differ with regard to the amount and kind of status afforded through organizational membership. Status may be considered as official and unofficial.

Official status is derived from the prestige of having a high job grade and salary or occupying a responsible position in the organizational hierarchy. Increased official status is an incentive for personal and professional growth for those who have the talent and desire to achieve it. But not every person wants a promotion in the sense of a higher job grade or becoming a supervisor or plant manager. However, every person does want the prestige of being a better craftsman and a valued member of his work group.

Unofficial status is a function of a person's contribution to the purposes of his work group, not only in achieving production goals, but also arising from such diverse factors as his skill with certain tools and equipment, his knowledge of a particular process or technology, his generosity, his ability to make others laugh, his contagious enthusiasm, his role as a sympathetic listener, or his willingness to accept an unpleasant task. The advantage of unofficial status is that it contains room for all; respect for a machinist does not detract from respect for a secretary, or engineer, or assembler. Nor does respect for one assembler preclude respect for another; each earns respect on the basis of unique competence factors.

Unofficial status leads to less rivalry and more satisfaction than official status based on power or wealth. Official status is more vulnerable to the whims of politics and happenstance, disappearing with demotions and organizational changes. Unofficial status is more intrinsic to the individual, is earned through personal achievements and attributes, and tends to go with him, granting him more lasting or permanent prestige. Further, unofficial status carries with it no authority-oriented status symbols. For the mature and accepted member of the work group, earned status (official or unofficial) is its own reward and needs no visible symbols. The flaunting of symbols, particularly the official reminders of inequality, is symptomatic of immaturity and serves only to undermine feelings of dignity and worth in persons who have lower official status—persons on whom those of higher official status depend for their continuing success.

Most people want to belong to a group and to be able to take pride in it. This belongingness and pride of membership constitute an opportunity and an advantage for the organization with a favorable company or product image. Attractive grounds and buildings and prestigious products are often symbols of status in a community and a source of pride at all levels of the organization. The attitude of the individual to his work group offers the key to filling jobs that would otherwise have low status, the key to getting people who will do the less attractive work. More important than the status of the job is the prestige of the group for which the job is done. Physicians and nurses, for example, have to do things that would disgust unskilled workers who did not see these actions in their professional context; yet the prestige of people in medicine is generally high. Hence, the prestige of the physician's work group and his needed contributions to it make such jobs acceptable. If the prestige of a person's group is high and he earns status by his membership in it, the unpleasant aspects of the work he has to do are of little importance.

Communication

The type and quality of communication within an organization are usually functions of the size and predominant managerial style of the organization. One consequence of the growth of an organization is the tendency to formalize communications. In the small organization, informal face-to-face communication usually finds natural expression, and managers who do not actively prevent it have the benefit of a well-informed work force. However, as the organization expands, relationships become more formalized and communications begin to lag.

A typical bureaucratic response to communication breakdown is the creation of the AVO (avoid verbal orders) and other formalized reporting processes for committing communications to paper. Though seemingly a harmless beginning, traffic in interoffice memos expands exponentially. The memo writer routinely prepares copies for his and the recipient's supervisor, and "for good measure" to others whose responsibilities are at least remotely related. These memos and their copies evoke responses in a reciprocating and exponential volume, to earn for the organization the self-imposed title of "the paper mill." The formalized communication process tends to reinforce an authority-oriented chain of command, quashing the spontaneous interactive process natural to the small organization and necessary for the functioning of a goal-oriented cohesive work force.

Apart from reasons associated with the size and complexity of the organization, communications may lose efficiency because of their defensive application against reductive managerial styles. When the interpersonal trust factor is low, "official" memos are written to provide instruction, obtain compliance, request approval, justify actions, and report progress. Informal oral commitment is no longer adequate, and rejected or unheard viewpoints find expression in the form of "letters to the file" as protection against the vagaries of the future. The massive flow of protective paperwork becomes known as the "paper umbrella."

Concomitant with organizational growth, computer technology is expanded and management systems applications are increased. The flow of memos, forms, and computer printouts increases, jamming in-baskets, filling file cabinets, and gradually encumbering the administrative process. The conformity demanded by these formalized systems takes its toll in freedom of action, administrative flexibility, and constructive expression of talent. As communications continue to fail, formalized communications increase in volume, only to increase the opportunity for, and the likelihood of, further breakdown.

Printed media seldom solve communication problems. No matter how formalized the organization, people rely on both formal and informal communication for job information. Attempts to "manage" information by publishing more communications tend to reduce the total percentage of information assimilated. In addition, the formalized management of information evokes reactive behavior and fosters the development of a reactive and hostile grapevine.

Stability

Organizational stability is a key climate factor, particularly for satisfying employee's security needs. Stability has many ramifications; for many employees it means trust in management, confidence that they will have a job as long as they do good work, or confidence that they will have advance knowledge of changes that may affect them. Ability to cope with instability is often a function of a person's role in the change. Unexpected or misunderstood changes may contribute to a climate of instability, but the same changes when evolved through understanding participation can enhance organizational stability. When people who are being affected by change have a hand in the management of the change, they are better prepared emotionally as well as intellectually to cope with it. In fact, predictable and constructive change is a welcome respite to the monotony of inescapable stability.

Instability is often a function of short-range planning. Layoffs, for example, are often followed in the near future by active hiring programs. Worse yet, a layoff in one part of an organization may coincide with an active hiring program in another segment of the organization. The coordinated efforts of managers in planning retrenchments can do much to preserve stability. Normal turnover may siphon off between 20 and 40 percent of a work force per year. An imaginative and active program for transferring, retraining, and upgrading can make this normal turnover an opportunity for upgrading and, when necessary, a constructive substitute for layoffs. Other actions for dealing with retrenchment include temporary reassigning and lending of employees within the organization, the splitting of shifts into half-day assignments, reduced hours, educational leave, rescheduling of vacations, early retirement, and other-company placement. Some companies have resorted to business diversification as a strategy for sustaining both the stability and the vitality provided through additional job opportunities.

35

The Enlargement of Competence

SAUL GELLERMAN

In the introduction to his book Management by Motivation, *Dr. Gellerman, a noted behavioral scientist, explains that he wrote the book as a practical sequel, of sorts, to one of his earlier, more theoretical works,* Motivation and Productivity *(New York: American Management Association, 1963). Although his earlier book was very successful at clarifying motivational theory for managers, it did not indicate how these theories might be applied in practical ways to specific problems.* Management by Motivation *deals with the major managerial problems to which the behavioral sciences and motivation theory address themselves. Dr. Gellerman does not seek to make an amateur behavioral scientist of the reader; rather, he attempts to train the reader to look at problems in the same way as does the behavioral scientist.*

"The Enlargement of Competence" deals with the process of individual growth and development. Dr. Gellerman begins by identifying the three primary strategies for developing managerial talent: the jungle theory, the education theory, and the agricultural theory. The jungle theory is based on the premise that talent will naturally make itself apparent, simply by outdistancing the competition. The essence of the education theory is that management consists of skills that can be taught in an educational program. The agricultural theory assumes that effective managers are grown, not born, and that job environments can be made very conducive to this type of personal growth. After discussing the limitations of the jungle theory and education theory, Dr. Gellerman concentrates on four essential characteristics of a growth-inducing environment: stretching, feedback, coaching, and career management. In the concluding portion of the selection, the author emphasizes the point that strong, decisive management action is required to remake the internal environment of a company into one that is conducive to personal growth.

There are, to oversimplify a bit, three main theories or strategies for the development of managerial talent: the jungle theory, the education theory,

Reprinted from Saul Gellerman, *Management by Motivation*, pp. 101-118, by permission of the publisher. Copyright 1968 by the American Management Association, Inc.

and the agricultural theory. Of these, the most popular and most widely practiced strategy is undoubtedly the jungle theory. It is also the least effective, and as time goes on it is likely to become even less useful as a means of providing an organization with the managers it needs.

The essence of *the jungle theory* is that talent will naturally make itself apparent, simply by outdistancing the competition. Therefore, the best way to discover it is to sit back and wait, hopefully, for some of its more obvious signs to appear. This is why managers are occasionally asked to "identify" their bright young men, on the theory that whatever it is that gives a man the potentiality for managing must surely be obvious to the man who supervises his work.

Unfortunately, the only thing that is reliably obvious to the supervisor of a man's work is the man's work. This causes no problem when management is looking for men to take over jobs that are no more than extensions of their present work. But it can lead to serious blunders when people are to be selected for jobs that are substantially different from what they are now doing. Managerial jobs are almost always substantially different from nonmanagerial jobs, and higher management jobs in particular are often quite different from lower management jobs.

The jungle theory has outlived its usefulness. In the days when most organizations had only modest managerial requirements, and when the available supply of men who were trained to think for themselves was rather thin anyway, it probably sufficed. Enough capable men came bobbing to the top, and were discernible enough by their distinctive attributes, to provide a company with all the talent it needed. This was the origin of management's gross overuse of the rating term "outstanding." This term used to refer to men whose qualities were so distinct from those of their peers that they almost literally stood out in bold relief from everyone around them. Today it has become simply a tired way of heaping an extra measure of emphasis into the ears of an audience that is already jaded by too many superlatives.

At any rate, the jungle theory is no longer equal to the task of providing a company with managers. The economics of the situation have changed. The demand for talent is greater; and, while the supply is also greater, the problem of distinguishing the potentially wise from the merely smart is too complex for natural selection alone to handle. Further, the ability to manage is not necessarily a weed; it often needs careful cultivation if it is to survive and grow to maturity. To sit back and wait for the talent to emerge by itself is to waste a precious resource.

The education theory is based on a recognition of the inadequacies of the jungle theory; it is very much in vogue in most companies that have management development programs. The essence of the education theory is that management consists of skills that can be taught, or at least induced to emerge, through an educational program. The result is often like an exclusive corporate prep school in which managers who have succeeded in attracting the attention of higher management are exposed to various internal and external programs and then turned loose to practice what they have learned.

In effect, "raw" managerial talent is passed through a management development mill in hopes of transforming it into a finished executive product.

The educational theory represented a significant breakthrough insofar as it made these points: that management skills could be deliberately developed, rather than merely harvested, and that this development was the responsibility of the employing organization rather than the local educational system or society at large. If it had not occurred, the resulting shortage of competent managerial manpower could by now have seriously curtailed industrial expansion. If this seems to overstate the case for an abundant supply of managers, one need only look at the economies of countries in which managerial talent is in shortest supply to see the results of such deficiencies.

The education theory has undoubtedly served us well. But, like most attempts to exploit a breakthrough, this one made the right diagnosis yet failed, in its first efforts, to find the most effective prescriptions. The problems have concerned what is to be taught, how, to whom, and when. None of these problems has been solved altogether satisfactorily, but we have learned a great deal about all of them.

In the early days of management development, it was assumed that whatever managers needed to learn in order to become better managers must be somewhere in the university catalogues. The courses to which aspiring managers were exposed were often lifted or adapted from curricula designed for much younger and less experienced students. The results were sometimes intellectually stimulating, sometimes bewildering, and seldom very productive of visible managerial improvement. In fact, the results were so disappointing that management development went into a temporary hiatus from which it did not emerge until it became fashionable to teach methods rather than content to managers.

This phase is still very much with us. We have attempted a more scientific approach to management development by subdividing the manager's job into its components and then teaching what are presumably the most productive approaches to those components. Thus we have the case and incident methods, in which managers are taught to trace the various causes of a problem and to compare the effects of various "solutions"; and sensitivity training, in which the manager is taught to improve his own ability to communicate, and to be communicated with, by learning about the ways in which other people react to him personally. We are concerned largely, in other words, with teaching managers how to use various techniques which are presumably useful, at least potentially, to all of them.

One of the main arguments advanced in defense of these programs when their results have been disappointing is that instruction has been wasted on the wrong students. It is not uncommon for line managers to meet their quotas for sending managers to training courses by providing those whose abilities are not too highly prized. They do this partly out of skepticism that management training courses can really add much to the abilities of managers who are already doing well, and partly out of a genuine reluctance to lose the services of such men while they are being "trained." The trainers regard these tactics as a not too subtle form of sabotage; it should hardly be surprising, they object, if when second-raters emerge from training programs they are still second-raters.

That argument has some validity, but not too much. On the basis of what we know today, it would be very difficult indeed to draw a sharp line between managers who stand to benefit from a management training course and those who are either too dull or too advanced to learn much from one. It would be equally difficult to draw such a line between training programs that should be helpful to most managers and those that will be helpful to only a few. Since neither line can be drawn with great accuracy at present, we are not likely to see the end of the assertion that the wrong people are being sent to management development programs, or of our inability to say for certain whether this is just a trainer's convenient rationalization or a valid complaint.

Actually, most training programs suffer not so much from the wrong trainees as from the wrong timing. As a rule, men are sent to these programs when they can be spared. This seldom occurs at points in their careers when the things they learn in training have much chance of becoming permanent additions to their repertories of managerial skills. They rarely get a prompt opportunity to practice what they have learned when they return to their jobs; hence the new ideas and techniques are usually forgotten rather quickly. Even if the manager does emerge from training a better man than when he entered it, the results are all too quickly dissipated. It is disturbing to speculate on how many second-raters have been prepared to become first-raters when they completed a management training course, only to lose whatever advantage they gained by the lack of an opportunity to put their new learning into practice.

The scheduling of management training has been treated as a mere administrative detail, but it appears to be every bit as important for the success of the program as course content and trainee selection. If management training cannot be scheduled at the right time in a manager's career, it probably should not be scheduled at all. The right time is when he is on the verge of a significant promotion—or immediately after such a promotion. That way he can apply whatever he has learned to the new job unencumbered by the dead weight of his old habits and preconceptions.

There should also be a motivational benefit from this kind of scheduling. If training is tied firmly to the promotional process, it will tend to become both a status symbol and a sought-after advantage. When training is applied to managers in general, as it usually is, it can hardly escape the connotations of a compulsory and profitless rest cure. Obviously, the trainees will learn more if they are pleased to have been sent to a course than if they regard it as an enforced preoccupation with irrelevancies. (As an additional side benefit, the selection problem would be solved automatically if admission to management training programs were restricted to the beneficiaries of recent or imminent promotions.)

One final point about teaching managers: The actual techniques of instruction—be they case histories, seminars, business games, or audiovisual methods—are perhaps less important in the long run than the frequency of instruction. We too often assume, wrongly, that learning takes place only when somebody is deliberately instructing. Much more managerial learning undoubtedly takes place in offices than in classrooms. But what managers learn on the job is necessarily narrowed by the limited perspectives of the job itself. They are seldom exposed *on their jobs* to new ideas or to the relationship of those jobs to other jobs. They seldom have eye-opening encounters with gifted teachers or thinkers to the extent that they can in a training course.

This is both the reason why training is given at all and the reason why its effects nearly always dissipate over time—even when the scheduling and selection are handled as they should be. If management training consists only of an isolated episode in a long career, it can scarcely be expected to have more than a minor and temporary influence on a man's competence to manage. This brings us to one of those uncomfortable realities which are too often ignored, simply because they were not obvious from the outset: *Management training is an open-ended investment.* If it is worthwhile at all, it is worthwhile only if it is repeated periodically. The course content itself can and should change, but the basic strategy of training—an interlude away from the job, devoted exclusively to the enlargement of competence—must recur fairly often to maintain lasting benefits. Ten times in the course of a career would not be too frequent an exposure to management training, especially for those men who rise to positions of higher responsibility.

If training should be timed to coincide with promotions, if training should be repeated periodically, and if training necessarily interrupts a busy working routine, it follows that there must be a centralized, high-level coordination of the training function. Whoever passes on promotions should also control entry into management training programs. In large organizations, this means that there will probably be several control points for both promotion and training, depending on the level and perhaps also on the functional specialization of the managers concerned.

The educational approach to management development therefore requires an extensive apparatus if it is to function well. Most of the complaints and disappointments that have been voiced about the results of this approach are probably traceable to a failure to provide enough of that apparatus; to trying, as it were, to buy management development at bargain rates. In this sense, the full potential of the educational approach has not yet been tapped, nor has a really definitive test of its potentialities yet been made.

The agricultural approach to management development is based on the premises that effective managers are grown, not born; and that, since most of this growth takes place outside the context of formal training programs, it is important that managers work in a job environment that is as growth-conducive as possible. Managers' jobs should be structured, in other words, not only to get the work itself done well, but also to increase the likelihood that the incumbents will qualify for promotion—and therefore for entry into formal training programs.

Competence can be encouraged to grow in the same sense that a tree can be encouraged to grow. This is not done by leaving it to develop as best it can in competition with others (the jungle approach), and not solely by giving it an occasional dose of fertilizer (which is the essence of the educational approach, and wags can do with that what they will). Rather, competence grows when it is systematically nourished, pruned of its errors, and transplanted, as it grows larger, to new ground on which it has ample room to flourish.

To get away from metaphor, what is a growth-inducing environment? It probably includes at least four factors: stretching, feedback, coaching, and career management. *Stretching* means assigning a man to responsibilities that are always a bit beyond those the man himself or any of his superiors feel he is ready for. Because we so often underestimate what a man is capable of doing, especially with regard to problems with which he has had little experience, stretching is much more likely to result in pleasant surprises than in disappointments. If it is gradual enough, the damage done by occasional disappointments can be minimized and easily remedied. Meantime, stretching not only accelerates the growth of competence but also delivers more productivity than would ordinarily be expected.

But there is a much subtler and more important advantage to stretching. It is often assumed that, when people achieve something of substantial importance, it is because they were highly motivated to do what they did. As far as cause and effect are concerned, the sequence is usually the reverse. That is, people who have achieved something of consequence for *any* reason frequently develop a taste for achievement. The process of becoming motivated to high achievement is not unlike the process of becoming motivated to eat salted peanuts: The motivation for the experience is touched off by the original encounter and sustained by further encounters. True, some people respond more strongly than others to having had to achieve something. But most people's interest in achievement can probably be increased by exposing them to what is, for them, a significant accomplishment.

There is a sense, then, in which people have to be thrust into achievement in order to awaken their appetite for more achievement, and this is precisely what stretching accomplishes. It also offers yet another advantage which can be of enormous motivational consequence for any organization. If stretching is used as a conscious policy for a period of years, it can eventually teach managers to stop underestimating people. It is precisely this habit which causes people to shrink—in despair, boredom, or frustration—to fit the undersized roles their superiors have conceived for them.

Feedback for managers is much discussed but still not really understood. First of all, there seem to be at least two kinds of information about themselves which managers need in order to develop optimally. Further, it is evidently important that these two kinds of feedback be given separately. One is the classical form of performance feedback in which a man is told how his work has been rated by his superiors. The second is less frequently provided, but it is at least equally important: periodic, frank reappraisal of the manager's promotion prospects.

When management people complain that they "don't know where they stand," they usually want the second kind of feedback (information on career prospects), but the nostrum that is usually prescribed is the first kind of feedback (performance appraisal). Not surprisingly, the complaint continues, and orthodox performance appraisal programs are regarded uneasily both by those who administer them and by those who are the presumed beneficiaries. There is no millennium in sight in the area of performance appraisal, but there does seem to be some merit in giving it in separate and clearly labeled doses. At least the man on the receiving end will then know what to expect.

By now it has been pretty well established that performance appraisal should deal largely with results rather than with ratings of such hard-to-define-or-measure qualities as "imaginativeness" or "aggressiveness." It is also preferable to measure results in terms of the extent to which previously agreed-to performance targets have been reached. It is generally considered wise to avoid having to appraise a man's personality in the process of appraising his work, since few people are capable (or, for that matter, desirous) of changing their fundamental make-up in order to please their supervisor. There is almost always room for more than one style or approach to any management job, and the appraiser should not quibble with style as long as the results are within range of target.

The function of performance appraisal is to teach, not to exhort or admonish. The manager can learn if it can be shown that his actions have been on or off target, especially when the target has been objectively defined. He can see the extent to which his actions have been effective or ineffective and adjust them accordingly. But he can hardly learn if the target consists of some vague adjective that can mean almost anything to anybody—if, for instance, he is told to become more "interested" or less "reserved." All such words point to is an image, not action, and that image is almost impossible to change without having enough clues to which kinds of action have created it and which kinds can dispel it.

Performance appraisal is on much firmer ground when it deals primarily with objectively defined operational results and when it deals with style or performance characteristics only to the extent that they can be shown to have affected results. It is better off when it deals with personality not at all. An effective performance appraisal statement—effective in the sense of promoting learning and growth—is really little more than a summary of what both parties should already know, since performance can be readily measured against objective targets. This gives rise to one of the most frequent criticisms of performance appraisal: that it should be unnecessary to summarize the obvious formally. But the truth is not so simple as that. If both parties are not aware that a summary will have to be written and discussed, the targets are not likely to receive as much attention; and the results, consequently, may not be so "obvious." There is also the question of authenticity: While higher managers often expect their subordinates to draw the "obvious" conclusions from their many day-to-day reviews during the year, the subordinates are likely to be much less impressed by their own conclusions than by a summary from the lips of the men who will have the most to say about their future. Lastly, a formal review of performance against one set of targets forms a logical and necessary basis for establishing a new set—especially if the manager is to be stretched.

A performance appraisal program would, however, be of comparatively little value if it stopped there. No human relationship is really quite so sterile as the restriction on "keeping personalities out of it" would seem to imply. The plain fact is that personality does enter into many decisions about a manager, especially promotional decisions. Further, since so much of a manager's time is spent in giving and receiving information, his personal impact on people can have a decided effect on his own effectiveness in higher positions. Therefore, while personality has no legitimate place in a review of what a man has accomplished, it inevitably enters into a consideration of what he will be permitted to attempt to accomplish.

This is why career counseling can be so difficult to bring off successfully. Perhaps it is also why we so seldom attempt to counsel our subordinates. Yet the costs of not making the attempt are often very high. When men are growing—that is, increasing their competence—they are naturally more interested in the future than in the past. The effect on their morale of an uncertain future, or a future that is simply not certain enough, can be profound. Some may decide that the gamble of staying in the company is not worth the risk of getting nowhere or of advancing too slowly. This is probably the main reason for the departure of high-potential managers. Other promising men who are faced with the prospect of slow or uncertain advancement simply lose their momentum and cease to grow as quickly as before. While most high-potential managers can tolerate some degree of ambiguity, few can endure too much of it for too long about a subject as close to their hearts as their own careers.

Career counseling is probably the most effective form of insurance against these risks. Its costs (in terms of bruised egos or personal animosities) can be minimized if the program is carried out with intelligence and discretion. To do this properly requires that certain ground rules be clearly established. At the very least, these should include three concepts: that the counseling is only advisory, not binding; that it attempts to forecast only the immediate future (say, the next two or three years), not an entire career; and that it is necessarily limited to generalities and estimates. These restrictions do not vitiate the program, provided the counseling is timed properly and, most important of all, is reasonably frank.

The best time for career counseling is when a manager is about midway to two-thirds of the way through a "normal" period of assignment to a specific job. This will vary from company to company and even, to some extent, within a single company. The important thing is that the issue be faced at about the time it usually tends to become uppermost in the manager's mind: when he can foresee the end of his present assignment or when he begins to feel that he has developed about as much mastery of it as he is likely to, so that the inherent challenge of the job is fading. That is when he will naturally wonder what is in store for him next. It is at precisely this point—and a similar stage will occur in every one of his major assignments—that *the manager's motives and those of his superiors are likely to be in conflict.*

His superiors, for their part, can now see the advent of a period of maximum return on their "investment," which is represented by the period during which the manager was learning to handle his job and gradually building up to top efficiency. They will naturally tend to feel that it is in the company's best interests to keep him there as long as possible. But the manager may feel quite differently about the matter. Instead of regarding the first phase of his assignment as a training ground in which he was prepared for a long and profitable tenure in one position, he probably will regard it as a proving ground on which he demonstrated his fitness to be advanced to another position. In other words, he may not want to be an expert in his present job—indeed, if he is strongly motivated to enlarge his managerial competence, he will probably look upon any opportunity to become an expert as a trap. He will want to broaden, not deepen, his experience so as to maximize his opportunities for further growth and achievement. As this conflict comes to the fore, he is likely to be increasingly disturbed by the possibility that the more effectively he handles his job, the more likely it is to turn into a trap instead of a stepping stone.

Career counseling that is timed to coincide with these natural periods of strain can serve three useful purposes. First, it can clear the air by demonstrating that management is neither oblivious nor indifferent to the problem. Second, it should aim to give the manager as realistic a perspective as possible of his own future, so as to prevent both gross overoptimism (which inevitably leads to disappointment) and gross overpessimism (which leads to needless demoralization). The third advantage is the most important of all: Career counseling compels both management and the individual to begin thinking seriously about the kinds of assignments for which he should be considered next. Failure to begin this kind of planning early enough leads to hasty and often ill-considered decisions later on.

The keys to effective career counseling, however, are frankness and realism. These must begin with a clear understanding that performance in a job at one level does not necessarily qualify a man for a job at a higher level.

Neither does a man "earn" the opportunity to try his hand at a higher-level job through his performance in a lower-level job. This distinction is seldom made very clear, perhaps because it seems to be in the short-range interests of both the manager and his company to leave it vague. Thus the manager may expect his present performance to weigh in his favor, even if he knows it does not necessarily give any clue to his capacity for handling a higher-level job. The company, for its part, is eager to preserve the manager's present performance by supporting his morale, even if that means letting him believe his promotability will be measured by a possibly irrelevant standard.

This mutual reluctance to dispense with a myth has prompted one seasoned observer of management, A. T. M. Wilson of Unilever, Ltd., to remark that

> It is difficult to avoid an impression that many systems of appraisal permit a collusive blurring, as between senior and subordinates, of the difference between, on the one hand, immediate level of performance and, on the other, potential for future performance in a different working milieu with different responsibilities which demand different skills.[1]

It is equally difficult to avoid the conclusion that the myth is unnecessary and even harmful. Illusions make poor motivators, if only because they inevitably turn a man away from his proper goal. The point must be made, and made clearly, that while current performance has a great deal to do with a man's pay and reputation, and even with his ability to attract the attention of executives who can influence his career, it does not *in itself* determine whether he should be considered for promotion. This is one of the reasons why performance appraisal and career counseling should occur separately: to emphasize that one does not necessarily determine the other. There are, of course, standards for judging promotability, and to some extent these may be observable in a man's current work. We will review some of these standards later in this book. The important point now is that believability is the essential element in career counseling, and in the long run believability rests on candor and on looking facts straight in the eye.

In any case, specific career plans will probably not have been made at this point, and no realistic manager would be impressed by such long-range prophecy. There are, however, three kinds of information which *can* be disclosed. Together they can achieve the motivational purpose of career counseling, which is to provide the growth-oriented individual with a yardstick against which to measure both his progress and his ambitions. The first kind of information concerns the relative speed of advancement which can be expected during the forecast period. This can be expressed in terms of

---

[1] A. T. M. Wilson, "Some Sociological Aspects of Systematic Management Development," *The Journal of Management Studies*, Vol. 3, No. 1 (February, 1966).

being faster than, slower than, or equal to the "average" rate—provided the average has been calculated and is generally known. The second kind of information concerns the range of organizational levels within which the individual can expect to be working during this period, usually expressed in terms of "example" jobs with which he is likely to be familiar. The third kind of information concerns functional groups and, when appropriate, geographical locations to which the individual might be assigned.

All this does is to give the manager some realistic parameters within which to focus his immediate hopes and plans. He knows that he must continue to deliver on his present job before any of the generalities expressed in his career counseling can harden into certainty. But he also knows that the opportunity for further growth is being held out to him. He knows which specific factors in his job or in his company may stand in his way and which ones are working for him. He knows, in a word, where he stands relative to the goals that matter most to him. Despite the fact that it has to be presented in a general and noncommittal form, this is precisely the kind of feedback he needs in order to maintain his motivation at a high level.

The third component of a growth-inducing job environment for managers is *coaching*. An opportunity to analyze problems, review plans, and "post-mortem" his mistakes can be invaluable for a manager. It sharpens his understanding of the environment in which he is working and fixes the lessons of his experience more firmly in his mind than they otherwise could be. This kind of relationship between a manager and an interested, well-informed associate is often found to have existed during the early phases of highly successful executive careers. It ought to be found throughout the careers of all managers, or at least of those managers who would appear to have more potential than most others.

Coaching is a valid but too often overlooked teaching tool. However, it is important to note that the function of a coach is quite different from that of a teacher. A coach does not give the manager the "right" answer to his problems; in fact, he may not even pretend to know it himself. Rather, he serves as a sounding board for the manager's ideas, as a friendly critic (when necessary) of those ideas, as a source of facts and ideas from his own broader experience, and sometimes as a sort of devil's advocate to test the strength of the manager's plans before they are formally implemented. The tactics used by the coach are not so important, however, as his basic commitment. He should be wholly committed to helping the manager to be as successful as possible, and this commitment should come from company policy, not personal altruism.

This is probably the main reason why coaching is so rarely used in industry. Most people in management are rewarded for making themselves successful, not for making other managers successful. In most companies there is simply no traditional role for a managerial coach: no job description, no compensation plan, no box on the organization chart. When coaching occurs, it is due to the wisdom and consideration of a thoughtful executive or sometimes to the efforts of a consultant who, usually, was retained for other reasons. Coaching seldom occurs as the result of a deliberate corporate policy to encourage it. But it should.

A tour of duty as a coach (perhaps "counselor" would be a more suitable title) could be highly productive for both a seasoned executive and his company. To be most effective, coaching should be a full-time job, not a secondary responsibility. An assignment to coaching should last at least a year, preferably two, and men should be selected for coaching on the basis of proven performance and experience at the level of the men they will be assigned to assist. Each coach should be carefully briefed by all the relevant executives—that is, those in the direct management line above the managers to be coached—both prior to, and periodically during, their assignment. This should serve the purpose of maintaining the perspective of overall company strategy, not "reporting" on the progress of the managers or evaluating their work. For reasons to be elaborated later, the coach's mission should be entirely to help the managers assigned to him; he should not give them marks for their work. Depending on the level, function, and location of the managers being developed, a well-organized coach should be able to work effectively with upward of half a dozen men simultaneously.

Coaching can and should be done by a manager's immediate superior, as well as by a specially appointed staff adviser. But, in the last analysis, the superior's main responsibility is to get the job done, and this is not always compatible with the patient and frankly partisan (pro-manager) role that makes the coach effective as a developer of managers. Because of the superior's fundamental commitment to line responsibility, he must regard each of the managers reporting to him as basically a tool for getting the job done—a tool which, if need be, can be discarded and replaced. To the coach, however, the manager is not a means to an end but a resource to be enriched and strengthened. It is in the company's interests that both of these functions, line management and management development, be performed and that neither have to suffer because of the other. This cannot be achieved by limiting either function to the part-time responsibility of anyone. There is room for full-time managerial coaching in addition to the necessarily part-time efforts of a manager's superiors. Indeed, it is probably no exaggeration to say that the function probably cannot be handled properly without full-time coaching.

All these considerations have profound implications for the ways in which companies are organized and managers are deployed.

Any organizational change in the direction of fostering a growth-inducing environment faces two major problems. The first is the obvious one of setting up the apparatus which will develop and administer programs designed to encourage men, and especially managers, to continually expand the range and depth of their competence. The second is subtler but at least equally important; and unless it is successfully solved, the effort expended in solving the first problem will have been to little avail. This is to make the shift toward a growth-inducing environment convincing by overcoming the notion, so widespread in most organizations, that despite occasional flirtations with new managerial fads the men at the top will always revert to a basically cynical and unresponsive style of management. Most companies, whether they like it or not, have been tarred with the same brush, simply because of the long tradition which holds that places of employment are meant for working and not for learning. That there is an enormous historical inertia to be overcome is evidenced by the gulf that separates work from growth in a great many minds.

Therefore, any company decision to treat the competence of its managers as an income-producing asset to be enlarged instead of, implicitly, as a commodity to be purchased will naturally create skepticism in the men it is intended to benefit. Strong, lasting, and convincing proof of a genuine conversion by top management to the cultivation of personal growth as a corporate way of life must be given. Otherwise, too many managers will find ways to circumvent or undermine the new policies; they will not want to be overcommitted to them when the "inevitable" reversion to the old philosophy occurs. Consequently, nothing less than a permanent change in the company's organizational structure, to accommodate a "career management" function with the avowed purpose of remaking the internal environment of the company, is likely to be capable of doing the job.

It may seem paradoxical to suggest that a growth-inducing environment is best established by executive fiat. There is little doubt, however, that a convincing commitment to personal growth as a company goal has to come from the top of the organization. So must the apparatus that can get the processes of growth into motion. This apparatus is more than an organizational necessity; it is tangible proof of the size of the bet that top management is willing to make on the potentialities of its own people. A growth-inducing environment can be created only when top management is sold on both the necessity and the possibility of doing so—and sold beyond lip service to the point of committing enough men, money, and power to the career management function to enable it to do its job.

Effective career management needs all three. Someone must be charged with administering these programs. In large organizations it may require several people or several decentralized departments; the responsibility, in any case, should be undivided. If career management is not somebody's full-time job and the principal basis for somebody's performance appraisal, it will stand in too great danger of not getting all the attention it deserves. Further, in order to insure that these programs are properly coordinated, without the tendency of so many well-intentioned personnel programs to be honored in the breach, the career management function should report to a high managerial level. At the very least it should report to a company's chief personnel officer; and if that official has only the modest organizational stature that many personnel managers have, the career management function should report instead to the same corporate officer to whom personnel ultimately reports.

This is not suggested merely for the sake of glorifying the career management function. Rather it is a matter of facing organizational realities. There is no point in establishing this kind of function if it is not to be given all the necessary means to accomplish its mission. Precisely because career management *must* intrude into so many citadels of traditional managerial prerogative—checking the timing of management training, for example, or reviewing assignment plans to insure that stretching takes place—it needs a sufficient measure of power to get its job done. To some extent, this kind of leverage may be earned by an incumbent who wins the respect of his fellow managers for his ability and fairness. But this is usually too slender a reed on which to allow the fortunes of career management to lean.

In most companies, power is represented mainly by the level of the executive whose wrath is likely to be incurred when a policy is ignored or circumvented, and the same principle undoubtedly applies to career management. The manager of this function must therefore be clothed with the authority to require, if necessary, that the company's career management policies be adhered to and that any exceptions to these policies be cleared with him. To those who object that this would alter the balance of power between line and staff in the direction of the latter, I can only agree that it does—and argue that the results would justify it. When a company is managed by men who are primarily motivated to increase their competence, rather than to guard their spheres of influence, the line-staff distinction becomes less important than the advancement of the organization as a whole—and the fun of being part of it.

There are at least seven functions whose control should be centralized in the career management group. These are:

1. Assessing the potentialities of managers for acquiring the competence to handle heavier responsibilities.
2. Appraising performance. This function is obviously related to the assessment of potential, yet there are important differences between the two functions which justify their being treated separately.
3. Reviewing individual development plans and promotion plans to insure that the stretching concept is being implemented judiciously yet without excessive timidity.
4. Scheduling, and helping superiors to prepare for, career counseling.
5. Determining the proper time for formal management training for each manager, as well as the types of course content most useful for him to study during each of his exposures to formal instruction.
6. Selecting, training, assigning, and evaluating management counselors (or coaches). Since the demand for coaches is likely to be chronically in excess of the supply, the career management group would also have to decide which managers would most benefit the company by being coached.
7. Maintaining an up-to-date, relevant, and reasonably complete "inventory" of managers.

Of these seven functions, undoubtedly the most important and most difficult to administer are the assessment of executive potential and the appraisal of executive performance. ...

36

The T-Groups

CHRIS ARGYRIS

This and the following two selections present a debate regarding the merits of sensitivity training as a management development technique. Although all three articles were written in the middle 1960s, the potential value of sensitivity training is still hotly debated. We have chosen these three selections because the participants in this particular debate, Dr. Chris Argyris of Yale University and Dr. George S. Odiorne of the University of Utah, pinpoint key issues clearly and concisely.

In recent years, sensitivity training, or the "encounter movement," as it is more popularly termed, has been receiving an increasing amount of publicity. Growing numbers of people have participated in encounter sessions, and this has precipitated growing debate on the pros and cons of this educational approach. In the selection that follows, Dr. Argyris, an early advocate of this approach, describes the educational benefits of sensitivity training.

A laboratory program is designed to provide as many experiences as possible where psychological success, self-esteem, and interpersonal competence can be increased; where dependence, control, can be decreased; and where emotional behavior when and if it is relevant can be as fit a subject for discussion as any "rational" topic. ...

THE T-GROUP

The core of most laboratories is the T-Group. ... Basically it is a group experience designed to provide maximum possible opportunity for the individuals to expose their behavior, give and receive feedback, experiment with new behavior, and develop everlasting awareness and acceptance of self and others. The T-Group also provides ... possibilities to learn the nature of effective group functioning. Individuals are able to learn how to develop a group that achieves specific goals with minimum possible human cost. ...

It is in the T-Group that one finds the emphasis on the participants' creating and diagnosing their own behavior, developing distributive leadership and consensus decision-making norms to protect the deviants, and, finally, sharing as much as possible all the information that is created within, and as a result of, the T-Group experience. ... We are not suggesting that organizations be administered like T-Groups. However, we are hypothesizing that they should include structures like T-Groups for certain selected decisions. ...

Mouton and Blake[1] describe the T-Group which they call a *development group* as follows:

The fundamental-dilemma-producing feature of a human-relations laboratory is the development group. The development group is composed of 8 to 12 members, whose explicit goal is to study their own interactions as a group. No leader or power structure is provided. No rules or procedures are given to structure interaction. No task, topic or agenda for discussion is inserted to serve as a guide for action. Thus, the group is faced with critical dilemmas in several fundamental areas of relationships in a group situation. What shall we do or talk about? How shall we relate to one another? What are our rules for interactions? What can we accomplish? How do we make a decision on any of these things? All of these issues and many more are dilemmas initially present in the development group. ...

In addition to group-level phenomena, much attention is centered on individuals trying out new and different ways of relating to each other. For example, an overbearing, long-talking person may try being silent for an extended period of time; a person who withdraws when under attack may experiment with more aggressive forms of reactions; feelings may be openly expressed. The dilemmas posed by the development group impel inventive, seeking, searching behavior on both the group and the individual level.

ORGANIZATIONAL DIAGNOSTIC EXPERIENCES

When a laboratory program is composed of a group of executives who work with each other the organizational diagnostic experiences are very important. Each executive is asked to come to the laboratory with an agenda or topic that is important to him and to the organization. During the laboratory he is asked to lead the group in a discussion of the topic. The discussion is taped and observed by the staff.

Once the discussion is completed, the group members listen to

[1] James S. Mouton and Robert Blake, *University Training in Human Relations Skill*, The University of Texas, mimeographed.

themselves on the tape. They analyze the interpersonal and group dynamics that occurred in the making of the decision and how these factors influenced their decision making. Usually, they hear how they cut each other off, did not listen, manipulated, pressured, created win-lose alternatives, etc.

Such an analysis typically leads the executives to ask such questions as: Why do we do this to each other? What do we wish to do about this, if anything?

In the cases known to the writer, the executives became highly involved in answering these questions. Few held back to cite interpersonal and organizational reasons why they feel they have to behave as they do. Most deplore the fact that time must be wasted and much energy utilized in this "windmilling" behavior. It is quite frequent for someone to ask, "But if we do not like this, why don't we do something about it?"

Under these conditions, the learnings developed in the laboratory are intimately interrelated with the every-day "real" problems of the organization. Where this has occurred, the members do not return to the organization with the same degree of bewilderment that executives show who have gone to laboratories full of strangers. Under these conditions it is quite common for the executive to wonder how he will use the information about human competence that he has learned when he returns back home.

Another frequently used learning experience is to break down the participants into groups of four. Sessions are held where each individual has the opportunity to act as a consultant giving help and as an individual receiving help; the nature of help is usually related to increasing self-awareness and competence.

One of the central problems of organizations is the intergroup rivalries and hostilities that exist among departments. If there is time in a laboratory, this topic should be dealt with. Again, it is best introduced by creating the situation where the executives compete against one another in groups under "win-lose" conditions.

37

The Trouble with Sensitivity Training

GEORGE S. ODIORNE

In this selection, Dr. George S. Odiorne, formerly of the University of Michigan and now Dean of the College of Business Administration at the University of Utah, discusses some of the problems associated with sensitivity training. He speaks of a sensitivity-training laboratory as a "psychological

Reprinted from George S. Odiorne, "The Trouble with Sensitivity Training," *Training Directors Journal* (October 1963), by special permission of the publisher. Copyright 1963 by the American Society for Training and Development.

nudist camp" where the trainee goes through an "emotional binge." Dr. Odiorne believes that laboratory education lacks sufficient direction. He prefers training that has specific goals, clearly identified terminal behavior, and a well-defined structure. He doubts that the T-Group is likely to have a permanent impact on trainees who return to their former environment. Although Odiorne believes that management training is vital for companies in our competitive economy, he is not at all convinced that laboratory training is the answer.

Is sensitivity training really training? Training should change behavior. How can we demonstrate changed behavior? We should be able to measure it. One of the most common outcomes of sensitivity training is that the people who undergo it describe the experience as one which "I am sure has had an effect on me but it's too early to tell just how." These are the fortunate ones.

Not long ago a large engineering company in the midwest was prevailed upon by a consulting firm to bring a group of their research executives to a lodge in Wisconsin for sensitivity training. The leader of the session had no prior training in the conduct of such sessions. During one horrible week-end he broke down the barriers of formal courtesy which had substituted quite successfully for human relations in this successful lab for many years. People spoke frankly of their hostilities. At this point they went back to the lab, their dislikes laid bare, with no substitute behavior being provided. Chaos immediately took over. People who had worked in good-mannered pomposity for years, turning out patents and papers at a prodigious pace, began to engage in organized politicking to get square. Senior scientists quit in droves and a major purge took place. Candid observations made up at the lake hung heavy between colleagues. ... People who had learned that they were seen as SOB's were somewhat less than grateful to the colleague who had enlightened them and had made them aware of this fact. ...

This is training? ...

TRAINING CRITERIA

To qualify as sound training, it would seem that these criteria should be met.

Criteria No. 1: In good training the desired terminal behavior can be identified before the training begins. Sensitivity training simply doesn't do this. ...

. . .

Criteria No. 2: The course of change is comprised of some logical small steps. ... In sensitivity training not only are the participants unaware of what the outcome will be, but in many instances, since there are no controls, neither are the trainers. In most labs, the coordination of what the respective trainers will do at what time is as vague at the middle and end as it was in the beginning. Typically, the staff of a lab is assembled by mail or phone from the in-group which conducts such sessions. They agree to gather one day ahead of the arrival of the subjects to be trained. They divide up the chores under the direction of the assembler of the program. There is little chance for any detailed checking of objectives of individual sessions, or any careful planning so that progressive stages of training will occur. Accordingly, most such sessions lack many of the elements of training which might change behavior, simply because they are so ineffectually run. If a general statement of objectives is made, it goes along the line of saying something like "open up their minds" or something equally vague. *How* open, or even what an open mind *is*, isn't defined. ...

... The only reinforcements which shape behavior are those randomly provided by a group of unknown composition. (The major criteria for admission being that of being able to pay the registration fee. This builds in a reinforcement of middle-class values and little more.)

Value changes are not based upon careful analysis of the present values which are to be changed, nor even explicit statements of desired terminal values sought. Since value changes could only be measured by verbal or written behavior at the end of the course, and no such values are clearly defined the effort at measuring behavior change runs into logical blocks. The few efforts at evaluation of behavior change from laboratories have not been clearly successful, and certainly are not wholly reliable.

... Because the T-Group is the major source of reinforcement, and their values are mixed, then the reinforcement of emitted behavior is just as likely to be for the wrong things as the right things.

Specific causes of changes unclear. More pointedly, there is no attempt to measure the relative effects of the different parts of the laboratory upon the learner. Are the T-Groups the crucial variable? How can we be sure the T-Group hasn't changed the trainee in one direction, and the lectures in another? Where observation and anecdotal evidence points to behavior change after a lab how can we know which training method effected the change; the role playing (which has been proven to change behavior even outside laboratory groups), the informal bull sessions, or simply the opportunity to live in a closed community for two weeks with others? Do different T-Group leader personalities (or reputations) or marvelously skilled lectures such as Argyris delivers have differential effects in changing behavior? Since we can't prove behavior change anyhow, all of these are merely speculative questions.

Criteria No. 3: The learning is under control. The major reason that control is not present in sensitivity training is that it is based on creating stress situations for their own sake which may go out of control and often do. ...

... The trainee has been through an emotional binge which has some totally unpredictable effects. The possibility that uncontrolled experience may be harmful is just as probable as it's being helpful. In any event it can hardly be called training.

. . .

Criteria No. 4: There are selection standards for admission. The more serious defects of sensitivity training relate to admissions standards. The present condition is such that anybody with the registration fee can attend. He may already be sensitive and aware, in fact may be too much so. You could make a good case that far too many people who are attracted to it are those who are emotionally high strung and overly sensitive. ... How about the overprotected individual whose pressing need is that he toughen up a bit because he is already a mass of quivering ganglions, thinking and feeling on several levels of perception at the same time, and therefore totally incompetent at the world of business infighting? For this one, the lab becomes a great psychological nudist camp in which he bares his pale sensitive soul to the hard-nosed autocratic ruffians in his T-Group and gets roundly clobbered. He goes away with his sense of inferiority indelibly reinforced. The bullies, of course, have also reinforced their roughneck tendencies upon him. ...

. . .

Criteria No. 5: Evaluation of results. ... Since the sensitivity trainers don't know what the goal of such training is, any road will get them there, and any outcome is exactly what can be expected. Small wonder nobody has yet done a rigorously executed evaluation of effect.

An experience it is, without doubt. Training, I'm afraid it is not, and the company that spends its cash on sending people to the more esoteric kinds is being unfair to their shareholders. No proof has been shown that it changes behavior on the job.

. . .

The real flaw in sensitivity training is that it isn't consistent with business and the economic world we live in. ... We may struggle through proofs that the new participative styles of management are more productive than autocratic styles, but then there crops up General Motors, which is built upon tight technical organization and tight discipline, being the most successful corporation that ever existed.

. . .

Survival of firms is serious business these days. Of the 4,500,000 companies in this country, the average length of life is seven years. ... Managers obviously need training in their jobs to help them and their firms survive. All too often they have learned their management by *imitation*. Behavioral science has much to offer in finding new and better ways of managing. This could be greatly accelerated if the new utopians could become more objective in their science. The great difficulty isn't whether they are right or wrong in their assumptions about participative versus autocratic management ... or liberty versus oppression. The point is that we can't trust them as being good scientists as long as every research proves *one position* to which our common experience tells us there are some startling exceptions that work even better.

Many businessmen know the true value of *situational thinking* in which you are sometimes autocratic or downright ruthless; coupled with other times when you are ... gentle ... with people's sensibilities. ...

A form of management training which has good guys and bad guys arbitrarily built into it to fit a utopian idea of panacean democracy is not safe for a business or any other form of administrative organization to experiment with.

Until the sensitivity trainers have come forth with a school which takes the overly sensitive man and toughens him up into a rough and ready model of man as well as the reverse, I can only suggest to businessmen that they avoid the entire cult.

38

In Defense of Laboratory Training

CHRIS ARGYRIS

In this selection, Dr. Argyris offers a rebuttal to the attack on sensitivity training that was made by Dr. Odiorne in the preceding reading. Near the end of this excerpt, after Argyris has responded to a question put to him by Dr. Jerry Rosenberg of the New York State School of Industrial and Labor Relations, Cornell University, Odiorne pointedly observes that the body of knowledge called management is fed by a number of disciplines, and the behavioral sciences are only some of these disciplines. Managers must, he concludes, keep the behavioral sciences in perspective.

Yesterday I received Odiorne's paper. I became—to use the laboratory language—hostile. I felt his attack should not go unchallenged. ...

Reprinted from Chris Argyris, "In Defense of Laboratory Training," *Training Directors Journal* (October 1963), by special permission of the publisher. Copyright 1963 by the American Society for Training and Development.

In my view, the problem with his presentation is not a disagreement with documented facts, because he presents very few. My problem is that I want to try to correct the distortions that he has made—distortions that he has been making throughout the country and that so far have gone unchallenged. ...

I have one other problem. It is never clear to which group Odiorne is referring. I will be speaking of the National Training Laboratories network.

Here are some of the facts as I see them:

1. I hope that my "Brief Description of Laboratory Education" made it clear that laboratory education *does* have objectives. Indeed, in every laboratory many hours are spent discussing and analyzing these objectives. However, as we shall see in a moment, the educators in a laboratory program do not try to jam these down the throats of the participants.

2. I agree that the Wisconsin incident was a horrible mess. But, my opponent failed to read the full text of his own manuscript and I quote, *"The leader of the session had no prior training in the conduct of such sessions."* (Italics mine.)

3. The experience of NTL as far as people having psychotic breakdowns is better than the population at large, and, at least, more than twice as good as the experience of students at Michigan and Yale. ... In over 10,000 cases, there have been about four individuals who have had psychotic episodes and who became seriously ill. All of these people had previous psychiatric histories. ...

• • •

4. Even though there is a lower level of research activity at laboratories than NTL staff wish, I think it is safe to say that more research has been conducted at, and about, laboratories than all the other executive programs combined—and this definitely includes the executive programs administered by my opponent. ...

5. The policy of NTL has been, and continues to be, to raise its standards of all its activities and this most certainly includes the development and choice of faculty. For example, for the last three years, in order for a new man to become a member of the NTL network, he has to have completed an approved professional graduate training (usually a Ph.D. program). Then he must take a rigorous three-month program. He participates as a member of a laboratory program and later, as a junior staff member. His training includes planning, developing, and executing an entire laboratory program under the guidance of a senior faculty member. Also, he attends a series of meetings during the remainder of the year. Finally, he serves as a junior staff member until his peers believe that he is ready to be voted as a senior fellow (which usually requires, at least, five years of experience).

6. NTL is not a profit-making organization. ... Actually, we underpay ourselves (in the executive labs) in order to help NTL pay for those labs (for example, for students and churches) that have gone into the red.

7. The majority of NTL labs have a Dean appointed from a year to six months before the lab is scheduled to take place. The staff is selected from the network of men available. Each individual is given an opportunity to state his preference for the lab he prefers to attend. The final selections are made by the Deans. The staff usually meets for three days at least four months ahead of time to plan the lab and to develop assignments to work on back at home. Later another three days are spent in planning for the lab. Also, it should be clear that by their very nature labs cannot be completely preplanned. When there are labs where the early planning is not done, it is primarily for the lack of money to pay for the expenses of these men to meet.

8. Before we—or General Motors—can believe in my opponent's generalizations about the effectiveness of ... authoritarian management we need to have much more information than he has just given.

For example, there are some data to suggest that ... [an authoritarian] company (and I can only take Odiorne's word that GM is such a company) gets away with being fully ... [authoritarian] by paying through the nose with a militant union, costly strikes, slowdowns, goldbricking, and by pouring oil over these troubled labor and management waters in the form of benefits and all types of social security services.

It is quite plausible that ... [such a company] can make much money at the same time it can be an excellent teacher to the American worker to accept socialism. ...

. . .

The logic used by my opponent is intriguing: describe a process that probably never existed; give no evidence for it; categorically state that this is *the* process; then conclude that it doesn't work. ...

. . .

Odiorne writes that there has not been any evidence of change in "back home" behavior as a result of the training. This is not true. ...

Miles,[1] Buchanan,[2] Boyd,[3] and Shutz[4] have conducted research in

[1] Matthew B. Miles, "Human Relations Training Processes and Outcomes," *Journal of Counselling Psychology*, Vol. 7, No. 4 (1960), 301-306.

[2] Paul Buchanan, *The Work Situation Questionnaire as a Measure of the Effect of Senior Management Seminar* (The New Jersey Standard Oil Co.).

[3] J. B. Boyd, *Findings of Research into Senior Management Seminars* (Personal Responsibility Department, The Hydro-Electric Power Commission of Ontario, June 22, 1962).

[4] William C. Shutz and Vernon L. Allen, *On T-Groups* (Berkeley, Calif.: University of California).

which they have asked others (than the subjects) to report on behavioral change. The positive as well as the negative results were reported. (In the first, third, and fourth studies appropriate control groups were used.)[5]

In the study that I conducted (and Odiorne quotes), I cited evidence for behavioral change.[6]

DISCUSSION

Dr. Jerry Rosenberg (assistant professor, New York State School of Industrial and Labor Relations, Cornell University): Is there any justification in the advertising of these programs primarily through brochures where they are labeled "Executive Leadership Programs" and "Management Development Programs" only to find when the person gets there, that it is something quite different from what had been anticipated? And had he known in advance that it was going to be a sensitivity program, would he have attended?

Dr. Argyris: First of all, I agree with you, there is that problem, but let me ask you something. Does this not happen to you every day with students who complain, "I never thought Yale or Cornell was going to be like this"? ...

However, I do not suggest that this should absolve us from trying to write more effective announcements. I think we can specify the end results of laboratory education as well as, or as poorly as, Yale University specifies its end results. When we hand our youngster (at Yale) a blue book, we give him no guarantee that he will learn anything by coming to Yale. So far as I can tell, we have tried to communicate as best we can what goes on during a laboratory. ...

Dr. Odiorne: ... There is a body of knowledge called management. There are the functions that a manager performs and then there are subsets of disciplines that impinge on them.

... [It has been said] that man is a political leader. He *is* at times. There are other times in which he is the passive watcher, and others when he is the democrat, and others when he is perhaps the overriding ruler. At Minneapolis-Honeywell I have heard it said, a manager is really the thermostat. He turns the heat on and off for the organization. Managers should keep behavioral science in perspective.

[5] Two sources of research in laboratory education, M. B. Miles, "Human Relations Training: Current Status," in E. H. Schein and I. R. Weschler, eds., *Issues in Human Relations Training* (National Training Laboratories), pp. 3-13, and D. Stock, *A Summary of Research on Training Groups* (New York: John Wiley & Sons).

[6] *Interpersonal Competence and Organizational Effectiveness* (Homewood, Ill.; Irwin-Dorsey Press, 1962).

FOR FURTHER READING

Argyris, Chris, *Executive Leadership: An Appraisal of a Manager in Action*. Hamden, Conn.: Shoe String Press, 1967.

Basil, Douglas, *Managerial Skills for Executive Action*. New York: American Management Association, 1970.

Bassett, G. A., "The Qualifications of a Manager," *California Management Review*, Vol. 12, No. 2 (Winter 1969), 35-44.

Bennis, Warren G., *Leadership and Motivation: Essays of Douglas McGregor*. Cambridge, Mass.: The M.I.T. Press, 1966.

Black, James Menzies, *Positive Discipline*. New York: American Management Association, 1970.

Blake, Robert R., and Jane S. Mouton, *Corporate Excellence Through Grid Organizational Development*. Houston, Tex.: Gulf Publishing Co., 1968.

Boyatzis, Richard E., "Building Efficacy: An Effective Use of Managerial Power." *Industrial Management Review*, Vol. 11, No. 1 (Fall 1969), 65-76.

Byham, William C., "Assessment Centers for Spotting Future Managers." *Harvard Business Review*, Vol. 48, No. 4 (July-August 1970), 150-160, 162-168, 171-172.

Calame, Byron E., "The Truth Hurts—Some Companies See More Harm Than Good in Sensitivity Training." *The Wall Street Journal*, July 14, 1969, p. 1.

Campbell, J. P., M. D. Dunnette, E. E. Lawler, and K. E. Weick, *Managerial Behavior Performance and Effectiveness*. New York: McGraw-Hill Book Company, 1970.

Carroll, Bonnie, *Job Satisfaction—A Review of the Literature*, Key Issue Series—No. 3. Ithaca, N.Y.: New York State School of Industrial and Labor Relations, Cornell University, 1969.

Carvell, Fred J., *Human Relations in Business: Social and Organizational Factors of Supervision*. New York: The Macmillan Company, 1970.

Coghill, Mary Ann. *Sensitivity Training—A Review of the Controversy*, Key Issue Series—No. 1. Ithaca, N.Y.: New York State School of Industrial and Labor Relations, Cornell University, 1967.

Cummings, L. L., and A. M. ElSalmi. "The Impact of Role Diversity, Job Level, and Organizational Size on Managerial Satisfaction." *Administrative Science Quarterly*, Vol. 15, No. 1 (March 1970), 1-10.

Cummings, L. L., and W. E. Scott, *Readings in Organizational Behavior and Human Performance*. Homewood, Ill.: Richard D. Irwin, Inc., and The Dorsey Press, 1969.

Drucker, Peter, *The Effective Executive*. New York: Harper & Row, Publishers, 1967.

———, *End of Economic Man: The Origins of Totalitarianism*. New York: Harper & Row, Publishers, 1969.

———, "Management's New Role." *Harvard Business Review*, Vol. 47, No. 6 (November-December 1969), 49-54.

———, *Technology, Management and Society*. New York: Harper & Row, Publishers, 1970.

Eddy, William B., ed., *Behavioral Science and the Manager's Role*. Washington, D.C.: NTL Institute for Applied Behavioral Science, 1969.

Emery, David A., *The Compleat Manager: Combining the Humanistic and Scientific Approaches to the Management Job*. New York: McGraw-Hill Book Company, 1970.

Estes, H., "The Modern 'Multiplier' Manager: Value-Added Approach to Managerial Work." *Business Horizons*, Vol. 13, No. 1 (February 1970), 79-83.

Evans, M. G., "Leadership and Motivation: A Core Concept." *Academy of Management Journal*, Vol. 13, No. 1 (March 1970), 91-102.

Fast, Julius, *Body Language*. New York: M. Evans & Co., Inc., 1970.

Fielden, John S., "Today the Campuses, Tomorrow the Corporations— Demand for Participation Can Be Good." *Business Horizons*, Vol. 13, No. 3 (June 1970), 13-20.

Fiedler, Fred E., "Style or Circumstance: The Leadership Enigma." *Psychology Today*, Vol. 2, No. 10 (March 1969), 39-43.

Ford, Robert N., "The Art of Reshaping Jobs." *Bell Telephone Magazine* (September-October 1968), pp. 29-32.

———, *Motivation through the Work Itself*. New York: American Management Association, 1969.

Freedman, Jonathan L., J. M. Carlsmith, and D. O. Sears, *Social Psychology*. Englewood Cliffs, N.J.: Prentice-Hall, Inc., 1970.

Gavin, James F., and Jeffrey Greenhaus, *Selecting Potential Managers*. New York: Life Office Management Association, 1969.

Gellerman, Saul W., *Uses of Psychology in Management*. New York: The Macmillan Company, 1970.

Gibb, C. A., *Leadership: Selected Readings*. Baltimore, Md.: Penguin Books, Inc., 1969.

Ginsburg, Woodrow L., E. Robert Livernash, Herbert S. Parnes, and George Strauss, *A Review of Industrial Relations Research*, Vol. 1. Madison, Wis.: Industrial Relations Research Association, 1970.

Grub, Phillip D., and Norma M. Loeser, eds., *Executive Leadership, the Act of Successfully Managing Resources*. Wayne, Pa.: MDI Publications, 1969.

Hill, Walter, "A Situational Approach to Leadership Effectiveness." *Journal of Applied Psychology*, Vol. 53, No. 6 (December 1969), 513-517.

House, R. J., "Role Conflict and Multiple-Authority in Complex Organizations," *California Management Review*, Vol. 12, No. 4 (Summer 1970), 53-60.

Huberman, John, "Discipline without Punishment." *Harvard Business Review*, Vol. 42, No. 4 (July-August 1964), 62-68.

Jennings, Eugene, *Executive in Crisis*. East Lansing, Mich.: Michigan State University Press, 1965.

_____, *Executive Success: Stresses, Problems, and Adjustment*. New York: Appleton-Century-Crofts, 1967.

Jones, John P., "Changing Patterns of Leadership." *Personnel*, Vol. 44, No. 2 (March-April 1967), 8-16.

Keisler, Charles, N. Miller, and B. Collins, *Attitude Change: A Critical Analysis of Theoretical Approaches*. New York: John Wiley & Sons, Inc., 1969.

Kelly, J., "The Organizational Concept of Leadership." *Management International Review*, Vol. 10, No. 6 (December 1970), 3-16.

Kipnis, David, and Joseph Cosentino, "Use of Leadership Powers in Industry." *Journal of Applied Psychology*, Vol. 53, No. 6 (December 1969), 460-466.

Kleinschrod, W. A., "Management and the New Humanism." *Administrative Management*, Vol. 31, No. 1 (January 1970), 24-25.

Kolb, David A., Irwin M. Rubin, and James M. McIntyre, *Organizational Psychology: A Book of Readings*. Englewood Cliffs, N.J.: Prentice-Hall, Inc., 1970.

Korman, Abraham K., *Industrial and Organizational Psychology*. Englewood Cliffs, N.J.: Prentice-Hall, Inc., 1971.

_____, "The Prediction of Managerial Performance: A Review." *Personnel Psychology*, Vol. 21, No. 3 (Autumn 1968), 295-322.

Labovitz, George, "Past and Future Management Priorities: Developing Theory for the Challenge of Change." *Management of Personnel Quarterly*, Vol. 8, No. 4 (Winter 1969), 20-26.

Laurie, J. W., "Leadership and Magical Thinking." *Personnel Journal*, Vol. 49, No. 9 (September 1970), 750-756.

Lawrence, Paul, "How to Deal with Resistance to Change." *Harvard Business Review*, Vol. 47, No. 1 (January-February 1969), 4-12, 116-176.

Lazarus, Harold, ed., *Human Values in Management: The Business Philosophy of A. M. Sullivan*. New York: Dun and Bradstreet, Inc., 1968.

Lennerlöf, Lennart, *Supervision: Situation, Individual, Behavior, Effect*. Stockholm: The Swedish Council for Personnel Administration, 1968.

Lerner, Max, "Creative Leadership in a Changing World." *Personnel*, Vol. 45, No. 3 (May-June 1968), 8-14.

Levinson, Harry, *Executive Stress*. New York: Harper & Row, Publishers, 1970.

Likert, Rensis, *The Human Organization: Its Management and Value*. New York: McGraw-Hill Book Company, 1967.

Lilienthal, David E., *Management: A Humanist Art*. New York: Columbia University Press, 1967.

Lopez, Felix M., *The Making of a Manager: Guidelines to His Selection and Promotion*. New York: American Management Association, 1970.

McDonald, J., "How the Man at the Top Avoids Crises." *Fortune*, Vol. 81, No. 1 (January 1970), 121-122.

McGregor, Douglas, *The Professional Manager*. New York: McGraw-Hill Book Company, 1967.

MacNamee, H., "Leadership for Tomorrow." *Conference Board Record*, Vol. 7, No. 1 (January 1970), 48-56.

Megley, John, "Management and the Behavioral Sciences: Theory Z." *Personnel Journal*, Vol. 49, No. 3 (March 1970), 216-221.

Miljus, R. C., "Effective Leadership and the Motivation of Human Resources." *Personnel Journal*, Vol. 49, No. 1 (January 1970), 36-40.

Mitchell, W. N., "What Makes a Business Leader?" *Personnel*, Vol. 45, No. 3 (May-June 1968), 55-61.

Mitton, Daryl G., "Leadership—One More Time." *Industrial Management Review*, Vol. 11, No. 1 (Fall 1969), 77-83.

Morris, DuBois S., Jr., ed., *Perspectives for the '70's and '80's: Tomorrow's Problems Confronting Today's Management*. New York: The Conference Board, Inc., 1970.

Morse, Gerry E., "Human Values and Business Leadership." *Personnel*, Vol. 46, No. 4 (July-August 1969), 15-20.

Muller, Helgaard P., "Relationship between Time-Span of Discretion, Leadership Behavior, and Fiedler's LPC Scores." *Journal of Applied Psychology*, Vol. 54, No. 2 (April 1970), 140-144.

O'Banion, Terry, and April O'Connell, *The Shared Journey: An Introduction to Encounter*. Englewood Cliffs, N.J.: Prentice-Hall, Inc., 1970.

Prahalis, C. P., "Crossing the Communications Crevice." *Manage*, Vol. 22, No. 5 (March 1970), 13-17, and No. 6 (April 1970), 13-16.

Rush, Harold M., *Behavioral Science: Concepts and Management Application*, New York: National Industrial Conference Board, 1969.

Schein, Edgar H., *Organizational Psychology*. Englewood Cliffs, N.J.: Prentice-Hall, Inc., 1965.

Sheriff, D. R., "Leadership Skills and Executive Development." *Training and Development Journal*, Vol. 22, No. 4 (April 1968), 29-38.

Steinmetz, Lawrence L., "Power to Ignore Power—A Hidden Factor in the Management of Change." *Personnel Administration*, Vol. 29, No. 1 (January-February 1966), 2-23, 25.

Sterner, Frank N., "Motivate, Don't Manipulate." *Personnel Journal*, Vol. 48, No. 8 (August 1969), 623-627.

Swope, George S., "Interpreting Executive Behavior." *Management Review*, Vol. 59, No. 4 (April 1970), 2-36.

———, "What's Your Leadership Style?" *Supervisory Management*, Vol. 15, No. 6 (June 1970), 12-17.

Thompson, D. W., "Selective Trait Matching Sequence: An Alternative Approach to Management Selection and Promotion." *Personnel Journal*, Vol. 49, No. 1 (January 1970), 45-49.

Uris, Auren, *The Executive Deskbook*. New York: Van Nostrand Reinhold Company, 1970.

_____, and Marjorie Noppel, *The Turned-On Executive: Building Your Skills for the Management Revolution*. New York: McGraw-Hill Book Company, 1970.

Van Dersal, William R., *The Successful Supervisor: In Government and Business*. New York: Harper & Row, Publishers, 1968.

Walker, C. R., *Technology, Industry, and Man*. New York: McGraw-Hill Book Company, 1968.

Walters, Jack E., *Research Management: Principles and Practice*. Washington, D.C.: Spartan Books, 1965.

Weisbord, Marvin R., "Management in Crisis: Must You Liquidate People." *Conference Board Record*, Vol. 7, No. 2 (February 1970), 10-16.

_____, "What, Not Again! Manage People Better?" *Think*, Vol. 36, No. 3 (January-February 1970), 2-9.

Whyte, William F., *Money and Motivation: An Analysis of Incentives in Industry*. New York: Harper & Row, Publishers, 1970.

Wytmar, Richard J., "Management Obsolescence." *Personnel Administrator*, Vol. 11, No. 1 (January-February 1966), 34-35.

PART SIX

Measuring and Controlling

Control is the management process designed to ensure that results conform to established goals. Control is a three-stage process: (1) Standards of performance that indicate desired results must be set. (2) Actual results must be compared to standards. (3) Corrective action must be taken if current activities are not leading to desired results. Control systems and the organizational problems that inevitably accompany such systems are discussed in selection 39, "Standing Plans and Controls."

A major pitfall of many control systems is that characteristics that can be tangibly measured, such as profits and market share, receive more attention than they deserve. We must be careful to develop a balanced control system that directs attention to intangible, difficult-to-measure characteristics as well as to quantitative results. Selections 40 and 41 deal with the need to develop balanced control systems. In "The Age of Anxiety at A.T. & T.," Alan Demaree describes how unbalanced control systems in some A.T. & T. operating companies contributed to the Bell System's current problems. "Measurement and Control: A Better Approach," presents E. Kirby Warren's recommendations for incorporating measures of long-range results into an enterprise's control system.

PERT and budgetary control are two valuable techniques for integrating planning and control. Although both techniques can be applied to a wide variety of situations, financial budgeting has been in use for a longer time and is more widely accepted.

The principal strength of budgetary control lies in its ability to convert many diverse actions into a single common denominator. Budgeting can also make use of existing records and systems and does not require the development of new records. Budgeting also has some important limitations. The first, and primary, danger is that the use of budgets will place unbalanced emphasis on the factors that are easiest to observe. Budgets also tend to generate internal conflicts and pressures. In selection 42, "The Game of Budget Control," Dr. G. H. Hofstede presents a set of practical recommendations designed to maximize the benefits of budgetary control while minimizing its negative features.

PERT (Program Evaluation and Review Technique) differs from budgetary control because it focuses on time control rather than on expense control. This technique, which was created to plan the development and production of Polaris missiles, is especially useful for planning and controlling large, complex, nonrepetitive projects. One variant of the PERT System that helps to control both time and cost throughout a project is a PERT/Cost System, which adds estimated costs for each activity in the network. Selection 43, "The PERT/Cost System," explains both PERT and the PERT/Cost Systems.

In addition to the mechanics of control—setting standards, issuing control reports, and taking corrective action—the behavioral aspects of controlling must be considered also in the design of a control system. Because the success of a control system depends on the willingness of people to alter their behavior, the reasons why people object to controls and methods for obtaining positive response to controls are of special importance. Common reasons for a dislike of controls include the failure to accept objectives, the feeling that par is unreasonable or that measurements are inappropriate, and a refusal to face unpleasant facts.

Managers have found that when they use "fact control," establish flexible control systems, and allow subordinates to participate in setting standards, they are more likely to elicit a positive response to controls. Participation has proved useful for securing the acceptance of objectives, performance standards, and methods of measurement. Most observers believe that the participative approach holds the greatest promise for improving human response to control. In fact, a significant outgrowth of the participative approach, called "management by objectives," or MBO, has received considerable attention from both academics and practitioners. Management-by-objectives systems vary considerably in practice. Some systems focus entirely on "results-oriented appraisals" while others use MBO to alter all aspects of managing—organizing, planning, leading, and controlling. The evolution of management-by-objectives systems is traced by Robert A. Howell in selection 44, "Managing by Objectives—A Three-Stage System." This general survey is followed by "Management by Objectives," a review of the relatively limited empirical data concerning the success of MBO systems.

39

Standing Plans and Controls

DAVID HAMPTON, CHARLES E. SUMMER,
AND ROSS WEBBER

As a firm grows, standing plans and controls emerge to provide the uniformity and predictability required by mature organizations. Standing plans, in the form of policies and procedures, seek to prevent people from "reinventing the wheel" each time a decision is made. Controls are designed to ensure that results coincide with plans. It is inevitable, however, that these attempts to provide direction and predictability will produce a new set of problems, namely, the loss of direction. In the following selection, David Hampton, Charles E. Summer, and Ross Webber provide a graphic description of this organizational phenomenon.

Using the Xerox Company as their example, the authors illustrate the positive features of standing plans and controls as they develop during the stages of organizational growth. Unfortunately, these same standing plans and control systems soon lose their connection with the true mission of the organization. The authors document this inversion of means and ends by citing some significant studies by Chris Argyris, Peter Blau, and others. Management plays a vital role in preserving organizational spontaneity and in avoiding negative responses to control systems.

Two key questions raised by this reading are: (1) Why do people respond negatively to control systems? (2) What methods should managers use to elicit positive response to controls? The second question will be treated in subsequent selections.

DEVELOPMENT OF STANDING PLANS AND CONTROLS

We have suggested that formulating operational goals, structuring duties, assigning people, and making unpopular decisions are primary functions requiring a formal organizational hierarchy. There are others, but all imply the need for a sense of direction in any organization. Therefore, the loss of awareness of purpose and direction is a major problem as an

Reprinted from "The Impact of Formal Organization," in David Hampton, Charles E. Summer, and Ross Webber, *Organizational Behavior and the Practice of Management*, pp. 192-198, by permission of the publisher. Copyright 1968 by Scott, Foresman and Company, Glenview, Ill.

organization matures and its hierarchy stabilizes. In its early days, a business may be quite successful by depending almost entirely on objectives, with few policies, procedures, or controls. Eventually, however, controls are necessary and they develop—and when they develop, there is danger of inverting means and ends. The Xerox Company offers an example.[1]

For more than a decade Xerox has been one of the most impressive organizations in American business. Between 1954 and 1964 the old family-dominated Haloid Company, manufacturing specialized photographic products, transformed itself into the modern Xerox Company—and jumped from 30 to over 300 million dollars a year in sales. In 1959 the company was chaotic. Offices were located all over Rochester, N.Y.—over delicatessens and in abandoned schools. Job descriptions were few, policies broad, procedures ignored, and controls weak. Yet the company was successful. And it was successful because of top management's ability to point out direction. Chairman Sol Linowitz and President Joseph Wilson saw their roles as the laying down of objectives—long, intermediate, and short range. Wilson spent much of his time selling the Xerox Company to his own managers, describing the revolutionary and beneficial impact of its information technology on society—and also pointing out how each manager's own interest would be served if the company advanced. Given the fantastic expansion, he was aware that it would be impossible to control the entire company from the president's office. In order to take advantage of a divergent market and to exploit their technologically superior product, it was essential that managers at all levels be committed to manufacturing the product and getting it out to the market as quickly as possible. Premature policies, procedures, and controls would have interfered with the spontaneous cooperation and initiative demonstrated by Xerox management.

Nonetheless, standing plans and controls did emerge in the Xerox Company—and for good reason. First of all, why go on reinventing the wheel? Why must a company handle every problem as unique? Sam Jones wonders how Gil Smith has handled the problem of quality control on his gears. He asks about it. Gil's answer seems reasonable, and rather than search for new alternatives, Sam adopts Gil's procedure. Or Mike Stratton has had great success in handling rush orders within his production area. How does he do it? Some questioning will disclose his methods. Why not let everyone know about it? So an information memo is drafted and distributed. The basis for standing plans and procedures, then, rests upon an awareness of the usefulness of past experience. There is no reason why one should repeat the same mistakes over and over again without taking advantage of the accumulated knowledge of people in the organization. The famous words, in another context, of Oliver Wendell Holmes apply: "Three generations of idiots are enough!" The company decides to make some rules that trade upon experience and give guidance to people facing similar problems for the first time.

[1] "Copy Machine Boom—And Xerox Boom." *Newsweek*, Vol. 66 (Nov. 8, 1965), 84-90.

So in the beginning these procedures and policies are developed from the organization's own experience. After a while, however, management may feel that they should take advantage of other people's experience instead of restricting themselves to their own company. Experts can provide this knowledge, and so specialists, advisers, auditors, and controllers are hired. Once they are hired, there is a natural tendency for management to see that they are used by giving them some authority to impose their experience on the rest of the organization.

At Xerox, the expansion of staff activities in the development of job descriptions, policies, and procedures was given impetus when management became concerned about internal efficiency. When their product is clearly superior and the market is fertile, management's main concern is getting the product made and out the door. Internal costs and efficiencies are of minor importance when production cost is a relatively small percentage of the selling or rental price. Xerox's main problem in the late fifties and early sixties was to get the jump on the competition and to put its machines into offices all over the world. Competition has developed, however, and although the price factor is apparently not critical yet, there has been increased concern within Xerox about manufacturing costs. Such concern inevitably means rationalization of production operations: rationalization means finding out what the best methods are, applying them throughout the organization, and seeing that people adhere to them—just as F. W. Taylor suggested many years ago.

A Xerox research and development engineer has indicated how such elaboration of procedures affected him. When he had an idea that required funds in 1959, he would walk into the office of the vice-president with a scratch pad and pencil, sit down, and sketch out the idea. A decision would be made quickly, and the researcher would go to work. In 1967, however, the same researcher must complete, in multiple copies, a prescribed project form indicating potential equipment cost, material requirements, potential return, cash flow, etc. This is not simply red tape; multiple forms are not required just to complicate the lives of people in the organization. The decisions that have to be made about fund allocation are much more complex than they were in a simpler day. More and different projects are involved; they must be compared with one another on some consistent basis; and priority decisions have to be made about organizational objectives. Specific procedures for allocating capital funds facilitate comparison, prediction, and control—essential functions of management in any organization.

This development of job descriptions, policies, and procedures aids efficiency by promoting coordination and predictability. However fine the initiative of Xerox managers had been in the expansion stage, it was stressful and unstable. For awhile, people will put up with instability, but order, regularity, and predictability become essential in the long run—especially if the rate of growth and promotional opportunities start to decline. Nor do managers necessarily dislike the development of standing plans and controls. Order will be brought out of chaos and predictability out of instability, and simple relief from making the same mistakes over and over again will be achieved. Indeed, many managers perceive the development of some control procedures as progress.

THE LOSS OF DIRECTION

However inevitable and necessary the development of standing plans and controls, equally inevitable is the development of problems with those plans and controls. One of the so-called management principles of long repute has been the rule that delegated duties should be explicit and specific—with no gaps or overlaps. If this is true, and if standing plans are inclusive, and if controlled measurements are feasible, theoretically each manager need only follow directions. No initiative is required.

Of course, we have described an impossible condition. Such perfect delegation, planning, and controlling is impossible. Therefore, spontaneity is essential. To a greater or lesser degree, every manager must fill in the gaps, work out the conflicts resulting from overlaps, and exercise discretion in following standing plans. If standing plans are followed blindly, the organization loses direction. There is an inversion of means and ends. To some people, rules, plans, and controls become ends to be followed without thought as to whether or not they contribute to the organization's objectives. Indeed, in the eyes of many, such inversion of means and ends is almost synonymous with bureaucracy in an organization. Most frequently, we assume such distortion to characterize governments and other public, non-profit institutions. The comments of John Knowles, former Director of Massachusetts General Hospital, are illustrative: "In the teaching hospital, it has become set that the patient exists for the teaching programs, and not that the hospital exists for the patient."[2] In his Pulitzer Prize-winning study of the Kennedy presidency, *A Thousand Days,* Arthur Schlesinger provides several, almost caricatured, examples of the loss of direction in governmental groups. ... A chapter from Schlesinger's book describes the organizational paralysis stemming from tradition and conservatism in the U.S. Department of State.[3]

Such inversion of means and ends, however, also occurs in business. An advertisement in a prominent management journal once showed a hand holding a fancy notebook entitled "Policy Manual" over a wire-basket incinerator in which several similar notebooks were burning. Who was the advertiser? A management consulting firm. Its message? That one shouldn't allow standing plans, policies, procedures, and controls to exist unchanged for too long because they get out of date and hinder the organization instead of helping—better to burn them (and call in a consultant to write a new set!).

---

[2] De Hartog, J. "What Money Cannot Buy." *Atlantic Monthly,* Vol. 218 (July 1966), 113.

[3] Schlesinger, A. *A Thousand Days.* Houghton Mifflin, 1965.

Once established and accepted, standing plans and controls tend to limit flexibility and initiative. In the beginning at least, standing plans are usually good, and an organization gains in coordination and predictability what it may lose in initiative. Nonetheless, it is difficult to keep policies, procedures, and controls up to date: policies no longer apply to new conditions; controls measure irrelevant factors; and those rational plans and controls which were developed to promote effectiveness begin to interfere with the accomplishment of objectives. If managers blindly follow these rules, spontaneity is lost. ...

RESPONSE TO MANAGERIAL CONTROLS

Spontaneity may be maintained but direction still lost if control standards are misplaced or overly tight. In this case, managers develop elaborate devices for adapting to controls by meeting the standards on paper but not necessarily in ways that contribute to organizational effectiveness. Therefore, overly restrictive control systems are one of the gravest threats to organizational initiative. People will try to meet the numbers they are measured by. If they cannot meet these numbers by accepted and desirable behavioral patterns, undesirable patterns will be attempted.

In a pioneering study, Chris Argyris examined the impact of budget controls on those being controlled. He gave repeated examples of short-run compliance with control standards that in either the short run or the long run had adverse cost consequences to the organization. He reported instances of people who worked under fixed quotas of output with some opportunity to select items to be worked on, choosing easy, rapidly completed jobs as fillers toward the end of a period in order to meet the quota.[4] Peter Blau reports similar behavior among law enforcement officials who maintain an established case load and who pick easy or fast cases towards the end of each month if they anticipate falling short of their quotas.[5]

... Frank Jasinski describes a similar adaptation by foremen of "bleeding the line" in assembly line production by stuffing all work in progress through the measuring point (using augmented crews) in order to meet a quota but losing efficiency in the succeeding period until the line is refilled with work in progress.[6]

An even more seriously distorting adaptive response to controls is reported by Blau in his analysis of a state employment service. The interviewers are appraised on the basis of the number of interviews completed. As a result they maximize the number of interviews but do not spend enough time determining the capabilities of their clients to fit them

[4] Argyris, C. *The Impact of Budgets on People.* Controllership Institute, 1952.

[5] Blau, P. *The Dynamics of Bureaucracy.* University of Chicago Press, 1955.

[6] Jasinski, F. "Use and Misuse of Efficiency Controls." *Harvard Business Review*, Vol. 34, No. 4 (July-August 1956), 105-112.

with available jobs—the obvious purpose of the interviews in the first place.[7]

Deliberate evasion is also a response. Jasinski describes "making out with the pencil" as a means of giving the appearance on paper of meeting expected standards without actually doing so. Melville Dalton reports a comparable instance of evasion where local plant officials through blandishment of, and subsequent conspiracy with, the central office representative were able to evade cost control checks imposed by the central office.[8]

Such managerial adaptation to controls is not culture bound. David Granick points out that monetary rewards and glory attend the Soviet plant manager who sets a new production record. There is pressure to set a record at the expense of operating repairs and preventive maintenance. The result is lower output in the subsequent period while the delayed maintenance is attended to—or its effects are felt in breakdowns, but the manager has received his payoff for the over-quota output of the earlier period.[9] In addition, Berliner[10] and Richman[11] note the practice in Soviet industry of "storming" production to meet output standards toward the end of a quota period, again at the expense of maintenance and balanced output.

Obviously there exists a strong tendency to meet formal performance criteria, even if high but hidden costs are generated in so doing. It also seems highly probable that the severity of penalities incurred for failure to meet control standards generates a proportional adaptive effort to make a showing of compliance, regardless of the other costs involved to the organization.

In all these examples, managers exercise spontaneous initiative to overcome control systems imposed on them. Perhaps even more dangerous for the organization is the disappearance of spontaneity. After a while under restrictive control systems, some managers don't care if mistakes are avoided. If they feel that punishment awaits an unsuccessful departure from procedure, they may do what the book requires—and that's all. No spontaneity will be demonstrated, and apathy will prevail.

. . .

SUMMARY

Hierarchy, control, and predictability are essential for organizational effectiveness. Managers must structure organizations, allocate people to jobs, fill communication links, and determine short-range goals. Standing plans, policies, procedures, and performance standards are means of reaching these

[7] Blau, P. *op. cit.*

[8] Dalton, M. "Managing the Managers." *Human Organization*, Vol. 14 (Fall 1955), 4-10.

[9] Granick, D. *The Red Executive*, Doubleday, 1960.

[10] Berliner, J. S. "A Problem in Soviet Business Management." *Administrative Science Quarterly*, Vol. 1 (June 1956), 87-101.

[11] Richman, B. M., *Soviet Management.* Prentice-Hall, 1965.

goals. In short, formal organization and structure are necessary to maintain a sense of direction and momentum for the achievement of organizational goals.

Yet hierarchy and formal organization create problems. They may be incompatible with the needs of individuals—although the conflict is possibly exaggerated. More detrimental to organizational effectiveness, standing plans and control standards get out of touch with the real needs of the organization. People may conform to rules without thought to their contribution to goals, and the organization loses direction. Rules usually work; that is, they influence behavior. People will try to follow prescribed rules in order to meet the numbers they are measured by. However, because of the expense and effort involved in continuous revision, these rules or numbers become obsolete. With time, all organizations face the problem of employees following rules without thought to their purpose. Personnel may sleepwalk through their jobs, responding blindly to policies without seeing the unplanned task that should be handled.

Every organization, with time and success, is in danger from the inversion of means and ends. Standing plans and controls are management's major tools for giving direction to organizational activities. They are imposed in order to promote goals. Yet, to the unspontaneous personnel, standing plans and controls become ends in themselves—to be followed without question. Narrow bureaucrats follow rules when all around them organizational effectiveness is being destroyed. Such a development is not uncommon. Such destructive stagnation is perhaps the businessman's primary vision of government organization. But business is not exempt. ...

No organization can fully plan the behavior of its members because not every necessary activity can be anticipated. Spontaneity, therefore, is essential. With good faith and ingenuity, managers must fill in the gaps. They must develop informal work practices that compensate for inadequate job descriptions and ambiguous organizational definition.

40

The Age of Anxiety at A.T. & T.

ALAN T. DEMAREE

This selection illustrates the difficulties involved in achieving effective control in a giant enterprise. The case in point is American Telephone and Telegraph, the world's wealthiest corporation ($47 billion in assets at the end of 1969) and the biggest monopoly in the United States. Alan Demaree

Reprinted from Fortune, May 1970, pp. 156ff., by permission of the publisher. Copyright 1970 by Time, Inc.

*describes how poor service, new competition, inexperienced workers, and the
Bell System's own life-style have combined to create "The Age of Anxiety at
A.T. & T."*

*The unprecedented decline in the quality of telephone service in New
York City and in other major cities across the nation has confronted A.T. &
T. with crisis, but it would be an oversimplification to single out any one
factor as the source of A.T. & T.'s problems. Mr. Demaree notes that "the
official view at A.T. & T. is that poor service resulted from strikes, difficulties
in hiring skilled workers in a tight labor market, and unanticipated growth in
demand." These problems are, however, only part of the story. Mr. Demaree
identifies some less publicized issues that are extremely relevant to our
analysis of the control process. First, there is the matter of developing
balanced control systems that give proper emphasis both to short-run profit
objectives and to long-run growth needs. The experiences of some A.T. & T.
operating companies demonstrate the dangers of giving undue emphasis to
short-run objectives. The second issue relates very closely to our previous
selection—avoiding the loss of direction. Mr. Demaree contends that A.T. &
T.'s comprehensive and tight measures of performance contribute to poor
employee morale and inefficiency.*

*Consider the following questions after reading this selection: (1) How
do we develop control systems that give proper emphasis both to short-run
and to long-run objectives? (2) How can we obtain more positive responses to
controls in an organization the size of A.T. & T.?*

On the brink of the Seventies, as trouble convulsed the once
well-ordered world of Haakon Ingolf Romnes, the tall, angular engineer who
heads American Telephone & Telegraph composed a letter to his managers.
He urged them to have confidence in the face of an uncertain future:
"confidence in ourselves—in each other—confidence in our ability to do the
kind of intelligent, realistic, and sensitive management job the times
demand." That uncharacteristic exhortation is light-years from the mood of
A.T. & T. a decade ago, when the formidable communications giant seemed
so impeccably managed and impervious to criticism that it did not permit
itself even the briefest moment of self-doubt. "It would be naive," wrote
Romnes, "to assert that the unclouded optimism with which we confronted
the Sixties would serve us well today."

So fundamental a change at A.T. & T. is epochal. For A.T. & T. is more
than the biggest monopoly in the U.S., a corporation controlling greater
wealth than any other in the world ($47 billion in assets at the end of 1969).
It is also a kind of subculture all its own, encompassing nearly one million
employees and filled with its own myths and mores, prides and prejudices,
that only momentous events can call into question.

Myriad events combined to confront A.T. & T. with crisis. An unprecedented decline in the quality of telephone service subjected the company to widespread criticism unparalleled in its history. Service in New York City is abominable, with lesser degrees of degradation in Boston, Miami, Detroit, Washington, and Pittsburgh. ... The reason for the service troubles was management's failure to anticipate demand, but the root cause of that failure stemmed from the interplay of many more subtle forces, both financial and psychological. The fortunes of the telephone business swing on management's ability to strike a precarious balance between profit and service, stockholder and customer, the efficient use of capital plant and the maintenance of enough spare capacity to meet unforeseen demands. And in the mid-Sixties, events conspired to knock that balance out of kilter.

As inflation drove up costs, profits came under pressure, and earnings on total capital declined steadily. Strangely enough, the operating companies were reluctant to seek rate increases, and in order to keep profits up telephone-company presidents felt increasing pressures to cut costs. These pressures were especially intense in companies like New York Telephone that had a low rate of return to begin with and, consciously or unconsciously, they began narrowing the margins of spare capacity and taking risks with the quality of service they provided.

Not even Bell's awesome technology could free telephone-company managers from their pains. Bell reaped the major gains of automation by 1963 in local service, the biggest chunk of the business, and it is back coping with people problems; its work force is increasing rapidly, reaching 956,000 at the end of 1969. The quality of that enormous force has declined dramatically as Bell has had to hire and train uneducated and undisciplined workers, causing efficiency to plunge and turnover to climb. At the same time, policy changes at the Federal Communications Commission opened the way for eager competitors, armed with technology that Bell itself had pioneered, to chisel away at multibillion-dollar hunks of the telephone empire. ...

The cumulative effect of these troubles has been to plunge A.T. & T.'s proud executives deep into introspection. Historically, the communications giant merrily expanded its monopoly, fending off would-be competitors with restrictive tariffs, refusals to interconnect, and selective rate cuts, which it could subsidize from its monopoly markets. Now groups of Bell officials gather in conference behind the classical granite façade of 195 Broadway, the corporate headquarters in lower Manhattan, to brood over the fundamental question: "What is our business?"

The answer is by no means clear; they are torn between pushing ahead and pulling back. The tug of war is waged not so much between individuals as within them. On the one hand, old-line telephone men reject, as if by reflex, the notion that they should cut back to their monopoly telephone business, leaving the rest of communications to others. "If we do, we'll make the same mistake the railroads did," says Vice Chairman John deButts, evoking an analogy to the railroad that is heard repeatedly in the Bell System. "Ours is a communications business, not just a telephone business."

On the other hand, the shock of severe criticism has increasingly brought telephone people to the realization that even Bell's vast reserves of capital, manpower, and management acumen are limited, and that the areas they serve on the periphery of their monopoly business must be judiciously chosen. "We can't be all things to all people," they tell one another, speaking softly lest the admission be heard outside. Thus, Bell is now wavering between its railroad syndrome and a new-found humility. If its actions are occasionally out of step with its words, or its words out of step with each other, the explanation is likely to be found in a kind of corporate schizophrenia.

Bell now faces many challenges, any one of which would sorely tax the resources of a lesser corporation. It must restore telephone service to the high standards its customers once expected. It must decide what markets it should serve beyond its basic telephone monopoly and cope with the competition there. And in an age of labor scarcity, it must hire, train, motivate, and keep more skilled men and women than ever before. How well it meets these challenges will depend largely on the unique culture of the corporation itself, a culture that contains great strengths and serious shortcomings.

The corporate empire of A.T. & T. comprises twenty-four operating companies, most of them big enough to rank on *Fortune's* list of the fifty largest utilities; Western Electric, A.T. & T.'s manufacturing arm, ranked eleventh among the 500 largest manufacturers; and Bell Telephone Laboratories, the biggest corporate research organization in the world. All these companies are majority-owned by A.T. & T. with three exceptions, Bell of Canada (2 percent owned), Southern New England Telephone (18 percent), and Cincinnati Bell (27 percent).

It would be natural to conclude that such concentration of ownership would yield concentration of control—that A.T. & T. is one great monolith, and that all the crucial decisions are made at the pinnacle of power. The truth is more complicated. Bell is a strange, perhaps unique, blend of independence and conformity. In mood and atmosphere, a great gulf separates the operating companies from corporate headquarters. Operating executives have the zest of men doing things—laying cables, installing phones, "operating in real time," as one of them puts it. A.T. & T.'s huge superstaff, entangled in task forces and committees galore, is far more contemplative, soul-searching, and all too frequently ponderous, deliberate, and painfully slow.

The conformity that pervades the Bell System has its dangers. Practices, habits, traditions, ways of thinking, inarticulate assumptions have overgrown the entire company and they are glacially slow to change. Not all, by any means, are bad. Older employees, especially, have an uncommon loyalty to the company and an unabashed pride in its traditional excellence of service to the public. But there is also the feeling, undisturbed for years, that the way Bell has always done things must necessarily be the best way. Someone once likened the Bell System to a great dragon: you could chop off its tail and it would take five years to feel it in the head.

This comfortable feeling of security and permanence has been reinforced by decades of inbreeding that virtually excludes all influence from outside the telephone business itself. Bell managers generally rotate through various companies and diverse jobs in the system, but few of those who reach the top have had much work experience elsewhere. They never seem to get fired, rarely are they demoted, and a shake-up is virtually beyond imagination. A.T. & T.'s twenty-one top officers average thirty-three years with the company. Of 148 top officers at Western Electric in 1968, all but one started their careers in the Bell System. "You're all right when you get hired," says a man who quit Southern Bell, "but as the years go by your head becomes more and more Bell-shaped."

Many dispassionate outsiders think it's high time for a breath of fresh air. "If I had a chance to make just one recommendation to Romnes," says Professor Richard Vancil, an expert in long-range planning at Harvard Business School, "it would be that he take a vice president from Xerox, I.B.M., even U.S. Steel, and make him president of an operating company. It would shake the industry to its boots." A.T. & T. has itself felt the need of outside advice. Upon occasion, operating companies have hired management consultants like McKinsey & Co., and A.T. & T. has its own board of independent economic advisers.

But "Hi" Romnes is not of a mind to make sweeping changes. His role, as he sees it, is largely advisory. He does not try to second-guess the top officers of the operating companies—indeed, he may not even talk to a company president for months at a time. "They don't have to check their decisions," he says. "Performance is what counts."

Bell measures the performance of each company and each area within each company by dozens of technical indexes that are compiled in green, orange, white, gray, and brown books, published monthly, quarterly, and annually, and distributed variously throughout the system. From headquarters pours volume upon volume of "Bell System Practices," of B.S.P.'s as they are called, prescribing everything from authorized methods for splicing cable to sales pitches for marketing switchboards. Conformity is not all bad. Because of standard procedures, emergency crews were easily borrowed from other Bell companies to repair the damage caused by Hurricane Camille. But many employees claim standardization is carried to the point of stultification. Operators are taught to get into their chairs on the left and out on the right, whether they work in New York or San Francisco. "If you figure out a better way of doing something," says an engineer from New York Tel, "forget it—they'd have to change all the manuals."

A GADFLY MEASURES BY THE CENT

For all this uniformity, the presidents of the operating companies still have broad discretion to make critical decisions affecting their business. The single most important decision they make is how much to invest in new capital equipment—the trunks that carry telephone calls, the central offices that switch them, and so forth. The capital budget, at least $6.5 billion this year for the whole Bell System, or 8 percent of all corporate capital expenditures in the U.S., determines the ability of each operating company to provide acceptable service. Solely responsible for their own forecasts of demand and investment projections, the operating companies submit these three times yearly to A.T. & T., beginning about two years before the equipment is slated for installation.

Albert M. Froggatt, sixty-three, a genial, English-born engineer in charge of A.T. & T.'s department of engineering economics, helps oversee the capital budgets.   Froggatt checks the companies' plans against past performance by a variety of indicators and jaunts around the country acting as the corporate gadfly, asking questions, offering suggestions. He knows it takes $1 of investment in telephone plant to earn 33 cents in annual revenue. So if a company forecasts 25 cents of new revenue for each dollar invested, Froggatt says: "I would yowl and look into it and see if I can find out what is wrong ..." Very frequently the companies are willing to make a further review of their program and modify it as they think it should be modified. But it is their ultimate responsibility.

When it comes to raising money for their investment programs, the operating companies must work closely with A.T. & T. They generate a little more than half their funds from depreciation and retained earnings. The rest comes from two sources—about one-third from issuing bonds and two-thirds from selling stock to A.T. & T. Since one Bell company or another is in the bond market every three weeks, the offerings have to be timed by John J. Scanlon, A.T. & T.'s treasurer. Scanlon, in turn, goes to the capital market on A.T. & T.'s behalf to help raise money to buy the operating companies' stock and to finance Western Electric, the Long Lines division, and Bell Labs.

What is truly surprising is that A.T. & T. has never directed its operating companies to cut back on capital expenditures. To keep from doing so, Scanlon has performed remarkable feats. A usually reserved fellow whose face seems cast in a perpetual smile, Scanlon glows with puckish delight when he talks high-flying finance. The nearly $1.6-billion package of bonds he put on the market last month is the biggest corporate debt financing in history, and the Bell System is expected to issue nearly one-fifth of the total long-term corporate debt this year. Since A.T. & T.'s investment plans will require $35 billion or more in new capital over the next five years, Scanlon will probably fashion another gigantic package of debt or equity next year. After that, Scanlon thinks, A.T. & T.'s use of accelerated depreciation, which it adopted for tax purposes this year, will begin generating enough cash flow to diminish its reliance on outside financing.

AS SOLID AS A POST IN CONCRETE

It might seem that any manager fortunate enough to enjoy an almost unlimited supply of capital is sitting in the catbird seat. But it doesn't work quite that way in the Bell family. If an operating-company president builds more plant than is needed to meet demand, service may be superb but excess capacity will devour his profits. If he builds too little, profits may be high but service will suffer the multitude of ills caused by overloads on the lines and switching centers. The act of balancing service against profit is never easy, and when costs rise, putting pressure on profits, it takes uncommon dexterity. Romnes himself concedes under questioning: "We talk and talk about service at every meeting we have, but I have to say there have been times when, in the minds of some, the investors were given greater consideration."

The official view at A.T. & T. is that poor service resulted from strikes, difficulties in hiring skilled workers in a tight labor market, and unanticipated growth in demand (e.g., some welfare clients received allowances for telephones, and brokerage calls increased as trading boomed on the New York Stock Exchange). All these had an important bearing, but they are only part of the story. The crunch was severe because the growth in demand came at a time when some operating companies were under intense pressure to cut costs and failed to invest enough money in new plant and equipment and in the people to maintain it. A.T. & T.'s reluctance to admit the extent to which cost cutting figured in its service problems is an understandable part of Bell System mores. "Service comes first," Bell people say again and again, and they honestly believe it. The thought is imbedded in their consciousness like a post in concrete, for providing good service is the *sine qua non* of Bell's legitimacy, the company's pledge of performance in return for the privilege of monopoly.

Saddled with fixed rates in a time of galloping inflation, the operating companies could, of course, have applied for increases. But telephone men have built up a psychological reluctance to go running to the regulators; they hate to admit that they can't keep ahead of costs. In startling contrast to electric utilities, the Bell companies averaged eleven years without rate increases before they started knocking on commission doors, late in 1968.

FORECASTING AND THE SHELL GAME

As the screws began to tighten, operating companies took risks with service in various ways. Some began adding equipment to meet only short-term growth. This saves money in the short run but ultimately increases costs and shaves the margin of spare capacity dangerously thin. Company presidents also cut back forecasts of future demand that were sent up to them from the field, thereby reducing the amount planned for investment. Since men in the field generally played safe by padding their forecasts, it was common practice for top executives to cut them; but when profit pressures mounted, managers tended to cut closer to the bone. In this world of imprecision, the risks executives took were frequently uncertain—hidden like the pea in a shell game.

"You start taking risks that you won't get greater growth than you think you are likely to get," says Alfred W. Van Sinderen, president of Southern New England Telephone. "We took some calculated risks in the latter part of the Sixties. Some paid off, some didn't. We knew we were doing it, but felt we had to." The results, while at first imperceptible to the public, could be statistically measured at some companies as early as 1966, when dial tones slowed and installation backlogs lengthened.

New York Tel appears to have been an extreme case of overzealous cost cutting, yet officials there seemed blissfully unaware of the risks they were taking. To start with, officials had an unclear idea of what their margins were because they kept only loose track of calling rates, which increased and cut into spare capacity more than they realized. Then they tightened maintenance budgets and cut back capital expenditures two years running, 1966 and 1967, even though their own forecasts predicted ever increasing demand. Thus the company's spare capacity had been chopped to the peril point when, late in 1968, it was hit with an unexpected surge of demand that overloaded nearly half its central offices in downstate New York.

William G. Sharwell, New York Tel's operating vice president, who was moved into that key post at the height of the crisis, now concedes, in hindsight, that the company put too much emphasis on earnings at the expense of service. "But at the time I didn't think they were doing wrong," says Sharwell. "I'm sure there was no sense of the enormity of risk involved—we were not playing it fast and loose—no one was conscious of taking any risk of particular consequence."

Pessimists see the mistake as fatal. "I don't think they're ever going to recover from it," says one of the most highly respected men at the FCC. A perceptive executive with another communications carrier foresees this scenario for A.T. & T.: increasing costs leading to a decline in service, declining service resulting in the loss of public sympathy, public criticism culminating in reluctance by the states to allow a fair profit—on and on in an ever descending spiral.

That dreadful specter is visible to Romnes, too, and he is pressing hard to avoid it: "I think we should put all our emphasis on the service side," he says. His view is widespread among telephone-company managers, many of whom are tasting severe public criticism for the first time and feel hurt, shaken, and challenged. Still, the tremendous increase in capital spending itself brings untoward side effects on service. The rapid buildup has siphoned some of the best skilled craftsmen into construction work and away from vital jobs in maintenance and repair. Many new workers have been hired quickly and efficiency has dropped. Productivity for the whole Bell System—measured in the number of employees per 10,000 telephones—declined last year for the first time since 1946. Unfortunately, both stockholders and customers will end up paying for Bell's error in judgment, and even if service is restored as predicted, Bell's vaunted reputation may be permanently marred.

· · ·

CASE OF THE CREEPING GIRDLE

As it struggled to meet new competition, Bell was beset by personnel problems. One of the largest employers of minorities, Bell hired black and Spanish-speaking workers whom its standards would have barred a few years ago. Many fledgling operators have never made a long-distance call before and some need speech therapy. Independent-minded young people with lots of job options are quickly dissatisfied with boring tasks and reject Bell's traditional regimentation. "If a girl's girdle is creeping up," says a union man describing the new attitude, "she's going to stand up and pull it down without asking the chief operator."

Turnover has shot up and is costing Bell dearly. Bell had to interview a million women last year, hired 125,000, and ended up with a net gain of 15,000. Operators are quitting at twice the rate they did in the early Sixties; switchmen, frame men, and other key craftsmen are quitting four times as fast. The money Bell has invested in training these workers is lost forever when they leave, and training costs are rising as equipment becomes more complex.

Efficiency has plunged as inexperienced and ill-qualified workers take the place of old-timers. More than a quarter of the craftsmen have less than two years' experience, up from 7 percent ten years ago. The drop in quality feeds back on morale. "The company puts more pressure on the supervisors for efficiency," says a former Ohio Bell manager, "but the supervisors have less dedicated people, so they get disgruntled."

Another cause of morale problems is Bell's most controversial management tool, the dozens of indexes it uses to measure performance. Observers tap the lines long enough to grade operators (Is she polite? Does she give correct information?), and electronic devices gather other data, such as dial-tone speed, that are used in the index ratings. Employees distrust the indexes and consider them dehumanizing. Supervisors complain that indexes are used too rigidly in judging their chances for promotion. Some managers won't take the risk of innovating lest it hurt their rating, and others over-react, such as the tense young supervisor who, upon seeing his service index drop, asked his workers to take a pledge to give good service or quit. The indexes' accuracy and effect on productivity are open to question because employees have found scores of ways to "game" them and cheat the system.

A.T. & T. is moving to combat its personnel problems. It has supplemented the indexes with new methods of measuring service quality, such as customer surveys, and officials report they use index ratings in determining promotions less than they did, say, five years ago. A.T. & T. has set up a manpower laboratory to learn how to cope with the changed attitudes of new employees. And Robert N. Ford, a personnel director who once likened Bell's problem of keeping people in dull jobs to "that faced by a general who commands mercenary troops," has run a number of trials to make jobs more interesting, abandoning pat routines and letting workers make better use of their native abilities.

The dimensions of A.T. & T.'s personnel problems are growing, however, as laborsaving automation, which cut the number of operators needed in the late Fifties and early Sixties, is now proving less potent. A.T. & T.'s projections show that by 1980 it must *increase* its complement of operators by 130,000, more than RCA's entire work force.

ADAPTING THE CORPORATE CULTURE

Beset by troubles at every turn, A.T. & T. is entering an age of anxiety. In the years ahead, its leaders will have to strike the tenuous balance between service and profits in an atmosphere of rising costs and intense public concern with the quality of the System's performance. They must cope with competition they never faced before and train new workers they wouldn't have hired a few years ago. The future of the Bell System hangs on its leaders' ability to adapt A.T. & T.'s great corporate culture to its emphatically new environment. Among the assets A.T. & T. brings to the task are the dedication of its management and the challenge its executives feel in the face of criticism. Change will come hard, however, because the company is slowed by great size, bound by tradition, encumbered by years of inbreeding. Overcoming these internal liabilities is the biggest struggle A.T. & T. executives face.

41

Measurement and Control: Developing a Better Approach

E. KIRBY WARREN

Now that we have learned of one organization's difficulties in balancing short- and long-run objectives in a control system, we turn to a set of prescriptions for developing a better approach. In preparing to write the book from which the following selection is taken, Dr. Warren studied planning and control practices in fifteen large corporations. His research involved some three hundred hours of interviews with more than a hundred corporate and divisional managers and additional hours of analyzing policy manuals and procedures.

After examining obstacles to sound long-range planning and means for solving them, Professor Warren presents an effective long-range planning process and describes the background, personality, and behavior of a fine director of corporate planning. (We are told that this man "adds to an engineering and accounting mentality a philosopher's temperament, a snake-oil salesman's pitch, and a missionary's dedication.") At the heart of this reading is an ideal approach to measuring the quality of long-range planning, plans, planners, implementation, and results. Long-Range Planning:- The Executive Viewpoint, the book from which this selection is drawn, won an Academy of Management and McKinsey Foundation award as one of the best management books published in 1966.

In attempting to formulate a better approach to measuring and evaluating the quality of long-range planning, one must begin by establishing the criteria by which to judge an effective approach. The approach must tend to minimize, if not remove, the numerous problems encountered in present practices. The following represents a summary of the problems which must be tackled and the means which must be developed to solve them:

1. The approach must reduce or overcome management's tendency to place little real time and talent on long-range plans, because short-term results tend to be the most powerful determinants of managerial success.
2. To do this, the approach must provide top management with the means of measuring the quality and soundness of the *plan* itself or, more indirectly, of measuring the quality and soundness of the planners and the planning process.
3. This must be accomplished in a way which permits management to determine with more accuracy whether undesirable results are the product of poor administration and implementation of sound plans or whether, *despite* good administration and implementation, results have been poor because of prior planning failures.
4. This evaluation must be accomplished by staff groups equipped to evaluate the soundness of plans, planners, and planning without compromising their relationship with divisions and subgroups of the company. In addition, the evaluation and recommendations of staff must be made in a way which does not permit lower levels of line management to abdicate from certain responsibilities by citing staff interference.
5. The approach must reflect the fact that while divisional personnel are asked to develop plans for five or more years, they will probably occupy their present position for less than four years.

If an approach which accomplishes these tasks can be developed and implemented, most of the remaining obstacles which are indirect products of present control devices will be reduced, if not removed.

The following proposal reflects an idealized version of what is now being tried on one of the survey companies. In addition, pieces of approaches employed in other companies have been added where appropriate. After an outline of this approach, the approach will be tested by the above criteria, in the final portion of this chapter.

THE "CONCURRENCE" APPROACH AT EDC, INC.

For the purpose of laying out this approach, let us call the survey company which follows it most closely the EDC Company. EDC is a successful producer of industrial products with sales of more than a billion dollars. The company began a formalized long-range planning program more than 10 years ago and appointed as corporate director of planning a man with rather unique qualifications. With background in both accounting and engineering, he gained marketing experience in product planning before being promoted to director of corporate planning reporting to the company's chief executive officer. In addition to his technical qualifications, he possesses a rare combination of personal attributes. He adds to an engineering and accounting mentality a philosopher's temperament, a snake-oil salesman's pitch, and a missionary's dedication.

In his first several years as director of planning, he did almost no planning himself but instead devoted his time to the following activities:

1. Developing a relatively simple yet comprehensive mechanism to be used by the divisions for writing, integrating and revising five-year plans.
2. Selecting the best people he could find to serve as his counterpart within the divisions.
3. Selling to both corporate and lower level management the importance of planning and the feasibility of the approach proposed.
4. Developing an approach to measurement and appraisal which put teeth into the activity.

The Planning Procedure

Before turning to the measurement and review techniques employed, it is necessary first to look briefly at the planning process employed at EDC. Each year all divisions are required to prepare a two-year operating plan and an equally detailed five-year plan. The two-year plans are submitted to corporate management for review and appraisal in November and, six months later, plans for years three through five, accompanied by 10-year forecasts on key activities. By separating the first two from the last three years of the five-year plan, the company feels it is able to spread the planning load over a longer time period. It is felt that when the entire five-year plan was prepared at one time, the pressures of work made it just that much more difficult to get a fair share of time and effort devoted at lower levels to *developing* plans and at corporate levels for *reviewing* plans for years three through five.

One possible drawback to this approach is that by reviewing plans for years one and two, prior to seeing what is planned for years three through five, it will be more difficult to judge the relevance of the two-year plan to the full five-year picture. In 1966, for example, when reviewing plans for 1967-1968, the company goes back, however, to the five-year plan submitted six months earlier and is able to use it as a fairly good basis for judging the 1967-1968 plan in the context of 1965's plan for years 1969-1970. Thus, even though the focus is on the two-year operating plan, its preparation and review can be related to the five-year plan which was submitted six months earlier. Similarly, when the plan for years three through five is reviewed in May, this review is related to a revised version of the two-year plan submitted in the previous November.

The actual preparation of both the two- and five-year plans follows basically the same procedure as practiced in all of the survey companies. Assumptions on external factors which might influence the divisions are circulated to the divisions along with tentative corporate goals and strategies for the time period being planned. Basic divisional objectives are formulated and tested as to feasibility and programs formulated and costed out. During the planning period, EDC follows, as mentioned, the same basic approach to planning as practiced in the other survey companies. There are two notable exceptions. First, throughout the planning period each division circulates its key assumptions, forecasts, and objectives to the other divisions. In this way, conflicts or possible opportunities for divisional cooperation are made visible before they become more difficult to spot in the summarized statements of detailed plans which will eventually emerge.

Several survey companies have attempted to get this horizontal transfer of divisional assumptions, forecasts, and objectives prior to the development of detailed plans. Unless there is time and incentive at the divisional level to use this interdivisional data, however, this step is wasted and interdivisional coordination must take place later at the corporate level. When this happens, after detailed plans have already been developed and fences built, it is much more difficult for corporate management working with summarized data to do the job effectively. The major reasons for EDC's success in getting interdivisional transfer of data are (1) the nature of the planning cycle leaves sufficient time to use the data and (2) the nature of the follow up review by corporate management allows them to find out whether the divisions made use of the interchange and if not, they will want to know why not.

The second difference in the EDC planning approach is that corporate staff groups play a very minor role in assisting the divisions in the *preparation* of plans. As in one other survey company, corporate staff groups will advise and council, will bring in survey material or relevant interdivisional viewpoints but are most careful *not* to give the impression that their major function is to be of help to the divisions. An adequate number of competent people are placed with division staffs, and it is the job of these division level staffs to devote their talents and allegiance to divisional needs. The function of the corporate staff groups is viewed as (1) carrying out corporate level studies, (2) assisting corporate management in formulating and communicating its viewpoints to the divisions, and (3) assisting corporate management in reviewing divisional plans and performance.

By keeping these points in mind, the corporate staff groups minimize the dilemma related earlier. Namely, the case where a director of corporate marketing, after working for years to build the trust needed to help a division, was forced to violate that trust to aid the president in reviewing the division's plans.

The Preliminary Review Procedure

As can be seen from the above, a certain amount of interdivisional coordination and review takes place in EDC while the plans are being formulated. In addition, by giving the division an opportunity to review major aspects of each other's plans, before many important premises and objectives are lost in the summary and consolidation process which follows, the divisions are more apt to uncover for themselves weaknesses and/or opportunities for improvement.

Once the divisional plans have been prepared and summarized (both the two- and five-year plans), they are submitted to the several corporate staff groups. Here, the procedure appears on the surface to be like those criticized in the other survey companies. There are several key differences, however. The financial elements of the plans are reviewed and consolidated by a budget and analysis group as before, but, then, each corporate staff receives not only the portions of the "prose" plan related to its activity but the entire "prose" plan and the financial plan as well. For example, the corporate marketing staff will receive each divisional plan and carefully analyze it in terms of how well it reflects sound long- and short-range thinking in the area of marketing. They must probe beneath the platitudes and seek to determine whether real planning is reflected. Then they must also evaluate the relationship between the prose plan and the financial elements of meeting it.

In theory, this is what might take place in any of the survey companies. Why it often does not lies in these differences:

1. In EDC, the corporate staffs have been built by selecting the very best men in the company in their specialties. The research staff is

headed by the most knowledgeable research man in the company. He is not viewed as too valuable to be in staff work. Instead, he is viewed as too valuable not to be. The only exception to this rule would be when the top man in terms of knowledge or expertise lacks the temperament and vision to be more planner and appraiser than doer. In these cases, EDC will settle for the best balance of knowledge and temperament. In many of the survey companies these were not the criteria used in selecting key corporate staff or when the selection was good, failure to provide the following conditions offset proper selection.

2. As noted earlier, EDC makes it perfectly clear that a corporate staff man's first allegiance is to corporate management and only indirectly shall he aid the divisions. While this necessitates capable staff talent at both corporate and division levels, EDC maintains that it cannot afford *not* to pay this price, since the responsibilities of the two levels are potentially incompatible. To ask a man to perform for both leads to built-in conflicts of interest.

3. The corporate staffs are made aware (at times painfully) that they will be evaluated on how well they have forced the divisions to balance their natural propensity to focus on the short rather than the long, on the tangible rather than the intangible. If subsequent review reveals that a division mortagaged its future in, for example, research, the corporate director of research will have a great deal of explaining to do. It is his charge to review division plans in such a way as to minimize the chances of this happening. Since the top corporate staff personnel in EDC are so carefully selected and highly rewarded they tend, if successful, to have a longer tenure in the same job than divisional counterparts. Thus, they know they are likely to be around when the mortgage comes due.

Given these three factors, corporate staffs carefully probe division plans before they are submitted to final consolidation and review. If one additional step had not been taken in EDC, however, this might be all for naught. The key lies in what happens when a staff head, charged with assuring that long-range excellence in his area is reflected in a division's plan, feels that the division fails to reflect this excellence in its plans. The general managers of most of EDC's divisions are charged with profit center responsibility. If they permit a staff request for change in plan, they *are not* allowed to use it as a reduction or abdication from responsibility. They must not be placed in a position where subsequent unsatisfactory performance can be blamed on the "staff's plan, not my implementation." If this were to happen, then it would be difficult to hold the staff head responsible because he will defend his "plan" and cite "the obvious lack of commitment and subsequent poor implementation of division management" as the reason for poor results.

To avoid this, both parties, corporate staff and divisional management, must come to agreement before the plan is approved and, when this is impossible, state for the record the basis for their disagreement. In so doing, the plan which ultimately comes to final review by the executive committee is one acceptable to both parties; one on which both parties are prepared to stake their futures.

The question which remains is what happens if they can't agree, or more often, prefer not to?

The Power of "Nonconcurrence"

Since the divisions are charged with profit responsibility and, thus, will take on the responsibility for making corporate staff recommendations work, they should not be forced to accept these recommendations. On the other hand, as has been noted, the staff head, charged with assuring long-run excellence in marketing or research, for example, will be held responsible if subsequent poor results are traced to failures in his area of expertise. Thus, the staff heads cannot be forced to accept a plan which they feel is deficient. Every attempt is made to have two parties who disagree work out a compromise acceptable to both. If this cannot be accomplished, the staff head attaches to the division plan a statement of "nonconcurrence."

In this statement he must indicate his reasons and document them. When this occurs, the head of the division in question will then be required to debate the issue with the corporate staff man before the division head's group vice-president. The group vice-president, serving as a mediator, seeks to work out an acceptable solution. Most "nonconcurrences" are settled at this level, but, when the two parties cannot agree, the process moves one step higher. The group vice-president, aided by the division manager, must now debate the nonconcurrence with vice-president of corporate staff, aided by the specific staff head in question. This debate is held before EDC's top management committee, and it serves as final arbitrator. Regardless of how the committee rules, the procedure has forced both the corporate staff head and the division manager to develop fully their positions and document not only their differing programs but the premises and forecasts which underlie them. In the future, when the impact of the decision begins to appear in performance, the availability of the debate records provides top management with a much better basis for judging whether unsatisfactory results stemmed from poor plans or poor implementation or some factor beyond the control of line or staff. This is done by comparing the premises and forecasts (and the methods used for developing them) to what history proved to be fact. It is only fair to note that relatively few disagreements reach the corporate management committee. Both sides in such a disagreement, rather than go through what has to be a harrowing experience, prefer to seek a mutually satisfactory solution. On the big issues though, since both parties know they will be held accountable, disagreements do and should come through this nonconcurrence procedure.

Given these several stages of financial and nonfinancial review, the final review of divisional plans by the corporate management committee is a relatively brief one. In theory, by this time, the top advisors to this committee, the corporate staff groups, through discussion and/or debate, have made their views felt. It remains for the committee to check the plans in the broadest terms against their over-all corporate aspirations and resources.

The Post-facto Review Procedure

It would be possible to go through all of the steps described above and still fail to measure accurately long-range planning efforts. The final phase of EDC approach is to review carefully plans submitted in prior years against both present plans and results. Deviations are expected. Only a most conservative or extremely lucky manager will have results which match his plan or will submit in 1967 for, say, 1968-71 a plan which is identical to the plan for that period submitted in 1966. As conditions change, premises and programs must change. Anytime a change is noted, anytime a difference between plans or between results and plans occurs, it must, however, be explained. If a goal for 1969 is set in 1966 and then revised in 1967, the corporate review committee will want to know why. If the manager can show that the premises he made in 1966 were sound, based on information then available, but that subsequent data make them unrealistic then he will have no problem. But, by requiring this explanation, it becomes that much riskier for a manager to throw together, arbitrarily, a plan for three years hence on the assumption that he will do the real planning in two years.

Whether true or not, there are two rumors which persist in EDC. The first has to do with the ex-corporate staff man, whose salary and bonuses had been in excess of $150,000 a year but who was demoted because subsequent reviews of plans he approved showed less than adequate effort on his part to assure long-run expertise in his area. The second rumor maintains that a division general manager who had been promoted to vice-president was demoted to general manager of a smaller division, when subsequent review of plans he had submitted three years earlier clearly revealed that his short-run success had been based on poor long-range planning. The record on two debates he had "won" supposedly showed that while he had been more persuasive, his premises and programs had not been soundly based. Despite his complaint that hindsight is always 20/20, the records and subsequent results indicated to corporate management that the ex-vice-president had had sufficient information when he submitted the plan to have made a better judgment. By not using that judgment, he saved his division three million dollars in costs in his last year as general manager, but as a result, it cost the company an estimated seven million dollars over the next two years and cost him his vice-presidency.

· · ·

There is no doubt that the attitude of EDC's top management and its ability to man its corporate staff groups with able people are key elements of its approach to appraising long-range planning. The nature of the mechanics of implementing this appraisal program, however, underlies and reinforces these attitudes and EDC's willingness to commit top talent to this appraisal program.

The process may in certain companies require modifications. EDC, despite its size, has a relatively narrow product line. As a result, it is possible for the several corporate staff groups to apply their expertise to virtually all divisions equally. In a more diversified company, divisional differences in product, market, or technology may make this impossible. In these cases, the role of over-all corporate staff in the detailed appraisal of long-range plans is greatly reduced, and there should be several smaller sets of EDC-type staffs located at the group vice-president's level. Where group vice-president levels do not exist and the staff must be located at the corporate level, then subspecialists must be found. The basic mechanism and philosophy of checks and balances leading to effective evaluation of plans as well as results and results in terms of plans remains the same.

Any corporation can, with modifications, develop these mechanics and take the first step toward creating the missing link: a soundly conceived and implemented approach to balancing short-term results with long-range plans through meaningful measurement and evaluation of the plan itself. Without such an approach, corporate long-range planning is doomed, at best, to isolated and limited success.

42

The Game of Budget Control

G. H. HOFSTEDE

Budgetary control is the principal control technique used in most organizations. Unfortunately, most of the literature on this subject emphasizes the technical aspects of budgeting rather than the human response to budgetary control systems. This selection is included because it concerns the human aspect of budgeting.

Reprinted from G. H. Hofstede, *The Game of Budget Control,* pp. 294-303, by permission of the publisher. Copyright 1967 by Royal VanGorcum Ltd., Assen, The Netherlands.

In his book The Game of Budget Control, *Dr. G. H. Hofstede reports on his comprehensive research study of behavioral response to budget systems in the Netherlands. He studied the budgets of six manufacturing plants in five different industries: printing, metal products, textiles, electronics, and food. Dr. Hofstede spent over four hundred hours interviewing approximately ninety first-, second-, and third-line manufacturing managers and approximately fifty controllers, budget accountants, and industrial engineers.*

This selection consists of the final two chapters of Dr. Hofstede's book, chapters in which he presents practical recommendations for those in business who have to work and live with budgets and budgetary standards. Separate recommendations are made for each level of line management and for those staff officials whose work is closely connected to the budget system.

Dr. Hofstede's recommendations are followed by his predictions concerning the nature of future budget systems. He notes that the key question in future systems will continue to be, "What is a desirable and proper balance between control and individual autonomy?"

PRACTICAL RECOMMENDATIONS

Recommendations to Company Top Management

These recommendations are aimed at top management of a manufacturing company, which for its manufacturing operations either uses budget control and wants to improve its functioning, or does not use budget control and wants to introduce it. The recommendations in this chapter go to some extent beyond the immediate conclusions of this study. This is unavoidable, as any researcher will realize when he steps into a consultant role. My recommendations to company top management are:

Realize that the budget control system is *your* tool to manage your company. Its functioning depends primarily on you, not on your controller.

When setting budgets, have the decisions which must be taken at your level, like the choice of product lines and production volume, taken first and then communicated to your subordinates. Then ask your subordinates to prepare the draft budgets at the lowest possible level of management and have them consolidated at each next higher level. If they cannot be accepted and have to be revised, take the time to discuss this with your subordinates and to explain the reasons. Make sure they do the same with their subordinates. Realize that budgets have a coordinating and a motivating function and that especially in the larger corporations the way the coordination is felt at the lower levels can easily destroy motivation. It is therefore necessary to explain much more than you think you should.

Realize that budgets only motivate when they are tight enough to be a challenge, and that they only offer a challenge if there is a risk that they will not be fully met. If some budgets are not met this is only a sign that the system is healthy and it does not mean that somebody is at fault. If you take the habit of interpreting it in this latter way, budgets will all soon be met, but they will not motivate.

Realize that the fact that motivating budgets are not always met means that the same budget cannot be used both for coordinating and motivating. It will be necessary to reserve a risk percentage for average underattainment of budgets to arrive at actually expected figures which can be used for coordination.

Decide beforehand which percentage variance from the various budgets you can leave to the discretion of your subordinates before you will intervene and let them know this. In other words, set their control limits.

Be sensitive to the reactions of your subordinates to the budgets set for them and keep open grievance channels for those who see their standards as impossibly tight. Be ready to change budgets if this is the case; if you do not do it, actual results will be worse than if you do.

Eliminate the taboo on communicating financial information about budget results to the lowest levels of management, including plant foremen.

Discuss the functioning of the budget system with your controller and make sure he sees his role neither as an auditor nor as a data processor but as a systems architect and educator.

Recommendations to the Top and Middle Management of the Plant

Realize that the budget control system is *your* tool to manage your plant. Its functioning within the plant depends primarily on you, not on the controller or his department.

If possible, see to it that budgets and standards are set separately for the responsibility area of each of your foremen, but at least for each second-line manager. Then have your foremen participate in the setting of their technical standards and make their own draft expense budget. Let them have the assistance from the budget accountant they need, but let them do the actual figuring themselves.

If draft budgets are changed afterwards or cut, discuss this with your subordinates and explain the reasons.

If you are running a shift operation so that more foremen are responsible for the same department, the budgeting effort should be done by the lowest level which covers all shifts, but only after consultation with the foremen in meetings. If results can be split by shifts, then again the individual foremen can be the budgetees.

Decide beforehand which percentage variance from the various budgets and technical standards you will leave to the discretion of your subordinates before you will intervene and let them know this. These percentages are their control limits.

Be sensitive to the reactions of your subordinates on the budgets and standards set for them and keep open grievance channels for those who see their standards as impossibly tight. Be ready to change the standard if this is the case.

Take account of the age and personality structure of each of your subordinates in setting targets and standards for them: what will mean a challenge for a young man can mean a discouragingly tight objective for an older man.

Show interest in your subordinates' budget results also when they do not transgress their control limits, but be sure this is seen as interest, not as intervention.

If you have to intervene, get the full story from your subordinate first. Center the conversation around what should be done to correct the situation, not on who is at fault.

Show your subordinates that you consider meeting standards as part of their performance but be careful not to appraise by budget or standards results alone. Realize that while from your point of view results may be the only important factor, in the eyes of your subordinate it is his efforts which determine his merit.

If you are under pressure from your superiors, consider whether it is wise to send this pressure down to your subordinates. Protect your subordinates against influences from above which will in their situation only discourage and demotivate them. Perform your umbrella function.

When budgeting is first started in your plant, do not expect results immediately. Give your subordinates the time to learn to use this tool and learn to use it yourself: this may take a few years. See to it that the budget accounting staff interprets its role not as auditing or policing but as supporting and educating the line in the use of accounting information.

Discuss with your subordinates and with the budget and standards staff which feedback information is desirable from a line management point of view and which is available from a data processing point of view. Try to unite the two. Resist attempts of the line to ask, or of the staff to supply, more information than a normal human being can digest. Review periodically the information received and stop whichever part of it you do not use. Realize, however, that there are key points in your production process about which you should be informed, even if they are never off-standard. They may be off-standard tomorrow.

Realize that the essence of good budget control is cooperation and that you must meet the budget challenge with your subordinates as a team. Realize that the performance of your plant depends on their motivation. Try to develop a game spirit among your team. Show your enthusiasm and respect the responsibilities of your subordinates. Mistrust and undue pressure will destroy the game spirit.

Be sensitive to any signs of passing the buck, scapegoating, fighting the system, or other wasteful activities among your subordinates. If these things happen it is a sign that *you* have failed in leading the game the right way. Try again.

Make sensible use of group meetings with your subordinates. Do not handle problems here which can better be handled on a man-to-man basis, such as budget performances of individual departments. Use them for informal contact and team-building. Use them to supply general information about cost. Let your subordinates use the meetings to help each other in giving meaning to the standards and using them as management tools towards their own subordinates. Meetings can be powerful tools to influence your subordinate's attitudes. However, if you feel your meetings are not useful, it is better not to have them; they will do more harm than good.

Discuss the reorganizations in your management structure with your controller before they are carried out, so that the responsibility and account structures can remain mutually adapted.

Recommendations to the Foremen
or First-Line Managers

Technical performance standards and budgets are a management tool for you to use. They are your guides in the management process and important yardsticks for your managerial achievement.

More and more the first-line manager will need the kind of information which is supplied by standards and budget systems. In many cases he will be able to do a better job if he gets insight into the financial results of his department as well as the technical results.

Although participation in the setting of an expense budget and sometimes other financial standards takes time and effort, this effort pays off in better budgets and a better understanding of how the business is run.

The foreman who is better informed himself will be able to do a better job at communicating results to the workers. There are many possibilities of involving the workers in the results feedback. The use of periodic meetings is one of them. This study has not included the cost-consciousness and standards fulfilment motivation of workers. From other studies it is clear that one important question is whether or not piece-rates or similar systems are used. Apart from this, the foreman is the key person in determining the cost-consciousness of his workers.

Recommendations to the Company
and/or Plant Controller

The success of a budget system does not primarily depend upon the controller, but upon the top line executive. The controller's role is hygienic: he has to satisfy certain minimal requirements but has more scope in making the system fail than succeed. If he considers not only the accounting part but also the human part of the system as his specialty however, he can become the systems architect, catalyst and educator.

The same budget cannot be used for coordinating and for motivating managers. Coordinating budgets should represent actually expected performance; but budgets can be shown to have a motivating effect only when they involve a risk of not being attained. Budgets that are really motivating should be increased with an average risk percentage to arrive at actual expected performance.

Consider the use of statistical techniques in cost control and budgeting. From a point of view of motivation it is desirable that, for each budget, control limits are set which guarantee a certain free scope for managers at various levels before their superiors intervene. From a technical point of view this can be solved by statistical techniques like those used in quality control. Controllers should familiarize themselves much more with the possibilities of these techniques.

Split the account structure if possible as far as the responsibility of the individual foremen. Let the foreman draft his own expense budget but have him supplied with all the support from the budget accountant he needs. Eliminate the taboo on financial information in the plant.

Both the system in which individual plant departments are full profit centers buying from and selling to other departments and the system in which they are only expense centers have their drawbacks. In the first case the system is difficult to understand and use for line management and a continuous effort at simplification and instruction is necessary. In the second case expense budgets should be kept flexible enough to adapt to changes in technical performance and line management should have more support in taking economic decisions.

Management information reports should be separated from accounting consolidation reports. In management information there should be a periodic weeding out of over-information, and periodic consultations with management of various levels down to the foreman level about the understandability of information and the desirability of other information.

Establish a close cooperation between work study engineers and budget accountants, although it is not essential that the work study engineers report to the controller.

Man budget accounting departments in such a way that about 25% of total time is available for personal discussions with and support to line management.

When appraising budget accountants and other staff people for salary increases and promotion, ask the line managers with whom they cooperate for their impressions. This has a beneficial effect upon staff behavior and line-staff cooperation.

The best service to the line is given by budget accountants and other staff people who are competent in their speciality and also tactful.

Develop a career planning for your people.

Recommendations to the Budget Accountant

When budgets have to be set, let the line managers make the drafts. Assist them with all the information they need. Develop special information sources for this purpose; but let the actual figuring be done by line managers themselves.

Design the management information system yourself after thorough discussion about what line managers at various levels, down to the foreman level, need to know and what you can supply. Do not use reports that serve for accounting consolidation simultaneously for management information. Give more detailed information to lower management levels and more general information to higher management levels.

Have periodic consultations with line managers of the different levels about the management information system: desires for new information, improvement of understandability, weeding out of unnecessary information. Beware of overinformation. Managers do not want to know everything; if they miss some information which they need, they will come and ask for it.

Make the management information reports yourself or if they are made by purely clerical people at least check them thoroughly before they are distributed. Managers will use figures only if they feel confident they are right. Frequent mistakes will spoil any information system.

Focus the information on efficiency variances. Omit variances that are caused by pure accounting causes.

Be informed about changes in the responsibility structure of the organization in due time so that you can adapt the account structure accordingly.

Budgets should always follow management responsibility.

Be critical as to the raw data you receive. Realize that if people feel they are measured by these data they will tend to make them look right. Data connected with a piece-rate system or which in another way directly influence pay are basically unfit for efficiency information. Always try to anchor the data you receive to actual cash movements, for instance wages paid, which cannot be faked.

Reserve about 25% of your time for personal contacts with the people who receive your management information. Take time to explain figures. Test whether they have understood the information. If they do not it does not mean that they are silly: it means that you have failed in speaking or writing a language they can understand. Try again.

Realize that the success of a budget and management information system is not in your hands: it is in the hands of line management. They will not be able to make it successful without your support, however. The success of *your job* depends on the quality of this support: upon your competence and the tactfulness with which you build up your contacts with line management.

430

Maintain good professional contacts with those responsible for the system of technical standards, such as work study engineers. Keep them informed about the financial side of efficiency results and always base your financial standards on their technical ones.

Recommendations to the Work Study Engineer

Set your standards always in close contact with line management. If line managers see you know your job and you behave tactfully, they will accept you. When they ask your support, always be ready to give it. A staff man should be happy when he is pulled and unhappy when he is pushing.

Base standards on external reference information wherever possible, but be careful about how you select these external reference points. If line management does not see them as legitimate and valid for their situation, they will do more harm than good. Take the time to discuss external data with the line managers and let them participate in finding valid reference points.

Realize that the success of your job depends to a large extent on how line people see you.

Maintain good professional contacts with the budget accountants and exchange information with them.

Recommendations to the Personnel Manager

Keep line management informed about any signs of discouragement of managers through standards that are seen as impossible, as well as about signs of interdepartmental conflict which may be adverse effects of the way the standards and budget system is used for management.

A system of job rotation between functions in line management or between line and staff can have its implications not only for the development of the people but also for the development of the control system.

Pay special attention to the development and career planning of staff people like budget accountants and work study engineers. For good line-staff cooperation it is not essential that staff people have line experience; it is more important that they are competent in their speciality and behave tactfully. Include staff people in management development courses and in training in interpersonal relations.

Design the performance appraisal system for staff people for salary increases in such a way that their line counterparts are asked for their impression about the support they get from them and that this impression contributes to the appraisal of the staff man.

• • •

The Budget System of Tomorrow

There is no doubt that the business of tomorrow will need financial planning and goal-setting. There will be more of it than there is today, including companies which could afford to do without it until now. The most significant development in business affecting the budget system is the application of Electronic Data Processing. Budget and management information systems will be more and more computerized and more and more integrated. They will probably be extended to non-accounting data, maybe even to data about employee attitudes and perceptions.

The challenge to business in this development is whether this will lead to increased pressure on the individual or not. The conflict between control and autonomy will be fought out in the process of computerization. The outcome of this battle has deep significance for both the individual and the business. What is the value of the Free Enterprise System if freedom exists only at the top? The modern free enterprise corporation is internally a highly guided economy. Will it do any thing better for the people in it than the State Capitalism it rejects?

This study suggests that it should be possible to deliberately plan a certain amount of scope for the individual, even within a system that is computer-controlled. ... 'calculated inefficiency' ... can save the humanity within the system.

· · ·

Suggestions for Further Research

There is a vast field for further research in management control systems. This study was necessarily still too exploratory. It is desirable to test the hypotheses developed on new data; in particular, to devote further studies to the game aspect of budgeting. ...

The study of budget control systems should be continued with better systems output measures than I was able to find; it should be extended to longitudinal studies (following the same system through time) and to field experiments. ... It should be extended outside manufacturing units to other functions of the business. How many studies have been devoted to quota setting processes for salesmen? It should be extended from the top management to the non-managerial employee level and to non-business organizations as well. With full acknowledgement of the work that has already been done by several eminent researchers, we have only just started.

432

43

The PERT/Cost System

DEPARTMENT OF THE NAVY

PERT/Cost is an integrated management-control system that attempts to achieve a proper balance of time, cost, and technical performance. In this selection staff members of the Special Projects Office of the Department of the Navy briefly describe Program Evaluation and Review Technique (PERT). With the use of graphs, they then present the limitations of conventional control techniques and show that redistribution of human, financial, and other resources can enable a project to look good until it is too late for corrective action. PERT/Cost is useful because it points out critical schedule slippages and cost overruns in time for correction.

The remainder of the selection is devoted to the procedure for constructing a PERT/Cost System.* One is invited to examine graphic presentations of critical and slack paths, and is encouraged to study the status reports that the system produces. Such reports are sent in appropriate detail to the various levels of management. Standard PERT/Cost outputs deal with time, cost, and manpower requirements. They are of interest to both contractor and customer.

Vice Admiral W. F. Raborn, Director of Special Projects for the U.S. Navy in 1961—when the PERT/Cost System was developed—believed that some of the most serious problems facing the United States were associated with planning and controlling large, complex weapons and space development programs. To solve these problems, managers had to have techniques that would provide continual balance of time, cost, and manpower. PERT/Cost is such a technique, a step toward an integrated management system that provides the contractor, as well as the customer, with the data required for effective decision-making and control.

Reprinted from "An Introduction to the PERT/Cost System," Special Projects Office, Department of the Navy, 1963. This material is not subject to copyright.

*The PERT/Cost System described in this selection was developed for the U.S. Navy Special Projects Office by a team consisting of members of Management Systems Corporation (formerly Management Controls Systems, Inc.) in association with Willard Frazar, project monitor, Hilda Callaway of the Special Projects Office, and William Hunter of the Navy Management Office. The system was pilot-tested at General Electric's Ordnance Department in Pittsfield, Massachusetts, and at Lockheed Missile and Space Company, Sunnyvale, California. General Electric and Lockheed participated in development of the system and contributed to the evaluation of its practicability.

PERT is not only used in defense industries, but is also employed in the construction of ships, buildings, and highways, in the planning and launching of new products, in the installation and debugging of computer systems, in the development of job corps training centers, in the publication of books, and even in the production of a Broadway play. Frequently, PERT systems are used in conjunction with computers. A computer program is employed that permits calculations to be made without reference to a flow chart or diagram. The printouts show job progress, departmental responsibility, and time schedules.

PROJECT MANAGEMENT

Early in the development of the Polaris Missile Program, the Navy Special Projects Office recognized the need for an integrated management system. As an early step in this direction, the Program Evaluation and Review Technique (PERT) was developed to aid in the planning and control of time schedules in the Polaris Program. Since its introduction in 1958, the PERT technique has received widespread interest and voluntary adoption throughout American industry as a significant improvement in project planning and control.

In addition to its use in schedule planning and control, the network concept in PERT provides the framework for treating a wide range of project management problems. Recognizing this fact, the Navy Special Projects Office [extended] the PERT technique to include the elements of cost and technical performance.

THE PERT/COST SYSTEM

A. What It Is

PERT/Cost is an integrated management system designed to provide managers with the information they need in planning and controlling schedules *and* costs in development projects. The system provides information in various levels of detail, thereby satisfying the needs of contractor management as well as the customer. It is designed both to mesh with existing management systems and to provide valuable new information.

The PERT/Cost System consists of a Basic Procedure for planning and control, and two closely related supplements setting forth more advanced planning procedures. The objectives of the PERT/Cost System are summarized in Figure 1.

The Basic PERT/Cost Procedure	Assists project managers by providing information in the varying levels of detail needed for planning schedules and costs, evaluating schedule and cost performance, and predicting and controlling time and cost overruns.
The Time-Cost Option Procedure (Supplemental)	Displays alternate time-cost-risk plans for accomplishing project objectives.
The Resource Allocation Procedure (Supplemental)	Determines the lowest cost allocation of resources among individual project tasks, to meet a specified project duration.

Figure 1   Objectives of the PERT/Cost System.

B. Why It Is Needed: Limitations of Conventional Techniques

The illustration in Figure 2 demonstrates the limitations of conventional planning and control techniques for determining project time and cost status, and for relating costs to progress.

- Figure 2 contains a standard milestone chart accompanied by its corresponding rate of expenditure display.
- The open triangles in the illustration are the milestones or events which are scheduled to be completed at a future time. The closed triangles are milestones already completed.
- The development work of Project "X" is planned for a nine-month period with six milestones scheduled throughout that period. The milestones scheduled during the first three months were the only ones completed at the time this report was prepared.
- The budget for Project "X" for the first three months was $100,000, and, in terms of the data represented in Figure 2, the manager would conclude that the project was on schedule and on budget.
- Project "X," however, is actually in serious difficulty. In order to identify this difficulty it is necessary to develop different kinds of information than that which is presented in Figure 2.

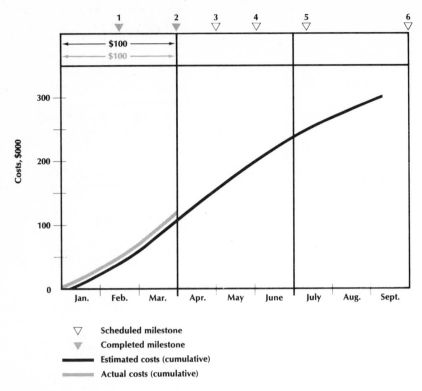

Figure 2   Conventional milestone and budget display.

A closer examination of Project "X" would have revealed significant information on a number of tasks that contribute to the accomplishment of the Project work (see Figure 3).

In task (I), milestone 1 was scheduled to be completed in February. Originally, $10,000 was estimated to achieve milestone 1, and $10,000 more for performing additional work on task (I) during the remainder of the first quarter. In task (II), milestone 2 was scheduled to be completed on 31 March at a cost estimated to be $20,000. Though tasks (III) and (IV) have no milestones scheduled during the first quarter, $30,000 was estimated to be spent on each of these tasks for ongoing work during the first three months. Thus, the total first quarter budget for Project "X" is $100,000.

As the project proceeded, task (I) expended funds and completed work as planned. Task (II), however, encountered difficulty. $50,000 was spent instead of the $20,000 estimated in order to accomplish milestone 2 on schedule. The added $30,000 came, in fact, from tasks (III) and (IV), which sacrificed labor and other resources to task (II). Thus, tasks (III) and (IV) face probable schedule slippages or cost overruns when attempting to meet their milestones later in the project year. Yet, in terms of the standard control techniques, all appeared to be fine.

Although conventional estimating procedures may require the preparation of estimates for all the tasks in a project, these tasks generally will not serve as cost accumulation centers. The estimates, therefore, cannot be used as a basis for control. The redistribution of resources to remedy the problem areas can continue to enable this project to "look good" in terms of milestone completion and rate of expenditure until the very last quarter in the project when it would be too late for effective corrective action.

The PERT/Cost System sets forth a procedure to identify critical schedule slippages and cost overruns in time for corrective action.

THE BASIC PERT/COST PROCEDURE

A. The Network and Time Estimates

The first step in the PERT/Cost System is the construction of a network consisting of the activities (project tasks) to be performed, and the events or milestones to be attained.

The network reflects the carefully developed plan for accomplishing the project, and identifies the interrelationships and interdependencies in the work to be performed. By so doing, the effects of any schedule slippages on the entire project can be readily determined.

Recognizing the need to express varying degrees of uncertainty about the work to be accomplished in the activities, the PERT System calls for an optimistic (t_o), most likely (t_m), and pessimistic (t_p) time estimate for each activity. From these estimates a statistically "expected" time estimate (t_e) is calculated.

Figure 3   The individual tasks in Project"X."

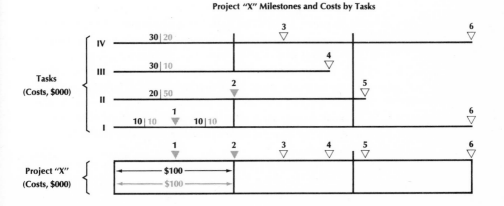

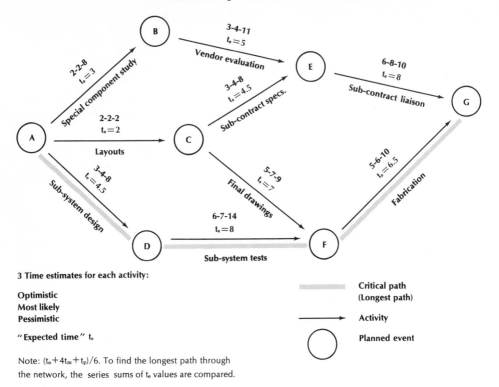

3 Time estimates for each activity:

Optimistic
Most likely
Pessimistic

"Expected time" t_e

Note: $(t_o + 4t_m + t_p)/6$. To find the longest path through the network, the series sums of t_e values are compared.

Critical path
(Longest path)

Activity

Planned event

Figure 4   The network of "expected" times.

- In the example shown in Figure 4, the "Subsystem Tests" activity time estimates are:

$$t_o = 6 \quad t_m = 7 \quad t_p = 14$$

- The calculated t_e is eight weeks. The longest path through the network is called the critical path. Any shortening of total project time must be accomplished by reducing the duration of the longest path. The critical path may be shortened by applying more effort to critical activities or by replanning the network to eliminate certain tasks or to perform more activities in parallel. Thus the network focuses management attention on those areas where corrective action is most needed and can do the most good. In Figure 4 the critical path is shown by the gray line. All other paths on the network are called, slack paths.

438

B. Cost Estimates

After the network has been prepared and time estimates developed for the network activities, the manager will establish a schedule. This schedule will be based on the critical path calculations, the directed dates and the manager's judgment concerning the goals to be established for accomplishing the activities.

Once the schedule has been established, resource estimates to perform each cost significant segment of the network (activity or group of activities) as scheduled are obtained. These estimates are then converted to total dollar estimates.

Figure 5 shows the PERT/Cost network with the scheduled time and estimated cost for each activity.

Figure 5   The schedule/cost network – plan.

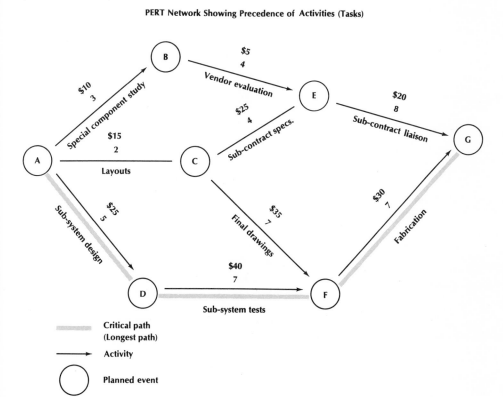

PERT Network Showing Precedence of Activities (Tasks)

C. Actual Time and Costs

Actual costs and times are collected separately for each cost significant segment of the network. These actual time and cost inputs are compared with estimates to indicate the project status. Figure 6 contains the sample network with estimated *and* actual time and cost information.

- In the example shown in Figure 6, the completed activities thus far include activities A-B, A-C, and A-D. Although activity A-B has consumed one week more than scheduled, it is on a slack path and the slippage will have no effect on the total program duration. This activity was budgeted for $10,000 and actually required only $8,000, a $2,000 underrun. Activity A-C was completed on budget and on

Figure 6   The schedule/cost network—plan and status.

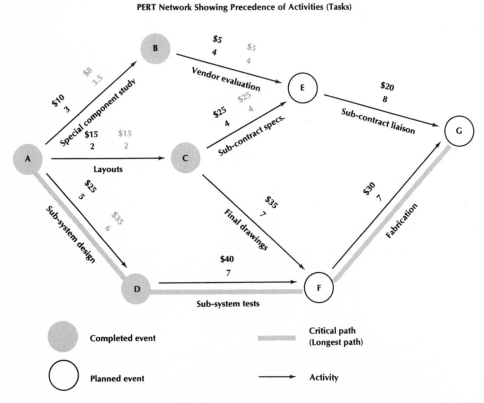

PERT Network Showing Precedence of Activities (Tasks)

PERT/COST ESTIMATING FORM							Date Prepared __23 JUNE__			

ACTIVITY DESCRIPTION _Design Simulator No. 5_		Activity Account No.	72345-01	PERT Time Est. (in weeks)	
Begin Event No. _191_	End Event No. _193_	Responsible Unit	5410	Optimistic	_5_
Beginning Event Date _10 JULY '72_	Ending Event Date _18 AUG.'72_	Estimator	_RJK_	Most Likely	_6_
		Approved	_TLM_	Pessimistic	_10_
Type Entry _1_	Scheduled Elapsed Time _6 WKS._	Date Approved	_6/27_	Expected Elapsed Time	_6.5_

Manpower Skill	ESTIMATED DIRECT MANHOURS BY MONTHS ELAPSED TIME												Total Man Hrs.	SUMMARY OF PURCHASES		
	MONTHS													Code	DESCRIPTION	$
	1st	2nd	3rd	4th	5th	6th	7th	8th	9th	10th	11th	12th				
D	200	60											260		Direct Material	
E	200	320											520	61	Eng. Dev. Material	400
M	180	360											540		Tooling Material	
S	80	40											120		Test Equip. Material	
															Insp. Equip. Material	
															Computer	
															Sub Contract	
															Total Purchases	400

Figure 7   The PERT/Cost estimating form.

schedule. Activity A-D encountered difficulty and incurred a $10,000 overrun in cost and a one-week slippage in schedule. The schedule slippage in this path required immediate management attention since A-D is an activity on the critical path.

• Note also that activity B-E and C-E have consumed both their time and budget, yet are incomplete. New estimates to complete are required for these activities.

D. Estimating Form

The PERT/Cost estimating form (see Figure 7) is used to develop the type of data needed for preparing the time/cost network plan for a project. Only the information appearing in the top half of this form is used until a satisfactory time plan and schedule have been determined. Once the schedule has been established, manpower and material estimates are entered in the manner indicated on the bottom half of the form.

The breakdown of manpower by skill categories provides the data needed to indicate the manpower requirements of the project. Conversion of manhours and material to total dollars is accomplished by applying the appropriate labor and overhead rates.

	IDENTIFICATION			TIME STATUS					COST STATUS			
PERT TIME AND COST STATUS REPORT — Project____ Contract No.____ Month Ending____	Begin Event No.	End Event No.	Activity Account No.	Expected Elapsed Time (t_e)	Scheduled Elapsed Time (t_s)	Scheduled Completion Date (T_S)	Latest Allowable Completion Date (T_L)	Activity Slack $(T_L)-(T_S)$	Contract Estimate	Actual Costs	Latest Revised Estimate	Overrun/ (Underrun)
BASIC / By Activities / (Direct Costs Only)	165	168	71829-01	5.0	5.0	9/8/72	8/25/72	-2.0	$20,000	$25,000	$30,000	$10,000
	168	182	71829-02	10.0	10.0	11/17/72	11/3/72	-2.0	35,000	18,000	30,000	(5,000)
	165	182	71829-03	8.0	8.0	9/15/72	11/?/72	7.0	15,000	6,000	25,000	10,000
									70,000*	49,000*	85,000*	15,000*
FIRST SUMMARY / By Individual Hardware Items / (Total Costs)	165	182	71829	15.0	15.0	11/17/72	11/3/72	-2.0	70,000 +105,000	49,000 +74,000	85,000 +128,000	15,000 +23,000
									175,000*	123,000*	213,000*	38,000*
SECOND SUMMARY / By Major Hardware Categories / (Total Costs)	051	325	718	30.0	30.0	1/26/73	1/12/73	-2.0	500,000	300,000	600,000	100,000

Notes:
+ = Indirect Costs
* = Totals

Figure 8 The time and cost status report with basic and summary data.

E. Time and Cost Status Reports

The PERT/Cost System provides time, cost, and resource reports for various levels of management. Some of these reports are shown on the following pages.

A typical comprehensive status report is one which combines time and cost information (see Figure 8).

The Time and Cost Status Report is a basic output of the PERT/Cost System. It is designed to assist the project manager in evaluating over-all time and cost progress and in pinpointing those activities which are causing schedule slippages or cost overruns, either actual or potential. The system permits this form to be printed in several degrees of data summation so that appropriate detail is presented to each level of management.

(The concept of summary reporting with detailed back-up reports applies to all PERT/Cost outputs.)

F. Manpower Requirements Report

This is a typical report that identifies the monthly manpower requirements to perform the project on schedule. The report is presented by total manpower and by individual manpower skills. An "Activity Slack" column provides the manager with a ranking of activities in the order of their importance to completing the project on schedule. The Manpower Requirements Report (see Figures 9a and 9b) is intended to point out those periods in the life of a project when manpower requirements for certain skill

Figure 9a   Manpower requirements report.

PROJECT MANPOWER REQUIREMENT By Skills					
Manpower Skill	Month	Manhours	Respons. Unit No.	Activity Acct.No.	Activity Slack
XX	XX/XX	XXXXX	XXXX	XXXXX-XX	XX.X
12	01/72	500	5410	72341-02	0.0
		1,000	5410	72344-03	10.2
		500	5430	72344-01	7.3
	02/72	720	5410	72341-02	0.0
		900	5410	72344-03	10.2
		400	5430	72344-01	7.3
		500	5430	72347-01	

Figure 9b   Manpower requirements histogram.

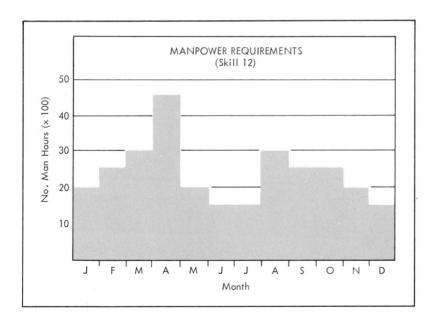

categories will exceed the availability, or where substantial idle time appears in the plan. This report will assist the line manager in leveling out peaks and valleys in his manpower loading plan.

G. Rate of Expenditure and Cost of Work Reports

These two summary reports, usually in graph form, present the manager with the over-all cost status of the project. The Rate of Expenditure Report, Figure 10, indicates the rate at which costs are budgeted and incurred over time. The Cost of Work Report, Figure 11, relates budgeted and actual costs to the amount of the work performed and indicates the estimated costs to complete the project. Together, these reports establish periodic funding requirements and show the trend toward total cost overruns or underruns. Both reports are prepared as standard PERT/Cost outputs.

THE PERT/COST SUPPLEMENTS

A. The Time-Cost Option Procedure

Most proposal requests today stipulate that the contractor prepare only one time-cost plan to complete the proposed project by a directed completion date. Although this "Directed Date" plan may be based primarily

Figure 10 Rate of expenditure.

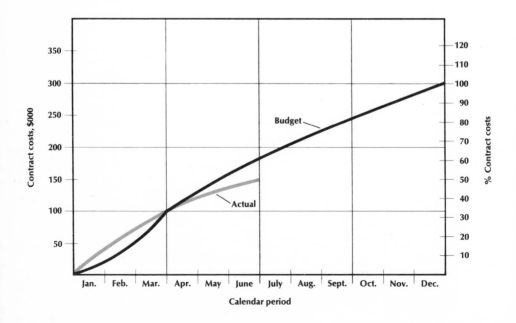

on a timed military requirement, the factors of cost and technical risk are frequently of major importance in selecting a particular development plan. With only a single time-cost alternative to consider, neither the customer nor the contractor can determine that a directed date plan is the "best" combination of time, cost, and technical risk for a particular project.

The Time-Cost Option Procedure calls for the preparation of three alternate time-cost plans for accomplishing the project (see Figure 12). At least one of these plans will be prepared to meet the Directed Date. In addition to the Directed Date plan, the procedure calls for: a plan to accomplish the project in the shortest possible time, and a plan for accomplishing the project in a time which will allow the contractor to achieve the project objectives in the most efficient manner.

B. The Resource Allocation Procedure

In a development project, there frequently are various levels of resources that can be applied to each activity. It is important for the manager to recognize what effect the different applications will have on the total time and cost of a project, especially when a speed-up or stretch-out is being considered.

The Resource Allocation Procedure identifies the specific allocation of resources for each activity that will yield the lowest total cost for one or

Figure 11   Cost of work.

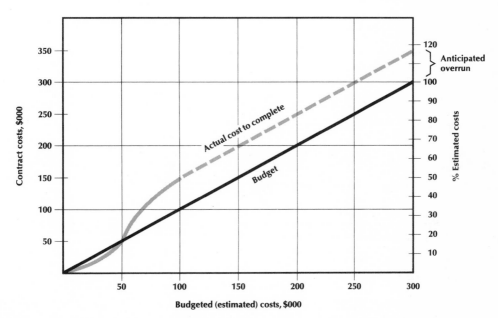

more specified project durations. To do this, the procedure calls for alternate resource/time estimates for performing each activity in the project.

The steps followed in this procedure are similar to the ones illustrated in Figure 13 and summarized below.

1. Construct network.
2. Obtain alternate time-cost estimates for each activity.
3. Select the lowest cost alternate for each activity.
4. Calculate the critical path and compare to directed date (duration).
5. If critical path is too long, select higher cost, shorter time alternates on critical path activities. These alternate points are picked where the ratio of increased cost to decreased time is least.
6. Repeat Step 5 until length of critical path conforms to directed date.

SUMMARY

The PERT/Cost System is directed toward the dynamic management of projects by the *contractor*, as well as toward the timely, accurate reporting of project status to the *customer*. The System specifies techniques and procedures to assist *project managers* in:

Figure 12   Three time-cost options. Selection of the "best" plan depends on the relative importance of cost, time, and risk in each program.

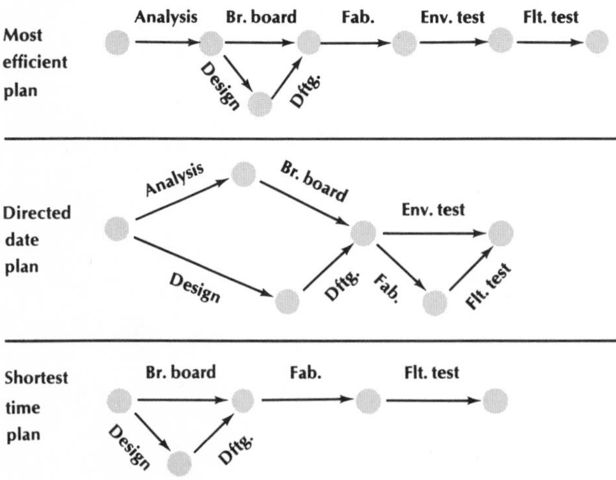

	Cost	Time	Risk
Most efficient plan	$1,000,000	100	Low
Directed date plan	$1,200,000	70	Medium
Shortest time plan	$850,000	65	High

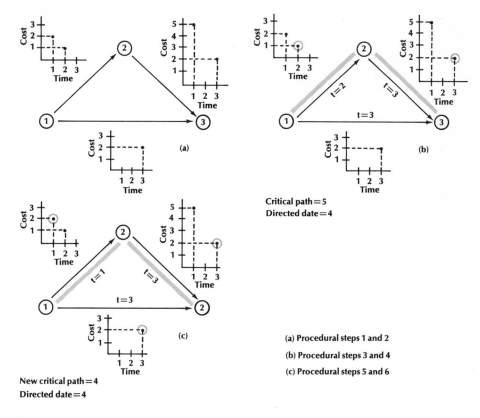

Figure 13 A summary of the resource allocation procedure.

- Planning schedules and costs
- Determining time and cost status
- Forecasting manpower skill requirements
- Predicting schedule slippages and cost overruns
- Developing alternate time-cost plans
- Allocating resources among tasks

44

Managing by Objectives—
A Three-Stage System

ROBERT A. HOWELL

Many observers believe that management by objectives (MBO) is the most promising new approach to building control systems that simultaneously satisfy organizational and individual objectives. Because of the wide variation in practices among organizations applying MBO, misconceptions have developed. In this selection, Professor Howell clarifies this variation in practice by explaining that firms normally go through three stages in the development of a management-by-objectives system.

The first stage he identifies is the performance-appraisal stage. During the late 1950s and early 1960s, the emphasis was on results-oriented approaches to performance appraisal. Practitioners realized, however, that the objectives of the individual manager should contribute to the overall objectives of the organization. Consequently, stage two developed during the mid-1960s. The emphasis at this point was on the need to integrate the objectives of the organization with those of the managers. But because management by objectives was too short-term oriented, many firms soon entered the third stage, namely, focusing on long-range objectives and action plans in order to make them a reality. Professor Howell expresses the belief that it is unlikely that a company can shorten the four- to five-year sequence required for an effective program.

A few years ago, in the article, "A Fresh Look at Management by Objectives," I contrasted two points of view regarding management by objectives that were prevalent at that time.[1] One took the position that the concept was basically an improved approach to performance appraisal; the second argued that it was much broader than performance appraisal and, in fact, was a total approach to managing a business, aimed at integrating the objectives of the business with the objectives of the individual managers in it. At that time, these seemed to be dichotomous views. I concluded that the

Reprinted from *Business Horizons*, February 1970, pp. 41-45, by permission of the publisher. Copyright 1970 by the Foundation for the School of Business, at Indiana University.

[1] Robert A. Howell, "A Fresh Look at Management by Objectives," *Business Horizons* (Fall, 1967), pp. 51-58.

performance appraisal viewpoint was very narrow, and that only the integration viewpoint would truly result in achieving the potential benefits to be derived from management by objectives.

Time marches on, progress is made, and we have learned something more about management by objectives. This article is addressed to the issue of the evolutionary stages of managing by objectives. I now see three of these stages. A manager, knowing what they are, should be able to put his own company into perspective. If he has gone through all three stages, great. If not, he will be able to see what he still must do, and get a feel for how long it will take to reap the benefits from managing by objectives that some companies already enjoy.

STAGE 1—PERFORMANCE APPRAISAL

During the late 1950's and early 1960's, the emphasis on management by objectives was directed toward its benefits in the area of performance appraisal. The argument went that traditional trait-oriented appraisals were unfair, failed to motivate the managers to whom they were applied, and were organizationally dysfunctional. Trait-oriented performance appraisals *were* unfair because they tended to measure a manager on how he approached his job rather than on the results he achieved. Characteristics such as enthusiasm, initiative, integrity, cooperation, judgment, and appearance frequently were used to assess performace. If a manager was motivated, it was toward appearing as a high performer. But traits are not something a manager can just turn on or off. Some managers are enthusiastic; others are not. Some managers are effective in groups; others are not. Some make a good appearance; others do not. Only those who met the various performance criteria would score high.

Either way, whether a manager was motivated to appear as a high performer or he just happened to possess enough of the success criteria to be judged a high performer, the total organization did not benefit very much. For under a trait-oriented performance appraisal system, there is virtually no emphasis on results achieved by the individual manager, nor on his contribution to the total organization.

"On the other hand," the proponents of management by objectives as a means of more effective performance appraisal would say, "if an individual manager designated those things he was going to accomplish (his objectives), reviewed them with his superior for approval, and then was measured accordingly, not only would the performance appraisal be perceived as fairer, but the individual setting the objectives and being measured against them would also be motivated to higher performance."

The results-oriented appraisal approach to management by objectives usually offered a manager a few weeks to develop his objectives and have them approved by his superior. A year later the objectives would be resurrected for appraisal purposes. This appraisal is fairer to the individual manager whose performance is being evaluated. It emphasizes accomplishments rather than approach. It is relatively unimportant how a manager approaches his job, provided that approach does not interfere with the progress of other managers toward their objectives.

Results-oriented appraisals also motivate individual managers. It emphasizes the accomplishment of those objectives that the individual manager previously established. To participate in the development of one's own objectives, to be given the latitude to accomplish them, and to know that one's performance will be measured against them is quite a motivator![2]

During this period, management by objectives programs were created in a number of companies. The programs were characterized by personnel department leadership, mildly supported by top management; booklets describing the virtues of the "program" and how the results-oriented appraisal system worked; and forms. It was not unusual for a single program to create a goals form, progress review form, performance appraisal form, and a skills inventory form. Walter Wikstrom of the National Industrial Conference Board and a leader in the area of management by objectives research has said that "management by objectives effectiveness is inversely related to the number of MBO forms," which he calls "artificial appendages." And I agree.

Something was still missing from the performance appraisal approach to management by objectives. This approach was clearly fairer to the individual manager, and it did motivate him to higher personal accomplishments as a result of setting objectives and knowing that he would be measured against them, but dysfunctionality still remained between the objectives of the individual manager and those of the organization. What was missing was the realization that the individual manager and subunits of an organization are part of the larger organization, and the reason a manager sets objectives is to contribute to the over-all objectives of the organization. Many management by objectives programs never gave dysfunctionality a thought, and as a result never progressed any further than stage one.

STAGE 2—INTEGRATION

Stage two of the evolution of management by objectives, occurring during the mid-1960's, emphasized the need to integrate the objectives of the organization with the objectives of the individual managers in it. The focus was on making management by objectives an integral part of the management

[2] There were a number of proponents for the performance appraisal approach to management by objectives. Among the more prolific writers on the subject were Douglas McGregor, author of *The Human Side of Enterprise* and the article "An Uneasy Look at Performance Appraisal"; Rensis Likert, *New Patterns of Management* and "Motivational Approach to Management Development"; and H. H. Meyer, E. Kay, and J. R. P. French, Jr., "Split Roles in Performance Appraisal."

process.[3] At this time, I was doing doctoral research on management by objectives, and reached the conclusion that what I now call stage one and stage two of an evolutionary process were two different approaches, and that the integration approach was superior to the performance appraisal approach. I still hold the same conclusions regarding the relative merits of stage one and stage two, but I now see the normal evolution more clearly.

With this new emphasis, management by objectives became quite a different program.

First, the impetus for management by objectives previously came from the top personnel official, but it now came from line management, especially the president. One company whose management by objectives system I have reviewed starts its objective setting process with the office of the chief executive—the chairman of the board and the president—and all subsequent levels of the organization's objectives emanate from this set.

Second, the objectives were no longer prepared outside the operations planning-budgeting cycle and time period. Instead, they became coincident with and an integral part of it. This meant that the objective-setting process became much more iterative and that more time had to be provided for the iterations, which resulted in the integration of objectives both vertically and horizontally.

Third, as a result of this integration, communication channels were opened; coordination between activities was improved; overlapping responsibilities and marginal activities were identified and eliminated; gaps were plugged; and organizations were modified to reflect the structure of objectives. Most important, managers were committed to organizational objectives.

In essence, the dysfunctionality that existed between organizational and individual manager objectives under the performance appraisal approach was minimized.

There were still disadvantages, however, related to the integration stage of management by objectives. For one, it was short-term oriented. Management by objectives programs aimed at better performance appraisals and the integration of the individual manager's objectives with the objectives of the organization both normally focused on the next year. To the extent that next year's performance is predetermined, based on the inertia that has already been built up, short-run objective setting adds little to short-run performance. In fact, the activity of objective setting may actually interfere

---

[3] Perhaps the most well-known proponent of the integration approach was Peter Drucker, author of many articles and books related to the subject, including *Managing for Results*. Others who shared his view include Charles Hughes of Texas Instruments, author of *Goal Setting;* Dale McConkey of United Fruit, *How to Manage by Results;* and John Humble of the British management consulting firm, Urwick-Orr, *Improving Business Results*. It is interesting to note that the appraisal proponents were, for the most part, behavioral scientists, and that the integrators were management consultants and practicing businessmen.

with the short-run future guaranteed by the inertia. In addition, if next year's operations are virtually set and the managers' objectives are integrated with the operating objectives, then the operations are leading management. This delegates management to a passive role.

If management is going to make an impact on the organization—that is, lead rather than be led—then it must set longer-term objectives and plan the ways to achieve them. This brings an organization to stage three of management by objectives.

STAGE 3—LONG-RANGE PLANNING

Many American businesses have entered the third stage in the evolution of management by objectives. Its focus is on long-range objectives and action plans to make them a reality for both the organization and individual manager, and on strategic planning for the organization.

One distinction, obviously, between long-range planning and operations planning is the time horizon involved. This, however, is a minor distinction. Long-range planning is not five-year budgeting, although part of the end product includes such considerations as profit objectives, capital investment plans, and expenditure programs. The major difference between long-range planning and budgeting lies in the number of alternative choices and, hence, decisions management can make that will have an effect in the time horizon covered by the plan. As pointed out earlier, short-run performance is, to a considerable extent, a function of the inertia that has previously been developed, and relatively little can be done to change that. Certainly discretionary expenses may be cut and sales "pulsed" by the introduction of specials, for example, but such actions as these are apt to have a negative effect on the longer run. On the other hand, management action can significantly affect the long run, and such long-range objective setting and action planning is the essence of stage three management by objectives.

The objectives that ultimately are set for the organization and the individual managers in it, and the action plans supporting the objectives, represent the culmination of extensive analysis of the variety of possible objectives open to the organization and the means to achieving them. The action plans are the result of the effort of specific managers upon whose shoulders the responsibility for achieving them rests. Those programs that last the test of planning time have gone through the series of iterations necessary for any integrated objectives program, and assure that effective communications, coordination, and commitment—basic to management by objectives—exist.

Long-range planning clearly is part of the evolution of management by objectives, but there are some limitations. Certainly the most important are the risks that long-range plans will make the organization inflexible to new developments and averse to creative ideas.

A second part of the current stage of management by objectives is strategic planning, which is aimed at the issue of changing the fundamental assumptions, policies, and direction of the business in question. A major emphasis of strategic planning is upon environmental analysis—customers and potential customers; competitors and potential competitors; basic fundamental shifts in the economy; and the implications of the findings on the need for change.

Strategic planning might be considered a fourth stage, but I think, in practice, as a manager begins to undertake comprehensive long-range planning, he must question the whole underpinning of his organization. But there are reasons for distinguishing between strategic planning and long-range or action planning. Strategic planning tends to focus on one aspect of the business at a time: a new product or markets, a new plant location, or methods of financing. Long-range planning focuses on the whole organization. Strategic planning, because it does focus on one aspect of the business at a time, tends to be unstructured in approach, whereas long-range planning may be routinized, allowing managers to follow prescribed procedures. Strategic planning normally involves a few top executives, whereas long-range planning involves all managers; and, most important, strategic plans show expected results whereas long-range planning leads to expected results. Another way to look at the distinction is that long-range plans must change if the strategies change; on the other hand, the strategies do not have to change if the long-range plans change.

Many companies have introduced long-range planning into their activities in the last few years. A number of these have done so as the natural evolution of management by objectives. Those that have, I feel, are truly profiting from managing by objectives.

GETTING STARTED

Some readers will appropriately wonder if their company might short-circuit the three stages of managing by objectives. I do not think so, though a company starting out may shorten the decade that the "bow-wave" has taken to pass through the stages.

Each individual manager has to go through the experience of setting objectives for his position, in collaboration with his superior, before a concerted effort can be mounted to achieve both vertical and horizontal integration of objectives. This obviously means that stage one must precede stage two. At least two years, and probably three, is necessary to achieve reasonably good integration.

Also, short-range objectives must be set first, even though they are "lagging" objectives, before longer-range "leading" objectives are set. Thus stage two must precede stage three. Possibly, however, efforts toward integration and the setting of longer-range objectives may be carried out coincidentally; to the extent that this is possible, the time to achieve a full management by objectives system can be reduced. Nevertheless, it will take four to five years to achieve a fully effective management by objectives system.

This article has attempted to trace the normal evolution that firms go through in the development of a management by objectives system. There are three stages: the performance appraisal stage, the integration of objectives stage, and the long-range planning stage. I can see no way to short-circuit this sequence, although possibilities exist for reducing the average length of time required to pass through the three stages. Regardless, it still takes four to five years to achieve a fully effective management by objectives system.

45

Management by Objectives—
Research Findings and Implementation

JAMES H. DONNELLY, JR., JAMES L. GIBSON,
AND JOHN M. IVANCEVICH

This second selection on management-by-objectives programs summarizes some important research findings relating to these programs. Professors Donnelly, Gibson, and Ivancevich briefly discuss the various forms that MBO programs have taken. They identify joint setting of goals by subordinate and superior and the joint review of performance to provide feedback to the subordinate as the common elements of all of these programs. The desired end results of these programs are improved performance, improved morale, and reduced employee anxiety.

Summaries of the following research studies are discussed: those by Raia at the Purex Corporation, by Meyer, Kay, and French at General Electric, by Tosi and Carrol in a large manufacturing firm; and by Ivancevich, Donnelly, and Lyon in two medium-sized manufacturing firms. All of these studies point up some key factors—among them psychological preparation of managers and a supportive managerial climate—that are needed for the successful implementation of management-by-objectives programs.

Reprinted from James H. Donnelly, Jr., James L. Gibson, and John M. Ivancevich, *Fundamentals of Management*, pp. 144-148, by permission of the publisher. Business Publications, Inc., Austin, Tex., 1971.

MANAGEMENT BY OBJECTIVES

One management technique which has acquired a legion of advocates since it was first introduced in the early 1950s is management by objectives (MBO). Exactly what MBO entails has been presented in slightly different styles by those who advocate its use. For example, Peter Drucker who first introduced the concept of MBO describes it as follows:

> ... the objectives of the district manager's job should be defined by the contribution he and his district sales force have to make to the sales department, the objectives of the project engineer's job by the contribution he, his engineers and draftsmen make to the engineering department. ...
> This requires each manager to develop and set the objectives of his unit himself. Higher management must, of course, reserve the power to approve or disapprove these objectives. But their development is part of a manager's responsibility; indeed, it is his first responsibility. ...[1]

Drucker believes that the greatest advantage of MBO is that it allows the manager to control his own performance. This self-control is interpreted to mean stronger motivation to do the best rather than just to get by.

Another slightly different presentation of the basic fundamentals and overall philosophy of MBO is provided by Odiorne:

> ... a process whereby the superior and subordinate managers of an organization jointly identify its common goals, define each individual's major areas of responsibility in terms of the results expected of him, and use these measures as guides for operating the unit and assessing the contribution of each of its members.[2]

An important factor, in Odiorne's viewpoint, is for the subordinate and superior to have an understanding regarding the subordinate's major areas of responsibility, what will constitute an acceptable level of performance, and what needs to be done to improve performance. A common thread found in both the Drucker and Odiorne conceptions is that MBO should lead to improved motivation of participants.

[1] Peter Drucker, *The Practice of Management* (New York: Harper and Brothers, 1954), pp. 128-29.
[2] George Odiorne, *Management by Objectives* (New York: Pitman Publishing Co., 1965), p. 26.

Other well-known scholars have also written extensively on MBO.[3] Their contentions are similar to those offered by Drucker and Odiorne. Synthesizing the works of these experts enables one to develop a set of three guidelines which will provide the reader with an operational understanding of the approach of management by objectives. The guidelines emphasize that, in MBO programs,

1. superiors and subordinates meet and discuss goals (results) for the subordinates which are in line with overall organizational goals;
2. the superior and subordinate jointly establish attainable goals for the subordinate;
3. the superior and subordinate meet again after the initial goals are established, and evaluate the subordinate's performance in terms of the goals. The essential feature is that *feedback* on performance is provided the subordinate. The subordinate knows where he stands with regard to his contribution to his organizational unit and the firm.

The exact procedures employed in implementing the goal-setting and performance evaluation program will vary from firm to firm or from organizational unit to organizational unit. The anticipated end results, however, will be the same: (1) improved participant contribution to the firm, (2) improved morale and attitudes of the participants toward the firm, and (3) reduced employee anxiety resulting from ambiguity as to where he stands with his superior.

SOME RESEARCH FINDINGS

A number of firms have implemented MBO-type programs on a company or departmental basis. A number of recent studies report some of the effects of such programs.

A two-part study of a form of MBO program referred to as "Goal Setting and Self Control" was undertaken during 1965 and 1966 at the Purex Corporation.[4] The result of the research was that, after the goal-setting program had been initiated, participants at Purex were more concerned about and aware of the firm's goals and future activities. In the initial study it was also found that the goal-setting procedure improved communications and understanding among those involved.

[3] See Douglas McGregor, "An Uneasy Look at Performance Appraisal," *Harvard Business Review*, vol. 35 (May-June, 1957), pp. 89-94; and E. C. Schleh, *Management by Results* (New York: McGraw-Hill Book Co., 1961).

[4] Anthony P. Raia, "Goal Setting and Self Control," *Journal of Management Studies*, vol. 2 (September, 1965), pp. 34-53; and Anthony P. Raia, "A Second Look at Management Goals and Controls," *California Management Review*, vol. 8 (Summer, 1966), pp. 49-58.

The follow-up study showed that many of the participants perceived the program as being a weak incentive for improving the performance level of participants. They had changed their attitudes about the program after it had been in operation over a four-year period. Their reasons for changing their opinions about the program were divided into five categories:[5]

1. Managers reported that the program was used as a whip.
2. The program increased the amount of paperwork.
3. The program failed to reach the lower managerial levels.
4. There was an overemphasis placed on production.
5. The program failed to provide adequate incentives to improve performance.

Another study was made on the effects of a form of MBO program known as "Work Planning and Review."[6] An experimental and a control group of managers were included in the research design. The control group operated under a traditional performance appraisal system. This involved an annual appraisal of a subordinate's performance by his manager. The experimental group was encouraged to prepare a set of goals for achieving improved job performance and to submit them for the superior's review and approval.

Managers using the goal-setting program (i.e., work planning and review) were compared to those operating under the traditional appraisal program. The managers using the goal-setting program expressed significantly more favorable attitudes. Specifically, their attitudes changed in a favorable direction over the one-year study in the following areas:

1. extent to which the managers made use of their abilities and experiences;
2. ability of the managers to plan;
3. degree to which the managers were receptive to new ideas and suggestions; and
4. degree to which they felt the goals for which they were aiming were what they should be.

A more recent study dealt with managerial reactions to management by objectives in a large manufacturing firm.[7] The researchers were concerned with the manager's perceptions associated with the MBO approach. The rationale of the program most cited by participants was that the

---

[5] *Ibid.*

[6] Herbert H. Meyer, Emanuel Kay, and John R. P. French, Jr., "Split Roles in Performance Appraisal," *Harvard Business Review*, vol. 43 (January-February, 1965), pp. 21-27.

[7] Henry L. Tosi and Stephen J. Carroll, Jr., "Managerial Reaction to Management by Objectives," *Academy of Management Journal*, vol. 11 (December, 1968), pp. 415-26.

objectives-setting process was intended to link the evaluation of an individual to his actual performance rather than to personality or other characteristics. It was also found that a majority of the participating managers believed that the most significant advantage of the program was that one was more likely "to know what was expected of him by his boss." A major problem cited by the managers was that excessive formal requirements were imposed because of the program; that is, the need to process, complete, and update forms, and to provide other data to the coordinator of the program were major irritants.

In the studies cited thus far, it was attempted to determine some of the effects of MBO programs rather than the impact of MBO upon managers. A recent study, however, was designed to determine the impact of MBO on participant job satisfaction.[8] In the study, the researchers administered a psychological test which measures an individual's perceived need satisfactions. It was found that the need satisfaction of participants was probably influenced by the MBO program. However, the findings indicated that the manner in which MBO was implemented in the two companies studied had some impact on the perceived need satisfactions of the participants. More will be said about this in the following section.

IMPLEMENTING MBO PROGRAMS

Despite the purported advantages of MBO, there are several key factors which should be considered in the implementation phase. For example, managers who are about to engage in MBO programs must first be conditioned and psychologically prepared.[9] With the introduction of MBO, changes will often occur in organizational variables such as the flow of communications horizontally and vertically, the intensity of intergroup interaction, and the number of personal contacts between superiors and subordinates. Thus, the dynamic nature of these variables and their impact on the functioning of the organization necessitate complete understanding of MBO by managers, to insure that managerial resistance to implementation and participation is minimal.

Another critical factor in the implementation of MBO programs is the supportive managerial climate which pervades the organization. In a study previously cited, two important conclusions were reached concerning implementation:[10]

1. Top management must not assume a passive role. The most effective manner to implement MBO is to allow the top-level executives to explain,

---

[8] John M. Ivancevich, James H. Donnelly, Jr., and Herbert L. Lyon, "A Study of the Impact of Management by Objectives on Perceived Need Satisfactions," *Personnel Psychology*, vol. 23 (Summer, 1970), pp. 139-51.

[9] Henry L. Tosi, "Management Development and Management by Objectives—An Interrelationship," *Management of Personnel Quarterly*, vol. 4 (Summer, 1965), p. 24.

[10] Ivancevich, Donnelly, and Lyon, *op. cit.*, pp. 148-50.

coordinate, and guide the program. When top managers were actively involved, the philosophy and mechanics of the program filtered through and penetrated the entire organization. Thus, a possible motivation strategy to improve need satisfaction at lower levels of management would be to involve the top-level management group in the MBO program.

2. Improvements in need satisfaction were higher in the company where the MBO program was instituted by upper-level executives than in the company where it was implemented by the personnel department.

Management by objectives is not being offered here as a cure-all for motivation problems in business organizations, but it is an approach which warrants careful consideration, especially since some evidence of its effectiveness is available.

FOR FURTHER READING

Anthony, Robert N., *Planning and Control Systems—A Framework for Analysis.* Boston: Graduate School of Business Administration, Harvard University, 1965.

Argyris, Chris, "Human Problems with Budgets." *Harvard Business Review*, Vol. 31, No. 1 (January-February 1953), 97-110.

Arrow, Kenneth J., "Control in Large Organizations." *Management Science*, Vol. 10, No. 3 (April 1964), 397-409.

Bacon, J., *Managing the Budget Function.* New York: National Industrial Conference Board, 1970.

Barkdull, Charles W., "Periodic Operations Audit: A Management Tool." *Michigan Business Review*, Vol. 18, No. 4 (July 1966), 19-25.

Beer, Stafford, *Decision and Control.* New York: John Wiley & Sons, Inc., 1967.

Becker, S. W., and D. Green, Jr., "Budgeting and Employee Behavior." *Journal of Business*, Vol. 4 (1964), pp. 230-244.

Bell, Gerald D., "The Influence of Technological Components of Work Upon Management Control." *Academy of Management Journal*, Vol. 8, No. 2 (June 1965), 127-132.

Blood, John, Jr., ed., *Management Science in Planning and Control.* New York: Technical Association of the Pulp and Paper Industry, 1969.

Bonini, C. P., R. K. Jaedicke, and H. M. Wagner, *Management Controls.* New York: McGraw-Hill Book Company, 1964.

Bowers, D. G., "Organizational Control in an Insurance Company." *Sociometry*, Vol. 2 (1964), 230-244.

Buiter, J. H., "Production Standards, Financial Incentives and the Reaction of the Workers." *Work Study and Management*, Vol. 8 (1964), 354-362.

Cook, Doris M., "The Impact on Managers of Frequency of Feedback." *Academy of Management Journal*, Vol. 11 (1968), 263.

Cooper, W. W., *et al.*, *New Perspectives in Organizational Research.* New York: John Wiley & Sons, Inc., 1964, Chaps. 13 and 14.

De Paula F., "The Implications of Real-Time Systems for Management Control." *The Computer Bulletin* (June 1966).

Eilon, S., "A Classification of Administrative Control Systems." *The Journal of Management Studies*, Vol. 1 (1966), 36-48.

————, "Control Systems with Several Controllers." *The Journal of Management Studies*, Vol. 3 (1965), 259-268.

Forrester, J. W., *Industrial Dynamics.* New York: John Wiley & Sons, Inc., 1961.

Glasner, D. M., "Patterns of Management by Results." *Business Horizons*, Vol. 12 (February 1969), 37.

Hall, W. N., "Methods of Evaluating Decentralized Operations." *Management Record*, Vol. 25, No. 1 (January 1963), 26-28.

Hicks, Herbert G., and Govonzy Friedhelm, "Notes on the Nature of Standards." *Academy of Management Journal*, Vol. 9, No. 4 (December 1966), 281-293.

Holden, P. E., C. A. Pederson, and G. E. Germane, *Top Management.* New York: McGraw-Hill Book Company, 1968, Chaps. 2, 5, and 6.

Howell, Robert A., "A Fresh Look at Management by Objectives." *Business Horizons*, Vol. 10 (1967), 51-58.

Hughes, C. L., *Goal Setting, Key to Individual and Organizational Effectiveness.* New York: American Management Association, 1965.

Ivancevich, John M., James H. Donnelly, and Herbert L. Lyon, "A Study of the Impact of Management by Objectives on Perceived Need Satisfaction." *Personnel Psychology*, Vol. 23 (1970), 139-151.

Jasinski, F. J., "Use and Misuse of Efficiency Controls." *Harvard Business Review*, Vol. 34, No. 4 (July-August 1956), 105-112.

Jerome, W. T., *Executive Control.* New York: John Wiley & Sons, Inc., 1961.

Kirpatrick, C., and R. Levin, *Planning and Control with PERT/CPM.* New York: McGraw-Hill Book Company, 1966.

Klein, L., "Rationality in Management Control." *The Journal of Management Studies*, Vol. 3 (1965), 351-361.

Knight, W. D., and E. H. Weinwurm, *Managerial Budgeting, A Behavioral Approach to the Successful Adaption of a Budgeting System from a Managerial Viewpoint.* New York: The Macmillan Company, 1964.

Levinson, Harry, "Management by Whose Objectives?" *Harvard Business Review*, Vol. 48, No. 4 (July-August 1970), 125-134.

Likert, R., and S. E. Seashore, "Making Cost Control Work." *Harvard Business Review*, Vol. 41, No. 6 (November-December 1963), 98-108.

Litterer, J. A., *The Analysis of Organizations.* New York: John Wiley & Sons, Inc., 1965, Chap. 13.

Mauriel, John J., and Robert N. Anthony, "Misevaluation of Investment Center Performance." *Harvard Business Review*, Vol. 44, No. 2 (March-April 1966), 98-105.

Marks, Leonard, Jr., "Air Force Financial Management and Control." *Business Topics*, Vol. 14, No. 1 (Winter 1966), 7-15.

Miles, R. E., and R. C. Vergin, "Behavioral Properties of Variance Controls." *California Management Review*, Vol. 8, No. 3 (Spring 1966), 57-65.

Miller, V. V., "Human Behavior and Budget Controls." *Advanced Management—Office Executive*, Vol. 12 (1962), 30-34.

Morse, G. E., "Pendulum of Management Control." *Harvard Business Review*, Vol. 43, No. 3 (May-June 1965), 156-157, 159-164.

Odiorne, George, *Management by Objectives*. New York: Pitman Publishing Corp., 1965.

Prince, T. R., *Information Systems for Management Planning and Control*, rev. ed. Homewood, Ill.: Richard D. Irwin, Inc., 1970.

Raia, A. P., "Goal Setting and Self-Control: An Empirical Study." *The Journal of Management Studies*, Vol. 1 (1965), 35-43.

——, "A Second Look at Goals and Controls." *California Management Review* (Summer 1966), pp. 49-58.

Schleh, E. C., "The Fallacy in Measuring Management." *Dun's Review and Modern Industry* (1963), pp. 49-54.

——, *Management by Results*. New York: McGraw-Hill Book Company, 1961, Chaps. 12-14.

Seashore, S. E., B. P. Indik, and B. S. Georgopoulos, "Relationships Among Criteria of Job Performance." *Journal of Applied Psychology*, Vol. 3 (1960), 195-202.

Shillinglaw, G., *Cost Accounting*, rev. ed. Homewood, Ill.: Richard D. Irwin, Inc., 1967, Parts III and IV.

Sord, B. H., and G. A. Welsch, *Business Budgeting, A Survey of Management Planning and Control Practice*. New York: Controllership Foundation, 1962.

Stedry, A. C., *Budget Control and Cost Behavior*. Englewood Cliffs, N.J.: Prentice-Hall, Inc., 1960.

——, and E. Kay, *The Effects of Goal Difficulty on Performance*. Crotonville, N.Y.: Behavioral Research Service, General Electric Co., Publication BRS-19, 1964.

Strong, E., and R. Smith, *Management Control Models*. New York: Holt, Rinehart & Winston, Inc., 1968.

Stewart, R. N., "Basic Reports for Management," *Advanced Management—Office Executive*, Vol. 7 (1963), 14-17,

Tannenbaum, A., *Control in Organizations*. New York: McGraw-Hill Book Company, 1968.

Vancil, R. M., J. Dearden, and R. D. Anthony, *Management Control Systems*. Homewood, Ill.: Richard D. Irwin, Inc., 1965.

Welsch, G. A., *Budgeting—Profit Planning and Control*, 3rd ed. Englewood Cliffs, N.J.: Prentice-Hall, Inc., 1970.

Wiest, J., and F. Levy, *A Management Guide to PERT/CPM*. Englewood Cliffs, N.J.: Prentice-Hall, Inc., 1969.

PART SEVEN

Managing: An Adaptive Process

The previous parts of this book have each contained reading selections dealing with a particular management process. In this concluding part, we turn to synthesis and stress the need for coherent management design. We first consider the need to link management design to management strategy and then examine the process of adapting management design to cultural differences.

A coherent management design is essential in order to carry out master strategy effectively. This means that a change in one phase of management must be supported by consistent changes in the other management processes. Each management process has certain key features that are most likely to be affected by the choice of a strategy. The degree of decentralization, the degree of division of labor, mechanisms for coordination, and the nature and location of staff are a few organization features that are likely to vary with a change in strategy.

With regard to planning, changes in strategy will affect the comprehensiveness and specificity of standing plans and single-use plans, the planning horizon, and the relative importance of intermediate versus final objectives. Although leadership style is not easy to change, variations in strategy have an impact on the amount of participation in planning, the degree of permissiveness in observing company plans and rules, and the closeness of supervision. Turning to the control process, shifts in strategy are likely to affect the choice of performance criteria, the location of control points, and the frequency of checks.

463

Technology is the intervening variable that directly relates management design to strategy. In this context, technology refers to the variety of methods that convert resource inputs into products and services. Technology bridges the gap between strategy and the work necessary to support that strategy. We then build a management design to fit the work to be done.

In Part One, we noted that the relationship between technology and organization structure has received increased research interest in recent years. Selection 6, "Empirical Research on Organization Structure," summarized the empirical work of Joan Woodward in Great Britain, Lawrence and Lorsch, and R. H. Hall in this country. To match management design to technology, we require a framework that distinguishes types of technology. One useful conceptual approach is provided by Charles Perrow in his book *Organizational Analysis: A Sociological View* (see bibliography at end of Part Seven).

It is important to recognize that the available evidence on the relationship between technology and organization structure is derived largely from studies of enterprises in Great Britain and the United States. Yet, a growing number of American companies are conducting operations abroad. In view of the accelerating pace of internationalization, attention must be given to ways in which management practices can be adapted for use in different cultures. Experts in comparative management have suggested for some time that cultural differences limit the universality of managerial philosophy and practice.

In order to focus on these differences, it is useful to examine some principal cultural assumptions that underlie American managerial concepts. The following set of assumptions differ markedly from attitudes and values in some other countries:*

1. A "master of destiny" viewpoint based on a belief that people can substantially influence the future.
2. A concept of a deliberately designed, independent enterprise that receives loyalty and willingness to conform to its managerial system.
3. A belief that personnel selection should be based on merit.
4. A belief that decisions should be based on the objective analysis of facts.
5. A belief that wide participation in decision-making is desirable.
6. A relentless urge for improvement that results in the acceptance of change as normal and necessary.

Each of these cultural premises has been an important factor in shaping management practices in the United States. The "master of destiny" viewpoint, for example, leads American managers to emphasize the

*For a more detailed treatment see Chapter 29 of William H. Newman, Charles E. Summer, and E. Kirby Warren, *The Process of Management*, 3rd ed. (Englewood Cliffs, N.J.: Prentice-Hall, Inc., 1972).

importance of planning. Similarly, the widespread use of decentralization in the United States is based on the assumption that personnel at all levels in an organization value self-determination. This strong dependence of management concepts on cultural premises suggests that management practice may have to be modified if cultural differences are significant.

The four reading selections in this part present a diverse view of management as an adaptive process. We begin with "Strategy and Structure," in which Alfred Chandler discusses the relationship between the strategy a business adopts and its organization structure. Whereas Chandler focuses on the link between strategy and organization structure, M. Y. Yoshino, in "Managerial Control for a World Enterprise," examines how the control process must be modified when a firm shifts to a multinational strategy. Selection 48, "Culture as an Intervening Variable," offers the view that culture must be considered an intervening variable between technology and organization structure. The final selection, "What We Can Learn From the Japanese," examines how some specific management practices vary with cultural differences.

46

Strategy and Structure

ALFRED CHANDLER

The majority of the selections in this anthology have been written by behavioral scientists, management theorists, business executives, management scientists, and economists. This selection, which is taken from the introduction to Alfred Chandler's book Strategy and Structure, *provides us with an opportunity to appreciate the perspective of a business historian.*

Professor Chandler examines the relationship between strategy and structure through an exhaustive historical study of organizational evolution at four industrial giants in the United States: du Pont, General Motors, Jersey Standard, and Sears, Roebuck. The expansion strategies followed by each of these firms demanded new organization structures to cope with rapid growth. These four firms were organizational innovators, in that each developed independently the modern, multidivisional structures that characterize large American enterprise today.

In this introductory portion of his book, Professor Chandler theorizes concerning structural responses to new organizational strategy. He seeks to answer two questions: (a) If structure does follow strategy, why was there a delay in the rate at which firms developed new organization structures? (2) Why did the new strategy come into being in the first place?

The thesis that different organizational forms result from different types of growth can be stated more precisely if the planning and carrying out of such growth is considered a *strategy*, and the organization devised to administer these enlarged activities and resources, a *structure*. *Strategy* can be defined as the determination of the basic long-term goals and objectives of an enterprise, and the adoption of courses of action and the allocation of resources necessary for carrying out these goals. Decisions to expand the volume of activities, to set up distant plants and offices, to move into new economic functions, or become diversified along many lines of business involve the defining of new basic goals. New courses of action must be devised and resources allocated and reallocated in order to achieve these goals and to maintain and expand the firm's activities in the new areas in response to shifting demands, changing sources of supply, fluctuating economic conditions, new technological developments, and the actions of competitors. As the adoption of a new strategy may add new types of personnel and facilities, and alter the business horizons of the men responsible for the enterprise, it can have a profound effect on the form of its organization.

Structure can be defined as the design of organization through which the enterprise is administered. This design, whether formally or informally defined, has two aspects. It includes, first, the lines of authority and communication between the different administrative offices and officers and, second, the information and data that flow through these lines of communication and authority. Such lines and such data are essential to assure the effective coordination, appraisal, and planning so necessary in carrying out the basic goals and policies and in knitting together the total resources of the enterprise. These resources include financial capital; physical equipment such as plants, machinery, offices, warehouses, and other marketing and purchasing facilities, sources of raw materials, research and engineering laboratories; and, most important of all, the technical, marketing, and administrative skills of its personnel.

The thesis deduced from these several propositions is then that structure follows strategy and that the most complex type of structure is the result of the concatenation of several basic strategies. *Expansion of volume* led to the creation of an administrative office to handle one function in one local area. Growth through *geographical dispersion* brought the need for a departmental structure and headquarters to administer several local field units. The decision to expand into new types of functions called for the building of a central office and a multidepartmental structure, while the developing of new lines of products or continued growth on a national or international scale brought the formation of the multidivisional structure with a general office to administer the different divisions. For the purposes of this study, the move into new functions will be referred to as a strategy of *vertical integration* and that of the development of new products as a strategy of *diversification*.

This theoretical discussion can be carried a step further by asking two questions: (1) If structure does follow strategy, why should there be delay in developing the new organization needed to meet the administrative demands of the new strategy? (2) Why did the new strategy, which called for a change in structure, come in the first place?

There are at least two plausible answers to the first query. Either the administrative needs created by the new strategy were not positive or strong enough to require structural change, or the executives involved were unaware of the new needs. There seems to be no question that a new strategy created new administrative needs, for expansion through geographical dispersion, vertical integration, and product diversification added new resources, new activities, and an increasing number of entrepreneurial and operational actions and decisions. Nevertheless, executives could still continue to administer both the old and new activities with the same personnel, using the same channels of communication and authority and the same types of information. Such administration, however, must become increasingly inefficient. This proposition should be true for a relatively small firm whose structure consists of informal arrangements between a few executives as well as for a large one whose size and numerous administrative personnel require a more formal definition of relations between offices and officers. Since expansion created the need for new administrative offices and structures, the reasons for delays in developing the new organization rested with the executives responsible for the enterprise's long-range growth and health. Either these administrators were too involved in day-to-day tactical activities to appreciate or understand the longer-range organizational needs of their enterprises, or else their training and education failed to sharpen their perception of organizational problems or failed to develop their ability to handle them. They may also have resisted administratively desirable changes because they felt structural reorganization threatened their own personal position, their power, or most important of all, their psychological security.

In answer to the second question, changes in strategy which called for changes in structure appear to have been in response to the opportunities and needs created by changing population and changing national income and by technological innovation. Population growth, the shift from the country to the city and then to the suburb, depressions and prosperity, and the increasing pace of technological change, all created new demands or curtailed existing ones for a firm's goods or services. The prospect of a new market or the threatened loss of a current one stimulated geographical expansion, vertical integration, and product diversification. Moreover, once a firm had accumulated large resources, the need to keep its men, money, and materials steadily employed provided a constant stimulus to look for new markets by moving into new areas, by taking on new functions, or by developing new product lines. Again the awareness of the needs and opportunities created by the changing environment seems to have depended on the training and personality of individual executives and on their ability to keep their eyes on the more important entrepreneurial problems even in the midst of pressing operational needs.

The answers to the two questions can be briefly summarized by restating the general thesis. Strategic growth resulted from an awareness of the opportunities and needs—created by changing population, income, and technology—to employ existing or expanding resources more profitably. A new strategy required a new or at least refashioned structure if the enlarged enterprise was to be operated efficiently. The failure to develop a new internal structure, like the failure to respond to new external opportunities and needs, was a consequence of overconcentration on operational activities by the executives responsible for the destiny of their enterprises, or from their inability, because of past training and education and present position, to develop an entrepreneurial outlook.

One important corollary to this proposition is that growth without structural adjustment can lead only to economic inefficiency. Unless new structures are developed to meet new administrative needs which result from an expansion of a firm's activities into new areas, functions, or product lines, the technological, financial, and personnel economies of growth and size cannot be realized. Nor can the enlarged resources be employed as profitably as they otherwise might be. Without administrative offices and structure, the individual units within the enterprise (the field units, the departments, and the divisions) could undoubtedly operate as efficiently or even more so (in terms of cost per unit and volume of output per worker) as independent units than if they were part of a larger enterprise. Whenever the executives responsible for the firm fail to create the offices and structure necessary to bring together effectively the several administrative offices into a unified whole, they fail to carry out one of their basic economic roles.

The actual historical patterns of growth and organization building in the large industrial enterprise were not, of course, as clear-cut as they have been theoretically defined here. One strategy of expansion could be carried out in many ways, and often, two or three basic ways of expansion were undertaken at one and the same time. Growth might come through simultaneous building or buying of new facilities, and through purchasing or merging with other enterprises. Occasionally a firm simultaneously expanded its volume, built new facilities in geographically distant areas, moved into new functions, and developed a different type of product line. Structure, as the case studies indicate, was often slow to follow strategy, particularly in periods of rapid expansion. As a result, the distinctions between the duties of the different offices long remained confused and only vaguely defined. One executive or a small group of executives might carry out at one and the same time the functions of a general office, a central office, and a departmental headquarters. Eventually, however, most large corporations came to devise the specific units to handle a field unit, a functional department, an integrated division, or a diversified industrial empire. For this very reason, a clear-cut definition of structure and strategy and a simplified explanation or theory of the relation of one to the other should make it easier to comprehend the complex realities involved in the expansion and management of the great industrial enterprises studied here, and easier to evaluate the achievement of the organization builders.

A comparative analysis of organizational innovation demands, however, more than an explanation of the terms, concepts, and general propositions to be used in assessing comparable experiences of different enterprises. It also calls for an understanding of the larger historical situation, both within and without the firm, during which strategic expansion and organizational change took place. The executives at du Pont, General Motors, Jersey Standard, and Sears, Roebuck did not solve their administrative problems in a vacuum. Other large enterprises were meeting the same needs and challenges and seeking to resolve comparable administrative problems. Their responses had an impact on the history of these four companies, just as the experience of the four affected that of many others.

The administrative story in each of the case studies falls into two basic parts: the creation of the organizational structure after the enterprise's first major growth or corporate rebirth, and then its reorganization to meet the needs arising from the strategies of further expansion. In developing their early administrative structures, these four firms were following accepted practices in American industry. Here the organization builders could learn from others. In fashioning the modern, multidivisional structure, they were, on the other hand, going beyond existing practices. Here others learned from them. An evaluation of the measures each took to improve the administration of its business requires therefore some knowledge of the methods and practices of business administration at the time when each built its major structure and began the reorganization that led to the fashioning of the multidivisional form.

47

Managerial Control for a World Enterprise

M. Y. YOSHINO

Studies of management as an adaptive process have tended to concentrate on organizing almost to the complete exclusion of other management processes, such as planning and controlling. Consequently, we have chosen to include "Managerial Control for a World Enterprise," by M.Y.

Reprinted from "Toward a Concept of Managerial Control for a World Enterprise," *Michigan Business Review*, March 1966, pp. 25-31, by permission of the publisher.

Yoshino, because the author considers the need to adapt the control process to a shift in master strategy. Specifically, Professor Yoshino outlines the requirements of a control system for use in managing multinational operations.

Professor Yoshino examines the setting of standards and the feedback phases of control. Exploring standards that may be used for evaluating performance of foreign affiliates, he recommends using adjusted profit-and-loss items over which local management has control. Attention is also directed to the environmental (social, economic, and political), competitive, and internal operating data that headquarters should receive from foreign affiliates.

How can top management encourage members of foreign affiliates to understand the headquarter's point of view? In addressing himself to this question, the author considers managerial control as an educational process, not a superior-subordinate authority relationship. This approach permits local managers to gain more realistic interpretations of headquarters policy and provides opportunities to participate in policy formulation.

Professor Yoshino concludes by emphasizing the need to understand cultural variables. He notes that cultural differences may block effective communication between foreign affiliates and headquarters and may also affect supervisory-subordinate relationships. Moreover, culture prescribes the standard of achievement and dictates the concomitant system of rewards. This timely discussion of cultural variables sets the stage for selections 48 and 49, both of which deal entirely with management adaptation to cultural differences.

.   .   .

One of the critical tasks of managing multinational operations is to design an effective managerial control system to allow top management to coordinate and guide activities of a large number of far-flung foreign affiliates into a unified whole. Since entirely new variables enter into the calculus of decision making in international business, the mere extension of a domestic control system is inadequate in meeting the demands of multinational operations.

This article seeks to identify major problems faced by corporate management in exercising managerial control over foreign operations and to offer some basic suggestions toward development of a more meaningful way of viewing managerial control in multinational ... contexts.

ALLOCATION OF DECISION-MAKING AUTHORITY

Though it is by no means unique to international business, one of the recurring issues raised by corporate management is the division of authority between headquarters and foreign affiliates. Some firms choose to centralize practically all decision making at corporate headquarters and to require from foreign units extremely detailed operating plans and reports with great frequency. As one would expect, this arrangement tends to dampen the enthusiasm and initiative of the management overseas and to limit its flexibility and freedom in meeting local problems and opportunities.

Excessive demand for information and reports not only has a demoralizing effect upon local executives, but it also diverts them from more pressing operating problems. Frequently, the headquarters staff are paralyzed by the sheer volume of information coming from foreign affiliates and fail to make effective use of it. Decisions are likely to be delayed, leading to losses in operating effectiveness.

Interestingly, tight control does not necessarily guarantee that local management will adhere strictly to the policies of the home office. I have observed some local executives who ostensibly comply with the requirements of headquarters but in reality deviate substantially from the policy directives of the home office.

Some firms go to the other extreme by almost completely delegating decision-making authority to local management. My recent field research has revealed that corporate headquarters of some international firms exercise virtually no control over their foreign operations, as long as the foreign units somehow meet the minimum sales or profit goal established by the headquarters. This approach is observed to be particularly prevalent among manufacturers of consumer products with many years of international experience. Some do it out of a conviction that it is impossible to manage daily affairs of overseas units from a headquarters located several thousand miles away, while others follow this practice out of negligence.

Though the laissez-faire approach gives maximum flexibility and freedom to local management, it suffers from two major weaknesses. Foreign affiliates which are virtually autonomous tend to generate subgoals not necessarily consistent with those of the headquarters. Also, extreme decentralization limits use of a wide variety of resources and experiences available at headquarters which are of potential value to foreign units. There seem to be nearly always some elements of a company's managerial competence that can be applied overseas. The latter point is particularly important inasmuch as the real strength of a world enterprise derives from its ability to integrate the activities of widely scattered affiliates.

Obviously, the optimum pattern lies somewhere between the two extremes described. Since the effectiveness of a particular pattern depends on such factors as nature of products, stage of organizational evolvement, size of the company, and availability of executive talents, it is impossible to prescribe a pattern that is equally suitable under any circumstances. However, it appears that distance, complexity, and instability in operating environments overseas tend to favor maximum decentralization of decision making. Only the very critical decisions should be reserved for corporate management. These are likely to be decisions involving such elements as major capital investments, selection of top managerial personnel, important government negotiations, and introduction of new products. This approach tends to maximize contributions that both headquarters and local management are best qualified to make. ...

ESTABLISHING MEANINGFUL
STANDARDS OF PERFORMANCE

A critical problem in planning managerial control for multinational operations is the determination of standards against which to evaluate the performance of foreign affiliates. In this regard, two points deserve careful consideration. They are (1) the appropriateness of reported profits as a measurement criterion, and (2) the need for multiple performance criteria. In multidivisional *domestic* operations, reported profit is generally accepted as the critical measure of managerial effectiveness. Each division is relatively self-contained, and interdivisional transactions can be adjusted through the mechanism of transfer pricing. Since general operating environments among various divisions are relatively homogeneous, top management can make some meaningful comparisons. In *multinational* operations, however, reported profit alone is quite inadequate as the measure of performance.

In the first place, the reported profit of a foreign operating unit is likely to be distorted by a number of external and internal variables that are absent in domestic operations. Because political and economic risks vary widely from country to country, what appears superficially to be high profit may, in fact, be quite unsatisfactory when risk factors are properly weighed. Foreign exchange regulations, legal restrictions, foreign tax structures, or unexpected political developments can have a decided impact upon the profit performance of a foreign affiliate. Yet the local management has virtually no control over these external factors.

Profit performance of a foreign affiliate can also be affected by intrafirm decisions that are beyond the control of local management. ... These factors provide convincing evidence that the reported profit-and-loss data must be carefully scrutinized and adjusted by removing various extraneous influences on the operations of a local unit. In so doing the following guidelines are important.

ENVIRONMENTAL VARIABLES

The most serious problem is determining the degree of controllability of the environmental variables. It is evident that local management can exercise no control over such developments as galloping inflation in a foreign economy or a surge of nationalistic feelings. However, it is possible to minimize the impact of these developments on the particular firm through careful planning and judicious actions. Corporate management must somehow determine the degree to which local management should be held accountable for these environmental variables.

... It must be noted that there is a ... tendency for management of most foreign affiliates to attribute poor performance mainly to hard-to-measure environmental variables or arbitrary decisions made by headquarters. Hence, each case must be reviewed carefully. Careless or arbitrary decisions in this respect contribute to poor morale among local government and relaxed control.

The next step involves technical adjustments of reported data. Here, two considerations are important. Since adjustments of profit-loss data of a host of foreign affiliates are highly complicated, time-consuming, and costly, they should be limited to major items large enough to make significant differences. ... Furthermore, it is important that the criteria and methods of adjustments be explicitly defined and understood by the management of foreign affiliates.

Removing distortions from the reported profit is only one step. Performance of all foreign units must be evaluated on a comparative basis. This is essential not only for the purpose of managerial control but for future decisions on allocation of corporate resources on a global basis. Establishing a comparative criterion of profit performance is extremely difficult because of a wide diversity in operating environments overseas. It is obvious that an investment in a high-risk country should earn a greater return than one in a stable economy. But is it possible to quantify the rather elusive political and economic risks?

· · ·

Now let us turn to the second basic issue. This involves the question of the relative importance to be attached to profitability as a performance criterion. ... Should the management of multinational operations rely predominantly or even exclusively on this single criterion in measuring managerial effectiveness of foreign affiliates? The answer is clearly negative when the following factors are considered. (1) Multinational operations are conducted in sovereign nations with diverse national goals and interests. (2) Foreign enterprise induces a potential conflict of interest between the American parent company, its local associates, and the governments of the host countries.

Any foreign enterprise that must rely heavily on local resources cannot expect to survive, let alone succeed, over the long run unless it is so structured and managed as to make the maximum contributions to the host country. This is particularly true in developing countries where productive resources are scarce and nationalistic feelings are rampant. Satisfaction of this requirement, however, may well conflict with the profitability criterion, at least in the short run. This conflict of interests must be recognized by top management in setting performance criteria for foreign affiliates.

· · ·

There is another area of potential conflict that must be recognized in establishing performance criteria. Many multinational operations involve joint ownership with local interests. Local investors can participate only in profits of the foreign enterprise, not those of the parent company located in the United States. ...

DESIGNING AN EFFECTIVE INFORMATION SYSTEM

The critical role of information in planning a managerial control system has been repeatedly emphasized in management literature. Distance, diversity, and instability in environments overseas place a premium on an effective information system in multinational operations. Information processing and analysis are much more complex and, correspondingly, more expensive in international business than in domestic operations. Top management, therefore, must balance comprehensiveness and speed on the one hand and the cost of information on the other.

Three basic considerations are important in designing an information system for a world enterprise. They are (1) the types of information sought, (2) the flow of information between headquarters and foreign affiliates, and (3) analysis of information for managerial planning and control.

... The informational needs of a firm ultimately depend on corporate strategies and goals. This basic consideration, however, is often ignored. Though the exact requirements vary from company to company, basically three types of information are needed by the management of multinational operations. They are environmental data (political, social, and economic), competitive data (real and potential), and internal operating data (both quantitative and qualitative). In many multinational firms, the only type of data systematically and regularly gathered is that related to internal operations. Even those data are primarily designed for accounting purposes rather than for decision making.

Since international operations are much more vulnerable to external variables than domestic operations, data on environmental and competitive conditions become all the more critical. ...

In view of their importance, it is dangerous to delegate over-all intelligence functions solely to foreign affiliates. Though foreign affiliates are unquestionably an important source of vital information for management, local executives are usually preoccupied with daily operating problems, and they may overlook subtle developments with far-reaching implications. Furthermore, there are other equally important sources of environmental and competitive data available to headquarters. For example, United Nations, United States government agencies, and trade associations can provide useful information.

THE FLOW OF INFORMATION

The second factor in designing a global information system is facilitating the flow of information between corporate headquarters and foreign affiliates. Two media of communication—written reports and personal visits—are available for this purpose. Though both serve useful functions, the balance between the two must be carefully considered. As noted earlier, excessive reliance on written reports tends to aggravate the already difficult and sometimes strained headquarters-foreign affiliates relationship. Action-oriented local executives find it time-consuming and difficult to prepare reports. Furthermore, foreign nationals are placed at a disadvantage because of language and cultural barriers. For these reasons, written communication should be kept to the minimum level. Headquarters must also standardize reporting procedures and methods to facilitate reporting and subsequent analysis.

Personal visits are used extensively by the management of most multinational corporations, though the character of personal visits varies widely as does their effectiveness. Too frequently, personal visits are used as a tool for trouble-shooting—to solve immediate problems occurring unexpectedly. Viewed in this fashion, personal visits have very limited educational value. Since face-to-face contacts can be useful in bridging the distance and cultural gaps that exist between headquarters and foreign affiliates, they must be well planned and made on a regular basis. Personal visits, if appropriately conducted, are useful in developing an insight into local problems, communicating policies of headquarters, discussing long-term plans, and sharing valuable experiences.

The most challenging area in designing an international intelligence system lies in analysis of data by headquarters staff for effective control and planning. Thus far, in many international firms relatively little has been done beyond the traditional accounting analysis. Comparative analysis of internal data is complicated by diverse environmental factors, as noted earlier; but this step is critical in identifying weak spots and unrealized opportunities. Some progressive firms have begun to make imaginative use of these ideas. For example, labor productivity, efficiency of logistics system, and effectiveness of a given marketing mix are analyzed and evaluated on a global basis.

UNDERSTANDING CULTURAL VARIABLES

Perhaps the most difficult and elusive aspect of managerial control in international operations is that control functions must be performed in a multicultural context. This is particularly significant when affiliates are managed by foreign nationals. Cultural variables affect managerial control in several ways.

First, culture may block effective communication between foreign affiliates and headquarters. Particularly serious from the viewpoint of managerial control are distortions introduced in reporting as a result of certain cultural values prevalent in some societies. Some cultures tend to emphasize politeness and agreeableness in superior-subordinate reporting relationships, even at the expense of accuracy and directness. Thus, local management may ignore or distort data deemed unpleasant to corporate headquarters.

Secondly, to a large degree culture prescribes the standard of achievement and dictates the concomitant system of rewards. Not every culture rewards what is considered to be productive achievement in advanced industrial societies, nor is the reward for similar achievements the same. For example, some traditional cultures place the ultimate reward upon loyalty, devotion, and contribution to the group rather than upon outstanding individual achievement. Thus, a system of motivations and incentives—an essential ingredient in managerial control—must be meaningful in terms of the local culture.

Culture also affects superior-subordinate relationships in an organization. As Professor Fayerweather concludes from his pioneering research, some cultures are prone to produce interpersonal relationships characterized by distance, distrust, and hostility; while others are more conducive to group-oriented, collaborative interpersonal relationships.[1] He further notes that the former type is relatively prevalent in more traditional societies, whereas the latter is predominant in Western societies, particularly in American culture. Though each pattern is meaningful and effective in its own cultural environments, difficulties are likely to emerge when control functions must be performed among men of diverse cultural backgrounds and orientations.

Finally, there is the problem of sensitivity often manifested by national executives toward control exercised by American executives. This is particularly prevalent among those in underdeveloped and former colonial countries.

The only permanently effective way to overcome these cultural gaps is to view managerial control as an educational process rather than a superior-subordinate authority relationship. Continuous educational effort is the only feasible way to provide management of foreign affiliates with the necessary background to understand the headquarters' points of view. With this background, local management could intelligently interpret policy directives from the home office as well as effectively participate in the formation of such policies. Such an educational approach would also minimize the sensitivity problem mentioned above.

. . .

[1] John Fayerweather, *The Executive Overseas* (Syracuse, N.Y.: Syracuse University Press, 1959), pp. 15-40.

48

Culture as an Intervening Variable

RICHARD B. PETERSON AND JAMES S. GARRISON

The central premise of this selection is that we presently lack sufficient knowledge about the role of cultural variables in the technology-organization structure relationship. Drs. Peterson and Garrison believe that empirical research on technology and organization, although valuable, is incomplete because the effect of culture has been ignored. All really significant empirical research on this subject has been conducted in Great Britain and the United States, both highly industrialized Western nations. They question whether—and if so, how—the results would change if the research were carried out in environments with significant cultural differences.

To guide research toward an analysis of the relative effects of culture and technology on organization, the authors propose four thought-provoking, although tentative hypotheses:

1. *Organizations using the same technology and found in the same culture will evidence similar organization patterns, everything else being equal.*
2. *Organizations using the same technology, but located in different cultures, will evidence different organizational patterns, everything else being equal.*
3. *Organizations using the same technology and found in the same culture will evidence different organizational patterns if the first group of firms is native-owned while the other group of firms are overseas subsidiaries or non-native-owned concerns, everything else being equal.*
4. *Organizations using the same technology that is adapted to the cultural values of the resident country will be more effective in meeting their organizational goals than those firms not adhering to the cultural values of the resident country, everything else being equal.*

The authors conclude by calling for research into these difficult and important questions.

Reprinted from "Culture as an Intervening Variable in the Technology-Organization Structure Relationship," *Academy of Management Journal*, March 1971, pp. 139-142, by permission of the publisher.

In recent years, there has been an abundance of discussion concerning the relationship between technology and organizational patterns or structure. Woodward and the Tavistock group have presented valuable empirical research on this relationship in Great Britain.[1] In the United States, Thompson and Bates, Sayles, Lawrence and Lorsch, and Perrow have dealt with this relationship through conceptual and empirical research.[2]

We should like to suggest that although the research on this relationship has been valuable, it is incomplete.[3] Additional information is required on the effect of culture as an intervening variable. To date, the work on technology and organization structure has been confined largely to Great Britain and the United States, both highly industrialized Western nations. Might we not expect different results in non-Western settings?

The growing literature in comparative management suggests the likelihood of modifications of the earlier findings when tested in firms operating in such areas as Asia and Latin America. Such writers as Hagen, Gonzalez and McMillan, Negandhi and Estafen, Farmer and Richman, and Whitehill and Takezawa, among others, have suggested that cultural relativism continues to limit the universality of managerial philosophy and practice. Perhaps Dubin has said it best when he states that although technology may, in the long run, determine the system of management, in the short run one would expect varied structures and modes of supervision as reflections of special cultural features.[4]

For instance, we would suggest that, viewed broadly, the United States and Sweden would exhibit the following organizational structure or pattern: fewer organizational levels; relatively high number of formal rules; wide span of control; moderately high specificity of job requirements; moderate decentralization of decision-making; and stronger knowledge-based rather than position-based authority.

[1] Joan Woodward, *Industrial Organization: Theory and Practice* (London: Oxford University Press, 1965), and Tom Burns and G. M. Stalker, *The Management of Innovation* (London: Tavistock Publications, Ltd., 1961).

[2] James Thompson and Frederick Bates, "Technology, Organization, and Administration," in James Thompson, ed., *Comparative Studies in Administration* (Pittsburgh: University of Pittsburgh Press, 1959); Leonard Sayles, *Managerial Behavior* (New York: McGraw-Hill Book Company, Inc., 1964); Paul Lawrence and Jay Lorsch, *Organization and Environment* (Homewood, Ill.: Richard D. Irwin, Inc., 1969); and Charles Perrow, *Organizational Analysis: A Sociological View* (Belmont: Wadsworth Publishing Company, Inc., 1970).

[3] As used here, "technology" is an organized body of technical knowledge about the firm's relevant environment. Our specific concern is the ability to specify and program the activities required to meet customer requirements. "Organizational patterns" or structure refers to such things as the arrangement and specification of formal relationships and rules, formal rules, operating policies, work procedures, and similar devices adopted by management to guide employee behavior (including that of executives) in certain ways. Scalar levels, span of control, etc., are subsumed in this broader category. "Culture" refers simply to the learned and shared behavior of a community of interacting human beings. For our purpose, the orientation of culture will be concerned with the attached values concerning the practice of management.

[4] Robert Dubin *et al.*, *Leadership and Productivity* (San Francisco: Chandler Publishing Company, 1965).

Because of the stronger value given to those in authority in France and Western Germany, we would expect: a larger number of organizational levels with close supervision; many formal rules, fairly high specificity of job requirements; highly centralized decision-making; and stronger accent on position-based authority.

Japan would represent the industrialized Oriental nation. The results of previous research there suggest the following organizational patterns: many organizational levels; narrow span of control; small number of formal rules (but high number of informal constraints); fairly strong specificity of job requirements; highly centralized decision-making (though appearance of group decision-making by means of ringii system); and finally, a strong accent on position-based authority.

We do not suggest that culture and technology are the only important variables relating to the organization structure of a particular firm. Such factors as the personality of the chief executive, size of the firm, age of the firm, market demands, etc., also play important roles in determining the organizational structure or patterns within a particular firm. Rather, we hypothesize that the organizational structure in a particular firm is a function of the interaction of the external culture and relative technology, everything else being equal. At this stage, we are unable to determine the relative weighting of culture and technology on the organization structure.

Some writers have suggested that technology is the key variable and that, over time, the technological imperative will supersede cultural forces. If so, the Japanese experience provides grounds for doubt. Japanese management has been very aggressive in absorbing Western technological advances, but still continues to retain certain traditional activities, such as lifetime employment, which may be questioned rationally. The technocrats may explain away this experience on the basis that sufficient time must be given for the technological imperative to negate the role of cultural forces. Furthermore, there is even the difficulty in our inability to differentiate rational technological imperatives from the Western cultural value system.

Given these problems, we should like to offer four tentative hypotheses for testing in the field so as to understand better the relative weighting of culture and technology as they interact to affect organizational structure and patterns. The first hypothesis would be:

1. H1.0: Organizations using the same technology and found in the same culture will evidence similar organizational patterns, everything else being equal.

   For example, if we are dealing with several Japanese firms using the same technological processes (unit, mass, or process), we would expect that the organizational patterns would be similar; much of the literature and previous research support this position.

   From this position, we can then offer a further hypothesis which states that:

2. H2.0: Organizations using the same technology, but located in different cultures, will evidence different organizational patterns, everything else being equal.

We might illustrate this hypothesis by using two modern chemical firms, one operating in West Germany, while another firm operates in Brazil under native ownership. We would probably see evidence of different organizational patterns because of the cultural differences between the two nations and the corresponding cultural effect on work roles and structure.

The third hypothesis would test the effect of the "third-world" culture on organizational patterns:

3. H3.0: Organizations using the same technology and found in the same culture will evidence different organizational patterns if the first group of firms is native-owned while the other group of firms are overseas subsidiaries or non-native-owned concerns, everything else being equal.

Here, we might compare two auto manufacturing firms in West Germany. The first firm would be owned by West German interests, while the other firm would be an overseas subsidiary of an American auto manufacturer.

To this point, we have not dealt with the issue of corporate effectiveness in our hypothesis formulation. How might congruency with cultural values relate to corporate effectiveness. We would suggest the following hypothesis:

4. H4.0: Organizations using the same technology that is adaptive to the cultural values of the resident country will be more effective (e.g., return on investment, etc.) in meeting their organizational goals than those firms not adhering to the cultural values of the resident country, everything else being equal.

This last hypothesis is more difficult to test because of the controversy concerning the recognizable standards or measures of effectiveness. We might compare two mining companies. One firm would be owned and operated by Japanese who conformed to their native value system. The second firm, on the other hand, would be a Japanese subsidiary of a British mining firm adhering to home country pressures in terms of organizational structure and patterns. Another possibility for the latter case would be a Japanese mining company adhering to Western values in structuring the organization.

No doubt it would be preferable to test the hypotheses over a number of firms so as to minimize the possibility of chance error. However, it is unlikely that we could find a number of firms in which other conditions were equal.

We realize the difficulties in carrying out this research, but feel that only in this way can we determine the relative weightings of culture and technological process on organization structure.

49

What We Can Learn from Japanese Management

PETER DRUCKER

Most literature on management adaptation to cultural differences considers how United States management practices can be transferred abroad. This selection departs from this tradition by discussing how American business may benefit from the application of Japanese management concepts. Peter Drucker is a distinguished management writer and teacher who has often visited and studied in Japan.

An abundant literature on Japanese management practices has accompanied that country's rapid economic growth during the last twenty years. Businessmen in the West are anxious to understand Japanese culture and management so that they may supply, purchase from, and compete and negotiate with, Japanese enterprises. A recent article on this subject is "Understanding the Japanese," by Robert Ballon (see bibliography at the end of Part Seven).

Professor Drucker urges businessmen to look at Japan also as a teacher. He believes that the principles underlying Japanese management practices could suggest solutions to some of American industry's current problems. The three specific areas of concern to management considered in the article are: making effective decisions, harmonizing employment security with other needs of employees, and developing young professional managers. Professor Drucker believes that the Japanese manager's use of decision by "consensus," lifetime employment, continuous training, and managerial godfathers is very relevant to current industrial problems in the West. He notes that these practices, which have frequently been criticized as nonrational or inefficient, are certainly not free of problems. Yet, the author suggests that the cultural premises supporting these practices deserve close scrutiny by American managers.

What are the most important concerns of top management? Almost any group of top executives in the United States (or in many other Western nations) would rank the following very high on the list:

○ Making effective decisions.

Reprinted from the *Harvard Business Review*, March-April 1971, pp. 110-122. Copyright 1971 by the President and Fellows of Harvard College. All rights reserved.

○ Harmonizing employment security with other needs such as productivity, flexibility in labor costs, and acceptance of change in the company.

○ Developing young professional managers.

In approaching these problem areas, Japanese managers—especially those in business—behave in a strikingly different fashion from U.S. and European managers. The Japanese apply different principles and have developed different approaches and policies to tackle each of these problems. These policies, while not *the* key to the Japanese "economic miracle," are certainly major factors in the astonishing rise of Japan in the last 100 years, and especially in Japan's economic growth and performance in the last 20 years.

It would be folly for managers in the West to imitate these policies. In fact, it would be impossible. Each policy is deeply rooted in Japanese traditions and culture. Each applies to the problems of an industrial society and economy the values and the habits developed far earlier by the retainers of the Japanese clan, by the Zen priests in their monasteries, and by the calligraphers and painters of the great "schools" of Japanese art.

Yet the principles underlying these Japanese practices deserve, I believe, close attention and study by managers in the West. They may point the way to a solution to some of our most pressing problems.

DECISIONS BY "CONSENSUS"

If there is one point on which all authorities on Japan are in agreement, it is that Japanese institutions, whether businesses or government agencies, make decisions by "consensus." The Japanese, we are told, debate a proposed decision throughout the organization until there is agreement on it. And only then do they make the decision.[1]

This, every experienced U.S. manager will say with a shudder, is not for us, however well it might work for the Japanese. This approach can lead only to indecision or politicking, or at best to an innocuous compromise which offends no one but also solves nothing. And if proof of this were needed, the American might add, the history of President Lyndon B. Johnson's attempt to obtain a "consensus" would supply it.

Let us consider the experience of Japan. What stands out in Japanese history, as well as in today's Japanese management behavior, is the capacity for making 180-degree turns—that is, for reaching radical and highly controversial decisions.

• • •

[1] See Howard F. Van Zandt, "How to Negotiate in Japan," HBR November-December 1970, p. 45.

Focusing on the Problem

The key to this apparent contradiction is that the Westerner and the Japanese mean something different when they talk of "making a decision." With us in the West, all the emphasis is on the *answer* to the question. Indeed, our books on decision making try to develop systematic approaches to giving an answer. To the Japanese, however, the important element in decision making is *defining the question*. The important and crucial steps are to decide whether there is a need for a decision and what the decision is about. And it is in this step that the Japanese aim at attaining "consensus." Indeed, it is this step that, to the Japanese, is the essence of the decision. The answer to the question (what the West considers *the* decision) follows its definition.

During this process that precedes the decision, no mention is made of what the answer might be. This is done so that people will not be forced to take sides; once they have taken sides, a decision would be a victory for one side and a defeat for the other. Thus the whole process is focused on finding out what the decision is really about, not what the decision should be. Its result is a meeting of the minds that there is (or is not) a need for a change in behavior.

• • •

Undertaking Action

When the Japanese reach the point we call a decision, they say they are in the *action stage*. Now top management refers the decision to what the Japanese call the "appropriate people." Determination of who these people are is a top management decision. On that decision depends the specific answer to the problem that is to be worked out. For, during the course of the discussions leading up to the consensus, it has become very clear what basic approaches certain people or certain groups would take to the problem. Top management, by referring the question to one group or the other, in effect picks the answer—but an answer which by now will surprise no one.

• • •

Increased Effectiveness

What are the advantages of this process? And what can we learn from it?

In the first place, it makes for very effective decisions. While it takes

484 Managing: An Adaptive Process

much longer in Japan to reach a decision than it takes in the West, from that point on they do better than we do. After making a decision, we in the West must spend much time "selling" it and getting people to act on it. Only too often, as all of us know, either the decision is sabotaged by the organization or, what may be worse, it takes so long to make the decision truly effective that it becomes obsolete, if not outright wrong, by the time the people in the organization actually make it operational.

The Japanese, by contrast, need to spend absolutely no time on "selling" a decision. Everybody has been presold. Also, their process makes it clear where in the organization a certain answer to a question will be welcomed and where it will be resisted. Therefore, there is plenty of time to work on persuading the dissenters, or on making small concessions to them which will win them over without destroying the integrity of the decision.

. . .

The Japanese process is focused on understanding the problem. The desired end result is certain action and behavior on the part of the people. This almost guarantees that all the alternatives will be considered. It rivets management attention to essentials. It does not permit commitment until management has decided what the decision is all about. Japanese managers may come up with the wrong answer to the problem (as was the decision to go to war against the United States in 1941), but they rarely come up with the right answer to the wrong problem. And that, as all decision makers learn, is the really dangerous course, the irretrievably wrong decision.

Improved Focus

Above all, the system forces the Japanese to make big decisions. It is much too cumbersome to be put to work on minor matters. It takes far too many people far too long to be wasted on anything but truly important matters leading to real changes in policies and behavior. Small decisions, even when obviously needed, are very often not being made at all in Japan for that reason.

With us it is the small decisions which are easy to make—decisions about things that do not greatly matter. Anyone who knows Western business, government agencies, or educational institutions knows that their managers make far too many small decisions as a rule. And nothing, I have learned, causes as much trouble in an organization as a lot of small decisions.

. . .

In the West we are moving in the Japanese direction. At least, this is what so many "task forces," "long-range plans," "strategies," and other approaches are trying to accomplish. But we do not build into the development of these projects the "selling" which the Japanese process achieves before the decision. This explains in large measure why so many brilliant reports of the task leaders and planners never get beyond the planning stage.

U.S. executives expect task forces and long-range planning groups to come up with recommendations—that is, to commit themselves to one alternative. The groups decide on an answer and then document it. To the Japanese, however, the most important step is understanding the alternatives available. They are as opinionated as we are, but they discipline themselves not to commit themselves to a recommendation until they have fully defined the question and used the process of obtaining consensus to bring out the full range of alternatives. As a result, they are far less likely to become prisoners of their preconceived answers than we are.

SECURITY & PRODUCTIVITY

Just as many Americans have heard about consensus as the basis for Japanese decisions, so many of us know about Japanese "lifetime employment" policies. But the common understanding of "lifetime employment" is as far off the mark as is the common interpretation of consensus.

Myths & Realities

To be sure, most employees in "modern" Japanese business and industry have a guaranteed job once they are on the payroll. While they are on the job, they have practically complete job security which is endangered only in the event of a severe economic crisis or of bankruptcy of the employer. They also are paid on the basis of seniority, as a rule, with pay doubling about every 15 years, regardless of the type of job.

. . .

But, while job security and compensation are quite favorable for Japanese workers as a whole, the picture does not have the implications a Western businessman might expect. Instead of a rigid labor cost structure, *Japan actually has remarkable flexibility in her labor costs and labor force.* What no one ever mentions—and what, I am convinced, most Japanese do not even see themselves—is that the retirement system itself (or perhaps it should be called the non-retirement system) makes labor costs more flexible than they are in most countries and industries of the West. Also, it harmonizes in a highly ingenious fashion the workers' need for job and income guarantees with the economy's need for flexible labor costs.

Actually, most Japanese companies, especially the large ones, can and do lay off a larger proportion of their work force, when business falls off, than most Western companies are likely or able to do. Yet they can do so in such a fashion that the employees who need incomes the most are fully protected. The burden of adjustment is taken by those who can afford it and who have alternate incomes to fall back on.

Official retirement in Japan is at age 55—for everyone except a few who, at age 45, become members of top management and are not expected to retire at any fixed age. At age 55, it is said, the employee, whether he is a floor sweeper or a department head, "retires." Traditionally, he then gets a severance bonus equal to about two years of full pay. (Many companies, strongly backed by the government, are now installing supplementary pension payments, but by Western standards these payments are still exceedingly low.)

Considering that life expectancy in Japan is now fully up to Western standards, so that most employees can expect to live to age 70 or more, this bonus seems wholly inadequate. Yet no one complains about the dire fate of the pensioners. More amazing still, one encounters in every Japanese factory, office, and bank, people who cheerfully admit to being quite a bit older than 55 and who quite obviously are still working. What is the explanation?

The rank-and-file blue-collar or white-collar employee ceases to be a permanent employee at age 55 and becomes a "temporary" worker. This means that he can be laid off if there is not enough work. But if there is enough work—and, of course, there has been during the past 20 years—he stays on, very often doing the same work as before, side by side with the "permanent" employee with whom he has been working for many years. But for this work he now gets at least one third less than he got when he was a "permanent" employee.

The rationale of this situation is fairly simple. As the Japanese see it, the man has something to fall back on when he retires—the two-year pension. This, they freely admit, is not enough to keep a man alive for 15 years or so. But it is usually enough to tide him over a bad spell. And since he no longer has, as a rule, dependent children or parents whom he has to support, his needs should be considerably lower than they were when he was, say, 40 and probably had both children and parents to look after.

. . .

Meeting Workers' Needs

In the West, during the last 25 years, more and more employees have achieved income maintenance that may often exceed what the Japanese worker gets under "lifetime employment."

There is, for instance, the Supplementary Employment Compensation of the U.S. mass-production industries which, in effect, guarantees the unionized worker most of his income even during fairly lengthy layoffs. Indeed, it may well be argued that labor costs in U.S. mass-production industries are more rigid than they are in Japan, even though our managements can rapidly adjust the number of men at work to the order flow, in contrast to the Japanese practice of maintaining employment for "permanent" employees almost regardless of business conditions. Increasingly, also, we find in the heavily unionized mass-production industries provisions for early retirement, such as were written in the fall of 1970 into the contract of the U.S. automobile industry.

Still, unionized employees are laid off according to seniority, with the ones with the least seniority going first. As a result, we still offer the least security of jobs and incomes to the men who need predictable incomes the most—the fathers of young families (who also may have older parents to support). And where there is "early retirement," it means, as a rule, that the worker has to make a decision to retire permanently. Once he has opted for early retirement, he is out of the work force and unlikely to be hired back by any employer. In short, the U.S. labor force (and its counterparts in Europe) lacks the feeling of economic and job security which is so pronounced a feature of Japanese society.

We pay for a high degree of "income maintenance" and have imposed on ourselves a very high degree of rigidity in respect to labor costs. But we get very few tangible benefits from these practices. Also, we do not get the psychological security which is so prominent in Japanese society—i.e., the deep conviction of a man of working age that he need not worry about his job and his income. Instead we have fear. The younger men fear that they will be laid off first, just when the economic needs of their families are at their peak; the older men fear that they will lose their jobs in their fifties, when they are too old to be hired elsewhere.

In the Japanese system there is confidence in both age groups. The younger men feel they can look forward to a secure job and steadily rising income while their children are growing up; the older men feel they are still wanted, still useful, and not a burden on society.

· · ·

More Meaningful Benefits

Today there is talk—and even a little action—in U.S. industry concerning "reverse seniority" to protect newly hired blacks with little or no seniority in the event of a layoff. But we might better consider applying "reverse seniority" to older men past the age of greatest family obligations, since so many labor contracts now provide for early retirement after age 55.

Under current conditions, these men may be expected to be laid off when they qualify for early retirement. Why not give them the right to come back out of early retirement and be rehired first when employment expands again? Some such move that strengthens the job security of the younger, married employee, with his heavy family burdens, might well be the only defense against pressures for absolute job guarantees with their implications for rigid labor costs.

Even more important as a lesson to be learned from the Japanese is the need to shape benefits to the wants of specific major employee groups. Otherwise they will be only "costs" rather than "benefits." In the West—and especially in the United States—we have, in the last 30 years, heaped benefit upon benefit to the point where the fringes run up to a third of the total labor cost in some industries. Yet practically all these benefits have been slapped on across the board whether needed by a particular group or not.

Underlying our entire approach to benefits—with management and union in complete agreement, for once—is the asinine notion that the work force is homogeneous in its needs and wants. As a result, we spend fabulous amounts of money on benefits which have little meaning for large groups of employees and leave unsatisfied the genuine needs of other, equally substantial groups. This is a major reason why our benefit plans have produced so little employee satisfaction and psychological security.

Willingness to Change

It is the psychological conviction of job and income security that underlies what might be the most important "secret" of the Japanese economy: cheerful willingness on the part of employees to accept continuing changes in technology and processes, and to regard increasing productivity as good for everybody.

There is a great deal written today about the "spirit" of the Japanese factory, as reflected in the company songs workers in big factories sing at the beginning of the working day. But far more important is the fact that Japanese workers show little of the famous "resistance to change" which is so widespread in the West. The usual explanation for this is "national character"—always a suspect explanation.

· · ·

The secret may lie in what the Japanese call "continuous training." This means, first, that every employee, very often up to and including top managers, keeps on training as a regular part of his job until he retires. This is in sharp contrast to our usual Western practice of training a man only when he has to acquire a new skill or move to a new position. Our training is promotion-focused; the Japanese training is performance-focused.

Second, the Japanese employee is, for the most part, trained not only in his job but in all the jobs at his job level, however low or high that level is.

. . .

Built-in Advantages

One result of the practices described is that improvement of work quality and procedures is built into the system. In a typical Japanese training session, there is a "trainer." But the real burden of training is on the participants themselves. And the question is always: "What have we learned so we can do the job better?" A new tool, process, or organization scheme becomes a means of self-improvement.

A Japanese employer who wants to introduce a new product or machine does so in and through the training session. As a result, there is usually no resistance at all to the change, but acceptance of it. Americans in the management of joint ventures in Japan report that the "bugs" in a new process are usually worked out, or at least identified, before it goes into operation on the plant floor.

A second benefit is a built-in tendency to increase productivity. In the West we train until a "learner" reaches a certain standard of performance. Then we conclude that he has mastered the job and will need new training only when he moves on or when the job itself is changed. When a learning curve reaches the standard, it stays on a plateau.

Not so in Japan. The Japanese also have a standard for a job and a learning curve leading up to it. Their standard as a rule is a good deal lower than the corresponding standard in the West; indeed, the productivity norms which have satisfied most Japanese industries in the past are, by and large, quite low by Western measurements. But the Japanese keep on training. And sooner or later, their "learning curve" starts breaking above the plateau which we in the West consider permanent. It starts to climb again, not because a man works harder, but because he starts to work "smarter." In my view, the Japanese pattern is more realistic and more in tune with all that we know about learning.

. . .

The concept of "continuous training" in Japan goes a long way toward preventing the extreme specialization and departmentalization plaguing U.S. business. Generally speaking, there are no craft unions or craft skills in Japanese industry.

. . .

Still, it is not really true, as Japanese official doctrine asserts, that "men are freely moved from job to job within a plant." A man in a welding shop is likely to stay in a welding shop, and so is the fellow in the next aisle who runs the paint sprays. There is much more individual mobility in office work, and especially for managerial and professional people. A Japanese company will not hesitate to move a younger manager from production control into market research or the accounting department.

The individual departments in an office tend to be rigidly specialized and highly parochial in the defense of their "prerogatives." Yet the tunnel vision afflicting so many people in Western business is conspicuously absent in Japan.

· · ·

Adapting the Concept

We in the West emphasize today "continuing education." This is a concept that is still alien to Japan. As a rule, the man or woman who graduates from a university there never sets foot on campus again, never attends a class, never goes back for "retreading." Normal education in Japan is still seen as "preparation" for life rather than as life itself.

Indeed, Japanese employers, even the large companies and the government, do not really want young people who have gone to graduate school. Such people are "too old" to start at the bottom. And there is no other place to start in Japan. Graduate students expect to work as "specialists" and to be "experts" rather than submit to training by their employers. Resistance to the highly trained specialist is considered by many thoughtful management people in Japan to be the greatest weakness of Japanese business—and of government. There is little doubt that, in the years to come, "continuing education" will become far more important in Japan than it now is, and that the specialist will become more important, too.

But, at the same time, Japan's continuous training has something to teach us in the West. We react to worker resistance to change and increased productivity largely along the lines of Mark Twain's old dictum about the weather. We all complain, but no one does anything. The Japanese at least do something—and with conspicuous success.

· · ·

With craft jurisdictions in the United States (and Great Britain) frozen into the most rigid and restrictive union contracts, continuous training is probably out of the question for many blue-collar workers on the plant floor. But it could be instituted—and should be instituted—for nonunionized employees. To be sure, many companies not only have massive training programs, but encourage their younger technical, professional, and managerial people to keep on going to school and to continue their education. But in all too many cases the emphasis in these programs is on a man's becoming more specialized and on *not* learning the other areas of knowledge, skills, and functions.

In most of the U.S. company training programs I know, the emphasis is entirely on the one function in which a young man already works; at most he is being told that "other areas are, of course, important." As a result, he soon comes to consider the other areas as so much excess baggage. And when it comes to education outside—in evening courses at the local university, for instance—a young man's supervisor will push his subordinate into taking more work in his specialty and away from anything else.

The approach should be the opposite: once a young man has acquired the foundations of a specialty, he should be systematically exposed to all the other major areas in the business—whether in company training courses or in "continuing education" programs outside. Only in this way can we hope to prevent tomorrow's professional and managerial people from becoming too departmentalized.

CARE & FEEDING OF THE YOUNG

The House of Mitsui is the oldest of the world's big businesses; it dates back to 1637, half a century before the Bank of England was founded. It also was the largest of the world's big businesses until the American Occupation split it into individual companies. ...

In the more than 300 years of its business life, Mitsui has never had a chief executive (the Japanese term is "chief *banto*"—literally, "chief clerk") who was not an outstanding man and a powerful leader. This accomplishment no other institution can match, to my knowledge; the Catholic Church cannot, nor can any government, army, navy, university, or corporation.

What explains this amazing achievement? In Japan one always gets the same answer: until recently, the chief *banto*—himself never a member of the Mitsui family but a "hired hand"—had only one job: manager development, manager selection, and manager placement. He spent most of his time with the young people who came in as junior managers or professionals. He knew them. He listened to them. And, as a result, he knew, by the time the men reached 30 or so, which ones were likely to reach top management, what experiences and development they needed, and in what job they should be tried and tested.

Appraisal & Assignment

At first sight, nothing would seem less likely to develop strong executives than the Japanese system. It would seem, rather, to be the ideal prescription for developing timid men selected for proved mediocrity and trained "not to rock the boat." The young men who enter a company's employ directly from the university—and by and large, this is the only way to get into a company's management, since hiring from the outside and into upper-level positions is practically unknown—know that they will have a job until they retire, no matter how poorly they perform. Until they reach age 45, they will be promoted and paid by seniority and by seniority alone.

There seems to be no performance appraisal, nor would there be much point to it when a man can be neither rewarded for performance nor penalized for nonperformance. Superiors do not choose their subordinates: the personnel people make personnel decisions, as a rule, often without consulting the manager to whom a subordinate is being assigned. And it seems to be unthinkable for a young manager or professional to ask for a transfer, and equally unthinkable for him to quit and go elsewhere.

This practice is being questioned by highly trained technical personnel, but it is changing very slowly. It is still almost unheard of for a young man to take a job in another company except with the express permission of his previous employer. Indeed, every young managerial and professional employee in Japanese organizations, whether business or government, knows that he is expected to help his colleagues look good rather than stand out himself by brilliance or aggressiveness.

This process goes on for 20 to 25 years, during which all the emphasis seems to be on conforming, on doing what one is being asked to do, and on showing proper respect and deference. Then suddenly, when a man reaches 45, the Day of Reckoning arrives, when the goats are separated from the sheep. A very small group of candidates is picked to become "company directors"—that is, top management. They can stay in management well past any retirement age known in the West, with active top management people in their eighties by no means a rarity. The rest of the group, from "department director" on down, generally stay in management until they are 55, usually with at best one more promotion. Then they are retired—and, unlike the rank-and-file employees, their retirement is compulsory.

Limited but important exceptions to this rule are made in the case of outstanding men who, while too specialized to move into the top management of the parent company, are assigned to the top management of subsidiaries or affiliates. In such positions they can stay in office for an indefinite period of time.

Informal Evaluators

To an outsider who believes what the Japanese tell him—namely, that this is really the way the system works—it is hard to understand on what basis the crucial decision at age 45 is made. It is even harder to believe that this system produces independent and aggressive top managers who have marketed Japanese exports successfully all over the world and who have, in the space of 20 years, made into the third-ranking economic power in the world a nation that, at the eve of World War II, was not even among the first dozen or so in industrial production or capital.

It is precisely *because* Japanese managers have "lifetime employment" and can, as a rule, be neither fired nor moved, and *because* advancement for the first 25 years of a man's working life is through seniority alone, that the Japanese have made the care and feeding of their young people the first responsibility of top management. ...

Today, of course, it is no longer possible for the chief *banto* of Mitsui to know personally the young managerial people as his predecessor did a few generations ago. Even much smaller companies are too large and have far too many young managerial and professional employees in their ranks for that to be done. Yet top management is still vitally concerned with the young. It discharges this concern through an informal network of senior middle-management people who act as "godfathers" to the young men during the first ten years of their careers in the company.

Managerial Godfathers

The Japanese take this system for granted. Indeed, few of them are even conscious of it. As far as I can figure out, it has no name—the term "godfather" is mine rather than theirs. But every young managerial employee knows who his godfather is, and so do his boss and the boss's boss.

The godfather is never a young man's direct superior, and, as a rule, he is not anyone in a direct line of authority over the young man or his department. He is rarely a member of top management and rarely a man who will get into top management. Rather, he is picked from among those members of upper-middle management who will, when they reach 55, be transferred to the top management of a subsidiary or affiliate. In other words, godfathers are people who know, having been passed over at age 45 for the top management spots, that they are not going to "make it" in their own organizations. Therefore, they are not likely to build factions of their own or to play internal politics. At the same time, they are the most highly respected members of the upper-middle management group.

How is a godfather chosen for a young man? Is there a formal assignment or an informal understanding? No one seems to know. The one qualification that is usually mentioned is that the godfather should be a graduate of the same university from which the young man graduated—the "old school tie" binds even more tightly in Japan than it did in England. Yet everybody inside the company knows who the godfather of a given young man is and respects the relationship.

During the first ten years or so of a young man's career, the godfather is expected to be in close touch with his "godchild," even though in a large company he may have 100 such "godchildren" at any one time. He is expected to know the young man, see him fairly regularly, be available to him for advice and counsel, and, in general, look after him. He has some functions that reflect Japanese culture; for instance, he introduces the young men under his wings to the better bars on the Ginza and to the right bawdy houses. (Learning how to drink in public is one of the important accomplishments the young Japanese executive has to learn.)

If a young man gets stuck under an incompetent manager and wants to be transferred, the godfather knows where to go and how to do what officially cannot be done and, according to the Japanese, "is never done." Yet nobody will ever know about it. And if the young man is errant and needs to be disciplined, the godfather will deal with him in private. By the time a young man is 30 the godfather knows a great deal about him.

It is the godfather who sits down with top management and discusses the young people. The meeting may be completely "informal." Over the sake cup, the godfather may say quietly, "Nakamura is a good boy and is ready for a challenging assignment," or "Nakamura is a good chemist, but I don't think he'll ever know how to manage people," or "Nakamura means well and is reliable, but he is no genius and better not be put on anything but routine work." And when the time comes to make a personnel decision, whom to give what assignment, and where to move a man, the personnel people will quietly consult the godfather before they make a move.

. . .

Implications for the West

In the West, though relationships are far less formal, we still need, just as much as the Japanese do, the senior manager who serves as a human contact, a listener, a guide for the young people during their first ten years or so in business. Perhaps the greatest single complaint of young people in the large organization today is that there is nobody who listens to them, nobody who tries to find out who they are and what they are doing, nobody who acts as a senior counselor.

Our management books say that the first-line supervisor can fill this role. That is simply nonsense. The first-line supervisor has to get the work out; all the sermons that "his first job is human relations" will not make it otherwise. A supervisor tries to hang on to a good man and not let him go. He will not say, "You have learned all there is to learn in this place." He will not say, "You are doing all right, but you really don't belong here." He will not ask a young man, "Where do you want to go? What kind of work do you want to do? How can I help you to get there?" In fact, the supervisor is almost bound to consider any hint of a desire to change or to transfer on the part of a young and able subordinate a direct criticism of himself.

As a result, young managerial and professional people in American business and industry—and in Europe too—"vote with their feet." They quit and go elsewhere. The absence of a genuine contact is an important reason for the heavy turnover among these people. Often, when I talk with them, I hear them make statements like these:

○ "The company is all right, but I have nobody to talk to."

○ "The company is all right, but I am in the wrong spot and can't get out of it."

○ "I need someone to tell me what I am doing right and what I am doing wrong, and where I really belong, but there isn't anybody in my company to whom I can go."

They do not need a psychologist. They need a human relationship that is job-focused and work-focused, a contact they have access to, a mentor who is concerned with them. This is what the Japanese have had to supply for a long time because of the impersonal formality of their rigid system. Because they cannot admit officially that the godfather practice exists, they have set it up in the right way. For it is clearly a strength of their system that the godfather function is not a separate job, is not a part of personnel work, and is not entrusted to specialists, but is discharged by experienced, respected, and successful management people.

But it is not only the young people in American and European companies who need a communication system. Senior executives could also make good use of it. Let me illustrate:

In a number of companies with which I have been working, an attempt has been made to have senior executives meet fairly regularly with younger men—outside of office hours and without respecting lines of function or authority. In these sessions the senior man does not make a speech, but asks, "What do you have to tell me—about your work, about your plans for yourself and this company, about our opportunities and our problems?" The meetings have not always been easy going. But the young people, though at first highly suspicious of being patronized, after a while have come to look forward to the sessions. The real beneficiaries, however, have been the senior executives. They have learned what the young managers are thinking.

The godfather concept of the Japanese may be too paternalistic for us in the West; it may even be too paternalistic for the young Japanese. But the need for some system enabling young managerial and professional people to become the special concern of senior men is especially acute in this age of the "generation gap."

CONCLUSION

Any Japanese executive who has read this article will protest that I grossly oversimplify and that I have omitted many salient features of Japanese management. Any Western student of Japan who has read this will accuse me of being uncritical. But my purpose has not been to give a scholarly analysis of Japanese management or even to attempt an explanation of Japan's managerial performance. ...

Whether anyone can learn from other people's mistakes is doubtful. But surely one can learn from other people's successes. While the Japanese policies discussed in this article are not the "keys" to Japan's achievement, they are major factors in it. And while they are not the answers to the problems of the West, they contain answers to some of our most pressing problems, suggest help for some of our most urgent needs, and point to directions we might well explore. It would be folly to attempt to imitate the Japanese; but we might well try to emulate them.

FOR FURTHER READING

Albrook, R., "Europe's Lush Market for Advice—American Preferred." *Fortune*, Vol. 80, No. 1 (July 1969), 128-131, 180-181.

Anderson, J. W., "The Impact of Technology on Job Enrichment." *Personnel*, Vol. 47, No. 5 (September-October 1970), 29.

Armstrong, John A., "Sources of Administration Behavior: Some Soviet and Western European Comparisons." *American Political Science Review*, Vol. 59, No. 3 (September 1965), 643-655.

Arning, H. K., "Business Customs from Malaya to Murmansk." *Management Review*, Vol. 53, No. 10 (October 1964).

Arthur, Thomas, Jr., "The Double Image of American Business Abroad." *Harpers Magazine* (August 1960).

Ballon, Robert J., "Understanding the Japanese." *Business Horizons*, Vol. 13, No. 3 (June 1970), 21-30.

Bell, Gerald D., "The Influence of Technological Components of Work upon Management Control." *Academy of Management Journal*, Vol. 8, No. 2 (June 1965), 127-132.

Blough, Roy, *International Business Environment and Adaption*. New York: McGraw-Hill Book Company, 1966.

Boddewyn, J., *Comparative Management and Marketing*. Glenview, Ill.: Scott, Foresman & Company, 1969.

Brabante, Ralph, and Joseph J. Spengler, eds., *Tradition, Values, and Socio-economic Development*. London: Cambridge University Press, 1961.

Burck, Gilbert, "The Challenging East European Market." *Fortune*, Vol. 71, No. 1 (July 1967), 122-124, 172-180.

Burns, Tom, and G. M. Stalker, *The Management of Innovation*, 2nd ed. London: Tavistock Publications Ltd., 1966.

Butler, Jack, and John Dearden, "Managing a Worldwide Business." *Harvard Business Review*, Vol. 43, No. 3 (May-June 1965).

Chandler, Alfred, *Strategy and Structure: Chapters in the History of Industrial Enterprise*. Cambridge, Mass.: The M.I.T. Press, 1962.

Clee, G. H., *et al.*, *International Enterprise—A New Dimension of American Business*. New York: McKinsey & Co., 1960.

Clee, G., and A. diScipio, "Creating a World Enterprise." *Harvard Business Review*, Vol. 37, No. 6 (November-December 1959), 77-89.

Conant, E. H., and M. D. Kilbridge, "An Interdisciplinary Analysis of Job Enlargement: Technology Costs and Behavioral Implications." *Industrial and Labor Relations Review*, Vol. 18, No. 3 (April 1965), 377-395.

Davis, Stan, "Cross-Cultural Management Quarrels." *Worldwide P & I Planning* (July-August 1967).

Duerr, Michael G., and James Greene, *The Problems Facing International Management*. New York: Holt, Rinehart & Winston, Inc., 1966.

Farmer, R. N., and B. M. Richman, *Comparative Management and Economic Progress*. Homewood, Ill.: Richard D. Irwin, Inc., 1965.

Fayerweather, John, *The Executive Overseas: Administrative Attitudes and Relationships in a Foreign Culture*. Syracuse, N.Y.: Syracuse University Press, 1959.

————, *Facts and Fallacies of International Business*. New York: Holt, Rinehart & Winston, Inc., 1962.

————, *International Business Management: A Conceptual Framework*. New York: McGraw-Hill Book Company, 1969.

Gabriel, Peter, *The International Transfer of Corporate Skills*. Boston: Harvard Business School, 1967.

Gonzalez, R. F., and L. G. Erickson, *International Enterprise in a Developing Economy*. East Lansing, Mich.: Michigan State University Press, 1964.

Gouldner, A. W., *Patterns of Industrial Bureaucracy*. New York: The Free Press, 1954.

Granick, D., *The European Executive*. New York: Doubleday & Co., Inc., 1962.

Grosset, S., *Management: European and American Styles*. Belmont, Calif.: Wadsworth Publishing Company, Inc., 1970.

Haire, M., E. E. Ghiselli, and L. W. Porter, "Cultural Patterns in the Role of the Manager." *Industrial Relations*, Vol. 2, No. 2 (February 1963).

————, *Managerial Thinking: An International Study*. New York: John Wiley & Sons, Inc., 1966.

Hall, Edward J., "The Silent Language of Overseas Business." *Harvard Business Review*, Vol. 38, No. 3 (May-June 1960), 87-96.

Hall, R. H., "Interorganizational Structural Variation." *Administrative Science Quarterly*, Vol. 7, No. 3 (December 1962), 295-308.

Harbison, F., and C. A. Myers, *Management in the Industrial World*. New York: McGraw-Hill Book Company, 1959.

Hayden, Spencer, "Problems of Operating Overseas: A Survey of Company Experience." *Personnel* (January 1968), 8-21.

Heck, Harold J., *The International Business Environment: A Management Guide*. New York: American Management Association, 1969.

Hickson, D. H., D. S. Pugh, and D. C. Pheysey, "Operations Technology and Organization Structure: An Empirical Reappraisal." *Administrative Science Quarterly*, Vol. 14, No. 3 (September 1969), 378-397.

Hoselitz, B. F., *Sociological Aspects of Economic Growth*. New York: The Free Press, 1960.

Katz, R. L., *Cases and Concepts in Corporate Strategy*. Englewood Cliffs, N.J.: Prentice-Hall, Inc., 1968.

Katzell, R. A., "Contrasting Systems of Work," in *Readings in Organization Theory*, ed. W. A. Hill and D. Egan. Boston: Allyn & Bacon, Inc., 1967.

Keller, Paul "The Transnational Company," *EFTA Bulletin* (July-August 1969).

Kindleberger, Charles P., *American Business Abroad*. New Haven, Conn.: Yale University Press, 1969.

Kolde, E. J., *International Business Enterprise*. Englewood Cliffs, N.J.: Prentice-Hall, Inc., 1968.

Kust, Matthew J., *Foreign Enterprise in India: Laws and Policies*. Chapel Hill, N.C.: University of North Carolina Press, 1968.

Lauterbach, Albert T., *Enterprise in Latin America: Business Attitudes in a Developing Economy*. Ithaca, N.Y.: Cornell University Press, 1966.

———, "Executive Training and Productivity: Managerial Views in Latin America." *Industrial and Labor Relations Review* (April 1964).

Lawrence, Paul R., and Jay W. Lorsch, "Differentiation and Integration in Complex Organizations." *Administrative Science Quarterly*, Vol. 11, No. 2 (June 1967), 1-47.

Lawrence, Paul R., and Jay W. Lorsch, *Organization and Environment*. Homewood, Ill.: Richard D. Irwin, Inc., 1969.

Leavitt, H. J., "Management According to Task: Organizational Differentiation." *Management International* (January-February 1962), pp. 13-22.

Lee, James A., "Cultural Analysis in Overseas Operations." *Harvard Business Review*, Vol. 44, No. 2 (March-April 1966).

Lewis, R., and R. Stewart, *The Managers: A New Examination of the English, German and American Executives*. New York: New American Library, Inc., 1961.

Lilienthal, David, *The Multinational Corporation*. New York: Development Resources Corporation, 1960.

Lorsch Jay W., *Product Innovation and Organization*. New York: The Macmillan Company, 1965.

McClelland, David, *The Achieving Society*. Princeton, N.J.: D. Van Nostrand Co., Inc., 1961.

Mace, M. L. "The President and International Operations." *Harvard Business Review*, Vol. 44, No. 6 (November-December 1966), 72-84.

McMillan, Claude, "The American Businessman in Brazil." *Business Topics*, Vol. 11, No. 2 (Spring 1963), 68-80.

Martyn, Howe, *International Business: Organization, Management, and Social Impact of Multinational Business Corporations.* New York: The Free Press, 1964.

———, "Social Benefits of Multinational Manufacturing." *Michigan Business Review*, Vol. 21, No. 3 (May 1969), 26-32.

Meyers, C. A., "Exportability of the American System of Industrial Relations." *Monthly Labor Review*, Vol. 86, No. 3 (March 1963), 268-271.

Miller, D. L., "The Honorable Picnic: Doing Business in Japan." *Harvard Business Review*, Vol. 39, No. 6 (November-December 1961), 79-86.

Morse, J. J., and J. W. Lorsch, "Beyond Theory Y." *Harvard Business Review*, Vol. 48, No. 3 (May-June 1970).

Murray, T. I., "The Global Company in a Changing World." *Duns Review*, Vol. 90, No. 2 (August 1967), 27.

Myers, C. A., "Management in Chile: Lessons from Abroad for American Management." *Journal of Business*, Vol. 33, No. 1 (January, 1960).

Perlmutter, Howard, "The Tortuous Evolution of the Multinational Corporation." *Columbia Journal of World Business*, Vol. 3, No. 1 (January-February 1968).

Perrow, C., *Complex Organizations.* Chicago: Scott, Foresman & Co., 1970.

———, *Organizational Analysis: A Sociological View.* Belmont, Calif.: Wadsworth Publishing Company, Inc., 1970.

———, "Technology and Structural Changes in Business Firms," in *Industrial Relations: Contemporary Issues*, ed. B. C. Roberts. New York: The Macmillan Company, 1968.

Polk, Judd, "The New World Economy." *Columbia Journal of World Business*, Vol. 3, No. 1 (January-February 1968).

Pym, D., "Effective Managerial Performance in Organizational Change." *The Journal of Management Studies*, Vol. 1, No. 1 (February 1965), 34-53.

Rice, A. K., *The Enterprise and Its Environment.* London: Tavistock Publications Ltd., 1963.

Richman, Barry M., "Significance of Cultural Variables." *Academy of Management Journal*, Vol. 9, No. 4 (December 1965).

———, *Soviet Management: With Significant American Comparisons.* Englewood Cliffs, N.J.: Prentice-Hall, Inc., 1964.

Robinson, Richard D., *International Management.* New York: Holt, Rinehart & Winston, Inc., 1967.

Robock, S., and K. Simmonds, "What's New in International Business?" *Business Horizons*, Vol. 9, No. 4 (Winter 1966), 41-48.

Rolfe, S. E., and W. Damm, eds., *The Multinational Corporation in the World Economy.* New York: Frederick A. Praeger, Inc., 1969.

Schmitt, Hans O., "Foreign Capital and Social Conflict in Indonesia." *Economic Development and Social Change*, Vol. 10, No. 3 (April 1962).

Scott, W. G., "Technology and Organization Government: A Speculative Inquiry into the Functionality of Management Creeds." *Academy of Management Journal*, Vol. 11 (1968), 301-313.

Servan-Schreiber, J. J., *The American Challenge*. New York: Atheneum Publishers, 1968.

Shearer, John, "Exporting United States Standards to Under-Developed Countries." *Monthly Labor Review*, Vol. 88, No. 2 (February 1965), 145-147.

Sturmthal, A. F., *Workers Councils: A Study of Workplace Organization on Both Sides of the Iron Curtain*. Cambridge, Mass.: Harvard University Press, 1964.

Teague, Frederick A., "Why U.S. Companies Fail Abroad." *Columbia Journal of World Business*, Vol. 3, No. 4 (July-August 1968).

Thompson, J. D., and W. J. McEwan, "Organizational Goals and Environment." *American Sociological Review*, Vol. 23 (1958), 23-30.

Thompson, J. D., *Organizations in Action*. New York: McGraw-Hill Book Company, 1967.

Thompson, V. A., "Bureaucracy and Innovation." *Administrative Science Quarterly*, Vol. 10, No. 1 (June 1965), 1-20.

Thorelli, Hans B., "The Multinational Corporation as a Change Agent." *The Southern Journal of Business* (July 1966).

Udy, S. H., Jr., "Administrative Rationality, Social Setting, and Organizational Development." *American Journal of Sociology*, Vol. 68 (1962), 299-308.

———, "Bureaucratic Elements in Organization." *American Sociological Review*, Vol. 23 (1958), 415-418.

Webber, Ross A., *Culture and Management*. Homewood, Ill.: Richard D. Irwin, Inc., 1969.

Whyte, William F., and A. R. Holmberg, "Human Problems of United States Enterprise in Latin America." *Human Organization*, Special Issue (Fall 1956).

Woodward, Joan, *Industrial Organization: Theory and Practice*. New York: Oxford University Press, 1965.

Wurfel, Seymour W., *Foreign Enterprise in Colombia: Laws and Policies*. Chapel Hill, N.C.: University of North Carolina Press, 1965.

Yoshino, Michael, "Administrative Attitudes and Relationships in a Foreign Culture." *MSU Business Topics*, Vol. 16, No. 1 (Winter 1968), 59-68.

———, *Japan's Managerial System*. Cambridge, Mass.: The M.I.T. Press, 1968.